Physio-medical Therapeutics

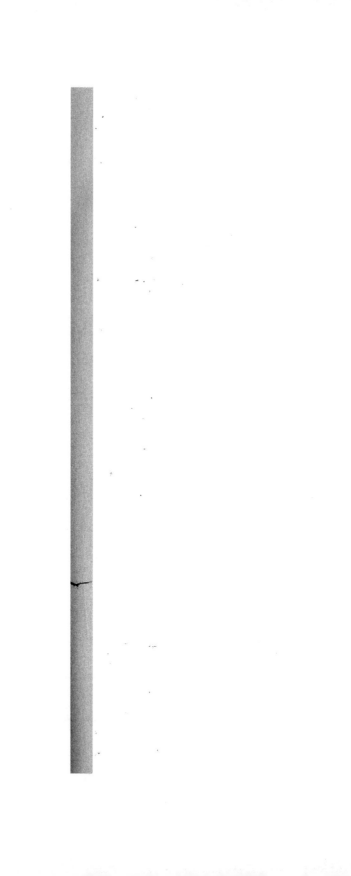

80

9-148164
5249-F

T. J. Lyle

Physio-Medical

Therapeutics

Materia Medica,

and Pharmacy

—BY—

T. J. LYLE, A. M., M. D.

Professor of Therapeutics and Materia Medica in the
Physio-Medical College.

Formerly Professor of Hygiene and Sanitary Science in
the Physio-Medical Institute, Cincinnati, Ohio.

—INCLUDING—

Many Valuable Articles from some of the

MOST EMINENT WRITERS IN

THE PHYSIO-MEDICAL SCHOOL OF MEDICINE

ILLUSTRATED

J. M. Stone and Son
Steam Printing and Publishers,
Salem, Ohio
1897

T. J. Lyle

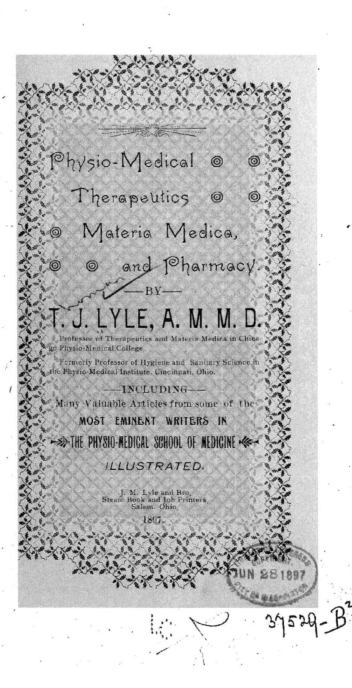

Physio-Medical

Therapeutics ◎ ◎

◎ Materia Medica,

◎ ◎ and Pharmacy

—BY—

T. J. LYLE, A. M. M. D.

Professor of Therapeutics and Materia Medica in Chicago Physio-Medical College.

Formerly Professor of Hygiene and Sanitary Science in the Physio-Medical Institute, Cincinnati, Ohio.

——INCLUDING——

Many Valuable Articles from some of the

MOST EMINENT WRITERS IN

⇒ THE PHYSIO-MEDICAL SCHOOL OF MEDICINE ⇐

ILLUSTRATED.

J. M. Lyle and Bro,
Steam Book and Job Printers,
Salem, Ohio.
1897.

R M133
.L91

➤❯❯PREFACE.❮❮◄

Gentlemen and Ladies of the Medical Profession

To you I offer this humble effort in the direction of an increase of Physio-Medical Literature. It is a necessity in order to successful Practice that we correctly understand Therapeutics, Materia Medica and Pharmacy from a Physio-Medical or Physiological standing point, where medicine administered to the organism shall not create disease but shall assist the Vital Force in maintaining its sovereignty over all the tissues of the body, enabling it to cast off impurities. To assist in properly selecting these agents to illustrate accurate combining and prescription so as to meet conditions as they may be presented. and to instruct in the preparation of these agents that they will be administered to the system in the most efficient form, are the objects of this Volume.

In what is presented I have avoided verbosity and aimed at the greatest brevity consistent with perspicuity. I could easily have doubled the size of this volume, but abundance of words do not always add thoughts. My object has been a Practical Hand-Book rather than a verbose elaboration. I have avoided the superfluous verbiage that necessarily surrounds fine-spun theories and have aimed to produce practical facts, the result of close observation and careful notings in the active Practice of Medicine in the last thirty years

In all things I have aimed to be practical rather than theoretical or dogmatic. The latter does not assist the physician when he stands at the bedside to lend the helping hand to struggling vitality in the battle between life and death. Facts, practical facts, are then needed.

I take pleasure in recording that among those who hold honorable Chairs in the Physio-Medical College of Indiana, Indianapolis, Prof J M Thurston, M D, Prof E Anthony, M D, Prof E G Anthony, M. D., Professor E M. Haggard, M D.; and among those who hold or have held honorable Chairs in the Chicago Physio-Medical College, Prof H A. Hadley, M D. Prof.A. A StoneBurner, M. D., M S E., Prof F O Broady, M. D., Prof A W. Kelly, A M., Ph D., M D and Prof 'W F. Pechuman, A M., M D, L L D, also G H. Mayhugh, M. D Editor of"Sanative Medicine," & J M Massie, M D, have each contributed valuable articles to this volume, while some have contributed some of their most valuable formulæ

I also take pleasure in mentioning the fact that some of our eminent and reliable Pharmacists have willingly given a helping hand

Medical Literature is immense, and I do not forget to acknowledge that in these many years I have gained much information from an extensive reading of Medical Journals of all Schools of Medicine, of Encyclopædias and various Medical Volumes: of Dispensatories and other volumes of Materia Medica and Botany

In all the departments of this book I have aimed to give the latest, the best and the most practical information Herein I have mentioned many new agents, some of which are very valuable and some not so valuable. I have spent much time and money with these agents and have patiently watched their influence under various conditions Some of these have not been equal to our anticipations, while others may now be considered among our best agents

Our ideas concerning some of our older agents have also changed, both with regard to their intrinsic worth and their relative application.

In the future as we shall know more of the knowable, we may think differently of some agents than what we now think I claim infallibility for neither myself nor this Book Careful investigation may cause us to change our opinions concerning the various influences of some of these agents, but the principles of Scientific Medication are the same yesterday, to-day and forever. No theory of Medicine can be Scientific which seeks to destroy or dethrone Vitality, hence Physio-Medicalism is *the* School of Scientific Medication; for Medicine is Scientific only as it seeks to sustain struggling Vitality.

One thing I earnestly ask of the entire Profession. Carefully note your investigations and whatever in the line of Materia Medica you find new and practical report to me. And as I propose to add to this Book an annual appendix, should encouragement favor, I shall be pleased to publish briefly the results of these investigations therein.

In reading these pages the critic's eye of course will be present. But while we pass along the road from Jerusalem to Jericho allow not yourselves to represent either the priest, the levite or the robbers, but act the part of the Good Samaritan.

Together we stand upon the same level, judged by the plummet of truth, and as we pass together along life's pathway we may by united effort bring forth the beautiful keystone for the triumphal arch of success.

As a student of Vitality, I have solved a few problems: I have gathered a few facts from the great ocean of truth that lies before us. These I hand to you in the hope that thereby you shall be able to drink the more deeply from the great fountains of Medical truth. Proclaim the truth to others, that they in turn may do good to succeeding generations.

> "Lives of great men all remind you
> You may make your lives sublime,
> And in dying leave behind you,
> Footprints on the sands of Time."

SALEM, OHIO.
March 4th. 1897.

PHYSIO-MEDICAL

THERAPEUTICS.

The true physician is a wonderful being, whose calling is second to none. He deals with human physical and more or less moral defects. Indeed, man's weal or woe to a great extent, is in his hands. If he ignorant, woe be to humanity. He cannot be too intelligent in his profession. He must be a continuous student, if he keeps abreast of the times. He must realize that there are others in the world who know some things as well as he, that there is room for him to improve, and that there is some information yet for him to gain. Let him be assured that there is room for him at the top if he will but put forth the effort to attain it.

Besides the knowledge of drugs, there are other things in which the physician must be proficient. He must be a thorough student of human nature and a thorough physiognomist. He must be wise in reading abnormal conditions, and be capable of reading character and of diagnosing on sight the conditions present in his patient. This will gain for him at once the patient's confidence and is extremely helpful in the physician's art.

Beware of deceptions, for remember you are everybody's confidante. Be swift to hear everything; be quick to observe everything; but be slow to speak anything. Always tell the truth, but not always the whole truth. Do not make light of your patient's ailments, they believe they are sick, and that itself is a disease and needs your attention. Book knowledge is good, but that gained at the bedside is frequently to be perfered. The results of a scientific experience are very valuable. The physician should have good common sense, good morals and a thorough medical and literary education. Then too he should have a true love for his profession, and possess a magnetic affability. A little fun, a good joke, a pleasant anecdote, and a little laughter will often do your patient good. Never approach your patient with a long face.

Be positively correct in your diagnosis, it is unpleasant to be compelled by force of consultation or otherwise to change your diagnosis of any case. Be scientific in the application of your remedies. "Be sure you are right then go ahead."

Physiology is the science of life, its normal development and preservation. Health is physiology as an art,—a sound, unobstructed condition of the organism. Disease is defection physiology,—an unsound and more or less obstructed condition of the whole organism or of some parts or part.

Study well the manifestations of the vital force in health as well as in disease. Carefully differentiate these manifestations, determine their signification and seek to restore to the normal condition. Let the manifestations of the vital force be your guide in diagnosis, in prognesis and in the art of curing.

Therapeutics relates to the discovery of remedies, the determining of their medical properties and of their application in restoring from diseased conditions to a state of health.

Medical history is full of therapeutical schemes — some very foolish and some seemingly very wise. Some practical, some impracticable, and some a mass of arbitrary dictums. It is not then surprising that some are unreliable. This unreliability has given unrest to the medical mind, and given rise to the assertion that medicine is not a science. Some minds have built up and some have torn down. The dethroning of one opinion has given room for the enthroning of another. The present stands upon the ruins of the past; and man is still searching for truth.

Many medical systems have been founded upon imperfect data, yet many have been their followers. All systems have had their gifted minds. But some preconceived fad, some false premis or some pre-desired conclusion have prevented these gifted minds from always reaching correct conclusions.

Because we differ from others, we do not brand them ignorant, but rejoice in the fact that we live in an age of great research and of wonderful knowledge. We are pleased to note the many intelligent persons who stand in the lead of other schools of medicine. We simply say these men are more or less mistaken, and hope that the day will soon come when they too shall behold the beautiful light of truth and pronounce medicine not a mass of arbitrary dictums, but in truth a science.

Since Hippocrates, who has been called the father of medicine, of 460 B.C. many systems have arisen. among those that remain, the leading are the Regulars or Allopaths the Homeopaths, the Eclectics and the Physio-Medicalists.

The Regulars would have us cure a diseased action by inducing a different kind of action, though not necessarily diseased action. They claim that therapeutics is not a science, that it is uncertain and dependent upon the skill of the practitioner. Once they called disease an evil spirit and attempted cure by incantations. Then they thought that the fluids and solids of the body had changed, and that the fluids had left their proper places in the body, or had become disproportioned. Then came experimental therapeutics, statistical therapeutics and experiments on the lower animals. All left them in more or less uncertainty, and hence to them medicine was necessarily somewhat empirical.

Galen was the man guilty of formulating the scheme of substituting an artificial diseased action for the disease itself. Such always led to the reduction of vitality, landed the patient into more or less asthænia, resulted in protracting the period of illness and led to so many heart failures. These are the men who seek the protection of Uncle Sam to prevent others from practicing medicine who do not believe as they.

Not unfrequently one extreme begets another. The Homeopaths under Hahnemann arose and shouted "Similia Similibus Curantur";—as medicines given to the healthy cause certain symptoms, they will cure disease showing similar or like symptoms. They would have you give arsenic or copper to cure diarrhœa, because such produce diarrhœa in the healthy. They would have you give strychnine for spasms beause it will produce spasms; or muriatic acid for hectic fever because it will produce similar results in the healthy. Why then not cure one drunk by inducing another drunk in the same person?

The Eclectics elect from each school as their experience seems to indicate. They give medicine because its effect is opposite to or opposed to the diseased action. They hold

that remedies contain a force which set free in the body
has the power to bring it back to that condition called normal. They call disease an excess, a defect or perversion.
They say a medicine lessens an excess, restores a defect or
changes a perversion to the normal standard.

Physio-Medicalism is medication in harmony with true
Physiology, recognizing in all conditions the indications
of the vital force and hence abstaining from all poisonous
medication, believing that *whatever has for its tendency to kill cannot have for its tendency to cure*.

In Anatomy, Chemistry and the use of the surgical knife
we hold a general agreement with other Schools of Medicine; but we differ more or less in Physiology, Therapeutics, Materia Medica, Medical Surgery and Practical Medicine. We teach Physiology as the basis of Medical Practice
and demand that the laws of human life and functional
activity must be thoroughly understood. The human
body must be regarded as a highly endowed vital independence by virtue of an inherent vital and living plastic matter, which is the sole causation of any function.

By virtue of this vital force and living matter, the body
is able to maintain its functional integrity against ordinary adverse influences. But when over-powered, functional work becomes more or less disturbed. Then the resistive effort of vitality is manifested in repelling or eliminating the producing cause To aid the vital force in
these restorative efforts is the work of true medicine from
the hand of a true physician. Toxics, irritants, or narcotics
tend to destroy bioplasm, to weaken functional power and
to foster chronic ailments in the body in place of the disease they were intended to remove and hence are improper
agents to be used as medicines. Anything that can deprive
the organs in part or wholly of their ability to act normally
is a cause of disease. That inability is the disease; and
the cure is the restoration of these organs and tissues to
their normal condition. Much has been said of bacilli, but
these are usually harmless; the posionous element in which
they thrive is the cause of further disease and is the contagium.

It is apparent that the mass of medical men are therapeutically at sea. In order that we may behold an appropriate superstructure it must be built upon a true foundation. See with what avidity medical men have allowed
themselves to run after therapeutical sensations. The

Brown-Sequard Elixir for the rejuvenation of the race produced a wild sensation; Koch's tuberculine was to be the eradication of consumption; and now antitoxine and serum theraphy are among the fading wonders.

I grant honor to him who for the welfare of man becomes a patient investigator But where is the trouble? Not in the intensity of the effort, but in the conclusions that are drawn from incomplete or incorrect premises. You need not search for gold in a dung hill; the proper place must be sought. Yellow glasses make all things look yellow; hence investigation must be conducted through the media of correct premises, in order to reach correct conclusions.

The physical basis of life is vital and not chemical The conservation of the vital force is the pivotal point in therapeutics No agent harmful to the physiological unit of animal life, the proto - plasmic cell, must find a place in our Armamentorium Medicorum

Medicine must have a rational and scientific basis a correct anatomy and physiology Physiological phenomena are dependent upon vital action. Chemical and other forces may and do act at times and under certain circumstances, within the organism, but their resulting phenomena do not constitute vitality.

Before us are two existing facts, matter and force Force is substantial, inherent with and inseparable from matter. Gravitation is the force one body has to attract another body in proportion to its size and density The force of gravitation is constant and the larger and denser the body the stronger the force, Then too, we have the force of electricity of magnetism, of heat, of light and of vitality Everything in the universe is in motion and governed by force of one kind or another, or by two or more forces combined. Heat is the great force in nature in opposition to gravity. Heat carries material things from the earth. can be seen, and is substantial. Heat is an attenuating force and is the most important remedial agent in the whole Materia Medica

The properties of a medicine constitutes its force: and so of a food The force of plant growth is absorption. The force of a substance gives character to that substance. The force of an agent when administered changes the condition of the man

Living matter is the seat of vital action, non-living matter is the seat of chemical phenomena When the vital force deserts living matter ,then chemical force decom-

poses and breaks it up into compounds. Matter assumes
one of three forms;

    Matter about to become living,

    Matter actually living, or

    Matter that has lived.

Such is the conversion ot pabulum into bioplasm and subsequently into formed material.

The first stage of life in all forms of organism is bioplasm
which is transparent, colorless, structureless and semi-
fluid, exhibiting certain peculiar motions, changes of shape
and dimensions as influenced by the vital force and surrounding circumstances. But the vital force dose not act
thus on any other form of matter. Pabulum is fluid, but a
reduction in volume takes place when converted into bioplasm, and a still further reduction takes place in being
converted into formed material, hence the necessity for
the regular supply of proper pabulum. In condensation
bioplasm is formed into cells or tissue elements. These cells
unite in definite arrangement and form tissues, structures,
organs and the living body.

The motion observed in living matter is vital action and
the result is function. There can be vital action and no
function, because there is living matter, where there is no
structure, without which there can be no function, and yet
there is vital action.

The ultimate intended result of all organism is the reproduction of its kind, and the starting point is bioplasm.

Food subtances are such as furnish proper pabulum for
the sustenance and reproduction of bioplasm during normal action.

Remedies are substances whose constituents are especially adapted to arouse and sustain extraordinary actions of bisplasm during disease.

A poison is a substance having an inherent deleterious
property, rendering it capable of destroying life in some
degree by whatever avenue it is taken into the system. A
substance ordinarily capable of destroying bioplasm can
not be classed as a true remedy. Poisons produce disease;
they are given for that purpose; hence their presence in the
system is physiologically criminal. True medicine acts in
harmony with the wants of the vital force in it's opposition
to disease. The one legitimate object of medicine is the restoration of the diseased body to a state of health. This is the
line of action of the vital force and when nature calls for

help, true medication must answer that call by harmonious
action Vital action arouses all its energies to resist disease and prevent death, thus frequently cures are effected
without medicine Blood, bone and muscle cannot be fur-
ished by any chemical process; but by suitable pabulum for
bioplasm which shall become formed material and organic
structures. In the blood we find fluid plasma holding in
solution nutrients for the white blood corpuscles which are
semi-fluid, converting digested food substances into its
own substance and finally into red blood corpuscles which
carry oxygen throughout the entire body and maintain
vitality.

All things influence the organism either favorably or un-
favorably, either increasing or diminishing the chances of
life by the supply of proper or improper pabulum These
chances are also varied by external circumstances, changes
of temperature, violence, habits and labor

In the work of restoration the attempt must be to restore to some extent the opposite condition of that abnormally existing If the parts are congested apply heat and
relieve the circulation. If the body is emaciated give
proper food and sustain digestion If there be too much
relaxation stimulate to the relief of such abnormal relaxation If there be too much rigidity, relax to the relief of
that rigidity

Diseased tissues are already weakened; and agents that
carry the tissues from the normal will act as still farther
causes of disease, because the diseased parts are more or
less incapable of resistance.

Narcotics benumb the body disable bioplasm, debilitate
the heart, weaken the nerves and interfere with a speedy
recovery Narcotics may and do ease pain; but they debilitate the vital force at the time she needs all her energies.
Do you recognize an imperfect or perverted act of the
vital force? Do not narcotize but determine the cause; ascertain the necessities of the vital force and medicate accordingly, with the utmost discrimination

Excitement is a function, excessive in action because of
some injurious impression having been made, but that excitement is the grand medium for the removal of obstructions, and for the maintainence of normal action So with
fever and inflammation They are but indications of nature for your guidance in order to proper medication. Nature throws her special energy where most needed, so

with a cough, it is a vital act for the purpose of removing some offending substances from the lungs, bronchi, or larynx. To narcotize the patient so that he cannot cough might leave nature helpless in the presence of dangerous substances she by that cough is trying to dislodge.

It is better that functional disturbances exalt the system above normal, then that the whole system be so depressed that the circulation be below normal. Either condition would respectively express the resistive power of the vital force. Departure from the normal may be in extremely varied degrees, and remedial measures must be similarly varied.

Different parts of the body may be in different conditions at the same time; the bowels may be tense and the skin lax; the head may be hot and brain hyperæmic and the feet cold; the heart pulsations may be much above normal and yet the surface may not be hot, even warm; there may be a tense uterus while the limbs are cold and clammy.

Some organs that are closely related may be either similarly or dissimilarly affected. Both liver and stomach may be relaxed, and yet we frequently find the stomach relaxed while the liver is tense and engorged. The uterus and urethra may both be influenced or the one only may suffer inflammation.

The human system is a most wonderful commingling of tissues, structures and organs demanding most careful study of him who would be a physician, and yet in the art of curing disease we can but influence to contract and relax with varied degrees of rapidity and energy in imitation of nature's way of useing these structures in health.

Remedies must be combined according to the structures to be impressed, and in strength or dose according to the remedial impressions desired. Make your compounds as simple as possible. Do not think that because from 25 to 50 drugs are combined in a preparation that it is a panacea.

Three principles of influence pervade the entire science of medicine *Relax, Stimulate, Astringe.* These three well applied are your passwords to the inner sanctum of success. The whole person or some of his parts may be too rigid as we find in hysteria, convulsions, chordee, tetanus, or stiff neck. Here our medication must be of a relaxing character. But the whole person or some part may be too much relaxed as in anæmia, night sweats, paralysis, chorea apoplexy, epilepsy, nervous prostration, diarrhœa. or leucorrhœa. Here there is a necessity for medication that will be stimulating and sustaining to nerve sensibility.

In the treatment of disease make your patient's food subservient to your medication. Have proper food, properly prepared and regularly given. Then both food and medicine will become instrumental under the vital force in the restorative act Some foods are stimulating in their nature as graham flour, beef, beets, cranberries, parsley, sour apples. pie plant. Some foods are astringent as boiled milk, thickened milk. fine flour, crab apples, arrow root Some foods are relaxing to the system, as turnips, sweet apples, asparagus Great care must be taken that the patient be not fed too much. More food can be given than can be assimilated, or the wrong class of foods may be given.

An excess of either food or medicine, or the wrong kind of either food or medicine though either in themselves may be innocent, may place tissues in such condition that for the time being they can be but imperfectly used by the vital force What folly it would be to use lobelia in paralysis or apoplexy, or to use asclepias tuberosa in malignant diphtheria; or to use tannin in case of constipation. Each food or medicine holds a more or less fixed relation to the organism, and expends its influence on particular tissues or organs Syi. juglans cinerea especially influences the lower bowel; léptandra virg influences the liver tubuli. ipomea jalapa influences the alvine mucous membrane, eupatorium purpureum influences the kidneys and asclepias tuberosa influences the skin This will ordinarily be as true if these agents, two or more of them, be combined as when used separate

But how shall we form a correct estimate of an agent as to its remedial effects in order to our selection of a sanative remedial agent. No correct estimate can be formed usually unless there be numerous observations of the influence of the agent by itself The effect of large and small doses must be carefully observed as also the cumulative effect of continuous doses. The patient must be carefully watched to see if the vital force gives a favorable or unfavorable response Can it be given persistently without any destructive influence to bioplasm Here the skillful use of the microscope is very valuable. Then too we must take into consideration that chemical union may have much to do in forming innocent compounds out of otherwise deleterious substances.

Let us take a few examples of substances that are ordinarily used as medicines.

Strychnine acts quickly, within ten or fifteen minutes.
The person first complains of stiffness about the neck and
presents the aspects of terror. There is an impression of
calamity or death. Soon the head is jerked back, the limbs
extended, the back tetanic and the mouth drawn, in a few
minutes these symptoms pass and there is rélaxation, but
on the slightest movements of the body these spasmodic
efforts return, and usually continue tell the body succumbs
in about a half hour. One forty-thousandth part of a
grain of strychnine will destroy living tissue. Such is its
action in death toxic doses. We could not recommend this
agent.

Aconite and its alkaloid *aconitine* will prove fatal in
1-16 gr. dose. It produces a peculiar burning, tingling and
numbness of the parts to which it is applied. Large doses produce violent vomiting and more or less paralysis of motion
and sensation, great depression of the heart and death from
syncope. Intelligence remains until the last. This drug
is not such as we could recommend.

Belladonna and atropine dilate the pupils, and give
a rapid pulse, a hot, dry, flushed skin, and an eruption similar to scarlatina, soreness of throat, difficulty of swallowing, intense thirst and a gay mirthful delirum. Neither
could we recommend this agent.

Chlorine & Bromine are powerful irritants. Inhaled
fumes provokes spasms of the glottis and then induces inflammation of the respiratory mucous membrane, which
may prove fatal. These drugs we could not recommend.

Mercury (Hydrargyrum) is given internally, chiefly for
two purposes, to check inflammation and promote absorption
and to antagonize syphilitic virus. In continued doses
it produces salivation, first giving a metalic taste, then
soreness of the gums, an undue flow of saliva and foetor
of breath. Then come swelling of the tongue, ulceration
of the mouth and disease of the jaw bones. The blood becomes impoverished and the loss of flesh and feverishness
ensues. Its action on the liver is uncertain. Inhalation of
its fumes gives tremor of the nerves.

Calomel (Hg. Cl.), subchloride of mercury is one of
the mildest forms of mercury. It acts on the secretory organs and stimulates the liver and intestinal glands to increased activity. Jalap is usually added as a purgative.

Calomel increases hepatic action and thence peristaltic action, but it exhausts the liver by excessive stimulation and leaves it more or less congested which may lead to to chronic enlargement, tenderness, hardening, abscesses and cancer Hence we could not make this agent a part of of our materia medica.

Opium gives at first a feeling of exaltation Then symptoms of cerebral congestion with face suffused or cyanosed and pupils contracted with skin hot and dry, breaththing slow, deep and finally stertorous In approaching unconsciousness the person may be aroused by shouting in the ear and then will respire more rapidly Then comes prostration, coma more or less profound, pupils become pinpoints and then widely dilated toward the end of life Respiration now slows, the face becomes pallid and cyanosed and a heavy perspiration follows which is at first warm and then cold and clammy. The pulse increases and then feebles Such is the action of opium in death-toxic doses It carries every tissue into a dangerous state of insensibility, and hence cannot be considered a part of our materia medica

From these illustrations it is evident that poisons destroy bioplasm and carry the organs farther from the normal standard, at least removes them more or less from under the control of the life power. Taken internally or applied externally they produce disease and lengthen the period of sickness We must confess that some poisons may be used for a time with seeming advantage. Calomel secures hepatic discharges and morphine usually secures sleep There are times when such results are necessities In fact many persons do take poisons and yet they live; and at times it would seem to be to some advantage in the restoration of certain faculties How is it possible that we should destroy true life to save life and yet assist nature by the process of that destruction? It is claimed that if a new disease can be produced in the exact site of the one already existing, it may possibly supercede the latter, and if the new disease subside without injury, the patient may be cured By other schools of medicine poisons are given to produce disease, not accidentally nor incidentally but with the fullest intent. Some of these produce diseased conditions which last through life, and the patients become miserable chronics. Frequently it is within the power of the organism to dispose of these poisons, but sometimes it results in death and then it is termed heart-failure.

A poison then has some deleterious property which renders it capable of destroying life by whatever avenue it is
taken into the system, whether by application, inhalation
or imbibition and whether they be in their nature corrosive,
inflammatory or such as effect the nerves of sensation
and motion.

I have given these few examples of agents that we do not
wish to recognize in our materia medica, in order that we
may see their unnatural influences and sequelæ, and realize
that they do not harmonize with vital efforts. Too often
patients are recovering from some sickness with aching
bones, stiffened joints, trembling nerves, and ruined digestion, abscesses on the lower limbs, decayed teeth or some
difficulty clinging to them the rest of their days as the result of poisonous treatment. Many a case is prolonged into
weeks and months which could have been cured by Physio-
Medical treatment in a much shorter period and without
leaving unpleasant sequelae.

To be able to relieve pain is both excellent and necessary.
To this end many drugs have been used as morphine, co-
deine, chloral, aconite, belladonna, the bromides, phenace-
tine, antikamnia &c. Morphine perphaps stands first and
is used to an alarming extent. If the ordinary Allopath
of to-day were debarred from using whiskey, morphine,
& quinine he would be almost compelled to give up business.

In health there is no pain. All is ease and comfort.
When some of the structures are not attuned to the vital
force, uneasiness ensues and pain results. The intensity
of pain will depend much on the tissues affected and the
severity of the cause. Pain is not the disease, but is a consequence of disease, of some injury received or of the accumulation of more or less morbific materials. The presence of dust in the eye may produce pain; the accumulation of fæces may produce enteralgia; and presence of gall
stone in the gall duct, or the descent of a calculus into the
urethra may produce pain in these localities. If any of
these conditions were present and no pain resulted, it
would most assuredly indicate that the parts were too nearly dead to recognize the presence of obstructions or make
any struggle in order to relief.

Pain is the announcement of something wrong in the
system; the relief of pain is to be sought in the removal of
that which gave rise to it. Morphine usually relieves,

but it is at the expense of vitality. It relieves no obstructions, re-establishes no suppressed functions, relieves the system of no offending substances, but usually leaves the nervous system much irritated and the whole system less able to eliminate the provoking cause, and less liable to recognize remedial measures Sensibility is benumbed and the causes of disease are left to care for themselves Benumbed sensibility is not natural sleep and hence not as beneficial as natural sleep In the latter the whole system is at rest; in the former the vital force is, so far as it is not benumbed in a state of resistance. Physiologically an exalted sensibility is to be preferred See the wrecks narcotics leave; with muscles weak and motion irregular, with nerves in universal tremor and nutrition impaired; with the foundation of intelligence prostrated they resemble the inebriate, poor emaciated wrecks, mentally and physically Insanity from this cause is least amenable to treatment

It is frequently urged that the size of the dose determines whether the agent be a poison But this is not possible Whether the dose be an infinitessimal one or one of allopathic proportions cannot change the real character of the agent. The results of either dose of the same strength of the agent will be proportionate to the size of the dose and of the ability of vitality to resist Quantity cannot alter quality The Homeopath understands this in the administering of his infinitissimal dose A small dose will excite less vital resistance and will be the more surely lodged in the system.

But we hear it said that some poisons provide certain needed elements to the body. They seem to forget that dead matter and not living matter or the living man, is the proper domain of chemistry

Because a substance is found in the gastric juice after death is not always evidence that the substance was there during life in normal action. Blood and bone and muscle are manufactured by no chemical process, but under the influence of the vital force in the distributing of proper pabulum for the growth of bioplasm, and thence formed material. Man is a vital structure and not a chemical labratory.

The Materia Medica of Physio-Medicalism is replete with agents that are perfectly safe and powerful in assisting the vital force in the work of restoration They cure rapidly, effectually and without benumbing the system or

causing disease. Such a system meets the approval of
every man's common sense, stands the surest test of scien-.
tific criticism and shows its superiority over all other systems. Indeed we plead a grand reform in the theory and
practice of medicine; a complete revolution in the art
of healing, and demand that true medicine is a science
and not a mass of arbitrary dictums. Physio-Medicalism
demands the highest place in Medical Education, requiring exact observation of all physiological phenomena, for
these are our accurate guide in all our efforts to cure.

Frequently you will hear it said by physicians of other
schools that your cases were not so ill as theirs. This is an
unintentional compliment. It is good evidence that their
use of poisons complicate disease and make their cases
worse. We medicate in harmony with nature and our
cases are soon cured.

All drugs do not influence the same class of tissues;
each agent has its favorite locality for its special influence
and each has its own peculiar mode of action. Leptandra
virg. influences the secretory tubuli of the liver, eupatorium purpur. influences the kidneys; arctostaphylos uva ursi
influences the urinary mucous membrane; solidago canadensis stimulates and tones the alvine mucous membrane;
cornus florida is an astringent to the mucous membrane;
asclepias tuberosa influences the skin and capillary circulation, lobelia inflata relaxes muscular and nerve tissue;
caulophyllum lends special influence to the uterine nerves,
while scutelaria is a general stimulating nervine, Thus
it is evident that the same remedy may be made to subserve
a valuable purpose in more than one disease.

The functions of organs and tissues are animal and veg-
etative or organic. Animal functions comprise locomotion
innervation and special sense. The organic comprise digestion, absorption, circulation, respiration, secretion, generation, and the developement of heat, light and electricity.
Medicine does not produce function; this is the work of the
organism. Each medicine makes its own peculiar impressions by going the round of the circulation. Contact, penetration and absorption must take place prior to complete
impression. Get your agents to the place where they are
most needed and by the shortest route possible. The nerve
structures and ganglia convey remedial impressions,
and by these and the circulation, the influence of some
medicines is almost instantaneous. This is well exempli-

hed in the influence of the third preparation of lobelia, wherein is combined intense stimulation and relaxation

Symptoms are abnormal functions dependent upon certain diseased conditions. The symptom is the sequent rather than the diseased condition. The symptom is not the disease and is not the thing to be medicated As soon as the diseased condition is removed the symptom is not present To medicate symptoms leads to narcotism and to specific remedies for special symptoms.

Each abnormal condition usually manifests a plurality of symptoms. The relation and inter-relation of organs, tissues and structures necessarily leads to the involving of adjacent and related structures.

Pain is not always manifested in the diseased part, but is sometimes felt at some distance from the part diseased A pain or uneasiness felt under the left shoulder blade will frequently be the result of a chronically inflamed ovary. The same cause has frequently given rise to a pain down the inside of the thigh or at the knee. The patient is more or less congested and a diarrhœa following a period of constipation is the result. Your patient needs not to be narcotized to relieve that pain, equalize the circulation, relieve the congestion, and the pain ceases without the use of narcotics Your patient has an aching back; it may be from some irritating cause in the kidneys, rectum, uterus or from one of several other causes. The cause must be sought and relieved. Your patient is nauseated or vomiting It may be from some injury to the extremities, from some condition of the stomach, from pregnancy or from other causes Ascertain the provoking cause and medicate accordingly, diagnose carefully the cause with the utmost precision. It may be that your patient has a headache. Such might arise from one or other of a dozen causes The ordinary headache powder may be far from relieving the cause of that headache

One thing is of especial importance, carefully differentiate between a normal vital effort, a vital effort resisting disease, and a vital effort under the influence of remedial measures Carefully differentiate between the disease and the efforts of the vital force in resisting disease. Inflammation, fever and pain are not diseases, but physiological manifestions of extraordinary bioplastic action They are indications of the degree of vital action in the effort to overcome disease, whether it be for the removal of obstructions, the replacing of destroyed cells, or other important aids to the restoring of a healthy condition.

Dysentery and diarrhœa are occasionally vital efforts to wash away through the alvine canal some offending substances.

Cough it a vital effort to cast off some material obstructing the bronchi or pulmonary tubuli.

In all cases of either extra or depressed vital effort, carefully diagnose what must be the conditions present that should cause the vital force to put forth such efforts for its relief. Such diagnosis will furnish you the indications for scientific medication. The heart as the center of the circulation feels to a greater or less degree all deleterious impressions; and the greatest care must be used in diagnosing the true cause of whatever trouble may be present. A stomach with fermented contents may make one feel as if there is heart trouble; and so may hysteria. The heart quickens its pulsations according to the arterial tension present. It is a great mistake to give antipyrine and drugs of that class, attempting to reduce fever by depressing the heart's action, instead of furnishing those agents which will relieve arterial and capillary tension, and thus relieve the necessity for the condition of the heart. Such drugs as antipyrine suppress vital manifestations instead of removing the causes. You are but a clerk about the vital establishment whose duty it is to act in harmony with the head of the firm in all its restorative acts, and not to attempt to paralyse its efforts.

It is usually true that an agent will similarly influence organs either similar in structure or intimately related Asclepias tuberosa influences the serous membrane, as well as the mucous membrane and the skin. Aristolochia serpentaria influences the circulation, the skin and the kidneys. Zingiber influences the circulation and the skin. Lobelia influences the nervous and muscular tissue.

'Many remedies influence more than one structure, some are quite general in their influence, and yet many confine their chief influence almost entirely to one structure.

Many agents having a general influence over the structures will expend their force either where most needed or in the directions whither they may be influenced by other medicines. In labor, lobelia will influence the os uteri more than elsewhere; while in croup, hepatitis, pleuritis,

bronchitis and pneumonia, lobelia will chiefly influence
the part that most needs to be relaxed. Lobelia combined
with honey or sugar, which are expectorants, will mostly influence the lungs and bronchi and is an expectorant
Lobelia with laxatives will assist in producing catharsis

In a sensitive and irritated condition of the stomach,
lobelia given in small doses and at regular intervals will
give gentle relaxation, ease and comfort   But should the
stomach be already too relaxed instead of irritated, lobelia
would be much out of place. According then to the conditions present and the mode of administering, lobelia will
either arrest emesis or produce emesis; leptandra will
either produce catharsis or check catharsis; capsicum
will either produce diaphoresis or check diaphoresis. But
these conditions are not diseases but efforts of vitality to
free the system of offending substances. The conditions
present and the necessities therefor govern the action of
the medicine.

In labor where the pains are inefficient, capsicum will
lend its principal influence to the uterus and become a
first class parturient   In conditions of extreme torpor of
of the liver, skin or bowels the influence of capsicum will
be felt as required in either direction.

In case of menstrual suppression cimicifuga racemosa
will chiefly influence the uterus, in case of nervous irritability it will influence the entire nervous system, assisting in the relief of the irritability present; and yet in
rheumatism its influence will be mostly felt by the serous
membrane the part then most needing relief

Some agents influence two or more organs or classes of
tissue   Such agents may be made to act principally on
either by properly combining with some agent which acts
more especially on one of them. Apocynum androsæmifolium combined with an excess of eupatorium purpureum
both will thoroughly influence the kidneys and be excellent for dropsy. It will do likewise if combined with serpentaria in cold infusion only, with a much more stimulating influence   Many agents that influence the generative
organs as caulophyllum, convallaria, mitchella, viburnum
prun and trillium, when combined with some agent or
agents in excess that especially influence the respiratory
organs, both agents will combine their influence upon the
lungs.

Some agents may be made to influence one of several or-

gans by thus combining. Capsicum with hepatics acts on
the liver; with cathartics influences the bowels; with
medicines that influence the uterus it will extend its influence in that direction; if the surface be congested capsicum with asclepias tub. will secure a good free perspiration; but if the skin be lax and the perspiration too free then
capsicum either alone or in combination with some tonic
will assist in stopping the excess. Uva ursi will assist in
cystic catarrh or in vaginal leucorrhœa as may be needed
or as influenced by other medicines. The same is true of
convallaria multiflora. It tones the mucous membrane of
the uterus or of the respiratory organs as required by
the vital force or as influenced by other remedies. Hydrastis is a very fine tonic to the stomach, but when combined
with diuretics it will tone the renal organs; combined with
cathartics it will tone the alvine canal; with hepatics it
will tone the liver and portal circulation; and so when
combined with agents that specially influence the generative or the respiratory organs.

In some spasmodic conditions as asthma large quantities
of lobelia may be given without producing emesis or even
nausea.

In case of gall stone large portions of saccharated podophyllin may be administered without nausea or excessive
catharsis as it would do under other circumstances.

Then too the mode of preparing a medicine and the
mode of administering it have much to do with produce-
ing the desired influence. Saccharated podophyllin acts
positively upon the gall ducts and gall cyst and tends to
liquify the gall, but non-saccharated podophyllin seems to
have a more direct influence upon the bowels and produces
catharsis. In hot infusion serpentaria influences diaphoresis, but cold preparations are diuretic.

In hot infusion aralia hispidia influences the circulation
and skin, but cold preparations are diuretic. In hot infusion anthemis nobilis influences the circulation, but cold
preparations are tonic to the mucous membrane.

The nearer the tissues are brought to the normal the
greater will be the influence of the remedies used, for then
the vital force makes the best use of these remedies.
Hence the nearer the tissues assume their normal condition
the less medicine will be necessary. and those medicines of
less power will be preferred. If the skin be but slightly inactive it will take but little ascleplas tuberosa and zingiber

to arouse capillary circulation and will be better than serpentaria for that purpose. If the liver be but slightly torpid, taraxacum will suit better than podophyllin If the kidneys be but slightly ailing eupatorium purpureum will will be better than juniper. The recognition of these facts will enable you to administer your remedies with greater accuracy, and with greater benefit to your patient. It is as important to know how and when to stop medication, as to know how to begin medication Never use strong medicines nor larger doses in the beginning of your treatment, if not adsolutely essential

It is also well that we carefully observe that indirect functional results may be due to vital action One part may be diseased through sympathy with other diseased parts Seek first to relieve the part first diseased and if the involvement of the second part be not of too long standing, it too will soon be relieved.

Cathartics as such do not act on the skin; and yet free catharsis will frequently be followed by more or less perspiration. In cases of congestion or inflammation such catharsis may very profitably be followed by a thorough course of diaphoretics Not unfrequently free catharsis will relieve a headache, especially if it be from a foul stomach or torpid liver but it should be followed by liver medicines rather than the use of quinine as is popularly practiced Hyperaemic conditions are best relieved by equalizing the circulation Catharsis and diaphoresis and sometimes emesis are the great means to be used for this purpose.

Medicines are specific to conditions and not to disease as such. Diseases are to be studied each as a combination or complication of conditions Remedies must be selected and used with reference to their ability to restore the tissues to their normal condition; medication must change as the conditions change. Treat the conditions as they are and change as developments may demand. Relaxation, stimulation and astringency are your watch words. These must be varied or combined to suit the conditions present at the time of prescribing In acute diseases the changes must be watched, for they will be more frequent than in chronic cases, where the changes are less abrupt and usually require more stimulation Some cases need relaxation only, some need relaxation and stimulation, some need astringency, some stimulation and astringency; some need stimulation and some need stimulation and relaxation.

Some agents are almost pure relaxants as asclepias tuberosa, cypripedium pubescens and leptandra virginica. Some agents are pure stimulants as capsicum. Some agents are pure astringents as tannin, and some agents have these qualities combined in various degrees as myrica, cornus, and hamamelis.

In selecting your agents as a rule use the depurative first to thoroughly cleanse the system. Then gently stimulate and tone as the case may demand. Relaxing agents expend their power more toward the surface, while the stimulating and astringent agents tend more toward the centres.

Leptandra virginica is an excellent hepatic favoring the secretion of bile, but it is nearly always best to add some diffusive stimulant as zingiber, or some stimulating and toning agent as euonymous atropupureus or taraxacum dens leonis. Even at times a little capsicum will assist. Capsicum is invaluable for its action on the heart and arteries, but in cases of nervous prostration its impressions are best diffused when combined with scutelaria.

Relaxants are rendered more active by the addition of a diffusive stimulant or a stimulant; as asclepias tuberosa and zingiber, or lobelia inflata and capsicum. In this last combination by the presence of the relaxant, the lobelia, the capsicum is rendered more diffusive; and its influence is felt more widely than had it been administered by itself.

Too much relaxation must be avoided, it may lead to exhaustion.

Hot water is a diaphoretic, hence the hot infusion of diffusive diaphoretics most readily secures diaphoresis. Capsicum is not a diaphoretic except in hot infusion; hot water gives it a diffusive tendency toward the surface from the heart.

In the use of alterants it is best to give them by themselves, using them in sufficent quantity to make a decided impression of whatever character is needed.

Physics as a rule should be separate and should be given only as occaion demands and in quantity sufficient to produce quick or tonic results as desired. Never allow the system to become accustomed to them. Instead thereof inculcate a positive habit of going to stool every morning immediately after the morning meal.

Some medicines when rubbed upon the skin will exert

more or less of their influence by being absorbed Lobelia
applied over the lungs is an admirable relaxant. Applied
over an ulcer or a denuded surface will produce nausea
This would readily prove the principle of absorption. Leptandra, apocynum androsæmifolium and capsicum·ap-
plied over the liver and gall cyst will powerfully influence
these organs This is just as true of poisons. Mercury
applied to the surface will produce salivation. Atropine
applied to the eye will widely dilate the pupil. Opium
will contract the pupil to a mere pin point. Cocaine will
benumb the surface to which it is applied The influence
of medicines by absorption is slower but more permanent
The same is true whether it be of the skin the rectum or
the vagina

Hypodermic injections produce more rapid effect Physio-medicalists need not throw aside the hypodermic needle
because it has been in bad company and been used to inject
poisons. Many of our agents may be used hypodermically
and with good success

Medicines in liquid form and especially in hot infusion
act with greater rapidity than those in solid or pill form
Resonoids usually require sometime to thoroughly dissolve
if taken in capsule or otherwise

Syrup forms are best for coughs Give in small doses and
frequently, and direct that no water be taken immediately
thereafter

In acute febrile cases the hot infusion surpasses all others
They open the pores and keep them open, so that an
amount of detritus escapes from the body which would
otherwise do mischief. The surface is more easily cleansed, and the patient is kept far more comfortable. The
temperature is more readily reduced and in accordance with
correct physiology the patient is more readily cured

Make your preparations as pleasant as possible Use little sugar except in cough syrups and liver medicines Use
as little medicine as you can, but as much as you must to
make your medicines effective Do not weary the organs by
continuing any medicine too long Be careful in your diagnosis, never fall into a routine practice; make your prescriptions with precision and confidence; keeping ever before
you the infallible standard of normal anatomy and physiology and carefully estimate the variations therefrom.

At times the stomach may be in such a condition as to
prevent the acting of some medicines in cold forms Then

give hot water, hot infusions, an emetic, a physic, or all of
them if needed.

Poultices, fomentations and liniments are very valuable aids in many conditions. In sprains, swellings, inflammations, congestions, abscesses or ulcers. Agents, relaxing, stimulating or astringent may be used as required by
the conditions present.

Rectal injections assist catharsis, relieve intestinal invagination, assist in emesis where you cannot give lobelia
per orem, and in tetanus to secure thorough relaxation,
Rectal injection is a valuable means of feeding and sustaining the system when food cannot be retained by the
stomach.

Small doses of medicine frequently given will accumulate
in force but each succeeding dose must be given before the
former dose has expended its force within the system.

Study well the temperament of your patient, the conditions of the structures affected, the age, the sex, the a-
mount of vitality possessed by the patient, the locality and
the general surroundings. Take all these things into consideration and then seek:—

1. To relieve the alvine canal and the secernents.

2. Equalize the circulation, relieving the surface and
sustain the heart.

3. Sustain and tone the nervous system:

Some one or other of the secernents may be too tense or
may be too lax, in either case torpor will arise and inac-
tivity of the organs will result in more or less toxaemia. It
may be from torpidness of the liver and result in cholaemia,
or from torpidness of the kidneys and uraemia be the result.
Indeed both may be present at the same time and great
prostration be the result.

In relieving the secernents, care must be taken to ascertain the condition of each class of tissue. Each must be
relaxed or stimulated as required. But no organ must be
overworked to accomodate the condition of torpor in some
other organ. It is frequently true, that the kidneys are
overworked to accomodate the torpor of the liver. perhaps
not intentionally, but nevertheless in reality. Frequently
the kidneys are found carrying off material that should
have been carried off by the liver.

Influence each secernent to a degree resembling the normal action of that secernent. In overcoming constipation
use only such medication as will assist in producing normal

action of the bowels once daily. Such action will be tonic rather than forced action. Positively demand that the patient shall accomplish daily evacuation by persistent regularity of habit. For chronic cases where it will be necessary to medicate for sometime, it is best to make some slight change in medicine so that the system shall not weary of the medicine nor become accustomed to it.

The system wearies of the long continued use even of the same diet The quantity of food required differs very materially in different persons, but it should be proportioned to the general vigor and relative waste in each case.

Some persons eat but little while others eat much and seem to be no better nourished Some persons seem to use up all the nutriment taken into the system, while others lay up much adipose material During sickness the former class will require a more liberal diet than the latter class who can live long on the adipose material scattered throughout the body. Such persons will eat but little and yet seem to be well nourished One trouble with such persons is that the secernents in fact all the organs are more or less prevented from doing their respective duties by being clogged with a superabundance of this fatty material.

Food substances contain starch, gluten and inorganic matter A positive food can be converted into pabulum.

Alimentation is the taking of food into the body whether it be per orem, per rectum or applied to the surface of the body Nutrition includes all the processes by which the body is built up and sustained. The process of digestion consists in dissolving food substances so as to be readily taken up and filtered through the walls of the blood vessels Reparation is the distribution of pabulum to the tissue elements and its being taken up by the living matter. Adipose tissue is composed of oil globules contained in dead cells In inanition the cell of the globule is taken up by the tissue and used and the oil is eliminated by the sebaceous glands It is this adipose tissue that gives rotundity to the frame and retains the animal heat.

The body is made up of different systems as the osseous, the muscular, the nervous and the articular.

The apparata are the circulatory, the digestive, the lachrymal, the urinary and the reproductive   .

The accessories are the nervous and muscular tissue.

The various tissues are bone, cartilage, fibrous, elastic, muscular, nervous, cellular and adipose.

Albumen, fibrin and earthy salts are the results of the death of living matter, and these can only become living matter by becoming suitable pabulum for other living matter.

The nutritious fluids are blood, chyme, chyle and lymyh.

The secretory fluids are saliva, gastric juice, bile, pancreatic juice, intestinal fluids, lachrymal, mucous and serous fluids.

The excretory products are sudoriferous and sebaceous perspiration and urine, carbonic acid gas from living air cells, billiary salts and lachrymal fluid.

Secretion is the taking of a fluid into the circulation with out causing any special disturbance. An excretion is not designed for the circulation, and is hence cast off. The mouth, stomach and intestines constitute one continuous canal.

That which influences the one either for good or for evil in any particular will more or less influence the entire tract. As all mucous tracts are external, food is not taken inside till it enters the circulation. The structural arrangement of all glands is the same whether secretory or excretory. The glands are emptied by the action of involuntary structures. Peyers patches are not glands as they have no ducts. They are poorly nourished and have but little circulation, and when this circulation is interrupted in the structures about them, their nourishment is cut off and results in sloughing as in typhoid fever, and may result in perforation of the bowel, and peritonitis and death soon follows.

The pancreas and liver are accessory to intestinal digestion. The gastric and peptic glands and juices are dissolvents. The pancreatic juice emulsifies the fats The bile is not well emulsified fat. The gall cyst is its receptacle, and the solidifying of the gall forms gall stones much as the accumulation of solids in the bladder forms calculi.

Starch is hydrated and then filtered into the blood. The intestinal juice converts the starch into sugar. The lymphatics are vessels situated in nearly all parts of the body and look knotted where the valves are located. Lymphoid bodies are capsules endowing parenchyma and celular tissue and in the channels of which are white blood corpusles.

The liver is the largest gland in the body. By fissures this gland is divided into lobes and these again are divided into lobules which are composed of hepatic cells fitting

closely together; polygonal in shape, one surface presenting to the blood vessels, portal veins, hepatic arteries and
veins. The billiary ducts are vessels between the hepatic
cells having racemose glands on the outer surface which are
secretory. The hepatic cells are excretory. The function of
the liver is to furnish bile and perhaps to secrete sugar.
Its physiological products are mainly secretory. There
are secretory lobules and excretory tubuli and ducts, and
a much larger venous than arterial circulation. Diagnose carefully the condition of each class of tissues and
medicate accordingly. Some remedies act mainly on the
secreting side of the liver, while others influence chiefly
the excreting department, while others influence both in
varying degrees. and others chiefly influence the portal
circulation. Whenever the secretory organs are affected
the circulation soon shows the effect in itself, and other
organs soon become affected. Torpor of the liver leads to
more or less disease throughout the body, and upon the relief of that torpor other abnormal conditions will begin
to subside.

Both the secreting and excreting functions of the liver
must be carefully watched. The secreting function may
be normal and yet there may be cholæmia. The excreting
function may be torpid and the bile though secreted in
quantity sufficient, hardens in the gall cyst and gall stones
may be the result.

The bile must now be quickly liquified or the most intense pain may result.

In cholæmia as well as in uræmia, not only is the circulation oppressed but the nervous system also deeply feels
its influence. The liver is usually the most torpid organ
of the body and usually requires more medication
than any other organ. Even after it has assumed its normal action it is frequently best to continue for a short time
a sustaining or toning treatment.

In the treatment of fever, whether of typhoid or mias-
matic origin this is especially true; for it must be remembered that a large amount of detritus and viri are eliminated through the liver and kidneys as well as by way of
the skin.

Medicines chiefly influencing the alvine tract have been
variously classed, but we shall here denominate them laxatives, carthartics and intestinal tonics, according to the
intensity of their ability to cleanse the intestines of their

contents and their ability to subsequently tone the mucous membrane.

Laxatives exert but a gentle influence upon the intestinal mucous membrane and are the best when that membrane is in a tense condition.

Cathartics are more powerful and are intended to thoroughly cleanse the alvine canal

Intestinal tonics are intended to stimulate and tone the alvine mucous membrane to normal action.

Those agents chiefly influencing the liver and assisting mainly in the secretion of bile are denominated hepatics; and those influencing the excretory function of the liver and gall cyst are denominated cholagogues. The bile excreted into the duodenum not only assists in the process of intestinal digestion but also influences normal catharsis. An excess of bile excreted at any one time may produce free catharsis.

Of those medicines that influence, the alvine mucous membrane, some are intestinal tonics and do not particularly influence catharsis, as hydrastis, some preparations of ferrum, gentiana, rhamnus purshiana and others Other agents are tonic cathartics, influencing the peristaltic action of the bowels; lead to catharsis and leave the bowels more toned for future action, as juglans cinerea. Still other agents are strictly cathartics and influence chiefly the cleansing of the bowels as ipomea jalapa, casia angustifolia, rhamnus catharticus and others. There results at times from persistent constipation or from other causes a semi-paralysed condition of the lower bowel. In such cases some positive stimulant or diffusive stimulant is needed to be combined with tonic cathartics.

One thing is positively essential; the exact condition of each tissue or class of tissues must be carefully diagnosed, and the abnormal condition relieved. The liver may be too lax or too tense to normally secrete bile: the gall ducts may be closed by hardened bile, or the mucous membrane may be too dry, irritated or sensitive. Catharsis merely will not relieve the liver except what may be derived from the relaxation following catharsis; neither will catharsis merely relieve the gall cyst; the thoroughly relaxing influence of lobelia may so relax the gall ducts as to relieve them of gall stone and yet lobelia is neither a cathartic, hepatic, nor chologogue.

Leptandra virginica influences chiefly in the secretion

of bile; podophyllin is a cholagogue; juglans cinerea is a tonic cathartic, while rhamnus catharticus is a cathartic.

Many agents have two or more of these qualities. Euonymous atropupureus and taraxacum dens leonis are tonics influencing both sides of the liver, and the gastric and intestinal mucous membrane as well. If the gall ducts are occluded, to give leptandra virginica would be to add to the misery of your patient by further distending the gall cyst. If the gall ducts are free, but the liver fails to secrete sufficient bile, then podophyllin would not be the agent to use; leptandra with some diffusive stimulant would be preferable, or some tonic agent might be better still as enonymous. Dyspepsia is not cured by mere catharsis, neither is chronic constipation. In dyspepsia, though the liver may be at fault, and there may be constipation, yet the mucus membrane itself is at fault.

Diarrhœa as well as constipation may either of them be a result of a failure of the liver to secrete and excrete bile. Do not expect to cure persistent constipation by the continued use of cathartics; these must be followed, when used, by alvine tonics.

Disease in one part of the alvine canal is not unfrequently felt throughout its extent. A sore throat may frequently be relieved by a good physic. In fact you need not ordinarily expect to cure throat diseases and torpid stomach troubles except by first thoroughly cleansing the intestinal tract, it may be by both emesis and catharsis. The same is true in the treatment of fevers, and indeed in the treatment of a majority of diseases; the alvine canal and its accessories demand first attention.

Here again we have certain agents that will extend their influence as the system requires or as influenced by other medicines. Capsicum is not a cathartic, but may be made to lend its stimulating power to cathartics in cases of extreme intestinal torpor.

Lobelia is not a cathartic, but may be made to lend its relaxing influence to cathartics in spasmodic conditions.

Normal secretion and excretion of bile is usually sufficient to stimulate to ordinary intestinal evacuations. An excessive discharge may produce a temporary diarrhoea.

Rectal injections may frequently be used to assist catharsis. These injections may be medicated and rendered stimulating or relaxing as desired.

Zingiber is not a cathartic, but is a fine diffusive stimulant to add to cathartics to prevent tenesmus and to render them more stimulating, diffusive and toning. Zingiber may be added to hepatics and tonic hepatics for the same reason.

Cathartics should only be occasionally administered; only when really demanded. Tonic cathartics are a better class of agents for persistent use, and these only as really demanded. When there is a weak stomach it is frequently best to administer the physic in broken doses. Excessive evacuations may lead to intestinal irritation. Aim to secure one free evacuation of the bowels each day. It is altogether probable that much of your practice will concern the digestive tract and hence it is well to be thoroughly prepared to meet every possible issue that may arise.

Diuretics induce a more or less increased flow of urine, which may or may not include much of the solids. Some agents increase the flow of the watery portion only, while other agents induce a marked increase of solids.

The fact that during diaphoresis the kidneys are less active is well worth noting when you have occasion to treat the opposite condition; in case of excessive or exhaustive renal discharges, diaphoresis to some degree should be induced. Resort may also be had to the vapor bath or to the hot water bath. During hot weather as a rule the flow of urine is less than in cold weather. So in case of general congestion, the kidneys are more or less burdened until the surface is relieved.

During the relaxation which follows a paroxysm or a hysterical convulsion there will usually be a free flow of urine. The same will frequently be a result following some considerable fright or excitement, whether of sorrow or of joy.

It is frequently true that too much medical attention is given to the kidneys. It is observed that they are not doing their duties properly, but we must not forget that when we search for a cause it will not always be found in the kidneys. The liver is frequently torpid and bile which should have been carried off by way of the gall cyst is eliminated by way of the kidneys. In such case the liver and not the kidneys is the organ to be medicated. As a rule the proper stimulation and relief of the liver is a great relief to the kidneys. Then too, constipation has much to do, when there is already irritation of the urinary tract, in increasing that irritation. Constipation will render a case of gonorrhea or gleet much worse than it would be otherwise. Keep the bowels free and the liver active and urethral irritation will be much less. Urethral irritation, if continued long, may induce vaginal and possibly uterine irritation.

The amount of excretion daily from the kidneys varies from 20 to 60 ounces. Its normal specific gravity is about 1020, but may range from 1010 to 1050. A specific gravity of 1030 or more indicates the presence of a superabundance of sugar, as in diabetes. A low specific gravity and diminished quantity indicates albuminaria. A persistent foam in urine indicates the necessity for a careful investigation for the presence of either sugar or albumen. Highly colored urine indicates the presence of an excess of solids, at times amounting to a so-called brick-dust sediment. In such condition the urine is usually scanty.

The reaction of normal urine when voided is acid, but after standing some time it becomes more or less alkaline.

Relaxing nervines as nepeta cataria, cypripedium pubescens or lobelia inflata usually increase the flow of urine upon the general principle of relaxation. Those agents gently stimulating to the mucous membrane as uva ursi, hamamelis, hydrastis or althea will usually increase the urinary flow.

In cases of more or less paralysis of the urinary apparata a diffusive stimulant as zingiber or serpentaria should be added to diuretics, and at times even the more positive stimulant capsicum, in order to secure a free flow of urine.

The female genito—urinary apparata are so situated and related that agents that influence the one will usually influence the other.

There may be a persistent scantiness of urine which may lead to an accumulation of solids and thence to the formation of calculi. Aralia hispidia, capsella bursa pastoris, agropyrum repens, mentha viridis, arctostaphylos uva ursi, eupatorium purpureum will each secure more or less freeness of urine and thus prevent the accumulation of solids. Juniperus communis, barosma betulina, sabal serrulata, piper cubeba are stimulating diuretics.

Urinalysis is a valuable aid in diagnosing the exact condition of each class of tissue and the microscope is a valuable assistant in determining the character of the solids evacuated. The diagnosis of disease by means of urinalysis and microscopy is an attainment worthy your best efforts. Each disease presents some more or less distinct appearances in the urine.

The liver, kidneys, and spleen are the cess pools of the body. It is of the greatest importance that these be kept well cleansed and sufficiently active to prevent uræmic or cholæmic poisoning to the general system. Typhoid fever requires some stimulation for the kidneys and so does dropsy; but in neither case would over-stimulation be appropriate. In typhoid fever it would be very likely to lead to depression. In dropsy the mere elimination of water would not be a cure of the condition present. The diet may have much to do with troubles of the urinary tract, and frequently a change of the daily dietary will be all that is necessary, or at least with but little medicine.

The *circulation* of the blood cannot be too carefully studied, and frequently demands the utmost care in medication. With the heart as the centre, the capillaries at the extremes and the arteries and veins connecting these extremes, each demands proper medication for the condition in which each may be found. The capillaries are the delicate vessels connecting the arterioles and venules and thus completing the circulation of the blood. Their walls are very thin and allow the exuding of the blood from the arterial to the venous system. The centre and propelling power of the circulation is the heart; the arteries convey the blood from the heart and the veins bring it back again for purification. The normal heart pressure on the capilaries is about 48 pounds to the square inch. The weight of blood compared to the weight of the body is about 12½ per cent., giving an average of about 18 pounds.

Anæmia is a more or less bloodless condition. Hyperæmia presents an abnormally increased supply of blood to a part. Congestion is an accumulation or overflow of blood in a part from mechanical obstruction, and precedes inflammation. It is an indication of bioplastic failure to withstand unnatural surroundings. The vital force has been compelled to more or less yield to some temporarily, superior obstructive influence.

Inflammation is increased vital energy in a part, resulting in more or less redness, swelling and pain. There is an increased nutritive activity usually according to the demand, and resulting in new formations. This in inflammation indicates the degree of vital resistance present, or

indicates the necessity therefor. The capillary walls being distended, their walls are much thinner and possess
greater transparency and hence show a brighter arterial
redness in the parts. The swelling is caused by the more
or less obstructed flow of blood through the parts, and the
still further increased flow as a result of increased vital
energy.

The epidermis is composed of dead cells in a more or less
mummified state. Some of these are constantly falling
off. The surface of the body needs very especial attention
from the physician. The skin has its circulation and its
two sets of excretory glands—the sudoriferous and the sebaceous.

A full, free and well proportioned circulation in all parts
of the body is essential to health and pleasure. Aim at all
times at the maintenance of such circulation. Let the
extremities be warmed by it, and the brain and trunk not
overcrowded. Relieve hyperæmia and anæmia so that the
blood makes its complete circulation in proper time, in
proper quality and in proper quantity, and the equilibrium is restored.

Each disease makes itself felt on the circulation in one
way or another. This is why we feel the pulse to discern
its character, and thus to diagnose the degree of vital resistance, the character of that resistance and the general
ability of the vital force to still further resist—whether
sthenic or asthenic. Thus it will appear that the vascular tissue may become too relaxed, too tense or more or
less irritable.

The pulse and the tongue are the two great indexes to
the abnormal conditions of the body. The former indicates
the degree that the abnormal condition is felt by the circulation, and the latter the degree that it is felt by the
digestive organs. It is not unfrequently true that if the
secernents are relieved, many other abnormal conditions
will cease. The cleansing of the liver, gall cyst, stomach,
bowels, kidneys and skin will secure normal action of the
heart and of the arterial and venous circulation. Especially do we find this to be true in the treatment of typhoid
and other fevers. This is the way to reduce the temperature physiologically. This leaves no depression of the
heart, but seeks to establish an equilibrium of the circulation, a thing which antipyrine, belladonna, aconite or
veratrum cannot do. These last agents leave the system

.more depressed and less able to care for itself. Such deleterious agents can but lead to more or less depression of the circulation and finally to heart failure.

If the secernents are not first freed, the blood current becomes more clogged with impurities, and the vital effort is necessarily more intense in action, the blood vessels become more irritated from the presence of abnormal contents and thence become abnormally tense and narrowed and able to carry only a smaller amount of blood at each pulsation. The blood current must have normal volume and force that it may properly nourish the entire body, and that it may also be capable of eliminating detritus or any impurity of its contents.

The secernents and the circulation may both be in a tense condition, then such agents as lobelia, eupatorium perfoliatum, cypripedium or some agent of similar influence will be needed. They will give general relaxation. But if both the circulation and the secernents be relaxed, then capsicum with some stimulating hepatics will be required. But occasions will arise when the circulation and the secernents may not be both relaxed nor both suffering from tensity. When such is the case each class of tissue must be medicated as they severally require.

This fact will also be observable. After the circulation and the secernents have been for some time abnormal the nervous system feels the effects, and this is perhaps nowhere more apparent than in typhoid fever where the pointed, quivering tongue is soon shown. In such cases the medication of the nervous system need only be such as is necessary to sustain.

As a rule some relaxation is necessary in the treatment in the beginning, while stimulation will be needed to continue throughout till each class of tissue shall have been toned to the performance of its respective duties,

The capacity of the capillary system is several hundred times that of the arterial system and hence the capillary requirements cannot be too carefully watched. A free capillary system is a necessity to a free arterial and venous circulation, and is frequently a great relief to cardiac excitement.

Cardiac stimulation must not be too strong; better give small doses and obtain an accumulative result.

Diffusives largely influence the arterial circulation but extend toward the capillaries.

Asclepias tuberosa, corallorrhiza odontorrhiza and sambucus canadensis in hot infusion are relaxing diaphoretics.

Xanthoxylum fraxineum aristolchia serpentaria, zingiber officinalis, polygonum hydropiper and asarum canadense in hot infusion are stimulating diffusives or stimulating diaphoretics They especially influence the arterial and capillary systems

Capsicum is the grandest of all cardiac stimulants and cereus grandiflora the greatest of all heart tonics.

If the capillaries are depressed as well as the heart, zingiber will sustain the arterial and capillary circulation, while capsicum will sustain the heart and arterial circulation. If more powerful stimulating diffusives are needed than zingiber then use serpentaria or xanthoxylum

The portal circulation and indeed the whole venous system is best sustained by hydrastis canadensis

In acute cases less stimulation and more diffusives are needed In chronic cases the stimulation will usually have to be increased, and tonics added

Hepatics, cathartics, stimulants and nervines will usually be more effective if combined with some diffusive, and a less dose will be required

Local applications will be found very efficient in influencing the capillaries, the secernents and the peripheral nerves A hyperæmic condition in many localities may be relieved by local relaxation and perhaps at times adding some stimulation Lobelia is one of the very best agents to be used as a local application to a tense surface It relaxes the capillaries and relieves the pain that would otherwise exist because of their distended condition

In a majority of the operations of surgery there is no better application than lobelia It relaxes the capillaries, relieves muscular tension and prevents hyperæmia to a considerable extent. So in dislocations, swellings, sprains and bruises. In thoracic hyperæmic conditions there is perhaps nothing superior to lobelia as an application, limiting the stimulation to a minimum proportion

Of course if the parts are cold, pale or relaxed then local stimulation is required Indeed local applications will be found beneficial to almost any part of the body, if the stimulation and relaxation be proportioned to the need of the respective parts, whether it be of the stomach, bowels, liver, spleen, peritoneum, ovaries, uterus brain, lungs or skin. Maintain the circulation by all possible means and prevent stasis of the blood. In some low conditions even a frequent change of the patient's position will for a time prevent stasis, which otherwise may be productive of much evil.

It must be remembered that all the parts of the vascular system may not all be in the same condition at the same time; so that the same quality of treatment that would be appropriate for one part of the system might not be appropriate for another part of the system. It is not unfrequently true that the capillaries may need relaxation and the heart need some degree of stimulation, as in most cases of eruptive diseases. But there are circumstances, many of them, when the body seems to have nearly all the circulation and the extremities are cold. This is especially true in parturition, gastritis, hepatitis, cystitis, pleuritis, &c.

With capsicum and cereus grandiflora for the heart; with hydrastis and gentian for the venous circulation; with xanthoxylum, myrica and polygonum for the arterial circulation; with ferrum for the intestinal circulation; with serpentaria, zingiber and asarum as stimulating to the capillaries, and with asclepias tuberosa, corallorrhiza and sambucus as relaxing to the capillaries you are well prepared to maintain the equilibrium of the circulation if it can be maintained.

As a rule medicines that influence the circulation, especially that of the capillaries, either by stimulation or by relaxation, more or less soothe the nervous system. This is especially true in diseases of an acute character. Other things besides medicine may influence the circulation. Mental confusion may bring a blush to the cheek. A hearty laugh or a vigorous exercise will give a better outward flow of blood, and so will a brisk rubbing of the surface. The application to the surface of an electric current will also induce a better superficial circulation. The process of mastication, digestion and reparation all influence the circulation more or less in those several directions. Fright or anger influence the circulation from the surface so that it will appear cold and pale. Shock of injury will lead to a somewhat similar result. Diseases of the nervous system, whether acute or chronic, also influence the circulation to a greater or less degree. But they are not always both influenced in the same direction. The one may require stimulation and the other relaxation. The demand of each condition must be met as required.

That class of agents which influence the circulation toward the surface are called diaphoretics. They are given in hot infusion and produce a warm perspiration. They may be either relaxing, as asclepias tuberosa, or stimulating, as serpentaria. Diaphoresis is one of the most valuable means of ridding the system of a large amount of offensive material, and of very materially shortening the duration of acute diseases. They are very valuable in all the eruptive diseases, and are not less important in typhoid and other forms of fever.

Diaphoretics primarily influence the surface but finally more or less influence the entire circulation. Capsicum primarily influences the heart but gradually proceeds toward the capillaries and especially so if a diffusive agent as zingiber is added.

If the whole system be hot, the skin dry, the heart impulse large, full and frequent; then relaxation is needed and relaxing diaphoretics alone are best. But if this condition of the skin be present and the heart impulse weak and wiry, then more or less stimulation must be added.

If the surface be congested diaphoretics of a more or less stimulating grade are required.

But another class of superficial glands demand our attention, the sebaceous or oil glands. These are especially deficient in action in scarlatina. The skin becomes intensely hot, dry and chaffy. Ordinary diaphoresis of the sudoriferous glands will not then suffice. The sebaceous glands must be stimulated to action. This is true to some extent in many eczemas. Such agents as arctium lappa semina, and helianthus annuus semina, and celastrus scandens cortex are among the best, and in order to accomplish the best results they should be given in hot infusion

Diaphoresis is one of the most valuable means of curing in a majority of cases. These millions of pores are the termini of a great human sewer system for the excretion of tissue detritus and various other injurious substances. If these remain closed the blood will soon be overwhelmed with deleterious accumulations, which will not only poison the circulation but may overwhelm the nervous system.

In acute febrile, inflammatory or congested conditions there is nothing equal to diaphoresis, whether accomplished by the steam bath, hot air bath or by diaphoretics in hot infusion. The two former means are rendered more effective by the addition of the latter in conjunction therewith. It matters little where the trouble may be, if the general circulation is involved, more or less diaphoresis is necessary. Whether the lungs, pleura, peritoneum, stomach, bowels, spleen, kidneys, bladder, uterus, brain, meninges, serous, mucous or muscular tissue, diaphoresis is essential. Equalize the circulation, sustain a full, free, superficial flow of blood and thus prevent hyperæmia in any locality. One of the best means for the relief of hemorrhage is the proper use of diffusive stimulants.

In acute dysentery and diarrhœa some degree of diaphoresis is frequently beneficial, and in dropsy and diabetes it is not unfrequently essential.

It must not be forgotten that surrounding circumstances, such as the proper warmth of the apartment, and the administering of the diaphoretic in hot infusion are points essential to be observed. Heat and hot water are themselves diaphoretics, but these are more fully discussed under the heading aqua. Heat, hot water, hot baths, hot broths and hot infusions are among our most powerful agents in this direction.

Sleep under certain circumstances will lead to more or less profuse perspiration. This however must be carefully watched. Under certain circumstances such perspiration if too profuse may be very weakening. This result must be guarded against. But while avoiding this extreme continue diaphoresis long enough and free enough to accomplish the required result.

Alterants are agents such as act on the blood current, toning the serous membrane and cleansing the current of some variety of impurity contained therein. In the broadest sense a large majority of our agents are alteratives, for they in some way tend to cleanse and tone the blood current. Indeed so do proper food, pure air, correct living and freedom from excesses in any direction.

Impurities may gain access into the blood current from many sources. It may be that the secernents are torpid and are not secreting or excreting in proper quantities. These secretions being retained in the system soon gain access to the blood current and some degree of septic influence is the result. It may be that the skin is retaining impure materials and these instead of being cast off, are retained and conveyed by the venous current again into the blood and constantly make it more foul. It may be that the lungs are being filled with impure air, or are supplied with an insufficiency of the same. In either case the blood becomes more or less deoxygenized, and worse still it becomes filled with still greater impurities. It may be that the food has been improper in preparation, in quantity or in quality, and thus improper pabulum has been conveyed into the system.

In order therefore that your alterative medicines may do the good intended to be accomplished, your patient must be supplied with proper food, proper air, proper clothing, proper exercise, and that he should have proper habits. and be given to no excesses. It will be your duty to see to those things and to administer your medicines so that the skin, stomach, bowels, mesenteries, kidneys and lungs are each doing their respective duties. Under these circumstances you can cleanse the blood current and your alterative medicines will be efficient. Else they will be more or less a failure in spite of your best efforts.

But remember that alteratives act slowly and promote a steady toning impression. It takes time for complete blood changes to occur. It sometimes takes months and even years to cleanse the blood current of some impurities. The quality of the whole blood current must be changed, and the secernents must be constantly toned to the ability of fully performing their respective duties.

To say then that an agent is an alterative is very indefinite. We must know the process or channels by which it accomplishes the elimination of any impurities from the system. Elimination may be either by way of the liver and bowels, the kidneys or the skin.

Alteratives may be relaxing, stimulating or toning. In chronic cases those of greater stimulating powers are needed than in acute cases. When eruptions of the skin are due to hepatic torpor, use such alteratives as have a decided tendency to influence the liver both in its secreting and excreting functions. General torpor of the secretions is more or less productive of impurity of the blood. So is idleness, a sedentary habit and constipation.

Physical activity in pure air and sustained by good food and pure water, and having good habits are the grand accessories to good health and pure blood.

To receive and to transmit impressions is pre-eminently the office of the *nervous* system. A leading manifestation of disease is pain, which is an exalted condition of the sen-

sory nerves arising from a greater or less degree of irritation which has been caused by the introduction of some
offending substance either locally or constitutionally.
Pain is an evidence of the presence of some disease, injury
or obstruction. Whenever and wherever there is loss of
sensibility from any cause, such part or parts or the whole
system is liable to suffer therefrom, because the vital force
is not or cannot be aroused to its proper protection, neither is there a proper supply of nutrition.

Pain is not only an evidence of disease but is a means of
arousing the vital force to some degree of activity for the
removal of the cause. When the abnormal condition sub-
sides the pain ceases. Do not be mistaken and demolish
your friend for an enemy. Forget not that the abnormal
reduction of sensibility is itself disease and is more or less
disastrous to the system. Narcotics do not remove the
conditions, that cause suffering. Instead of narcotizing
administer such agents as tend to remove the cause.

The cause of pain is not always directly in nerve tissue.
It is more frequently elsewhere, and the nervous system
is then but the transmitting medium. Yet the long continuance of such may become a source of nerve irritation.

The pain is usually confined to the part or parts affected,
but in time other parts suffer therefrom.

Then too the pain is not always located at the point diseased. This is frequently true with ovarian and uterine
pains. You cannot be too careful in the study and diagnosis of transmitted pain. Many a time pain under the left
shoulder blade, down the thigh or at the knee is from the
ovary or ovaries. Many a time a headache is from constipation, hepatic torpor, improper mastication or imperfect
digestion. Many a case of chronic sick-headache is cured
by the use of a new set of teeth when the natural set had
become decayed.

Insanity is not unfrequently due to chronic torpid conditions of the secernents, first resulting in hypochondriasis.

Therefore carefully diagnose the cause of the symptom.
Each disease and each injury in each different part gives
its own peculiar suffering. If the pain proceeds from irritation then relaxing and soothing medication is needed as
given by cypripedium, lobelia or ulmus.

The pain due to hyperæmia is very frequently relieved
by external local applications of relaxing agents, and the

use internally of a hot infusion of diffusives and relaxants.

The pain due to sprain is frequently relieved by the stimulating and relaxing influence of hot water continued for some hours and of the use internally of diffusives and relaxants.

For the relief of the pain due to gangrene the strongest stimulants and antiseptics are necessary until the separation of the parts dead and living is complete.

Neuralgia is more or less an irritation of the nerve structures themselves, and yet this irritation not unfrequently arises from some secernent or circulatory cause. In the treatment of such it is not only necessary to relieve the secernents and the circulation but also to sustain the nerves with agents of a more or less stimulating influence, as dioscorea villosa, caulophyllum thalactorides, ferula fœtida, sorbilin, salicine, scutelaria, or quinine.

Restlessness is usually a result of long-continued irritation of the nervous system leading to general weakness. Here you require a gently stimulating class of nerve tonics.

Convulsion is a very much over-stimulated condition of the nervous system. In some children the cause of convulsion is the approach of some eruptive disease, the presence of worms, teething or some stomach or bowel trouble. Convulsion may also be the result of cerebro-spinal disease, or of some injury; or it may arise from some weakness of the nerves as in hysteria.

In all such cases more or less relaxation is need at first. In tetanus especially use the most powerful relaxants. Lobelia in large quantities will probably have to be used per rectum. But as the system becomes relaxed, more stimulating and toning nervines are required to sustain the system.

The nerves and circulation frequently run side by side and reciprocate each other's action. Carefully diagnose which may be primarily at fault. Ascertain whether pain arises from acute irritation in any respect or from hyperæmia in any part. Investigate as to whether it be from congestion, suppuration or from gangrenous destruction. Ascertain whether the pain arises from some failure of the secernents, the circulation or the nervous system, or from two or more of them combined.

Estimate carefully the degree of vitality present and the necessities in each direction. Then select your medicines and combine them accordingly. In the treatment of some pain stimulating agents will be required, while other cases will require relaxation and still others astringency. Inflammatory effort will require relaxation; a depressed effort will require more or less stimulation; irritation requires demulcents and a very relaxed effort will require some degree of astringency and it may be of stimulation also.

All pain therefore cannot be treated alike. While lobelia would be very suitable for the relief of arterial pressure in an inflammatory effort, it would be worse than nothing in the vital failure of gangrene where the most positive stimulation is needed. Cypripedium pubescens will relieve the pain due to some irritated condition of the nervous system, but in a depressed condition it would be a failure. Here more positive stimulating nervines as scutelaria, quinia or sorbilin are essential.

Impacted fæces may be the cause of pain. Not nervines then, but the removal of the cause is the thing required. Caulophyllum, polygonum, ferula, valeriana are both stimulating and relaxing in varying proportions. The third preparation of lobelia is the climax in this respect.

Tonics are intended to give fuller vigor to the system and are more or less stimulating.

An emetic, a bath, a cathartic or a diaphoretic is each a depurative measure, assisting in cleansing the system of whatever impurities may be present. Subsequently tonics are needed to slowly and permanently assist in giving greater firmness to the tissues. Tonics are especially used to restore general strength and vigor to the digestive apparatus, upon which depends the vigor of the entire system. Care must be taken not to use more stimulating agents than are necessary, nor should they be used in stronger or more frequent doses than required. Care must also be taken that the alvine canal and its accessories are cleansed and active, for then a tonic will do most good. Without taking these precautions tonics will be of little value.

Demulcents may be applied as poultices. They may be either relaxing or stimulating according to the agents selected or incorporated and according to the necessities requiring such. They should be kept warm. Poultices or fine powders may be used to absorb discharges from sores, the better to prepare the surface for further local treatment.

Demulcents given to the stomach soothe the mucous membrane and relieve irritation of the stomach and bowels. Per vaginam and per rectum they are very soothing to the mucous surfaces, and assist in relieving irritation.

Demulcents may also be used as a vehicle for the conveying of more stimulating agents either into the stomach or rectum.

Demulcents are also useful in the formation of pill mass in the manufacturing of pills.

When required demulcents are excellent for the relief of bronchial and pulmonary irritation or inflammation. In such cases they are very important both applied externally as a poultice and taken internally either alone or in combination with other agents that influence the respiratory organs.

Demulcents are also of great value in the covering of abraded surfaces, burns or scalds, especially when combined with some suitable oil. They prevent exposure to the air and pain ceases.

Fruit acids are of great benefit in the treatment of bilious troubles and in convalescence therefrom. Avoid using them too frequently or too freely. A wash of vinegar and water will be both pleasant and profitable at times in cleansing the tongue of foulness.

Alkalies as soda, potassa, magnesia and lime are at times needed to correct acidity of the stomach. Cautiously avoid giving more than enough to relieve the acidulated condition present. Sometimes sores having an ichorous discharge may be relieved by an alkaline wash applied as needed. Such wash may also be applied to the tongue to cleanse it of foulness.

Escharotics are not strictly remedies, but as the surgical knife, may be applied to the surface for the destruction of abnormal growths. Cautiously limit their use to the parts to be destroyed.

PHYSIO - MEDICAL

MATERIA MEDICA.

he following pages will be devoted to the consideration of such agents as we deem *Physio-Medical* both old and new: In presenting some new agents it may be that we shall in future years change our views somewhat as we have concerning some of our older agents. We are in for advancement. We believe in employing the very best agents and the most efficient preparations the world can furnish.

In this consideration of our *materia medica* I have excluded to a great extent botanical description, and I have included but little concerning pharmacy, because an excellent article has been furnished by Prof. J. M. Thurston. His pharmacy is peculiarly physio-medical, and such as we need, and I ask for this article the attention of the profession.

Prior to introducing the first subject of materia medica I have deemed it proper to give some instructions as to gathering your material. In each locality this will be valuable concerning some agents.

ROOTS.

The roots of *annual* plants should be gathered just previous to flowering.

Those of *biennial* plants should be gathered shortly after the leaves have fallen in the autumn of the first year.

Those of *perennials* are the most active after the fall of the leaves and flowers in the autumn.

BULBS.

These should be gathered as soon as matured after the plant has lost its foliage.

STEMS.

Herbaceous stems should be gathered after the foliage appears and before the blossoms have developed.

Ligneous stems should be gathered after the falling of the leaves.

BARKS.

These should be gathered in the spring before the flowering season or in the autumn after the foliage has gone.

LEAVES.

These should be gathered as soon as matured, in the time between the flowers and the maturing of the fruit.

Biennials do not perfect their leaves during the first year.

BERRIES, SUCCULENT FRUITS AND SEEDS.

Should be gathered when ripe or nearly so.

FLOWERS.

These should be gathered when about to open from the bud. Sometimes the buds themselves are collected.

Leaves, flowers and herbs should gathered in dry weather.

Aromatic Plants are best after the flower buds are formed and ready to open.

DRYING.

Those agents which are to be dried, should be put into a room where they will be much in the shade. They should not be dried to quickly so as too dissipate any of their qualities, nor left long enough to mould.

RULES FOR PRONUNCIATION.

The following rules are applicable for the pronunciation of medical terms of latin origin. Of course there will be many exceptions which could not be considered here.

1.—Words of two syllables receive the accent on the penultimate; as cortex, radix, vera, alnus, carum etc.

2.—Words of more than two syllables receive the accent on the penultimate, if the vowel be long; as palmatum, vulgaris, acetum, etc.

3.—If the penultimate vowel be short; then the antepenultimate receives the accent; as acidum, krameria, kalmia, cataria etc.

4—If the antepenultimate vowel is followed by a single consonant, that consonant usually receives the accent and the vowel preceeding is rendered short; as hepatica, nobilis, nepeta, etc.

5—If the antepenultimate vowel be u it usually receives the accent instead of the consonant following; as punica, aluminum etc.

Words derived from the Greek language are pronounced according to the rules of pronunciation in that language.

ABIES BALSAMEA

Balsam Fir, Canada Balsam

The bark of this tree when punctured yields a thick and more or less transparent *balsam,* which is moderately stimulating to the mucous membrane throughout, especially influencing that of the renal apparatus. It is quite persistent and in large doses nauseates If the mucous membrane be irritated it is inappropriate but is best in relaxed and torpid cases, as in gleet, cystic and renal congestions In bronchial and pulmonary congestions it is a stimulating expectorant, but its influence is best felt in this direction when combined with some agents which especially influence the respiratory organs It gives very favorable results when combined with syrups for chronic coughs.

F E. Abies Bal.	dr. ii
Acetous Syr Lobelia Sem.	oz. iiss
Mel	q. s oz iv

This may be used for colds, coughs, croup. asthma and bronchial catarrh.

F E Abies Bal.	dr ii
Glycerin	
Mel	aa oz. ii

This makes a good cough syrup.

This balsam may also be incorporated with vaseline and used as an ointment for old sores and ulcers.

Yolk of Egg

Fresh Balsam

Triturate thoroughly and apply.

It may also be used as a plaster and applied to some weak or painful part, especially in the region of the kidneys

The *bark* is also used either in infusion or in fluid extract for the same purpose as the gum which exudes therefrom.

ABIES CANADENSIS.

Hemlock Spruce   (Pinus or Tsuga Canadensis)

The bark of this tree is used for tanning purposes By incising the bark the tree yields a heavy black pitch or gum

The *inner bark* is a drying and gently stimulating astringent, useful in hemorrhages and for diarrhœa Locally it may be used as an astringent wash wherever needed, as in cases of sore mouth or other ulcerous parts. Its action is mostly local and is valuable in the treatment of rectal ulcers. It checks the excessive discharges and the ulcers heal under it. It is good also for buboes.

Dr. C. B. Riggs advises the following for rectal suppositories for internal hemorrhoids:

Gum Tragacanth

Glycerine q. s. ad. to make a thick syrup.

Powd. Pinus Can.   2

"   Hydrastis Can.

"   Myrica Cer.

"   Boracic Acid

Wheat Flour   aa. 1

q. s. ad. to make the former stiff enough to form suppositories the size desired.

Sig. One suppository each night on retiring. This has proven very successful, especially when the rectum is lax, and the tumors protrude. Rectal pain and tenesmus will be quickly relieved, and hemorrhoids soon cured and remain so until the liver becomes torpid and the bowels constipated.

The *leaves* are more stimulating and less astringent than the bark. In hot infusion it is diaphoretic and may be used for the relief of colds and for dysmorrhœa; but it is not best to use this agent where the patient is inclined to constipation. They are valuable in hot fomentations for sprains, rheumatism, and inflammations.

The *oil* of hemlock is obtained from the leaves and is far more stimulating. It is a useful addition to liniments, but is not used internally.

The *resin* is sometimes incorporated with oils and formed into a plaster.

ABIES EXCELSA.

Norway Spruce.

From the little drops on the bark we get our frankincense; and from incisions in the wood flows the pix burgundica. This incorporated with sweet oil forms an irritating plaster which may only occasionally be used. To irritate the surface is seldom the part of wisdom.

ABRUS PRECATORIUS.

Jequirity.

This is a stimulating and toning agent to the mucous

membrane. It cleanses the parts and leaves them invigorated. The *seeds* reduced to a powder and mixed with
hydrozone is excellent in the treatment of uterine ulcer,
abrasions, excoriations, polypoid excrescences, and in
somewhat similar conditions of the rectum. It completely exfoliates morbid tissue and leaves the parts underneath
toned. It may be used in capsule, powder, suppository or
cerate.

The infusion of the seeds is best in granular ophthalmia,
in opacities of the cornea and in some varieties of cata-
racts.

Make the infusion of one drachm of the beans crushed
to one pint of boiling water. Two or three drops put upon
the inner canthus of the eye two or three times a day
should be continued until complete exfoliation takes place.

In diphtheria spray the throat with the ozonized jequirity and this will cause immediate exfoliation.

For eczemas it may be used as a salve.

ACACIA CATECHU.

Catechu.

This we obtain chiefly from the East and West Indies
in the form of an extract which is a powerful astringent
somewhat similar to tannin, and may be used for the same
general purposes locally and internally.

ACACIA VERA.

Gum Arabic.   Arabia and Northern Africa.

The *gum* exudes freely from the bark of the trunk and
larger branches, soft and nearly fluid. Exposure hardens
it.

Acacia Vera is a pure mucilage, nutritious and demul-
cient; and may be used to excellent advantage in all irritated conditions of the mucous membrane whether it be of
the alvine canal, the bronchi or of the renal apparatus.
Its chief influence is most felt where most needed or
whether influenced by some other agent. It is quite serviceable in bronchial inflammation or irritation, in dysentery and diarrhœa.

Gum Arabic   oz. i
Water, Vinegar, or Lemonade   oz. vi

Do not use enough to clog the system but merely to
soothe as a mucilaginous drink. This gum plays an im-

portant part in the manufacture of pills, troches and emulsions.

ACETUM.

Vinegar.

The juices of various fruits after having undergone some degree of fermentation and having become sufficiently sour is called vinegar. The best vinegar is obtained from apples. Though there is a small proportion of acetic acid in vinegar, yet it is improper to manufacture vinegar from acetic acid and water.

Acetum influences the mucous membrane chiefly, promoting the increase of saliva; and is an expectorant to the respiratory mucous membrane.

Vinegar, sugar and water in appropriate combination form a pleasant acidulated drink when indicated in fevers to allay thirst and to promote a flow of saliva.

Acetum in hot water is diaphoretic, and if inhaled when the head is somewhat covered is valuable for the relief of colds in the head and nasal passages, the throat and bronchi. As a stimulating antiseptic it is valuable in various forms of sore throat, especially if combined with more stimulating and toning agents. It may be used as a gargle or be atomized into the throat in diphtheria, pharyngitis, laryngitis, aphonia or tonsilitis. A favorite home gargle is acetum, sodium chloride and capsicum in boiling water for various forms of mild sore throat. With verbascum thapsus its influence is excellent as a fomentation for sprains and swellings. With lobelia it decreases its nausea, yet its influence is more permanent.

Acetum with sanguinaria and lobelia may de administered with very favorable results in membranous croup in connection with gently stimulating diaphoresis. The acetous tincture of lobelia much less readily nauseates but is more persistent than the ordinary tincture.

With capsicum the influence of both is intensified. Locally acetum increases the power of any agent with which it is combined. If acetum is brought to the boiling point and poured over the crude ingredients as lobelia or sanguinaria the full strength of the agent will be more readily gained.

In case of delirium tremens a wine glass of strong vinegar will soon restore sense and locomotion.

ACHILLEA MILLEFOLIUM.

Yarrow

This *herb* is a mild, slow, stimulating astringent tonic; influencing the mucous membrane of the alvine canal, and gives favorable results in chronic dysentery and chronic diarrhœa It stimulates the appetite and tones the digestive organs It is of much importance as a tonic to the general system Combined with uterine tonics its influence will be felt upon the generative organs and will be serviceable in lucorrhœa, gleet and vaginal laxity

In hot infusion it arouses the capillary circulation and is somewhat antiperiodic, and assists in the relief of hemorrhages.

In cold forms it is useful as a tonic in convalescence from fevers, from nervous prostration, in phthisis and night sweats.

ACORUS CALAMUS

Calamus, Sweet Flag.

The *root* when green is rather pungent but when dry is a pleasant, mild, aromatic stimulant. It is mildly warming to the stomach and is frequently used to relieve the flatus and colic of children. It is best for this purpose combined with zingiber and dioscorea, and it may be used as a carminative vehicle for other drugs

ADIANTUM PEDATUM

Maiden-hair.

This *herb* is a mild, pleasant, demulcent, stimulating astringent It influences the mucous membrane throughout In combination with agents that influence the bronchi its action will be determined in that direction; as with aralia racemosa or symphytum officinale With hydrastis or gentian its influence will be most felt on the alvine canal With uva ursi its influence will be felt by the kidneys, the uterus, bladder and urethra, assisting much in the relief of cystic catarrh and scalding urine

AGAVE AMERICANA

American Agave

The *juice* of this plant forms a lather with water and has been sometimes used as a substitute for soap, and forms a good cleansing application to the surface Internally it influences the mucous membrane and is somewhat laxative. It also influences the urinary and generative organs, increasing the flow in either direction as needed or as directed by other agents.

AGAVE VIRGINICA.

Rattlesnake Master.

The *root* is a bitter, tonic carminative and is useful in flatulence and colic, and is recommended as an antidote for snake bites.

AGRIMONIA EUPATORIA.

Agrimony.

The *herb* is a gently stimulating, aromatic astringent, acting mainly on the mucous membrane. In hot infusion it influences diaphoresis. Cold preparations influence the kidneys and other urinary apparata, imparting a gentle tonic influence, and will give favorable results in enuresis and relieve milky urine.

With hepatics its chief influence is given to the intestinal mucous membrane in cases of dysentery and diarrhœa, acute or chronic. Dr. F. G. Hoener recommends it in hepatic abscess, mesenteritis, anæmia, atrophy of the liver, albumenaria, cirrhosis of the liver, marasmus, peritonitis, and stomatitis

With uterine tonics its chief influence is given to tone the generative organs, slowly toning them and relieving leucorrhœa.

With agents that influence the bronchi its influence will be expended in toning the mucous membrane in that locality, and is valuable in excessive expectoration. Dr. F. G. Hoener recommends the following in incipient consumption, colds and coughs:

Elix. Agrimonia Eup.
" Chrysanthemum Leucan. aa. oz. iss
" Verbena Hast. oz. iiiss
" Sabbatia Ang.
" Veronica Off.
" Verbascum Thap. aa. oz. ii
" Helonias Dio. oz. iiss
Syr. Marrubium Vulg. oz. iss

M. S. A teaspoonful to a dessertspoonful every 2 or 3 hours.

With more stimulating agents its influence when needed by the vital force will be exerted upon the pharynx and larynx.

With ulmus oi other mucilaginous wash it is good in ophthalmia.

AGROPYRUM REPENS

Tri icum, Couch Grass (Triticum Repens.)

The *root* is a pleasant diuretic, and is excellent for the relief of irritation of the bladder and urethra. It is valuable in gonorrhœa in the inflammatory stage. It increases the flow and relieves the irritation It is also valuable in cystic catarrh and renal congestions. In dropsy it gives favorable results, also in nephritis, cystitis and urethritis it may be used to good advantage.

—— ALCOHOL ——

By W F. PECHUMAN, A M. M. D LL D.

Late Professor of Histology, Physiology and Pathology, Clinical Professor of Surgery at the Chicago Physio-Medical College and Secretary of its Faculty Member of the Medical and Surgical Staff of the R R Hospital and Militant Church Hospital, Chicago Lecturer at St Paul's College.

This is a subject on which much has been written, and yet there is room for much more to be said

We would like to go into a more lengthy article but time and space will not allow; so we will content ourselves with as short an article as possible, giving only enough to have our readers understand the main ideas and facts we wish to impress upon the minds of honest men and women, who read with an unprejudiced mind, to get a knowledge of truth wherever found

This subject is becoming more and more important to the the honest investigator It is high time that the truth should be known, concerning this much argued question.

Honest ,conscientious, scientific experiments and investigation is the only way to find the right use and disuse for alcohol.

This agent has become an important article of commerce. It is used as a medicine and as a food It is much used in pharmacy and in the arts.

There is hardly a country on earth where alcohol is not known and used to a greater or less extent It is shipped by tons to even barbarous nations High taxes are paid for license, to allow the sale of it.

At present it is not only a question in the medical profession, whether or not it is useful as a medicine, but it is seriously discussed from a legal and religious point of view. So if we come to think of it as it stands to-day, we find that it is one of the great questions to be scientifically solved and understood.

It is claimed by many that we cannot do without alcohol as a medicine; by others that it is absolutely injurious in all conditions and under all circumstances, in quality as well as in quantity.

That alcohol has ever saved a human life is a question, that it has destroyed the lives of thousands is no question at all.

An old adage might well come in at this point: "have a place for everything, and everything in its place." So we will try to find the right place for alcohol.

The name alcohol is supposed to have its origin from the arabic language. The word is now used to designate a highly rectified spirit.

History: — It is believed that alcohol was distilled from rice, many years before rice was introduced into Europe. We read of it being known in Bagdad in the ninth century. It is spoken of as known to the moors of Spain and by them the knowledge of its production and use was spread into Europe.

It was known to the early Romans for Pliny wrote of "a strong kind of wine that was inflammable," which shows that a knowledge existed of distillation in the first century.

A description was given in about 1280 by a western writer who wrote of a "burning water."

But we find that it was used much earlier in the form of beer, by the ancients; whether they knew it by itself as alcohol we cannot say.

As early as 700 B. C. Archilocheus referred to *wine of barley*. The king of Egypt, Osiris is credited by Diodorus Siculus, who wrote 630 B. C., with having introduced into that country, a fermented drink made of barley, as early as 1900 B. C.

In 400 B. C. both Æschuylus and Sophocle speak of *wine of barley*.

In the writings of Julius Cæsar we find mention of beer, in the year 50 B. C.

Egypt is credited with the discovery of a fermented

drink - beer; yet it seems that for a long time the manufacturing of it ceased till it was reintroduced by the French
army.

The Germans introduced it to the Gauls.

We also find drunkenness spoken of in such expressions
as — "staggered like a drunken man," as early as 1520 B·
C. "He is a glutton and a drunkard ' in 1451 B C "And
he drank of the wine an l he was drunken", about 2347
B C "Drinking himself drunk" in 930 B. C "I am like a
drunken man" 599 B C   "These are not drunken" and
"drink with the drunken" 33–54 A D.

Now then, if there was drunkenness at those times there
must have been something that made them drunk; and as
we have no evidence that they used other drugs that could
produce drunkenness. we conclude that it was alcohol in
some beverage that made them drunk.

Paracelsus who lived from 1490—1541 introduced alcohol
into medical use" Paracelsus of old who wasted life in trying to discover its elixir, which after all turned out to be
alcohol, and instead of being made immortal upon eartlf,
he died drunk on the floor of a tavern."

There is quite a large number of articles that have been
classed under the generic term of alcohol. We have about
twelve of the alcohol family The common or ordinary
alcohol is the ethylic, sometimes known as spirit of wine
and vinici alcohol

Absolute alcohol is pure alcohol entirely free from water.

Alcohols are also known according to the number of hy-
droxyl groups they contain A group of alcohols may be
given as follows — The Methylic, Ethylic, Propylic, But-
ylic, Amylic, Caproic alcohol &c

Lime is generally used to make the absolute alcohol for
commerce

The chemical formula for alcohol is (C_2H_5OH)

It is a liquid that is very volatile; is entirely volatilized
by heat; is colorless, inflammable, of a hot, pungent, burning taste and a sweetish penetrating odor Has great
affinity for water, even abstracting water from the air if
left in an open vessel It boils at a temperature of 173.3
degrees F It has never been frozen by any cold hitherto
produced At a temperature of 130 degrees alcohol becomes
of an oily consistency: at 146 degrees it assumes the aspect
of melted wax, and at 166 degrees it gets still thicker, but
it does not congeal at the lowest attainable temperature.

Alcohol does not conduct electricity.

The specific gravity of absolute or anhydrous alcohol at a temperature of 60 degrees Fahr. is 0.820.

We cannot get pure alcohol by the ordinary way of distillation. The rectified alcohol or spirit of the United States pharmacopœias is composed of 91 per cent. by weight of ethyl alcohol, and 9 per cent by weight of water.

It is a powerful solvent for the alkaloids, resins, essential oils, and many fats; also for gasses and minerals. It is very readily absorbed by all organic structures. It is a powerful antifermentative when stronger than 18 per cent. It is also an antiseptic agent, in the way that it stops fermentation, absorbs fats, coagulates albuminous substances, in having an intense affinity for water, and its power for destroying all living micro-organisms: it is therefore also a preservative for animal tissues.

We may take dilute alcohol and distill it with chloride of lime and obtain chloroform. It reacts upon acids in such a way that water is eliminated, and ethers are produced. Alcohol is in itself an anæsthetic It is alcohol in alcoholic beverages that intoxicates; even if the vapor of alcohol is inhaled, it will produce intoxication.

The Source of Alcohol.—We produce alcohol from sugar, but many other articles can be changed into it, by first converting them into sugar; such as the grains, fleshy roots, beets, potatoes, &c., the fruits, and even woody fibres.

The fermentation of sugar and other saccharine matter is the only source of alcohol. Sugar is the product of the vegetable kingdom. Some plants contain sugar while many more contain starch, which can be converted into sugar. Therefore those vegetables that contain the greatest amount of sugar or starch will yield the most alcohol.

Alcohol is then a chemical product, produced by fermentation of vegetable tissue from degeneration; a breaking down of organized matter; which is a backward process or a dissolving of matter into its primitive elements or atomic state, and then rearranging them into an entirely different compound or compounds.

We have said that the chemical formula for alcohol is (C_2H_5OH): that of starch is $(C_6H_{10}O_5)n$ and of sugar is $(C_6H_{12}O_6)$. So we see that the same elements are found in the three entirely different compounds—starch, sugar and alcohol—which are carbon, hydrogen and oxygen; only in different proportions. Yet starch is not sugar, nor is sugar alcohol.

We do not find starch in the human body, only when it has been taken in as food.

We believe that all chlorophyll-containing plants, at some period of their existence, contain starch. Starch is the first organic substance produced by the vegetable kingdom from the mineral or inorganic matter.

Animals cannot live on inorganic matter; such matter must first pass through the vegetable kingdom.

Plants form starch from carbonic acid and water, which are taken out of the air and the soil. This process is expressed by the following chemical formula:

$$(6CO_2 + 5H_2O)n = (C_6H_{10}O_5)n + On.$$
$$\text{carbonic acid} \quad \text{water} \quad\quad \text{starch} \quad\quad \text{oxygen}$$

In the hydrolytic action or change of starch into sugar we have:

$$(C_6H_{10}O_5)n + H_2O = C_6H_{12}O6.$$
$$\text{starch} \quad\quad \text{water} \quad \text{inverted sugar}$$

In producing common alcohol it is supposed that the cane-sugar first passes into grape-sugar; and in forming alcohol from cane-sugar, maltose and grape-sugar, carbonic acid gas is set free.

$$C_6H_{12}O_6 = 2C_2H_5HO + 2CO_2.$$
$$\text{grape-sugar} \quad\quad -\text{alcohol} \quad \text{carbonic acid gas}$$

It is claimed by some that alcohol is found in corn and in other grains; to substantiate their false theory that all things are poison, and that poisonous agents are medicines. They argue that we get alcohol from corn, therefore it exists in corn; just as if alcohol was mixed with other ingredients in corn, and then all that would be necessary to get alcohol, is to extract it as you would acid from the lemon. But that is an erroneous idea, and it cannot be upheld by scientific investigation. Alcohol can no more be taken directly out of these bodies than vinegar out of the apple, prussic acid out of the peach, tartaric acid out of the grape, or a deadly poison out of an animal body; unless we first add heat and moisture to produce fermentation—a chemical change to disorganize the elementary substances put together by *vital force* or life.

Heat is the great disintegrative force; it separates the atomic structure, so that the atoms lose their affinity for each other and in that way the tissue is disintegrated—separated; and as these atoms now set free cannot exist in a free state long, they unite with other atoms that are found in the disintegrated mass, and according to natural law form a new compound or compounds, entirely different from what existed at first.

The Action of Alcohol.—This is generally spoken of as the physiological action. but by the physiological action we understand it to "pertain to or of the nature of physiology; of or pertaining to the functions of living organisms. Physiology treats of the vital phenomena manifested by animals or plants; the science of organic functions." —*Standard Dictionary.*

It then means, to act in harmony with life or with the vital phenomena, or the functions of living organs.

Alcohol does not do this; it does not act in harmony with life, therefore its actions are not physiological.

Pathology teaches of morbid disease conditions, their causes, symptoms and nature; alcohol causes morbid, disease, or pathological conditions; therefore the proper term would then be, its pathological instead of its physiological action.

Before we speak of the action of alcohol, let us first look at the human body as it is, from the microscopical, histological and the chemical point of view.

When we examine the human body we find that it is made up of bones, muscles, bloodvessels, lymphatics, nerves, etc. When we examine these tissues under the microscope, to study them histologically, we find that they are composed of many small particles, called *cells*. When we make closer observation we find that all living cells contain a nucleus, a central germinal spot, which is alive It is the matter, and the only matter through which life can manifest itself.

This central germinal spot which is found in every living cell in every living tissue of the living body, is the matter that performs all the functions of that tissue. All organs of the body are made up of these cells, and the functions of all the organs—the brain, muscles, liver, stomach, etc.— is the result of the action of this living center of the cell that composes the organ.

If we go still further into the mysterious work of nature, and examine one of these little cells, or the entire human body, chemically, we then find that it is composed of about fourteen elements, which are: Oxygen, hydrogen, carbon, nitrogen, calcium, sodium, potassium; phosphorus, magnesium, iron, sulphur, chlorine, fluorine, and silicon. These are not always the same but are constantly changed by new ones, taken from the food we eat. In the healthy normal body they are so combined that they are, as a whole, nonpoisonous; but when the body is dead and acted upon by decomposition, a deadly poison may be produced; as, for example. in dead bodies in the dissecting rooms

The central germinal spot or bioplasm in the cell is of an albuminous consistency, resembling the white of an egg. All food that nourishes the body is assimilated by the cells. and the living matter transforms such food into its own substance In this way the body is built up and kept in repair . The waste material is thrown off from the cell in a molecular and atomic form.

A good example of this living matter, which we find in all living bodies, is found in the blood—the white blood-corpuscles or leucocytes If we take one of these white blood-corpuscles—or any living matter wherever found—and place it under the microscope, we see that it is a colorless, semi-gelatinous mass, spherical in its natural state; but it can change itself into almost any shape, reaching out here and there, and moving from place to place. Under favorable conditions this bioplastic mass will divide and subdivide, so that a large number may be produced It takes up pabulum and converts it into its own substance, throwing out all foreign material that is not suitable for its nourishment.

It seems as if the human body has been looked upon as a chemical laboratory medicines were given—and are only too often given yet--without knowing anything about their true physiological or pathological action

The only true and scientific way to determine the action of any drug is on the bioplasm or living matter To do this we should proceed as follows First take a bioplastic body and place it under the microscope, let the fluid in which the bioplasm is immersed be of the right kind: also the temperature should be just right Then take your agent to be tested; take for example capsicum, which is known to be the purest and most powerful stimulant in the materia medica, and place a small amount under the microscope with a mass of living matter, and we can soon see it begin to act more freely it will take up more pabulum, and divide and subdivide more readily It has been stimulated to increased action This can be kept up for some time, and the experiment will always show the same result.

We next take lobelia inflata, a most powerful relaxant (and it is by some badly informed practitioners called poisonous) and put some of it with the living matter, in the same way as before, and we see that the active mass will begin to move very slowly, and then spread itself out so thin that it can hardly be seen for its transparency. Its movements become very slow and may cease altogether for a while; and now, while it is in this relaxed condition, should you add a little capsicum, or any other true stimulant, you would soon see it begin to resume its original shape and action. It would do so without the stimulant, but it would take longer. When hydrastis is used the living matter becomes more firm and yet it is very active under the tonic effect of this agent. When an astringent is used it will be seen to contract into a spherical mass and remain in that condition for a time, according to the character or strength of the agent used; but if the agent is sanative, the bioplast will in time resume its action as before. Some agents induce the living matter to throw out more material to form a cell wall.

We now take a very weak solution of alcohol, and add it to this living particle of matter which has just preformed so wonderfully under our very eyes, and we see it change almost instantly according to the strength of the alcoholic solution into a spherical mass. So here we might conclude that alcohol is an astringent as the former agent was. We wait but there is no return to activity, we add stimulants as in former cases but still no sign of action. We repeat our experiments over and over again but we get the same result, no activity, no life, but death.

When a strong solution of alcohol is used the amœba or or bioplast will remain almost in the shape it was in when the alcohol struck it, only a little smaller. When we examine it closely we find that some have undergone a granular and others a fatty change.

All our experiments with alcohol on living matter show that it so changes the bioplastic matter that life cannot manifest itself through such matter. All vital phenomena cease, death is the result. So we declare alcohol to be an irritant not a stimulant in any sense of the word, no more than a whip is a stimulant to a hungry, tired and sick horse. Alcohol is a narcotic poison.

When the alcoholic preparation is very weak it only injures to a less extent, accordingly, but if even this small amount is kept up any length of time, the pathological conditions that are set up will in time produce death Therefore alcohol is injurious in quantity as well as in quality, under all conditions and under all circumstances.

The question is often asked Why is it a man can drink much more of the alcoholics after he is used to them, than he could when he began? Our answer is nature has adapted itself to surrounding circumstances Send a small boy out, in the spring barefooted on a rough road for miles, and he will come back with his feet bruised, torn and bleeding, but let the boy go a short way every day with care, and in time he will be able to run over the roughest road without injuring his feet· here nature throws out more formed material to protect the living ·particles within, a thick skin was formed, strong and tough In the same way each bioplast is protected from the ravages of poisonous drugs, alcohol, opium morphine, chloral, .&c. &c. Nature throws out more formed material to make a stronger and thicker cell wall, so as to protect the living centre within

The drunkard's fatty tissue is nothing but dead, waste material, caused by disease not health; death, not life

After experimenting with alcohol we try other drugs that are known to be poisonous, and we always get the same result—death. It has been proved that one seven-millionth of a grain of strychnia will kill bioplasm.

There is a universal law in the physical world and that is, a poison will kill, no matter what the poison may be. Poison may whip up the system to action, it may bring out the latent force to activity, yet it can only do harm in the end Why should such drugs be made use of, when nature has supplied, so abundantly, agents of life? Agents that act physiologically, in harmony with nature, in harmony with life.

Alcohol can destroy a white blood-corpuscle in more than one way First, because of its great affinity for water; second, on account of its power to coagulate albuminous substances; third, by its inherent power or property to destroy life

Now the question comes, what is a poison? Many of the old definitions given do not throw much light on the subject. Some would have us believe that everything may be a poison. We will here quote from the *Literary Digest* on "What is a poison?" "This question is propounded to the editor of *The National Druggist* by a correspondent who criticises the definition of the word 'poison' as given by many of the dictionaries. Says this correspondent: 'Webster says a poison is any agent which, when introduced into the animal organism, is capable of producing a morbid, noxious, or deadly effect. Now, should there not be a limitation as regards quantity of the substance? It seems so to me; because there is scarcely a substance known which, if taken too freely, will not produce morbid, noxious. and even deadly effects.'

"To this query *The Nat. Drug.* replies editorially as follows: 'Your criticism of the definition given by Webster is entirely justifiable. The definition of the word given in Dunglison's Medical Dictionary is almost identical with that of Webster, and so is that of Dr. Billings in his great Material Medical Dictionary. An English authority, whose name escapes us, defines a poison as 'a drug that kills rapidly when administered in small quantity;' which, while it gives the element missing (the limitation referred to by the querist) is far more liable to criticism than those quoted. All poisons are by no means drugs, as witness the poison of typhus, of malaria, etc. [No poison should be used as a medicine.] A celebrated English toxicologist, recently deceased, we believe Dr. Melmott Tidey, defined a poison as "any substance which, otherwise than by the agency of heat or electricity, is capable of destroying life by chemical action or its physiological effects upon the system." This, too, is not entirely satisfactory, as admitted by the author, who confessed the difficulty of giving a true and comprehensive definition. If it were true, there is scarcely a substance in the whole armamentarium of medicine that would not fall under the term.

"Nobody, for instance, thinks or speaks of quinine as a poison, and yet there are numerous instances recorded wherein it has caused death, to say nothing of the morbid and noxious effects of which we have ample evidence every day. Glycerine, too, merely a feeble laxative when taken into the stomach through the mouth, when introduced into the animal organism by direct injection into the blood causes extreme nervous perturbation, and in the lower animals, death.

"It would seem to us, therefore, that the following definition would be more nearly correct and comprehensive: 'Any substance which, if introduced into a living organism in small amount, or quantities beyond and over a certain definite limit, which latter is variable in each substance and for each class of organism, is capable of destroying life, either by chemical action or by its physiological effects.' Like Dr. Tidey, we believe that 'if a substance is a poison it is deadly, if it is not deadly it is not a poison' Substances which do not kill are merely noxious or hurtful "

"Whatever tends to taint or destroy character or mislead."—R. Ogden Doremus' letter to the Standard Dictionary, January 22, 1896.

What agent does more of this than alcohol?

The Standard Dictionary gives: "Any substance that when taken into the system acts in a noxious manner by means not mechanical, tending to cause death or serious detriment to health." This does not give us any definite answer.

Dunglison's Medical Dictionary gives the following "All substances which, when introduced into the animal economy, either by cutaneous absorption, respiration, or the digestive canal, act in a noxious manner on the vital properties or the texture of organs."

In Dutton's "Key to Medicine" we find that "any substance whose nature is injurious or destructive to health and physical manifestations of life. Something that cannot be taken into the body without physical injury Food tends to support physical life; poison tends to destroy it."

Any substance that has a power or inherent property to so change matter that life cannot maintain itself through such matter

Any substance that has an inherent power or property to destroy bioplasm; or perhaps the best definition would be Any substance that has the power or inherent property to kill, quantity does not change quality Poisons kill

Then we learn that all poisons have a tendency to destroy life, and sanative medicines have a tendency to assist the vital phenomena—or life.

It is a fact that all food made use of by the human body is taken up by the central germinal spot, the bioplasm of the cell; and likewise the medicine that influences the living matter to perform its functions normally and harmoniously. All foods to a certain extent are medicine, and all true medicines are foods.

No inorganic substance can become a part of the animal tissue, until it has first passed through the vegetable kingdom. If this is true—and all physiological research will substantiate this assertion—then a great many articles used by many, are not only unscientifically applied, but are detrimental to the human organism; such agents are mercury, arsenic, zinc, iron, etc. Those that are poisonous kill; and those that are not poisonous, as iron, act as foreign substances, or irritants.

All true medicines should be of a vegetable nature.

Bi-carbonate of sodium will neutralize the acid conditions; sub-sulphate of iron will stop hemorrhage; these act locally, and should be given for that purpose, and as far as it goes, do well. But there are vegetable remedies that will do just as well, and better.

The curative effect of all mineral waters is only local, a washing out of the various canals, as it were; and in that way may do some good, if they are free of noxious matter.

Alcohol can be used as an antiseptic. It dissolves fatty matter, absorbs watery excretions, coagulates albuminous matter, and destroys all germs. On this account it can be used to good advantage to wash the hands in before a surgical operation, and it is well adapted to immerse the instruments in before and during the operation.

Old putrid sores are sometimes washed with alcohol before applying the regular remedies. In fevers where the body is very dry and hot, alcohol is used to evaporate the heat and to dissolve the fatty waste material.

It is often used in combination with chloroform and ether as an anæsthetic.

While alcohol is used in the above mentioned circumstances, yet we would not recommend it for such use. The hands harden when washed in alcohol. Hot water and soap is better. Your instruments immersed in hot water or some non-poisonous antiseptic, will produce better results.

Old sores are washed with alcohol, yet we have many superior articles that will do better. Alcohol would extract the water from the delicate blood-vessels, destroy healthy granulation, and do much harm generally. To wash the skin in fevers is not always best; it hardens and weakens the skin. It is no tonic to the skin, as is believed by many. Warm water with sanative agents is best.

We believe that alcohol destroys many of the medical properties in extracting them from plants; therefore alcoholic preparations cannot always be depended upon

Very often symptoms of depression, which are supposed to be caused by an innocent agent is caused by the alcohol in the medicine

Alcohol given internally will arouse to action many organs; but this action is of an irritating nature, and function is performed normally. Its injurious effect begins as it enters the mouth. The mucous membrane is loose, soft and far more delicate than the external integument. Much is absorbed by the numerous small capillaries of the mouth, and here it begins its work of destruction

In the stomach where the surface is large, and the small blood vessels near the surface, much more harm is done; the alcohol absorbs the water of these tissues, coagulates their albuminous substance,—and we know that animal tissue contains a very large per cent. of albumen—injuring or killing the living matter of the cell, and in that way disintegrating the organized tissues, causing ulcers, much inflammation and fever; which naturally produces a desire for drink

It destroys the digestive fluids, and causes the food already in the stomach to become almost indigestable.

What remains unabsorbed passes on to the smaller intestines Here among the delicate villi, much harm is done in the same way as above described.

But all this in one sense is only local When it enters the blood it at first injures or entirely destroys the white blood corpuscles The red blood corpuscles which are the oxygen carriers suffer much.

The plastic material is hardened in them, and when examined under a microscope we can see some of them shriveled, others much enlarged and still others in a state of disintegration, so here we have disturbed one of the most important functions, that of supplying oxygen to the blood and the removing of carbon dioxide, And yet more, the blood contains the food for all the tissues of the body, and much of this is albuminous this food is deranged and made unfit for the use of the animal economy

When alcohol has once reached the blood it passes to all the tissues of the body Some receive more than others. The brain, heart, liver, kidneys and stomach suffer largely, but more or less all of the organs of the body.

The child nursing its mother's breast gets a certain per. cent. of alcohol; and even the unborn, that is nourished by the blood of its mother can become drunk before it opens its eyes to light, and be born a degraded wreck both physically and mentally

What a curse this common belief that the mother must use some alcoholic beverage — and it is for the alcohol in any of these liquors, that they are given, the other material in them is only like the aromatics in medicine to help it down to keep up her strength. How many poor beings are born with the alcoholic habit, how many with a weak nervous system, how many insane or become so during life, how many idiots, how many cripples, and how many with some other constitutional disease?

We believe that alcohol causes the greater number of nervous diseases; insanity, mental debility, melancholia, hysteria, convulsions, vertigo, chorea, paralysis of all forms, hysterio-epilepsy, nervous fits, infantile cerebral hemiplegia, cerebral atrophy, athetosis, imbecility, cerebral sclerosis, epilepsy, apoplexy, congenital imbecility, pachydermic cachexia, arrested development and perversion of instinct, alcoholism, tobacco and other degrading and deadly drug habits. It lays the foundation of many other diseases such as lung troubles, diseases of the heart, liver and kidneys.

A drunkard cannot withstand any disease or injury as well as an ordinary temperate man. It has been known that the scratch of a pin has proved fatal to a drunkard. As to the degree of drunkenness, depends a great deal on the amount taken, and on the resistive power in each body. When a person takes a teaspoonful, he is a teaspoonful drunk; if he takes a "modest" drink, he is "modest" drunk; if he takes a gallon, he is a gallon drunk.

The greater amount of crime, suicide and murder comes through the portals of alcohol.

Alcohol is not a food; most of it is thrown off as alcohol through the lungs, skin and kidneys. It is possible that some of it becomes disorganized and passes out of the body with other excretions as a waste. The false theory as to nourishing patients with alcohol is of a very badly informed, unscientific nature. If patients live on a compound containing alcohol, it is not the alcohol that keeps them up, but they live in spite of the alcohol. It has been

demonstrated over and over again that alcoholic liquors
contain no, or but very little, nourishment, and such
nourishment does not come from the alcohol.

Alcohol does not stimulate, but depresses and paralyzes.
The warmth felt is only of an irritating nature, from
the vital efforts to rid the body of an offending object

The flushed face or surface is caused by partial paralysis
of the nerve peripheries, and if this is continued will cause
congestion, the vessels become dilated, the surface blue,
and breaking down of the blood and blood-vessels will take
place—which can be seen so well in the nose of a drunkard.

The heart beats faster, but it throws less blood than before, because the nerves that control the heart are in a
paralyzed condition. More waste is formed everywhere
and less is thrown off The lungs do not oxydize the
blood sufficiently, because these nerves too are in a paralyzed condition, so, often a drunkard dies of suffocation

Locomotion is interfered with. The mind becomes be-
wildered, deranged or entirely confounded, because the
brain is badly affected

We would like to go on and take up each department
more thoroughly but our article would be too lengthy; so
we will quote from many eminent writers on this subject,
and in that way will bring out other points and also give
other authority than our own

If an honest observer will but take time and carefully
investigate the teaching that 'poisonous drugs are curative agents,' he will learn that such teaching is full of
"absurdity, contradiction and falsehood.,' Such systems
do not agree with themselves Take for example Dr. Robert Bartholow of Philadelphia, in his Materia Medica:
"In small doses not too frequently repeated, alcohol increases the digestive power by stimulating [it does
not stimulate] the flow of blood and soliciting a greater
supply to the stomach-juices " This is mere guess work;
but he goes on and tells us that "large doses impair digestion directly by precipitating the pepsin, an albuminoid
ferment." He does not tell us what a *small* or large dose
is, and should he do so it would not change matters any.
What would be a small dose for one would be a large dose
for another Alcohol is generally given in some alcoholic
beverage, and you can never tell just how much alcohol
the liquor contains, or of what strength the alcohol is

itself, say nothing about the other injurious articles contained in many of the alcoholic liquors. We claim that a
small amount of alcohol will produce the same effect as a
larger dose; only, of course, not to so great an extent. But
he says: "The structural alterations induced by the habitual use of alcohol, and the action of this agent on the pepsin, seriously impairs the digestive power." Then again
he dares to say that, "Alcohol in small doses is a useful
stomachic tonic. It is especially serviceable in the feeble
digestion of old people, the atonic dyspepsia of the sedentary, and in the slow and inefficient digestion of convalescence from acute diseases." Again he says: "It should
be prescribed with caution in these cases, especially in the
atonic dyspepsia of women and of sedentary men, because
of the danger that an alcohol habit may be formed." It
is well that he should take notice of such a fact, but how
can Dr Bartholow or any one else know who is or who is
not easily predisposed to the alcohol habit? Many people
condemn alcoholic liquors when they are well, but as soon
as they get sick they must have it in some form; yet who
can blame the people? The blame rests on the false
teachers; and above all the false teachers are the doctors
who so recklessly prescribe it for almost every known human ailment. As Dr. Cheyne, of Dublin, Physician to the
Forces, says: "The benefits which have been supposed,
from their liberal use in medicine, and especially in those
diseases which depend upon mere weakness, have invested
these agents with attributes to which they have no claim,
and hence we ought not to rest satisfied with mere ac-
knowledgement of error, but we ought also to make every
retribution in our power for having so long upheld one of
the most fatal delusions that ever took possession of the
human mind." But we must go on and quote. He says:
"Excellent results are obtained from the use of brandy in
the apepsia of infants. The summer diarrhœa, both of
children and adults, may be arrested by a *full dose of
brandy*." He tells us how brandy is made: "Brandy is
also a solution of alcohol in water (48 to 56 per cent.). It
contains a volatile oil, an ether peculiar to wine (œnanthic
ether), coloring matters, tannic acid. aldehyde, and acetic
ether. The odor is usually factitious; in pale brandy the
color is derived from the cask; in dark brandy from cara-
mel Brandy is made artificially from high wines by the
addition of an ether (cognac, acetic or nitric), of coloring

matter (burnt sugar), and an astringent to give it the necessary roughness of taste (logwood, catechu, etc.) " And this mixture to go into the delicate stomach of a weak and depressed infant ! But when given by a "self-styled practitioner" it *must* be swallowed, even if it does contain alcohol in water 48 to 56 per cent , say nothing about the other injurious "stuff"

Then he goes on and recommends "alcoholic stimulants to counteract the depressing influence of certain agents on the action of the heart—as, for example, aconite. veratrum viride, conium, digitalis, and the poison of venomous snakes." These are all used as medicine. yet he speaks of them as "depressing influence " and recommends one of the most depressing agents to overcome the depressing influence of other deadly drugs What kind of a being can understand such reasoning ?

Again: "Alcohol in some form is constantly prescribed in low conditions in fevers, acute inflammations, and depressing maladies of all kinds " To contradict this he says. "As respects its action on the nervous system, alcohol is a narcotic." Well, if this is true, how can a sane man possibly prescribe alcohol ' in low conditions of fever," where the nervous system is always depressed, "and depressing maladies of all kinds ?"

"It is directly indicated in chronic wasting diseases, especially in phthisis " Then again: "It is an interesting fact that an intractable form of phthisis is induced by alcoholic excess " "Before commencing the inhalation of chloroform, an ounce or two of whisky or brandy should be given to the patient." If chloroform depresses, alcohol does the same, only more so Then, "With the increased action of the alcohol on the cerebrum the excitement becomes disorderly, the ideas incoherent and rambling, the muscular movements uncontrolled and inco-ordinate (over-stimulation of the cells of the gray matter)." [More properly over-depression—paralysis of such cells] We could go on and quote much more, but this is sufficient to show the inconsistency of such teaching Many others that recommend alcohol in the treatment of disease contradict themselves likewise.

With all due respect for such men, we feel sorry for their convictions, but more sorry for the thousands that suffer through such false theories. It is only *alos*, another, and *pathos*, suffering

Listen to Dr. J. W. Turner, of the Royal College of Surgeons, who confirms the statements of Dr. Beale, of England. He says: "From my own experience, after thirty years' practice, I positively declare my opinion that half the untimely male deaths (innate phthisis excluded) are owing to the abuse of alcohol [in the use of it]; and I judge it incumbent on the medical profession, as guardians of the public health and well-wishers of their fellow mortals, to make this evil of alcohol drinking better known."

"Let us ask," he says, "the cause of a vast amount of kidney and liver diseases, diseases of brain and nervous system, insanity, paralysis, and idiocy? From what cause more than one-half the accidents which fill our hospitals? What number of suicides occur in the depressing stage following over-excitement of alcohol? How many murders in the non-natural state produced by it—not to mention the many cases of assaults which appear before our police courts and crowd our prisons? How many miserable alcoholic dyspeptics apply daily to the profession for aid, and too often confirm their ill health by persisting in the use of stimulants [irritants, narcotic poison] that have brought them to their wretched condition? Can we imagine that the public is fully aware of these facts, and that from alcohol or spirits of wine in small doses a person is quickly placed in such a non-natural position as will excite him or her to commit such acts as in their normal state they would shudder to think of? Not a day passes without such sad evidences of spirit drinking being brought to the direct knowledge of medical men, and they, of all classes, I think, should give utterance to their opinion on this subject."

This idea that alcohol is beneficial to the human body is so deeply rooted in the minds of the people that Prof. Bunge would say: "Nothing gives us such a perception of the selfishness of the human heart as an attentive attitude in regard to the alcohol question." Says Dr. Albert Day: "The drinking customs of society have developed very strange theories in order to sustain the custom, and in most cases they are the offspring of gross ignorance, or a mind befogged by alcohol. No matter how healthy a man is, if he indulges in alcohol even moderately, physical and mental degeneration will follow."

Is Alcohol a Food?—No. It is a common belief that, when a patient gets down so low that he cannot take nourishment very well, then alcohol in some beverage must be given to support life

Says one. "The chief utility of alcohol in these forms of disease is not as a stimulant, but as a food."

Prof. Charles A Cameron, Royal College of Surgeons, Ireland, says "That alcohol is incapable of forming any part of the body is admitted by all physiologists. It cannot be converted into brain, nerve, muscle or blood "

Writes the editor of *The British Medical Journal*: "The clinical facts which some writers have produced as demonstrative of the food-nature of alcohol, are, as such, worth absolutely nothing We have no hesitation in saying that to call alcohol food. in the present state of our knowledge of its effects,is an abuse of language."

We possess no particle of satisfactory and scientific evidence to show that it is such Those who affirm that it is should give us something beyond the mere vague surmises of their own opinions

Dr Robert Bartholow, M. A, M D, LL D, says "The diminished power of resistance to cold shown by drunkards, has conclusively demonstrated that alcohol does not supply the place of other foods "

Prof G. Bunge, Professor of Physiological Chemistry in the University of Basle, Switzerland, says. "We do not know that alcohol burning in the system gives any strength to any muscular fiber, or nerve cell Our tissues are not so created that every pleasant tasting substance will feed them. * * It is a deep-rooted belief that alcohol strengthens the weary to new exertions and efforts. * * The error that alcohol strengthens the weary is most fatal in the class to which the largest part of the population belongs. Poor people whose income scarcely holds out for the supply of the barest necessities, are led by this mistaken notion to spend a very important part of their wages in drink. rather than in providing plentiful and nourishing food. which alone can fit them for hard work. * * It is the same with other poisons The opium eater cannot work, or eat, or sleep on giving up his drug—he is 'strengthened' by opium [so he thinks], but the man who is entirely free from narcotics is the stronger, more capable man Better than any scientific deductions however, one learns the real uselessness—nay, the actual damage even—of moderate drinking, through the thousands of experiments made with the army and which go to show, all of them, most conclusively, that soldiers in peace and in war, in all climates, in heat, rain and cold, best endure the hardships of their labor and discipline when all kinds of intoxicating drinks· are withdrawn from their supplies. *. * Alcohol strengthens no one. It only dulls or deadens the feeling of fatigue."

Dr. Frank Hamilton speaks as follows: "It is greatly to be hoped that these experiments may not be repeated in. the United States army. We have reached the firm conviction, through observation and experience, that the customary use of alcohol is under no circumstances necessary for healthy persons. We make no exception for cold, rain, heat, nor even for the habits of former drinkers, when once they have enlisted."

Prof. Beale, of England, says: "Alcohol is not a food, but is absorbed as alcohol. It does not act as a food; it does not nourish tissue. * * It cuts short the life of rapidly growing bioplasm, or causes it to live more slowly, and thus tends to cause a diseased texture in which vital changes are abnormally active, to return to its normal and much less active condition. It is easy to prove that by these measures many cells that were alive are killed, and that those that escape death live and grow more slowly than before."

Prof. N. S. Davis, A. M., M. D., LL. D.; of Chicago, says that alcohol "is not assimilated, but is thrown off unchanged. As it is not assimilated, it cannot be a food."

Dr. James Ross was told by a medical man that he kept a prematurely born child alive for the first three weeks by feeding it with whisky toddy. Seven years later the child was a puny little idiot. In nearly every instance where alcohol is given it is given with some nourishing food, as milk, and it is this that keeps the patient alive, not the alcohol. The patient lives in spite of the alcohol.

Sir Ashley Cooper, England, an undisputed authority in his day, denounced habitual beer-drinking as noxious to health. Referring to his experience in Guy's Hospital, he declared "that the beer-drinkers from the London breweries, though presenting the appearance of the most rugged health, were the most incapable of all classes to resist disease; that trifling injuries among them were liable to lead to the most serious consequences; and so prone were they to succumb to disease that they would sometimes die from gangrene in wounds as trifling as the scratch of a pin "

Dr John Higginbottom, F. R. S., after more than fifty years of practice, said. "Alcohol is neither food nor physic."

The eminent German chemist Baron Von Liebig says, "If a man drinks daily eight quarts of the best Bavarian beer, in the course of twelve months he will have taken into his system the nutritive constituents contained in a five-pound loaf of bread, or three pounds of beef"—730 gallons—23½ barrels—nearly three tons in shape of beer against three to five pounds in ordinary foods. During that time he would pass through his system about one barrel of absolute alcohol; and this nourishment in shape of b er would cost about $300.00.

Is Alcohol a Stimulant ?—Alcohol is not a stimulant but an irritant, a narcotic poison .

The eminent Dr. Semnola, Professor in the College of Medicine at Naples, says: "I am of the opinion that alcohol is simply a toxicative, like many other antipyretics, as digitalis, phenic acid, etc , which poison the patient and those organs or tissues which are the necessary instruments of febrile manifestation '

Dr. Reynolds· "It has been proved to be a true narcotic poison, of the same class as the so-called anæsthetics, chloroform. and sulphuric ether * * Its influence is entirely in the direction of paralysis—suspension of nervous activity—a source of deficient vital power ''

In Schmiedenberg's First Principles of Pharmacology, Leipsic, we read "In general let it be understood that all the workings of alcohol in the system which usually are considered as excitement or stimulant, are only the indication of paralysis "

Prof. Bunge "The benumbing of all sense of fatigue or weariness belongs also among the tokens of paralysis so commonly attributed to stimulation "

Prof. R W. Wilcox, M. A., M. D , LL D , in his Materia Medica· "In many campaigns and Arctic expeditions it has been found that although at first the men, after taking alcohol, could do more work [so it would seem, in the stage of excitement], yet soon they felt so tired and exhausted, that on the whole they could do much more without than with the alcohol "

Dr. Elisha Chenery, of Boston, author of a fine work—

"Alcohol Inside Out"—says: "Though alcohol may excite for a while a portion of the mind, it is always the lower faculties; while the higher, such as the judgment and reason, are always lessened: so that by this abeyance of the higher powers, the wise and learned, though they cease not to speak when drunk, they babble as fools; and not infrequently have decrees been issued and armies marched under the authority of this species of stupidity."

Prof. N. S. Davis, A. M., M. D., LL. D., of Chicago, says that alcohol "does not stimulate or strengthen, but depresses and weakens."

Alcohol is an irritant, a narcotic poison.

Prof. William Hargreaves, M. D., of Philadelphia, in his fine paper on alcohol, says: "For alcohol, in all its forms, instead of nourishing, poisons; instead of stimulating, narcotizes and paralyzes; instead of increasing the vital forces, diminishes force; produces disease, and is an agent of degeneration and death."

Dr. F. R. Lee, of England, says: "All poisons lessen vitality and deteriorate the ultimate tissue in which force is reposited. Alcohol is an agent, the sole, perpetual and inevitable efforts of which are to avert blood development, to retain waste matter, to irritate mucous and other tissues, to thicken normal juices, to impede digestion, to lower animal heat, to deaden nervous sensibility, to kill molecular life, and to waste, through the excitement it creates in heart and head, the grand controlling forces of the nerves and brain."

Reynolds says: "It has been proved to be a true narcotic poison. * * Its influence is entirely in the direction of paralysis—suspension of nervous activity—a source of deficient vital power."

Sir William Gull, M. D., states that "the commonest thing in British society is that people are injured without being drunkards. From my experience, alcohol is the most destructive agent that we are aware of."

Dr. Desquin, of Antwerp, in a paper published in the *Bulletin Generale de Therapeutique* for October 25th, 1875, said: "Two phases should be distinguished in the physiological action of alcohol and alcoholic drinks. The first is characterized by excitations of all parts of the nervous system, ganglionary as well as cerebro-spinal; the second, by the depression of all the acts of organic and animal life."

Dr J. Mathews Duncan. "That alcohol does not produce equally palpable evidence of poisonous effects on all, argues no more against its poisonous nature than the different effects of opium, arsenic, or lead on different persons"

Dr. W. B Richardson, F. R S. "The true character of alcohols is that they are agreeable temporary shrouds"

Dr N S Davis says· "Alcohol is a poison"

Dr Dunglison says "That alcohol in large doses is such a poison admits of no question. All medical and medico-legal writers so classify it; and all practitioners become painfully familiar with the fact * * It is in any form and dose noxious to the body"

Prof'T. L. Mason says that "alcohol is a poison inherently, absolutely, essentially; in a drop or in a gill, in a pint or in a gallon, in all quantities and in every quality, it is a poison Its quantity does not alter its chemical constitution"

Prof Willard Parkes. "Alcohol has no place in the healthy system, but is an irritant poison, producing a diseased condition of the body and mind."

In Health. —There is no human body so healthy or strong that it will not in time be ruined by the continual use of alcohol, even moderately Some can stand more of the degenerating effect than others, just as many can withstand cold, heat and rain better; yet all must in time be bent low by the depressing effects In the United States Dispensatory we find the following. "As an article of daily use, alcoholic liquors produce the most deplorable consequences."

Prof. E A Parkes, Netley, England· "Experience decidedly shows that the highest health, the greatest vigor and long life are quite compatible with entire abstinence from these liquors"

Dr W Parker says "Alcohol has no place in the healthy system."

Dr Hudson says "By continuing our alcoholic stimulants [not stimulants] we retard the process, thus acting contrary to the indications of nature."

Dr George M Beard, of New York, says of alcohol that it "in every way works more injury than benefit"

Prof Sydney Ringer, M D , says "There can be no doubt that healthy persons, capable of the fullest amount of mental and physical exertion without the stimulus of alcohol, not only do not require it, but are far better without it."

Alcohol Causes Diseases of a Great Variety.—

James L. Perryman, A. M., M. D., of Illinois, says that "alcohol is no more the gift of a beneficent Creator than small-pox, yellow fever, diphtheria, measles, typhus. typhoid, leprosy, or any contagious or infectious disease. Alcohol passes through the animal economy unchanged, scorching, burning, disorganizing, paralyzing, and breaking down sooner or later every tissue it comes in contact with."

Prof. N. S. Davis says alcohol "disturbs physical processes and lays the foundation of disease."

Alcohol causes cirrhosis of the liver. Of twenty cases of this disease seen by Prof. Austin Flint, seventeen admitted intemperance, and another was not an abstainer. Of twenty-four cases caused by liquor, he found twenty-three drank spirits and one beer.

Dr. Loomis, in his "Practice," states that "those who take alcohol before breakfast as well as through the day are almost certain to develop cirrhosis of the liver."

Dr. H. F. Formad, of Philadelphia, found that of 250 bodies of chronic drinkers examined, 220 or 88 per cent. had fatty livers that were more or less enlarged.

According to Dr. Edward Goodeve, "atrophy of the liver, which is so frequent in Europe, is to be ascribed chiefly to the use of alcoholic drinks among the people."

Dr. S. J. Goodfellow, Physician to the Middlesex Hospital, regards it an unquestionable fact, that alcoholic compounds are a very frequent cause of kidney disease and albuminous urine.

Alcohol is Given in Consumption.—

Dr. Lebert, who has seen much practice in Germany, France and Switzerland, strongly condemns alcohol as a cause of consumption, and never intimates that it will help cure it. And no less an authority than Dr. Austie insists that no form of consumption is so utterly fatal as that arising from alcohol. This form is usually what physicians call the "fibroid" consumption, corresponding to cirrhosis in other parts.

The Effect of Alcohol on the Heart —

Prof. R. W. Wilcox, M. A., M. D., LL. D., in his Materia Medica, says: "It has been repeatedly proved that these good results are but transitory. The heart, although at first stimulated [irritated], is more exhausted after the stimulation has passed

' off, than it was before This is also true of all the organs."

Dr. B. W. Richardson, of London, studied the heart with the aid of instruments of precision, showing that the heart beat was decidedly altered in persons much short of inebriety. Total abstinence and time were both necessary, to restore the heart to normal function again

Dr. Aitken asserts that ' alcohol acts specifically on the heart, and the powers of the heart are often permanently augmented, whilst the coats of the arteries, thickened, thinned or ulcerated, have their elasticity destroyed and thus the tendency to hemorrhage in the brain is increased "

Dr Thomas Sewall, who has held many autopsies on the bodies of the intemperate, observes: ' I am inclined to think that the heart seldom escapes injury."

Dr Marvand of France, and Dr Zimmerberg of Germany, through their experiments made with the sphygmograph, or pulse-writer, have learned that "large doses increase at first and then diminish the heart's action, and very large doses depress from the first "

Prof. Martin, of the John Hopkins University, one of the foremost experimenters in physiology in this country, aided by the fine instruments of precision of that highly endowed university, has made many experiments to demonstrate the action of alcohol on the heart, and has found by comparison that an ounce of whisky or brandy always lessens the force of that organ, though generally increasing its frequency But frequency is often only the indication of weakness, as is so often seen in disease and when the physical powers are going out in death. This weakness so clearly made out from an ounce of such spirits, becomes more and more decided as the dose is increased. This is an unequivocal demonstration which must be accepted.

Prof A B Palmer, M D, who was president of the medical department of the University of Michigan up to his death, made the following remarks in an address

"We thought, and we may sometimes still think, alcohol makes us witty. We know from observation it makes men silly We thought it brightened the intellect and might make men wiser; we find that in the long run, at least, it dulls the intellect and makes men foolish Wine has been called the 'milk of age,' and we thought it supported advanced life; we know that the aged live longer and retain their powers better without their use. As a medicine, we thought it protected against epidemic diseases; we know now that it invites attacks. We thought it prevented and even cured consumption; we know it is the almost frequent cause of at least one form of that disease. As our scientific knowledge of alcohol advances, our practice with it and our language respecting it should change. As to its physiological effects, we have certainly in many respects been mistaken in the past. We have said it excited the vaso-motor nerves of the surface and thus increased vascular action in the cutaneous circulation; we know now it depresses these nerves and causes passive dilatation of the surface vessels. We thought it increased animal heat; the thermometer shows it diminishes it. We thought that, from more blood coming to the surface and sometimes causing a feeling of warmth, it would diminish the danger from exposure to cold; we find that, from less heat being produced in the centers, and more being lost from the surface by the increased blood in the superficial vessels, the danger of exposure to cold is greatly increased. We said the alcohol taken was oxydized in the lungs, and that increased heat and other forms of force were thus produced; we find that it is not thus oxydized, and that under its influence heat and the other forms of force are lessened. We thought it increased muscular strength, and it was taken to aid men in their work; we find that it diminishes muscular power, both for immediate action and with reference to endurance. We said it was a direct heart excitor; we now know it is a direct heart depresser. We said, and nearly all the text-books still say, it is a cardiac stimulant; we know from most conclusive experience it is a direct cardiac paralyzant."

Alcohol in Cholera, Yellow Fever and all Intestinal Diseases.—Dr. Christison mentions a case where the whole lining coat of the stomach was in a gangrenous state, and the large and small intestines were red or inflamed their whole length. Dr. Jacobs confirms these observations.

Remembering that fact and knowing that alcohol is one of the principal agents of many practitioners in the treatment of cholera, yellow fever and allied diseases, we will listen to those who have had much experience in this line. When cholera was prevailing in 1832, *The London Morning Herald* put forth this announcement: "Intemperance is a qualification it never overlooks. Often has it

passed harmless over wide population of temperate country people, and poured down, as an overwhelming scourge,
upon the drunkards of some distant town."

The testimony of Dr. Mackintosh, of the extensive cholera hospital in Edenbury, is this   "Drunkards were the
persons generally attacked; and, above all, the first victims
are the dissipated, particularly those addicted to the use of
ardent spirits "

Dr Bronson, who has treated many cases of cholera in
Montreal, said   "The disease has searched out the haunts
of the drunkard, and has seldom left it without bearing
away its victims, even moderate drinkers have been but
little better off."

Under the false theory that alcohol is a preventive of
such diseases, and especially cholera, many persons resorted to their bottle, but, says Dr. Bronson, "they did it at
their peril "

It is a stated fact that out of one thousand deaths in the
city of Montreal only two were members of temperance
societies of any kind   "During this same time there were
5,000 members of temperance societies in the city of Al-
bany, N Y, and Dr Mussey testifies that only two of
them fell by that disease "

There were 204 cases in Park Hospital in New York, and
Dr. Sewall, who came from Washington on a visit, made
inquiry and reported that only six of them were temperance men, and they all recovered, while those who
used alcoholic drinks all died   "(On account of this
scourge the grog-shops were closed, as a nuisance to public
health)"

In 1853 nine hundred persons died in Rotterdam of the
disease, and only three were total abstainers

In Tifflis, in Asiatic Russia, a city of 20,000 inhabitants,
Mr Huber reported that "every drunkard has fallen; all
are dead; not one remains "

What is true of cholera is also true of yellow fever

Dr. James Rush, who was a witness to a fearful outbreak
of this plague in Philadelphia said:— "Every species of
inflammatory and putrid fever is rendered more frequent
and dangerous by the use of spirituous liquors   This has
been remarked in all the yellow fevers which have visited
the United States   Hard drinkers seldom escape and rarely recover "

Dr. G. Dowell of Texas, who has had very large opportunities for observation, writes:— "All habitual drinkers died, none recoverd who were taken while drunk."

In New Orleans 5000 died of the disease ere one sober man was touched.— "Alcohol inside out."

The alcoholic liquors are taken to keep the cold out in winter, and to keep the heat out in summer. They are taken for colds and when a man is out in the cold weather he takes it to prevent taking cold. When a man is nearly frozen to death, it is given to warm him up. When a person is overcome by heat or burning with a fever, it is given to revive him or to reduce the fever.

With us on the Congo "says Henry M. Stanly" where men must work and bodly movement is compulsory, the very atmosphere seems to be fatally hostile to the physique of men who pin their faith on whisky, gin and brandy. They invariably succumb. And again in the Journal of Balneology we read that Stanly very positively declares that Englishmen can keep their health under the Equator only on condition that they entirely relinquish alcohol even the use of light-wine or malt liquor is followed by the most unfavorable effects, and in course of a few months or a year the health is broken down and death or invalidism follows.

Greely, the great Arctic explorer said that:— "Those who used alcoholic drinks could not stand the cold as well as those who used no alcoholic drinks of any kind, stood much more cold, hunger and hardships than those who did. The latter soon gave out, froze or died of exhaustion."

Soldiers in peace and in war, in all climates, in heat, rain and cold, best endure the hardships of their labors and discipline when all kinds of intoxicating drinks are withdrawn from their supplies. ** Results like these are also to be seen in the navy, as well as among merchantmen, thousands of which go to sea from America and England without a drop of spirits on board and it matters not whether in the tropic, temperate or friged zones.— Prof. Bunge.

As the result of a great many observations taken in conjunction with Dr. Richards, every quarter of an hour, for several hours, on persons of all ages, we found that alcohol, brandy and wine, diminished temperature. ** These observations have been confirmed by Prof. Bing of Boner, and Dr. Richardson, who asserts that all alcohols reduce the animal temperature."— Ringer.

Dr. Davis - "It diminishes nervous sensibility, reduces temperature, and retards molecular change."

The general idea that mothers who nurse their children should use some alcoholic beverage is wrong; and very injurious to both mother and child

The milk of a drinking nurse is prejudicial to infants. The observing Scotch doctor Macnish, says.–Such children are almost always sickly; subject especially to derangements of the digestive organs and to convulsive affections."

Dr. North has been obliged to discharge such nurses, transfering the children to the breast of abstaining women with immediate benefit.

Prof. J. Redding, M. D author of Physiology, it science and Philosophy," says;– "But worse than all else—yea a thousand fold more disastrous in its damnable influence, it even penetrates into the pregnant womb and there grasps the unborn babe in a vice-like grip, and sad to say may never let go either throughout time or endless eternity "

What Life Insurance Statistics show

President Green, of the Connecticut Mutual Life Insurance Company, says.— "The degree to which many diseases commonly referred to as malaria, overwork and other vague general scape goat causes, are actually grounded in what would almost invariably be called a temperate use of drink by persons of reputed temperate habits, would be incredible to the mass of people unaccustomed to careful observation and comparison of related cases".

Mr John Rutherford, some years ago, made the following statement. a certain assurance office with which he was connected, issued 30000 policies to moderate drinkers, and 10,000 to teetotalers, excluding all publicans, brewers, and free - drinkers, and the mortality of the two classes was kept separate During the first thirty years the mortality of the teetotalers was 9 per cent less than that of the moderate drinkers, while for the last eight years it has been 25 per cent less.

In 1886 the Total Abstinence Department of the Sceptre Life Association of England had at risk 3901 lives, of whom only 14 died, being less than four per 1000 During the last 21 years this association should have lost 361, but as a matter of fact only 163 died, less than $\frac{1}{2}$ the usual death rate where drinkers are insured.

Dr. W B Carpenter says.— "The average mortality for

the whole population of England is twenty-three per thousand. Those insured in life insurance companies, eleven per
thousand, those insured in Friendly Societies (Masonic,
Odd Fellows, and others) ten per thousand; in the Rechab-
ites, who are total obstainers, seven and one half per thousand.

The Pennsylvania Insurance Report of 1874 gives the
following rate of death during the preceding year.

Western Masonic, R. A.,	death per 1000,	14.
Odd Fellows,	" " "	6·
United Brethren, (M.)	" " "	8.
Temperance Mutual,	" " "	4.

Alcohol as a medicine:— Dr. Davis, who has had many
years of experience, gives his testimony as follows:- I have
demonstrated by the last forty years of actual experience
that no form of alcoholic drink, either fermented or distilled, is necessary or desirable for internal use, either in
health or any of the varied forms of diseases: but that
health can be better preserved, and disease be more successfully treated, without the use of such drinks."

The theory that alcohol is necessary in treatment of
pneumonia has received a death blow from Dr. Bull of New
York, who finds that in the New York Hospitals sixty-five
per cent of the pneumonia patients die under alcohol treatment, while in London, at the Object Lesson Temperance
Hospital, only five per cent die.

S. Wilks, M. D., Physician to Guy's Hospital, London,
says:- "To my mind, the most important question in therapeutics at the present day is the value of alcohol in disease. If it be said that its frequent use is an evidence of
its potency, this is the more sufficient reason why its administration should be watched with the extremest care.
So wedded, however, are some to an idea of the absolute
necessity of stimulants, that they have expressed almost
incredility when they have heard it stated that fevers
would terminate favorable without them. Young persons
with typhus and typhoid do far better without them. **
It is also a fact that in bronchitis I have repeatedly seen
improvement after stimulants [irritants] have been omitted; and, as regards heart disease, I am convinced that
the amount of mischief done is immense. In the case of
fevers and bronchitis, the weak pulse is often but an indication of extreme capillary congestion, and a stimulus to
the heart often aggravates the evil; and in the case of a

diseased and weak heart, where repose is indicated, a constant stimulation by alcohol [not stimulation but depression, paralyzing, poisoning] adds immensely to the trouble

* * Do not then assume that alcohol is an equivalent to a tonic, and that it must be necessarily administered because your patient is weak. It may be that that very weakness is due to the long-continued pernicious effect of this same stimulant indeed. as you have often heard me say in the out-patient room, it a man comes into our presence with a tottering gait, a bloated face, and his nervous energy all gone, you may be quite sure that he has been taking 'strengthening' things all his life

John Higginbottom, F R S . F R C S   "I gave alcohol in my practice for twenty years, and have now practiced without it for thirty years or more. My experience is that acute disease is more readily cured without it, and chronic diseases made much more manageable   I have not found a single patient injured by its disuse, or a constitution requiring it. indeed, to find either, although I am in my 77th. year I would walk fifty miles to see such an unnatural phenomena."

J. W. Beaumont, M D , L R. C. P , Edenboro   "I have treated several thousands of cases off all kinds occurring in general practice without alcoholic liquors of all kinds The medicines take effect more potently, and answer their end better. Patients get well much sooner, and, as a natural consequence, my bills are considerably less "

Sir Henry Thompson regards it as · a luxury, and not in any sense a medicine."

Dr Callenette, of the Isle of Guernsey, writes, 'For twenty-one years I have banished all intoxicants from my practice, and during that period I have made not fewer than 180,000 medical visits. and I hesitate not to say that the recoveries have been more numerous and more rapid than they were during the five years I followed the usual practice and administered brandy, wine and beer "

Dr Austie, of London, speaks of the alcoholic system of treatment, that "it is a system fraught with danger of the gravest kind "

Dr B. W. Richardson (*London Lancet* 1876): "As a medicine it has no place."

Dr Henry Leffman condemns it on scientific grounds, and turning the tables on those who prescribe it makes them responsible for a large proportion of the misery it occasions and declares the time come when the profession should take a stand for abstinence. Years ago Dr. R. D. Mussey insisted that so long as alcohol retained a place among sick patients so long would there be drunkards.

Dr. Davis: "There is no disease that cannot be better treated without than with it."

Alcohol Causes Insanity.—Dr. Ogston teaches that "the nervous centres present the greatest amount of morbid change, the morbid appearance within the head extending to over 92 per cent, of cases examined by him.

Dr. Behics, a French physician, reporting on the physical causes of insanity in that country, puts down 34 per cent. of 8,800 lunatics of alcoholic liquors; and no doubt but what the percentage is much higher.

Dr. Romberg, of Berlin, having passed an army of 50,000 of his insane countrymen under his eyes, speaks thus: "The diseased condition of the blood and its vessels exerts an undoubted influence on the mind. The affections of the brain, such as vertigo, dizziness, fear, terror, etc., are caused in a great measure by the continued use of spirituous liquors and other narcotics, that influence the blood-vessels of these parts. So, after a time the mind becomes clouded, and sopor-drowsiness. paralysis and death supervenes."

Dr. D. H. Tuke, in "Manual of Psychological Medicine," states that "insanity produced by intemperance is unfavorable, and when it does not assume an incurable form, manifests a strong tendency to relapse after recovery."

Dr. Harlow, of the Maine Insane Hospital. says: "It is quite a frequent occurrence to have patients brought in to us. between the ages of 50 and 70, who in early life were given to the use of alcoholic drinks, but had reformed and lived temperate lives ten, twenty or thirty years prior to the appearance of their malady, showing conclusively, to my mind, that the alcohol taken thus early left a damaged brain, doubly susceptible to mental derangement."

Dr. Contesse, Superintendent of the Bicetre, near Paris, states "that over 25 per cent. of cases received are due to alcoholic drinks."

Dr. Harlow: "The brain and nervous system of men. when acted upon for a considerable length of time by alcoholic drinks, by narcotics, as tobacco, opium, chloroform, chloral hydrate, or any of the nerve stimulants [nerve de-depressants], are pretty certain to give forth uncertain and unreliable mental manifestations which soon ripen into unmistakable disease—insanity."

Lord Shaftesberry, in his evidences before the Committee on Lunatics, in 1859, expressed his opinion that fifty per cent. of the insane admitted into English asylums owed the cause of their mental state to intemperance, and quoted the authority of Esquirol in support of the statement.

We now come to one of the most serious questions—that of *heredity.*

The alcoholic liquors may dull the intellect—the face of a bright, intelligent young man may be disfigured, so that he will stagger along the street with blinded and bleared eyes, with red congested nose, bloated face; and long before he enters the good years of old age, to go down as a miserable wreck, into ruin and disgrace, and end in a drunkard's grave, from whence there will be no return All alcohol drinkers are walking advertisements for alcohol. showing the way to misery, to degeneration and to death.

The grog-shops may hang out bright glittering bottles, to waylay the virtuous and innocent passer-by, and even succeed to entice him through the doors that lead to eternal darkness, and keep him there—for "brigands, gangs of robbers, prostitutes, cannot dispense with alcohol " It may be given to the father to so derange his reasoning faculties that he will slay his whole family. It may be forced down the throats of helpless invalids, who cry for mercy and for health, but only to be held down with that powerful arm of destruction, that will take the very food in their system and destroy it; that will depress, paralyze, irritate, poison and destroy life Yet all is not one-half so sad as to be born with the alcohol habit. What curse on earth can there be worse than to be born with the disease of alcoholism ? No matter how good a man may be, how determined his intentions, he is bound to fall sometime No matter how high an office in life he is holding he will fall in spite of all he can do. into the bottomless abyss of the "outcasts of society," and go friendless, homeless and Godless into the dark avenues of death.

This, above all. should make sane people think—to have mercy on the generations to come, if indeed they do not care for their own welfare How few—even people who class themselves among the good on earth—will not turn away from the voice of an honest teacher, whose heart is breaking within him to tell his fellow men of the dangers of alcohol poisoning. Much blame rests on them who would know truth only so far as not to interfere with their own selfishness.

Then we would most earnestly appeal to the medical profession, who should be guardians of public health, to study this question more carefully, and we are sure, when the medical profession will come out *right* then the alcoholic liquor, with all its branches, will become less, year by year, till at last the thousands on earth can shout as with one mighty voice, "Hallelujah! The agent that was the greatest curse to humanity with many of its branches is dead." Such a time will come when the doctors will tell the truth concerning alcohol.

The term alcoholism was coined by Magnus Huss.

All ancient authority who had any occasion to speak on the propensity for strong drink, whether they were philosophers or physicians, noted its transmissibility from parents to offspring.

Dr. J. D. Steele, in his "Hygienic Physiology," says: "The alcohol craving may be transmitted from father to son, and young persons often find themselves cursed with a terrible disease known as alcoholism."

Gall, an authority of note, admits the transmissibility of the propensity for strong drink.

Giron de Bonzareinque, in his book on Procreation, says that he knows of families where this morbid, unfortunate fondness for alcoholics was transmitted from generation to generation through the mothers.

Thonreuf (thesis 1859), Conlesse (thesis 1882), also Marce, admitted fully the heredity of alcoholism.

Lancereaux and Fournier suggest that the proneness in certain cases to alcoholic excess "is the result of an innate vitalized predisposition, and that habitual drunkenness is, in some cases, certainly the outgrowth of a morbid transmission."

Tagnet ("Heredity in Alcoholism," Ann. Medic. Psycho, 1877, Vol. II., p. 5) admits, "for alcoholism, as in all other diseases, is transmitted from the procreators." He dwells particularly upon the morbid manifestations produced by alcoholism of the procreators upon the constitutions of their progeny.

Dr. Paul Sollier, resident physician in the Paris Hospi-

tal, tells us in his admirable article on "The Influence of
Heredity on Alcoholism," that "We have found some very
interesting inferences from the discussions of our present
point in two recent theses by Grenier and by Legrain.
Grenier, studying the progeny of alcoholismics, shows by
numerous instances that weak minded subjects are very
much inclined to abuse of strong drink, and that from being at first hereditary alcoholismics, they become inebriates by the same sequence as their procreators. We see
alcoholics not only generating feeble offsprings, but im-
planting in them also the taint of alcoholism Hard
drinkers procreate hard drinkers in a notable proportion
of cases."

Legrain (thesis 1886) says "If there are any two propositions that we have the right to formulate at the present
day, the following are the two 1.—Cerebral inferiority,
the direct cause of excesses in strong drink, has its origin
most frequently in heredity; that is, excessive drinkers
are degenerates 2.—Alcoholism is one of the most powerful causes of mental degeneration that is, the sons of
inebriates are degenerates The relations between alcoholism and mental degeneracy are comprised within this
vicious circle, which is irrefutably traced out and confirmed
by innumerable most eloquent medical observations."
Further he says. "There are but few cases of degenerates
in the careful study of which we may not discover, some-
where, evidences of excessive addiction to strong drink.
On the other hand, it is notorious that in the category of
confirmed inebriates we find their progeny to include cases
of idiocy, imbecility, weak-mindedness, and various neu-
ropathies, of which the most frequent is epilepsy "

Dr Crothers says. "In many cases alcoholism has a
preliminary period, varying in duration, before the addiction to strong drink develops itself; and in some cases
before the initiation by the first alcoholic indulgence.
Alcoholism then makes itself known under shelter of the
reparatory measure against the wear and waste of years,
or after a nervous shock, or some sickness, entirely outside
of all temptations and simply from the habitual use of
stimulants The patient commences to drink for relief to
his suffering; then he increases his potations; and finally
he cannot do without them. Such a subject has started
with latent alcoholism."

Sollier shows that "in 141 cases the alcoholism was

linked with conditions of heredity, viz., in 106 cases by heredity in similars and in 35 cases by heredity in dissimilars. * * If we analyze the cases of heredity in similars we find:

Transmission to 2 generations. 93 cases.
"　　　　　" 3　　　" 　　　10 " .
"　　　　　" 4　　　"　　　 3 "

In certain cases we have observed that alcoholism, after having been transmitted directly to two generations in one branch of the family, has been transmitted indirectly in skipping from the first to the third generation, tainting a member of another branch of the family. In one case the alcoholism, after being transmitted directly to the first two generations, was transmitted collaterally to the third and fourth generations, among which it was again transmitted directly."

According to Darwin (Zoonomia) alcoholism is transmitted through three generations, "after having gradually sunk in the scale of degeneration both physically and mentally."

Morel, in his "Degenerations" (p. 114), gives the following:

"First generation--alcoholic excesses, depravity, moral turpitude, brutal instincts.

"Second—habitual drunkenness. attacks of mania, general paralysis.

"Third—hypochondriacal, thoughts of suicide, thoughts of homicide.

"Fourth—undeveloped intelligence. stupidity, idiocy, and finally, probable extinction of the race."

Dr. Tarquet says that "the children of drunkards are not all of necessity idiots, lunatics or epileptics, but there are few that present nothing abnormal; and in those of seeming freedom, the germ may be late in developing itself."

Fusch speaks of three young men whose father was a drunkard; two of them followed his example quite early, and the other one became a drunkard very suddenly at the age of thirty.

The Herald of Health speaks of startling results of a study of the posterity in ten families of drinkers and ten families of non-drinkers; "The direct posterity of the ten families of drinkers included 57 children. Of these 25 died in the first weeks and months of their life, six were ‑

idiots, in five children a striking backwardness of their longitudinal growth was observed, five were affected with epilepsy, five with inborn diseases   One boy was taken with cholera and became idiotic.

"Thus of 57 children of drinkers only ten, or 17.5 per cent. showed a normal constitution and development.

The ten sober families had 61 children. Five only died in the first weeks four were affected with curable diseases of the nervous system, two only presented inborn defects The remaining fifty—81 9 per cent —were normal in their constitution and development "

But alcoholic heredity carries with it more than the mere taking to the cup; it leads to suicide and to every namable crime   Nowlin was a drunkard, a dipsomaniac, and is dead.   His second son, aged seventeen, expiated on the gallows a horrid murder, while two younger sons have received sentences. Dupuy mentions four brothers, sons of inebriety, all of whom took their own lives

The following shocking facts are by Tarquet: "The head of the family was a drunkard and a debauchee His wife, though remarkably sober herself, was the daughter of a drunkard and had two brothers, both drunkards.

"These parents brought five children into the world, three sons and two daughters The oldest was like his father, married and had three dissolute children The second boy has been twice sent to the asylum for mania and homicidal impulses. The third was a debauchee, and died of consumption, of which there was none in the family, at the age of twenty-one.

"The oldest girl married, and is the mother of a licentious, drunken thief The second girl, though married, has lost all moral sense and decency, and is leading a most irregular life."—*Alcohol Inside Out*

Now for just one point more   After reading this article there may still be some who will tell us that there are other physicians who administer alcoholic liquors, and that "they know all about it "   The time has not long passed when just as able and wise physicians used for medicine, powder of viper's flesh and bones, volatile salts of earth worms, man's hair, powdered negro skull and dried human flesh, crab's eyes, hog and dog excrements dried and roasted—by such men that reason as all alcohol doctors do.

We will show that the alcoholic liquors are bad, and are

dangerous in the treatment of disease, in another point of
view.

1st. No one can tell just how much to give; just what
is a small or a large dose in many cases.

2d. You can never tell just how much alcohol the liquor
contains, or of what strength the alcohol is itself.

3d. You can never tell of what the liquor is made.

It has been proved that the alcoholic compounds are not
very often what they are represented to be.

Dr. Messner said: "The lager beer sold in New York is
not by any means a healthy drink."

A malster confessed that if his customers knew what he
really does they would all leave him.

Another asserted that there is hardly an exception to
some form of cheat. Take for example whisky and brandy,
which are so much used for medicinal purposes.

Some whisky was seized near Newton for examination,
and in some way the recipe was obtained, which was as
follows:

10 gallons of kerosene;
3 pounds of potash;
1 oz. of strychnine.

Mix with soft water. If you want gin, add *quantum sufficit* of oil of juniper.

"The State Chemist of Ohio, in the course of two years,
made about six hundred inspections, and found ninety per
cent. spurious.

"Two samples bought for the best, for medical purposes,
were examined by him in the court room at Cincinnati,
and the polished blade of a knife was placed in it for fifteen minutes, when it changed the blade to the color of
copper, and the liquor became black like ink. Nitric acid,
sulphuric acid, prussic acid, Guiana pepper and fusel oil
were among its ingredients."

That nearly all the alcoholic liquors are fraudulent concoctions there is no doubt.

United States Consul George Gifford at Bordeaux, wrote
from La Rochelle in 1882: "All French brandy might,
and perhaps ought to be, excluded from the United States
on sanitary grounds. * * They are only counterfeit
chemical compounds." It is a noted fact that much more
"wine" is shipped from France than is grown there. So,
much of their "wines" are fictitious compounds. It is so
the world over. We cannot trust the manufacturers of

these liquors, to risk the lives of the sick and dying by giving them as curative agents; say nothing about the deadly poison alcohol, there is enough noxious material in them to condemn them forever, in sickness or in health

In conclusion we will say that we have written this arti-cle with the view to bring out some more truth on this vital question, and not for any credit on our own part. To make our points as strong as possible, we have made many references to the experiences of noted men of science on this subject, so that we may convince our readers that we do not stand alone in condemning the alcoholic liquors, but that many of the world's greatest scholars concur with us in such condemnation.

With this we close our arguments, hoping that many may hereby learn the true use, disuse and place of alcohol.

ALETRIS FARINOSA.

Star-Grass, Unicorn Root.

The **root** of this plant is a gently stimulating and toning agent, chiefly influencing the female generative organs It is gently laxative to the bowels In dysmenorrhœa it stimulates and tones the uterus to normal action and thus frees the parts from pain. In menorrhagia it stimulates to the relief of the excessive flow It is an excellent, perhaps the best, preventive of miscarriage, and may be given during any portion of the pregnant period or during the whole period of pregnancy; and is an excellent preparatory parturient. Many a case of impotency and barrenness has been relieved by its use continued for some weeks or months Given during pregnancy in small doses two or three times a day gives relief to much of the dyspepsia of this period, and with mitchella is a superb female tonic In amenorrhœa it stimulates to normal action If anæmia be present proper medication must be added. It is not best to use this agent with married ladies who are given to too frequent pregnancies In such cases mitchella repens is to be preferred.

F E Aletris Far
" Viburnum Op
" Cauiophyllum Th aa dr iss
" Mitchella Rep. dr. iii
Syr Simplex q s oz. iv

F. E. Aletris Far.
" Viburnum Op.
" Caulophyllum Thal.
" Serenoa Serrulata aa. dr. iss
" Mitchella Rep   dr. iii
Syr. Simplex   q. s. oz. iv
Either of these formulæ makes a good female tonic.

F. E. Aletris Far.
" Viburnum Op.
" Scutelaria Lat.
" Dioscorea Vil. aa. dr. ii
Syr. Simplex   q. s. oz. iv
This is a good nervine tonic in depressed and irritated
conditions.

F. E. Aletris Far.
" Phytolacca Rad. aa. 1
" Arctium Sem.   2
This is a preparation used by Dr. J. E. Roop for ovarian
irritation,

ALISMA PLANTAGO.

Plantain.   (Plantago Major.)

The fresh *leaves* bruised and applied to the surface are
moderately stimulating as a poultice to bruises, sprains
and swellings. When dry a hot infusion is diaphoretic
and is soothing to the nerves. Cold preparations increase
the flow of urine and allay irritation of the urethra. To
the alvine mucous membrane it is stimulating, toning and
demulcent.

ALLIUM SATIVUM.

Garlic.

The *bulbs* are a diffusive stimulant to the mucous membrane throughout, and their influence will be most felt
where most needed. In case of coughs and colds their influence will be felt most upon the lungs and bronchi, for
which they may be given internally and applied as a fomentation or poultice. They are stimulating to the alvine
mucous membrane throughout, and are sometimes used to
expel the stomach worm.

The warm juice may be dropped into the ear in case of
otalgia and in dryness of the wax.

The ordinary onion (*Allium Cepa*) is of less strength but
may be used in the same manner and for the same purposes

as the garlic bulb. The onion poultice applied over the chest of children in case of cold, bronchitis or pneumonia is of much benefit

They also soothe the kidneys and increase the flow of urine.

Expressed juice of Allium Sat   1 part

　　　or of Allium Cepa   3 parts

　　Acetum   1½ parts

Granulated Sugar enough to make into a good syrup is an excellent cough syrup for children's coughs

Allium Vineale or wild garlic seed tincture, says Dr. F. G Hoener, mixed with a little sweet oil and injected 5 or 10 drops into the ear passage will give instant relief in some cases of otalgia

ALNUS SERRULATA.

Tag or Small Alder.

The *bark* is a mildly stimulating and gently astringing tonic alterative, influencing mainly the cutaneous and renal secretions, glands and lymphatics; and is therefore valuable in scrofula, glandular swellings, skin diseases and mercurial cachexia. It is also valuable in chronic diarrhœa, sore mouth, sore throat, especially when arising from some impurity in the blood. In the treatment of dyspepsia it influences the flow of gastric juice and invigorates the appetite. Its action is excellent on the mucous membrane in catarrh of the stomach or bowels Acting as it does on the circulation it is valuable in rheumatism, and in the treatment of syphilis and in chronic and acute inflammation of the stomach and bowels and in cases of hemorrhages. It is a gentle stimulant of the kidneys and absorbents.

ALOE SPICATA AND SOCATRINA.

Aloes.　　　　　　　　　　　　　　　South Africa.

The *leaves* furnish a juice which when expressed and evaporated gives the aloes of commerce.

It is stimulating to the alvine mucous membrane, is somewhat hepatic and considerably cathartic. It is not suited to irritated or inflamed conditions of the mucous membrane, and may under other circumstances create more or less irritation of that membrane Sympathetically it is stimulating to the vagina and uterus and may promote menstruation. It is usually best to combine it with less irritating agents.

It eradicates pin-worms when given in doses of 1 grain every three hours, for three ci four doses only.

Aloes is very bitter and is usually best given in pill form.

F. E. Aloes   dr. ii
    " Taraxacum   dr. vi
    Syr. Zingiber   q. s. oz. iv

This is a good hepatic and cathartic preparation.

Aloes
Myrrh
Glycyrrhiza

in equal parts is another preparation somewhat more cathartic.

ALTHÆA OFFICINALIS.

Marshmallow.

The *root* contains much mucilage which is quite soothing to the mucous membrane and skin, and is valuable in the treatment of irritated conditions especially in pharyngitis, laryngitis, bronchitis, pneumonia, dysentery, diarrhœa, typhoid fever, diphtheria, gonorrhœa, cystitis, urethritis and nephritis. Its influence to soothe will be used by the vital force wherever needed, or where its influence may be determined by other medication.

With lobelia it forms a good wash and poultice in ophthalmia.

Althæa Off.   oz. i
Rubus Strigosus dr. iv

Boil in 1¼ pints soft water down to 1 pint, and strain. Bathe the eyes 4 to 6 times a day for inflamed sore eyes.

With raw linseed oil it forms a good covering for burns, scalds, and denuded surfaces. The mucilage is best prepared by boiling the root a short time.

Dr. F. G. Hoener says it enriches watery milk of mothers nursing and makes it come more freely.

ALTHÆA ROSEA.

Hollyhock.

The *roots and flowers* are demulcent and are frequently substituted for the althæa officinalis. They are soothing to the mucous membrane and may be used for the same general purposes. It does not yield so much mucilage as the officinalis, but its influence on the kidneys and urinary tract is more marked.

Aqueous Hydrastis
"   Hamamelis
Mucilage Althæa Off. or Rosea q. s.

This is a good preparation for gonorrhœa. The hydrastis should be used in excess in the primary stage and the hamamelis should be in excess subsequently.

With aralia rac. and prunus it forms a good cough syrup for irritable coughs and colds.

With celastrus scandens it gives favorable impressions in diabetes

ALUMEN

Alum $Al^2O_3, 3SO_3+KO, SO_3+24HO$.

The Sulphate of Alumina and Potassa   Volcanic and rock alum are found in some parts of Italy nearly pure. It is purified by solution and chrystalization It is a rather powerful astringent, but is somewhat irritating and stimulating. Many persons use it in croup but it is not the best agent that could be used ·

Locally as a wash it quickly allays the irritation due to rhus tox. poisoning, especially if applied soon after contact. Keep the parts moist with a strong solution. It also gives good results when applied to sore nipples, apply a strong solution and wash off before the child nurses.

Burnt alum or alum deprived of its water by heat is mildly escharotic.

Mutton Tallow	oz xiv
Cera Flava	oz. ii
Resina	dr. i
Pix Liquida	oz. ii
Carbolic Acid Crystals	oz ss
Alumen	
Glycerine	aa oz viii

Dissolve the alumen in the glycerine and add to the former ingredients in a heated state and stir till cold This forms an excellent ointment for application to piles, either externally or by capsule internally. If more relaxation is needed add to the capsule some pul. lobelia seed This ointment may also be used upon eczemas, tetter, and with a small portion of sulphur added is useful in scabies.

Alumen Exsiccatum Vel Ustum
Acidum Tannicum

In equal parts; apply twice a day to venereal warts.

Talcum 5
Alumen 1
Use this for foot sweat.
Alumen
Chloride Sodii aa. one teaspoonful
Aqua Fervens   oz. xvi
Use this as an injection for pin worms.

AMARANTHUS HYPOCHONDRIACUS.

Prince's Feather.

The **leaves** are a stimulating astringent to the mucous membrane but especially influencing the generative organs. It readily checks uterine hemorrhages, and gives favorable results in diarrhœa, dysentery and leucorrhœa.

AMBROSIA ARTEMISIÆFOLIA.

Rag-weed.

This **herb** is a mild, stimulating, astringent tonic. A hot infusion relieves the circulation, giving a good outward flow of blood, and gives very favorable results in dysentery, diarrhœa and in feverish conditions where the bowels are too free, A strong infusion makes an excellent wash in case of relaxed vagina, prolapsus uteri and leucorrhœa. It is the equal if not the superior of hamamelis virg. In case of weakened digestion with laxity of the bowels ambrosia is a good tonic to the mucous membrane throughout. Zingiber renders it of more importance to the circulation, and taraxacum or euonymous renders it of more importance to the hepatic apparatus and alvine canal in chronic dysentery and diarrhœa.

It is claimed that during the season of the wafting on the breezes of the pollen of ambrosia that hay fever is more perplexing.

The fresh juice of the ambrosia gives good results in cases of rhus poisoning.

Dr. F. G. Hoener recommends the ambrosia as a good tonic, and for the removal of the after effects of quinine.

AMPELOPSIS QUINQUEFOLIA.

American Ivy.   (Vitis Quinquefolia.)

The **bark** of the root and vine and the **twigs** are mildly stimulating and toning, influencing mainly the mucous membrane and lymphatic structures, imparting tone and

vigor and increasing the absorbing function of the vessels
and hence is very valuable in scrofula, in enlargement of
the spleen and lymphoid bodies. It greatly assists in both
gastric and intestinal nutrition It is valuable in enlarged
mammæ or testes, and gives strength and tone to the generative organs.

Ampelopsin

Apocynin   aa, grs ii to iv

This is very useful in case of congestive chill and enlarged spleen. Repeat as occasion demands, or give the
apocynin alone

Inasmuch as it influences the mucous membrane it tones
the bronchi and is a good addition to cough syrups where
there is too free expectoration and especially for scrofulous
cases.

AMPHIACHYRIS DRACUNCULOIDES.

Broom-weed.

By J. M. Massie, M. D., of Dallas, Texas, by whom it
was introduced to the profession

The following is the botanical description furnished by
Miss Ora Crawford, Dallas, Texas

Family—composite; genus—amphiachyris; species—dra-
cunculoides.

Plant from one to three feet high, pheogamous, exogen-
ous, herbaceous; small yellow flowers, blooms in Autumn,
grows in the waxy, heavy soil of Texas; root, primary tap,
many rootlets, annual fibrous; stem, erect; herbaceous,
smooth, naked 6 to 8 inches, then bears many branches,
leaves, simple and bract like, sessile, linear, with strong
mid rib; flowers, intermediate inflorescent in panicled
raceme clusters, composite, irregular and unsymmetrical;
involucre of two rows of needle shaped scales 7 to 11 in
number, ray flowers number 7 to 10, are pistillate style,
two cleft, gamopetalous 3 petals included; imperfect calyx
polysepalous, modified into a pappus of hairy bristles, head
of velvety flowers 7 to 18, corrolla gamopetalous, 5 petals,
5 stamens; anthers syngenesious; pistil with style bearing
one stigma, perfect involucre downy.—[*Physio-Medical
Journal.*]

The *leaves, flowers* and *tender branches* are used in
medicine They contain a somewhat volatile oil, and a
resinous gum as well as extractive medicinal matters. It
is difficult to grind on account of its gummy nature; and

an alcoholic strength of 50 per cent. is required to extract all its properties.

It is a pleasant and decided diffusive stimulant to the intestinal, bronchial and circulatory nerves. It promptly soothes all irritated mucous membranes, is carminative and stimulating to peristalsis which may lead to evacuations It is instantaneous in relaxed intestinal catarrh, and is a specific in cramp colic in doses of 15 gtta. to dr. i of the fluid extract from two to four hours A pleasant warmth follows its administration; more pronounced than that of the mint family.

Its local effect is well observed in nasal catarrh, where it stimulates the mucous membrane, relieves it of viscid secretions, leaves the surface clean and permanently tones the relaxed palatal muscles. A most valuable property is its influence upon the mucous membrane of the bronchi when taken per orem, for irritable coughs depending upon a relaxed state, where a prompt stimulating and soothing expectorant is desired. The amphyachyris promptly cleanses and tones the bronchial membrane. It is also a valuable local application to the vaginal membrane where it cleanses and tones and is one of our best agents for the treatment of a degenerate leucorrhœa.

It influences the entire mucous membrane and may be made to give its especial influence to some part of the mucous membrane by being combined with other remedies having special local influences.

This agent may be relied upon for its specific action described. It is excellent in bronchitis, bronchial asthma, broncho-pneumonia, and catarrh of all the mucous membranes. This is a new agent that fills a place in our materia medica unoccupied by any other agent. It is a sanative agent perfectly harmless, and may be administered to patients in all stages of vitality with perfect safety.

Dr. F. O. Broady gives the following recipe for a Neutralizing Cordial which he says is superior to all others:

I.   Amphyachyris Dra.   oz. viii to iv
     Reum Pal.   oz. viii
     Xanthoxylum Frax. Cort.   oz. iv

Pulverize the Rheum and grind the others for percolation.

II. Prunus Virg. Cort.
     Chelone Glabra   aa. oz. viii
     Hydrastis Can.   oz. iv

Grind for percolation.

Percolate I with 50 per cent. alcohol q. s. ft fl. ext

Percolate II with glycerine oz. viii, water oz. xxiv till two and one-half fluid lbs. have passed   Add sod bicarb. oz. iii to percolate II., and saturate the latter, cold, with granulated sugar   Add percolate I ; add syr. simplex to'' . make one gallon if necessary; finally add ess. mentha pip. dr. iv

Normal Tincture Amphiachyris Drac (Broom Weed) standardized to represent 16 ounces per pint, as made by C T Bedford, is a good representative preparation of the agent, and con'ains all its valuable properties, and is in most cases the best and most convenient method of using it. Can be used i i ground and powdered form if preferred

This valuable agent was discovered and introduced by Dr J. M Massie, of Dallas, Texas.

After a years' experience with it in bronchial, pneumonic and catarrhal troubles, and in là grippe, it has been found to fully justify the praise and recommendations bestowed upon it by Dr Massie. (See P. M. Journal and Sanative Medicine, December, 1894).

Dr P. Holt says the following formula is splendid for catarrh, the only objection to it being that it will stain the handkerchief, but not permanently:

F. E Amphiachyris Drà   oz vi
. Tr. Myrrh et
    " Mentha Piperita   aa oz. iv
Soda Bicarb et.
    "   Biboras et.
Glycerine   aa oz. vii
Aqua   qs   gal. i

Mix as follows:— use a large open vessel – a shallow pan. Dissolve the sodas in the water then add the other agents which have been previously mixed. Filter through a closely woven cloth. When used as a douche or spray add an equal portion of water.

Dr. P. Holt also recommends the following vaginal powder.

Powd. Amphiachyris Dra et
    "   Alumen Com.   aa oz. viii
    "   Boracic Acid   oz. xvi
    "   Tannic Acid   oz iv

Mix Sig. one teaspoonful to a pint of boiling water, steep 30 minutes, strain and inject to the vagina once or twice a

day as indicated. This is valuable in all cases of leucor-
rhoea, erosions and ulcerations of the os uteri. He says, we
would not be without this preparation. The fact is, the
longer we use amphiachyris, the better we like it and the
more we use of it, we average a pound a day.

The permanganate of potash and amphiachyris make a
good wash for old sores.

A combination of amphiachyris, sassafras and eucalyptus
has been recommended for asthma.

AMYGDALUS COMMUNIS DULCIS.

Sweet Almonds.

They are a nutrient aromatic demulcent. They may be
eaten or emulsed and used to cover other remedies. They
are somewhat diuretic, but chiefly lubricate and nourish
the bowels in cases of debility. They yield an abundance
of oil which may be used for the same general purposes.

AMYGDALUS COMMUNIS AMARA.

The bitter almond is more tonic that the sweet.

AMYGDALUS PERSICA.

Peach.

This is an excellent *fruit* of fine flavor and taste and is
quite nourishing in its ripe state and is somewhat laxative
to the bowels. But the canned peach is a dangerous article of diet to the sick. The dried peach is far better. Soak
it for twelve hours and then cook. This is best when the
peach is out of season.

The kernels or peach *pets* are a mildly stimulating tonic
to the stomach; and if a diffusive be added its influence
will be felt more generally throughout the alvine canal.
If these be given in infusion care must be taken that fresh
infusion be made every ten or twelve hours, and taken
cold. This must be done in order to prevent the formation
of hydrochloric acid.

This same precaution should be observed in the use of
the *leaves*, which are moderately stimulating, and demulcent to the mucous membrane throughout the alvine canal.
the kidneys, ureters, bladder and urethra, and may be used
to good advantage in the treatment of catarrh of the alvine
and urinary tracts, for the relief of irritated conditions,
and for the cleansing from accumulated mucous.

A hot infusion will influence the circulation toward the

surface and produce diaphoresis, except for which cause cold preparations are best A diffusive renders them more active The *bark* of the tree is also useful and is a stronger tonic than the leaves It is excellent in catarrhal indigestion. The fresh bark and leaves are much to be preferred, but if carefully dried they will still be of some importance The green leaves are excellent applied as a hot fomentation in cholera infantum, inflammation of stomach, bowels or bladder

ANACYCLUS PYRETHRUM.

Pellitory.

The *root* is quite stimulating to the mucous membrane and circulation It creates a tingling sensation in the throat and excites a good free flow of saliva. It is valuable in chronic rheumatism and facial neuralgia For semi-paralysis of the tongue and a relaxed palate, uvula or pharynx it may be used as a gargle very frequently.

ANÆSTHETICS AND ANÆSTHESIA.

By Prof E Anthony. M D.

Professor of Surgical Pathology Applied, in the Physio-Medical College of Indiana, Indianapolis

To relieve suffering and prolong life is one of the first duties of man to his fellow man The office of the physician and surgeon is among the most important in a philanthropic sense in which man can engage As far back in antiquity as the scientific investigations have penetrated the chaos of thought, agents were discovered that would relieve pain and suffering, regardless of the causes that give rise to disease The ancients were comparatively ignorant of anatomy, physiology and pathology, consequently could not explain the effects of their remedies, or give a solution of their mysterious action in relieving pain Yet they were hailed with delight and accepted as gift's from the gods, and even at the present time, opium is considered as the greatest boon that a beneficent Creator ever bestowed on man

As the light of science has beat back the powers of darkness, and the human body has been searched as by a lighted candle, the deep recesses of this wonderful structure have been made to stand forth as in the brightest light, while the keen eye of perception and the intuitive powers of the

mind of man has wrought out the philosophy of life, and
is now able to explain the mode of operation by which the
various functions of the body are performed. A deviation
from this regular line of motion constitutes disease, and is
considered pathological in contradistinction to the normal
actions which are called physiological. Remedies have
been discovered which will correct these deviations from
the standard of health, and are not destructive in their
tendencies, this being so, any one of these medicines that
brings back the tissues to their natural state and allows
the functions to go on regularly relieves all pain and suffering, this is the highest point of attainment in the healing art at the present time.

This kind of application of remedies which restores
health without impairing the integrity of the tissues
or weakening the vital functions should and will relegr-
ate to oblivion all remedies that bring relief by destroying
or paralyzing structures and sensibilities of the human
frame; but this requires years of study, first of the bodily
mysteries as they are revealed in the study of anatomy,
physiology, therapeutics and materia-medica. Great as
this task may be, it should be accomplished before the
the physician should be allowed to take the responsibility
of caring for the lives and health of men, and the physician
who is thus not qualified to treat disease, and still resorts
to destructive agencies and narcotics, should be discarded
as a man unworthy the high calling in which he is engaged.
The fact that he cannot do better than to administer them
should be taken as a confession of his ignorance.

The century that is just closing has been marked by the
greatest development of medical knowledge that has characterized any age, in all departments of the healing art,
but especially in general medicine. The perfection that
has been born of accumulated experience of all the ages
past, laid the foundation for a system of therapeutics,
and the acquisition of a materia medica, that will enable
any physician who will apply himself to the acquirement
of such knowledge, to treat his patients and relieve them
of their pain and suffering without the use of poisons.
These latter, instead of prolonging life, leave dangerous
effects on the constitution and tend to multiply suffering
in after years and shorten life rather than lengthen it.

In the past centuries when little was known of the
structure and uses of the different organs of the body, any

agents which relieve pain and suffering were hailed with unbounded enthusiasm; but experience in the use of them has shown that while they bring relief, they also are productive of very deleterious results not only to life, but to health in after years. This coupled with the fact that disease can be more successfully treated without, than with them renders the physician inexcusable who goes on prescribing them because he is too ignorant to be able to do without them, and too indolent to learn better methods

Surgeons of the past centuries were not so successful in discovering agents that would relieve pain while they made operations. It was not till near the close of the first half of this century that anæsthetics were discovered and used. Until that time surgery was regarded as an opprobrium of the healing art Few men had the courage to withstand the cries of their patients, and witness the writhing with agony from the effects of the knife or cautery So terrible was the suffering that an eminent surgeon of those days was wont to remark that it was not a question of whether they could withstand the suffering, but whether they could live without the operation Operations were undertaken only as a dernier ressort, and then generally too late

The discovery of agents that would render the patient unconscious while the severest and most prolonged operations were being made gave to surgery an impetus that has never been witnessed in any other of the sciences or arts. The darkest recesses of the body have been penetrated by the surgeon's knife. The brain, the spinal cord, the lungs and contents of the abdominal and pelvic cavities, and even the heart, have experienced the surgeon's touch, and life that receded apace has been wooed, so to speak, back to its wonted habitation. And yet, we must remember, as remarked Samuel D. Gross, one of America's greatest Surgeons, that "immunity from suffering is purchased at the expense of vitality." It is a fact recognized by most prudent surgeons that the poisonous influences of anæsthetics upon the system produce depression and weaken vitality, and that many patients succumb to this cause and die, that would live if a painless operation could be made under the influence of agents that left no deleterious results after them Physio-Medicalists use anæsthetics in surgical operations because they know nothing

better to lessen the mental and physical impressions that
necessarily attend all surgical procedures, and because it
has been abundantly proven that the deleterious effects of
the anæsthetic is far less than the shock of the operation
would be without it; also that under its influence operations can be made that no man would have the hardihood
to undertake, and from which no living, being could survive. Nevertheless we approach this crisis with fear and
trembling because we know that lives are lost by its use.
It is the duty of the surgeon to surround his patient with
all influences that can possibly add to his safety, and to
arm himself with all the knowledge and appliances that
can be commanded to combat the accidents that mometa-
rily may arise. Having done this, he can only acknowledge
his ignorance of a better and safer method, and hope that
the time may come when methods will be discovered that
combine relief from suffering and avoid deleterious results.
This result has been accomplished in medicine; so may we
hope for it in surgery.

CHLOROFORM.

"Discovery.—This agent was discovered by Mr. Samuel
Guthrie, of Sackett's Harbor, N. Y., in 1831, and about the
same time by Soubeiran in France and Liebig in Germany." From that time to the present it has been administered internally as a remedy in asthma, spasmodic
cough, scarlatina, atonic quinsy with favorable results,
has been used in hysteria, cancer, neuralgia and painful
gastric disturbances.

It was first employed by inhalation in 1832 in a case of
pulmonary disease, and was said to give relief from the
difficult respiration. In 1847 its action on the lower animals was tested by inhalation by M. Flourens and Dr.
Simpson, of Edinburgh, in surgery, as a substitute for
ether.

Physical Properties.—"Chloroform is a heavy, clear,
odorless liquid, having a pleasant ethereal odor, a burning
sweet taste and neutral reaction; specific gravity 1.485 to
1.490 at fifteen degrees C., fifty-eight F. It boils at 140 to
142 F."--*U. S. Dispensatory.*

If the greatest care is not exercised, it is likely to contain foreign elements, introduced during its manufacture;
of these, water, alcohol and ether are most common. If
pure, it will not have a density of less than 1.38. When
impure, it will float on the surface of a mixture of concen-

trated sulphuric acid and water in equal parts, after it has
cooled. Numerous tests are in use for impurities, but the
most convenient is that of Mialhe. This consists in dropping a quantity of chloroform in distilled water If pure,
it will remain at the bottom of the glass, but if impure, it
will either float on the top, or turn the water milky.

The composition of chloroform is very unstable. It decomposes quickly in direct sunlight, or even diffused day-
light.   The presence of a very small quantity of water
causes it to decompose, the resulting compounds being
hydrochloric acid and phosgene gas It is of the utmost
importance for the safety of the patient that it should be
pure and of a known strength. Squibb's chloroform and
ether are now supposed to be the best; to be sure of this
even, it should be obtained of the most reliable druggists,
on whose knowledge and integrity implicit reliance can be
placed

The local action of chloroform is that of an irritant
When applied to the skin and evaporation is prevented,
vesication is produced   On the mucous membranes it
exerts about the same effect as excessive heat, or acro-
narcotic poisons. In a case of poisoning from an overdose
reported by the U. S Dispensatory, "Death took place in
about thirty-four hours. The lining membrane of the larynx and trachea was found inflamed, the bronchi were
loaded with a dirty-gray purulent fluid, the lungs were inflamed as in the first stages of pneumonia and the brain
and its membranes congested."

The smallest dose reported to have produced death was
one teaspoonful, the subject a boy about eight years old
Larger doses may be taken and the person survive, but the
irritant effect on the stomach leaves the organ weak for a
long time, and in some instances they never recover.
When an overdose is taken by accident or for suicidal purposes, they soon begin to feel its influences, if walking
about, the first sensation is a dizziness, they stagger and
fall semi-unconscious and soon fall into a state of coma,
with stertorous breathing, dilated pupils, pulse imperceptible, cold skin, anæsthesia and sometimes convulsions
Occasionally there will be momentary flushing of the face
and vomiting, but this does not retard the action of the
poison The temperature falls and respiration is slow and
shallow. If called to a case of the above description, the
breath will form a guide to the cause; if called after death

and a post mortem is made soon, the poison will be found
in the stomach; if called very late, say several days after
death, only the corrosive action will be left, and the absence of any other poison, together with any other circumstances that point to chloroform as the agent, may lead to
tolerable certainty as to the cause of death.

Treatment.—As with any other acro-narcotic poison,
the first thing should be to evacuate the stomach with a
stomach pump if possible; if not, then by such agents as
ipecacuanha, given in thirty grain doses with an infusion
of aristolochia serpentaria. Large draughts of water,
with salt or mustard, will also be effective in the absence
of ipecac. After free emesis has been produced, if the
patient can be induced to drink freely of a solution of bicarbonate of soda or magnesia, they should be directed to
do so. If the patient is stupid or comatose, "flicking"
with the end of a towel dipped in cold water may answer a
good purpose. But far the best is an enema of half an
ounce tincture of myrrha compound in half pint of warm
water. After recovery has progressed so far as to establish the circulation and sensibilities, a cup of strong coffee
is said to be good. The gastric disturbances that follow
in such cases should be met with mild alkalies to keep the
contents of the stomach as nearly neutral as possible, except during the period of digestion. Persistence in the
above line of treatment will in time restore a natural state
in most cases, but in bad cases and those who are debilitated from other diseases, perfect health will never be
restored.

Chronic chloroform poisoning affords one instance of the
many that attest to the incontrollable influe ce of narco-
mania. Its victims are mostly medical practitioners.
The habit is solitary and usually periodical at first, but
soon becomes constant. The most prominent symptoms
are the gastric disturbances: the nervous symptoms are
also prominent, especially during the intervals. Nervous
depression soon manifests itself. Languor, tremors and
loss of interest in everything, drowsiness and stupidity, a
slow and weak circulation, coldness of the skin and great
emaciation are usually present in the last stages, and
death may take place at any moment from inefficiency of
heart action. Alternating sensations of heat and cold are
present, but the general temperature is lowered and at all
times below the normal standard. This is caused by the

contracting influence on the capillaries through the vaso-motor system Through this state of the circulatory system, nausea, chills and pallor are present in nearly all cases. The habit is very seldom cured Despite his own efforts and those of his friends, he continues his downward course until death relieves him of his suffering. There' are no well-established pathological conditions except that there is a general failure of all the nutritive functions. Every tissue of the body, but especially the heart, is found in a soft and relaxed state, and reduced in size No change of structure has been found to account for the symptoms that are seen in life, except that stated by Tillman, who says "Winogradow found granular degeneration of the ganglia of the heart brain and spinal cord in both men and animals after death from chloroform " It was thought by Von Lagenbech and Pirogoff that death may be caused by the presence of gas in the large venous trunks and in the right ventricle of the heart; but it has since been shown that this condition is not peculiar to persons who have died from chloroform, and in some cases at least is produced by decomposition after death Not infrequently the above changes are present and may be assigned as the cause of death in those who have been addicted to its use for a long period of time. In sudden death from chloroform, the blood is usually found dark-colored and uncoagulated, much as it is after death from the inhalation of carbonic acid gas. which no doubt is the cause of death in many cases; but microscopic examination shows no alteration in the constituents Chemical analysis, however, shows the blood overloaded with carbonic acid and the products of waste from the tissues which could not be eliminated in consequence of the failure of the respiratory process

ÆTHER.

The ethers are a class of liquids discovered by chemists as early as the thirteenth century. The method of preparing them was given by Valerius Cardus in 1540. They were known to Boyle and Newton, and were usually prepared by distilling alcohol with some acid. They receive various names according to the method of preparation; thus we have nitric ether, acetic ether, sulphuric ether, etc.

Ether puris, or commercial ether, as it is commonly called, is sufficiently pure for all pharmaceutical and remedial purposes; but for surgical purposes, the stronger sulphuric ether, or ether fortior, prepared by Dr. Squibb, is perhaps the best that can be obtained at the present.

Physical Properties.—"A thin diffusive and colorless liquid, possessing an aromatic odor, a burning and sweetish taste, leaving a slightly bitter sensation in the mouth. It is soluble in all proportions of alcohol, and the fixed volatile oils; also in benzoin, benzol and chloroform. It may be dissolved in eight times its volume of water at fifteen degrees C. (59 F.) Ether is very inflammable; when its vapor is mixed with air and brought in contact with flame, it explodes with great violence. To preserve its purity, it should be kept in well-stoppered bottles, or in soldered tin cans, and kept in a cool place out of the light and away from fire or flame. It is extremely volatile and evaporates rapidly when exposed to the air with the reduction of the temperature. The simplest test of its purity consists in dropping a small portion on paper, and when it has evaporated it should leave no odor."

Ether, as a medicine, is chiefly used for its anæsthetic properties, and may be used locally, or taken into the system by the stomach   When used locally, its evaporation should be prevented. When taken into the stomach, its first manifestation is that of a stimulant, which soon gives way to narcosis. It is used as a stimulant in cases of sudden nervous depression, fainting from mental shock, hysteria and all suspension of animation, in neuralgia and painful gastric disturbances; also in the nausea of flatulent and biliary colic.

When ether is taken into the general system, it causes an increase in the force and frequency of the heart and vaso-motor system; the pulse will be full and strong, the capillaries in the skin will be filled with blood, which gives a florid appearance resembling that of health. Given in larger doses, the skin will assume a dark livid color, showing that the respiratory center is being influenced by it; there will be anæsthesia, but not always loss of consciousness. This state will continue until death takes place, in some cases; while in others there will be paralysis of the vaso-motor system and collapse of the capillaries. In such cases the skin will become blanched, and cold perspiration stand upon the surface; but the heart will continue to act and the radial pulse can be felt beating several moments after respiration has ceased and life is extinct in all other parts of the body

The dose of ether taken internally is from fifty drops to one teaspoonful, to be repeated frequently when its full effects are desired It may be dropped on the surface of cold water, or rubbed up with spermaceti, in the proportion of two grains for each fluid drachm of the ether It can also be given in capsules, usually known as pearls of ether Given in this way, the mouth and throat are not irritated, but the full irritating influence is soon felt on the stomach It is said they can also be introduced into the bowel and vagina, but for what purpose is not stated. Gelatinized ether may be prepared by placing ether fortior and white of an egg in a bottle, stoppering the bottle tightly and shaking rapidly Four parts of the egg and one of the ether are the usual proportions used This may be spread on linen and applied locally for the relief of pain To prevent rapid evaporation, the parts should be covered with oiled silk. The French Codex gives directions for making a syrup of ether They take 440 parts of sugar, 490 parts of distilled water, 50 parts of alcohol 90 per cent , pure ether 20 parts. If the above ingredients are represented by grains in the same proportion, the whole of this might be taken at one dose This is a very convenient method of administering ether for tape worm. This agent also enters into several anthelmintic compounds for the same purpose.

The symptoms and treatment of the acute ether poisoning are about the same as those of chloroform poisoning Chronic ether and chloroform poisoning, or narco-mania, is an abnormal and in many cases an irresistible desire for the influence of some narcotic. This appetite may be acquired by the constant use of some narcotic prescribed, possibly, as a medicine, until the will power is broken down by the overwhelming desire, or rather longing for its effect to quiet a feeling of unrest, that is many times worse than death itself; in fact, the monomaniacs will risk their lives and take the potion, well knowing that the sleep may be the last on earth. It may be hereditary, or may be acquired by the constant use of ether taken by persons desirous of concealing the fact that they are addicted to the drink habit.

Norman Kerr in the *Twentieth Century Practice of Medicine* tells of an epidemic of etherism that swept over

a large portion of Ireland and extended to London, some
parts of Germany, France and even to New York, U. S. A.
He says: "About 1838 a Catholic priest commenced a cru-
sade against alcohol, and within three years had administered the teetotal pledge to millions of his countrymen."
Following this tidal wave, equally as bad, if not worse,
came the ether habit. "A medical man gave a drachm of
ether, which was not believed to be a violation of the
pledge, to each one of a few of these abstainers. It was
like applying a flame to highly combustible matter. In a
short time it extended over an area of nearly 295 square
miles with a population of more than 79,000 people. In
one instance a village of 300 inhabitants had one shop to
every 23 persons, for the sale of ether. The intoxicant
was brought to the doors of the people by hawkers, was
sold in sheebeens and groceries, being often exchanged in
barter for eggs and other produce of the farmyard. This
was suppressed by law, but the drink habit of Ireland is
now, in proportion to the diminished population, nearly as
great as ever. Fifty years of observation of these subjects
confirms the above statement." I have known many persons to acquire the ether habit from taking the drug to
disguise the use of spirituous liquors. I have also known
others to acquire the habit from inhaling small quantities
to relieve some transient neuralgia, or perhaps toothache.
I once knew a physician who when called to attend an obstetric case, and while waiting for the tardy labor pains to
become severe enough to require his assistance, would lie
down, saturate a handkerchief with ether or chloroform,
place it over his face and go to sleep till aroused by the
attendants and informed that his services were needed at
the bedside. Of all the other anæsthetic agents used to
produce anæsthesia in surgery, none, so far as the writer
knows, are used as remedies and given internally.

A brief account of these agents, showing their use by
those who are the advocates of such remedies, was thought
to be proper in the present connection, but it can be seen
from the foregoing account of them that Physio-Medicalists have no use for them as remedial agents. It will also
appear from their use and action when inhaled, that the
internal administration of them is attended with far more
deleterious results than when they are inhaled under
proper care.

ANÆSTHETICS AS AN ADJUNCT TO MEDICINE

The action of anæsthetics on the human body is peculiar when the vapor is inhaled. We have seen from the above that when applied direct to the tissues by actual contact, or by absorption from the stomach, it is an acro-narcotic, producing actual destruction of tissue in a few minutes; but when applied to the mucous surfaces in the form of vapor, as by inhalation, its presence can be tolerated for hours, or even for days, without producing any serious results. The same is true of its presence in the blood, and through this medium on the nervous system. The writer has witnessed its use in puerperal convulsions, where the patient remained unconscious several days, and ultimately recovered; and only recently a case occurred in Indianapolis where a patient was under its influence thirty-six hours and that too under the most unfavorable circumstances. The case was one of typho-malarial fever on the twenty-first day of the attack. There had been a tendency to cardiac paralysis from the onset; for two weeks it was with the utmost difficulty that the circulation could be kept up. The suffocation was so urgent that the room had to be kept open, and he was fanned constantly for two weeks. During the third week the action of the heart improved, but he showed symptoms of disturbance of the brain. Delirium, sleeplessness and subsultus came on and gradually grew worse until on the twenty-first day, when at 3 o'clock P. M. he had the first convulsion, followed by another in thirty minutes. For twelve hours they increased in violence until there was no complete intermission, and the remissions were only momentary. Physio-Medical remedies were used energetically by "*Physio-Medicalism's Most Skillful Hand;* but it seemed to avail nothing. Chloroform was given until the convulsive movements ceased and a quiet sleep came on; for a short time the spasm of the muscles ceased, but the sleep was broken by the convulsions, and again were checked by the chloroform, and sleep was again obtained; thus sleep and convulsions alternated for thirty-six hours. During this time the chloroform was not discontinued long enough to allow the system to be free from it, and when the last muscles ceased to contract and there was complete relaxation, life seemed almost extinct. He was watched with the most tender and skillful care for another twenty-four hours by the physicians, and the most careful and scientific medica-

tion was directed; at length life seemed to return to him
and he rapidly recovered, and is now convalescent, October
20th, 1896. It will be natural for the reader to inquire
what part the chloroform performed in the case, since
other medicines were given with an unstinted hand. In
answer to this anticipated question, will say that its action was not curative: it acted as an adjunct, relieving
violent convulsions and relaxing the spasms of the muscular system, which were driving the blood with such violence into the brain, that no medication now known could
counteract, and the congestion was momentarily increasing. It held the convulsive movements in abeyance and
gave the medicines time and opportunity to remove the
obstruction to a free circulation; and by so doing the cause
was removed and the effect ceased. This use of chloroform, as an adjunct to medicine, is the same as the use of
it by the surgeon to obviate the muscular contractions
while he does his work.

THE INHIBITORY ACTION OF ANÆSTHETICS.

It is an established fact chloroform exerts such an influence on organic matter without producing any destructive
changes. "If an aquatic plant be placed in a watery solution of ether or chloroform, its absorption of carbonic
anhydride and its exhalation of oxygen ceases. The plant
does not die; it merely sleeps. The germination may also
in a similar manner be arrested by surrounding it with an
anæsthetic atmosphere. Irritability of the protoplasm in
the cells at the base of the petioles in the leaf of the sensitive plant is in like manner inhibited by anæsthetic vapors.
A vigorous specimen of this species placed for half an hour
under a bell glass, with a sponge saturated with ether,
will no longer exhibit any irritability. Its healthy appearance remains unchanged, but it no longer absorbs carbonic anhydride, and its leaflets will not shrink when
touched. Restoration of the plant to a pure atmosphere
is soon followed by complete recovery of all its natural
functions. The addition of ether to an infusion containing yeast at once arrests the process of fermentation. On
removal of the anæsthetic by evaporation, or by filtration,
the activity of the yeast fungus is renewed and fermentation is again resumed." (See Anæsthetics and Anæsthesia
by Henry M. Lyman, International Surgery.)

Anæsthetics do not destroy living matter directly when
taken by inhalation. Postmortem examinations have

thus far shown no changes in the tissues of the bodies where anæsthetics given by inhalation have caused death. That anæsthetics do sometimes produce death is not denied; but when it does occur, it is by the inhibitory effect on the nerves controlling circulation or respiration, and not by any direct destruction of tissue, like other narcotics with which they have erroneously been classed.

The action of chloroform and ether seem to be much the same in producing temporary relaxation of muscular spasm and loss of sensibility; but very unlike so far as their effect upon the general circulation is concerned. The former lessens the quantity of blood circulating in the brain, while the latter increases the quantity   This property renders chloroform applicable where there is hyperæmia of the encephalon and in all cases of plethoric habit without any weakness of the heart   Ether is more applicable where there is anæmia of the brain, or weakness of the heart.

ANAESTHESIA IN OBSTETRICS.

Ether, chloroform and many other agents have been used in obstetric practice; but one after another has been abandoned, until at the present, chloroform is the only one used. It is claimed for it that it is more effective and certain in in its action and causes less irritation than ether.   It also counteracts the determination of blood to the head, a condition which is present in greater or less degree in all cases of childbirth.   The use of chloroform as an adjunct to labor is popular with the profession and people, and it seems at times to be productive of the most gratifying results. The Physio-Medical physician, however, has but a limited use for it.   Labor is a physiological process, but is attended with more or less pain even in the most natural state.

It is a matter of common observation that the nearer a labor approaches the normal, the less there is of pain and suffering and the better will be the recovery after confinement.   In nearly all cases, the cause of laceration of the cervix and perineum is to be found in conditions that antedate labor, and should be removed before the labor comes on; or if the physician is not consulted previous to the confinement, as soon as called, he should make a thorough examination and at once institute measures for restoring the parts to a normal state, and continue treatment after confinement until health is restored   These means, properly

directed, will at the time of confinement usually place the
patient in a normal state, and then the suffering will be
at a minimum, the parts concerned will be in a favorable
condition for recovery, by a recognition of those methods.
If chloreform is administered without a recognition of
these conditions, the patient is greatly benefitted in some
cases; but a failure to recognize the abnormal conditions
and remove them allows the patient to relapse into a bad
state of health·that may last for months or years. Added
to this, the fact that it interferes with the natural process
by producing relaxation of contracting muscles,·which are
necessary for the expulsion of the child, under its influence
labor is in at least half the·cases retarded; there is no sufficient vital action to expel the child, when even a small
part of the force is destroyed by the chloroform and consequently instrumental interference is rendered necessary.
In the other class of cases, where the constution is vigorous, and the expulsive force is very great, the relaxation of
a part of the muscles by chloroform seems.to facilitatethe
labor; but the same thing might be accomplished by other
remedies just as well, and leave the patient in a more favorable condition to recover.

  It is said that even small quantities given just as the
pain begins will take off the sharp excruciating suffering,
but this is only imaginary, as the time that the pain lasts
is not sufficient to get any of the chloroform, at least, not
enough to do any good; it is only a placebo. Its use is also
recommended during the last expulsive pains. Anything
short of insensibility at that moment will avail nothing;
and to render a patient insensible at that time is to deprive the case of one of the most important factors in the
safe termination of labor, that·is, the loss of the will power
at the time when it is most needed. If the perineal structures receive proper attention during the hours preceeding
delivery, there will be no excessive pain at that moment
and the risk of laceration will be greatly reduced.

  A proper study of the physiology, pathology and mechanism of labor will justify the conclusions: first, that chloroform in obstetrics should be used only as in other surgical
cases; second, that it may be used in some cases without injury, and with *apparent* benefit; third, that while this
may be the case, it dose not justfy the general use of it in
obstetrics by Physio-Medicalists, because they have other
means far more efficient inasmuch as they operate in har-

mony with the physiological laws that govern the mechan
ism of labor

ANEMONE PULSATILLA.

Pulsatilla, Pasque Flower. Europe

This species of the anemone has violet blossoms, having
the outer surface hairy This plant prefers a calcareous
soil

The *herb* is stimulating and relaxing, influencing the
skin and mucous membrane In large doses it may produce nausea and vomiting It is also quite cathartic and
unless combined with zingiber or mentha it may produce
considerable griping

In hot infusion it influences the circulation and relieves
the skin and nervous system. Cold preparations will occasionally prove diuretic

It is a valuable agent in the treatment of skin diseases,
in some stages of syphilis, ophthalmia, and eczema. It is
also recommended in whooping cough and bronchitis especially when there is some impurity of blood present.

ANETHUM GRAVEOLENS

Dill

The *seed* is a warming, diffusive, stimulating, aromatic
and carminative principally used in compounds to relieve
the unpleasant taste of medicines.

ANGELICA ATROPURPUREA.

Angelica Seed. American.

The *seed* of the American angelica are more diaphoretic
than the German, but are used for the same general purposes They are valuable in acute febrile cases and zy-
motic diseases, coughs and colds They are antiperiodic,
and in hot infusion are valuable in dysmenorrhœa and
especially with nervous females

ANTHEMIS COTULA.

Mayweed

The *flowers* and *stems* of this plant are diffusive stimulants to the circulation, tending the blood toward the surface In hot infusion it is decidedly diaphoretic and
somewhat emmenagogue

A hot fomentation of the green herb is excellent for
sprains and inflamed extremities; for pelvic and abdom-

inal peritonitis; for cystic, pelvic, abdominal or thoracic congestions and for local neuralgias.

This herb is best adapted to torpid or congested conditions of the mucous membrane.

ANTHEMIS NOBILIS.

Chamomile, Roman.

The *flowers* are more relaxing and less stimulating than the anthemis cotula. In hot infusion they induce diaphoresis and a good outward flow of blood. To the nervous system and the mucous membrane they are very soothing and have a decided influence upon the uterus, relieving congestion and promoting the menstrual flow. They are valuable in amenorrhœa and dysmenorrhœa when there is a scanty flow and nervous irritation. It is a good agent to be used for nervous and hysterical persons. Large and frequent doses.may prove nauseating and result in emesis, but this will be no detriment in such cases, but rather an advantage.

F. E. Anthemis Nob.   dr. iii
" Caulophyllum Th.   dr. ii
" Liriodendron Tul.   dr. iv
Syr. Zingiberis   q. s. oz. iv

Sig. Teaspoonful four times daily as a tonic in dysmenorrhœa.

A hot infusion is an excellent diaphoretic for the relief of colds especially if zingiber be added, and will be found very valuable in bilious fever.

Cold preparations are quite tonic to the stomach and uterus, giving tone and vigor to the stomach, increasing the appetite and improving digestion. It is best for this purpose combined with some diffusive stimulant or some mild hepatic. In convalescence from fevers chamomile is a fine tonic especially if combined with hydrastia sulphate.

F. E. Anthemis Nob,   dr. iv
" Liriodendron Tul.   dr. iii
" Scutelaria Lat.   dr. i
Hydrastia Sulp.   gr. i
Syr. Zingiberis   q. s. oz. iv

This is an excellent tonic in nervous prostration and in hysteria.

F. E. Scutelaria Lat.   dr. ii
" Liriodendron Tul.   dr. iv
Hdyrastia Sulph.   gr. i

Ferri et Potassæ Tart, grs. x
Infusion Anthemis Nob oz iv
Mix.

When there is any danger of hemorrhage or when the periodic flow is too free or too frequent this is not the best agent to be used. In sluggish cases some diffusive stimulant should be added

The inhaling of the acetous infusion of chamomile is very beneficial in quinsy and colds in the head or nasal passages. A hot poultice of the same may be applied to the forehead or over the lungs; stomach or bowels for congestions in these regions.

With aralia rac. the influence of chamomile is valuable in cough syrups where a soothing expectorant is needed.

APIUM GRAVEOLENS.

Celery.

The *seed* is a moderately stimulating tonic nervine. It is useful in depression or prostration of the nervous system, whether it be from general prostration, general debility or from overtaxing of the nerve centres by over brain work. It is best used with some toning hepatic as euonymous or taraxacum

With viburnum opulus it is good for pregnant females with a nervous temperament and a tendency to cramping. Aletris or helonias may be added if there is a tendency to miscarriage.

The *vegetable* is a soothing nervine but is less stimulating than the *seed*. In convalescence it is especially valuable in the treatment of those of a nervous temperament.

Apium Grav. et
Kola Ac. et
Cocoa in equal parts, or
Apium Grav. et
Kola Ac et
Cocoa et
Viburnum Op. in equal parts are each good nervine tonics

McCoy, Howe Co., Indianapolis, Ind , prepare an elixir of celery and guarana in equal parts by direct percolation. Dr. N D. Woodward recommends it as an agreeable and reliable nerve stimulant in nervous prostration and migraine.

APOCYNUM ANDROSÆMIFOLIUM.

Bitter Root.

The intense bitter taste of this *root* is difficult to be gotten rid of. It requires but little to produce a lasting nausea. It influences the mucous membrane, is quite stimulating to the gall ducts, influencing especially the excretion of bile. It influences the alvine mucous membrane as well as the gall ducts and in large doses will produce watery discharges. Its best influence is shown in torpid rather than in sensitive conditions.

In jaundice 2 to 5 drops every 2 or 3 hours will work well especially if combined with capsicum. Where the jaundice is from occlusion, podophyllin is to be preferred.

Apocynin 1
Quinine 10

given one to three hours is excellent for chronic cases of ague.

In ague-cake give apocynin 1 to 1½ grs. every 2 hours.

In combination with triticum, juniper, or eupatorium purpureum, it is a good diuretic and is one of the most serviceable articles to be used in dropsy, F. E. 5 to 8 gtta. every 2 to 4 hours.

Apocynum may be combined with lobelia in dry forms of catarrh, and used as an infusion to cleanse the parts.

It is valuable in syphilis, scrofula and eczema where the hepatic apparata are sluggish.

With or without hydrastis it may be used as a vermifuge.

Apocynin is a good resonoid preparation. In small doses it is a tonic to the stomach, promotes digestion and influences the appetite.

The taste of apocynum may be moderately well covered when needed by comp. syr. rhei et potas.

Tr. Capsicum et.

F. E. Leptandra et.

F. E. Apocynum, in equal parts applied over the liver is excellent in cases of congestion; or the powders may be used in the form of a liver pad, and occasionally moistened with tr. capsicum, or with the fld. exts. combined, and worn in cases of extreme torpor.

Apocynin
Leptandrin   aa gr. ¼
Podophyllin   gr. ⅛
Ampelopsin

Oil Capsicum   aa gr. 1-16
This makes an excellent pill.

APOCYNUM CANNABINUM.

Canadian Hemp.

The *roots* are a stimulating alterant, quite cathartic
and largely influencing the glandular system,

    Apocynum And et
    Apocynum Can. in equal parts in
    Syr Zingiberis is good for dropsy.

In large doses it produces emesis, which is followed by a
free diaphoresis, especially if given in hot infusion

Cold preparations produce free diuresis.

It hastens disintegration of the nitrogenous elements of
the body and eliminates solids freely through the
kidneys It is of value in atonic dyspepsia, in scrofula,
rheumatism, phthisis, sluggish condition of the kidneys
and a clogged conditions of the lacteal vessels

It is excellent for the destruction of the ascaris vermicul-
aris

In hot infusion it is diaphoretic and expectorant and
hence good in rheumatism and acute febrile disorders with
clogged secernents

AQUA-WATER, H_2O.

BY PROF E. G ANTHONY, M D

Professor of Didactic and Clinical Ophthalmology, Otology and Rhinology
in the Physio-Medical College of Indiana, Indianapolis

A study of the physiological uses of water in the human
organism, will show it to be one of the absolute necessities
for life For the purpose of slaking thirst, the lower animals
use nothing else, and even man, in his primitive state desired no other drink. But, in our modern life, as a result
of what might be termed moral retrogression, a large share
of the populace indulge too freely in drinks, of which,
water, of necessity, is the staple ingredient Among drinkers of beer and other alcoholic liquors, some bloated men
will swallow many pounds of liquid daily. This greatly
distends the vascular system, weakens the walls of the
blood-vessels and keeps the tissues constantly distended
with fluid These weakening influences in connection
with the still more deleterious effects of the alcohol on the
assimilative and disassimilative processes, renders such in-

dividuals very prone to attacks of congestion of any of the vital organs upon the slightest provocation.

A lack of water in the dry seasons leads to the generation and accumulation of impurities of various kinds. Cooking is interfered with, dirt and filth collect about the home, streets are not washed and sewers not flushed. By virtue of the decomposition of such offending material, noxious gasses and specific poisons are formed which contaminate the very air itself. Hence the state of health of the people inhabiting such an unfortunate district, is greatly lowered. And in most instances, if conditions are properly investigated, it will be found that the direct cause of this lowered state of health of the community at large, is the small amount of rainfall and the bad quality of drinking water, instead of the "high temperature" as is sometimes supposed.

DRINKING WATER.

The supply of drinking water may be obtained either from rain "which the clouds do drop and distill upon man abundantly," or from springs, wells, rivers and lakes.

The quality of drinking water depends to a great extent upon the amount of oxygen it contains. And the amount of this element found in water is dependent upon the good quality of the air. After distillation water is almost free from air. It is tasteless and very unpalatable. When taken into the stomach an unpleasant sense of heaviness is experienced. These disagreeable properties will be found to have disappeared after aeration. This may be accomplished by shaking or spraying the distilled article in air, allowing it to absorb oxygen.

In hot weather, ice water is more frequently the cause of stomach and bowel troubles than the heat. This is due partly to the fact that in the process of freezing, the air is expelled, and thus the product is unwholesome. Some germs which are found in water survive after having been subjected to a freezing temperature and are a great source of danger. And it may even be suggested that the vessels in which water is frozen in the manufacture of artificial ice, are not always thoroughly cleansed and freed from impurities even though the water be previously distilled.

PHARMACOPOESE.

In the preparation of medicines, water is a valuable menstruum. It is principally used in preparing decoctions, infusions and syrups It is also used extensively as a diluent and solvent in the manufacture of tinctures and fluid extracts. The vast majority of Physio-Medical remedies possess a combination of properties, some of which alcohol will extract while others can only be dissolved and held in solution by water, So to have a preparation that will represent all the properties of such drugs. these menstrua must be combined in various proportions

For all ordinary purposes in pharmacy. common drinking water will answer But since such water generally contains a greater or less amount of organic matter and calcium compounds, causing precipitates and holding in abeyance the dissolvent properties, it is better in many instances to use aqua that has been subjected to a process of purification

Of the various processes distillation is undoubtedly the best. However, it has been suggested that in this plan, foul gasses and even *bacteria* may be carried over in the attempt at vaporization and condensation, but this is exceedingly doubtful It is always well to test distilled water by adding to three or four drachms a small amount of nitrate of silver. If it turns turbid or milky, it has become charged with impurities

Pure distilled water should always be used in preparing lotions for the eye Especially should this be the case in solutions of nitrate of silver, cocaine, atropine, homatropine and various other drugs which are to be applied to the delicate tissues of the organ of vision It should always be kept tightly corked, for it is easily contaminated by mixing with impure air.

Next to distillation comes boiling It is said that this process kills most fungus spores, precipitates lime products, gets rid of iron in part and very markedly lessens the amount of organic matter An absence of these elements increases the solvent power of the article Hence it is better adapted for use in pharmacy. In surgical operations and the dressing of wounds, by being boiled several times, water can be successfully sterilized and its use is quite safe.

Filtration through sand and animal charcoal is another method quite satisfactory for removing organic and mineral matter, especially if such material is not held in solution. In case sand is used it should not be too fine. and should be cleansed often; for the particles soon become encrusted with the impurities.

A good charcoal filter is one of the best means for the purification of water by the removal of both organic and mineral suspended matters. But the water must not be kept in contact with the charcoal any longer than is absolutely necessary for it to filter through. If allowed to remain in contact too long it will again take up the matter which has already been deposited. While this method makes water quite pure, yet it cannot be depended upon, for if allowed to stand any length of time, evidence of its containing low forms of organic life will begin to show.

MINERAL WATERS.

In filtering through the earth, water becomes loaded with the mineral salts and gases which are peculiar to the soil through which it passes. When impregnated with these salts and gases to such a degree as to be unfit for the ordinary uses in life, it is spoken of as mineral water.

Aqua mineralis derived from springs may be hot or cold, and in making use of it, there is no doubt but that the temperature of the article has much to do with the good effect. The deeper the source of the water the higher its temperature. It has been estimated that for every sixty feet in depth, there is an increase in temperature of one degree F. So, if this be true, the springs of Arkansas and other localities well known, must derive their water from a great depth.

Furthermore, mineral waters may be either natural or artificial. The former are preferable, and to get the best results the user must drink and bathe in them at their source, since imported waters, drank and used at home, will not have the same effect. The chemist can imitate some of the waters quite well. But in no instance can the same effect be obtained from artificial as from natural mineral waters.

Mineral water baths act very similarly to ordinary water baths, although much of the good results depends upon the temperature of the water. It is true also that the stimulating effect on the skin is enhanced by the mineral salts which are held in solution.

When given internally, mineral water often acts as a diuretic, diaphoretic and sometimes purgative. Torpid livers are stimulated to increased activity and rheumatism and gout are frequently relieved. In reality, these waters,

of which there are several varieties, may be considered
medicinal. Some physicians are in the habit of prescribing them for a remedial effect, while others discard them
altogether as medicament.

The classification of mineral waters is difficult. The
different salts and gases are so intermingled, that the varieties are exceedingly numerous But for the sake of brevity, they may be grouped into four classes, as follows·

(1) Gaseous or carbonated.
(2) Chalybeate—containing iron.
(3) Saline—containing salt.
(4.) Sulphurous—containing sulphur.

Gaseous or Carbonated water is strongly impregnated
with carbonic acid gas This gives to the water a "live,"
sparkling effect, and by chemical action helps to hold in
solution other elements, chief among which are carbonates
of iron, calcium and magnesia.

Carbonated mineral waters are often applicable in chronic cases of gastritis where there is considerable irritability
of the stomach. Their influence is modified by the salts
which they contain, but they are generally soothing and
grateful to the stomach. Kidney secretion is often stimulated and constipation due to defective peristaltic action
is many times relieved, since the carbonic acid water aug-
ments peristaltic movement.

Chalybeate water is generally impregnated with carbonate of iron. This is held in solution by the carbonic acid
gas which the water contains. Iron mineral water has an
astringent taste and although when taken from the spring
it is perfectly clear, if exposed to the air any length of
time, the iron precipitates and is deposited on the sides of
the vessel.

Carbonate of iron is a Physio-Medical remedy and a
strong tonic. Hence chalybeate waters are applicable in
all cases where a tonic effect is desired. In atony of the
stomach, menstrual derangements and many nervous conditions a beneficial influence may be secured

Saline waters, for the most part, contain chloride of
sodium. Magnesia and iron are found in some of them.
They are principally used in stomach troubles. Cases of
intestinal catarrh often derive benefit from their use.
They are generally recommended in diseases of the alimentary canal and even hemorrhoids are sometimes
relieved.

Sulphur water contains sulphuretted hydrogen together
with saline matter. This makes it quite applicable in all
chronic affections of the mucous membrane of the digestive tract. Many diseases of the skin are relieved under
the influence of sulphur mineral water. Especially is this
the case when sulphur baths are applied.

Speaking in general terms, the use of mineral waters of
various kinds, in properly selected cases, is often followed
by good results. At any rate they may be considered an
auxiliary to medical treatment. But in no case should
they be used indiscriminately, for each kind of water has
its peculiar properties, and like any sanative remedy has
its indications for each use and must be prescribed in accordance with those indications.

BATHING.

For simple ablutionary purposes, water devoid of mineral
matter is best. The good effect of the bath depends upon
the thoroughness of skin cleansing. The body must be
soaped and thoroughly washed. And since the mineral
matter in water interferes with the soaping process, it is
better to use rain water or other water that has been
boiled. Subsequent rubbing with a rough towel removes
the epidermic scales, opens the ducts of the sweat glands,
induces perspiration, brings a glow to the surface, fills the
vessels of the skin with blood, renders the integument soft
and pliable and enables the individual to experience a feeling of comfort throughout his general economy.

The remedial effect of water when applied to the surface
of the body, depends (1) upon its temperature and (2) upon
the vital powers of the individual. Each must be carefully
considered and one adapted to the other. We often hear
the cold plunge, the cold sponge and the cold shower baths
condemned. The bad results which are sometimes obtained come from a misapplication of the bath. Every
bath, no matter what its temperature may be, has its indications for use and its field of application. And if not
selected in accordance with these indications, taking into
consideration the vital resistive powers of the patient,
harm will of necessity be the consequence.

The temperature of the ordinary water bath will vary
from 32 to 112 degrees F., or even higher.* So according to
the sensations of the bather. baths are classified between
these two extremes as follows:

(a.) Cold bath 32 to 60 degrees F.

(b.) Cool bath 60 to 75 degrees F

(c.) Hot bath 98 to 112 degrees F.

(d) Warm bath 92 to 98 degrees F.

(e.) Tepid bath 75 to 92 degrees F.

It must be remembered, however, that the bather is not capable of judging as to the temperature of the water. Water, the temperature of which is pleasant and agreeable to the extremities, will feel cold when applied to the abdomen and other parts where the temperature of the body is higher. If the body be allowed to remain in the bath until an equilibrium is effected between the temperature of the skin and that of the water, the coolness is no longer experienced. This being a fact, in regulating the temperature of the different baths it is better to depend upon the thermometer

THE COLD BATH.
32 to 60 degrees F.

On suddenly immersing the body in cold water, the bather experiences some very unpleasant sensations. The water being so much colder than the body absorbs heat very rapidly. This abstraction of heat is perceived by the peripheral fibrillæ of the sensory nerves of the skin as a shock. The impression is conveyed to the centre, where it is reflected to the vaso-motor constrictors of the tegumentary structure. This transient influence causes a contraction of the skin and its vascular structures, effecting an unequal distribution of blood throughout the general vascular system.

By virtue of these facts the derma appears contracted; shriveled and pale. As a natural consequence the bather feels as though all the blood had been forcibly driven to the internal organs, particularly the viscera of the thoracic cavity. There is sudden and spasmodic gasping for breath. The respirations are increased in frequency and the individual feels like he would certainly suffocate. Pulse small, hard and not easily compressed. Muscles and tissues in general seem drawn together, rigid and tense.

After the body has remained in the water a few minutes a change takes place. The bather feels like new life had gained possession of his tissues. A sense of nimbleness is experienced. He moves with the greatest ease and enjoys in the highest degree the feeling of flexibility.

The skin is now full of blood. There is a glow. Reaction has taken place, and there is a determination of blood to the surface, relieving the pressure on the internal organs. Pulse full and strong. He can breathe deep and his respirations are regular. In short, he enjoys a great sense of comfort, ease and juvenility.

At this moment, when reaction is established. he must leave the water and rub the surface thoroughly with a crash towel to assist Nature in her efforts to throw the blood to the surface. Upon the completeness of reaction depends the good effect of the bath. If the bather remains in the water very long after reaction. he again becomes cold and is seized with cramps. When this condition obtains harm always results from the bath.

A vigorous constitution is the essential requisite to a beneficial effect of the cold bath. If the individual has strong vital powers. the bath will give increased tone, strength, flexibility and firmness to the vascular structures, skin and nervous system, enabling him to endure vicissitudes of temperature without so markedly disturbing the equilibrium of the circulation. And thus he can withstand a greater amount of exposure with less danger of taking cold.

It is a principle in physiology that "the growth of a part from undue exercise of its functions is always, in itself, a healthy process." While the force of the heart's action alone is sufficient to propel the blood the rounds of the circulation, there are other forces which act as helps. The arteries perform their part of this function. For this purpose they are provided with an elastic and muscular coat. The former is predominant in the larger arteries but gradually diminishes in thickness as the vessels get smaller, until finally the muscular coat is thickest and most developed. These two coats are the ones by which the arteries are enabled to influence the onward flow of the life sustaining fluid and at the same time assist in keeping up the blood pressure. Aside from this, their elasticity allows them to receive more than an average amount of blood, either from an increased quantity, or from an unequal distribution.

The first effect of a contracted surface from the application of cold. is a determination of blood to the heart and larger vessels. This sudden accumulation of blood gives the heart more work than it can perform for the time being. There is also a greater dilatation of the vessels than they are accustomed to in the performance of their ordinary function Hence the heart's action is feeble In two or three minutes, nature supplies the heart and arteries with energy necessary to perform their extra amount of work, and soon the peripheral vessels are filled, equilibrium is established and reaction is complete.

The performance of this increased function—which is physiological—is what leads to the development of a strong heart, strong blood-vessels and increased tone of adjacent tissues, which also exert an influence on the onward flow of blood Thus the circulatory apparatus is strengthened and better adapted for its function. The circulation is more active and the tissues in general more hardened and more capable of resisting the influence of sudden changes in temperature

Although the cold bath does not receive much favor from Physio-Medicalists, there are individuals whom it will benefit. In its recommendation it is well to observe the following conditions.

(1.) Where there is disease of the heart or large blood-vessels, or exhaustion from any cause, or disease of any organ or organs causing the walls of the blood-vessels therein to be thinned and weakened and unable to withstand increased blood pressure, the bath will prove injurious

(2.) Where there is an absence of these conditions and a strong nervous system, with vital powers capable of reacting quickly and thoroughly, the bath may be recommended.

(3) In the beginning the water should be tepid and its temperature gradually lowered at each bathing until the cold bath is reached

(4.) The stimulating effect is greatest and reaction comes up best when the bath is taken quickly The longer the bather is in the water the slower and weaker is the reaction which follows.

(5) A warm diffusively stimulating tea should be given before entering and after leaving the bath.

THE COOL BATH.

60 to 75 degrees F

The cool bath has a much wider field of application than the cold bath Its physiological action is much the same, except as to the degree of shock and intensity of reaction, which are much less. This makes baths between the above temperatures applicable in cases where the vital powers are weak. Old people and children may take them. The cool bath answers a good purpose in disease, for if due care be exercised the degree of impression induced will not be too great for the patient's vital resistive powers. And it is altogether probable that, if the truth were known, the good results which have been reported as due to the action of the cold bath, were, in reality, a consequence of a cool bath, since many times the temperature of the water is judged by the patient's sensations, in the absence of a thermometer. In recommending the cool bath to individuals suffering from disease, the temperature of the room in which the bath is taken must be properly regulated. Subsequent rubbing of the surface must be practiced until reaction comes up thoroughly, for in this as in the cold bath, the good effect is in direct ratio to the completeness of reaction. In cases where complete reaction is not established, particularly if the bath is followed by chilliness, tired feeling and loss of appetite, its use should either be discontinued or the temperature of the water raised.

This bath is not applicable in all cases. But when it does prove beneficial, rheumatic and neuralgic pains are often greatly relieved. Some nervous troubles like hysteria, and spasmodic croup will quickly yield upon the application of a cool bath followed by brisk rubbing with a crash towel. In some cases of rickets, if due care be exercised, good will result. It has a tonic effect upon the skin and the tissues become firmer. But in all such cases, the condition of the bath room as regards temperature and ventilation, as well as subsequent rubbing of the skin to aid reaction, must be carefully looked after.

THE HOT BATH.

98 to 112 deg. F.

The effect of this bath is therapeutically opposite to that of the cold bath. Yet they both bring about the same result, which is increased capillary circulation of the skin. One is the extreme of the other. Both have a field of usefulness, the former being applicable in those people who have enough reserve force to allow the performance of increased function, the latter where there is a delicate constitution, lowered vitality, poor circulation, and bad resistive powers, engendering an inability to overcome influences demanding strong reaction. While the hot bath is one extreme, it invites blood to the tegumentary vascular structures, thereby relieving internal pressure without calling into requisition the vital powers

In the first stages of pneumonia, when congestion and engorgement are marked but as yet no actual inflammatory lesion, the hot bath, by inviting a flow of blood to the vessels of the derma, lessens the amount of that fluid at the diseased point in the thoracic viscus. This does much toward aborting the attack, or at least greatly modifying its severity. Likewise, in an acute inflammatory condition of any of the internal organs, its use is not contra-indicated although care must be exercised lest the patient take cold.

An external application of hot water brings the blood to the surface. The skin becomes red and has a puffy appearance The conjunctiva is hyperæmic and there is a tendency to lachrymation. The derma of the face is turgid. Increased heart action causes the pulse to be full and frequent The temporal arteries throb and the bather complains of a heaviness in the head with confusion of thought. Breathing is somewhat difficult and there is a feeling of oppression in the chest.

Soon a profuse sweat begins, much to the relief of those unpleasant feelings At this moment it is best for the bather to leave the water and take a cool or tepid shower followed by brisk rubbing If he remains in the bath too long he has a subsequent feeling of fatigue and loss of energy The pulse continues rapid, he feels weak and the extremities are swollen. In some cases, however, this degree of relaxation is desired, especially when the muscular system is to be relaxed in cases of dislocation, rupture and many other conditions In these cases the hot water may be applied to a circumscribed portion of the body by saturating cloths and applying to the part.

In cases of keratitis, iritis and many other acute inflammations of the eye or its appendages, the local application of hot water does much to relieve the pain and suffering

After bathing in hot water the skin is much relaxed and in a very delicate and susceptible condition. To avoid a state of extreme contraction of the vessels of the skin, endangering violent congestion of the internal organs, the bather must be placed in a warm room or in bed to favor perspiration.

THE WARM BATH.
92 to 98 deg F.

The warm bath has a most soothing effect. There is no

shock, no extreme redness of the skin and no hyperaemia of
the conjunctiva. The face is only slightly flushed and the
respirations are normal. Pulse a little quickened but full
and strong.

This the bath for the feeble; the ablutionary wave for
the convalescent. Instead of securing its results by calling
into action nature's dormant powers, it assists lowered vitality and deficient nerve force in soliciting a full and free
circulation to the skin. The cuticular layers absorbing the
liquid are softened and subsequent rubbing removes the
loose ones, opens the ducts of the glands, induces perspiration and imparts renewed vigor and increased tone to the
integumentum and underlying tissues. Irritability of
the nervous system is relieved and neuralgic and muscular
pains are allayed. So that, after a long and tiresome journey, the weary traveler secures from the warm bath a tran-
quilizing effect to his living economy.

It will be found that the warm bath is much more useful
in disease than the cold bath. Those old rheumatic cases
in which there is inflammatory thickening of the ligaments
and other structures of the joints, will derive much benefit.
In cases of paralysis of syphilitic origin where the cause is
removable the warm bath is a valuable accessory to treatment. In the very first stages, Bright's disease will yield
more readily to the influence of medicines if the skin be
stimulated to a better performance of its function.

In many forms of skin disease the continuous warm bath
is made use of and recommended by Hebra of Vienna a
prominent writer on skin disease. The vessel in which the
bath is given is so arranged that the water flows constantly
and is kept at a certain temperature. At first the patient
is kept in the bath only two or three hours. The time is
gradually lengthened until he is made to remain under
water several days. He can eat, sleep and drink while in
the water and the processes of nutrition, secretion, excretion and respiration are carried on normally.

In psoriasis the continuous bath softens the scales and
keeps the part cleansed. Burns are treated with the greatest success. The water keeps the air from the burned surface and cleanses the part so that resolution is soon complete. While this bath cannot be well used except in hospitals, and but few if any Physio-Medicalists have used it,
good results can no doubt be obtained in properly selected
cases.

THE TEPID BATH
75 to 92 deg F

Water, between these temperatures, has no special remedial effect when applied to the surface of the body   It is used more for cleansing purposes   And since the oily filth can not be removed from the derma without the use of soap, soft water is preferable

There are people who go months and even years, without having their bodies subjected to the cleansing influence of water   Yet these undeserving creatures pass through life seemingly healthy and robust   In most such cases however the individual indulges in such physical procedures as excite free perspiration and thus the sudoriferous glands are continuously flushed   Were it not for this fact, these anti-ablutionists would certainly suffer the dire consequences of surface suffocation

It is necessary to take a good cleansing bath oftener in Summer than in Winter   During the hot months the sweat glands are constantly at work   The watery portion of the cutaneous excretion evaporates leaving the solid constituents and sebaceous matter in contact with the skin This, together with the dried epithelial scales forms a uniform coating over the entire surface of the integumentum The mouths of the gland ducts are clogged and this product undergoes decomposition   Thus very offensive odors are exhaled. The bath should be taken often enough to prevent the collection of such foul material and the skin should be thorougly rubbed afterwards to stimulate capillary circulation

THE SPONGE BATH.

One of the simplest and at the same time most effective methods of applying water to the surface of the body is by the use of the wet sponge   One part should be bathed at a time and thoroughly rubbed and dried, then another until every part of the body has been bathed   The water may be used at any temperature that the condition of the the patient and the state of vital resistive powers seem to indicate

The cool sponge bath upon arising in the morning, is a luxury which but few of us enjoy. Yet it is a process which is cleansing, stimulating, bracing and if not carried to excess, conducive to health   While at first the cool water may feel unpleasant, in a short time it becomes more agreeable And if followed by brisk rubbing, a warm glow o'erspreads the surface and a thrill of vigor permeates his entire organism.

The warm sponge bath is especially applicable in febricula, typhoid fever, pneumonia, and acute inflammatory conditions of any internal organs attended by an elevation of temperature. The temperature of the water is below that of the body and yet it does not produce shock when applied, but absorbs or becomes charged with heat from the body. Thus by the sponging process, radiation of heat is favored and the temperature of the patient can be reduced several degrees, great care must be exercised in fever cases to sponge and dry one part of the body at a time. And this must be done under cover to prevent taken cold.

THE SITZ BATH.

In taking this bath the patient sits down in a vessel of suitable size and depth. Enough warm or hot water is then poured into the vessel to come well up on the hips, Hot water must be added every few minutes to maintain proper temperature. The patient may remain in the bath from twenty to thirty minutes.

This process of local bathing is very relaxing to the pelvic organs and, has a tendency to attract blood to their vessels. It may be used to advantage in cases where the menses are checked from cold. In all such however, diffusively stimulating emmenagogues which have a tendency to aid in bringing on tardy menses must be administered internally.

If persistently applied in connection with internal relaxation and stimulation, in cases of renal colic, being careful to have the vessel deep enough to allow the water to come well up on the back, its relaxing influence will do much to lessen the tension and allow the offending material to pass into the bladder, much to the relief of the patient's suffering and physicians anxiety.

In acute inflammations of the kidney and bladder as well as neuralgic affections of the uterus and ovaries, its soothing effect will be greatly appreciated.

THE FOOT BATH.

This bath is very frequently made use of for the relief of pain and suffering due to severe congestion and inflammation of internal organs attended by febrile movement. It should always be used as hot as the patient can bear it and the water should be heavily charged with a powerful and

persistent stimulant   Mustard or an infusion of capsicum
is generally used

The vessel in which the bath is given should be deep
enough to allow the hot water to come well up to the knees
and the feet should remain in the bath until the capillaries of the skin are full of blood and the surface of the feet
and legs intensely red   This lessens the blood pressure at
the diseased point and makes the bath of special benefit in
all acute inflammations of the lungs, liver and bowels
The sharp cutting pain due to acute inflammation of the
membrana tympani and purulent accumulations in the
cavity of the tympanum, is often greatly relieved   In the
first stages of meningitis, this bath together with the
internal administration of diffusively stimulating remedies
which have a tendency to strongly favor an outward circulation, will do much to abort the attack, or at least lessen
the danger of subsequent serious results

THE SHOWER BATH

The apparatus necessary for the bath consists essentially
of a funnel-shaped cup the large end of which is covered
with a perforated sheet of tin or other metal   The small
end is attached to a common pipe to which two other pipes
are attached   One of these serves for the passage of hot,
and the other for cold water.   Properly arranged stop-
cocks allow a mixture of the hot and cold aqua and thus
any temperature can be used from hot to cold   In passing
through the perforated sheet, the flow of water is broken
up into small streams

The advantage of this bath is that there is a constant
change of water   The bath may begin with tepid water
and gradually increase to hot   After the effect of the hot
bath has been secured, the water may be gradually cooled
until finally a shower of cold water may be passed over the
body   This closes the ducts of the sweat glands and
brings up reaction   Then there is no danger of the bather
taking cold upon leaving the bath

THE PACK BATH

Packing the patient with a wet sheet is a method of applying water quite different from those which have been
considered   The water may be either cold or warm.   But
since the temperature of the water and that of the skin
quickly approximate, it is better to begin with warm water

Oil-cloth is placed on the mattress to keep it dry   The
patient is stripped naked and wrapped in a sheet which has

been dipped in warm or hot water. If it is the wish to encourage perspiration, a blanket may be applied also.

Great care is required in giving a cold pack for there is danger of doing the patient considerable injury. Even a warm pack requires close attention. When properly given a warm pack is a valuable help in the treatment of malarial fever. The patient has a chill. After the chill comes the fever. The tongue is dry and the pulse quickened. He is in no condition to stand a shock. So, we place him in a warm pack having the temperature of the water about 98 deg. F. Slight diffusive stimulation or in some cases nearly pure relaxation are given internally. Bottles of hot water are placed to the feet and sides. The bath may be continued until free perspiration is secured. Then the temperature begins to drop and the patient may be removed from the pack and rubbed briskly. As long as the fever remains high the pack may be continued. Prof. Davidson, one of the ablest men, most successful practitioners and deepest thinkers ever known to Physio-Medicalism, once said that he had continued the pack in these cases two or three hours with the happiest results.

If the patient is a child, a partial pack may be applied over the organ or part affected. It acts well in cases of pneumonia, dysentery and derangements of the bowels. In cases of erysipelas the warm pack answers a good purpose.

In applying the pack bath to patients suffering from chronic troubles it must be applied quite hot to arouse them thoroughly. But it must be remembered that a person in a hot pack is very easily scalded. The water must not be too hot.

If an emetic has been given, the patient should not take a bath that day. He must wait until he has thoroughly recovered from the effects of the emetic.

It is always well to stimulate patients before they enter and during the time they are in the pack. And subsequent friction until the surface is dry must always be practiced.

THE MOIST VAPOR BATH.
90 to 150 deg. F.

For its hygienic effect, vapor bathing has been practiced from time immemorial. Hippocrates recommended simple watery vapor. The ancient Romans used it extensively. But their use of it was more for enjoyment and a preventive influence than any therapeutic effect.

In the United States, Physio-Medical physicians have

been given the credit of first using the vapor bath for therapeutical purposes And although in his effort in this direction Samuel Thompson was classed as an empiric, the best writers of to-day must acknowledge that as a sudatory process it is far superior to any yet known

The placing of the body in a medium in which there is suspended watery vapor, is called a moist vapor bath Directly opposite to this is the dry vapor bath in which the medium consists of heated air.

The temperature of a steam bath will vary from 90 degrees to 150 degrees F. When the entire body, with the exception of the head, is surrounded by steam having a temperature above that of the body, a portion of the water is taken up by the absorbents of the skin. Indeed, in the very beginning of a vapor bath the absorbents are often so active that they will take up the greater part of the water. After the blood-vessels and absorbents are full, and the steam has lost some of its caloric by contact with the body which has a lower temperature than that of the vapor, large drops will trickle down the skin.

When the head is surrounded by vapor and the latter inhaled, there is great augmentation of fluid absorption and at the same time increased stimulating effect. The vascular system is filled with water The heart's action is increased and the pulse full There is corresponding increased fullness of the cerebral vessels. This extra quantity of fluid in the cranial cavity has its effect on the encephalic function, hence there is a feeling of drowsiness and indisposition

In due time, profuse sweating begins The delicate vessels of the skin are filled with blood At the same time the absorbent vessels are filled with water By virtue of these two conditions the integument has a swollen, plump appearance immediately after the bath

The patient may remain in the steam from ten minutes to two hours, owing to his temperament, habits and sensitiveness. Therapeutically speaking, as soon as perspiration is thoroughly established, the full effect of the bath has been secured If continued too long, drowsiness and other unpleasant symptoms supervene and prostration is the sequence And in some cases, if the steam is applied still longer, the blood becomes heated to such a degree that the results may be quite disastrous

The simplest way to give a vapor bath, especially in

certain acute cases where it is necessary to give it at the patient's home, is to seat him in a chair, nude. A blanket is thrown around him, pinned sufficiently tight around the neck and allowed to reach the floor to prevent any draught from striking him. The feet are placed in hot water to keep them warm. Under the chair sits an alcohol lamp and over the flame rests a small basin or cup filled with water. During the time he is in the bath, warm diffusively stimulating drinks should be administered to favor an outward circulation and call into action the sweat glands.

Although very simple and seemingly rude, when better apparatus cannot be made use of, the good effect of a moist vapor bath may be secured in this way.

In chronic cases where the patient can come to the office more expensive apparatus may be used. A box large enough to allow the patient to enter, should be secured. This box may be made of hard wood nicely finished. A stool which can be raised or lowered must be placed in the box. The lid of the box is made in two sections. A circular opening is cut through these sections, allowing half to be removed from each section. This opening should be sufficiently large to receive the patient's neck. Thus the attendant may enclose the patient's entire body in the box with the exception of his head.

The steam may be generated either in the box or out of it. If generated in the box an alcohol lamp should be placed under the stool, and the basin containing the water suspended over this. If formed outside of the box the water may be heated in a closed boiler and the steam conveyed to a point beneath the stool by means of a pipe.

The interior of the box may be lined with zinc. An opening at some point in the bottom will allow the escape of water. A shower bath may be attached in such a way that when the steaming process has been completed, the lid of the box may be removed and a shower bath given. This should be given with warm water and its temperature gradually lowered until the cool bath is reached.

A fan attached to the box and operated by means of a crank is a valuable accessory. Or, in cities where an electric current may be made use of, an electric fan is more convenient. The patient's head can then be kept cool while his body is subjected to the influence of the steam.

The best time to give a vapor bath to get the most beneficial effect, is when the stomach is empty. For this reason in some cases it is well to give an emetic previously. It is good practice also to cleanse the lower bowel by enema to prevent the absorption of any offending material.

In many forms of disease, restoration of suppressed perspiration is the desideratum, and this is one of the first effects of the vapor bath To assist in accomplishidg the object, warm diffusively stimulating diaphoretics, such as zingiber tea, or an infusion of myrica comp , or sierra salvia in hot lemonade, should be given at the time. The next effect of the vapor bath is a softening of dried epithelial scales, together with relaxation of the skin   After being exposed to such high temperature the skin is open and very susceptible to influences   This calls for a cool shower which will close the pores Subsequent rubbing aids in bringing up reaction, and places the skin in such a condition as will prevent the taking of cold

THE DRY VAPOR BATH OR HOT AIR BATH
100 to 120 deg F

The dry vapor bath, or Turkish bath, excites profuse sweating, without necessitating an exposure of the body to the influence of moisture   And although its consideration has no direct connection with water, it may be well to give the hot air bath brief mention.

To give a thorough Turkish bath, three rooms are necessary   One serves for a dressing room   Another having a higher temperature is used for a cooling room. while the third, having a temperature of from 100 degrees to 120 degrees F., is the bath room proper. In this room is a marble slab on which the bather reclines. The attendant rubs him thoroughly during the time he is in the hot room. After perspiring freely for a short time. he is washed with warm water and soap and then rubbed with a crash towel. To prevent taking cold, he remains in the cooling room from thirty to sixty minutes

The Turkish bath arouses the sudorific glands powerfully and fills the tegumentary vascular structures with blood. But since this bath is not always available, a patient may be sweated just as effectively by means of hot air, at the office   The same box in which the moist vapor bath is given, may be used for a dry vapor bath   The alcohol lamp should be much larger and several wicks are necessary   A thermometer may be placed in the box and when the temperature is raised to 100 degrees F the pa.

tient should enter. In some cases the temperature may be raised as high as 120 degrees F. But in no instance should the patient be allowed to remain in such hot air without having his head kept cool by fanning.

Sulphur fumes add very much to the good effect of a hot air bath. These fumes may be applied by placing over the flame of the lamp, in a metallic cup, about two drachms of sulphur. If not heated above 232 degrees F. the sulphur passes into a vapor. But if heated above this point, and a current of air strikes the sulphur, it burns and sulphurous gas is formed which is very irritating. Care must be exercised not to have the temperature of the cup in which the sulphur is burned too high.

After the patient has been in the bath a few minutes, his face becomes flushed and the conjuctiva hyperæmic. Soon slight perspiration appears on the body and in a short time it becomes profuse. In most cases the respirations are increased and the pulse quickened and full.

It is very necessary to be careful, especially with weakly persons, for there is much excitement of the cerebral circulation, often dizziness and sometimes syncope. If the patient be allowed to remain in the bath until these symptoms appear, there is a subsequent feeling of exhaustion which neutralizes to a certain degree the good effects of the bath.

After remaining in the sulphurous vapor fifteen or twenty minutes, the lamp should be removed from the box and a shower bath applied, beginning with warm water and gradually lowering its temperature to that of a cool shower. Then rub the patient thoroughly with a crash towel.

The dry vapor bath with sulphur fumes is one of the best baths that can be made use of in chronic cases. Long standing intersticial hepatitis, chronic bronchitis, gastric difficulties and rheumatism will be greatly relieved. In fact this bath is applicable in almost any chronic case where there is not too much prostration. Many forms of skin disease are improved and diseased conditions of the mucous membranes at any point will yield to the influence of medicinal treatment more readily, if this bath be applied. It has one marked advantage over the moist vapor bath in that there is little or no danger of the individual taking cold upon leaving the bath, even in damp cold weather. I have known weakly people to leave the bath at once and drive several hours, cold, windy weather days, and not take cold. This may be due to an astringent which is deposited upon the skin, closing the pores; for if the attendant rub the bather's skin with his hands it feels as though his integument were bathed in alum water

In the preparation of this article the writer has availed himself of many excellent works, chief among which may be mentioned, Ravogli on The Hygiene of the Skin, Parkes' Practical Hygiene by Notter, Wilson's Handbook of Hygiene, Kirk's Manual of Physiology, Carpenter's Human Physiology, Bell on Baths, Phillips' Materia Medica and Therapeutics, and others

ARALIA HISPIDA.

Dwarf Elder.

The *bark* of the roots and stems are mildly stimulating and tonic diuretic   In hot infusion it influences the blood toward the surface, but cold preparations influence the kidneys and procure a good flow of urine, and yet leaves the parts toned   To the stomach they are a warming, pleasant, bitter tonic.

For its tonic diuretic properties it is excellent in dropsy, renal torpor, renal congestions; and where there is scanty and scalding urine with aching of back or bladder.

With females, while it is valuable for its action on the renal tract it also influences the uterus, relieving uterine torpor and assisting in the promotion of the periodic flow.

```
F  E  Aralia Hisp.          dr. ii
"   Taraxacum Dens Le.      dr  iv
"   Mitchella Rep.          dr  iii
Syr  Zingiberis             q. s  oz  iv
```

Sig. Teaspoonful three or four times a day as a female diuretic tonic

```
F. E  Aralia Hisp et
"   Capsella Bur Pas  aa  oz  ss
Potassa Citralis            dr  ss
Syr. Zingiberis             ad  oz. iv
```

Mix   Sig.   Teaspoonful every three hours for cystic congestion.

ARALIA NUDICAULIS

American Sarsaparilla

The *root* is a pleasant and gently stimulating diuretic, influencing all the mucous membrane, but especially that of the renal organs   In hot infusion it influences the cir-

culation toward the surface very favorably and may be
used for the relief of colds whether of the head, lungs,
stomach, bowels or uterus. It is stimulating and soothing
to the mucous membrane.

    F. E. Aralia Nud.   dr. ii
    "   Celastrus Scan. dr. ii
    "   Taraxacum   dr. iv
    "   Menispermum C. dr. i
    Syr. Zingiberis q. s. oz. iv
This is a valuable alterative.

ARALIA RACEMOSA.

Spikenard.

This *root* is mildly stimulating, demulcent, warming,
sustaining and toning to the mucous membrane especially
that of the respiratory organs. In hot infusion the circulation and skin feel its influence.

It allays irritation of the respiratory mucous membrane,
and is a soothing expectorant. It is of much value in
allaying spasmodic cough and in the relief of inflammations
and congestions of the thoracic organs, whether they be
bronchial, pleuritic or pulmonary. It is valuable in the
treatment of the irritation subsequent to eruptive diseases.
It soothes the mucous membrane throughout the stomach
bowels and bladder also.

Inhaling of a vapor or spray of aralia is valuable and
pleasant in irritated conditions of the lungs.

    Aralia Rac.   2
    Symphytum Off.
    Mitchella Rep.
    Eupatorium Purp. aa. 1
forms a valuable tonic for ladies having a weak and irritated mucous membrane, whether alvine, renal, respiratory or uterine.

    F. E. Aralia Rac. et
    "   Inula Hel. et
    "   Symphytum Off. et
    "   Marrabium Vulg. aa. dr. i
    "   Sanguinaria Can. gtta. xv
    "   Prunus Virg.   dr. ii
    "   Glycyrrhiza Glab. dr. ss
    Syr. Simp.   q. s. oz. vi
This is an admirable tonic cough syrup for chronic cases
with more or less debility. If needed it can be made more

relaxing by the addition of F. E. Lobelia Inf.

F. E. Aralia Rac.   dr. vi
"   Lycopus Virg.   dr. iv
"   Polemonium Rep. dr. ii
Syr. Zing.   q. s. oz. viii
Sig Half to one teaspoonful as required.

F. E. Aralia Rac. et
" Symphytum Off   aa. dr. iss
" Inula Hel. et
" Sanguinaria Can. aa. dr. i
" Lobelia Infl. et
" Cephælis Ipecac. aa. dr. ss
Tr. Capsicum   gtta. v
Syr. Prunus Virg.   q. s. oz. iv
This is a stimulating cough syrup.

F. E. Aralia Rac. et
" Symphytum Off. aa. dr. ii
Syr. Prunus Virg.   q. s. oz. iv
Add to this F. E. Lobelia Inf. or Sanguinaria, or both to suit the case,

F. E. Aralia Rac.   dr. iii
F. E. Symphytum Off. et
" Caulophyllum aa. dr. i
Syr. Prunus Virg.   q. s. oz. iv

Aralia Rac.   8
Symphytum Off. 4
Viburnum Opu. 2
Inula Hel.   1
Mitchella   3
Prunus   10
This forms a good female tonic and cough syrup combined.

F. E. Aralia Rac.   dr. iii
" Eupatorium Perf. dr. ii
" Lippia Mexicana dr. ii
" Cimcifuga Rac. dr. ss
Syr. Prunus   q. s. oz. vi.

Aralia Rac.   oz. xvi.
Convallaria Mult. oz. vii.
Prunus Virg.   oz. iv
Capsicum   dr. i
Lobelia Herb   oz. i
Amphiachyris Dr. oz. iv

Grind all for percolation, using as a menstruum:

Glycerine   oz. vi
Alcohol   oz. xiii
Soft Water   oz. xx

Percolate till 2 fluid pounds pass. Set this aside, and continue the percolation with water till 2 fluid pounds more pass. In this dissolve sugar at slow heat. When cool add:

Alcohol   oz. l
Ol. Wintergreen et
Ol. Sassafras   aa. dr. i

Then add the first percolate.

This is Dr. F. O. Broady's formula and he says it takes the palm as a pleasant and efficient cough syrup. The broom weed makes it especially valuable.

ARCHANGELICA OFFICINALIS.

Angelica.   German.

The **root** is peculiarly aromatic, oleaginous and of rather a pungent taste. It is moderately diffusive and stimulating to the mucous membrane. In hot infusion it is diaphoretic, and relieves the uterus in case of suppression from cold. It is also valuable in flatulence.

Cold preparations act well on the kidneys and tone the entire pelvic apparata.

F. E. Archangelica Off.   dr. iv
  "   Dioscorea Vil.   dr. ii
  "   Caulophyllum Thal. et
  "   Leonurus Card.   aa. dr. i
Syr. Zingiberis   q. s. oz, iv

This is a fine uterine antispasmodic and tonic where there is a deficiency of the menstrual flow and it may be also dysmenorrhœa.

ARCTIUM LAPPA.

Burdock.   (Lappa Major.)

The **root** is a soothing demulcent tonic alterative. It slowly and steadily influences the skin, soothes the kidneys and relieves the lymphatics. It is of great importance in all skin diseases and in scrofulous affections. It is very soothing to the mucous membrane throughout and is hence valuable in irritated conditions. Its soothing character is also extended to the serous membrane and is valuable in rheumatism, and also in venereal diseases especially if combined with more stimulating agents, and notably in the inflammatory stage of such diseases.

Dr. F. G. Hoener recommends the following alterative:

Elix. Arctium Lap. et
" Rumex Crisp.   aa. oz. ii
" Aralia Nudic. et
" Iris Vers. et
" Stillingia Syl. et
" Trifoliata Pra. et
Syr. Podophyllum   aa. oz. i

M. S. One teaspoonful or more 4 or 5 times a day as needed.

He also recommends the following hair tonic to be used to prevent the falling off of the hair during or subsequent to convalescence from typhoid fever, also to cleanse and cure sores on the scalp especially of infants:

Lappa Major   oz. xvi
Salvia Officinalis   oz. viii
Cydonia Vulgaris et
Lycopodium Comp.   aa. oz. iv

M. Make into two quarts of decoction and add
Succus Betula Lenta   oz. xvi
Bay Rum   oz. xvi
Take
Alcohol 45 per cent.   oz, xii
Ess. Hiliontrope   oz. iv

Mix well these last and then add all together and let stand for several weeks, or it may be immediately filtered.

The *seed* are somewhat more stimulating than the roots, and are quite oleaginous. The seed should be ground in order to obtain their properties quickly. In hot infusion it influences the sebaceous glands, and is of superior importance in scarlatina, and other exanthemata, and in typhoid fever.

Cold preparations influence the kidneys, increasing the flow of urine and relieving irritation of the urinary tract.

In skin diseases the seed are to be preferred to the root.

A teaspoonful of the ground seed to a teacup of boiling water, after standing half an hour may be drank during the forenoon and the cup with the same seed filled with boiling water again and drank off in the afternoon. This is excellent in ophthalmia, as a good hepatic alterative.

With zingiber it is more diffusive; with hydrastia sulphate it is rendered more tonic; with taraxacum or euonymous they are more hepatic and give favorable results in eczema and jaundice; with mitchella its influence is given to the generative organs; and with triticum repens, juniper or eupatorium purpureum it influences the kidneys and may be used to good advantage in dropsy.

The green *leaves* applied in hot fomentation are an excellent application to sprains. They have the same general properties as the roots. In the green state they are more active than the roots upon the alvine canal and the hepatic organ. A fluid extract of the leaves, smaller branches and seeds shortly before ripe is an excellent preparation.

ARCTOSTAPHYLOS UVA - URSI.

Uva-Ursi.

The *leaves* are a mild, soothing, bitter. astringent, tonic diuretic. It influences the mucous membrane, but especially that of urinary and genital structures, increasing the flow of urine, relieving congestion and toning the parts.

It is valuable in leucorrhœa, gonorrhœa and gleet. The discharge is lessened and the parts toned.

    Infusion uva - ursi.   oz. ss
    Bicarbonate Soda.   grs. x

M. Sig. Take this every two hours. This gives quick relief in cystitis, aching of the back or of the bladder, and gives good results in enuresis given occasionally. Dr. F. G. Hoener recommends the following for bed wetting children.

    Elix. Uva - Ursi   oz. ii
     "   Achillea M.   oz. i
     "   Rhus glabra bacca   oz. iss

M. Sig. One teaspoonful or desertspoonful every two or three hours during the day according to the case, and a hot sitz bath daily.

    Uva-Ursi et
    Mitchella aa 2
    Taraxacum 3

forms an excellent pelvic tonic for the relief of prolapsus uteri, relaxed vagina, cystic catarrh and aching of kidneys and bladder.

For the relief of congestion of the mucous membrane uva-ursi is best in hot infusion; but its toning effect is best obtained from cold preparations.

ARISTOLOCHIA SERPENTARIA.

Serpentaria, Virginia Snake Root.

The *root* is a bitter, warming, aromatic, diffusive stimulant

In hot infusion it influences the capillaries and thence the arterial circulation It is quite stimulating to the gastric membrane and should not be given too strong nor too frequently else it may produce nausea and vomiting. In this way it is decidedly valuable in the promotion of stimulating emesis

It is stimulating to the mucous membrane throughout and large and frequent, doses may prove irritating especially if the alvine canal be already more or less irritated In such cases more soothing agents will be better. But in languid and sluggish conditions it arouses promptly and fully

In eruptive diseases, before the appearance of the full eruption it is excellent, especially in languid conditions, but where milder agents will do the work. I prefer them

In the treatment of nettle rash or rhus poisoning give freely and fully for a few hours and then stop, it will do good work

Its influence is primarily toward the surface, but soon its influence is felt by the whole arterial system, and the heart's impulse becomes stronger and fuller By its stimulating action upon the arterial side of the circulation and the whole nervous system is aroused by its influence. Even the uterus feels its influence and its use is valuable for the relief of colds suppressing the periods

Given during parturition when the feet are cold and there is a general receding of blood from the surface and where the pains are inefficient, this agent will have an excellent influence It will also anticipate flooding.

Cold preparations quite freely influence the kidneys and relieve congestion and renal torpor

It is best to use serpentaria thoroughly and then discontinue its use for a time

Occasionally in atonic dyspepsia, and gastric catarrh it arouses the mucous membrane and relieves the surface of viscid mucous

ARTANTHE ELONGATA.

Matico   (Piper Angustifolium) Persia

The *leaves* are a pleasant, soothing, diffusive, stimulating and gently astringent tonic.

In hot infusion it influences the circulation toward the surface, and its action on the mucous membrane is excellent throughout. It is of much importance in pulmonary hemorrhages, relieving them by relieving the circulation. Given shortly before parturition it pleasantly anticipates post-partem hemorrhage, it stimulates to better contractions and facilitates labor.

Its influence upon both mucous membrane and the circulation gives it a very positive influence in diarrhœa and dysentery, cholera infantum and cholera morbus,

ARTEMISIA ABSINTHIUM.

Wormwood.

The *leaves* and *flowers* are an intensely bitter stimulant decidedly influencing the mucous membrane, and is somewhat cholagogue.

In very small doses it is a tonic and improves the appetite and assists digestion; in large doses it is quite cathartic. It is anthelmintic, but it is too intensely bitter to be very frequently used. Its influence is best felt in torpid conditions of the mucous membrane. It is too stimulating for irritated conditions.

In hot infusion it best influences the circulation, and is best for the relief of menstrual suppression from cold.

The *oil of wormwood* is valuable in intensely stimulating liniments; and for enuresis two or three drops may be given for a few days.

ARTEMISIA VULGARIS.

Mugwort,

This is not so intensely better as the artemisia absinthium, but is more tonic, and has a more decided influence on the uterus as an emmenagogue.

ARTEMISIA ABROTANUM.

Southern-wood.   American.

The *flower buds* have the same influence as the artemisia santonica as a tonic vermifuge.

ARTEMISIA SANTONICA.

Santonica.   Russia.

The *flower buds* are anthelmintic especially in case of the round worm, or stomach worm.

Santonine is the principal form in which this ingredient comes into the medical market. It appears in small white crystals almost tasteless making a strong gastric tonic. It is gently stimulating and is very suitable for children, because of its tastelessness. Give one or two grains in a little water morning and evening for three days and follow on the third day with an appropriate dose of antibillious physic. The worms usually pass from the child as a mass of mucous. Santonine in a few hours colors the urine quite yellow.

A solution of two to four grains in water injected once or twice a day for a few days usually puts an end to pin worms

When either pin or stomach worms have been the cause of enuresis santonine will relieve this condition

ARUM TRIPHYLLUM.

Indian Turnip   (Arisæma triphyllum.)

The *root* when fresh is quite biting and pungent, and within a short time after being dried it is almost inert.

The *fresh leaves* bruised and used as a hot fomentation on scrofulous sores is excellent to cleanse and tone

The bruised pulp of the rootmay also be used to excellent advantage as a poultice in the same class of cases   At the same time use sanguinaria canadencis internally   Perseverance will here effect a cure

The fluid extract of the arum more or less dilute may be used for the same purpose

ASARUM CANADENSE.

Wild Ginger, Canada Snake Root   America and Europe.

The *root* is a mild, aromatic, diffusive stimulant. It is somewhat less stimulating than zingiber and is more soothing to the nerves, and they about equally influence the circulation when given in hot infusion. It gives very favorable results in eruptive diseases, in colds, coughs, suppressed menstruation from colds, and in dysmenorrhœa.

Large doses may in the sensitive stomach create nausea and emesis, which in chronic coughs and gastric catarrah when the mucous membrane needs to be aroused it is valuable, and it increases expectoration.

In irritated or inflamed conditions of the mucous membrane, other agents are to be preferred.

parturition it is valuable when the surface is cold, and in all languid conditions of the mucous membrane. In insomina it gives excellent results.

ASARUM EUROPÆUM.

Asarabacca.

. The *leaves* are slightly aromatic, bitter, acrid and nauseating. They especially influence the gastric and alvine mucous membrane, and prove emetic and cathartic. In hot infusion they may be used in rheumatism and colds.

ASCLEPIAS CURASSAVICA.

Blood-flower.

The *roots* are relaxing, chiefly influencing the mucous membrane, and proving cathartic and emetic in large doses.

In combination with zingiber they are more diffusive and influence a good outward circulation. It may be used for the arrest of light hemorrhages, and in the acute stage of gonorrhœa.

ASCLEPIAS INCARNATA.

White Indian Hemp.

The *root* is chiefly relaxing to the mucous membrane, is mildly laxative and may prove cathartic when given in large doses. Under such circumstances it may also provoke emesis. It is sometimes used to exterminate the stomach worm and is useful in acute catarrh and rheumatism.

ASCLEPIAS SYRIACA.

Silkweed.

The *root* is a relaxant, especially influencing the genito-urinary organs. It soothes the renal organs and relieves the aching back. It increases the flow of urine and leaves the parts soothed and somewhat toned. To the bowels it is rather laxative. In hot infusion it may be used in acute bronchial or nasal catarrh. It promotes expectoration and assists in relieving the cough. It is also valuable in hot infusion in fevers.

Asclepias Syriaca 3; Phytolacca Dec. Rad. 1. Make into an infusion for dropsy.

ASCLEPIAS TUBEROSA.

Pleurisy Root, White Root.

The *root* is a relaxing agent, influencing chiefly the skin, and mucous and serous structures

In hot infusion in combination with some diffusive or stimulant or diffusive stimulant, as zingiber, it is a diaphoretic of much importance It influences a flow of blood toward the surface and relaxes the capillaries in the producing of good free diaphoresis.

By itself it is of but little use, but with zingiber it is a most valuable agent

Asclepias Tub	4
Lobelia Infl.	½
Zingiber	1

in hot infusion is excellent in bronchitis, pleuritis, peritonitis, pneumonia, acute catarrh, membranous croup, colds, &c.

Asclepias	4
Zingiber	1

in hot infusion is an excellent fever powder for children or adults If more positive stimulation is needed add capsicum in small proportion.

Dr F. O. Broady recommends the following mixture for fevers and says "I used it for five years in Chicago with great confidence "

Pulv Asclepias Tub.		3
" Pterospora And.		2
" Cypripedium Pub	et	
" Zingiber Jam.	aa	1½
" Lobelia Inf. Fol		1
" Saccharum Album		5

M Trit. Bene Dose 5 grs every hour

When there is a tendency to decay or slough asclepias is not the proper article to be used It is useful in tonsilitis rather than in diphtheria; in feverish and inflamed conditions rather than in congestions; and in cases possessing a sthenic rather than an asthenic pulse

Powd. Asclepias Tub	et	
" Solidago Can.	aa.	4
" Zingiber Off		1
" Capsicum in proportion as needed.		

This is a most excellent formula for la grippe given freely in hot infusion, also in typhoid and bilious fevers I use some such preparation from beginning to end of the fever stage. In preparing this compound I use more asclepias toward the first and more of the capsicum as the case progresses, if needed.

Asclepias and Zingiber is a most excellent compound in all the eruptive diseases. Capsicum may be added to suit. It is also important in dysentery and diarrhœa, uteritis, urethritis, cystitis and nephritis, and in irritable conditions of the nervous system.

In dysmenorrhœa or amenorrhœa, give in hot infusion.

Powd. Asclepias Tub.   4
    "   Zingiber Jam.   1
    "   Caulophyllum Th.   2

It is antispasmodic and increases the periodic discharge.

Powd. Asclepias Tub.   4
    "   Zingiber Off.   1
    "   Mentha Vir.   2

This influences the kidneys and secures a good free flow of urine.

ASPIDIUM FELIX-MAS.

Male Fern.   Europe.

The *root* is anthelmintic. It is an old-time remedy for tape worm, but is not always certain. A few hours subsequent to the administering of this agent free catharsis should be secured. Repeat if found necessary in two or three days. It may be given in the form of infusion or in capsules upon an empty stomach.

The *oil* may be used for the same general purposes. Give ½ to 1 dr. in some emulsion.

ASPARAGUS OFFICINALIS.

Asparagus.

The *root* is a pleasant diuretic. It should be used in the green state as the dry root is nearly inert.

The young shoots are an excellent food as well as a demulcent diuretic.

Guaiacum Off. et
Asparagus Off. et
Petroselinum Sat. Sem.   aa. grs. xxx
Viburnum Op.   grs. Lx

to the fluid oz.

Give according to the severity of the pain in cases of dysmenorrhoea, leucorrhœa, and as a preventive of miscarriage.

ASTER CORDIFOLIUS.

Starwort.

The *root* is a very mild, aromatic stimulant. In hot infusion it influences the circulation and with it the nervous system. It allays irritation, soothes and tones In rheumatism and hysteria it may be used with good effect If combined with zingiber it will be valuable in dysmenorrhœa. With mitchella repens it will be excellent in hysteria and be rendered more toning to the nerves

ASTER PUNICENS

Cocash Root.

Dr. F G Hoener recommends this for rheumatic headache, and as a suitable agent to be used in proper combination with other agents for nervous debility.

ASTRAGALUS VERUS

Gum Tragacanth

This is used but little as a medicine, except in the manufacture of pills, troches and suppositories

AVENA SATIVA.

Oats

This is a soothing, demulcent, gently stimulating, nutritious nervine tonic

In cases of irritability of the nerves or a deficiency of nerve power avena is valuable In the irritability resulting from nervous prostration, from paralysis, from the use of opium, or alcohol, in chronic sick-headache, in chorea and in the irritation and depression resulting from dysmenorrhœa.

If given in hot water its effects are noticeably quicker, and its influence on the circulation more rapid and complete.

In hysteria and for insomnia it is valuable, as well as in convalescence from many acute cases It should be used at short intervals to maintain its cumulative force

With helonias dioica, aletris farinosa or mitchella repens it is an excellent nervine tonic for females, especially where there is a tendency to excessive flow and more or less during pregnancy, especially by those who are weakly, anæmic and nervous

With hydrastia sulphate it is excellent in nervous dyspepsia.

Hydrastia Sulph	1
Avena Sat.	10
Podophyllin Sacch	20

This is a nervine tonic hepatic.

F. E. Leptandra Virg. et
"   Euonymous At. et
"   Avena Sat.   aa. dr. ii
"   Taraxacum Dens L.   dr. iv
Syr. Zingiberis   q. s. oz. iv

This is a good nervine hepatic.

Helonias Dio.   3
Viburnum Op.   4
Dioscorea Vil.   5
Avena Sat.   6

This is an excellent female tonic.

BALSAMODENDRON MYRRHA.

Gum Myrrh.   (Commiphora Myrrha.)

Abyssinia, Arabia.

This *gum* is a slow, mild, stimulating, antiseptic tonic. It gives a pleasant gastric warmth, and stimulates the circulation in assisting a flow of blood toward the capillaries, especially when given in hot infusion. Locally it is an excellent application on ulcers and foetid sores, as a gargle in diphtheria, as a wash in sore mouth, and as a powder applied to the umbilicus of the infant immediately after the removal of the cord. In all these cases it assists in removing foul odors and arrests putrefaction.

With hydrastia sulphate it is excellent in gastric catarrh.

Pul. Balsamodendron M.   grs. x
Hydrastia Sulphate   grs. ii
Ferri et Potas. Tartr.   grs. xx
Syr. Zingiberis   oz. i
Aqua   q. s. oz. iv

This is a good tonic for a relaxed and debilitated stomach, water brash, anæmic dyspepsia and chronic enteralgia.

F. E. Balsamodendron M. et
"   Cypripedium Pub.   aa. dr. iv
"   Xanthoxylum Frax.   gtt. xx
Syr. Zingiberis   q. s. oz. iv

This is an antiseptic, diffusive tonic to the circulation and the nervous system.

F. E. Myrrh   oz. iv
Tr. Capsicum   dr. ii
Syr. Simplex   oz. i

Or

Pul Myrrh   oz xvi
" Capsicum   oz 1
Alcohol 60 per cent.   oz LXIV
Sugar   lbs 4 to 5

Or

Pul Myrrh   oz. iv
" Capsicum   dr. ii
Sugar   oz. i

Triturate

Either of these preparations will constitute No. 6 The last may be denominated Saccharated No 6. This is a fine formula and a valuable stimulating antiseptic I always use a few drops of No 6 in some water a few times before administering an anæsthetic. It sustains the heart, and steadies the nerves, and frequently your patients will come out from anæsthesia with a fuller and better pulse than when you began.

One drop in a little water, repeated as needed, is an excellent parturient. It equalizes the circulation, sustains the contractions, relieves irritability and anticipates flooding. But do not give it or any other stimulant unless needed In shock from injury there is nothing better

Dr. F O. Broady advises the following formula for Tincture Myrrh which will mix with water without precipitation.   It is valuable and practical

Pul Gum Myrrh   1 lb
Alcohol   1 qt
Glycerine   13 oz
Water   16 oz
Carbonate of Potash   3½ oz

M. Macerate for 2 to 4 weeks with frequent shaking

Gum Myrrh   oz. ½
Gum Guaiacum   oz. ½
Gum Camphor   oz ¼
Oil Capsicum et
Oil Anise   aa dr ss
Alcohol 50 per cent. q. s

This is recommended as a pain killer

BAPTISIA TINCTORIA

Wild Indigo

The **root** is a stimulating antiseptic alterative, especially influencing the glandular system Wherever there is a retrograde tissue, a tendency to putrescence, the metamorphosis in typhoid fever, this agent holds a valuable position.

In erysipelas an infusion given freely will soon reduce the inflammation.

    Baptisin et
    Pul. Sanguinaria aa 1
    Vaseline   3 to 4

Apply this in cases of erysipelas or other inflamed eczemas.

Baptisia may be used on all kinds of ulcers, sprinkled on the surface or made into an ointment or mixed with an elm poultice. It removes foul odors and assists in the reparative process.

Baptisia is stimulating to the liver and to the bowels and in large doses is freely cathartic. In typhoid fever, in peritonitis, in puerperal fever, typhus fever, syphilis and gangrene it is very valuable, as also for a wash for mercurial sore mouth. The powdered drug in hot fomentation will give good results when applied upon scrofulous swellings or abscesses. In arresting putrescence balsamodendron myrrha will be a valuable addition.

BAROSMA BETULINA AND CRENULATA.

Buchu.   South Africa.

Buchu *leaves* are an aromatic, diffusive, stimulating, toning diuretic. The short leaves are superior to the long. It chiefly influences the urinary tract, increasing the quantity of water excreted and cleansing and toning the urinary mucous membrane. It soothes the pelvic nerves and relieves the aching back and hips and especially so when influenced in that direction by some uterine agent as mitchella repens or alteris farinosa; it then assists in toning the generative organs.

In hot infusion it is somewhat diaphoretic and soothes the nerves and influences the mucous membrane throughout. In cystic catarrh, in congestion of any of the pelvic organs, gleet, gravel, dropsy, prostatic affections, spermatorrhœa and mucous discharges in the urine buchu will be of good service.

    F. E. Barosma C.   4
      "   Eupatorium Purpur.   8
      "   Hydrastis Can.   1

Give of this three times a day, and use one of the following powders three times a day for ascites:

Leptandrin	gr. i
Apocynin	grs. iv
Capsicum	gr. ½

With an excess of convallaria mul. you will have favorable results in leucorrhœa. With an excess of liriodendron or cypripedium it is an excellent nervine.

Liriodendron TuL	4
Barosma C.	1

This is a mildly stimulating nervine and diuretic.

Cypripedium Pub.	6
Barosma C.	1

This is a relaxing nervine diuretic.

Caulophyllum Th.	5
Barosma	1

This is an antispasmodic diuretic

The following formulæ are more or less stimulating diuretics:

Buchu	9
Juniperus Com.	4
Piper Cubeba et	
Sweet Spirits Nitre	aa. 1½

Buchu	4
Juniperus Com. et	
Piper Cubeba et	
Arctostaphylos Uv. Urs.	aa. 1

Buchu	4
Collinsonia Can. et	
Chondodendron Tom.	aa. 1
Juniperus Com.	2

McCoy, Howe Co. prepare by direct percolation an elixir, an efficient and reliable diuretic and valuable in many ailments of the bladder and kidneys.

Buchu	grs. x
Juniper Berries	grs. v
Uva-Ursi	grs. v
Acetate Potash	grs. iii

BERBERIS AQUIFOLIUM.

Oregon Grape Root.

This is a mildly stimulating tonic hepatic and alterative. It influences the alvine mucous membrane and is mildly cathartic. In syphilis and other blood diseases especially those which influence the genitals it gives excellent results.

BERBERIS VULGARIS.

Barberry.

The *bark and leaves* are intensely bitter, and form a good stimulating tonic hepatic and alterative; influencing the alvine mucous membrane, the kidneys, liver and spleen. It improves the appetite, digestion and assimilation, and is especially useful in debilitated conditions. It is mildly laxative to the bowels as well as hepatic and hence is valuable in jaundice.

It may be added to other alteratives with excellent results.

In small doses it is a valuable tonic in convalescence, and is of especial value in bilious attacks. The following formula is excellent for debilitated and bilious cases:

Berberis Vulg.	1
Populus Trem.	2
Prunus Virg.	3
Acetum	q. s.

BETA VULGARIS RUBRUM.

Red Beet.

This is a much used vegetable. When cooked it forms a delicious dish.

The *fresh juice* of the red beet has many a time cured thrush, and relieved irritated conditions of the mouth and throat. It is soothing and stimulating to the entire alvine mucous membrane.

BETONICA OFFICINALIS.

Wood Betony. (Betonica Lanceolata.)(Stachys Betonica.)

This is a gently stimulating tonic to the mucous membrane and is valuable in catarrhal conditions, whether of the nose, stomach or bladder. It is useful in the treatment of la grippe, gastralgia, neuralgia, hysteralgia, prostatitis, pruritus, varicocele, dyspepsia, chronic rheumatism, malarial jaundice, syphilis, scrofula, and renal and nephitic colics, and onanism.

Dr. F. G. Hoener recommends the following for sciatica:

Elix. Betonica Lanc et		
" Cimicifuga	aa. oz. iss	
" Helonias Dio. et		

" Scutelaria Lat   aa oz. i

Sig. One teaspoonful every two or three hours and use hot sponge baths to the parts affected.

Dr. Hoener also recommends the following for peritonitis

Elix Betonica Lanc. et ·

" Agrimonia Eup.   aa. oz. iss

·' Aralia Rac   oz i

Sig. One tablespoonful every two hours.

He also recommends the following for phrenitis

Elix Betonica Lanc   oz ii

" Cimicifuga Rac et

" Verbena Hast   aa. oz i

M. S. One tablespoonful every thirty minutes to one hour with mustard bath, and keep the bowels open with enemata

BETULA LENTA.

Black Birch.

The *bark* is a mild relaxing and stimulating nervine. In hot infusion it promotes diaphoresis.

It soothes the gastric membrane, relieves nausea and tones the mucous membrane.

The *leaves* are somewhat more diuretic and are very soothing to the entire urinary apparata in case of renal or cystic irritation or inflammation They are cleansing to the mucous membrane, and in hot infusion produce diaphoresis.

BIDENS BIPINNATA.

Spanish Needles.

The *seeds* are a mild diffusive stimulant, very slightly astringent, influencing especially the mucous membrane and the circulation, and thence the nervous system partakes of its influence when administered in hot infusion. In this form they are also valuable in dysmenorrhœa.

With aralia racemosa it is a valuable expectorant.

Dr F. G. Hoener says it has proven itself to be a specific for hay asthma.

BIGNONIA CATALPA.

Catalpa Tree.

The *bark* is a bitter stimulating tonic, especially influencing the mucous membrane In hot infusion it influences the circulation and induces a good outward flow of blood, and also soothes and tones the nerves.

Combined with other agents especially alterative in character it is valuable in syphilis, in scrofula and some eczemas.

The *seeds* are more demulcent and are valuable in cough syrups. It relaxes the respiratory mucous membrane and is a good expectorant.

The *leaves* in hot infusion form a good preparation for colds, coughs, and may be used as a hot fomentation upon swellings, abscesses, &c.

BISMUTHUM.

Bismuthi Subnitras.

This is a very mildly stimulating and soothing astringent. It is valuable in irritations of the gastric and intestinal mucous membrane. It soothes the membrane and relieves irritation. It relieves the nausea of pregnancy and the irritation of gastritis and the intestinal irritation of cholera infantum. It is also successful in the treatment of ulcerous sore mouth, and for diarrhœa and dysentery.

Applied locally as a powder it is splendid for the relief of the chafing of children.

Iodoform
Bismuthi Sub.
in equal parts is good to fill syphilitic ulcers.

BISMUTHI SALYCILAS.

Bismuthi Saly.	1
Fuller's Earth	4

This makes one of the most soothing and the most rapidly healing of baby powders. It is my favorite. I have cured cases in a few days with this powder that have baffled other physicians for months.

It is also an excellent application in cases of pruritus vulva and in cases of eczemas or other irritations of the skin.

BRUNFELSIA HOPEANA.

Manaca.   Brazil.

In Brazil manaca is regarded as a specific for the cure of rheumatic affections. The results obtained have been good. The fluid extract may be used or the elixir which combines also the virtues of the salycilates of sodium, potassium and lithium, and is hence valuable in the treatment of lithic diathesis.

Manaca et
Syr Simplex   aa. oz ii

Sig. Teaspoonful every three hours in the treatment of rheumatism

CAFFEA ARABICA.

Coffee.

Coffee is a cerebral stimulant, largely used as a beverage. It is stimulating to the nerves and tonic to the muscular systems. It stimulates the circulation and is more or less of a tonic diuretic. If taken late at night it is apt to produce sleeplessness by its cerebral stimulation. In the morning it assists digestion.

This is a stimulating nervine which disposes to wakefulness, and is frequently used for the purpose of resisting the stupefying influence of alcohol and of opium. It stimulates the circulation and the digestive function. But care should be taken that when this is used as an article of diet that it be not used too strong, as a persistent use of any stimulant is apt to produce finally more or less depression and possibly dyspepsia

Caffein does not appear to undergo any material change. in the roasting process and is extracted unaltered from the roasted coffee. It stimulates the liver and promotes the secretion of bile. It is a stimulating nervine.

Dr. J O Morrison recommends the following for headache

Caffein et
Quinine et
Salycilate of Sodium et
Trit Oil Capsicum aa. equal parts.

Fill No 2 capsules and give one or two as required. This is good to clear up the mind and brace up on.

CALENDULA OFFICINALIS

Marigold

The *flowers* are a very mild diffusive stimulant.

In hot infusion it influences the circulation toward the surface and is diaphoretic. It is also a soothing antispasmodic nervine, and gently influences the menstrual flow. It is also useful as an alterative to cleanse the blood in strumous troubles

An infusion forms an excellent wash in ophthalmia and

it may be made into an ointment for bruises and sprains. Used in cases of otorrhœa an infusion lessens the discharge, and applied to sores, ulcers, or wounds it cleanses the surface and promotes the process of granulation and healing. Even cancerous sores are much benefited by its use.

CALX (Ca O).

Lime.

That derived from white marble or from oyster shells gives the purest lime. When cold it absorbs carbonic acid gas. Lime is quite alkaline and caustic, but when hydrated or slacked it is much less caustic. When an excess of lime is mixed with water it is called milk of lime.

Liquor calcis or lime water is a mild ant-acid, slightly astringent. It is made by slacking ½ ounce of lime in one pint of water. Allow this to stand an hour. Then pour off and retain the sediment to which add one gallon of water and bottle for use. This preparation neutralizes the acid present and absorbs the carbonic acid gas arising from fermentation.

Lime Water	2
Linseed Oil	1

thoroughly mixed forms a covering for burns, scalds and denuded surfaces.

Calcii chloridum Ca O, Cl is a compound resulting from the action of chlorine on hydrate of lime containing at least twenty-five per cent. of chlorine. It is a valuable disinfectant.

Potassa cum calce forms an officinal caustic.

Sulphas calcis or plaster of Paris is used much in surgery.

Sulphis calcis 1-10 grain doses 4 to 6 times daily will usually stop the continuance of boils.

Creta Præparata. Prepared chalk is a good quality of chalk (carbonate of lime) powdered, hydrated and thoroughly triturated. The water is then poured off and the precipitate dried.

This is principally applied to the surface, either as a powder or incorporated into a salve, or compounded with liquids or oils for covering burns. The powder is an excellent absorbent and is very soothing to an irritated surface.

CAPSELLA   175

CANELLA ALBA.

Canella.

The *bark* is a moderately stimulating aromatic

It warms the gastric membrane and influences the blood toward the capillaries especially when given in hot infusion   It is a good adjuvant for bitter medicines and is principally used for this purpose

CAPSELLA BURSA-PASTORIS

Shepherd's Purse

This *herb* is mildly relaxing and gently stimulating to the kidneys and urinary tract   It increases the flow of urine and relieves atonic and sluggish conditions. It is quite prompt in the relief of the aching back and of the irritated urethra in cases of scalding urine   It is quite efficient in the relief of renal catarrh   It allays nervous irritability, irritable spermatorrhœa.   Directly or indirectly it is beneficial to the whole pelvic viscera, and is one of the best agents to be used for irritable conditions of these parts   It is more stimulating than eupatorium purpureum, but not near so stimulating as juniperus communis or barosma crenulata.

Concentrated Tincture Shepherd's Purse (from the green) as made by C T Bedford, is a strong tincture, of a rich brown color made from the green herb, 8 ounces to the pint, and represents all the virtues of this valuable agent for urinary troubles.

CAPSICUM FASTIGIATUM

Capsicum, Red Pepper   Africa, New Mexico.

The *fruit* is a most positive, pungent stimulant   It is an excellent antiseptic and is very nutritious   It is the most powerful and persistent heart stimulant known   It increases arterial force, enlarges its calibre and slightly increases its frequency   Its influence is permanent and reaches every organ through its primary influence upon the circulation—the heart first, then the arteries, the capillaries and the nerves

Its constituents are extractive and oleaginous.   Alcohol holds the gum in solution   This alcohol may be evaporated which leaves the extractive gum, which is excellent when triturated on sugar   If you allow the tincture to settle you will observe two grades of tincture, the upper is light colored and is best as a rubefacient.

    Tr. Capsicum et
    Oil Cinnamon et
    Oil Cloves   aa equal parts.

This is an intense stimulant needed only perhaps in extreme cases.

The lower half of the tincture is more or less filled with extractive and is not best for liniment purposes, as the gum is not absorbed and it flies around the room and causes the patient to cough.

Capsicum by itself is not very diffusive. It is quite local in its influence, but is gradually permeating.

Lobelia renders it much more diffusive and this compound is a much better application for colds, chills, congestions, congestive chills, pneumonia, rheumatism, neuralgia, sciatica, lumbago, pleurisy, peritonitis, uterine and ovarian congestion, congestion of liver, spleen, or kidneys. But by itself it is a valuable application in failing circulation, sinking spells, dysentery, bilious colic, cholera infantum, paralysis, diphtheria, aphonia, gastric catarrh, gangrene and typhoid fever. The tincture made of

    Pul. Capsicum   oz. i
    Alcohol 98 per cent.   oz. xvi

is an excellent preparation for application where and when needed. The powder may be made into a poultice or prepared in a pad form and applied to the surface where needed. In this way also the capsicum may be combined with such agents as leptandra and apocynum and for the liver, and occasionally moistened with the fluid extracts.

With more relaxing agents the pad may also be used for sciatica and for ovarian troubles.

In cases of severe congestions capsicum may be added to a water bath very profitably.

In nervous depression capsicum given in very small doses is very sustaining. Given with medicines that influence the alvine canal, it increases catharsis, prevents griping, and assists in relieving rectal paralysis.

In old ulcers lobelia and capsicum may be used. Put in enough to get up a good circulation.

    Oil Capsicum   gtt. i
    Aqua   dr. i

may be used in cases of ulceration of the cornea.

    Tr. Capsicum et
    Spts. Camphor   aa. 5

Gum Camphor	2
Alcohol	3
Aqua	10

Tr. Capsicum	oz 1
Spts Camphor	oz ½
Tr.Guaiacum	oz 1
Alcohol 45 per cent.	

Oil Capsicum	
" Sassafras	
' Origanum	
" Horsemint	
" Cedar	aa. dr i
Alcohol	qt 1

These are excellent stimulating liniments, especially the last mentioned.

Internally capsicum may be taken in infusion, in mucilage, in syrup, in fluid extract in water, or the oil may be triturated in sugar or lactin and given Give small doses frequently and wait for the cumulative results. Large doses may produce hiccough and cramping.

In all putrescent stages whether of typhus or typhoid fever, in diphtheria, scarlatina malignans, erysipelas, gangrene and wherever there is absorption of pus, capsicum must be given in quantities to meet the conditions present In all such cases the result will be a lessened frequency of the pulse and its volume, force and firmness will be increased It is a most powerful antiseptic and may be used more or less in gonorrhœal, syphilitic and mercurial poisoning It is of importance in torpor, sluggishness and loss of sensibility, but for permanence of action it is best to combine it with tonics.

In typhoid fever with hepatics and hydrastis it sustains the portal circulation and increases the power and value of the hepatics used; and with diuretics its influence in that direction will also be quite marked.

In yellow fever, cholera, shock of injury and where there are cold and clammy sweats capsicum is an agent of much importance.

Capsicum with lobelia is a most excellent antispasmodic. With nervines it is valuable in delirium tremens. With diffusives and hepatics it will do good service in ague-cake, and applied locally it will give good results in case of habitually cold feet, gastritis, enteritis, and cystitis. If the application of capsicum gives much burning sensation use over the surface some lard or other oil.

As a rule increase the dose of capsicum as vitality decreases.

Do not forget its excellent service as a parturient and as a preventive to post-partem hemorrhage.

In diphtheria and scarlet fever it is valuable as a gargle or to be used with the atomizer and to be taken internally.

Powd. Myrrh et
"   Hydrastis Can.   aa. oz. ii
"   Capsicum et
"   Chloride of Sodium aa. oz. i
"   Solidago Can.   oz. iv
· Acetum   q. s. oz 32

This forms an acetous tincture which for diphtheria, scarlatina and some other forms of weak and sore throat cannot well be surpassed. It may be used as a gargle or with the atomizer, or the ingredients may be used in infusion and some acetum added. With that which is to be swallowed use no vinegar; and that which is to be used as a gargle prepare as above. Then apply a strong tincture of capsicum over the tonsils externally. ·

Oil of Capsicum   dr. i
Alcohol   oz. iv to viii

This is a good rubefacient.

The dose of the oil of capsicum is 1-10 to 1 drop triturated on sugar or lactin and thence dissolved in water.

A very little capsicum renders quinine a much better antiperiodic.

Dr. F. O. Broady recommends the following as a sure cure for chills:

Pulv. Capsicum   grs. x
· Quinia Sulph.   grs. xx
· Pulv. Myrica Cerif
"   Hydrastis Can.   aa. oz. i
Ol. Sassafras   gtta. xxx

M. Trit. bene, ft. cht. No. 20 for an adult.

Sig. One powder in cold water 3 times a day before the chill, preceded by an active cathartic. This recipe is reliable but the dose is a little large.

Ol. Capsicum
"   Origanum
"   Abies

```
   " Sassafras            aa  1
   " Olives                    2
   Alcohol                    32
```
This is a powerful stimulating liniment
```
   Tr. Capsicum           dr. ii
   " Myrrh
   F E Xanthoxylum Fr
    " Hydrastis Can
    " -Cypripedium Pub aa dr. i
    " Hemlock            dr ss
    " Myrica             dr ii
   Syr Zingiberis       q. s. oz iv
```
This may be termed a cholera mixture, and may be used in proper proportions where such a stimulating preparation is needed
```
   Tr. Capsicum           oz iiss
   Oil Sassafras          dr ii
   " Hemlock
   " Origanum             aa dr. i
```
This is a stimulating liniment for application when much stimulation is needed
```
   Tr Capsicum
   F. E. Lobelia Infl     aa 16
   Ol Wormwood
   " Rosemary
   " Spearmint            aa. 1
```
This is excellent for sprains, bruises, rheumatism or neuralgia

Tinct, Myrrh Compound. (No. 6) is a reliable and superior article made from the best quality of gum myrrh and Zanzibar capsicum is always in stock by C. T. Bedford

Oil capsicum made from purest Zanzibar capsicum will not dissapoint you when you want stimulation in concentrated form. That sold by C T Bedford is made according to Prof. Davidson's formula for making oils.
```
   Powd Myrrh             .2
   "  Capsicum            1
   Alcohol                16
   Sugar                . 8
```
This is Saccharated No. 6   Without the sugar it is the ordinary No. 6, one of the preparations of the immortal Dr. Samuel Thompson   In suspended animation from any cause No. 6 may be injected hypodermically with most excellent results   The giving of a few drops diluted with

water is an excellent preparation for anæsthesia; if needed it may be injected hypodermically to assist in resuscitation.

CARBENIA BENEDICTA.

Blessed Thistle.   (Centaurea Benedicta.)

The *leaves* are a relaxing diaphoretic when given in hot infusion. They are somewhat stimulating and will induce nausea and vomiting. Its relaxing influence is well felt by all the secernents and the alvine mucous membrane and while it is emetic, it also proves hepatic and cathartic,

In cold infusion it is much like eupatorium perfoliatum, a wortby tonic for billious conditions, and may be used with profit in remitting and intermitting fever.

Menispermum Can.

Carbenia Ben.   aa equal parts.

or Smilax and Carbenia in equal parts, or Stillingia and Carbenia in equal parts are good alterative compounds.

Carbenia   1

Mitchella repens   2

forms a good preparation for females with pelvic weakness and constipation

Carbenia Ben.

Aralia Rac.

Symphytum Off. in equal parts, in Syr. Prunus is a good expectorant especially when hepatic torpor is present.

CARBO.

Carbo Animalis or animal charcoal is used for deodorizing purposes.

Carbo Ligni or wood charcoal it best for medical purposes and is used chiefly for absorbing gases. Slowly it absorbs carbonic acid gas from the air till it is replete, but heat will drive that carbonic acid gas off again. In order to keep carbon pure it must be kept tightly corked. It is an antiseptic and an absorbent of gasses.

Internally it may be used in dyspepsia where there is foul breath and gaseous eructation, with flatus and pains therefrom, also in water brash, nausea and vomiting. It is best given in capsules in doses of from to two five grains taken one hour after meals.

Powd. Charcoal   50

"   Myrrh   10

"   Capsicum   1-20

Hydrastia Sulphate   1

This given in capsules is excellent in the treatment of fermentative dyspepsia   Charcoal may be applied dry on the surface of an ulcer before applying a poultice   It arrests decomposition and deodorizes

CARTHAMUS TINCTORIUS.

Safflower.

The *flowers* are a family remedy to be used in measles In hot infusion they are a moderately relaxing diaphoretic influencing the circulation toward the surface   In strong infusions it colors the urine and fæces

CARUM CARVI.

Caraway.

The seed, the oil or the fluid extract are mainly used as an aromatic adjuvant in the administering of hepatics and cathartics   They are gently stimulating

CARUM COPTICUM.

Ajowan, Bishop's Weed   East India

This is an old remedy in India where it is much used and much cultivated

The *fruit or ajava seed* is an aromatic, diffusive, stimulating tonic influencing chiefly the mucous membrane imparting a warming pungent taste   It contains an oil that much resembles thymol, and the fruit is now largely imported into various parts of Europe for the manufacture of that article. ' The seeds somewhat resemble those of parsley.

A poultice of the crushed seed is said to relieve pain when applied in case of neuralgia, rheumatism or inflammations.

A weak infusion makes a good wash in case of inflammations or congestions of the eye or conjunctiva

A hot infusion may be used successfully in cholera morbus and in some cases of gastralgia and enteralgia, especially when from congestion

Its influence upon the nervous system is soothing and stimulating.

To the dipsomaniac the bitter taste, the pleasant warmth it imparts to the stomach and its soothing and toning influence over the nervous system, removes that unpleasant gnawing so well known to him.

CARUM PETROSELINUM.

Parsley.   (Apium Petroselinum)

The *root and seed* are an aromatic, relaxant and mildly stimulating diuretic increasing the urinary flow and giving relief to the aching back. When the urine is scanty, this makes a valuable addition in the treatment of dropsy.

The fluid extract may be used for all the purposes of the plant.

CARYA ALBA.

Shag-bark Hickory.

The *middle bark of the trunk* when fresh is quite acrid. The dry bark is a permanent bitter stimulating tonic. It is quite warming to the stomach, slightly elevating to the circulation and stimulating to the gall cyst and ducts. A strong infusion is an excellent antiperiodic in chronic ague Given in strong decoction a tablespoonful five or six times a day is very efficient as an antiperiodic.

Where there is a strong uterine or pulmonary hemorrhagic diathesis this agent is successful.

It also forms a good cough syrup, and at the same time influences the appetite, and tends the whole system to general improvement. In languid conditions with soft sluggish pulse and torpid secernents it brings good results.

    Carya Alba   1
    Taraxacum D. L.   2

forms a very serviceable combination for chronic billiousness and jaundice.

CARYOPHYLLUS AROMATICUS.

Cloves.   (Eugenia Aromatica.)

The *buds* are a stimulating aromatic. The *oil* is a diffusive stimulant. It is an ordinary remedy for toothache and is frequently used as a specific for an offensive breath. It is principally used as an adjuvant to bitter tonics.

CASSIA ANGUSTIFOLIA.

Senna.   (Cassia Acutifolia.)

The *root, leaves and pods* are a prompt stimulating cathartic. It is antibillious, antiperiodic and tonic. Catharsis is usually produced in two to four hours, thoroughly influencing intestinal peristalsis. Mentha piperita or zingiber prevent griping. Small doses may be continued for some time without tiring the system

Powd Cassia Ang.	4
" Ipomea Jal.	8
" Zingiber	4

This is an excellent antibilious physic. It may be given in such doses as may be required by the conditions present. If quick catharsis is needed give a large dose and have the patient recline and keep quiet. It will thoroughly cleanse the alvine canal in two or three hours, and will assist in relieving engorgement of the liver and gall ducts. But should you desire its action less upon the alvine canal and more upon the liver give small doses every three hours. I have aborted many a case of tonsilitis by a large dose of this compound, and in diphtheria and many other acute cases where the bowels are constipated this is my first dose. I have treated successfully many a case of typhoid fever with no other hepatic than this compound in small doses every 3 hours. It stimulates and cleanses the alvine mucous membrane

In jaundice where the overflow is not from gall stone it gives good success. In all eruptive diseases you will find a less virulent course and a more favorable termination by the use of a good dose of this compound in the beginning. In the treatment of chronic constipation there are few compounds that will do their work more completely and of which the system will become less weary. At first give dose sufficient to procure a complete evacuation, then give smaller doses and gradually decrease the frequency and quantity And during the time of this temporary treatment strive to educate the system to habitual regularity In the treatment of remittents and intermittents this compound is very important; regulate the doses as required to keep the alvine canal free, but not too free. Many a case may be aborted by the use of this compound, taken in time. Cassia is an excellent antiperiodic. Many a time a good size dose of antibilious physic will anticipate and prevent a chill and frequently will do it more permanently than quinine It will certainly prevent the necessity for giving so much quinine as would otherwise be required In giving large doses of this compound let the patient recline for an hour This will usually prevent nausea and vomiting which may otherwise occur It may be given in capsule or in fluid extract form, but neither are so good.

A dose of the compound should usually be given after the use of anthelmintics. Small doses given every three hours will soon relieve hemorrhoids and frequently prevent their recurrence.

In case of constipation either acute or chronic this compound may be given in suitable doses to infants.

Dr. C. B. Riggs' antibilious compound is as follows:

Powd. Senna
  "   Jalap   aa. oz. i
  "   Ginger
  "   Mandrake   aa. oz. ss
  "   Sanguinaria   oz. ¼

Mix. Sig. No. 1 capsule two or three times daily. This is a splendid cathartic and strongly influences the liver. It will be found useful especially in sluggish cases.

CASTANEA DENTATA.

Chestnut.   (Castanea Vesca.)

The *leaves* are a mild, stimulating, astringent tonic.

This is a home remedy for whooping-cough, but is not so successful alone as in combination with the acetous syrup of lobelia.

CASTELA NICHOLSONI.

Chaparro Amargoso.

This is a thorny shrub indigenous to Texas and Mexico.

The *bark of the stem* is an intensely bitter stimulating and astringent tonic, antiperiodic and antiseptic.

By the people among whom it grows it is considered a specific in the treatment of acute and chronic dysentery and diarrhœa, and of remitting fever. Let an infusion be given plentifully and it seems never to fail.

It influences the mucous membrane, improves digestion, tones the alvine mucous membrane, soothes and tones the nerves, relieves insomnia and builds up the general system.

CAULOPHYLLUM THALICTROIDES.

Blue Cohosh.

The *root* is a gently diffusive, relaxing and stimulating nervine and excellent antispasmodic especially in uterine irritations. Its principal influence is expended upon the generative system and the sympathetic nervous system connected therewith, soothing each and imparting tone and vigor.

In amenorrhœa its influence is felt favorably, increasing the periodic flow. The addition of leonurus gives a more stimulating compound. In dysmenorrhœa it is an excellent antispasmodic. In vaginitis its influence is good both per oram and per vaginam. In urethritis whether of the male or of the female, it prevents too frequent urinating and soothes irritation. In the irritation of the nerves that frequently occurs during parturition and for false pains and the restlessness during pregnancy and for after-pains caulophyllum is superior.

In acute rheumatism it gives ease, and it is valuable as an antispasmodic for whooping-cough and asthmatic and catarrhal coughs.

It may be added to aralia racemosa and prunus virginiana or other agents used in cough syrups.

In hysteria it allays nervous irritation but frequently needs such an addition as scutelaria to furnish greater tonicity.

It may be used in puerperal convulsions, as an antispasmodic and to assist in relieving the flow which is usually suspended at that time.

Dioscorea Vil	3
Caulophyllum Thal.	2
Scutelaria	1

may be used in cases of chorea, after-pains, nervousness during parturition, and with a little lobelia inflata it is excellent for rigidity of the os uteri.

Caulophyllum may be added in the treatment of an irritated stomach, and to the third preparation of lobelia for sick-headache.

Dr F. G Hoener recommends that the leaves be combined with asarum canadense and says that then it is a specific for whooping-cough.

F. E Caulophyllum Thal.
Tr Lobelia Inf.　　　　aa. dr. ii
Syr Zingiber　　　　q. s oz. iv

Use half a teaspoonful every two to four hours for bronchial catarrh. The fluid extract quite fully represents the drug.

CEANOTHUS AMERICANUS
New Jersey Tea

The *root and leaves* are a mildly stimulating tonic, quite soothing to the mucous membrane.

It may be used to good advantage in diarrhœa; and with aralia racemosa or other agents that especially affect the respiratory mucous membrane it is excellent in bronchitis and in the convalescent stage therefrom; also in pneumonia when the membrane is relaxed and weak and the discharge moderately free.

F. E. Ceanothus Am.
" Aralia Rac.   aa. dr. ii
" Symphytum Off.   dr. i
Syr. Prunus Virg.   q. s. oz. iv

This is an excellent cough syrup.

Lobelia or sanguinaria in small quantities may be added as the mucous membrane may require.

CELASTRUS SCANDENS.

False Bitter-Sweet.

The *bark of the root* is a mild, slow, relaxing and slightly stimulating alterant. It chiefly influences the secernents and the glandular system and the skin. It soothes the nervous system and is just in place when used in the treatment of nervous irritation with skin or glandular troubles, as in scrofula, glandular swellings, general struma. But its best influence is usually felt when combined with more stimulating agents especially when it is to be used for chronic cases.

F. E. Celastrus Scan.   dr. iii
" Alnus Serul.
" Stillingia Syl.   aa. dr. i
" Taraxacum D. L.   dr. iv
Syr. Zingiber .   q. s. oz. iv

Celastrus Scan.   30
Menispermum Can.   10
Rumex Crisp.   15
Xanthoxylum Frax. Bac. 1
Syr. Zingiber   q. s.

These are good alterative compounds.

Celastrus Scan.
Arctium Sem. aa. equal parts
may be used for a scaly skin.

With agents that influence the genital organs its alterative influence is exerted upon the ovaries; and with diuretics its chief influence is conveyed to the urinary organs. With aralia racemosa it influences the lungs; and with

hepatics it influences the liver. It is useful in syphilis
and gonorrhœa, especially in the fever stage; and with
agrimonia it soothes and strengthens the kidneys in cases
of irritable spermatorrhœa

F. E. Celastrus Scan.	oz. 1
Hydrastia Phos.	grs 11
Ferri et Potas Tartras	grs. x
Syr Zingiber	q. s oz iv

This is a good alterative for the alvine tract and will be
found valuable in diabetes.

Celastrus	3
Helonias	1
Eupatorium Purpur.	2

gives favorable results in albuminaria.

A hot infusion especially if combined with zingiber is
felt more directly by the skin and surface circulation. It
is also a good wash for a chaffy skin, and for scaly eruptions In cases of piles it slowly promotes absorption;
and with caulophyllum it is quite relieving to epilepsy.

With tallow or cosmoline it makes a good ointment suitable for application to piles, rectal fissures, ulcers, glandular troubles, chaffy skin and scaly eruptions.

Simple Cerate —	16
F. E Celastrus	4
Ol. Olives	2
Hydrastis Can	1

Dissolve, strain and stir till cold

Celastrus Scan	4
Mutton Tallow.	6
Cera Alba	2
Rosin	1

Simmer three hours, strain while hot and stir till cold.

CEPHÆLIS IPECACUANHA.

Ipecac

The **root** is a powerful and positive relaxant. It does
not cause nausea so quickly as lobelia, but the nausea once
produced is more persistent. It is frequently used in
bronchitis, pneumonia or asthma in combination with
other medicines that influence the bronchi or lungs and
freely increases expectoration. Given with diaphoretics
in hot infusion it increases diaphoresis.

If you want to make a drunken man sick of liquor give

him a glass of liquor with a dose of ipecac in it. For a time it creates a disgust, and it will soon straighten him up.

In a majority of cases the influence of lobelia is to be preferred to that of ipecac, though the wine of ipecac gives favorable results in the preventing of membranous croup.

CEPHALANTHUS OCCIDENTALIS.
Button Bush.

The *bark* is a moderately stimulating tonic influencing chiefly the alvine mucous membrane and the secernents.

In hot infusion it promotes diaphoresis. With eupatorium purpureum it assists in diuresis. With helonias dioica, aletris farinosa or mitchella it influences the generative organs, relieves the aching back, tones the uterus and vagina and increases the general tone and vigor of the whole system. With taraxacum or euonymous it influences the liver, promotes digestion, increases appetite and is somewhat antiperiodic.

Dr. F. G. Hoener says it will remove hydro-pneumonia and chronic hydro-asthmatic spasms and thereby reduce swelling of the chest.

CERA FLAVA AND ALBA.
Beeswax.

Cera Alba	3
Cetaceum	1
Ol. Olives	4 to 6

This forms simple cerate, gently heated and then stirred till cold.

Cera Flava	1
Ol. Linum	2

is a good application for swollen breasts.

Borax	1
Glycerine	5
Cetaceum	
Cera Alba	aa. 20

Dissolve these and while cooling add

Rose Water	30
Oil Almonds	10
Attar of Roses	q. s.

This is an admirable cold cream.

Cera Flava
Bos Taurus

Resina Pinus   aa. oz. 1
Pul Ulmus Fulva
" Chionanthus   aa. oz. iv
Ol. Lini Usi.   oz xvi

This is Dr. F G Hoener's salve for the instantaneous relief and radical cure of burns, scalds, wounds, boils, cuts, sores, ulcerated breasts, poison oak, tetter, poisonous insect bites, and syphilitic, gangrenous or scrofulous sores

CERASTIUM VULGATUM.

Chickweed.

This **herb** is a soothing, stimulating and relaxing agent influencing the skin and mucous membrane. An infusion forms a valuable wash in some skin diseases of an inflamed character, rhus poisoning, erysipelas, inflamed and chafed surfaces, stomatitis and pharyngitis A hot fomentation gives good results when applied to inflamed or swollen parts, abscesses, &c.

Dr. F. G Hoener says either prepared as an ointment or as a wash this will cure any kind of erysipelas

CERASUS VIRGINIANA.

Choke Cherry.

The **bark** is a mildly stimulating and relaxing tonic slightly astringent It is antispasmodic and antiperiodic. It is very useful in the treatment of intermittents. Some claim that it is preferable to quinine as an antiperiodic; but like the latter it needs the addition of hepatic tonics. In general debility and indigestion this is quite a powerful tonic In hysteria it gives very favorable results. as also in enuresis in weakly children. In spermatorrhœa it will be found to be one of the best agents. For coughs with excessive and weakening expectoration and in chronic diarrhœa, chronic dysentery and cholera infantum it tones the mucous membrane and gives very favorable results In vaginal weakness and leucorrhœa it may be used both locally and constitutionally

CERCIS CANADENSIS.

Judas-Tree

The **leaves** are a moderately stimulating, astringent tonic Its chief influence is toward the mucous membrane and glandular system. It is valuable in scrofula when the

bowels are weak and inclined to diarrhœa or dysentery.
Locally it forms a good wash for sores and swellings.

Cercis Can. Cort. Rad.   3
Populus Trem. Cort.   1

Dr. F. G. Hoener recommends this in chronic diarrhœa

CEREUS GRANDIFLORUS.

Night-blooming Cereus.   (Cactus Grandiflorus.)
    (Cactus Mexicana.)

The *flowers and stems* applied locally are non-irritants. Per oram it accelerates the pulse, increases its fulness, elevates arterial tension and is truly a stimulating cardiac tonic. It is also stimulating to the spinal nerves and motor centers. It is toning to the heart in simple dilatation and muscular atony from deficient innervation and nutrition without organic lesions. It is sustaining in valvular disease with dilatation. In cardiac and general muscular relaxation with impaired nerve energy cactus is toning and strengthening to both heart and nerves. The irritable alcoholic and tobacco heart is sustained by its use and perhaps mainly by its stimulating the spinal motor centers and by its continuous stimulation of the heart's muscular action and thereby increasing its nutrition and development. Chewing tobacco may not produce organic disease of the heart, but it affects the gastric membrane and nerves; and in smoking, carbonic oxide, ammonia and nicotine are inhaled. The ammonia acts on the blood and makes it alkaline and more fluid and hence impairs its nutritive properties. Tobacco leaves the stomach dyspepsied and debilitated. The heart becomes weak, irregular and intermitting. Palpitation, pain, faintness and vertigo follow. Tissue is degraded, vision is more or less impaired, the hands become tremulous and there is a dragging feeling or pain in the region of the heart about the size of a silver dollar.

Cereus may be used continuously without exciting any gastric irritation. Small doses of two to five drops repeated every fifteen to thirty minutes as long as needed will usually give the best results, yet a teaspoonful may be given if required without any inconvenience or adverse symptoms. Its action is favorable. It regulates the pulse, promotes diastole and diminishes peripheral resistance. In organic cardiac diseases, excluding arythenia, when prompt action is desired and when other cardiac remedies fail cereus is a most effective agent.

It is equally useful in functional troubles, regardless of cause, particularly of nervous origin.

It may be taken before, during or after meals, but its influence is best on an empty stomach.

Cereus is quite efficient in mitral and aortic insufficiency, in mitral stenosis and exophthalmic goitre, rheumatism, chorea and mild anæmia

CEREUS BONPLANDII

This agent once considerably used is giving way to the use of cactus grandiflorus. Prof. H. J. Treat reports having used this agent for some years especially in iritic affections In iritis and in irido-cyclitis and especially in that form known as sympathetic ophthalmia that he has used it in seemingly hopeless cases; that it greatly allayed irritation and toned the parts He pronounces it a specific in this condition

F. E Cereus Bonplandii   oz. ss
Aqua Dist.   oz iss

Sig   One teaspoonful four times a day, before meals and before retiring   This dose may be increased if found necessary. It strengthens the heart and circulation, relieves the blood current of impurities and cleanses the mucous membrane

CETACEUM.

Spermaceti.

This is used as a basis for ointments

Cetaceum   1
Ol Linum   5
Pul. Ulmus   2
Rose Water   4

Melt together and add the rose water, stirring till cold. This is an excellent preparation for burns, scalds, irritable sores, chapped hands and denuded sores and wounds

CHAMÆLIRIUM LUTEUM

Helonias, False Unicorn.   (Helonias Dioica)

The *root* is a positively stimulating uterine and ovarian tonic for all depressed conditions of these organs It is useful in prolapsus uteri, uterine atony, barrenness, relaxed vagina, post-partem hemorrhage, excessive menstruation and leucorrhœa. In cases of liability to miscarriage it is excellent. I have prevented scores of miscarriages by its use, even after pain was prominent and hemorrhage had made its appearance. It is a reliable agent. But this agent should not be given to weakly married ladies who are liable to very frequent pregnancies.

It is also toning to the mucous membrane throughout. In gastric torpor and gastric irritation it soothes and tones the membrane, promotes appetite and assists digestion. It is frequently tolerated by the stomach when but little else will, and hence is valuable during pregnancy as a gastric and uterine tonic. It is stimulating to the assimilative organs throughout

It is also a stimulating diuretic of great value in albuminaria and diabetes. It is stimulating and toning to the kidneys, bladder, uterus and urethra, and is serviceable in gleet.

Helonin in 5 to 10 grain doses may be used with much advantage in Bright's disease. Helonias gives very favorable results in enuresis. It is a toning and strengthening agent to the generative and urinary organs of both sexes.

Its tonic properties are also well marked in the treatment of dyspepsia and for the expelling of the stomach worm.

With aralia racemosa and agents of similar influence it acts on the bronchi as a stimulating expectorant and tonic.

Helonias is best administered in small doses three to six times a day, but in cases of threatened miscarriage the fluid extract may be given in doses of from five to ten drops in water every fifteen minutes to one hour.

Helonin is a good preparation and represents the drug quite fully.

        Helonin
        Viburnin   aa. 24
        Dioscorein   4
        Avenin   12
        Caulophyllin   1
This is a powerful uterine tonic.

CHELIDONIUM MAJUS.

Garden Celandine.

This *plant* is bitter, rather acrid when green but not when dry, somewhat demulcent and stimulating to the mucous membrane. It proves cathartic and somewhat

diuretic In hot infusion it is diaphoretic and expecto-
rant· In large doses it is nauseating. It exerts also a
favorable influence upon the mesenteric and lymphatic
glands and the skin.

Dr. F G Hoener recommends the following formula·

Chelidonium Maj (green root)
Glechoma Hederacea
Chrysanthemum   aa equal parts

for the curing of inflammation of the eyes, conjunctivitis,
scaly eruptions and gonorrhœal ophthalmia. He reports
one case as having been blind by the last trouble. but by
washing the eyes with an infusion of this agent three to
five times a day, in six weeks she could see as well as before

CHELONE GLABRA.

Balmony

The *herb* is a mild stimulating tonic to the mucous
membrane It stimulates the appetite and tones the
stomach. It is excellent in the treatment of dyspepsia
and may be used freely for atonic conditions. It influences
the liver and is a moderately stimulating cholagogue. It
is chiefly through its action in this direction that it produces moderate catharsis The bile itself is a cathartic,
hence when properly excreted it becomes a valuable assistant in the relief of chronic constipation This influence
also renders this agent of much service in the treatment
of chronic jaundice As a mild hepatic tonic it does well
in convalescence from fevers and other diseases where the
liver has been involved In mal-assimilation it is one of
our best agents, and it does excellent service in ridding
the system of stomach worms. In general debility, at
times accompanied with more stimulating agents chelone
is one of the best for its general tonic influence Indeed
this makes chelone an excellent addition to most alteratives, especially where there is much depression and
hepatic torpor.

Combined with diuretics its tonic powers are exerted in
the direction of the kidneys; and in dropsy where there is
chronic hepatic and gastric torpor the influence of chelone
will give very favorable results

Combined with syr juglans it will be found very serviceable in chronic constipation better than either agent by
itself.

F. E. Chelone Glab.
" Gentiana Och.   aa. 3
" Hydrastis Can.   1
This is useful for congestion of the liver.

CHENOPODIUM ANTHELMINTICUM.

American Wormseed.

The *oil* in doses of ten to twenty drops on sugar or in some emulsion and followed by a cathartic is a vermifuge.

Dr. G. H. Mayhugh recommends the following anthelmintic preparation:

Ol. Chenopodii   gtt. xxx
" Anise   gtt. vi
Sacch. Lactin   dr. i
M. Trit. Fiat. Chart. No. 6.

Sig. One or two powders every three hours. Follow at night by a cathartic.

The oil of wormseed is also an emmenagogue and should not be used during pregnancy.

An infusion of the *leaves* is a far more pleasant stimulating aromatic anthelmintic. A hot infusion may be used to relieve and increase the menstrual flow in case of cold, and the relief of dysmenorrhœa incident to such cases.

CHENOPODIUM BOTRYS.

Jerusalem Oak.

This is the foreign species but the properties are so near like the American that it needs no separate description.

CHIMAPHILLA UMBELLATA.

Pipsissewa.

The *leaves* are a mild stimulating and relaxing alterative, influencing especially the glandular system, the lymphatics and secernents.

As a good cleansing agent it carries off effete matter and relieves the liver, kidneys and skin. In scrofula it is one of the best agents. Use it quite freely.

In phthisis and cancer it assists much in the relief of the blood current from impurities and waste material. Give it in large quantities if needed. In dropsy it relieves and tones the kidneys. In gonorrhœa it is soothing to the mucous membrane and cleansing to the blood current. In syphilis it is of no little importance, but in certain stages may have to be combined with more stimulating agents.

It is also useful in vaginal and uterine weakness, and in leucorrhœa; in rheumatism especially when it arises from some impurity of the blood; in cystic catarrh, spermatorrhœa, typhoid and other fevers, in urinary obstructions, and coughs and colds   It is valuable not only for its alterative influence but for its diuretic action in cleansing the mucous membrane of accumulated solids or mucous.   Combined with uterine tonics it does well in leucorrhœa and gonorrhœa

In depressed and very debilitated cases it is best that more stimulating agents be added

Combined with syrup macrotys you have a good remedy for coughs and colds

It may be used in place of uva-ursi   The fluid extract is more astringent than the infusion.

CHIONANTHUS VIRGINICA.

Fringe Tree

The *bark of the root* is a gently relaxing and stimulating hepatic and alterative   It is rather bitter and influences the liver, gall ducts and kidneys   These qualities make it a valuable antiperiodic, and is useful in typhoid, bilious and intermitting fevers, and in jaundice, hepatic torpor and constipation.

Chionanthus Virg
Euonymous At   aa. 10
Podophyllin   1
will be found to do you good service.

CHONDODENDRON TOMENTOSUM

Pareira Brava.

The *root* is a relaxing and very mildly stimulating diuretic   It is useful in enlargement of the prostate and engorgement of the urethra from any cause. It mildly increases the urinary flow and cleanses the mucous membrane, and hence should be used in cases of cystic catarrh, gonorrhœa, leucorrhœa, and in congestions of the mucous surfaces.

CHRYSANTHEMUM LEUCANTHEMUM

Ox-eye Daisy

The *flowers* are relaxing and mildly stimulating to the circulation and in hot infusion prove diaphoretic. It also influences the mucous membrane and the nervous system.

They have a decided influence upon the uterus in the relief of congestions and in the promoting of the menstrual flow in dysmenorrhœa with scanty flow and especially so in cases where this is habitual. It is an excellent agent for the hysterical, especially if there be a foul stomach and nervous tendency. This given freely in large doses, emesis will be a result, which will leave the nerves soothed and the whole system at rest, as well as the decided benefit of having the stomach well cleansed.

Zingiber may be added if a diffusive be necessary in order to a free perspiration.

Bilious cases need the extra use of hepatics, and constipation the addition of syr. juglans.

In bilious fever after the tongue has been cleared chrysanthemum may be used in convalescence. It is a mild somewhat bitter and good tonic to the mucous membrane.

Hot fomentations may be used over the lungs, where relaxation and gentle stimulation is needed as in colds, bronchitis, pneumonia. Sometimes an acetous infusion inhaled will readily relieve a cold in the head or nasal passages, and such vapor is very soothing to the throat and bronchi.

Dr. F. G. Hoener says this has proven to be a specific for night sweats.

CHRYSANTHEMUM PARTHENIUM.

Feverfew.

This *plant* is a diffusive, mildly stimulating and relaxing and influencing the skin, nervous system, the circulation and the genito-urinary organs.

In hot infusion it is diaphoretic and is excellent in equalizing the circulation and relieving the head, brain and nerves of pressure and excitement. So in pleuritis it relieves the hyperæmia present and reduces the inflammatory excitement. In parturition by equalizing the circulation the pains become more regular, the contractions firmer and the rigid os uteri relieved of its tensity. In cases where the menses are suppressed from cold it quickly relieves the hyperæmia present and the flow assumes its normal condition. Its influence upon the circulation tends toward the surface and with proper hepatics it assists in relieving the circulation of impurities especially in uræmia and cholæmia. It is a superior tonic to the stomach, relieving hyperæmic conditions of the mucous membrane, and is serviceable in colic, flatulence, eructations and general indigestion   With proper hepatics it assists in the relief of engorged liver, whether it be from congestion or inflammation   In bronchitis and pneumonia it dispels hyperæmia and tones the mucous membrane   In hysteria it relieves the nerves as well as the circulation. In puerperal fever it does its work well, but at times needs more stimulation. In combination with cactus it is excellent for the nervous, unstrung condition resulting from the use of tobacco or liquor.

In hot fomentation this herb may be applied with good results over the lungs, stomach or abdomen in cases of either congestion or inflammation.

The F E may be used instead of the herb in either hot or cold preparations.

CIMICIFUGA RACEMOSA.

Black Cohosh

The *root* is a relaxing and stimulating, diffusive nervine and alterant. It is a powerful agent   The green root has a nauseating odor which is almost entirely absent when dry.

Large doses especially of the fluid extract influence the brain and produces dizziness, which however lasts but a short time

Age impairs the value of this agent, and heat materially changes some of its properties   It then does not influence the brain as much as the glandular system, the uterus and the mucous membrane throughout   A strong decoction is an excellent antiperiodic, but it is still better when combined with small portions of quinine

A syrup made by boiling the green or dry root and then adding enough sugar to keep it   This may be used as a base for alterative preparations and gives very favorable results in eruptive diseases and scrofula

The fluid extract and the resonoid producing headache as they do, cannot be used in large quantities, sufficient to produce the required alterative effect, but of the syrup you can give as much as is required. It acts well on the secernents throughout, the liver, kidneys and lymphatics   It does well in all bad contaminations of the blood.   It is a good remedy in syphilis   If it attacks the joints apply a strong infusion of cimicifuga to the parts   The syrup of cimicifuga makes an excellent base for other alterative preparations, tonics and antispasmodics. It tones and prevents waste, soothes and stimulates the nerves; is a good antispasmodic and is useful in whooping-cough, asthma, hysterical convulsions, hysteria and chorea.

    Cimicifuga Rac.
    Caulophyllum Thal.
    Cypripedium Pub.
    Helonias
    Leonurus Card.   aa. equal parts. Or

    Cimicifuga Rac.
    Aristolochia Serp.
    Asclepias Tub.
    Lobelia Infl. aa. equal parts. Either of these formulæ is good in the treatment of chorea.

Dr. F. G. Hoener recommends the following for epilepsy and chorea:

    Elix. Cimicifuga Rac.   oz. iv
      " Scutelaria
      " Verbena Hast.   aa. oz. ii

M. Sig. One tablespoonful four times a day. All meats and heavy digestible foods to be strictly avoided.

Dr. Hoener also recommends the following for apoplexy. If life is not too near extinct, rub the whole body with hot water and give

    Elix. Cimicifuga Rac.
      " Betonica Lan.   aa. oz. iss
      " Cunila Mar.   oz. i

M. Sig. One tablespoonful every thirty minutes. When the patient improves lengthen the time to one hour. When it cannot be administered per oram it may be used by enema.

Cimicifuga soothes the serous membrane and gives a fullness to the pulse and is hence of much importance in acute and chronic rheumatism. In dysmenorrhœa, amenorrhœa and in parturition its influence is valuable. It soothes the uterus and gently increases the periodic flow. It relieves after-pains and maintains the lochial discharge. In case of a sudden check of the lochia it will influence a gentle return of the lochia, and affords relief to the uterine and general circulation.

    Macrotin
    Humulin
    Acacia   aa. grs. x

Camphora

Trit. Ol. Cinnamon   aa. grs v

Make into from five to eight powders and use in dysmeuorrhœa every half hour for two hours.

In all eruptive diseases the syrup of cimicifuga freely given will tend to purify the blood current and given'in hot water or an infusion of the root, is diaphoretic. It cleanses the circulation so that the eruption will not be so virulent and the surface inflammation not so intense

In bronchial congestion or inflammation in hot infusion it is an alterative expectorant which readily allays irritation of the respiratory mucous membrane, and especially is this true when combined with such agents as aralia racemosa, or prunus virginiana,

Cimicifuga Rac

Aralia Rac.

Lycopus Virg.

Anthemis Nob. aa in equal parts. Use a heaped tablespoonful of this combination to one pint of barley water Sweeten with honey. and use for a bronchial cough.

With the superior influence of diuretics the action of cimicifuga is well marked upon the kidneys and urinary mucous membrane

The influence of this agent upon the nervous system much depends on the grade of nervines with which it is combined, and so with its influence on the serous tissue and the secernents generally

CINCHONA

Peruvian Bark

Cinchona Calisaya is the yellow bark.

Cinchona Officinalis is the pale bark.

Cinchona Succirubra is the red bark

All these varieties are stimulating nervines It is from the cinchonas that quinine, the popular antiperiodic, is derived

Cinchona includes in its range of influence the entire nervous system, the sympathetic as well as the cerebral and spinal, the peripheral as well as the central nerves.

In large doses especially quinine causes much buzzing in the ears and may so stimulate the auditory nerves as to cause temporary or permanent deafness according to its extravagant use.

The red and pale varieties are considered most astringent, but it is claimed that the yellow furnishes most quinine in proportion to bulk.

All the varieties tend to increased sensibility and excitement, even inducing tension, a dryness of the mucous membrane and of the surface, also inducing constipation, warmth, and hardening of the pulse. Given during febrile excitement it increases that excitement, and gastric and intestinal tenderness follow its excessive use.

The fluid extract of the bark is a good antiperiodic and a tonic to the nervous system.

Spasmodic condition arising from weakness may be quieted by cinchona

At times very simple things may create a shock to the system and become as good an antiperiodic as cinchona. I have known a half teacup of raw corn meal taken before breakfast to do as well as quinine to prevent a chill. And so with a tablespoonful of ginger in a pint of milk. The eating of a pound of raisins has done the same thing, and so will asafœtida taken at the right time. Even the eating of a raw egg in a tablespoonful of vinegar sometimes forms a good antiperiodic.

In the giving of cinchona or any of its preparations it is absolutely necessary that you look to the cleansing of the system of morbific materials. If this be first done the necessity of quinine will be much less, and smaller doses will be required. It should then be given in small doses hourly for three or four hours prior to the time of the expected chill

If the occasion for quinia is upon your patient and you have not time to prepare your patient, then give your cleansing material with your quinine, if necessary a good dose of antibilious physic. See that the stomach, liver, bowels and circulation are doing their respective duties.

Quinia sulphas is an alkaloid, a neutral salt, odorless, white, silky crystals. Its action is identical with the bark except that it possesses less astringency and is more stimulating to the auditory nerves than is the bark.

Per rectum two or three times as much quinia as per oram may be given for the same purpose.

In typhoid fever when occurring in typhoid regions, small doses of quinia should be given throughout the whole course of treatment.

The cinchona bark is more of a general tonic than the quinia.

It may be that in some extreme cases large doses may be
admirable, but these cases are very seldom   When large
doses are deemed necessary you may avoid much of the inconvenience by filling the ears with cypripedium and lobelia, and this repeated at intervals as needed   It prevents
the presence of the extreme tension upon the auditory
nerves

. Quinia sulphas is so intensely bitter that many preparations have been made to cover the taste. An alkali to
some extent does this without much injury to the effects
of the quinine.

Cinchona	12
Lactin	60
Bicarb Soda	1

forms a tasteless cinchona. Fluid extract of glycyrrhiza
to some extent relieves the bitter taste of quinia, and so
will cinnamon.

McCoy, Howe Co., of Indianapolis, manufacture a Quin-
ia-Masque a syrup yerba santa aromatica   A teaspoonful
will disguise 2 grs. of quinine   It disguises without impairing solubility or efficacy.

Cincho-quinine throws the blood to the surface, fills the
capillaries and causes redness of the surface, but without
extra heat

Quinia may be given in small capsules but pill form is
usually too slow

Chinoidin is a preparation strongly antiperiodic. It is
very liable in large doses to cause nausea and starts a free
flow of bile. One to three grains is an ordinary dose   It
is best given in a little lemonade   On account of its action on the secernents it is a desirable preparation in the
treatment of intermittents and neuralgia.   The fluid
extract of the bark is an excellent preparation for the
treatment of intermittents and it does not give the inconvenience that some other preparations do

Red Cinchona	6½
Bitter Orange Peel	5½
Aristolochia Serpen.	1½

Or

Red Cinchona	8
Bitter Orange Peel	4
Aristolochia Serpen	2
Carthamus Tinct.	1

Or

Cinchona Pale	12
Sweet Orange peel	2
F. E. Cardamon Comp	2

These are all good tonic nervine compounds involving cinchona.

| Quinia Sulph. | gr. i |
| Aqua | oz. ii |

forms an appetizing tonic for many cases of convalescence.

There is now prepared a F. E. cinchona detannated for use in the manufacturing of elixirs and for combining properly with iron preparations.

CINNAMOMUM CASSIA.

Cassia, Cinnamon.   (Laurus Cinnamomum.)
                          Ceylon and China.

The *inner bark* of the branches is a warming, diffusive, stimulating, aromatic and astringent tonic. It is rich in oil, upon which its properties largely depend. It influences chiefly the alvine mucous membrane, and is one of the best agents in cholera infantum and in all cases of diarrhœa. But in all such cases care must be taken to keep the liver and gall ducts in proper action.

It promotes digestion, soothes the nerves and stimulates the circulation, but it is mostly used as an adjuvant in the administering of other medicines.

The *oil* of cinnamon is more stimulating and less astringent than the bark and is very useful in liniments.

Ol. Cinnamon	
" Capsicum	aa. 1
" Sassafras	3

This makes an excellent liniment, one of the very best for a very stimulating influence. It is powerful, but it may be diluted and used as a liniment of whatever strength required. In one drop doses in water it may be used internally for colic, cholera morbus, flatus, cholera infantum, and in such cases it may be diluted and also used as a liniment over the abdomen.

Cinnamomum Zeylan.	
Zingiber	aa. 5¼
Myristica Frag.	
Elettaria Repens	aa. 2¼

Triturate on sugar.

This is an excellent aromatic stimulant to be used in

faintness and prostration, a cold surface. nervous depression or sympathetic vomiting.

CIRCIUM ARVENSE.

Canada Thistle   (Cnicus Arvensis)

The *root* of this agent is a mild, stimulating, astringent and somewhat demulcent influencing chiefly the mucous membrane. and quite favorably so in the treatment of dysentery and diarrhœa.

It also influences the nervous system, assists in parturition, anticipates post-partem hemorrhage and relieves after-pains

An infusion forms a good wash in relaxed vagina, prolapsus uteri and leucorrhœa.

The whole plant boiled in lard makes a good ointment for some forms of eczema, pruritus, irritable hemorrhoids and rectal fissures and ulcers in various parts

Dr F. G Hoener recommends its use in strong decoction in cases of tuberculosis of the lungs and for its desirable action on the kidneys   In either case it may be combihed with suitable agents.

CITRUS AURANTIUM

Orange

The *peel* is a mild diffusive, stimulating aromatic tonic It contains some oil   It warms the stomach, relieves flatus and improves the appetite and digestion

In convalescence the fruit is refreshing, and a small portion of the dried peel chewed slowly is a good tonic to the gastric membrane

Grated Fresh Orange Peel   1
Granulated Sugar   3

Triturate thoroughly   This is a good vehicle for quinine and other bitter tonics.

Citrus Aur Peel   12
Caryophyllus Arom.
Carum Carvi
Cinnamonum Cas
Pimpinella An   aa. ½

This is an excellent compound which may be made into a syrup or used as a powder triturated on sugar   It is a vehicle of no little importance for the administering of bitter or unpleasant drugs.

CITRUS VULGARIS.

Bitter Orange, Seville Orange. France.

Aurantii Floris Aqua is chiefly prepared from this variety and is used as a perfume.

The **oil neroli** is obtained from both varieties by distillation from the flowers. That from the bitter variety is the best.

The **peel** of this variety has about the same medical properties as that of the sweet variety except that this variety is more bitter.

CITRUS LIMONUM.

Lemon.

The outer peel contains the oil of lemon. It is a warming aromatic. Hot lemonade is a diaphoretic. Cold lemonade is an excellent refreshing drink, very agreeable and very useful in proper quantities in billious fever, in rheumatism and in many other conditions. It is a pleasant tonic to the stomach.

A syrup made of lemon juice is a good temporary cough syrup.

Citric acid is fermented lemon juice and is very much stronger than the fresh lemon juice.

Fresh lemon peel grated	2
Strained lemon juice	16
Granulated Sugar	36

This forms an excellent syrup as a vehicle for bitter medicines

In the use of the lemon, care must be taken that the acid shall be used by the patient in moderation, for even a good thing used to excess may do harm.

Lemon juice	1
Granulated sugar	3

forms a good syrup for ordinary purposes.

In cases of epistaxis cleanse the nostrils of clots and spray the inner surface with lemon juice.

COCCULUS PALMATUS.

Calumba. (Jateorhiza Palmata.)

The **root** is a mild, stimulating, bitter tonic, slightly dumulcent, influencing chiefly the mucous membrane of the alvine tract. It invigorates the stomach, improves the

appetite and assists digestion and assimilation. It is soothing to the mucous membrane, and it allays the vomiting of
pregnancy and other weak and irritable conditions of the
stomach and alvine canal.

In convalescence from fevers when the alviue mucous
membrane is left irritated. In combination with some astringent agents it is valuable in dysentery and diarrhoea.
With hydiastis it is toning to the alvine canal. Calumba is
one of those agents which by combining with various other
agents may be made to influence any particular part of the
mucous membrane. Thus its chief influence may be felt
on any particular part, on the stomach, the bowels, the
urinary tract or the generative organs

COCHLEARIA ARMORACIA.

Horse Radish   (Nasturtium Armoracia.)

The *fresh roots* will blister the surface and so will the
leaves. I have used them frequently for neuralgia where
mustard might be used. Relief has usually resulted. Do
not allow it to remain long enough to blister.

The root grated in vinegar is a good table relish for the
torpid stomach.

When dry the roots are a rather pleasant stimulant to
the kidneys, the skin, the stomach and the circulation. It
arouses a gastric warmth, gently relieves the gall ducts
stimulates alvine action, increases urinary flow, tones the
mucous membrane, produces a fullness of the pulse, and
leaves a warmth of the surface.

In atonic dyspepsia and bilious, sluggish conditions it is
best, and in gastric and intestinal catarrh it is of much
importance; also in dropsy, jaundice and chronic rheumatism

    Tr or F. E. Cochlearia   dr ii
    F E Taraxacum   dr. vii
    Syr Citrus Auran   q s oz. iv
M. S Teaspoonful with meals is good for a torpid
stomach and liver with constipation

    Cochlearia
    Sinapis Alba Sem
    Juniperus
    Berberis Aquifol
    Citrus Auran   aa oz ii
    Cider Vinegar   pints 3
Allow to stand a week and press. The result is a good

tonic for a very torpid digestion and poor assimilation, with biliousness, as found frequently in cases of dropsy.

COCOS NUCIFERA.

Cocoa-nut Tree.

From the *nut* of this tree by expressing is obtained, a fixed oil. The oil is white and about of the consistency of lard. It is much more palatable than cod-liver oil and has frequently been used as a substitute. Occasionally it has been used in the culinary art as a substitute for lard. Its use in pharmacy is far superior to lard.

COLA ACUMINATA.

Kola Nut.   Africa, West Indies.

The *nut* is a mild stimulating, astringent tonic. The African kola nut is more astringent than that from Jamaica, and is more valuable for diarrhœa. It checks nausea and vomiting, soothes the gastric and intestinal mucous membrane and assists digestion when used in moderation. Kola is of the tanno-caffeic order. It is stimulating to the mucous membrane throughout and toning to intestinal digestion. Kola contains a high percentage of caffein, but it is far more tonic than caffein.

Kola is also quite sustaining to the nervous system especially the cerebral and spinal. It sustains, tones and rests the brain during continued intellectual labor, and is valuable in convalescence and neurasthenia, and some neuralgic conditions especially of a chronic character.

Kola is also a tonic diuretic and may be used in diabetes.

In parturition kola is sustaining to the nervous system and relieves fatigue. It sustains the body well during physical exercise.

In anæmia it stimulates the appetite, improves the flesh and assists sleep. It also gives favorable results in melancholia.

It is claimed to give favorable results in loco-motor ataxia, pulmonary tuberculosis and carbuncle.

The Jamaica kola forms a pleasant beverage and is sometimes called kola coffee. Taken at night it will produce wakefulness and may be important to the student when there is a necessity for the burning of the midnight oil.

The infusion is the preferable form for the use of this agent.

COLLINSONIA CANADENSIS.

Stone Root.

The **root** is a gently stimulating diuretic and tonic alterative slightly astringent, influencing the mucous membrane throughout In diarrhœa and dysentery it stimulates, cleanses and tones the alvine membrane and materially aids digestion and soothes hemorrhoids In cystic catarrh it assists in diuresis and stimulates and cleanses the membrane. In leucorrhœa it may be used as a wash and per oram with good results Combined with agents that influence the respiratory organs it is valuable in cleansing and toning the bronchi. In hot infusion its influence is decidedly toward the surface, and is valuable in acute and chronic peritonitis, pleuritis, and acute and chronic endo-carditis In influencing the circulation it influences the nervous system and gives favorable results in nervous irritation and nervous depression.

F. E. Collinsonia Can.
"   Leptandra Virg   aa. 1
- Syr. Juglans   2

This is an alterative, hepatic, tonic cathartic and nervine.

Dr. C B Riggs recommends the following for hemorrhoids

Syr. Juglans   oz lii
F. E. Collinsonia Can (green) oz. i

M. S Teaspoonful often enough to keep the bowels acting gently.

Dr. Riggs also advises the following diaphoretic compound as a most excellent preparation in the producing of diaphoresis in such troubles as la grippe, colds, and fevers·

F E. Collinsonia Can. (green)   oz. viii
"   Lobelia Inf.
Comp Tinc. Myrrh   aa. oz iv
Sodium Salicylate (Wintergreen) oz. i

Mix Sig. Ten to thirty drops in warm water every ½, 1 or 2 hours

Collinsonin   4
Juglandin
Euonymin   aa. 2
Leptandrin   1

This may be used in capsules for indigestion, hemorroids , &c

F. E. Collinsonia
"   Avena Sativa aa. equal parts.
Mix   Sig.   Twenty drops every 3 or 4 hours for infant paralysis.

Dr. F. G. Hoener recommends the use of this agent in cholera infantum, cholera morbus, diarrhœa, dysentery, gastro-enteritis if accompanied with diarrhœa; entero-colitis, and persistent vomiting.

COMPTONIA ASPLENIFOLIA.

Sweet Fern.   (Myrica Asplenifolia.)

The *leaves* are a mild aromatic, stimulating, tonic alter-ative, chiefly influencing the mucous membrane. It stim-ulates the appetite and promotes digestion and assimila-tion. It is valuable in scrofula, tabes mesenterica and tuberculosis.

F. E. Comptonia Asp.	oz. i
Hydrastia Sulph.	gr. i
Ferri et Pot. Tart.	grs. xv
Syr. Zingiberis	q. s. oz. iv

This is a valuable compound in tabes mesenterica.

With aralia racemosa it acts well in bronchitis.

With helonias and leonurus it does well in vaginal and uterine weakness.

CONVOLVULUS SCAMMONIA.

Scammony, Man Root.   (Convolvulus Panduratus.)
                          (Ipomœa Pandurata.)

The *resin* is rather a pleasant stimulating cathartic, but in large doses like other cathartics it is quite griping, which is much lessened by the addition of zingiber in some form. Its most profitable influence is when combined with some appropriate hepatics.

COPAIFERA OFFICINALIS.

Copaiba.   West Indies and South America.

Incisions in the copaiba tree yield an oleo-resinous excre-tion of balsamic odor and nearly colorless. It is warming and rather nauseating and is usually administered in sealed capsules or in some form of emulsion, or triturated on lactin and reduced to a powder. It is best in soft cap-sules because of the volatile oil evaporating and leaving little but the resin which is comparatively of little value.

Copaiba is a stimulating diuretic strongly influencing

the mucous membrane, especially that of the urinary organs. Its use is best adapted in languid and sluggish conditions, chronic congestion and weakness of the mucous passages as in gleet It is not suited to inflamed and irritated conditions of the mucous membrane, because of its stimulating ,properties It is frequently combined with barosma or uva-ursi.

COPTIS TRIFOLIA

Gold Thread.

The **root** is a gently stimulating bitter tonic to the mucous membrane throughout. It is valuable in convalescence from fevers, is a good appetizer and gently tones the gastric membrane. In many respects it has nearly if not quite fully as good influence as hydrastis canadensis

It is valuable as a wash for sore mouth, a vaginal wash and as an injection to the urethra in gonorrhœa. It tones the mucous membrane and enables it to cast off impurities.

CORALLORHIZA ODONTORHIZA.

Crawley·Root   (Pterospora Andromedea)

The **root** is a pleasant, prompt, diffusive, relaxing diaphoretic, slightly stimulating and somewhat demulcent. It influences the circulation, allays nervous irritability, induces free diaphoresis and relieves the capillaries.

It is a superior agent in febrile conditions, and in eruptive diseases If needed, more stimulating agents may be added. With zingiber its influence is valuable in bronchitis, pneumonia, pleuritis, peritonitis and nephritis, and in this combination it promotes the menstrual flow in cases of congestion, by relieving the circulation and promoting an outward tendency of the blood By equalizing the circulation it is valuable in puerperal fever, in ovaritis, uteritis, and for the relief of hyperæmic conditions wherever found. By its use also after-pains are relieved and the lochia increased

Pul. Pterospora And	dr. iss
" Asclepias Tub.	dr. i
" Xanthoxylum Frax	dr ss
" Capsicum	grs x
" Dioscorea Vil	dr i
Aqua Bullens	oz viii

Sig. Tablespoonful hourly for peritonitis.

CORIANDRUM SATIVUM.

Coriander.

The *seeds* are a mild, pleasant, aromatic carminative, chiefly used as a vehicle for bitter tonics and cathartics.

CORNUS CIRCINATA.

Green Osier Bark.

The *bark* is a bitter, gently stimulating and slightly astringent tonic, influencing chiefly the mucous membrane. It is useful in dysentery, diarrhœa and cholera infantum. In hot infusion it somewhat influences the circulation and the nervous system, gently stimulating, soothing and toning.

CORNUS FLORIDA

Dogwood.

The *bark* is rather a pleasant stimulating and astringent tonic chiefly influencing the mucous membrane. In hot infusion it influences the circulation. It is a good antiperiodic especially with small portions of quinine, but its best influence is upon the alvine mucous membrane in cases of laxity of the bowels. Even here its best influence is felt in combination with suitable hepatics.. With comp. syr. rhei et pot. it is very useful in cholera infantum.

An infusion is a good wash for sore mouth and tender gums. For vaginal weakness and leucorrhœa it is one of the best for injections or may be used in capsules.

An infusion forms a good wash for the cleansing of foul ulcers, or the dry powder may be used as an absorbent.

In chronic and debilitated conditions of the mucous membrane with a tendency to diarrhœa it is just the agent wanted.

The *flowers* are a mild and valuable stimulating tonic, not astringent like the bark. They are soothing and sustaining to the nervous system and to the circulation especially when given in hot infusion, when it is also somewhat diaphoretic.

The *berries* are also a pleasant mild bitter tonic similar to the flowers.

These flowers and berries possess a mildness and effectiveness that makes them a favorite for convalescence and indeed wherever a mild tonic is needed.

Cornin is a better antiperiodic than any other preparation of this agent

CORNUS SERICEA.

Red Osier Bark, Swamp Dogwood

The *bark* is a stimulating astringent It is useful in stopping hemorrhages whether from the nose, lungs, uterus or bowels. In parturition where there is a hemorrhagic tendency, and where the pains are inefficient, and the parts lax, this agent will be very valuable It will anticipate flooding, increase pains and add general vigor to the system

Dr. F G. Hoener advises the use by injection of the following for the cure of uterine ulcers   It also checks the vomiting incident to pregnancy

    Cornus Ser

    Viburnum Prunif. aa. equal parts

COTO AND PARA-COTO BARK

These are two distinct barks brought from Bolivia under the name of coto-bark They are now distinguished as above. In physical appearance these two barks are strikingly different, but their therapeutical properties are very similar.

The *bark* is a gently stimulating, tonic astringent. Its influence is especially felt by the alvine mucous membrane. and is very useful in dysentery, diarrhœa and cholera infantum   In hot infusion of zingiber it is excellent in the exhaustive discharges of cholera morbus and to quiet the pain incident thereto. With xanthoxylum, capsicum and hydrastis it will be found very valuable in cholera.

Coto tones the digestive tract and is especially valuable in all lax conditions of the mucous membrane It influences a good flow of blood toward the surface. It is very successful in the treatment of sore and spongy gums. toothache, sore mouth, sweating of the feet and the night sweats incident to phthisis

It may be used locally upon ulcers and old sores, and is valuable to be used as an injection to the vagina in case of excessive discharges whether lucorrhœal or from ulceration.

In nasal, gastric, intestinal and bronchial catarrh it will

be found very valuable in cases where the discharges are
in excess.

In typhoid fever and in the excessive discharges from
the bowels in phthisis this is a superior agent.

F. E. Para-Coto Cort.

Tr. Cardamon Comp.	aa. dr. i
Acacia Mucilage	dr. iii
Syr. Simp.	dr. ii
Aqua	q. s. oz. iv

Sig. Teaspoonful or more as needed to arrest diarrhœa.

CROTON ELUTERIA.

Cascarilla.   Bahama Islands.

The *bark* is a pleasant, mild, aromatic, stimulating tonic,
chiefly influencing the mucous membrane. In hot infusion
it is diaphoretic, soothes the nerves, gently quiets the
whole system and gives a good flow of blood toward the
surface.

In convalescence it is gently sustaining and if needed
may be combined with stronger tonics, or combined with
some diffusive, as required.

If combined with aralia racemosa or some other agent
influencing the respiratory organs it lends its influence in
that direction. It is a good tonic addition to some cough
syrups, especially when the expectoration is already too
free. It will be found valuable in phthisis for such condition.

In combination with uterine and vaginal tonics it is
useful in the treatment of leucorrhœa, prolapsus and vaginal weakness.

CUCURBITA CITRULLUS.

Water-melon.   (Citrullus Vulgaris.)

The *seed and husk* are a moderately relaxing and stimulating diuretic. It influences the mucous membrane
throughout, but especially that of the kidneys, promptly
increasing the flow of urine. In nephritis, cystitis and
urethritis it is one of the best agents. It relieves scalding
urine and soothes the entire urethra.

Its influence may be partially felt on other parts of the
mucous membrane when properly combined with other
agents.

An infusion of the seed gives best results when freely
drank.

CUCURBITA PEPO

Pumpkin.

The *seed* without the husk is bruised in a mortar or ground and then emulsed in water. This is oily and sweet and influences the mucous membrane throughout, but especially that of the kidneys, bladder and urethra, and promptly relieves scalding urine.

It is a pleasant anthelmintic for the expulsion of the tape worm. Emulse two ounces of the peeled seed in water and drink early each morning for three mornings, eating but little during these three days, and follow their use with a full dose of antibilious physic

The *oil* may be used for the same purpose in doses of from 20 to 60 drops

CUNILA MARIANA.

Dittany

This *plant* is a pleasant diffusive aromatic stimulant.

In hot infusion it is diaphoretic and gives a good outward circulation. In recent colds, in tardy exanthems, headache, hysteria, cramping, gastralgia, enteralgia, remitting and continued fevers and in tardy menstruation caused by congestion · In all such it stimulates the capillaries, relieves nervous irritability and sustains the circulation. It stimulates the mucous membrane, relieves flatulence and assists digestion.

Cunila Mar.

Cypripedium Pub aa equal parts

makes a good relaxing nervine for irritated conditions

Cunila Mar

Caulophyllum Thal

Dioscorea Vil. aa equal parts

makes a good antispasmodic preparation for dysmenorrhœa.

Cunila Mar

Scutelaria Lat aa. equal parts

makes a stimulating nervine

The *leaves* yield an oil which is a carminative essence.

CURCUMA LONGA

Tumeric.   ·

The *root* is a diffusive stimulating aromatic tonic to the alvine mucous membrane   Its chief use is as an adjuvant for the administering of bitter tonics and cathartics.

CUSPARIA TRIFOLIATA.

Angustura.   (Galipea Cusparia.) South America.

The **bark** is a mild, diffusive, stimulating, tonic nervine.

It relieves the heart by promoting an outward circulation. It influences the alvine mucous membrane and large doses are cathartic. It more or less influences all the secernents, and is valuable in the treatment of intermittents, remittents and typhoid.

It cleanses and tones the gastric and intestinal mucous membrane and is very serviceable in convalescence from typhoid and other fevers, in gastric, intestinal, cystic, nasal or vaginal catarrh. It is an agent that may be influenced in different directions by being combined with different agents, and yet it maintains its general character of influence. It is positive in its infusion and is a valuable agent used in the relations mentioned.

CYDONIUM VULGARIS.

Quince.

The **seed and covering** yield a mucilage very soothing to the mucous membrane and to the surface as well. It is excellent in cases of irritation or inflammation of the kidneys, bowels, bladder or urethra. To the stomach it is a very grateful bitter tonic, more pleasant than most demulcents.

Hydrastis Aq. Dis.	6
Hamamelis Aq. Dis.	4
Cydonium Mucilage	22

This forms a good injection for gonorrhœa.

The **mucilage** is an excellent wash for ophthalmia.

Dr. F. G. Hoener says that quince **leaves** either as a local steam bath or taken in hot infusion per oram in four cases out of five will prove emmenagogue in cases of temporary suppression.

CYNOGLOSSUM OFFICINALE.

Hound's Tongue.

Dr. F. G. Hoener says, this has given good effects in bronchitis, dentition and coughs and colds of infants.

CYPERUS ARTICULATUS.

Anti-emetic Root, Adrue.   Tropical.

The **root** possesses an aroma somewhat resembling that of calamus. It is a gently stimulating, warming, and diffusive agent, soothing to the mucous membrane In Jamaica a strong infusion has been used successfully to stop the black vomit incident to yellow fever It may also be used in the vomiting incident to cholera infantum, cholera morbus, atonic dyspepsia, and the vomiting incident to pregnancy. It is a pleasant aromatic and creates a feeling of warmth and comfort in the stomach It is a fine tonic to the gastric and alvine mucous membrane

In hot infusion it influences the circulation toward the surface and soothes the nervous system.

The *mucilage* is an excellent wash in ophthalmia.

CYPRIPEDIUM PUBESCENS.

Lady's Slipper

The *root* is almost if not quite a pure relaxing nervine. It is less positive and less stimulating than lobelia It is antispasmodic by inducing nerve relaxation, and thus freeing the nerves from irritability and excitement

In typhoid fever it decidedly influences the brain and relieves delirium to a great extent The more your patients can naturally sleep and the less the brain is allowed to be irritated the better

Of course cypripedium in typhoid fever is not best alone. More or less capsicum or other stimulant is necessary

    Cypripedium Pub
    Lobelia Infl. aa equal parts
is excellent in many cases of insanity where there is much restlessness and inability to sleep Business men who are overworked or worried and unable to sleep can take with much benefit small and frequent doses of cypripedium with excellent quieting effect

If it is to be used on the surface, capsicum should be added; and in depressed cases it is best to add a small portion of capsicum for internal use

    Cypripedium Pub
    Lobelia Infl   aa 5
    Capsicum   1
Make into a pill with extract of eupatorium perfoliatum.

These may be used in febrile delirium, insanity, dysmenorrhoea and uterine irritation.

    Cypripedium Pub   2
    Cimicifuga Rac.
    Zingiber Off   aa 1

Give an infusion of this for dysmenorrhœa.

In cases of insomnia give an injection of cypripedium or of cypripedium and lobelia at night on retiring. Do not give enough to nauseate but simply to quiet. This process may also be used in nymphomania and used on retiring to prevent seminal emissions.

Cypripedium Pub.   6
Lobelia Infl.   5
Eupatorium Perfol.   2

This makes an excellent suppository to be used for irritation of the nervous system, or the ingredients may be used in infusion per oram, in hysteria, chorea, nervous headache, neuralgia, nervous irritability, nervous debility when from irritability, dysmenorrhœa and epilepsy.

For delirium or insanity from nerve irritation there is nothing better to relax them. Give such doses as are required to produce the desired result. As the case progresses other nervines may be added to sustain the nerves after the stage of excitement has passed.

If cypripedium be given in hot infusion, especially if some zingiber be added, a warm and gentle perspiration results. Its relaxing effect upon the nerves is felt by the circulation, and the secernents are also relaxed and relieved. The kidneys and bowels are also relieved. Indeed the whole system is left in better shape for future activity.

In dysmenorrhœa ascertain if the patient has been given to too free discharges or as is usual to too scanty discharges. If the latter use in hot infusion the following:

Cypripedium Pub.
Anthemis Nob.   aa. 4
Caulophyllum Thal.
Leonurus Card.   aa. 2
Zingiber   1

In parturition cypripedium relieves the rigid os uteri and the nervous irritation that is frequently present. Of course this does not apply to cold, slow cases that need some degree of stimulation.

Cypripedium Pub.   3
Dioscorea Vil.   2
Zingiber   1

gives very favorable results in colic and after-pains, but in cases of post-partem hemorrhage omit the zingiber and add either trillium or capsicum or viburnum prunifolium as required.

The above preparation may also be used in rheumatism, but must be combined with some degree of stimulation.

In a dry and irritable form of catarrh cypripedium is useful to cleanse and to relieve irritation.

In the convulsions of hysteria use a large injection of
    Cypripedium Pub
    Lobelia Infl. aa equal parts
and if needed give a second smaller injection.

Cypripedium is not a diaphoretic, but in cases where there is feverishness with irritation of the nervous system some diaphoretic agent as zingiber or serpentaria should be added.

Cypripedium is not a tonic, and yet after the system has been brought well under its influence, the entire system is relieved and toned

In the presence of putrescence this agent has but little value unless combined with very positive stimulation In such cases it is simply of value to relieve irritation of the nervous system
    Cypripedium Pub.   2
    Scutelaria   1
is an excellent combination for a case of irritable nervous depression In nervous headache this will give good results If the stomach is involved it may be used by enema,
    F E Cypripedium Pub.   dr iv
    ``   Scutelaria Lat
    `   Nepeta Cat.
    ``   Dioscorea Vil.   aa. dr. i
    Syr Zingiber   q. s oz. iv

This is a soothing nervine for child or adult for cranial or abdominal pain

Cypripedium is one of our best agents when properly used

CYSTISUS SCOPARIUS.

Broom Tops, Scotch Broom.   Europe

The *young shoots* are a stimulating and relaxing diuretic, securing a free flow of urine.

With hepatics and tonics this is of much value in dropsy. It gives good results.
    Cystisus Scop.
    Euonymous Atr.   aa 3
    Zingiber.   1
This is a successful combination for dropsy.

Dr. F. G. Hoener recommends the following for general dropsy:

Elix. Cystisus Scop.
" Celastrus Scan. aa. oz. iss
" Agrimonia Eup. oz. i
M. S. One teaspoonful every two hours.

DAUCUS CAROTA.

Carrot.

This vegetable is of some importance as a medicine. Finely grated it is a stimulating application for sores, ulcers, abscesses, carbuncles, and scrofulous and cancerous sores. It cleanses the surface and stimulates to sound granulation, after which other applications will make more favorable impression.

The *seed* are a pleasant, mild, diffusive, aromatic, stimulating diuretic. It increases the watery discharge and with hepatics will, be found valuable in some forms of dropsy.

Dr. F. G. Hoener recommends the following for severe cases of general dropsy. To be used in conjunction with steam baths.

Elix. Daucus Carota Sem.
" Polytrichum Juniperinum aa. oz. iss
" Cucurbita Citrullus oz. i
M S. One tablespoonful every hour.

DELPHINIUM CONSOLIDA.

Larkspur.

This *plant* is a moderately stimulating diuretic and is somewhat emmenagogue. It influences the alvine mucous membrane and in large doses may produce emesis and catharsis. Dr. F. G. Hoener says an infusion washed over a child's head, a few times will destroy insects.

DENTARIA DIPHYLLA.

Pepperwort.

This *root* is a pleasant, diffusive, stimulating, tonic nervine. It influences the sympathetic and the peripheral nerves.

In hot infusion it influences a good outward flow of blood and stimulates the capillaries. It is valuable in dysmenorrhœa, colic, hysteria and general nervous weakness. It warms the surface and tones the nerves.

DICENTRA CANADENSIS

Turkey Corn.

The *root tubers* are a positive systemic, stimulating alterant which influences the stomach and mucous membrane throughout, the secretory organs and the skin. It is stimulating to the salivary glands, warming to the stomach and invigorating to the whole circulation. In hot infusion it influences both the sudoriferous and the sebaceous glands. It is one of the best of stimulating alteratives In fact all the excretive avenues of the body are more or less emptied of injurious and impure contents and all the secernents are rendered more active. It is just the agent for torpid, sluggish or depressed conditions. It is especially valuable in secondary syphilis, scrofula, chronic eruptive troubles and chronic rheumatism. In all such conditions it is one of the most valuable of stimulating alterants

F, E. Dicentra Can   dr. iv
'   Arctium Lap Sem.
"   Taraxacum Den. L. aa. dr. ii
"   Xanthoxylum Frax   gtta. xx
Syr. Simplex   q. s oz. iv

F E Dicentra Can⁻   dr iv
"   Iris Versicolor   dr ss
"   Euonymous At.   dr. iii
"   Celastrus Scan   dr. ii
"   Xanthoxylum F.   gtt xx
Syr. Simplex   q. s oz. iv

F. E. Dicentra Can.
'   Alnus Ser.
"   Menispermum Can.
"   Arctium Lappa Sem. aa dr. ii
Syr Zingiberis   q. s oz iv

F E Dicentra Can   dr. iv
"   Iris Vers.
"   Jeffersonia Diph.   aa dr. ii
"   Xanthoxylum Frax.   gtta. xx
Syr Simplex   q. s. oz iv

These are all good stimulating alterant preparations suitable for the treatment of secondary syphilis, scrofula and chronic eczema.

F. E. Dicentra Can.   dr. iii
"   Taraxacum Dens. L.   dr. iii
"   Xanthoxylum Frax.   gtta. xx
Inspissated Juice Phytolacca Bac. q. s. oz. iv
This is a good preparation for syphilitic rheumatism.
F. E. Dicentra Can.
"   Rumex Cris.   aa. dr. ii
"   Arctium Sem.   dr. iv
"   Zingiber   q. s. oz. iv

This is a good preparation for scaly eruptions, secondary syphilis and scrofula.

DIERVILLA TRIFIDA.

Gravel-weed.

The **bark** is mildly stimulating to the mucous membrane, the skin and the kidneys. It is useful in the treatment of gonorrhœa, gleet, scrofula and skin troubles. It is best administered in an infusion of zingiber.

The **leaves** are a mild stimulating diuretic.

DIETETICS.

Digestion, assimilation and disassimilation are purely vital acts. In no sense are they chemical. Chemistry is essentially integrative, but digestion is disintegrative through heat force.

There is perhaps no subject of more importance for us to consider than that of food. It is that upon which we live and when properly selected, properly digested, properly assimilated and properly disassimilated adds length to our days and obtains for us much bodily and social pleasure.

There is scarcely a subject of more importance to the physician or to the nurse. What shall be our food? How shall it be prepared and given to meet the requirements of the patient? It is often of principal importance that the physician give proper instructions to the nurse upon these questions. Sometimes it is of as much importance as medical discrimination. An error in food may prove as disastrous as an error in the administering of medicine, and may prove fatal to the patient of the otherwise most skillful physician. Especially is this true in typhoid fever.

Of all things, proper feeding is of principal importance with the infant, and more especially in the summer season when there is so great tendency to cholera infantum. The great mass of cases of cholera infantum and summer dyspepsia come from administering improper food and from improper feeding

Nature has provided us with many foods; the industrious housewife and nurse have provided us with many more; and wherein these sources lack, the inventive genius of the pharmacist has come to our aid with a variety of prepared foods.

Many a person has been rendered dyspeptic more or less through life by the way that person was fed during infancy and childhood, or if we may be permitted to go one step further back and say, by the way that person's mother lived and ate when he was en utero.

To-day as a rule we are a race with rotten teeth, partly because our mothers lived on food that did not provide material out of which nature could manufacture tooth material, and partly because of our improper feeding during infancy and childhood, and partly because of the amount of destructive calomel and other poisons taken into the system that have been destructive to bioplasm and impoverishing to the blood current.

Sugars, candies, pies and cakes are not the proper materials out of which to manufacture children, whether it be pre-natal or subsequently

Proper feeding may do much for those children whose misfortune it has been to have one or both parents consumptive Let the consumptive pregnant be properly fed and it may perhaps be a means of saving the child

Let every pregnant be instructed as to how she may escape the greater or less unpleasantness of the pregnant state, and that she is now manufacturing a human being, and that that being's future earthly happiness depends upon two things: the manner in which she lives, acts and feeds herself during this allotted time; and the manner in which she takes care of the child after birth, as to its feeding, clothing and association During this allotted period her mental, physical and moral powers should be used for the development of that new being Many a noble, patriotic and positive man came from humble parentage, because these elements were pre-natally established by a true mother. The question has been asked, how shall we prevent our jails and penitentiaries being filled with criminals One answer is evident. "Stop breeding them." This is theoretical but not practical.

Health is thoroughly and practically the antithesis of

disease of every form and of every degree. The blood current is the citadel of life and of the great power of vital
resistance and for bodily cleansing through its capillaries.
Nutrition is life itself and is the result of alimentation,
digestion, absorption, secretion and circulation. In proportion as any of these functions fail, nutrition becomes
impaired. In the blood current we find the elements of
nutrition necessary for the support of life, both the nitrogenous and the carbonaceous elements; the nitrogenous
necessary for the supply of muscular force and the carbonaceous for the supply of animal heat. Proper food must
be supplied in proper proportions of these elements.

If there be an inherited tendency to mal-nutrition, the
blood is more likely to become contaminated and a weakened digestion established. The continuance of acute and
chronic ailments furnishes a similar result. A deficient,
excessive or improper supply of food will produce indigestion. So will the habitual use of alcoholics, opiates or
tobacco.

Food is either inorganic or organic. The inorganic consists of water and various saline elements. The organic
are either nitrogenous or non-nitrogenous; and the non-
nitrogenous are either hydro-carbons or carbo-hydrates.
The nitrogenous contribute to growth and nutrition and
furnish the active agents of the secretions. The hydro-
carbons or fats are for the production of heat force. These
are the basis of adipose tissue and are essential more or
less to tissue development. Carbo-hydrates as starch and
sugar assist in the formation of fats and are force producing. Thus there is constantly developing new cellular
growth, and new formed material is added to the body.

Of some persons the nitrogenous element of food may be
deficient, and even if the carbonaceous be abundant, debility ensues. He may seem well and have sufficient fat
about his person, but he will lack resistive ability. He is
not muscular and has not the power of endurance. His
development is chiefly adipose.

But suppose the carbonaceous element is wanting while
the nitrogenous is sufficiently prominent. The heat giving element is deficient and he is chilly and soon becomes
emaciated In some way to such a person fats must be
supplied, whether per oram, per rectum or as a rubifacient.

It must not be forgotten that a proper amount of exercise is absolutely essential in order to a proper assimilation

of nitrogenous food   Else it will not contribute to muscular vigor so fully   The indolent person consumes more food, as a rule, than the man who toils hard from morning till night

The excess of the nitrogenous is eliminated by way of the bowels and kidneys and the excess of the carbonaceous forms adipose tissue, an excess of which is likely to produce more or less debility which may lead to some disease or at least degeneracy of tissue.

Deficient or improper nutrition may render the system more liable to contagious maladies   It leads to degeneracy of tissue.

Again let the general system be blockaded, the stomach foul, the liver torpid and bowels constipated, and such a one is a fit subject to contract almost any contagious disease   Such a one has prepared a nest that germs love to revel in   Micro-organisms of one variety or of another are more or less everywhere, in some things we eat, in some water we drink and in some air we breathe. When these find a proper soil in which to propagate within the system they multiply with wonderful rapidity.   For the time being such conditions of indigestion more or less control the system and the degree of resistive vitality is lowered Defective, improper or perverted nutrition here plays the disastrous part

Whether the defective nutrition be inherited or arising from some acute or chronic disease, such failure of assimilation results in an impoverished condition of the blood current which thus becomes more or less loaded with impurities

Carefully diagnose wherein the blood current is deficient or abnormal; ascertain the needed elements and administer the proper food and medicine to meet the requirements of the case. But do not forget that man is vital and the supply should be such as the vital force can cheerfully recognize   Supply those materials in that form in which they will most readily be assimilated   Some propose to give the fresh blood itself, others prefer it in some manufactured form   I believe I have seen some cases where such have furnished good results

All the digestive fluids are alkaline except the gastric juice   The final mixture results in a neutral compound, else the blood plasma being slightly alkaline, an acid coming into contact therewith would derange the blood and render it incapable to properly nourishing the body.

Moleschott gives the following as an estimate for average daily alimentation:

Albuminous matter	oz.	4,587
Fatty matter	"	2.964
Carbo-hydrates	"	14.250
Salts	"	1,058

	oz.	22.859
Add to this the water in this food	"	22.859

	oz.	45.718
Then add to this the extra water drank	"	45.718

	oz. 91.436

This will be about the average amount of solid and liquid consumed daily by an adult in health. Of course this amount will differ in different persons, of different ages, under different circumstances and in different climates.

Some nations are largely vegetarians. It has been said that the Brahmans lived entirely upon roots and vegetables and that their longevity was very great. Some nations use chiefly the cereals, while others use largely of meats. Within the tropics man's living is mainly vegetable, but in the arctic regions it is chiefly oleaginous; while in the temperate zones these two extremes are more or less combined.

The laboring man requires more food and different food from that required by persons of sedentary habits. Many athletes while in training confine themselves to some form of prepared beef. But under normal conditions some substantial foods varied are best for the ordinary person in ordinary employment.

In the reduction of fatty tissue the diet must be cut down to some prepared food, and that must be given only in such quantities as to relieve the system of hunger and to maintain the general vigor. The corpulent should avoid fat meats, butter, cream, sugar, sweetmeats, pastry and starches. The better foods for such persons are lean meats, eggs, green vegetables, fruits and these in very limited quantities.

In the treatment of acute diseases frequently it is almost impossible to do otherwise than to seek some carefully prepared food. A good cook is a queen in the sick-room, in fact almost anywhere   But in the sick-room you do not always find a good cook   Sometimes your cook is worse than no cook at all   Then prepared foods are a necessity, indeed then they are a boon to the sick, and a relief to the physician

Physical exercise by the healthy must be proportioned to the quantity eaten, and vice versa. The sick who are not exercising at all must eat but little—just enough to maintain the general system, and to prevent debility. Else the case may be prolonged and debility increased by the system being unable to dispose of the quantity of food supplied. It is then more a burden to vitality than a benefit

In chronic cases many times it has been found necessary to put the patient upon some prepared food before you can see any important change in his condition toward improvement   In anæmia, chlorosis and consumption, prepared foods are very essential

An irritable or very debilitated condition of the stomach not unfrequently renders rectal alimentation a necessity. In this way fatty, albuminous and mucilaginous matters may be introduced into the system and some of it taken up into the circulation   Milk, beef, starch, etc , may be thus used.

The following makes a very nutritious injection for rectal alimentation: *

Beef finely cut and blood warm	oz xxxii
Water	oz xvi
Hydochloric Acid	gtta. xxv
Pepsin	dr ss

Keep this mixture at a temperature of 100 degrees F Shake it occasionally and when disintegrated strain and add half a teaspoonful bicarbonate soda to neutralize the acid

Or the following may be used   Beat one egg well and add four tablespoonsful of beef essence.

Always, if they will, let the bowels move first before giving rectal nourishment

Milk porridge by the using of graham flour may also be used in this way

Eggs and milk contain the elements of normal food perhaps more fully than any other edibles, whether animal or vegetable   The constituents of milk are usually stated about as follows

Water	88 per cent.		
Oleaginous matter	3 " "	Cream and butter.	
Nitrogenous matter	4 " "	Cheese and albumen.	
Hydro-carbons	4½ " "	Sugar.	
Saline matters	½ " "	Phosphate of lime, chloride of sodium, &c.	

Man survives longest and develops best physically and intellectually upon a mixed diet.

Of the foods taken from the animal and vegetable kingdoms, that taken from the animal kingdom is as a rule the more easily appropriated by man's vital organism and more fully satisfies hunger at the time of participation and for a longer period of duration than do those foods taken from the vegetable kingdom.

If we compare the nitrogenous elements in bread with that in milk, eight ounces of bread would be equal to a pint of milk, but the carbonaceous element in the bread exceeds that in the milk.

Wheat is an excellent article of diet, but fine flour is constipating. Potatoes have about eighteen per cent. of starch and two per cent. of albumen. The sweet potato has about ten per cent. of sugar and about the same proportion of starch. Fruits contain more or less sugar. In milk, eggs, and meat the albumenoids predominate. Butter contains mostly fats. The starches should not be omitted from our food. They have done much toward the eradication of scurvy at sea.

Good cooking is an important factor, but to eat slowly to solicit the aid of all the saliva possible, and to rest for a short time after each meal are quite important. The American people are always in a hurry. This renders them nervous and any abuse tells more quickly on them than on those of easier habits.

The Romans usually ate but twice a day. The English and the Germans eat from three to five times a day.

The following animal foods are considered to be easy to digest: Raw eggs beaten to a froth, eggs soft boiled, beef tea free from fat, fresh milk, boiled mutton, boiled venison, boiled white part of the chicken, boiled rabbit, boiled fresh fish if not fat, etc.

The following vegetable products are considered easy of digestion: Stale bread, graham bread, rice well boiled, tapioca, sago, corn starch, oatmeal porridge long boiled, dry toast, graham mush, cracked wheat, cauliflower, asparagus, some preparations of beans, baked apples, strawberries, whortleberries, grapes without seeds or skins, oranges, etc

The child should not be nursed longer than from eight to ten months, and during this time the nursing mother should be well and properly fed. Her daily diet should be about as follows:

Meats	oz. 14½
Fats, butter and sugar	oz. 13
Farinaceous foods and vegetables	oz 20
Salt, etc	oz ½
Aqueous fluids	6 pints.

If it agrees with the mother, cow's milk may be used, or a prepared milk if preferred.

The milk as it flows from the mother's breast into the infant's mouth may be said to be still alive and it quickly becomes living blood in the infant's circulation. For the first six months the infant usually requires nothing else By this period of nursing the uterus is better relieved, becomes more contracted, ovulation is usually though not always longer deferred, and the whole pelvic viscera is better prepared for the future

But if the mother be suffering from any specific or other blood or lung trouble, or from general debility, the child should not nurse the mother at all If she be otherwise healthy but does not herself furnish enough nurse for the child, a suitable substitute should be chosen for that part she is unable to furnish

One thing must never be forgotten The child must not be nursed while the mother is overheated Many a case of cholera infantum has been induced by inattention to this, and such cases are usually very intractable

Cow's milk is richer in all its essential constituents than woman's milk and goat's milk is richer still than cow's milk. Each of these if used as a substitute for mother's milk must be toned down with water more or less according to the age of the child Allow the milk after being poured into a vessel to stand for an hour or more, then take of the upper half for the infant's food. If the infant be quite young add as much water as milk. As the child grows older the quantity of water may be slightly decreased. Then too the child should be fed with as much regularity as possible

At the conclusion of parturition the child should not

ordinarily be separated from the mother until the pulse in the umbilical cord has ceased to beat. Many a child has been robbed of some vitality that it might have had, had it not been cut off too soon from the source of its fœtal nutrition.

It has been said that those children born in Winter and Spring have the greatest vitality.

During the first days of the infant's life it seems to lose weight some little, at least it does not perceptibly gain in weight.

In proportion to weight the infant takes four times as much food as the adult. Ordinarily if it be overfed of proper food it will vomit the superabundance. The danger is when it is fed an excess of improper food.

At first the babe should nurse, if awake, every two hours during the day and once or twice during the night. At each nursing during the first day the babe will take about from one to two drams. This quantity will be increased on the second day to five or six drams, and on the third day to an ounce at each nursing. By the fourth day this quantity will be increased to two ounces and thenceforward for perhaps three or four weeks it will range from two to three ounces, and this quantity will be taken from six to ten times in twenty-four hours. During the second month the child will take about four ounces and by the fourth month it will be increased to five or six ounces, but the frequency of nursing will now be reduced to from four to six times in twenty-four hours.

Children require less variety of food and more in quantity than do older persons. Meat then once a day is enough. Milk, bread and butter are the requisite diet, with vegetables and fruits.

Neglect not one thing. Instruct them positively to cultivate the habit of obtaining one good free passage from the bowels regularly every morning.

From two to five years of age about twelve hours sleep are required. At seven or eight years of age the child's appetite is capricious and does not appreciate so much a plain diet, but care more for fruits and confections, much of which is more or less injurious.

Rachitis is the result of improper feeding and of the use of improper food.

Food or drinks much above 98 degrees F. retard digestion. Meats usually should be warm because digested largely by the gastric juice Farinaceous foods should be well boiled and then cooled. Foods at a high temperature are injurious to the teeth Use sufficient water but not too much. Do not over-cook food, a too concentrated food is liable to produce indigestion

The nitrogenous element is essential for the day laborer, but for mental work an easy soluble mixed died is essential Never overload the stomach Than to do this you will find it preferable to arise from the table slightly hungry Rest half an hour before meals, eat slow and enjoy pleasant conversation, then rest for a half hour subsequently. Never partake of a meal when you are overexcited, angry or overheated, indigestion will be the result.

In sickness avoid such articles as will in any way increase the severity of the conditions present. If possible cause your foods to be curative as well as your medicines.

In old age there is less growth and hence a less demand for food.

In hysteria, hypochondriasis and insanity correct feeding is very important. And daily exercise and temperate habits are no less so

In febrile and acute inflammatory troubles, especially where there is a failure of digestive power, care must be taken not to administer too much food, and that proper food be administered regularly and in proper quantity Beef-tea, mutton, veal or chicken broth, barley water, rice mucilage, fruit jellies, lemons and oranges are good, and in convalescence a raw egg in milk or wine, stale, bread, fish and game

In typhoid fever the stomach and bowels must scarcely be looked upon as digestive organs, but better as receptacles for food that has been more or less pre-digested. Thus absorption will quickly take place In typhoid fever the stomach and the upper half of the smaller bowels are least affected, and from these portions most of the absorption of food takes place In catarrhal conditions more or less of this power of absorption is lost Fatty substances are rejected because principally absorbed by the lacteals. Boiled water improves digestion and prevents emaciation if systematically given.

Raw white of egg and pepsin dissolved in cold water is very acceptable, being wholly digested and absorbed from the stomach.

Raw milk is not the thing to be used in typhoid fever;

boiled milk is better, but even then it can only act as a salt and water, as neither the fat nor the casein can be fully absorbed. Hence if milk is given it is best in some pre-digested form. Junket or milk digested with rennet will give good results.

In acute rheumatism and acute gout avoid nitrogenous foods. Albuminous foods contain nitrogen and are not to be used in rheumatism. The use of an excess of meats gives an excess of uric acid in the blood. A vegetable diet and alkaline waters are then to be preferred.

In the treatment of gravel restrict to about the same diet as in rheumatism.

In Bright's disease, atrophied liver and all the other degenerative diseases alcohol is very injurious, tending to greater arterial tension. Pre-digested milk and stale bread are best. Use mostly a vegetable diet and in cases of threatened uræmia add some little fats and carbo-hydrates may be added. Throw as little burden on the kidneys as possible.

A weak and slow digestion demands great care of food and feeding. In cases where there is a deficiency of nerve power debar food for about from seven to nine hours between meals. In other words, such should eat only when they must eat and not because it is meal time. Two meals are better in such cases than three meals. Mutton, chicken, venison, lamb and beef are digestible in the order here given. Oatmeal gruel, chicken broth, meat jelly, meat soups supply the nitrogenous.

In dyspepsia reduce the amount of food and the kinds of food to that which will be best suited to the particular case. Give the stomach but little to do, and yet sustain the general system. Avoid that which seems to hurt and use in great moderation that which agrees. In some cases it is best to give only one kind of food at a meal. Say partake of one meal in the day of vegetables, one of meats and one of bread. The starches are dissolved by the alka-line saliva, and meats are dissolved by the acid of the gas-tric juice.

In diabetes melitis there is a want of assimilative power over the saccharine and starch elements, therefore avoid adding these as food. Animal food increases the acidity of the urine, and vegetable food decreases it. Hence care-fully examine the urine and feed the patient accordingly.

In dysentery and diarrhœa use boiled milk, thickened

milk, fish, fresh game, boiled eggs, boiled meat, boiled rice, boiled barley, toast, crackers.

Avoid salted or dried meats and vegetables Use but little fluid

Add a few drops of gentian in a glass of water and give a teaspoonful every three hours.

Scurvy has usually been the result of an improper diet, dry food, and improper water Vegetables, fruits generally and lime-juice are best here

In habitual constipation prescribe graham cracker, or bread without fluid, oatmeal, corn meal, barley meal, or fruits. Such coarse foods irritate the mucous membrane sufficiently to start secretion and muscular contraction

The treatment of consumption is largely dietetic. Consumptive mothers should not be allowed to nurse children The greatest care must be taken to use nothing that will spoil the appetite Watch the assimilative process and make everything tend to improve the appetite

I now take pleasure in introducing some digestive preparations from some of our most reliable Manufacturing Chemists These preparations are especially valuable in wasting diseases and where there are digestive failures.

PROTONUCLEIN

Manufactured by Reed and Carnrick, New York

Protonuclein is derived from all the available lymphoid structures of healthy bullocks and pigs The brain substance, salivary, thyroid, thymus, gastric and intestinal glands, pancreas and spleen are used The cellulary active constituents are separated by a mechanical process, which does not alter the form in which they exist in the living glands. Metchinkoff, who discovered the nature and function of the leucocyte, stated that in his opinion "the secret of health will have been discovered when science learns how to increase the number of white corpuscles at will.' Protonuclein produces leucocytosis as soon as taken into the organism, and in this way becomes nature's tissue builder and antitoxic principle.

Protonuclein is indicated in all forms of wasting diseases and asthenic conditions It rapidly restores the vitality of all the tissues by stimulating and supporting assimilative nutrition It is also indicated in all diseases due to toxic germs, and in the treatment of neoplasms, ulcers and all surface lesions, malignant or otherwise; also as prophylactic in exposure to contagion or infection.

Protonuclein is prepared in three forms, Tablets and Powder, prepared especially for internal use, and Protonuclein Special for local applications and for hypodermic use.

Nutrition is the important factor both in growth and in the prevention of disease. There is no doubt that the leucocytes of the blood have much to do with nutrition, and by properly sustaining their number and vitality, physiological conditions are restored.

Protonuclein may be administered in doses of one to three tablets, or three to nine grains of the powder, every three or four hours. It is valuable in bronchitis, tonsilitis, laryngitis, pneumonia, diphtheria, typhoid fever, ovarian troubles, abscesses, anæmia, Bright's disease, cancer, neurasthenia, phthisis, etc.

PEPTENZYME.

This is a perfect digestant, a prompt and efficient physiological remedy for dyspepsia, vomiting, cholera infantum, malnutrition in its various forms. It contains all the ferments furnished by nature for the digestion af all kinds of food. The best results are obtained by administering it about twenty minutes before and immediately after meals.

CARNRICK'S SOLUBLE FOOD.

We have used this food for years, and know it to be excellent for children, a preventive of cholera infantum or a cure for it. It will not fail you.

Anæmiol is made by H. K. Wampole & Co., It is a distinctive preparation of beef containing hæmoglobin and albumin, highly nutritious, restorative and tonic.

It contains all the nutritious albuminous constituents of meat tissue unaltered. The bright red arterial color of the preparation is due to hæmoglobin, the natural proteid of iron contained in blood and meat, which has been proven by clinical tests to be more readily and completely absorbed than any other form of iron known. This is one of the best, if not the best preparation on the market. It is easily digested and absorbed without forming hard fæces, and hence is especially valuable in typhoid fever, chronic diarrhœa, gastric catarrh, sickness of pregnancy, phthisis, anæmia and chlorosis.

H. K Wampole & Co 's Liquid Wheat is an excellent preparation. Each teaspoonful represents one ounce of the whole wheat grain in perfect solution and ⅛ grain of pepsin containing over seven per cent. of the nutrient vitalized hypophosphites and oleo-nitrogenous hypophosphites obtained solely from wheat, principally from the germ and cortical portion. It is rich in gluten and albumen and contains over four per cent. oil of wheat, and the wheat starch is converted into maltose, a direct force and fat producer.

It is an ideal nutrient for anæmic cases, a fat and flesh producing food.

It contains all the elements of nutrition easily assimilated without digestive effort. It is a brain and nerve food, valuable in nervous prostration and debility, fatigue of body and mind, lassitude, insomnia and for anæmic pregnants.

It enriches the milk of the nursing mother and assists the babe in cholera infantum.

Why is it that we have but few children over eight years old who have perfect teeth?

There has been something wrong in the material out of which they were made and grew

Liquid wheat is a palatable and nourishing food, it gives to the system those valuable organic and vitalized phosphatic elements so deficient in the food which children and the sick will ordinarily eat.

McCoy, Howe Co . Indianapolis, manufacture liquid acid phosphates, a brain and nerve food for mental exhaustion, insomnia and melancholia

Pepsin is the active digesting principle of gastric juice, mostly obtained from the stomach of the hog. This is much stronger than that obtained from the stomach of the calf, but call pepsin is best for children It is best triturated on sugar, and in conjunction with tonic medicines. It is best dissolved in a little lemon juice, vinegar or glycerine

Dr. G. H Mayhugh uses the following

Pepsin C. P.	grs. ii
Pancreatine C. P.	gr. i
Diastasi	gr. ⅓
Lactic Acid	gr. 1-16
Hydrastin	gr. 1-16

M. Trit. Make into one tablet

Sig One to three tablets after meals.

Sacch. Pepsin	gr. i
Charcoal	grs. ii
Soda Bicarb.	grs. ii

This forms an absorbent for dyspeptics troubled with fermentation.

| Sacch. Pepsin | 3 |
| Sub. Nit. Bismuth | 2 |

may be used in summer complaint of children.

Lactopeptine is pepsin and lactic acid with sugar of milk.

Ingluvin from the ventriculus callosus gallinaceous is a superior digestant, and is much used for the vomiting of pregnancy and with good success.

Pancreatine is a similar preparation to pepsin only prepared from the pancreas instead of the stomach. It is frequently combined with pepsin and gives excellent results.

Many of the malt preparations also serve an excellent purpose.

I conclude this article by appending some excellent dishes for the sick and the convalescent.

Beef Tea.

Take one pound or more of lean beef, cut into small pieces, add salt and put into a self-sealing glass jar. Cover tight and put the jar upon a thin piece of wood in a kettle of cold water filled as high as the beef in the jar. Boil from two to four hours, adding water to keep it as high as at first. This prepares an excellent essence.

Mutton Broth.

Take one pound of lean mutton, cut small; one quart of cold water; one tablespoonful of rice or barley soaked in a little warm water; four tablespoonsful of milk, salt and pepper to suit. A little parsley finely cut may be added.

Boil the meat covered and unsalted in the water until it falls to pieces. Strain it out, and add the barley or rice. Simmer a half hour and stir in the seasoning and milk. Then simmer five minutes. Some crackers may be added if desirable.

Chicken Broth.

Make the same as the above.

Chicken Jelly.

Take half a raw chicken, pound with a mallet and add

water to cover. Heat in a covered vessel for about two
hours, until the liquid is reduced one-half Press through
a colander, salt to taste and then simmer five minutes·
Keep on ice and use on stale bread.

Chicken Panada

Boil a chicken, take the breast and pound it fine. Season with salt, nutmeg and lemon-peel, and boil gently until
a little thickened but so that it can be drank.

Calf's Foot Jelly.

Take one pair of calf's feet and put into a gallon of water. Boil down half, skim, strain and cool.   Take the fat
off the top Then warm and add sugar, the juice of three
lemons, one pint of wine, the whites of seven eggs Boil
half an hour, strain and cool.

Milk Gruel

Take one pint scalding milk, two tablespoonsful of fine
oatmeal, one pint of boiling water Cook until done.

Milk Porridge.

Soak two teacupfuls of oatmeal in water over night. In
the morning strain and boil the water half an hour, add
two cupsful of milk and a little salt and boil well. Eat
warm Sweeten a little if desired

Thickened Milk.

Mix well a little milk, a little flour and a little salt
Add a quart of boiling milk. Stir well and bring to a boil.
Serve alone or with dry toast If it is to be used during a
case of diarrhœa, scorch the flour before mixing with the
milk

Rice Milk

Boil the rice in a water bath till it swells and softens.
Add some milk, sugar and nutmeg and if desirable add a
little well dissolved flour or beaten egg.

Egg and Milk. ·

Take the white of an egg and milk Beat the white of
the egg to a froth and stir quickly into a glass of milk.

Egg Cream.

Beat a raw egg to a stiff froth, and add a tablespoonful of white sugar and two tablespoonsful of blackberry wine and half a glass of cream. Beat all well together.

Wine Whey.

Sweeten one pint of milk to taste and when boiling throw in two glasses of sherry wine. When the curd forms, strain the whey through a muslin cloth into glasses.

Lemon Whey.

Take the juice of two lemons or twice as much vinegar to a quart of milk heated till the curd is well formed. Then strain. This whey is a pleasant and nourishing food. A little powdered cinnamon and sugar makes an excellent drink to be given during the treatment of dysentery and diarrhœa.

Egg Wine.

Break a fresh egg into a glass, beat until very light, sweeten and add a tablespoonful of wine and beat again.

Egg-Nog.

To the yolk of an egg add a tablespoonful of sugar, the ½ of a pint of new milk, and two tablespoonsful of sherry wine. Beat the white of the egg separately and stir into the mixture.

Egg and Water.

Stir the white of an egg into water as warm as it can be without coagulating. This is excellent for infants or adults where there is a disordered digestion.

Egg Gruel.

Beat the yolk of one egg with one tablespoonful of sugar. Pour on one teacup of boiling water. Beat the white of the egg to a froth and add. Take while warm.

Soft Boiled Eggs.

Put the eggs into a pan of boiling water and put on the stove where they will not boil and keep them there for several minutes. Such eggs will be much like jelly, soft and very digestible.

Oatmeal Gruel.

Soak a handful of oatmeal over night in water. In the morning pour off the water and add a pint of fresh water. Stir well, add salt and boil an hour and a half.

Or cook two tablespoonsful of oatmeal in a quart of water at least two hours by simmering

Corn-Meal Gruel.

Thoroughly mix one tablespoonful of fine corn-meal in water. Add a little salt and a pint of boiling water and boil half an hour Add a little more water as it boils down. Frequently stir and add a tablespoonful of cream.

Arrow-Root Broth

. Put a little lemon-juice, sugar, nutmeg and salt in half a pint of water. Dissolve a tablespoonful of arrow-root in a little water and add. Then boil five minutes and take warm

Arrow-Root Jelly

In one pint of water boil a little cinnamon or lemon-peel, and add two tablespoonsful of arrow-root dissolved in a little water Boil ten minutes, strain, salt and add sugar, wine and nutmeg. —

Barley Water.

Cook the barley five or ten minutes, strain and add two quarts of boiling water. Boil to one quart and flavor with lemon-juice. More water may be added if desired.

Or,

Soak 1 pt of barley in lukewarm water a few minutes and drain off. Add three quarts of cold water and cook slowly till soft. Skim occasionally and when cold flavor with jelly or lemonade

Cracker Panada.

Split half a dozen crackers and pile in a bowl in layers with a little salt and sugar Cover with boiling water and set on the back part of the stove for an hour. Then add sugar to suit the taste.

Bread Panada.

Into a little water add some wine, sugar, nutmeg and lemon-peel, The moment it comes to a boil stir in a few crumbs of stale bread. Boil about five minutes.

Soft Toast.

Toast well some thin slices of bread. Put them upon a
warm plate and pour a little boiling water over it, cover
quickly with another plate of the same size and drain off
the water. Then remove the upper plate and butter the
toast. Put now into the oven for one minute and then
take out and cover again with the plate and serve at once.

Toast Water.

Toast stale bread brown, but do not allow it to burn.
Break into a bowl and pour on boiling water. Then allow to cool.

Lemonade.

Slice two or three lemons into one quart of cold water.
Add four tablespoonsful of granulated sugar. This should
be used occasionally at dinner during the summer season,
also in some cases of rheumatism, in malarial and typhoid
fevers and in convalescence therefrom.

A hot lemonade may prove diaphoretic in cases of colds.

Cracked Wheat.

Put a teacupful of cracked wheat and a little salt into a
quart of hot water. Boil slowly for one hour. Then add
sugar and cream.

Onion Soup.

Slice sufficient onions, fry brown in a little butter and
fine flour. Pour into a saucepan and add q. s. milk, three
parts milk and water one part. Season to suit the taste
and add one grated potato. Then cook some ten minutes
and add some sweet cream.

Roasted or Baked Potato.

Wash well and bake with skins on till well done.

Rice and Apple.

Cook apples to a pulp and sweeten. Boil the rice in milk
till tender and mix the two.

Appleade.

Cut two large apples in slices and pour on one pint

of boiling water; strain, sweeten and cool before drinking.

Apple Water.

Roast two large, tart apples until soft Put into a
pitcher, and add a pint of cold water, and stand in a cool
lace for an hour

Roasted Apples.

Take large, tart apples, wipe clean, extract the core and
put into a pan. Then partly fill with sugar the opening
out of which the core was taken and bake for one hour.

Dried Fruit Water

Several of the dried fruits, as apples, peaches, apricots,
etc , may be washed, and then stand in water over night
Then stew The water will be found quite pleasant and
nutritious.

Jelly Waters.

A little jelly may be added to some water It is a good
appetizing drink. Such jellies as currant, cherry, plum,
elderberry, grape or apple may be profitably used in this
way

DIOSCOREA VILLOSA

Wild Yam

The **root** is a gently stimulating and relaxing, antispasmodic nervine. It is quite positive in character and its
action is peculiar to itself

In bilious colic it is a superior agent, also in cholera
morbus, flatulence, and in almost any painful condition.
In neuralgia of almost any part of the body it affords wonderful relief In facial neuralgia it affords quick relief
and that relief is quite permanent. In nervous rheumatism it soothes, relaxes and tones.

    Dioscorine
    Salicylate Sodium aa equal parts
    Or
    Dioscorine
    Sorbilin aa equal parts

Either of these preparations gives admirable results in
rheumatic pains

For uterine pains but few things equal it and for after-

pains it is surpassed by no other agent. For uterine neuralgia use the following:

    F. E. Dioscorea Vil.
      "   Valeriana Off.   aa. dr. vi
      "   Cimicifuga Rac.
      "   Xanthoxylum Frax. aa. dr. ii
    Ess. Anise q. s.
    Syr. Simplex   q. s. oz. viii

For nervousness, restlessness and pains incident to pregnancy there is nothing equal to dioscorea. It may be given
throughout the whole period of pregnancy with the very
best of results. It gives ease and comfort and quiets nausea. Especially to nervous females it is quite relieving in
the preliminary stage of parturiency. It quiets the nerves
and enables the patient to do more vigorous labor. It is
also a superior preventive of miscarriage.

    Dioscorea Vil.   4
    Zingiber Off.   1

The diffusiveness of the zingiber added to the antispasmodic influence of the dioscorea, especially if given in hot
infusion, gives admirable results in dysmenorrhœa, relieves
the uterine hyperæmia and produces a good outward flow
of blood, both to the surface and also locally as a menstrual flow.

Dioscorine is a good preparation of this agent. For
quicker results this may be used in hot infusion of zingiber or even alone in hot water.

The fluid extract is a good preparation but it is very liable to gelatinize.

    F. E. Dioscorea   dr. i to ii
      "   Zingiber   gtta. v to x
    Comp. Syr. Rhei et Potas. q. s. oz. iv

Sig. Half teaspoonful as needed for the colic of children.
It is a good remedy.

    F. E. Dioscorea Vil.   3
      "   Viburnum Op.   1
      "   Mitchella Rep.   4

This is a splendid female tonic for crampings, pains and
nervousness.

    F. E. Dioscorea Vil.
      "   Mitchella Rep.
      "   Aletris Far.   aa. 2
      "   Viburnum Prunif.   1

This is an excellent preparation for the preventing of

miscarriage and the relief of the pain premonitory thereto

DIOSPYROS VIRGINIANA

Persimmon.

The *bark* is a bitter, stimulating and astringent, nervine tonic.

Small portions are a good appetizer and a sustaining nervine. It is a pleasant tonic for convalescence, especially when there is a tendency to too much freeness of the bowels In chronic diarrhœa its nervine tonic influence is very favorable. It possesses not only the necessary astringency, but has the influence of a permanent tonic. In phthisis where there is a general laxity of the system, more or less diarrhœa, too free expectoration, night sweats and poor appetite this is just the agent. Of course the continued use of this agent must depend, like that of other agents—upon the necessity therefor

DISINFECTION AND DISINFECTANTS.

The Latin *contagium* indicates that material in which resides the infective power of certain diseases This power of contagiousness pertains to quite a number of diseases and is not alone confined to man. Domestic animals and even the vegetable kingdom are each more or less subjects of special contagious diseases. These latter phases of contagion we shall not here discuss, nevertheless they are interesting to us in many ways.

The word contagion (*contingo*) implies the existence in some way of material contact. Whenever this material, whatever it may be, finds admission to the system and finds therein suitable substance adapted to its growth, it grows, and multiplies as rapidly as the conditions will permit. Why not then assume that *contagia* are material in some way endowed with life? Whether this be true of all or not, it certainly is true of some at least

Some parasitic diseases spread by direct contagion or ordinary contact; as by the acari in scabies, and by the spores of the microphyte in tinea capitis

Trichiniasis is produced by the eating of raw or imperfectly cooked pork affected with trichinæ Thus the parasite eggs or larvæ still living are introduced into the system.

Those persons given to the eating of raw beef occasionally suffer from attacks of tænia.

In all cases of contagion the severity of the disease contracted is largely due to the clogged condition of the
person's system and to the ability of his vitality to resist
such incursion

Each contagium propagates itself in its own form and
never in any other form. As in small-pox. measles, scarlatina, whooping-cough, typhoid fever, typhus fever, yellow
fever, cholera, mumps, syphilis, gonorrhœa, venereal soft-
chancre, chicken-pox, diphtheria, erysipelas, hospital gangrene, purulent and other ophthalmia, puerperal fever,
phagedænia, tuberculosis, cancer and hydrophobia.

Tuberculosis and some other forms of disease are occasionally derived from milk taken from diseased animals.

Some contagia show a particular affinity for some organs
or parts, though the whole system may become affected by
it; as small-pox for the face, mumps for the parotid glands,
syphilis and gonorrhœa for the genitals. and typhoid fever
for the bowels.

Different persons and different families show different
susceptibility for contagion and in fact for all diseases.
Some are more susceptible than others and some have more
vitality to resist disease or to endure its influence

Then too there is in some persons and in some families
an inherited tendency to consumption, cancer or some
other form of disease

In all these contagia we find a more or less definite
course of duration.

It is also true of some contagia that those who once suffer with it have immunity from it for the future; as scarlatina; while in other diseases having been once affected
gives a liability to a second or further attacks

We also find that a contagion may be worse in some communities than in other communities; that it may be of a
more malignant type some years than other years

In the passage of contagia various media may be instrumental, as bedding, towels, dirty hands, unclean instruments, cooking or other utensils, foul or deficient water
supply, cohabitation, house drains, contaminated food or
the atmosphere

The disengagement of infectious products from the body
of the sick and the establishing of communication with
a diseased body bringing its products into relation to the
healthy person is pathalogically the one influential factor.

The air seems to purify space from the presence of some

contagia and in other cases the air seems to be the means by which contagion is spread, as in la grippe

. Tuberculosis is conveyable to the fœtus by cohabitation and so are alcoholism, syphilis and other forms of disease that have become thoroughly septic to the blood of a progenitor

Much trouble may be caused by continually inhaling in a close room the breath of a consumptive, a typhoid or a diphtheritic case Ventilate thoroughly but cautiously

In treating cancerous, syphilitic or other sores possessing some degree of malignancy great care should be taken that your own hands are free from any denuded surfaces, else inoculation to some extent may take place.

But the broken skin or the denuded mucous membrane are not always necessary to transmitting, as in cases of ophthalmia from one eye to another on the same or on different persons And also in the transmitting of gonorrhœa and syphilis In all such the mucous membrane being very thin, and the discharges in either case being very irritating, the mucous membrane soon becomes irritated and absorbs the virus

In vaccination the surface is denuded and the virus is absorbed; and if the vaccine be pure bovine vaccine virus the inoculated disease will be much lighter than the disease itself But vaccination from virus taken from other persons has many a time inoculated some disease worse than small-pox.

Periods of incubation differ in different diseases In hydrophobia it is usually one or more months. In syphilis it is from two to five weeks, and nearly three months elapse before the appearance of the roseola In small-pox the incubative period is about ten or twelve days and the eruption appears some two or three days later Measles and scarlatina have about the same length of incubative period, some nine or ten days; but while the eruption does not appear in measles until the fourth day, that of scarlatina appears on the second day of the fever stage.

During epidemics usually but one contagious disease prevails and nearly every other disease will be found to partake more or less of the characteristics of that contagion. This is especially true of la grippe.

Sporadic cases if not properly cared for may lead to epidemics, and these epidemics may be local or extend over one or more nations.

In order to establish the proper means for preventing the spread of contagious diseases we must consider the means by which they are spread, whether it be the air, the drinking water, the food, the surroundings, or whether it be transferred direct from one person to another. The following will do much toward checking the spread of contagion:

1. Isolation of the sick.

2. The use of more or less continuous disinfection during the continuance of the diseased condition.

3. Maintain cleanliness of the person and the apartment Maintain a proper temperature and give good ventilation.

4. The physician should make his visits short, and the nurses should be careful not to mingle with the rest of the family.

5. Food and medicine should not be long exposed to the air of the room; they will absorb contagious effluvia.

6. Oiling of the surface of the body in scarlatina will be of great benefit to prevent the scales from being carried by the air. In small-pox it will prevent pitting.

7. Thoroughly disinfecting the room and the entire house and all things that had any relation to the room or the patient, when the patient shall have been ready to leave the room.

8. In venereal troubles positive abstinence must be maintained.

Disinfectants are agents employed in preventing the spread of contagion.

The efficiency of any disinfectant is due to its power to destroy or at least to render inert whatever specific poison or disease germs may be exerting an influence in each particular case.

Deodorizers act by oxidizing or otherwise changing the chemical constitution of volatile substances disseminated in the air. Such also prevent noxious exhalations from organic substances. Hence deodorizers may be disinfectants in certain diseases, but all deodorizers are not necessarily disinfectants.

A free atmosphere, pure water, dry earth, heat and cold are very powerful disinfecting media.

Artificial disinfectants are either vaporizable and cleanse the air, or are chemical agents for rendering inert all infectious discharges.

The use of sulphurous anhydride gas obtained by burn-ing sulphur is unequalled as a means of purifying the air and of thorough disinfection.

Disinfectants may be classified as *solid, liquid* and *gaseous.*

To the *solid* belong dry earth, quicklime, charcoal, cal-cium, magnesium carbonate, a mixture of lime and coal tar, etc

To the *liquid* belong solutions of potassium permanga-nate, zinc chloride and lead nitrate.

To the *gaseous* belong ozone, chlorine, iodine, bromine: nitrous, sulphurous and hydrochloric acids; carbolic acid, tar fumes, acetic acid, ammonia

Deodorizers do not always disinfect. They may absorb offensive gasses and liquids as when water absorbs hydro-gen sulphuret or the earth absorbs foul drainage, but heat may drive the hydrogen compound again into the air.

Rain may wash impurities into open wells, or wells may be so nearly dry as to become more or less putrid.

The boiling of water is one of the best means of purify-ing it.

Instead of throwing disinfectants into manure heaps, pile them so that they will quickly heat, and they will soon be disinfected —'

Heat is one of the most powerful of disinfectants This is true whether it be dry or moist heat. An intermitting high temperature is best. It need not exceed 220 degrees F for one hour.

Clothing may be baked thus or they may be boiled in water with some soda; or any of the following may be added Either commercial chloride of lime, 2 ounces to the gallon of water, or 1 ounce of sulphate of zinc, or half an ounce of chloride of zinc. or a five per cent. carbolic solution may be used

Sulphate of Zinc	oz. iv
Salt	oz. ii
Water	1 gal

This also may be used to disinfect clothing. It must be used boiling hot.

Sulphur dioxide in aqueous solution contains sulphu-rous acid. It is one of the most powerful of disinfectants. It destroys sulphuretted hydrogen and combines with am-monia As to its disinfective power there is no question. Its suffocative odor is the chief objection to its use. The solution can be made by deoxidizing hot concentrated sulphuric acid with copper turnings or charcoal.

Sulphur dioxide should not be used in conjunction with either chlorine or permanganate of potash for they mutually destroy each other

The room to be thoroughly disinfected should be kept saturated with the gas for not less than an hour.

For general disinfecting purposes the sulphur may be burned in small quantities every six to nine hours during the continuance of a contagious disease It is especially valuable in diphtheria, scarlatina and small-pox. In thoroughly disinfecting a room one pound of sulphur should be used for each 1,000 cubic feet. One pound when burned it has been estimated produces 11 7 cubic feet of sulphur dioxide gas.

Chlorine is most easily obtained from chloride of lime by adding either hydrochloric or sulphurous acid; or some crystals of potassium chlorate may be placed into a widemouth bottle containing dilute hydrochloric acid. This allows the gradual discharge of euchlorine or protoxide of chlorine, which is more agreeable and more effective than chlorine. Chlorine is soluble in water to the extent of $2\frac{1}{2}$ volumes in one, and this solution will be found valuable for disinfecting purposes. As a deodorizer enough euchlorine may be expelled from moist chloride of lime by the carbonic acid of the air for most purposes.

The *chloride of lime* or bleaching powder gives off chlorine easily It forms a cheap and valuable disinfecting powder.

Quicklime does well as a disinfecting whitewash and for drains

Carbolic acid solution 5 per cent is a good disinfectant. The chief objection to it is its odor

Ozone is a powerful agent It oxidizes organic matter and so destroys odors and organic germs It is produced by half immersing a stick of phosphorus in tepid water, or by gradually mixing two parts of permanganate of potassium with three parts of strong sulphuric acid

Permanganate of potassium is non-poisonous and is a good deodorizer. It is odorless and its aqueous solution loses its color as it becomes exhausted. It should be dissolved in water and used in plates or other large open surfaces.

It is an absorbent of gasses as well as a deodorant. It

oxidizes and destroys contagia and putrid matters, but its best use is as a deodorant

Charcoal is a powerful absorbent of gasses and is valuable for drains, water closets, etc

Bromo-chloralum is a non-poisonous compound, a disinfectant and deodorizer of some merit

Smoke from burning wood, paper or green coffee forms good deodorizers. The last mentioned is especially valuable during the continuance of small-pox

The *hyposulphite* and *sulphite of soda* arrest putrescence and can be used internally if desired .

Sulphate of copper or blue vitriol dissolved in water is a good, cheap disinfectant for vaults, drains, privies and bed-vessels.

Pul. Copperas	1
Fresh Pul Charcoal	2
Or	
Copperas	¼ lb
Water	1 gal.

Either of these is cheap and reliable

Dissolve nitrate of lead	dr i
in boiling water	pt i
Add to this	
Salt	dr ii

in a bucket of water

This gives chloride of lead, which is excellent for the fœtor of gangrene and small-pox It sweetens the air immediately

DOREMA AMMONIACUM.

Gum Ammoniacum.   Persia

The *juice* is gathered from incisions in the bark and when this becomes dry it assumes the form of a gum-resin. It is a diffusive of moderately stimulating and relaxing power, influencing the mucous membrane, and in hot infusion it influences the skin and general circulation.

The odor is rather disagreeable and the taste is rather bitter and nauseating. In large doses it is cathartic By the combining of particular agents it may be made to be diaphoretic, expectorant, diuretic or emmenagogue

DORSTENIA CONTRAYERVA

Contrayerva .

The *root* is a diffusive, stimulating, mucilaginous tonic.

In hot infusion it sustains the capillary circulation and promotes diaphoresis and thence soothes the nervous system.

In scarlatina, measles, small-pox and other exanthemata it arouses the circulation and hastens the eruption. It is also valuable in typhoid and other fevers as a stimulating diaphoretic.

In local and general congestions it relieves the surface by relieving the capillary circulation, if given in hot infusion.

In cold infusion it influences the alvine mucous membrane and the kidneys.

DROSERA ROTUNDIFOLIA.

Sundew, Youthwort. Eastern and Southern U. S.

This *plant* grows in marshy places and peat bogs, and is covered with a chaff-like coat. Its flowers are white.

It is considerably valued in pertussis, where from 2 to 4 drops may be given every 3 or 4 hours. It is also recommended in asthma, chronic bronchitis, dry hacking coughs, nervous or sympathetic coughs arising from pulmonary, cardiac or gastric disease. It is also spoken of in gastric troubles where there is flatulence, catarrhal or ulcerous conditions.

ECHINACEA ANGUSTIFOLIA.

Echinacea, Black Samson. Western U. S.

This is a perennial herb with thick black roots and pungent taste.

The *root* is a stimulating, antiseptic alterative, somewhat like xanthoxylum.

In puerperal septicæmia give half to one teaspoonful every four hours, or a half teaspoonful from two to four hours.

F. E. Echinacea Ang.　　　dr. ii
Ess. Pepsin　　　　　　　oz. ii

Give a teaspoonful every four hours in cases of pelvic abscess.

Echinacea and lycopodium make a very good application for carbuncles and boils. Then give

F. E. Echinacea Ang.
Syr. Simpl.　　　・　　aa. equal parts.
M. Sig. One dram three to six times a day.

This may be alternated with

Lycopodium	gtta v
Peroxide Hydrogen	dr. ss.

3 times daily.

Apply a poultice of flaxseed, lobelia, ulmus and capsicum wet with echinacea twice a day for four days. Put a napkin ring around the carbuncle and pour in a dram of peroxide hydrogen and let it foam for a few minutes twice a day.

In consumption give of echinacea 10 to 15 drops three times a day, and also the peroxide of hydrogen in dose of half to one dram three times a day. Lycopus virg. may be added five or six times a day in doses of ten drops.

For black tongue use

F. E. Echinacea Ang.	dr. i or more
Aqua Dis.	q. s. oz. iv

Sig. One dram may be given every three hours for low septic conditions.

In case of scorpion sting apply. fld. ext. echinacea ang every 10 or 15 minutes and give per oram also

F. E. Echinacea Ang.	gtta xx
Aqua	oz. iv

M. S. Teaspoonful every 15 or 20 minutes till the patient rests. Or the fresh root may be scraped and given the person bitten. It then induces an excessive flow of saliva and perspiration.

ELECTRO-THERAPEUTICS.

By A. A. Stoneburner, M. D,, M. S. E.,

Professor of Electro-Therapeutics in Chicago Physio-Medical College and Proprietor of the Electro-Therapeutical Institute of Chicago.

To wade into the general scope of Electro-Therapeutics would require more space than we are allotted in this volume, and we shall endeavor to be as concise as possible, trusting our efforts will be appreciated by our many Physio-Medical friends.

Electro-Physiology is that science pertaining to the action of electricity on the human body, animals and plants.

Electricity as a factor in medicine is measurable with the milliamperemeter. It is portable as in case of the secondary battery, and many of its various phenomena on the human body are manifest.

With the use of electricity in medical science as a remedial agent it has been found necessary to employ currents of different qualities, electrodes or conductors of varied styles and various applications are made   Each individual case requires specific treatment

Now in order to utilize this agent with success, we should know something of its physiological action, that we may apply it to every individual case requiring electrical treatment scientifically

The advancement made in Electro-Physiology has been very slow, but much credit is due Baird and Rockwell for the noble fight made by them against the old country granny, the egotistical professor of medicine. the ignoramus, and the practitioner who used it simply for a fake. They have placed Electro-Physiology on a scientific basis where it should have been many years ago, and too much cannot be said in praise for their noble efforts in their behalf, for the noble sacrifices made by them in their efforts to advance medical electricity

While we have some practitioners using electricity in their practice with something like success, without knowing anything about its physiological effect, yet it is not the way to apply it   We should know beyond a question of doubt where to apply the current, in what direction it should flow, and what quality should be used.

The electro-therapeutist should know every action that should manifest itself in its application on the human body; at least he should know its action on the brain, spinal cord, sympathetic system, nerves of motion and of common and special sense; also of the conductivity of the body, besides electro-physics   When we become masters of these points, electro-diagnosis is made easy, and the interpretations of the various complicated ailments readily understood and treated scientifically with proper apparatus   When we become master of electro-physiology, we are then electro-therapeutist in a strict sense of the word.

When we put a drug into a human being's stomach, chemical action takes place, after which we have a physiological effect; this effect may be on one particular organ or part, and when this takes place, it is due to the inherent affinity for such organ or part. So can electricity be localized, and with greater certainty; its action can be recorded with some hopes of accuracy, while with drugs when internally administered, its action is always clouded with uncertainty

Matteucci discovered that muscles would with the

interrupted galvanic current become affected, but DuBois-Reymond more fully investigated these effects, and he has accomplished a great deal in his investigations

It was proven that all the animals, both warm and cold blooded, contain animal electricity, toads, salamanders, fresh water crabs, addlers, lizards, glow-worms, and tortoises, as well as rabbits, rats sparrows, etc. Animal electricity like mechanical, is due to action, and we find when a chemical decomposition or chemical change takes place, electricity is always produced This electricity is found in the muscles, nerves, brain, kidneys, liver, lungs, testicles, spleen etc Matteucci and DuBois-Reymond are the founders of electrology

Electricity in mankind, while the cutaneous currents in the human being have certain laws made concerning the direction in which this current flows, we sometimes find the reverse condition exists

Dr C R Radcliff says that during sleep the sheaths of fibres, of nerves and muscles are charged with electricity the same as a Leyden jar This change is brought about by the development of electricity, either positive or negative through oxidation, or some form of chemical action on the outside of the sheaths of fibres, through the di-electric sheath, and have opposite condition as in the Leyden jar, which would be in a static condition The nerve-current and muscle-current are purely incidental phenomena, resulting from applying the electrodes to points of unequal electric tension or potentiality That the passage of a nerve or muscle from a state of rest to that of action is accompanied by a discharge similar to that of a torpedo. The arguments in favor of this view are, that the anatomical and physiological apparatus of the torpedo closely resembles the muscular apparatus of all animals: that the nerve-current nearly disappears from the nerve, and the muscle-current from the muscle, when nerve and muscle pass from rest into action, and, finally, that the phenomena of induced or secondary contraction cannot otherwise be explained The discharge takes place between the sheaths of fibres, which are very elastic, and are capable of being elongated during rest by mutual attraction of the opposite electricities with which they are charged

When a nerve or muscle passes from action to rest, it resumes its condition of charge. Elongation therefore is the result of charge and contraction of discharge. This point is illustrated by the following experiment: A narrow band of rubber is covered on both surfaces very near the edge with gold-leaf, so that it can be charged or discharged with electricity, similar to the Leyden jar. By a simple arrangement of a grooved wheel, and an apparatus that multiplies and records the movements, it can be shown that when the band is charged by a few turns of a frictional or static machine, it elongates, and when discharged it contracts. It is believed that the muscle behaves in precisely this manner. If the nerves are not affected in the same way, it is because their fibres are not sufficiently elastic.

The acceptance of this view explains many interesting facts in pathology. It explains the fact that diseases that are accompanied by a deficiency in the nerve currents, as neuralgia, spinal irritation, hysteria, tetanus, epilepsy, usually manifest themselves by morbid activity, by increased and unnatural movements of muscles and nerves.

This theory of current production in the human body may be correct, but the theory of destruction of a cell structure or chemical decomposition looks more reasonable, for we find in chemistry that when a chemical change takes place a current of electricity is generated.

We find electricity prevailing in all the organs of the body and are in opposite electrified state. We find the hand is negative to the elbow, and the palm of the hand is negative to the back. The foot is negative to the chest, and the sole of the foot is negative to the back. The elbow is slightly positive to the chest, and the hand is sometimes negative to the foot, and sometimes the reverse.

Apparatus for Studying Animal Electricity, as Recommended by Du Bois-Reymond.

A delicate galvanometer or milliamperemeter registering only a few milliamperes in its full circle, in order to detect the most feeble current present. Two cushions, as they are called, made of layers of blotting paper soaked in a solution of sulphate of zinc, are laid in the edge of each vessel, with their ends in the liquid. The whole is enclosed in a moist chamber in order to protect the tissue.

Professor Trowbridge, in the description of his experiments, says that he is satisfied that the deflection produced by DuBois-Reymond is mainly due to the soaked cushions used by him, and in his experiment with natural and artificial muscle, says that he is convinced that when there is an absence of saline solution, no deflection takes place, and when present a perceptible deflection is manifest He therefore comes to the conclusion that there is no such thing as muscular current, properly speaking.

In all these experiments made by different authorities, we should expect different results would be obtained when different methods are used. whereas if they were continued to the end, they would all arrive at the same conclusion It is natural therefore to find sodium chloride in the blood, hence the saline solution, and according to Trowbridge's theory and DuBois-Reymond's electricity should be present in all parts of the body, and no doubt of it electricity prevails in all animal life It is more perceptible in the muscles, on account of there being the best conducting path in them

Irritability or electrotonus is a condition of altered functional activity The electrotonic state is produced by the passage through a nerve of a constant polarizing current

The passage of the constant current produces a change in the electromotive force of that part of the nerve traversed by the current This alteration in muscular excitability may consist in either an increased or a decreased functional activity. The decreased functional activity occurs in the neighborhood of the anode or positive electrode, and is called electrotonic state. The increased functional activity occurs in the neighborhood of the cathode or negative electrode, and is called catelectrotonic state

The altered activity affects not only the intra polar parts of the nerve, or that part between the electrodes, but also the extra polar portions, or the remainder of the nerve

The electrotonic state is characterized by two varieties. Those in which the electromotive force is decreased, and those in which this force is increased These conditions are called positive and negative phases.

. A decrease in the electromotive force of a nerve affected by sending a current through the nerve in opposite direction to the nerve current is called negative phase, and by sending it through the nerve in the same direction it is called positive phase

Anelectrotonic zone, and catelectrotonic zone, are terms used for that region surrounding the electrode. Positive and negative regions

The electrotonic condition not only remains while the current continues. but a considerable time afterwards, or it remains in a charged condition after the current ceases. Dead nerves, or nerves that have lost their irritability, electrotonus effects connot be accomplished.

In a comparative illustration, the disturbance that takes place in a magnet are similar to the action of the nerve.

DuBois-Reymond says that the nerve is always in the condition of a closed circuit, since electric currents are produced by the connecting layers surrounding the molecules with their molecules; and secondly, that current obtained from an animal as indicated by the galvanometer is only a small portion of the entire current that it contains.

While it is true that contraction is not so marked at midway as at the anelectrotonic or catelectrotonic zones, yet there certainly cannot be any neutral point. This chemical or mechanical stimulation of the nerve must be proportionate throughout its entire length, according to the amount of current traversing it. We must remember that in the electrical zone region the current is confined to the surface at conducting terminal, and after penetrating the body it diverges and again contracts to suit conductor at the terminal. The portion of a nerve near the positive pole has its conductibility diminished, while that portion of a nerve near the negative pole has its conductibility increased.

Some authorities claim that we have a neutral point in the contraction of a nerve by electricity: they say that the anelectrotonus meets catelectrotonus at about midway, and at this point there is no irritability, and this is called neutral point, or intra-polar region. While a nerve when acted upon by the electric current is in a polarized condition, it does not necessarily follow that it is exactly like a magnet, having a neutral or dead point at the intra polar region, for we notice when a death occurs caused by the electric fluid, we find a uniform condition between the terminals, that is, when the stroke is distinctly marked. We have deaths from the physiological shock, sometimes its action on the repository centres, or on the nerves and muscles, etc., but when we have a distinct rupture of the body by it, we do not find any neutral points.

While it is true we have positive and negative terminals, and at the anelectrotonus zone we find oxygen gas and at the catelectrotonus zone we find hydrogen, we would also find if we had some means of making the examination correctly that when electrolytic action takes place, that the hydrogen while accumulating at the negative pole, has a flow extending to the anelectrotonus zone, we would also find the oxygen extending to the catelectrotonus zone. This does not prove that we have a neutral point. Now while we are satisfied that at midway of intra-polar region we have less irritability, this is due no doubt to it being the highest point of diverging.

The nerve when in a catelectrotonus condition is greatly modified by the breaking of the current, its irritability is diminished thereby. This is called negative modification. At the positive pole an increase of irritability is manifest, and is called positive modification.

The restoration of irritability is accomplished with a suitable faradic current, and when we find patients whose condition is such that they cannot take the faradic current, or no faradic current is at hand that would have the desired effect, then the interrupted galvanic will often restore irritability, even when the faradic sometimes fails. When the muscles are affected, a faradic coil should be used of coarse wire and to have a slow vibrator, so as to allow saturation to be completed before the current is broken. If the sympathetic are affected, a finer wire and a finer interrupter should be used in order to produce the best results. Many experiments have been tried for the restoration of the muscle and nerve irritability, but nothing is so effectual as the properly applied and correct faradic current.

The theory of analectrotonus and catelectrotonus is, when a current from a battery of voltaic cells is passed through the nerve, the irritability diminishes at the anelectrotonus zone region and increases at the catelectrotonus zone region. This may be explained by the physical effects of the current in the tissue. We have seen in electrolysis that acids go to the positive or anelectrotonus zone, and the alkalies to the negative or catelectrotonus zone. It is a well known fact in physiology that acids diminish nerve irritability while alkalies increase it.

In Coyn's experiments of Paris on the ulner nerve, Pfluger's Laws and the action of electricity were proven, which are as follows.

The nerve is excited by the appearance of catelectrotonus and disappears on anelectrotonus. Coyn has shown in his experiment that after closing the circuit, the irritability is increased near the negative pole; that is, this condition increases as the current runs up to a certain point; that on breaking the current the negative modifications or conditions of diminished irritability appears for a moment and then disappears near the positive pole, on the other hand the irritability is diminished at and after closing the circuit. On breaking the circuit there is an increase of irritability or positive modification, which appears to be greater when the current has been allowed to run a long time.

Action of Electricity in Brain and Spinal Cord.

It has been shown by Fritsch and Hitzig that in the cerebral convolutions there are centres for the production of voluntary muscular movements in various parts of the body These investigators took off the upper part of a dog's skull, and by means of a weak galvanic current, excited the exposed brain, locating the current in small portions They found that when certain definite portions of the anterior convolutions were excited, movements were caused in certain groups of muscles on the opposite side of the body. Continuing their researches, they showed that there are definite nerve centres for the nerves that preside over the muscles of the neck, the foot, and the face, for the extensor and adductor muscles of the forearm, and for the flexor and rotator muscles of the arm.

Ferrier, of King's College, London, performed similar experiments. He studied the cerebrum, the cerebellum, the corpora, etc Electrization of the optic thalami produced no result; of the corpora striata caused the limbs to be flexed; of the anterior tubercles of the corpora quadrigemina caused dilatation of the pupils and apisthotonus, while electrization of the posterior tubercles caused the animal to make all sorts of noises.

Dr. Beard has carefully studied the action of electricity on the cerebellum in dogs, rabbits, cats, and pigeons, and he has come to the conclusion that the surface of the brain was electrically excitable; that the theory advanced by Dupuy and others, that the excitation was due to the diffusion of currents to the central ganglia, was not tenable.

In the external application of galvanism to the brain, it is somewhat different If we should place an electrode to the forehead and the other on the back part or occiput and use from ten to twenty milliamperes, the sensation would not be as marked as five milliamperes from temple to temple, when the sensation would be that of vertigo.

Hitzig says when the current passes from forehead to occiput, the right and left lobes of the brain and all that pertains to them are equally or symmetrically influenced, and little if any dizziness is perceived; but when applied to the temples, dizziness is at once produced if the current be sufficiently strong   It will be readily perceived the dissimilarity in the region of the zones, one hemisphere being in anelectrotonus condition and the other catelectrotonus, or diminished irritability on one side and increased irritability on the other.

And we must have falsification of the muscular sense.

Hitzig indicates several degrees of galvanic dizziness:

1   A mere sense of fullness in the head is caused by a mild current when broken, but not usually when the current is running nor so marked when closed; certain temperaments however experience this feeling, not only when the current is broken, but also when it is running.

2   Apparent movements   These are produced by stronger currents; objects when the current is passing appear to go from positive to negative pole, and when the circuit is broken, the movement is in opposite direction.

3   Staggering is produced by still stronger currents. Luschka says there are anatomical reasons for supposing that the brain can be more easily affected in the mastoid and occipital regions than in the anterior portions   A large vein connects the transverse sinus with the posterior auricular veins, and with the posterior meningeal artery into the skull through the mastoid foramen. In the occipital region a vein connects the transverse sinus with the venacervicalis profunda through the posterior condyloid foramen

If an electrode is placed upon either end of the spinal cord, contraction of the muscles of the trunk and the extremities follows   If one electrode is placed upon the centre of the spine and the other on the lower extremity of the cord, only the muscles of the lower limbs will be contracted: and if the upper half of the spinal cord be electrized, the muscles of the arms only will be affected.

When we break the circle of a galvanic current, the spinal cord being part of it, the contraction of the muscles in the body manifests its presence; but if this current be not so broken, no contractions are observed and a paralyzing effect takes its place. The cord remains insensible to any

stimulus that may be applied to it as long as the current
is passing, but at its cessation mechanical irritation will
give rise to the usual tetanic convulsions This diminution
of excitability is confined to the spinal cord   The long
continuation of galvanic treatment of about twenty milliamperes on the spinal cord is liable to produce paralysis

Centrum cilio spinale, as designated by Budge and Wal-
ler, a ganglion near the fifth lumbar vertebra, which, on
being electrized in animals produces contraction of the
rectum and bladder   And when we electrize the spinal
cord at the sixth dorsal vertebra in the human body, excitation is transmitted to the cervical sympathetic nerve,
and thence to the iris, producing dilatation of the pupil

The Action of Electricity On the Skin.

In the application of electricity to the human body, it is
done by the way of electrodes on the skin or epidermis
mostly, and when it is so done it requires a large electrode
externally and a much smaller one internally   The reason
for this is due to the high resistance ot the external coating of the body   This resistance of the skin is subjected
to marked difference in some individuals and different in
each individual, according to their condition in life.

While this resistance is great, it can be materially reduced in two ways; one is by washing the skin with lukewarm vinegar, and the second way is to increase the size
of the electrode.

So in the application of electricity, either galvanic or
faradic, to the human body, we must take into consideration the resistance interposed, the individual's susceptibility to the electrical stimulus, etc

We find young and old are more susceptible than middle
aged persons. Brain working classes more so than laboring or uneducated classes   Women more so than men.
Hence, the difficulty of electrical formula

The application of electricity, galvanic or faradic, to the
cervical sympathetic may cause in one individual symptoms of cerebral congestion. and in another cerebral anæmia, so each individual case must be carefully diagnosed
before application is made, then carefully watched.

The action of static electricity when applied to the skin
has a pricking sensation, and has a tendency of making
the skin red If the patient be placed upon an insulated
stool or platform, and is charged with static electricity,

and a negative conductor be placed near the surface of the skin, a small lump will be produced by the jumping shock, which resembles that of a mosquito bite This would soon disappear by a little friction, but it is a very unpleasant sensation.

The action of the faradic current on the skin is somewhat similar, but more pleasant than that of the static current On account of the resistance of the skin a moist electrode is preferable for most work, but when faradization of the skin is desirable, then a dry electrode should be used, or the hand of the operator The action of the dry electrode is, that the high resistance of the skin is maintained, the electricity fails to penetrate the deeper tissues, unless the current be very strong The calibre of the blood-vessels is narrowed through its action on the vaso-motor nerves They first have anæmia and then hyperæmia Hyperæmia will not be noticeable for several minutes, but it will make its appearance soon, according to the strength of coil and the size of wire and interruption made.

The fine wire coil with a high tension interruption has a more marked effect on the sensory nerves than the muscular or intermediate coils And the negative pole has a more marked effect on the sensory nerves than the positive The forehead and the region of the scapula and tibia are very sensitive to faradization. Electricity penetrates the skin through the sudoriferous and sebaceous glands, and the smaller these apertures are, the greater the resistance

The action of the galvanic current on the skin differs from that of the faradic and static currents very materially. When a few cells are applied, no sensation is manifest, but when about twenty or thirty milliamperes are applied it is noticeable, and the sensation is like that of a mustard plaster

When a moist electrode is placed upon the skin and a current of galvanic electricity of about twenty milliamperes is passed, through it, there appear small pale vesicles at the negative pole that are transparent and are not raised much above the surface These are produced by the alkalies and hydrogen gas, and as the current continues, the epidermis becomes brown and the serum comes to the surface and assists in producing these ugly electrical sores

Electrical Action of the Sympathetic and Pneumogastric.

The action of electricity on the sympathetic and pneumogastric region should be used with care or intelligence, on account of its action on all of the ganglia of the body, for none of the ganglia can escape its influence, when applied internally or externally. We should know beyond a question if the case in hand is one for electrical treatment or not, and if we should use galvanic or faradic currents. If galvanic, how strong and how shall we apply the electrodes, and in what direction should the current flow, and if faradic, what kind of faradic, etc. These are essential points when the electrical treatment is to be used near the pneumogastric.

When we make an external application, the effect is not so marked as when we apply direct to the nerves themselves, on account of its absorption by surrounding conductors, but as external application is the practical way of applying electricity to the pneumogastric region, we should only consider this one. If a current of sufficient power was conveyed so as to saturate the surrounding conductor, then the same effects would be obtained on these nerves as if a direct contact was made by the electrode, but this is not possible with the galvanic current, on account of the resistance of the skin.

When we place one electrode on the nape of the neck, and the other at the anterior of the sterno-cleido-mastoid muscle, the current will diverge from a direct path, but it will traverse the sympathetic and pneumogastric. While the surrounding tissue is almost as good a conductor as the nerves are, yet we will have a distinct action when a current of electricity is applied by this method, on both pneumogastric and sympathetic nerves, and it is impossible to act on one without affecting the other.

The anatomical relation existing between these two great nerves is such that, no matter where we place the electrodes, one or the other will be affected, which will be carried to the base of the brain, where the pneumogastric, the phrenic and other nerves centre, hence through the other nerve to the electrode.

In Baird and Rockwell's experiments on these nerves, they were laid bare and isolated, the cervical ganglia of the sympathetic receiving the most attention, and distinct action on one could not be obtained without affecting the other

M M Arloing and Tripier have shown that section of the pneumogastric below the medulla so far modifies its contraction that the action of the heart is not arrested, or but for a short time, with the faradic current whèn applied to the distant end of a cut pneumogastric   Also weak faradic currents affect the heart's, action; by the contraction of a nerve the free flow is checked, elevating the blood pressure in the arteries.

They also found that the right pneumogastric has a more powerful influence over the heart than the left. Faradization of the peripheral end of the divided pneumogastric causes arrest of the action of the heart, sudden irregularities of its rythm, with slightly reduced pressure.

They also found that the left pneumogastric has a more powerful influence over respiration than the right.

Masoin found that the movements of the heart were stopped by galvanization of the left pneumogastric   It was possible to restore heart action by mechanical movement, such as striking the heart with the fingers, but after the movements were stopped by galvanization of the right pneumogastric. it was not possible to restore them in that way

I have observed that when an electrode is placed upon the nape of the neck and another under the feet, and a strong faradic current is used, with sensitive patients a severe attack of coughing is produced, and lasts while the current is flowing

Also, I have observed with external applications the following results; one of the electrodes being placed in the mastoid fossa, and the other over the seventh cervical vertebra, and the current used was from one to ten milliamperes from one to ten minutes duration·

A young lady whom I was treating for facial acne by central galvanization, was frequently put right to sleep within one minute after application, and she would awake but slowly as if from a sound sleep, and in a number of cases this drowsiness was manifest when the electrodes were so applied

I find the following laws in reference to the action of electricity on the retinal circulation through the neck are correct·

1   Galvanization or faradization of the region of the

cervical sympathetic has a marked temporary influence over the retinal circulation. It may cause contraction of the arteries or dilatation of the veins.

2. The faradic current produces precisely the same effects on the retinal circulation as the galvanic, only more slowly. The physiological difference between the currents in this respect is therefore a difference of degree and not of kind.

3. Mild currents of short duration caused contraction of the blood-vessels of the retina, while strong currents and long applications caused dilatation. Much seemed to depend upon the temperament and condition of the individual. What would cause contraction in one would cause dilatation in another. These varying effects correspond with clinical experience.

In conclusion we would say that it is a difficult matter to localize a current of electricity from external application without affecting the sympathetic or pneumogastric by external application near the medulla oblongata.

The Nerves of Special Sense.

Optic Nerve.—The galvanic electrodes when placed upon the temples cause both light flashes and a perception of color.

The faradic current has very little effect on the retina. A coil of very fine wire as made by some of the best makers has a decided action on the retina.

Auditory Nerves.—The action of a faradic current when the electrode is applied to the ear, or in the vicinity of the ear, causes a ringing or rumbling noise, according to the method of application, which no doubt is due to the contraction of the muscles and the disturbance of susurri.

The galvanic current acts on the auditory by certain fixed laws, and various sounds are produced. A distinct accented sound, a sound that gradually fades away, a whistling sound, a ringing sound, a hissing sound, and many more different sounds are produced.

These sounds vary according to the individual and strength of current. With the healthy ear, the anelectrotonus effect is always the same.

All these various sounds, no doubt, are due to the auditory nerve.

Olfactory Nerve.—When a galvanic current is applied to this nerve or to the Schneiderian membrane, an odor resembling sulphuretted hydrogen is produced   This is no doubt due to the liberation of ozone

Gustatory Nerve.--The action of two dissimilar metals producing a sensation when in contact with the tongue was discovered by M. Sulzer in 1754. This taste was similar to the vitriol of iron   If we placed zinc on top of the tongue and silver underneath, an acid taste would be experienced under the zinc plate, and a slight alkaline taste under the silver plate. This action of the gustatory nerve varies with different individuals but the majority say it is a copper taste.

It is not necessary to send the galvanic current through the tongue or through the chorda tympani nerve, or even through the face   An electrode placed upon the neck or any part of the spine will produce this effect,

This coppery taste is due no doubt to electrolytic action, the acids and alkalies forming at their respective poles.

Voluntary and Involuntary Muscles.--In the excitation of the involuntary muscles by faradism, the contractibility continues during its entire application, while with the continuous galvanic current the muscles relax after the first shock, and again contract upon breaking the circuit. If we should pass the current through the intestines, stomach, œsophagus, etc , which are composed of involuntary muscular fibre, excitation does not take place until the parts become saturated or charged, in which case excitation continues after cessation of the current.

Stomach.--In electrization of the stomach with the interrupted galvanic or muscular faradic current a shortening of the transverse and longitudinal fibres in the direction from the cardiac to the pyloric orifice takes place. In the treatment of paralysis of the œsophagus associated with a sort of atony of the stomach, we have frequently had occasion to observe the readiness with which this phenomenon took place

In the shortening of these fibres, close adhesion with the serous coat is prevented   It also prevents and will assist in the destruction of the solid adhesion of any of the four layers of the stomach: areolar, mucous, muscular or serous.

Bladder.--When electricity is applied to the bladder when partially filled, a painful sensation is manifest, caused by the contraction of the whole bladder.

Intestines.--In the contraction of the intestines by electricity, strong currents are generally used, on account of the tardiness of the intestine contraction, and when the passage of the current ceases, relaxation takes place slowly.

The duodenum responds most readily, almost instantly, and the lower bowel is a little less responsive.

Uterus.—The contraction of this organ is similar to that of the bladder.

Gall Bladder.—The contractions are similar to those of the bladder.

Heart.—The direct electrization of the tissues of the heart is somewhat different from that of the aorta and its direct branches. We can apply a much stronger current to the heart before cessation is accomplished than when the aorta is contracted. It is also possible to restore the heart's action by a weak current momentarily applied, and again stopped by a strong current of long duration.

The *liver* and *lungs* are very little affected, so far as the contractibility is concerned. A congested liver may be restored by a continuous treatment of a muscular faradic current daily at a fifteen minute seance.

Its Action On the Blood.

The action of the galvanic current on the blood is a subject that has received considerable attention from Baird and Rockwell, Rollet, Neuman, Parsons, Hutchinson, Hayes, and others.

While the conclusions arrived at by these several investigators are not in unison, they are nearly so.

While the blood corpuscles are variable in size, they are fairly uniform in appearance, and the average length would be about 1-2400 of an inch, If it would be possible to pack together 8,126,464 they would occupy space the size of a pin head. (This is for human blood). Dr. R. K. Browne has calculated that these corpuscles move 400 times their own length in a second of time. If we should take a weak solution of blood and put it into a test tube over heated mercury, it reduces itself to a state of oxidation of venous cruorine and a spectroscope would show that it was purple cruorine, but if we should add one drop of distilled water, the color of the cruorine will be restored to its scarlet state. In the higher animals we find the composition of the blood is very complex. We find water, albumen, fibrin, and coloring matter, also several fatty substances, such as cholesterine, cerebrine and some salts, chloride of sodium, sulphate of potash, carbonates of soda, lime, and magnesia, and no doubt there are many more substances that we do not know are contained in the blood. We have in the globules 79 per cent. water, 19 per cent. albumen, and one of salts

Now when a galvanic current of electricity is applied, and it be strong enough to produce electrolytic action. we have chemical decomposition. If its strength were about twenty milliamperes this would be sufficient to coagulate albumen. Now the presumable phenomena that take place in the blood would be as follows:

In the decomposition of the blood, water is paramount to all the rest of its composition as previously shown, two gasses are given off, the lighter is carried to the negative pole, and the oxygen accumulates at the positive pole. In this decomposition the electrolyte is broken into atoms or groups called *ions*, which are of two kinds, electro-positive or cathions, and electro-negative *ions*, or anions

The decomposition that takes place is greater at the positive than at the negative electrode, and we would naturally infer that the anelectrotonus zone being gradually dried up, a clot formation would take place without the assistance of any other agent, but the oxygen that is liberated performs an important part Acids are formed and they gradually disappear, leaving a charged mass, which would adhere very closely to the electrode. Where these acids are formed, coagulation takes place with the albumen, while at the catelectrotonus zone we find very little coagulation has taken place, but what there is, are yellowish, light and bulky

If a large clot is desired to obstruct the passage within a blood-vessel, about forty milliamperes is preferable

The following rules in regard to electro-coagulability of the blood:

1 At both galvanic terminals, clot formation takes place.

2 At the positive terminal is the hard black clot, and at the negative it is light, soft and bulky

3 When the galvanic terminals are located within a blood-vessel, and when in close proximity, the coagulation is most satisfactory, the duration is very short compared with the time of a separation

4 In blood electro-coagulation, the larger the volume of current, the quicker coagulation takes place.

The Human Body as a Conductor.

The composition of the human body is such that it is a better conductor than water, but is variable in different parts of the body, on account of different quantity of saline constituents.

Proportionately, adults have about 80 per cent. of water, children under one year about 85 per cent. The blood has about 78 per cent., gray matter of the brain 85 per cent., white matter of the brain 75 per cent.; the spinal cord, gray 72 and white 67 per cent.; muscle 82 and nerve 77 per cent. These figures are variable in different individuals. The water in the tissue is very uniform. The bones, like the skin, are a very poor conductor, and when the epidermis is in a dry state, little or no current will pass, it, but when moistened it will conduct fairly well.

We would call the attention of the medical student to the complex condition of affairs, which we will find on studying the dosage of electricity. In drugs, the physician has only to know the absolute strength of the extract or tincture he is using; but in electricity we must take into account volume, pressure, or current strength, in relation to the work to be performed. These conditions are explained by the following expressions, which we call electrical units: The volt, ampere, ohm, coulomb and watt. We have about forty electrical unit phrases, but the above are about all that are necessary for our purpose. Hitherto the student has found difficulty in studying these terms, as in the various text-books on the subject, the meaning of the authors has been obscured by abstruse mathematical problems. Physicists, like lawyers, seem to try to promulgate laws that are incomprehensible. In as concise a manner as possible, we will endeavor to translate these specific terms and render the explanation easy of comprehension.

A thorough understanding of the effects of electricity on the body is as necessary as the study of general materia-medica, and in order to become familiar with the subject, the student must thoroughly understand the symbols, words, and phrases used in expressing the condition of the current.

Electricity is analogous to other manifestations of force, and is capable of being generated, measured, and put to work or utilized, similar to steam power. In the first place we must consider force as unliberated pressure, or energy of suspended action, ready for motion and easily changeable into energy of action   Engineers express the amount of energy of suspended action that can be generated in a given boiler, by saying it represents ' so many pounds pressure," and in fact we habitually compare pressure and weight   Thus we say the thermal unit can perform 500 foot-pounds of work, which means that the potential so situated as to be easily changeable into kinetic energy would equal 500 foot-pounds   In a similar manner another arbitrary work-unit is established to which we give the name of horse-power   We can and must therefore fix upon a unit to express electrical energy, and the term volt-coulomb has been adopted, which corresponds to the caloric (or any other) arbitrary unit.

The electrical units are all based, upon the C. G. S. system, or centimetres grammes and seconds, adopted in September, 1881, at the Paris Electrical Congress

Volt, or Unit of Force —To explain the meaning of volt let us perform the following experiment: Take a standard voltaic cell and an unknown cell   Couple the zincs of each cell together, and attach the copper of negative elements to a galvanometer.   Now as a result we will have the galvanometer or needle deflected or remaining at rest.   Should we find the needle remaining quiescent, then we have a condition of equilibrium, the electromotive force of each cell being identical, but should the needle be moved, then there is a difference in the strength of the current from the different cells   Should we make a battery on the same plan as the Daniel cell, and of the same materials, but only as large as a thimble, and connect it with an ordinary sized one, we will find no deflection of the needle   This shows that the larger cell has no more pressure than the smaller one, which is, as far as pressure is concerned, an equivalent of the larger   We therefore say it has the same voltage.

In order to measure the pressure or the voltage definitely, we must use a comparative test of some kind   It is to be understood therefore that when two bodies having different electrical potentials are connected by a conductor, the quantity of electricity present must occupy a certain time in passing from one to the other, hence if there be a certain difference of potential, we have a difference in the transfer of a given quantity of electricity as regards time or duration of flow.

If we should take a voltaic cell and connect the terminals to a galvanometer, we would find the current flowing from the negative element to the positive, through the circuit. Should we place a magnetic needle near the conducting wire, it would be deflected. Now should we add another cell to be connected up in series, that is, carbon of one cell to zinc of the other, we would have double the previous force, but not double the deflection of the needle The reason for this is that, while we have increased the pressure or E. M. F., we have also increased the resistance. which has destroyed the volume equivalent to one cell's production, but the E. M. F. is never destroyed.

Now these cells being connected with a galvanometer and add 2,000 ohms resistance when we find a certain deflection, and on taking one cell away the deflection is reduced. Should we take 1,000 ohms from the circuit, we have then half of the previous resistance, and we get a corresponding increase in the needle's deflection. From this we infer that the current that is passing is inversely proportional to the resistance. This is called strength of current.

We now take a standard cell and connect it with the instrument having a thousand ohm's resistance, when we will get a deflection that we take note of, and we can then calebrate the unknown cell accordingly.

The volt is being considered the unit of potential, the electro-motive force and means energy. The Daniell's standard cell is usually used for comparison, the electro-motive force being 1.079 volts or E. M. F.

The second unit we will consider is the *coulomb* or unit of quantity, or the ampere measure. For example, it would require a quantity of galvanic electricity equal to two coulombs to supply a current of two amperes for one second, or a five ampere current will give twenty-five coulombs in five seconds. Each coulomb of electricity liberates 0.1176 C. C. of hydrogen, and 0.0568 C. C. of oxygen or a total of 0.1764 C. C. of mixed gasses. It also requires 95,000 coulombs of electricity to decompose nine quarts of water. We think these experiments explain the coulomb distinctly, but rather than be obscure in any way, we will explain farther. The coulomb was first used to measure frictional electricity, and it was found very useful, because in that case there is a surface current to deal with, and all that had to be done was to measure the surface of a plate containing metal, Boit's hemispheres or a Leyden jar, etc., and note the number of coulombs.

In the coulomb as we use it in galvanism, we must look upon it from a different standpoint   In frictional electricity we do not have a continuous flow, while in galvanism we get no flow or current unless the circuit is complete: we then have a continuous flow or momentum, and the method of measurement must be different.   It must be multiplied or divided by something before it means anything in particular; it is simply a flowing current of a certain strength   It the strength of current in a circuit is one ampere and is flowing for three seconds, we would say that three coulombs of electricity have passed.

A coulomb then is simply an ampere multiplied by time; it is an ampere which lasts one second of time.   The coulomb alone means nothing, we must introduce another factor and that is the volt.   We then have the volt-coulomb, which means the electrical unit of work or energy.

Ampere Unit —The ampere is the unit of current, and is equal to the quantity of electricity which will pass during one second through a circuit having a resistance of one ohm, when the energy is one volt

The usual method of obtaining the actual value of the ampere is by electro-chemical deposit of electrolysis.   A metal plate is used, the weight is first ascertained, and the plate is then put in the circuit with the positive terminal, a similar one is placed on the negative with a suitable solution interposing   The metal from the positive is deposited on the negative by the passage of the current   The results in this way obtained by different authorities are very nearly if not entirely similar.

The ampere is represented by that quantity of current which is capable of depositing 4 025 grammes of silver per hour or 0 001118 grammes per second.

The *milliampere* is the one-thousandth part of an ampere   The ampere or unit of current, to sum up, is the strength of current that is required to produce 0 172 C. C. of O and H. in one second at 0 degrees C and· 760 m m pressure   An ampere is approximately equal to the current of a Daniell's cell through one ohm resistance

Ohm's law may be briefly stated as follows: The strength of the electric current in any circuit is found by dividing the value of its electro-motive force by the value of its total resistance.

All electrical phenomena are susceptible of measurement. The essential properties of an electric circuit may be said to be, first, the difference of potential included or contained within it; second, the resistance which it offers to the passage of the electric current; and third, the magnitude of the current traversing the circuit, as determined by the relation which the difference of potential bears to the resistance.

When any two of these three properties have a known value, the value of the third may readily be calculated.

This calculation is done by Ohm's law. This law is nearly always expressed in mathematical formulæ.

The resistance in any circuit is found by dividing the value of its electro-motive force by the value of its current.

The electro-motive force in any circuit is found by multiplying the value of the resistance contained in it by the current traversing it.

The quantity of electricity produced in any circuit is found by multiplying the value of the current by the time during which the current flows.

The mathematical formulæ so often employed in electrical works are nothing more than an abbreviated manner of expressing the same thing, thus:

Let Q denote the total quantity of electricity generated in any circuit.

Let E. denote the electro-motive force in the circuit.

Let R, denote its resistance.

Let C. denote the current flowing.

Let T. denote the time during which it flows.

We may then write down the above four rules of Ohm's law thus:

$$(1)\ C=\frac{E}{R}; \quad (2)\ R=\frac{E}{C}; \quad (3)\ E=RC; \quad (4)\ Q=CT.$$

For the benefit of those not familiar with mathematical notation, it should be explained that when two letters standing in the place of numerical quantities are placed one above the other in the form of a common fraction, it is signified that the quantity above the line is to be divided by the quantity below the line. Thus $\frac{E}{R}$ signifies the same as E divided by R.

The sign = denotes equality, or that the quantities on the right hand of the sign are equal to those on the left hand.

When two or more letters standing for numerical quantities are written together, one after the other, it signifies that they are to be multiplied together. Thus, in the above case, the expression E=RC means that E is equal to the product of R multiplied by C; or, in other words, that the electro-motive force (E) is equal to the resistance (R) multiplied by the strength of current (C), which is exactly what was stated above in the third section of Ohm's law, only in the former case it required twenty-six words to explain it, while by the latter method we express precisely the same thing by means of three letters and one arbitrary sign. This explanation may perhaps serve to give the student some idea of the reasons why persons who understand the notation prefer to use it, as a matter of convenience, when circumstances permit, instead of entering into a labored explanation and elaboration in every case.

Ohm's law as explained by Mr. Pope is very clear, and so we publish it in full. We have another way of explaining it, and that is this. The strength of current varies directly as the E. M. F and inversely as the resistance. This resistance is the total resistance of the circuit, including the internal resistance of the cells or generator and the resistance of the external circuit.

$$\frac{\text{volts}}{\text{ohms}} = \text{amperes; or } C = \frac{E}{R}. \quad E = CR. \quad R = \frac{E}{C}.$$

Ohm's law is used in solving nearly every problem in relation to electricity.

If we had a potential that secures an E. M. F. of eighteen volts and if the total resistance of the circuit be three ohms. the strength of the current will be six amperes.

To give a better idea of an ohm we will use the following example. A galvanized iron wire four millimetres in diameter and one hundred metres long is one ohm, a copper wire one millimetre in diameter and forty-eight metres long represents an ohm. Or 130 yards of copper wire 1-10 inch in diameter represent one ohm; 20 yards of platinum wire 0 016 inches in diameter is 27 ohms; 46 feet of No. 32 German silver wire of American gauge represent 100 ohms.

The Farad.—This is a unit of capacity, and is of little

or no importance, except to telegraph electricians. A
farad will contain one coulomb of electricity at a potential of one volt. If the potential be raised to two volts,
the same condenser will hold two coulombs, and so on.
The farad being too large for convenient use, it was reduced to the microfarad, which is the one-millionth part
of a farad, and nearly all that use the farad, use the latter
as their unit. The microfarad is equal in capacity to
about 5.6 kilometres (3.5 miles) of ordinary submarine
cable. We do not think it necessary to dwell longer on
this unit, as we do not see the utility of it as an electro-
therapeutic agent.

Potential is something that may be, a possibility, a reserve. The potential in a voltaic cell is the force that
may be liberated.

Watt.—The unit of electrical power or volt-ampere. A
power that is developed when 44.25 foot-pounds at work is
done per minute, or 0.7375 foot-pounds per second, or it is
1-746 of a horse-power. That is, 746 volt-amperes are equal
to one horse-power.

Prof. Liemens was the first to make use of the name of
watt for the electrical dynamic unit, and it is now universally adopted as the unit of electrical work. A watt
defined electrically is the rate at which work is done when
a current of one ampere is maintained in a resistance of
one ohm. We have three equations that give the value of
watt, viz.:

(1) $C E =$ the watt.

(2) $C_2 R =$ " "

(3) $\dfrac{E^2}{R} =$ " "

where $C =$ the current in amperes; $E =$ the electro-motive
force in volts; and $R =$ the resistance in ohms.

The watt may be called electrical energy, for it is the
power which electricity possesses of doing work. The
current in amperes, multiplied by the difference of potential in volts, divided by 746, equals the rate of doing work
in horse-power. Thus, if .7 ampere is required to operate
a 16-candle lamp on a 110-volt circuit, it requires 4.8 watts
per candle.

Accordingly the electrical power is proportional to the
product of the quantity of electricity per second that

passes, in amperes, and the difference of electric potential or level through which it passes in volts

The watt or the electrical power varies as to the amount of resistance, when the current is constant, or as the square of the current; that is to say, if with a given resistance the power of a given current has a certain value, and the current flowing through this same resistance be doubled, the power is four times as great or is as the square of the current. .

A current of one ohm resistance will have a power of one watt, when under an electro-motive force of one volt ampere is flowing through it If the resistance be halved or become five ohms, then two amperes pass or a power equals two watts, or two amperes and two volts in a circuit of one ohm resistance gives a power of CE=2x2=4 watts If the electro-motive force be raised to four volts, and the current to four amperes, we would have CxE=4x4=16 watts.

Joule —The unit of electric energy The volt-coulomb, the amount of electrical work required to raise the potential of one coulomb of electricity one volt

The joule may be regarded as a unit of energy or work in general, apart from electrical work or energy The British Association proposed to call one joule the work done by one watt in one second of time.

Recapitulation.—The several units in themselves do not signify anything, but collectively they mean a "watt," a "watt" being the unit of work done, or "watts" as the case may be The strength of current is "ampere" and the symbol is S The electro-motive force or potential is "volt" and the symbol is E The quantity is "coulomb" with the symbol Q. The resistance is "ohm." having R for a symbol, and capacity is the farad with the symbol C. These units look much brighter now than when we first started, but we will endeavor to make them still a little clearer

Potential is, as we have seen, a possibility, and when it is an accomplished fact we call it voltage or electro-motive force or volt-coulombs

Now to give the student a better idea of these terms, we will use the following illustrations; they are not correct, but they are as near so as any illustration can be

First, you must look upon the word volt as indicating pound pressure; the ampere as a volume of water in a tube on a level, with the pound pressure back of it; the coulomb as the area of pipe in which the fluid flows; the ohm as the length of pipe or resistance. Now we have one volt or pound pressure in the water column, or ampere of current passing through one ohm of pipe, at the rate of one coulomb or amount in one second

If we should take ten Daniell's cells, the energy of which is one volt per cell, the total number of cells would then be equivalent to ten volts   Now we connect these cells in series, the internal resistance we say is two ohms per cell or twenty ohms in all; then we have twenty ohms placed in the circuit which would represent forty ohms in all for the current to pass through, and we would find a current of 0 25 amperes.

This is expressed in Ohm's law as follows.

$E = 10$ (volts)
$R = 40$ (ohms)

and $\dfrac{E}{R} = \dfrac{10}{40} = 0.25$ amperes.

Should we reduce the resistance say 20 ohms we would have the following.

$E = 10$ (volts)
$R = 20$ (ohms)

and $\dfrac{E}{R} = \dfrac{10}{20} = 0.5$ amperes.

This shows that we have a much stronger current than before   If we should take four voltaic cells having an electro-motive force of four volts with internal and external resistance of 40 ohms, we would have 0.1 ampere

With a few more words on the practical use of positive and negative poles, we have finished

All acutely inflammatory affections are electrically *positive* in excess, having too much vital action, being *overcharged* with electro-vital fluid, while all paralytic diseases are those of sluggish character are electrically *negative*, having too little vital action.

When we wish to repress or repel inflammation. which is electrically positive in excess, we put the positive pole to it or as near to it as possible. by applying this positive current to a diseased part, we drive away the condition by the repelling influence of the positive battery current, while the negative pole is upon some more healthy portion of the body; also, we find *spinal irritation* and at the same time a stomach afflicted with chronic dyspepsia, accompanied with constipation of the bowels We place the positive pole at the spinal nerves, because we know that from its irritation that there is an excess of electro vital fluid in the part making it improperly positive, and with the negative electrode we will at the same time treat over the stomach, bowels, and liver, because we know from the inaction of the organs that there is a lack of the vital force there, and that consequently they are too negative.

Now if we find inflammation or enlargement of the spleen as is commonly the case with chills and fever we place the positive pole upon the spleen and the negative pole upon the liver

The positive repels the excess of electro-vitality away from the positive spleen, and so reduces the improper excitement there, while at the same time it rushes by attraction to the negative liver under the negative pole or electrode and makes that more positive and so more active

In this way we change the polarization of the parts, and in so doing remove the sustaining cause of the disease Thus you see we may treat different functions of the body with correspondingly excellent results. Of course, as soon as the object in view is attained, we change the location of the electrodes, as long continued actions of the current would not be desirable in the same direction and location

Again, in treating a case of enteritis (inflammation of the intestines) we would place the positive current over the bowels and the negative over the lumbar region.

Mechanical Effect of Each Pole

The mechanical effect of the negative pole or negative current on that part of the body under the negative electrode is to relax, expand. When, therefore, we wish to relax a muscle that is unnaturally contracted by rheumatism or otherwise, we must bring it under the negative electrode. If we desire to contract ligaments or muscles that are abnormally relaxed (not atrophied) as in prolapsus uteri, we must subject them to the positive current or bring them under the positive electrodes Parts that are unnaturally contracted are electrically negative in excess, and need to be made positive Parts that are unnaturally relaxed are too positive and should be made more negative

We make a part more positive by applying to it the negative pole and more negative by applying the positive.

Parts *spasmodically* contracted are acute and positive. Those *permanently* contracted are chronic and negative.

Inflammatory affections should be treated by a downward current in most cases. In treating a paralyzed organ, the current should be run through a healthy part to it, with negative electrode over the affected part.

Acute diseases are to be regarded as electrically positive, and chronic affections as negative.

Alkaline affections, those causing excessive alkaline secretions are electrically positive, and *acid or acidulous* states are negative. Recent wounds, contusions, and burns are positive. Old ulcers and irritations are generally negative.

With a few brief quotations from celebrated writers on therapeutic electricity, who testify to its value as a remedial agent, we will conclude:

"Electricity," says Matteucei, "is the only irritant which can excite at one time, sensation, and at another, contraction, according to the direction in which it traverses a nerve."

Dr. Phillips remarks that in cases "where there is a failure in the secreting power of the liver, or a defective action of the gall tubes, I have repeatedly seen from galvanism the same effect on the biliary system which arises from calomel; a copious bilious discharge from the bowels, coming on a few hours after the employment of galvanism."

Says Golding Bird, "It is the only direct emmenagogue which the experience of our profession has furnished. I do not think I have ever ever known it to fail to excite menstruation, where the uterus was capable of performing this office."

"The beneficial effects of galvanism," says Sturgeon, "in asthma and bilious complaints, have several times come under my notice."

"Mr. Cole, house-surgeon to the Worcester Infirmary," according to the Dublin Medical Journal, "informed Dr. Phillips that no other means employed there have been equally efficacious in relieving asthma, as galvanism." -

The same paper observes that "Dr. Marcus reports several instances of the successful application of galvanism in the great hospital of Bamberg. One was a case of paralysis of the arm, in which a complete cure was effected. Another was one of violent headache after a remittent fever, which could not be subdued by any medical treatment."

"The same reason" says Smee, "for which electricity is valuable in amenorrhœa, might lead us to expect that it would tend to rectify the state of barrenness in the female; for, by causing it to act directly upon the uterus, it is calculated to increase the supply of blood, and thus remedy the deficit." I might here remark that I have been successful in curing several cases of barrenness, of many years standing, by the application of electricity.

"One of the most important and curious of the physiological properties of the galvanic influence," says M. Donavan, "is its power over the peristaltic motion of the intestinal canal, and the consequent evacuation of the fæces. The power over the peristaltic motion, denied by Volta, was, I believe, first observed by Grapengiesser; but the resulting effects were discovered by M Le Roy d'Etiolle."

"Costiveness in the bowels," says Sturgeon, "however obstinately it may resist the usual remedies, very soon yields to the galvanic treatment; and by a similar process, constipations generally may be readily vanquished "

"In diseases of the eye" says Donavan, "the application of galvanism has been of the greatest service; there are many cases of cure on record."

The experience of many others might be added, equally commendatory of the therapeutic power of electricity; but as our object in making these quotations is merely to show what many eminent physicians of the *old school*. across the Atlantic think of it, these are sufficient.

PHYSIOLOGICAL ELECTRO-THERAPEUTICS

The Physio-Medical Idea of Medical Electricity.

By J. M. THURSTON, M. D.

Professor of Applied Physiological Anatomy of the Nervous System and Electro-Therapeutics in the Physio-Medical College of Indiana, Indianapolis

It is an historical fact not at all flattering to the Medical Profession in general, that the large volume of our Therapeutic agents were discovered and used by the nonprofessional laity; so also we have the singular historic fact that the fathers of Medical Electricity were nonmedical men. For instance: Michael Farady was an English chemist; A. Volta was an Italian physicist;

Charles Augusta Coulomb was a French philosopher; Andris M. Ampere was a French physicist; Georg Simon Ohm was a German physicist. And so cf our own Benjamin Franklin, and our up-to-date Edison and Tesla. Most fortunate for science and far more fortunate for humanity's weal, there were no "State Boards of Health" in those days to throttle progress in medical science, else Benjamin Franklin could never have used statical electricity Therapeutically. And indeed the early history and development of Medical Electricity owes not its origin to what is to-day styled the "Regular" medical profession. The fact is, that like the most of the so-called new Materia Medica of this school of medicine which have been regularized by a singular process of piracy upon the Materia Medica of the New Schools, and likewise Electro-Therapeutics, has received its baptism into Regularism only within the last two decades. By this we do not wish to be understood as refusing full credit to our Regular brethren for the many good things they have developed in the way of Electro-Therapeutics, but we do mean to here enter our protest against their appropriation of the valuable fundamental truths of Electro-Therapeutics, which cost the pioneers of medical reform so many years of patient perseverance and untiring experimental work, without giving them the least credit for their life work, but on the contrary boasting that they have rescued Medical Electricity from the hands of ignorant empirics and charlatans.

The question which the Physio-Medical school of medicine must first answer before recommending the use of electricity therapeutically is, what is the inherent tendency of electricity upon the living matter of the tissue elements of the organism; in other words, is its influence sanitive, in harmony with the physiological actions in the human body? If we seek an answer to this question in the literature of the "Regular School" of medicine, as Physio-Medicalists, we will be compelled to answer this question in the negative.

When the attention of the so-called Regular School of medicine was directed per force to the "irregular" medical electricians, because of their enviable reputation for curing diseases wholly beyond the control of the "Regular" methods of treatment, and when it became apparent that they must adopt this wonderfully successful remedy, or go to the wall for want of business, they found themselves in a dilemma; for the medical electricity of the "Irregulars" would not fit the central idea of *alos pathos.* that is, they could not use the "Irregulars'" electrical currents with the idea of making disease to cure disease, because they were not "strong" enough. So that they must either abandon their cherished philosophy of *"contraria contrarius curanter,"* or else they must adapt electricity to the disease-producing therapy. The latter they had little difficulty in achieving. so that their medical philosophy was really in no danger. For electricity is the most versatile and eccentric force of the universe, and we now know that its influence upon the living organism can be made as various and opposite in nature as there are means and methods of varying its force or voltage. its quantity and intensity—amperage, and its modification by magnetism, etc. In other words, that we can produce every effect upon the living tissue from that of a gentle stimulating and tonic influence upon the whole great process of general nutrition, to that of complete disintegration, as by nitric acid or caustic potassa electrolysis So that it was only necessary in order to adapt electricity to their idea of therapeutics to administer it in heroic doses; and thus we find their whole system of Electro-Therapeutics is based upon the fact of electrolysis. Dr George Apostoli, one of the early baptizers of electricity into "Regular" medicine, used immense electrodes of potters' clay to diffuse the force of the current, so as not to burn a hole straight through the patient. or produce electrolysis of the tissue from one pole to the other, and then would turn on 250 milliamperes, believing that he actually produced electrolysis of fibroid tumors of the uterus

We have said the whole theory of "Regular" Electro-Therapeutics is based upon the fact of electrolysis. Let us examine their literature upon the subject and see if we are misstating their position On page 108 of "Electricity .in Diseases of Women and Obstetrics," by Benjamin H. Martin, M D., "Professor of Gynecology Post-Graduate Medical School of Chicago, attending surgeon Women's Hospital of Chicago. Gynecologist to Charity and Post-Graduate Hospitals, member of the Chicago Gynecological Society, etc , etc ," says, "Electrolysis is the power possessed by the voltaic current of chemically decomposing a compound body into its constituent elements. An *electrolyte* is that body or substance which is capable of being dissolved into its several elements by means of the electric current. The *ions* are the product of electrolysis or the constituent parts into which an electrolyte has been divided by the current of electricity. When the two electrodes from a galvanic battery are plunged into a solution containing electrolyte to be decomposed, definite proportions of the *ions* are attracted by the positive pole, while the remainder are attracted by the negative pole. Those which are deposited or attracted by the positive pole or anode are called *anions,* while those which are deposited or attracted by the negative pole or cathode are called *cathions."* After thus explaining what electrolysis really is, on page 110, he says, "That electrolysis does occur, however, in living tissues, we have obtained proof. When it is remembered that from one-half to two-thirds in bulk of the human tissue of the body is water, we can, at least, readily understand why electrolysis should occur under proper influences. While the galvanic current passed through a soft living tissue, has not an uninterrupted fluid medium, it has practically a fluid medium divided into innumerable compartments, each one separated from the other by a thin wall of solid. During the passage of the current, each of these particles of solids, acts as a positive electrode on the fluid between it and the solid particle in front of it. Each molecule of fluid in a conducting solid, therefore, in the line of a galvanic current, may become electrolyzed." And on page 111, he says, "Now, are we not in a position to explain how tissue-change, or absorption even, may be promoted by these two factors alone, when applied to living normal tissues? A galvanic current of moderate or decided strength is made to traverse a portion of living tissues and the most susceptible molecules in the course of the current become broken into their original elements. (1.) These liberated elements immediately make a similar or different combination with neighboring elements of opposite electrical tendencies, making thereby new compounds which act as foreign particles; as foreign particles, they are promptly removed by the nearest absorbent. (2.) Other elements, as they become free from their original molecules, make combinations with elements which are already leaving the tissues through one of their innumerable minute vascular or absorbent canals. (3.) Many in the form of gas, pour into the atmosphere beneath and surrounding the electrodes.

(4.) Others attack the electrodes and are disposed of in the form of deposits on their surfaces. (5.) The current by its cataphoric action, produces an engorgement of the tissues at the negative end of the circuit. The absorbents in that portion of the tissues will promptly make an effort to establish an equilibrium, and by a direct action of endosmosis, they are filled and the excess is carried away in their currents." On pages 121-2 Dr. Martin gives a concise summary of their whole philosophy of Electro-Therapeutics, as follows:

"1. Electrolysis in living tissues, is in direct proportion to the strength of the current and direct proportion to its density.

"2. Electrolysis may occur at any or all the points in the line of the tissue current, as well as at the external poles.

"3. Electrical osmosis, or the cataphoric action of the galvanic current, causes a direct transference of the fluids of the body through the tissues in a direction from the positive to the negative pole.

"4. The products of interstitial electrolysis of living tissues, are removed by the absorbents of the tissue in which the action occurs.

"5. When a portion of living tissue becomes overcharged with fluids from the effect of electrical osmosis, it is unloaded by the absorbents of the part acted upon.

"6. The polar effect of an electrode upon the living tissue with a concentrated electrode, varies with the polarity as well as the strength of the current.

"7. The *cathode* acts locally like the varying effects of an alkali of different strengths, from (a) a slight burning with accompanying redness of the parts; with a mild current, (b) a more decided burning sensation with a local destruction of the superficial tissue, leaving a white scar; with a medium current, to (c) a severe burning pain accompanied with an active and deep destruction of tissues, a perceptible gathering of fluid products, and an active escape of gasses through the fluids, with a strong concentrated current.

"8. The *anode* acts locally like the varying effects of a deep penetrating acid of different degrees of concentration, from (a) a slight feeling of discomfort with a local redness of the tissues; with a mild current, with (b) a decided feeling of discomfort, a tendency to numbness, and a superficial hardening of the portion of tissue in contact with the electrode; with a medium current, to (c) a severe local pain accompanied with numbness, and an effect of coagulation and hardening of the tissues for some considerable distance around the electrode, with a strong concentrated current."

In the paper on treatment of stricture, in the International System of Electro-Therapeutics, Robert Newman, M. D., gives a thorough exposition of this philosophy of Medical Electricity, from which we quote at some length, as we do not want to misrepresent the status of their fundamental theory of electrical action.

"Electrolysis is the decomposition of a compound body by electricity—a chemical decomposition. The body to be decomposed must possess certain elements to be an electrolyte, and, as a compound body, must contain water and salt. A simple element cannot be further subdivided, and, therefore, cannot be an electrolyte. Tissues of the human body have all the properties of an electrolyte, and therefore electrolysis can be applied there, and electrolysis as a chemical action is an indisputed fact.

"Nicholson and Carlisle discovered this process of electrical decomposition in 1800, and successfully electrolyzed water into oxygen and hydrogen; therefore the theory is not new, and the explanation can be found in any text-book on elementary physics and chemistry. In combination with this chemical action is the cataphoric, which by some authors is considered an important factor of electrolysis. The explanation lies in the direction of the current interpolar, between the elements from zinc to carbon, or the current from electro-negative to the electro-positive. In the external current between anode and cathode the direction of the current is positive, and the particles of the fluid gather at the electro-negative pole, which is the cathode. The galvanic current only produces the desired result."—M.—1, International Therapeutics.

"*Meat Test.*—The poles of the battery, in the shape of two needles (platinum are best) are inserted in a piece of fresh raw meat. After electrolytic action has been allowed to take place for a while, the difference in pole action can readily be seen. The positive pole almost destroys it; at the negative pole the color is nearly white, and bubbles of hydrogen appear. In electrolysis the action of the poles is very different, each having its own function. The positive pole attracts

the acids and the oxygen from the tissues and coagulates
the blood. The negative pole attracts the alkalies, hydrogen and the base of the salt, dissolves blood (but forms a
plug from froth of the hydrogen), coagulates albumen,
and causes absorption. The positive pole acts like an acid
and burns like fire, which is not only exceedingly painful,
but may leave a hard, resilient cicatrix The negative
pole acts more like a caustic alkali, which should not hurt
so severely during the application, and leaves, if carried to
excess, a cicatrix which is soft and not retractile Thus it
is evident that for the immediate destruction of tumors
and for the treatment of strictures the negative pole
should be selected Electrolysis requires the presence of
water and that is present in every tissue of the human
body.   It is vitally important to distinguish the poles,
and, as we cannot trust to the marks of the instrument-
maker, we must always ascertain which is the positive and
which is the negative pole The positive pole is noiseless,
the litmus-paper applied to it shows an acid reaction, and
the needle adheres firmly to its surroundings in the meat;
the needle of the negative pole sticks loosely in the meat,
can easily be removed and during electrolysis a hissing
sound proceeds from it   A piece of fresh meat still contains enough water to become an electrolyte, while the
living body, in which the circulation is active, is better,
a dried up piece of meat is not an electrolyte The author
has made practical experiments on dogs, on pieces of meat,
and pathological specimens, particularly with carcinoma.
From among them the following are mentioned.   (a) Into
a piece of fresh raw pork two large platinum needles were
inserted, at a distance of three inches apart.   The current
of thirty-five cells from a galvanic battery was allowed to
pass for fifteen minutes, after which the meat between
and around the needles was thoroughly changed into a
soft pulp   A weaker current caused changes proportionately; the current of five cells produced distinct effects in
five seconds, twenty cells in one second. (b) Into a piece
of meat, containing a bone in the centre, the needles are
inserted at a distance of two and a-half inches from each
other   One large platinum needle was then connected
with the positive pole, while with the negative pole two
small steel needles were connected   These needles were
inserted close to the bone, and one direct into the bone
cells.   The negative current of thirty-five cells in fifteen

minutes produced changes in the entire tissue, so that the
bone around one negative needle was entirely destroyed."
—Ibid. M.—2 and 3.

Here then is the philosophy of electrical action upon the
living tissues of the human organism, based upon the
electro-chemical phenomena which take place in water
in fresh meat, and in short, all organic or inorganic sub,
stances, when a current of sufficient electro-motive force
and intensity is sent through them to disintegrate their
molecular integrity; in other words, to wholly destroy the
organic conditions of an organic body, and break up
present molecular relations in an inorganic body, when in
either case chemical laws instantly go to work to construct
new atomic relations; and the new product is builded on
chemical laws wholly, whether the electrolysis occurred in
an organic or inorganic body.

Why did not these experimenters complete their experiments, and subject the whole human body to the same
proportion of current that it takes to decompose water,
and a piece of fresh meat?,

The recent claims of D'Arsonval, who announces that
electricity does not electrocute the criminal, throw a ludi-
crous halo around our friends, to say the least; he says the
criminal is not killed, but his physiological functions are
inhibited—simply the functions of the body are brought
to a standstill by the powerful action of electricity upon
the nerves, the criminal being in a trance—electric trance,
as it were, and death really occurs, he says, from the surgeon's knife at the autopsy! This is certainly a startling
announcement to the advocates of electrolysis, as well as
to the humane society; for if electricity does, as so positively averred by our above quoted eminent authors, produce electrolysis throughout the whole interpolar region,
certainly no power could resuscitate the criminal, and if
electrocution only inhibits the functional activity of the
body, it is in order for the advocates of the "Therapeutic"
electrolysis theory to arise and explain the explanation as
to why the whole patient does not become raw meat under
a "medical" electric current which produces chemical decomposition. Then, if D'Arsonval is correct, the theory
of therapeutic electrolysis is disproved without further
argument, and if he should be wrong, then the very fact
of patients surviving the therapeutic electric currents is

proof in itself that electrolysis cannot occur   There is no
attempt to explain—in fact there can be no possible explanation—why electrolysis, if it occurs in the living tissues
in th interpolar region, should be in any way different
from the electroiytic phenomena that occur in the elements of the battery cell, in fresh meat, in salt water, or
in any other substance, whether it is organic or inorganic,
the fact is, that if electrolysis occurs in the application of
electricity to the living tissues of the body it simply means
disintegration (destruction) of the organic continuity, and
reconstruction of molecular conditions by the chemical
changes and interchanges which instantly ensue, which
new molecular constitution must necessarily be inorganic
The very fact then that patients not only live under the
application of medical electricity, even by the advocates
of the electrolysis theory, but actually improve, and their
ailments disappear, is proof positive that this theory is
false, and electrolysis cannot occur in therapeutic electricity   This is one of the many singular instances of the
inutility of theory, when not in accord with practical results.   Here is an agent producing valuable results in
many cases, applied upon a false and harmful dogma.
Certainly if such good results so often follow the application of this agent upon such a false idea, how much more
good can be accomplished with it if used in accordance
with the true philosophy of its physiological action and in
harmony with the normal functional activities of the body.

Physio-Medical philosophy rejects this idea of electrolysis as the fundamental basis of Electro-Therapeutics.
That electrolysis can be produced upon the living tissues
of the body it does not deny, indeed it is willing to make
use of electrolysis to get rid of superfluous offending tissues
or new growths, but it admits electrolysis as it admits the
surgeon's knife, as a last resort, and as an acknowledge-
ment of final failure to redeem and restore the organic
integrity of tissues, by most thorough sanative therapeutic means.   We accept electricity as a Physio-Medical
agent because its current force for all necessary practical
medical uses is perfectly sanative, and in line with the
vital endeavors to restore and maintain the physiological
equilibrium   All who use electricity to any extent in the
cure of diseases, regardless of school or theoretical belief
as to its action, must admit that under its influence in
proper current, intelligently applied in accordance with

the conditions, that nutrition is promoted; that the circulation, local or general, is increased; that the functions of assimilation and dissimilation are rendered more active; that nerve energy is increased and equalized; and that the patient experiences a strengthening and invigorating effect from its application. Upon these results we establish the Physio-Medical philosophy of Electro-Therapeutics. The term "catalysis" was used by the old electricians—who are now called empirics—on the above idea with the enumerated beneficial results which have been so frequently observed and lauded by all alike, regardless of school, or theory, since its discovery. This term, as well as these facts which are incontrovertible, it is now sought by the advocates of the new Electro-Therapeutics to relegate to the realms of empiricism and obsolescence.

Static electricity was the first form of electricity discovered, and the only kind used for medical purposes for a great many years. Any one at all acquainted with its nature knows that it is impossible to produce electrolysis with static elecricity. This form is in fact nascent electricity, yet it is not the result of chemical action. Great confusion has arisen from the close resemblance of electrical and chemical forces and phenomena; the fact is that writers upon the subject seem to make no distinction between chemical action and electrical force, notwithstanding the fact that a correct understanding of the same constitutes the basis of all correct Electro-Therapeutic investigation. In the galvanic battery we have first the chemical action of the fluid upon the metal (zinc), its chemical molecular disintegration, and the liberation of atoms which instantly seek new combinations. As a result of this general breaking up of the old, and formation of new atomic relations, as far as affinities permit, there are atoms, or, perhaps, atomic constituencies, combined into kinetic energy, constituting the subtile ethereal force which we call electricity; which now seeking a level of potentiality, readily traverses any conducting media from one element of the battery out through all intermediate or interposed substances forming a circuit as it returns to the other element of the battery, which is of less potentiality, thus constituting the electric current. Thus while chemical action creates the conditions from which arises electrical force, we must not confuse the conditions with the result itself, for the chemical action and the electrical

force are certainly two entirely different things As proof
of this, in statical or mechanical electricity we have no
chemical action or disintegration from which the electrical force is generated; here the electrical force is obtained
simply by agitation of the atmosphere from which it is
liberated, and seeking the balance of potential as before,
is taken up by the proper conducting media and constitutes the static electrical current Therefore this the-
'ory of chemico-electro-therapeutics, which is assumed,
perhaps, in order to harmonize electricity with the modern chemico-therapeutics, is as fallacious as the idea of
electrolysis.

A few experiments with the electrical current under
proper conditions will demonstrate our theory of physiological electro-therapeutics. With the lite-slide, place under the microscope an amœba; attach about No 30 wire
electrodes, bringing the poles a little distance at opposite
points from the amœba, and turn on with a good current
controller first an exceedingly mild galvanic current After a few seconds the amœba will exhibit more activity, it
will move with greater vigor and seemingly increase in
bulk Now increase the current slowly and very gradually; the amœba exhibits correspondingly increased activity, but when the current has reached a certain degree of
strength, it exhibits symptoms of exhaustion, and finally
assumes a spherical form, all motion ceases, and it is apparently dead; but with a very mild faradic secondary
current from coarse wire it can be resuscitated; if, however, the galvanic current is continued five minutes longer
after assuming the spherical form, it remains motionless
despite all efforts to resuscitate it, and in the course of
twenty minutes to an hour disintegration has taken place;
it is reduced by chemical action back into the simpler ele-
-ments, and as an amœba is gone forever

If the faradic current, exceedingly mild, is used instead
of the galvanic, and not increased, the amœba will live and
seemingly do well under it for an almost indefinite time,
but if this current is increased gradually as with the galvanic current, the same result occurs, though not nearly
so soon The same phenomena exactly will be observed in
experiments with the white blood-corpuscles. Now, certainly, electrolysis has not occurred in the amœba or white
blood-corpuscles when they can be resuscitated with the
mild faradic current, and chemical disintegration and de-

composition does not occur until a considerable period
after all life manifestations have ceased. Then what does
kill the amœba and the white blood-corpuscles ? Exactly
the same thing that would cause the death of the complex
organism of the human body under proportionately the
same force. It is essential that we bear in mind the proportionate relation between micro-organism and the vol
ume of electric current. We have a being so minute that
it must be increased in volume several hundred times to
come within the region of our optical power, consequently
electro-motive force and current quantity must be proportionately diminished. Now apply the same proportion to
the whole human organism, or in other words, take the
same amount of current strength that would kill an amœba or white blood-corpuscle and multiply it by the number
of living bioplasts in the human organism, and we would
have enough electrical force to kill a billion men ! And
yet they undertake to base Electro-Therapeutic hypothesis
upon such data. The fact is that the most harmless and
beneficial substance used by man would, if applied in the
same ratio, become a huge sum of evil. Let us undertake
to use bread for instance in the same proportion as the
electric current required to kill the amœba and the white
blood-corpuscles, and we would be crushed under the
weight of billions of loaves, much less attempting to eat
them.

Adjust the web of a frog's foot under the microscope
with a magnifying power of 900 or 1,000 diameters, and
arrange the poles of the battery under a current controller, turn on—what is best for this experiment—the
faradic current coarse secondary coil with rapid interruptions, bring on the current exceedingly mild at first,
gently increasing it to the current strength that would
be barely perceptible through the little finger. Watch
carefully the change that takes place. The accompanying
cut, which is partly diagramatic, gives only a faint illustration of what can be seen under proper conditions after
the current has been applied for from twenty to thirty
minutes. The first thing to be seen is an increase in the
circulation as evidenced by the rapid movement of the
blood-corpuscles. There will be an increase in the number
of red blood-corpuscles seen in the vessels near the positive
pole, which will finally extend toward the negative till it
covers nearly half of that polar region. Now after start-

ing the current again, with a camel's hair brush apply to
the surface both above and beneath, close to the positive
pole, a very small quantity of staining fluid, analine blue,
for instance; after the current is continued for perhaps
five or ten minutes, the white blood-corpuscles and the
extravascular interspaces (areolæ) will be seen to become
filled with the coloring matter; and gradually the staining will move like a cloud through the areolar interspaces
toward the negative pole, and remain collected in a dense
cloud about this region. Now reverse the poles, and after
the current has continued for from ten to twenty minutes
the whole process is reversed; the vessels at the other pole,
now negative, become richer in blood-corpuscles, and grad-

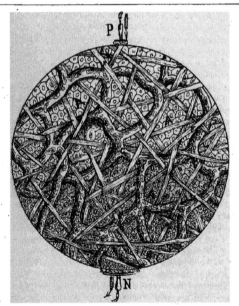

THE WEB OF A FROG'S FOOT UNDER THE FARADIC CURRENT,
AS SEEN UNDER THE MICROSCOPE, plus 1,000.

Partly diagramatic; that is, the electrodes P and N of course were not
in the microscopic field; and the fibrous net work F is introduced to show
the form and limits of the extravascular space-, A.

ually the cloud of color traverses to the negative pole
again. There is nothing resembling electrolysis in this
phenomenon; the current is a faradic secondary, with
which it is impossible to produce electrolysis in any substance, and there is no disintegration of tissue elements or
tissues; on the contrary there is every evidence of increased vital activity, and all the conditions favorable to
the great physiological process of nutrition and growth.

The lesson we learn from these experiments with the
amœba and white blood-corpuscles, and the webb of the
frog's foot, is one of vast importance.   Not least of which
is, that electricity applied in accordance with the physiological demands of deranged tissue conditions, and perverted functional actions, it exerts a mild stimulating,
toning effect upon the living matter of the tissue elements,
and from the initial increase and strength of vital actions
arises a general equilibrium of nervous action and circulatory volume and strength, favoring all the important steps
of assimilation, reparation, and disassimilation.

Upon these facts as observed by the application of electricity and the web of the frog's foot under the microscope,
and which can be further extended by experimenting with
the mesentery of a young mouse, the cornea of a frog, and
patches of epithelium scraped from the tongue, etc., subjected to the same electrical current under the microscope,
we base our philosophy of Physio-Medical Electro-Therapeutics.

As a basis, then, of our theory of Electro-Therapeutics,
and for the want of a better term, we have coined the
word "*Electrosmosis.*" By this term we mean the sanative influence of properly applied electrical currents, of
mild and harmless strength and volume, that shall act in
the line of the resistive and reconstructive efforts of the
Vital Force. In fact the term is synonymous with that of
"catalysis" as used by the older electricians.

The contenders for therapeutic electrolysis are compelled
to admit all these facts as to the increase of all the nutritive functions, the general invigorating, tonic, and stimulating effect of electricity upon the system; but they
allude to it in a vague way, exactly as they admit the
"vital force" in the living organism whose actions "are
sometimes constructive, sometimes destructive;" but
when pressed as to what is really meant by the term "vital
force," no definite answer is elicited. It seems then that

the term electrolysis being more in harmony with the idea of induced diseased conditions to remedy existing pathological states, it is desirable to do away with all ideas of sanative influences of mild electrical therapeutical currents

"We are aware that tissue changes are produced, that nutrition is promoted, that obscure nervous tendencies are transformed by the mildest application of the faradic, static or galvanic form of electricity. * * * These effects of the current, then, including the refreshing and invigorating effect often experienced from the application of the above forms of electricity, which cannot be the effects of electrolysis, but which may be due to the mechanical effects of the current, which, like massage or other form of mechanical treatment, favors tissue changes, are included under the convenient name catalysis, a term which it is to be hoped may rapidly become obsolete, with many other terms connected with empiricism."—*Electricity, Diseases of Women and Obstetrics. F. H. Martin, M. D.*

And why, forsooth, should this and other terms of "empiricism" become obsolete, if they express exactly what takes place under "the mildest application of the faradic, static, or galvanic form of electricity?" In the absence of any reason given by the above, or all other authors of that school, are we not justified in presuming that the term catalysis and all that it implies being directly opposed to the fundamental basis of the medical philosophy of *"contraria contrarius curanter,"* and *"alos pathos,"* it is desirable to get rid of it and base Electro-Therapeutics upon electrolysis, which means electro-chemical disintegration of the living tissues—destruction of diseased tissue elements in the hope that in the reconstructive efforts of the vital force the diseased conditions may be eradicated? We are justified further in this conclusion from the fact that hundreds of terms far more empirical are still retained and continually used For instance, the terms inflammation, artery, diaphragm, Bright's disease, have all arisen from the most empirical and erroneous ideas of anatomy and pathology; they are meaningless and arbitrary in the light of advanced sciences, yet are continually used in all their original glory of "empiricism;" whether thus kept in use purposely or not, they are certainly in accord with the traditions of the "Regular" medicine as expressed in its present medical philosophy.

Physio-Medical Electrical Dosage.

Then as we have already seen, from the Physio-Medical standpoint the current quantity, intensity, and work, are all-important, and summed into one word mean *dosage.* And our dosage means mild sanative currents as applied to the organism to correct departures from normal physiological functional actions. In other words, we seek and use those electrical currents that act in harmony with the vital force in maintaining the vital integrity of living matter and tissue elements, purposeful and harmonious functional activities, the constructive and sanative efforts of the vital force generally—*Sanative Electro-Therapeutics.*

Our dosage being mild and sanative. it follows that our most valuable current quality is the induced; the faradic apparatus and faradism being the basis of Physio-Medical electricity. Not that the galvanic does not afford us valuable sanative work in proper dosage, but the faradic secondary is the most valuable.

The Faradic Current.

It is not necessary here to describe minutely the faradic apparatus, much less attempt to refer to the numerous faradic machines on the market. We therefore content ourselves with briefly classifying the current qualities and the Electro-Therapeutic effects of each.

From the faradic apparatus, as generally constructed, we get three qualities of current, each of which may be varied and multiplied by special construction of the apparatus. These, mentioned in proper sequence of their occurrence, are:—

1st. Primary faradic.

2d. Induced, or secondary faradic.

3d. Electro-magnetic.

Primary Faradic.—This is the current coming from one element of the cell, or battery, traversing the first or primary wire coiled around a soft iron core, and after traveling through whatever essential media there may be in the circuit of the faradic machine—current controller, switches, etc., and the interposed media—the patient—finally returns to the other element of the cell.

As the current travels around the coils of the primary wire encircling the soft iron core, it induces a static force

in the core called magnetism and it becomes a magnet
This fact is taken advantage of to mechanically interrupt
the current—break it up into exceedingly short waves. A
little metal hammer on a spring or flexible post is placed
in front close to the end of the core, so that when it becomes magnetized this hammer or "rheotome" is attracted
to it and drawn away from a screw point in an adjacent
stationary post which is bringing the current to the coil
This movement of the rheotome breaks the current, when
the core is instantly demagnetized, releasing the rheotome,
which flies back, receiving the current, again magnetizing
the core which attracts the rheotome to again break the
current and demagnetize the core, and thus the current
is more or less rapidly interrupted according to the rapidity of the vibrations of the rheotome.

The wire of the primary coil is quite coarse, which offers
less resistance and affords a greater volume of current.
Therefore we have two essential qualities of current, viz
high volume and *low tension.*

To these may be added a third quality, that of *rapidity
of interruptions.*

Therapeutically we get from the primary faradic current
muscular stimulation, by the large volume, low tension
and slow interruptions · *Vaso-motor stimulation*, by
the large volume, very rapidly interrupted, giving a greater intensity

Secondary Faradic or Induced Current —This is our
most valuable current, especially as afforded by the recent
improvements in faradic machines. We have a variety of
current qualities, which in their sequence may be classified as follows.

Large volume (voltage) and high potency   This is obtained from a coarse secondary coil of moderate length,
whose potency may be varied by the character of the interruptions, as follows: *Slow interruptions*, stimulates muscular tonicity, voluntary and involuntary: increases local
nutrition by increasing the circulation—vaso-motor stimulation. *Rapid interruptions*, vigorous muscular stimulation, and increased nervous circulation

*Smaller volume (amperage) and higher tension (poten-
cy).* This is obtained by a secondary coil of fine wire (No. 20)
and considerable length (1,500 feet) This may be varied by
the character of the interruptions as follows. *Slow interruptions*, stimulates deep muscles, and increases vaso-

motor action. Moderately applied for thirty to forty minutes with 600 or 800 interruptions per minute, it leaves a general pleasantly stimulated sensation, and an invigorating effect. *Rapid interruptions*, from 1,000 to 1,500 per minute. This current will exert a still more soothing influence upon the nervous system if applied generally, say at the back of the neck and to the feet; at the same time it increases the vaso-motor functions generally, so that after thirty or forty minutes or an hour's sitting the patient is in a general warm perspiration, and no matter where or how many aches and pains, acute or chronic, he is in a most agreeable state of perfect ease and quietude; if he has lost sleep from pain he will go to sleep under the treatment, and awake at the end of it with a feeling of deep rest and refreshment. *Very rapid interruptions*, 3,000 to 5,000 per minute, increases the above effects, and is best in cases of extreme nervousness, with acute pain and tenderness locally.

Very small volume (amperage) and exceedingly high tension. This most valuable current is obtained with a very fine wire (36 or 40) and 2,500 to 3,000 feet long, and is usually used with very rapid interruptions, 3,000 to 5,000 per minute. It is the nervine current. Used with the positive pole at the back of the neck and the negative at the feet, with a sitting of forty to sixty minutes, it most effectually relieves all nerve tension, pains, aches, and general muscular soreness.

Applied locally it relieves local congestions, engorgements, tenderness, and irritation. In ovarian irritation, congestions acute or chronic, hypertrophies, or other enlargements of uterus and appendage; chronic enlargements of the liver, spleen and kidneys; congestion, pain and tenderness of the stomach and bowels.

Electro-Magnetic Current.—When the soft iron core in the primary coil of the faradic apparatus is unmagnetized by the sudden stoppage of the current through the primary wire as the rheotome strikes it, breaking the connection between it and the screw post, as in the ordinary arrangement of the machine, the static magnetic force instantly pours out of it in every direction, as light, or heat-rays would emanate from a radiant or a heated body; and obeying the physical law of electricity, it seeks a media of less potential, which would be the wire coils. Now it is natural to suppose that in seeking its potential level the magnetic current would lodge in the secondary coils, because they are of much lower potential than the primary wire; second, because the initial force of the escaping magnetic volume is the greatest at the start and this would project at least its main volume through the primary coil out to the secondary wires, to which it is drawn by the additional force of potential attraction. This would add to the secondary faradic currents, already described, more or less magnetic current, making it an electro-magnetic current. With our present means of investigation it is impossible to determine the proportion of these two forces—electric and magnetic—in this combination, much less to determine which is the greater or less factor in the therapeutic effects of this current.

Magnetic-electric machines have been variously devised, affording a current in which the magnetic largely predominates, but so far they have not yielded therapeutic advantages over the faradic currents, and consequently have not come into general use.

The Galvanic Current.

This is simply the constant stream directly from the batteries or cells through switches, current controller, milliamperemeter, and. any other essential media constituting the board of galvanic apparatus, and the interposed media as the patient. From this current we get the largest current force. amperage, from a medical standpoint at least, and therefore it should be used moderately.

The most useful form of galvanic current is the interrupted. It is found that by mechanically breaking the current flow into exceedingly short waves or rapid interruptions a very large amperage or current quantity can be used without producing electrolysis of the tissues; indeed the application soothes irritation, relieves pain, the structures being in a state resembling anæsthesia for some little time after the current is discontinued.

The best, cheapest, and simplest galvanic interrupter is a small electric motor; the toy motors which range in price from $1.50 to $5 00 are quite sufficient. The little metal pulley-wheel is divided into about three or four equal segments insulated from each other by filing broad grooves and fitting in them segments of wood or other non-conducting material. The motor is run with about three small cells which can be thrown on in succession by a selector or double switch. The first cell runs the motor at a moderate speed; by adding to it the second it runs at a rapid speed; and adding the third, exceedingly rapid revolutions are attained. It is now only necessary to bring the galvanic current to the pulley by spring bearings so that one bears against the end of the metal pulley, and the other bears on the segmented surface of it, sliding alternately over a wooden and a metal segment, thus breaking and making the current with proportionate rapidity to the revolutions of the pulley.

The galvanic current thus interrupted is better than the constant current for fibrous and fibroid tumors; for cysts of very fluid contents, such as ovarian cysts; and for pleural and abdominal effusions, etc.

For vascular tumors and cheesey cysts the constant current should be used.

No Heroic Dosage.

In all currents, but especially the galvanic constant, mild amperage should be used; the current strength need never exceed fifteen or twenty milliamperes. It is just as grave a mistake to believe that heroic electric dosage is necessary, even in the removal by absorption of fibrous tumors, as to administer heroic therapeutic remedies and dosage, such as strychnia, aconite, dynamite, etc. For we insist, as has been amply proved herein from the best authority, viz., its own advocates, that electrolysis never occurs in the interpolar region; and these growths are removed by the physiological process of absorption, which is simply increased to its highest activity by the sanative stimulating influence of the electric current upon the living matter of tissue elements.

Let us here impress upon the Physio-Medical beginner in the use of electricity, that a good knowledge of physiology, the Physio-Medical philosophy of Electro-Therapeutics, and a little patience and perseverance will accomplish far greater curative results with mild and persistent currents of electricity, than by the painful and dangerous heroic dosage.

The author has followed the simple rule for twenty-five years of using no current of electricity stronger than the patient can agreeably bear. Our milliamperemeter for practical dosage is the patient. Briefly stated our method is as a rule, mild currents, stationary large electrodes, and long sittings, from 30 minutes to one hour. Seated in an easy upholstered chair wired for the purpose, we place our re-enforcement pads, (see Max Wocher & Son's catalogue, Cincinnati, Ohio,) upon the patient at the required points, hand them some interesting literature to entertain themselves with. turn on the current with a Massey controller till the patient says, ' That's about 'right," and then go about our business, probably attending to five or six other office patients in the mean time

To the honest critic who believes the above method old-fashioned, "empirical," and "too weak" to accomplish anything, we have only to say that, although we never take "certificates," we can furnish ample proof of the removal of an ovarian cyst, large as the gravid uterus at full term, by the faradic secondary current, an hour's sitting every third day for three months   The removal of numerous fibrous and fibroids, from the size of a hulled walnut to a cocoanut, with the faradic secondary, and also the galvanic, of not over ten milliamperes, rapidly interrupted.

Surgical Electricity.

As already stated we use electrical currents to the extent of producing electrolysis, only as we use the scalpel—after all sanative resistive and constructive vital efforts, aided by sanative therapeutic means, have failed, and it becomes necessary to remove an obstructive perverted growth.   In such cases, where inconveniently situated, and there is danger of excessive hemorrhage with the knife, electrolysis becomes a valuable surgical means   Deep electrolysis of dense growths, deep or superficial is accomplished by introducing silver or platinum needles, and using the constant galvanic current of sufficient amperage to cause disintegration or electrolytic action upon the fluids of the areolar interspaces, extra-vascular spaces, and living matter of the tissue elements at each polar (not interpolar) region.

Electro-cautery is produced by passing the constant galvanic current through variously-shaped platinum cautery-knives, which are constructed so as to form a circuit of sufficient intensity to bring the knife to a white heat.

With our modern aseptic surgical technique, and our means of controlling hemorrhage with compression forceps and the Esmarch bandage, surgical electricity can never attain a very prominent position

However for facial blemishes electrolysis has a field that

is fast bringing it into prominence. Warty growths, moles, nevi, etc., and superfluous hairs, can be removed by the constant galvanic current. But here, as in the general use of electricity, much harm has been done by heroic dosage amounting to actual cautery, producing a wound exceedingly hard to heal and leaving a cicatrix much more unsightly than the original blemish. Mild current with low tension, which effects electrolysis of the fluid plasma and living matter, and not actual cautery, though the treatment requires a little more time and patience, will accomplish the work more effectually and leave no cicatrix.

ELETTARIA REPENS.

Cardamon. •   Malabar.

The *seeds* are a stimulating, aromatic, warming carminative. They are chiefly used as a vehicle for cathartics to prevent griping and nausea; and with bitter tonics, especially with quinia sulph, gentiana and apocynum androsem. It partially covers the bitter taste.

Cardamon Seed
Caraway Seed   aa. oz. 1
Cinnamon Bark   oz. 2
Raisins, Seedless   grs. 8
Or
Cardamon Seed
Cassia Cin.   aa. oz. 2½
Caraway Seed   oz. 1½

Either formula makes one pint of fluid compound cardamon. Either forms a good vehicle for bitter medicines.

EMBELIA RIBES.

Babarang.   India, Malaga, China.

This climber is native to the forests of Bengal.

Its *seed* is similar in appearance to pimento seed and is slightly aromatic. It is a pleasant, mild, stimulating, astringent, alterative tonic, influencing the mucous and serous membranes. It is considered a specific in the treatment for the expulsion of tape worm. A teaspoonful twice a day followed by a cathartic is sufficient for a child while a dessertspoonful is required for an adult. It usually expells the worm dead.

In small doses it improves digestion, relieves flatulence, tones the stomach, soothes and stimulates the nerves, and soothes and tones the serous membrane.

Its alterative quality is best realized when combined with some such agent as iris versicolor.

With salicylate sodium it gives good results in rheumatism and dyspepsia

EPHEDRA ANTISYPHILITICA.

Brigham Weed.   Western U. S.

This *herb* grows in Arizona and the surrounding States. It is a mild but positive stimulating alterative, slightly astringent

By the people among whom it grows it is recognized as a very efficient agent in the treatment of gonorrhœa, syphilis and various eczemas. It is certainly an admirable alterant. It soothes, stimulates and tones the general system, but its depurative properties are aided by combining with such agents as syr. juglans or iris versicolor.

It is also valuable in scrofulous diarrhœa and the diarrhœa sometimes incident to phthisis and in cholera infantum in scrofulous, syphilitic and rickety children. It eliminates impurities, cleanses the blood current, and tones the mucous membrane.

EPIGÆA REPENS.

Gravel Plant.

The leaves are a mild stimulating and astringing diuretic.

In sluggish renal action they stimulate, sooth and tone the kidneys and promote diuresis. They relieve the aching back and stimulate the prostate gland. This agent is of much value in gonorrhœa and cystic catarrh

F. E. Epigæa Rep.	3
" Mitchella Rep.	2
Fld Hydrastis Can.	1

This is a good remedy for gonorrhœa.

F E. Epigæa Rep.	dr. iv
" Celastrus Scan.	dr. i
" Mitchella Rep.	dr. ii
" Althæa Ros	dr. ii
Syr Simplex	q. s. oz. iv

This is a valuable prescription for spermatorrhœa and all irritable troubles of the urinary apparata.

    F. E. Epigæa Rep.   dr. iv
       " Liriodendron Tul.   dr. ii
       " Eupatorium Purpu.   dr. ii
    Hydrastia Sulph.   gr. i
    Ferri et Pot. Tart.   grs. iii
    Syr. Zingiber   q. s. oz. iv

This is a good tonic for prolapsus uteri, chronic cystitis and general pelvic weakness.

    Epigæa Rep.   4
    Amygdalus Pers. Fol.   6
    Cypripedium Pub.   2
    Zingiber   ½

This in cold infusion is a good preparation to be used for weakness of the bladder, and for gleet.

EPILOBIUM ANGUSTIFOLIUM.

Willow-herb.   (Epilobium Spicatum.)

The **root** is a pleasant astringent tonic, chiefly influencing the mucous membrane and useful in cases of dysentery, diarrhœa and cholera infantum.

The **leaves** are more diuretic and influence the entire pelvic viscera. They are useful in chronic cystitis, cystic catarrh, leucorrhœa, gonorrhœa, vaginal weakness, and uterine hemorrhages. In severe cases it may have to be combined with more positive agents.

EPIPHEGUS VIRGINIANA.

Beech-drop.

This **plant** is a stimulating-astringent. When applied to the surface of foul and indolent ulcers and gangrenous sores it arouses and cleanses the surface ready for the application of an appropriate dressing. Internally or externally it may be used for the relief of hemorrhages.

ERECHTHITES HIERACIFOLIA.

Fireweed.

The **leaves and flowers** are a mild bitter, stimulating, astringent tonic. Its chief influence is expended upon the mucous membrane and are best in relaxed and sluggish conditions, as in chronic diarrhœa.

In combination with uva ursi it is valuable in cystic catarrh.

Combined with agents that chiefly influence the generative organs it is useful in vaginal weakness and in prolapsus uteri.

It is also of service in hemorrhages of the lungs and of the bowels, as well as in menorrhagia and in post-partem hemorrhage.

Incorporated into an ointment it is a good application for old sores, for hemorrhoids and for rectal ulcers

The *oil* of fireweed more or less diluted with olive oil forms an excellent application for hemorrhoids.

ERIGERON CANADENSE.

Canada Fleabane.

This *herb* is a diffusive, aromatic, stimulating, astringent It is best administered in small and frequent doses

In hot infusion it influences the circulation toward the surface and is of advantage in hyperæmic conditions.

In diarrhœa. dysentery and cholera infantum it is a superior remedy. Repeat small doses as the conditions require.

It is quite effective for the relief of hemorrhages, whether from the lungs, nose, uterus or bowels.

Dr F. G Hoener recommends an infusion to be used as an injection in cases of gonorrhœa.

The *oil* of erigeron is very diffusive and has almost entirely superceded the use of the herb for hemorrhages. A good fresh article is a success, age impairs the quality of both the herb and the oil. Give one to four drops on sugar and follow with a little hot water. This is the ordinary dose of the oil, but do not depend too much upon this agent unless you know the quality of the oil you are using. You can better depend on capsicum and lobelia or on capsicum alone The following is a good preparation to be used in such cases.

Oil Capsicum
'   Erigeron   aa. 1
Sugar or Lactin   10

Triturate thoroughly and administer from one to three grains every ten minutes for two or three doses and then lengthen the time as the conditions require. If it be post-partem hemorrhage give only as required or you may check the flow so completely as to give trouble in the opposite direction

For metrorrhagia Dr G. H Mayhugh advises the following.

Oil Cinnamon
" Erigeron .   aa. gtt. 5 to 10
M. Sig. Give in hot water every five or ten minutes
till the flow is checked, then give every half hour till relief
is had.

In cases of anal fistula apply erigeron throughout its
entire length. It will cure it.

In cases of rectal ulcer, it will arouse the parts, but it
will cure the ulcer.

ERIGERON PHILADELPHICUM.

Philadelphia Fleabane.

This *plant* is a stimulating diuretic.

Dr. F. G. Hoener says: This agent, combined with some
good alterant preparation, will cure those afflicted with
syphilitic ulcers on the lungs.

ERIGERON STRIGOSUM.

This is another species of the fleabane. The *leaves and
flowers* in medical properties much resemble the erigeron
philadelphicum. They are valuable, says Dr. F. G. Hoener,
for coughs, colds, sores in the mouth or on the tongue or
tonsils. It may also be used as a gargle for the throat, and
as a wash for foul ulcers, sores and old wounds. It may
also be used as an injection for gonorrhœa in severe cases,
and gleet.

ERIODICTYON GLUTINOSUM.

Yerba Santa.   Northern California.

This is of thorough balsamic properties and quite stimulating to the bronchi, trachea and larynx. It is a superior
agent to be used in cases of chronic congestions and sluggish conditions, chronic laryngitis, aphonia, paralysis of
the vocal chords and chronic bronchitis.

In inflamed and irritated conditions it is best combined
with more relaxing agents.

It is a good agent to add to cough syrups when there is a
dry, hacking cough, a constant desire to clear the throat,
with sputa scanty and dry.

It almost completely disguises the bitter taste of quinine
and an aromatic syrup is an excellent vehicle for the administering of quinine in the proportion of about 8 to 1.

ERYNGIUM YACCÆFOLIUM.

Water Eryngo,   (E. Aquaticum.)
Button Snake Root.

The **roots** are a moderately diffusive stimulant, somewhat relaxing. It influences the mucous membrane, the circulation and the secernents.

In hot infusion it promotes diaphoresis, and increases expectoration.

Large doses prove emetic and cathartic. It is useful in the exanthems to bring out the eruptions, as in cases of small-pox, scarlatina and measles.

It is claimed that it will eliminate the viri of snakes. For this purpose it should be used internally and applied externally.

It influences the kidneys, the bladder and the urethra in the relief of chronic congestions and gleet. Combined with epigæa repens it is a superior tonic diuretic, useful in dropsy and nephritis. It also lessens erections and prevents seminal emissions. It lessens urethral, vaginal or rectal irritation and is valuable for diarrhœa, leucorrhœa, and hemorrhoids.

It makes a good addition to some alterative medicines for the elimination of impurities from the circulation, as in scrofula and syphilis.

ERYTHRONIUM AMERICANUM

Adder's-tongue.

The **leaves and roots** lose much of their power by drying. In the green or recently dried state it is a moderate stimulating antiseptic and astringent.

Dr. F G. Hoener recommends this agent in hæmatemesis and hæmaltirrhœa and says that it is a very cooling antiseptic.

ERYTHROXYLON COCA.

Cuca, Coca   South America.

The **leaves** of this plant somewhat resemble the leaves of the tea plant. The leaves are dried in the sun and are much used by the inhabitants of Peru, Ecuador, Columbia and Rio Negro, in which countries it grows wild, and it is also much cultivated and used in Bolivia

The Peruvian Indians use from one to three ounces a

day and seem to be well sustained by its use. When used in moderate quantities it increases nerve energy, removes drowsiness, gives an indisposition to sleep, much as tea or coffee. It enlivens the spirits and enables the Indians to bear cold, wet, bodily exertion, and even the want of food for whole days with apparent ease. But they will eat freely in the evening. But they find it necessary to use in conjunction therewith some alkali, as ashes or lime.

When well dried they have an agreeable odor and in infusion have a peculiar taste somewhat bitter and astringent.

Cocaine $C_{16}H_{19}NO_4$ or $C_{17}H_{21}NO_4$ is the alkaloid. It induces a series of symptoms affecting the nervous, respiratory, circulatory, vaso-motor and glandular systems.

Cocaine is a local anæsthetic.

Cocaine Hydro-chlorate.—This salt of cocaine usually comes in the form of crystals. Useful in ophthalmology, especially the large crystals. 1½ grs. to 1 dr. dis. water equals a 2 per cent. solution. Add 2¼ grs. for a 4 per cent. solution, and double this for an 8 per cent. solution.

These solutions should always be properly prepared.

The following is recommended as a dental sedative:

  Hyd. Cocaine   gtta xx
  Oil Cloves
  Chloroform   aa. dr. i
  Alcohol   oz. i

Dry the gum and apply a few drops around an aching tooth. Squeeze the gum between the finger and thumb for a few seconds. This will paralyze the gum. Then extract the tooth immediately. It may also be injected into the gum.

Coca Cordial or F. E. may be used.

Coca.—The leaves in a remarkable degree possess the power of sustaining the vital powers, under conditions of extraordinary fatigue and privation. Useful in nervous exhaustion, sleeplessness, mental depression, and in relieving the opium habit.

EUCALYPTUS GLOBULUS.

Eucalyptus.

This is an evergreen which grows vigorously in Australia and California. The leaves contain numerous pellucid glands filled with an essential *oil* which is quite diffusive, having a strong, penetrating, disagreeable odor. This

odor assists respiration and neutralizes marshy miasms
The tree is of very rapid growth and has been very fie-
quently planted for the latter purpose. The bark, flowers
and fruit are covered with glands containing the oil,
which is denominated eucalyptol This is an antiseptic
in fevers and catarrhal affections, in odontalgia, in gonorrhœa and gleet, in gastric ulceration and in diphtheria.

Dr. J E. Roop uses locally the following for endo-metri-
tis:

    Eucalyptol
    Fld Hydrastis   aa 1
    Glycerin   2 ·

For nasal catarrh use with the nasal douche or atomizer
two to four times a day.

    Eucalyptol
    Sodæ Bicarb.   aa. dr ı
    Glycerin   oz 1
    Aqua   oz xvı

This may also be used as a wash to cleanse offensive discharges from sores.

In hot infusion the *leaves* form a fine febrifuge and antiperiodic. They contain a resin which is precipitated when
water is added The infusion is quite stimulating to the
throat and fauces and is serviceable in membranous croup.

    F. E. Baptisia Tinc   dr. i
     "   Eucalyptus Gl.   dr ıss
    Aqua .   q s oz. ıv

Gargle with this every hour and swallow a half teaspoonful for sore throat

    F. E. Eucalyptus   oz. ı
    Aqua   q s. oz ıv

This is a good antiseptic gargle for diphtheria and scarlatina, or

    Eucalyptol   gtta xv

may be added to half a glass of water and used for the
same purpose

    For membranous croup use

    F. E. Eucalyptus   oz ı
    Syr. Simplex   oz ııı

Ten drops or more of the fluid extract or of the oil four
times a day will be found serviceable in dropsy

Dr. Hunter recommends the following in teaspoonful
doses every two or three hours for a dry, tickling cough
and in bronchitis:

Elixir Eucalyptus
F. E. Grindelia Robusta (soluble)
" Cypripedium Pub.   aa. oz. ss
Syr. Simplex   q. s. oz. iv
Tr. eucalyptus gtta. xx to xxx used three times a day is a specific for cystitis.

Eucalyptus, benzoate soda, boracic acid, yerba santa, yerba reuma, vaseline. Apply locally for nasal catarrh.

The following forms a good local anæsthetic: Cocaine, hydronaphthol, eucalyptus, mentha arvensis, baptisia, gaultheria, thyme, benzo-boracic acid.

Euthymol (eucalyptus and thymol antiseptic), a liquid preparation of wide utility. It is neither poisonous, irritant nor escharotic and is perfectly safe in any form of administration, whether internal or external. It possesses an agreeable odor and may be used instead of iodoform and carbolic acid. It equals either as an antiseptic and does not possess their objectionable characteristics. Each fluid ounce contains:

Oil Eucalyptus	3-8 M.
" Gaultheria	9-32 "
F. E. Baptisia Tinctoria	1 1-4 "
Boracic Acid	10 15-16 grs.
Menthol	5-64 "
Thymol	15-32 "

This article should not be exposed to the cold. It should be used as a spray or internally in doses of a fluid dram three or four times a day.

EUGENIA CHEQUEN.

Chekan.   (Myrtus Chekan) Chili.

The *leaves* are slightly stimulating, astringing and toning to the mucous membrane especially of the respiratory organs.

It contains a good percentage of volatile oil.

Chekan is tonic, expectorant, diuretic, and antiseptic.

It is chiefly valued in purulent bronchial inflammation, bronchial and cystic catarrh, emphysema, winter-cough, phthisis where the expectoration is too free, catarrhal conditions where the expectoration is difficult of removal and pneumonia.

Through its toning power it decreases purulent expectoration.

It also influences the serous membrane and is valuable in the treatment of rheumatism

EUGENIA JAMBOLANA

Jambul, Java Plum.   East Indies.

This is a tree of some considerable size, yielding an abundant crop of a pleasant and a much esteemed sub-acid fruit. In the East Indian peninsula it is abundant in both the wild and the cultivated states.

The *fresh bark* and the *leaves* yield a juice that is valued in the treatment of acute and chronic diarrhœa both of children and of adults.

The use of the *root* and of the *seed* give similar favorable results.

The bark and especially the seeds seem to have the property of arresting the excessive formation of sugar in cases of diabetes mellitis.

The physicians of India claim that not only does it cure diabetes, but that it enables the patient to continue to eat anything without augmentation of sugar in the urine

It arrests emaciation, assists in the general improvement of nutrition, giving natural sleep and a less tendency to micturation. It diminishes the density and quantity of urine and relieves the intolerable thirst of which those patients suffer.

It influences intestinal digestion and thus prevents excessive saccharification. It influences the vaso-motor centers and is hence useful in cases of diabetes of nervous origin. Large doses may produce nausea in some patients In order to better prevent the tendency to glycosuria the diet should be watched and restricted to skimmed milk, gluten bread and meat.

The powdered extract may be given in dose of 5 grs 3 times a day, or 5 to 8 grains of the powdered seeds may be given, or 6 to 8 drops of the fluid extract These doses may be much increased if desired It is usually best to begin with small does, say 5 drops of the fluid extract one hour after each meal and this dose increased one drop per dose per day or given as required

EUGENIA PIMENTA

Allspice   (Pimenta Officinalis)

The *berry* is a mild diffusive. stimulating, astringent aromatic

It is chiefly used as a vehicle for cathartics and bitter tonics.

In cholera infantum it is used to good advantage, relieves colic incident to cold and in hot infusion gives a good outward circulation and relieves irritation of the nervous system.

EUONYMOUS ATROPURPUREUS.

Wahoo.

The **bark** of the root is stronger than that of the trunk and twigs but all are used. It is a reliable, gently stimulating, bitter tonic hepatic. It is antiperiodic and laxative, and in large doses cathartic.

It will abort mild cases of ague. It may cause nausea but does not usually cause emesis.

It is positive in its action on the liver both as secretor of bile and as an excretant of the same from the gall cyst. Its tonic influence is extended throughout the mucous membrane. As a tonic hepatic it is a superior agent. Its mildness and yet positiveness are properties in such degree as, possessed by but few agents. It improves appetite and gastric digestion and slowly but persistently relieves cholæmic poisoning. Its qualities in billiousness and jaundice are not surpassed by scarcely any agent. In hypochondriasis it exerts a gentle depurating influence and gives relief to the nervous system. This depurative power makes it a good antiperiodic, persistingly relieving hepatic torpor. It is one of those agents that may be used for a long time without wearying the system by its use.

Large doses will prove cathartic, but for this purpose it is best combined with syrup juglans.

For chronic coughs where there is hepatic torpor it may be added to cough syrups with excellent results.

It may be added to alteratives especially in torpid conditions of the digestive tract.

In dyspepsia it is a tonic to the gastric membrane, but should be given in small quantities and in frequent doses.

In dropsy it is best combined with apocynum androsæmifolium or with some diuretic as triticum.

In rheumatism with suitable agents it is a favorite. But it must be remembered that the excellency of this agent lies in its gentle persistency and not in its excessive action.

F. E. Euonymous Atrop.　　　oz. i

Syr. Juglans Cin.　　　　q. s. oz. iv

Sig. Teaspoonful morning and evening or evening only for the relief or habitual constipation

F. E. Euonymous At.	dr v
" Leptandra Virg.	dr. ii
Podophyllin	grs iii
Syr Zingiberis	q. s. oz. iv

This is a stimulating hepatic and may be used in teapoonful doses once to three times a day.

EUPATORIUM ALTERNIFOLIUM.

False Boneset.

This *plant* grows on dry hillsides The leaves are lighter colored than the true boneset, but the flowers are very similar. The leaves have the same shape, but are loose around the stem, and gummy to the touch

Dr. F G. Hoener says he has employed this for many years with good success in typhoid and typhus fevers especially where there was much tympanitis, also in typhoid pneumonia and meningitis. He recommends the following for typhoid fever, to be taken in dessertspoonful doses every two or three hours.

Elix. Eupatorium Alter	oz. ii
" Betonica Lanc.	
" Chionanthus Virg	aa oz i

If desirable the eupatorium perfoliatum may be used instead of the alternifolium

EUPATORIUM AROMATICUM.

White Snake-root   (E Agertoides).

The *roots* are a pleasant stimulating and relaxing diffusive.

In hot infusion it influences a good flow of blood toward the surface, soothes the nervous system and increases expectoration It relieves the heart and brain from the pressure due to congestion by promoting and outward circulation and securing of an abundant warm perspiration in ague. congestive chills and billious fever it sustains the circulation, relieves restlessness and headache. In the treatment of eruptive diseases it is valuable in assisting in bringing out the eruption. It is also useful in typhoid fever, pneumonia, bronchitis and pleuritis Its being antispasmodic renders it useful in hysteria, dysmenorrhœa and in tardy parturition Cold preparations give a warming feeling in the stomach promote appetite. influence the salivary flow and materially increase the   renal flow. Combined with eupatorium purpureum it is a valuable diuretic. The stimulancy possessed by this agent makes it adapted to languid conditions of the mucous membrane.

EUPATORIUM PERFOLIATUM.

Boneset.

This *herb in bloom* is positively relaxing to the mucous membrane throughout, slightly stimulating, toning and antispasmodic. It is best when it first blooms. It is slow in its action but almost certain to relieve the liver. It is a favorite remedy for the prevention of fever. In large doses it is gently cathartic and gently tones the bowels throughout.

Boil the herb down to a solid extract, and this makes an excellent pill for indigestion. Night sweats yield to this better than to almost anything else even in phthisis. The relaxing properties are to some extent dissipated by the heat and the stimulancy, antispasmodic and tonic properties are left. I have frequently stopped night sweats in three or four days and in some cases in less time. And they are not likely to return. Give a pill from 1 to 3 hours. For chronic ague it cannot be excelled, but it is good for all fevers. Other medicines may be incorporated into this extract if needed when it is being formed into pills.

Eupatorin moderately represents this agent and the fluid extract is good also.

Whenever needed a large injection of this agent in infusion may be used to cleanse the bowel. It does well. In hot infusion in large doses it is nauseating and may be emetic. Small doses continued at short intervals prove diaphoretic.

I have no doubt that the persistent use of this agent has prevented many a case of typhoid and of remitting fevers, and if not entirely prevented, it has made them very much lighter than they would otherwise have been.

Dr. F. G. Hoener recommends the following for enteric fever:

Elix. Eupatorium Perfol.
     "   Jeffersonia Diph.
     "   Xanthoxylum Frax.
     "   Helonias   aa. oz. ί

M. S. One teaspoonful in as much sweetened water every hour or two according to the conditions present.

In hot infusion it is good for a cold especially when the tongue is foul and the liver torpid.

Eupatorium promotes the secretion of bile by the liver also its excretion by the gall cyst. This makes it valuable in many liver complaints especially in general biliousness.

In habitual constipation it is best when incorporated with more or less of syr juglans cinerea as required.

In skin diseases of hepatic origin it is of much importance if persisted in.

    Eupatorium Perfol.   5
    Zingiber Off.   1

gives a preparation for infusion far more diffusive and better in some cases of considerable torpor

    F. E. Eupatorium Perfol   oz. i
    Syr. Zingiber   q. s oz. iv

may be used for the same purpose.

As a rule this agent is not best when the bowels are too free, except when such is the result of torpor of the liver In such cases the last mentioned formula will be preferable.

This agent is also valuable in some forms of jaundice, both acute and chronic

    F. E. Eupatorium Perf.   oz i
      "   Zingiber   gtta x
    Syr Juglans Cin.   q. s oz iv

This is a reliable preparation for persistent constipation. It is rather pleasant and may be continued as long as needed

The fluid extract may be added to cough syrups when a more free expectoration is needed. In colds, bronchitis and pneumonia, especially if the patient be inclined to biliousness and constipation, a large injection may be given to free the lower bowels Then give hot infusion per oram till free emesis takes place. Relaxation of the mucous membrane generally will follow with good results. Subsequently smaller doses may be continued and the mucous membrane will become toned thereby The producing of a free outward circulation relieves the hyperæmic condition

If used in the eruptive fevers more stimulation is necessary. Eupatorium perfoliatum is valuable in the treatment of rheumatism especially of the gouty and bilious classes. In the former it cleanses and tones the gastric membrane and in the latter it relieves the liver and gall-cyst.

When you have an irritable condition of the stomach and nervous system with biliousness and constipation, small enemas of this agent may be used with much profit to the stomach and nerves. In whatever manner this agent is given it influences an outward circulation, soothes the mucous membrane and relieves nervous irritation.

Dr. F. G. Hoener recommends the following for cerebro-spinal meningitis:

 Elix. Eupatorium Perfol. oz. iii
  " Verbena Urtic.   oz. iss
  " Cypripedium
  " Cimicifuga Rac.
  " Leptandra Virg. aa. oz. i
  " Xanthoxylum Frax. oz. ss

M. S. One dessertspoonful every two hours. Give a hot sponge bath, and if the bowels are constipated use enemata.

The Doctor also says, In the last epidemic (1891) of la grippe, influenza, catarrhal fever or epidemic catarrh as you please to call it, I cured over seven hundred cases with the use of the following prescription:

 Elix, Eupatorium Perfol.
  " Eupatorium Alternif. aa. oz. iiss
  " Agrimonia Eup.
  " Verbena Hast.
or " Betonica Lanc.
  " Leptandra Virg. oz. i

M. S. One dessert or tablespoonful every two or three hours according to the case. I did not lose a case by heart failure as others claimed in their practice with the use of their agents.

EUPATORIUM PURPUREUM.

Queen of the Meadow.

The **root** is a relaxing and very mildly stimulating diuretic. It chiefly influences the urinary and genital organs. It relaxes, gently stimulates and tones the pelvic viscera and influences the sympathetic nervous system. In the suppression of the menses it is splendid and always safe. It needs to be given in large quantities, but always leaves a toned condition. It is valuable in uterine and vaginal irritation. It is very soothing to the kidneys and gently toning by the relief of irritation and increasing the flow of urine. In these respects it is one of the most reliable agents. It tones the urinary mucous membrane and enables by the process of relaxation and some stimulation to cast off sediments that may have accumulated upon its surface. Thus it is that after taking some large doses of this agent that the urine will be found full of deposit of one kind or of another

In typhoid fever it needs to be combined with more stimulating agents as juniper or barosma.

When needed it is an excellent addition to alterative compounds. In spermatorrhœa, irritable prostatic troubles, painful or scalding micturition, gonorrhœa, urethral irritation, aching back, and general pelvic weakness it is one of the best agents It may be thoroughly relied upon.

Eupatorium Purpur. 3
Epigæa Rep. 2
Mitchella Rep. 1

This makes a good compound for such pelvic troubles.

With helonias or aletris it is excellent in barrenness. These three agents are among the most powerful in that direction. They positively tone the uterus and ovaries, and neither of them should be used much by ladies who are given to frequent conceptions.

EUPHORBIA HETERODOXA.

Alveloz.

The *milk juice* of this plant applied in cancroid ulceration promptly destroys the affected tissues layer by layer. It produces profuse suppuration and some degree of irritation and dermatitis with but little pain It acts as an irritant and escharotic and results in the destruction of morbid tissue, which is replaced by healthy granulation. It is of importance in cancroid and syphilitic ulcers, lupus of the nose, epithelioma of the lip, ulcerated epithelioma of the nose, malignant ulceration of the os uteri. In cases that have become thoroughly constitutional there is no cure, but this agent will even then make life somewhat more endurable.

EUPHRASIA OFFICINALIS.

Eye-bright.

The *leaves* are a mild, stimulating, astringent tonic, influencing chiefly the mucous membrane, and useful wherever there is too free discharge, whether it be of the bladder, urethra, bowels, or bronchi. In cholera infantum when there is an excessive greenish mucous discharge, in leucorrhœa, gonorrhœa, cystic catarrh, and catarrhal ophthalmia this agent may be used with profit.

In cases of congestions and inflammations of the eyes, especially of any torpid grade, it is valuable as an eye-wash.

In nasal catarrh when the discharge is too free it may be used with the douche or atomizer and is a good cleansing remedy. It is an astringent but is not drying and hence is more toning to the membrane.

FABIANA IMBRICATA.

Pichi.   South America.

The *leaves* of this plant are a relaxing and stimulating tonic diuretic.

I have never used this but in one case of cystic congestion and then with excellent results. The case was one of much severity. The local spasms were terrible. I had usually relieved such by the use of eucalyptus, but this was in the night and I had no eucalyptus. I had an ounce of fabiana and believed here was a case for a fair trial. I used it in small doses every five or ten minutes. It was not long till the patient quieted down, and began to pass urine in small quantities and was soon relieved of both the pain and the congestion.

I administered the F. E. of the agent in some hot infusion of zingiber. I have no doubt it is also valuable in cystic catarrh. It is soothing and cleansing to the urinary mucous membrane.

FAGUS FERRUGINA.

Beech.

The *leaves* are a relaxing, demulcent, slightly stimulating and toning diuretic. They influence the mucous membrane and especially that of the kidneys. They are useful in cystic catarrh, cystitis, nephritis, urethritis, scalding urine. It relaxes, soothes, gently stimulates and gently increases the quantity of urine.

A hot fomentation of this agent is valuable to be used over the bowels, lungs, stomach or bladder in cases of inflammation and also to be applied over painful swellings.

Dr F. G. Hoener says

Fagus Ferrugina Cort

Rhus Glabra Bac. aa. in equal parts

is a good recipe for diabetes.

FERULA FŒTIDA.

Asafœtida.

The roots yield a thick, milky juice of a peculiar fœtid odor. When dried this *gum-resin* is a penetrating diffusive, stimulating and relaxing, antispasmodic nervine

It is best given in pills or capsules, but nothing will disguise it fully

Though a nervine, its influence is extended to the circulation and to the mucous membrane.

It is an excellent antispasmodic and it is a pity that its odor cannot be disguised so that it can be administered in some unobjectionable form In nervous irritability, in hysteria, in hypochondria, in convulsions, in meningitis, in double vision, in spermatorrhœa, in restlessness, in insomnia and in dysmenorrhœa it is one of our very useful agents.

For colds it is a good remedy, and in bronchial troubles it is a good expectorant It is a good remedy to be used for nervous females with scanty or tardy menstruation. It gradually increases the flow

It may be dissolved and used per enema and thus influence the bowels and the pelvic nerves If it be retained its influence will extend through the entire system Give it in the evening and allow it to remain all night. By morning the nerves will be thoroughly quieted. This is an excellent way to treat the hysterical and those habitually nervous. The whole system will thus slowly feel its effects and be calmed and toned thereby. Triturate one-half to one dram in four ounces of tepid water for enemata

Even the odor is soothing and stimulating to the nervous system. These little asafœtida and camphor bags that many times we find put on children's necks and hung next to their bodies, though we smile at it, I have no doubt they have a soothing and stimulating effect on those wearing them, especially so if it be hung over the child's stomach in a thin cloth.

Even though the odor is unpleasant it is not so unpleasant to the stomach In fact though some ladies become nettled because it is prescribed for them, many others soon become accustomed to it and do not dislike it. It may be administered in some wine one-half ounce to eight ounces and triturated thoroughly

A syrup may be formed by thoroughly triturating one ounce of the gum in boiling water and then adding two pounds of sugar, and enough water to fill one pint

Asafœtida	oz. i
Valerian	dr. ii
Capsicum	grs x

This is a good antispasmodic and may be made into pill form or used in the form of syrup. It will be found useful in congestion of the brain, inflammation of the brain, meningitis and the double vision at times incident thereto. It is a superior remedy in such cases.

FERULA SUMBUL.

Musk root.   Central and Northeastern Asia

The **root** has a strong, pleasant, musky odor It has a faintly sweetish taste which soon becomes a slightly bitterish aromatic It is a rather positive stimulating and relaxing antispasmodic   It arrests spasms and relieves and tones the muscles.

Ferula Sumbul
Piper Meth.
Rhamus Pursh. aa. equal parts.

This is rather effective in the treatment of epilepsy and hysteria

Sumbul hardens the muscular fibres of the arteries and stimulates and soothes the blood current.

With lobelia it is valuable in the treatment of asthma, and with aralia rac. it will be found useful in bronchitis

This agent will also be found useful in gastralgia, enteralgia, and dysmenorrhœa

FERRUM

Iron

Some preparations of iron are harmless, some are not so harmless and some are very injurious

Chalybeate waters are chiefly valued because of the iron and sulphur ingredients they contain.   These waters largely influence the kidneys and tend to cleanse both the urinary and the intestinal tracts, and leave these parts more or less toned.

The chief value of sanative iron preparations is that they are stimulating to intestinal digestion. Some of them more than others, some of them influencing in one way and some in another.

Beware of compounding the iron preparations with vegetable astringents. Such will give you inky results.

Detannated prunus may be combined with iron.

All the iron preparations are used for one or other grade of gastric or intestinal indigestion, and the accompanying anæmia.

Ferri et Potassæ Tartras is soluble in water and is laxative to the bowels, usually coloring dark the stools. It is an excellent preparation for anæmia and intestinal indigestion, especially when there is a tendency to constipation.

Ferri et Pot. Tart.	grs. x
Hydrastia Sulp.	gr. i
F. E. Zingiber	gtta iii
Aqua	q. s. oz. iv

Sig. Teaspoonful before meals, between meals and before retiring.

Ferri et Potassæ Citras is more soluble in water than the above but may be used for the same purposes. The slight acidulation in this preparation may be more suitable to some stomachs. Either of these preparations makes a good tonic for depressed conditions.

Ferri Carbonas Præcipitans is a stimulating astringent useful in more or less debilitated conditions complicated with dysentery or diarrhœa in either acute or chronic form. It is useful in gastric and intestinal dyspepsia, cholera infantum, chronic dysentery and chronic diarrhœa.

Precip. Carb. Ferri	dr. ss
Tr. Kino	oz. iv
F. E. Zingiber	gtta. v
Comp. Syr. Rhei et Pot	q. s oz viii

This is an excellent compound for the conditions above named.

Ferri Carbonas Saccharatus is a grayish brown preparation which may be used in two to four grain capsules three times a day for the same purposes as the last mentioned

Ferri Pulvis is a gray powder, one of the best of the powdered forms. It may be given one to two grains with each meal. This is also denominated hydrogen iron. It is quite stimulating and is best for debilitated conditions.

Ferri Oxidum Hydratum is frequently used as an antidote in cases of arsenic poisoning.

Munsel's Solution of Iron (Perchloride of Iron) is a fluid preparation of iron of the strongest styptic powers for the arrest of hemorrhages.

Thiana is a good preparation of ferrum manufactured by the Yale Chemical Co., Atlanta, Ga., and for sale by C. T. Bedford of Indianapolis, Indiana.

Thiana   3
Hydrastia Sulph.   1

Given in capsules is a good aid in the treatment of indigestion, colic pains, diarrhœa, flatulence, and insomnia.

Dialyzed Iron is the result of dialysis. A vessel containing the required salts of iron is closed by a membrane of parchment and placed in a vessel of distilled water with the orifice downward. Part of the liquid in the upturned vessel passes through the membrane and mingles with the distilled water. The separation will be complete. The acids will be transmitted to the water and leave the oxide of iron in the dialyzer. In this way dialyzed iron is obtained. It is very soluble in water devoid of styptic properties, almost tasteless and readily made into a syrup.

Chloro-Ferrine is made by McCoy, Howe Co., Indianapolis, Ind., for the treatment of diphtheria and acute diseases of the throat. It is a combination of chlorine, ferric iron, chlorates, etc., in conjunction with an agreeable menstruum, valuable for diphtheria, follicular tonsilitis, thrush, ulceration of the mouth or tonsils, syphilitic ulceration, chronic pharyngitis, enlargement of the tonsils and ordinary sore throat.

It is used internally, locally or both as conditions indicate. It is best undiluted. The dose for an adult internally is one teaspoonful every three or four hours. In diphtheria the parts should also be frequently atomized, or the patient may swallow some after each local treatment.

FŒNICULUM CAPILLACEUM.

Fennel Seed.   Europe.

The *seed* are a relaxing and stimulating, aromatic, diffusive carminative. They are chiefly used as a vehicle for the administering of bitter tonics and cathartics.

The *oil* may be used for the same general purposes.

Fœniculum Cap.	1
Sweet Orange Peel	½
Carbonate Magnesia	3
Sugar	2

Triturate thoroughly and give in hot water to increase the lacteal fluid.

Fœniculum Cap.	1
Parsley Root	½
Licorice root	½
Carbonate Magnesia	3
Sugar	2

This is another formula used for the same purpose

FRAGARIA VESCA

Strawberry.

The *leaves* are a pleasant, mild, astringent tonic to the mucous membrane. In diarrhœa and dysentery it is soothing, toning and strengthening but not drying. It is an excellent remedy for children's diarrhœa and intestinal debility. If given in hot infusion they influence the circulation toward the surface and soothe and quiet the nerves.

The *berries* are a pleasant vegetable acid for convalescence when an acid is proper An excellent syrup is made by expressing a pint of juice and adding a pound of granulated sugar This may be used as an acid vehicle in bitter medicines and the juice unsweetened makes a nice acidulated drink in convalescence from fevers The berry itself is not admissible until seeded.

FRASERA CAROLINENSIS,

American Columbo

The *root* is a reliable mild, stimulating and slightly astringent tonic. It is moderately bitter but not unpleasantly so. Its chief influence is expended upon the alvine mucous membrane as a tonic. Its best use is for that class of persons who have a weak digestion and are more or less subject to an extra freeness of the bowels. It is an excellent tonic in typhoid fever and hastens convalescence, but other agents had better be used when there is a tendency to constipation If diarrhœa be troublesome throughout the course of typhoid, frasera will give good results.

In gastric ulceration this agent will usually be well

received. In gastric catarrh you will find frasera one of your most valuable and most reliable agents.

It improves the appetite and assists digestion.

In combination with uterine and vaginal tonics it extends its influence in that direction and becomes a very excellent addition in cases of uterine and vaginal ulceration, prolapsus uteri and vaginal weakness.

This agent may be used with excellent effect with children having a weak digestion and a chronic diarrhœa.

It is also a good wash for aphthous sore mouth.

An infusion forms an excellent vaginal wash for a weak vagina, prolapsus uteri and leucorrhœa. The fluid extract of this agent may be used for all the purposes of the agent.

Frasera Car.
Leonurus Card.
Anthemis Nob.
Cypripedium Pub.   aa. 4
Citrus Auran. Cort.   1

This forms an agreeable nervine tonic for chlorotic ladies.

Frasera Car.   4
Aletris   3
Hydrastis Can.
Citrus Auran Cort.   aa. 1

This forms an excellent tonic for weakly ladies with a tendency to miscarriage, and for those having a poor digestion, a degenerate leucorrhœa, general pelvic weakness and more or less menorrhagia:

FRAXINUS AMERICANA.

White Ash.

The *bark* of the root and the inner bark of the trunk yields a mild, persistent, stimulating tonic alterant influencing chiefly the digestive apparata. The mucous membrane and secernents all feel its effects. It influences the liver both in the secretion of bile and in its excretion from the gall cyst   It also influences the peristaltic action of the bowels in defecation. It increases the flow of urine and cleanses and tones the urinary tract.

In chronic jaundice and chronic biliousness, chronic hepatic congestions and general hepatic torpor and skin eruptions arising therefrom.

With diuretics and hepatics it is valuable in dropsy. It is a slow, steady, cleansing and toning agent to the whole system. Its steady, persistent toning influence makes this agent very valuable in its influence on the kidneys.

The nervous system also feels its influence and it is of much importance in the treatment of insanity. It depurates the whole system and tones and strengthens the nerves, sympathetic, cerebral and spinal In hysteria, hypochondria, cholæmia and uræmia there are but few medicines that will do better work.

Fraxinus Am.	6
Aralia His.	3
Gentiana Lut	2
Taraxacum D. L.	4
Xanthoxylum Frax. Cort	1

This forms a preparation excellent in chronic biliousness, jaundice, habitual constipation, hypochondria, anæmia, chlorosis, insanity.'

It forms a good addition to cough syrups for chronic coughs when there are bilious conditions to be met.

FRAXINUS SAMBUCIFOLIA.

Black Ash.

This *bark* is about the same as the americana and may be used for the same general purposes. It is said by some to have a slight degree of astringency.

Fraxinus Sam. Cort. Ashes	2
Acacia Vera	
Valeriana Off.	aa 1

Make into pills to be used night and morning for sleeplessness.

An infusion is said to be good for the expelling of pin worms.

FRAXINUS ORNUS.

Flowering Ash, Manna Tree.

This tree yields a light yellowish, sweetish exudation from its stems. When treated with alcohol it is white sweet, odorless and soluble in hot water

The *manna* is a mild laxative, one of the most pleasant agents to be used for the relief of constipation, especially of children. For adults it is best used as a vehicle for some bitter remedy

When an infant which nurses the bottle is chronically constipated, manna may be dissolved and added to the milk

FUCUS VESICULOSUS.

Bladder-wrack.

This *plant* has a reputation as an antifat, claiming that it diminishes the fat without in any respect injuring the health. It influences the mucous membrane, the serous membrane and the lymphatics. It is a gently stimulating and toning alterant. It is one of those slow, persistent agents that require time to accomplish the desired results. It is stimulating to the absorbents and especially influences the fatty globules. Its best action is observed in individuals having a cold, torpid, clammy skin and loose flabby rolls of fat. It is an agent that gives better results in cases of morbid obesity than in those cases of a healthy character. When using it as an antifat it is best to exclude farinaceous foods and beer and prescribe an active life. It is best to begin with small doses and gradually increase to larger doses. Soon the urine becomes more abundant and the stomach is invigorated by its use.

By its influence on the serous membrane it is valuable in cases of gout, rheumatism and dropsy especially for those of plethoric habit.

It may be used in form of pill, fluid extract or infusion.

This agent seems to influence the starches and prevents their being formed into fats.

Where there is a tendency to constipation in cases of obesity the following will be found best adapted: '   -

Fucus Ves.
Juniperus Fructu. ∖
Juglans Cin.   aa. in equal parts in infusion.

GALBANUM OFFICINALE.

Galbanum.   Persia.

The *gum* has a disagreeable, fœtid odor, an acrid, pungent and unpleasant taste. It may be dissolved by trituration in water or vinegar. It much resembles asafœtida. Its use is almost entirely superceded by that agent.

GALIUM APARINE.

Cleavers.

This *herb* is a soothing, relaxing, diffusive diuretic. It materially increases the urine and relieves irritation. It is valuable in scalding urine, and irritable bladder and urethra; in the inflammatory stage of gonorrhœa it relieves the irritation and soothes the nervous system.

In hot infusion this is a diaphoretic and may be used to good advantage in fevers where there is a necessity to favor a good free outward circulation and it relieves the nervous system An inspissated juice of the fresh herb is a valuable agent in acute gonorrhœa given every 3 hours.

GALIUM VERUM.

Yellow Ladies' Bed-straw.   Europe.

The *flowers* have an agreeable odor, and are antispasmodic. They are useful in nervous affections.

The *herb* is inodorous and a mild, bitter, stimulating astringent, influencing the mucous membrane and the nervous system The bruised plant has been used to color cheese yellow. The *roots* dye red

It is a valuable tonic in dyspepsia, and is an emmenagogue of some importance. For this last named purpose it is best used in hot infusion, when it is also valuable for dysmenorrhœa.

GARCINIA MANGOSTANA.

Mangosteen.   India, Malay.

This is a very handsome tree growing from twenty to thirty feet high. It has beautiful dark green foliage. It bears a finely flavored and most palatable fruit about the size of an apple. Near the equator it fruits twice a year.

The *bark* is a stimulating, antiseptic, astringent tonic to the mucous membrane, but does not seem to produce constipation It can be used as a valuable aid in acute inflammation, typhoid fever, cholera infantum and diarrhœa.

In cases of uterine inflammation, and ulceration of the cervix, paint the cervix with the full strength of the fluid extract, or make an infusion to be used by injection. This will overcome very obstinate cases.

It lessens catamenial pain, cures leucorrhœa and diminishes the menstrual flow.

In nasal catarrh spray the mucous surfaces thoroughly. It will be very beneficial in the more moist forms

It may be employed in the treatment of hemorrhages from either uterus. bowels, or lungs, and it also lessens muco-purulent discharges from either of these sources.

In light forms of diphtheria the fluid extract in full strength may be sprayed into the throat, or it may be diluted as required for inflamed or irritated conditious of the pharynx.

It forms a good antiseptic wash for ulcers. It cleanses and tones the surface. It will also give good results in dermatisis.

The *leaves and flowers* form a good wash for sore gums and sore mouth.

F. E. Garcinia Mang.   1
    Aqua   5 to 10

M. S. One teaspoonful every one to three hours.

In small doses this is easily taken and causes no gastric disturbance. Its action is rapid and positive. In cases of uterine hemorrhage, whether from threatened or actual miscarriage, from the presence of uterine tumors or during the menopause, this may be considered a specific.

It is also very valuable in the treatment of dysentery and diarrhœa, acute or chronic, and especially where there is indigestion and more or less debility.

GARRYA FREMONTII.

California Fever Bush.   California.

This is an ornamental evergreen shrub growing from five to ten feet high. The *leaves* excite a profuse saliva, give a sense of gastric and intestinal warmth and impart a persistent bitter taste closely resembling that of cinchona.

It is a gently stimulating tonic and antiperiodic.

It stimulates the circulation and especially so when used in hot infusion. In large doses it creates a cerebral fullness and tinnitus aurium somewhat similar to those symptoms when induced by quinine. It leaves no other unpleasant after-effects.

In dysentery and diarrhœa where these conditions show some signs of malaria this agent will give good results.

In hot infusion it will abort many a case of malarial fever, and cases of chronic ague soon yield to it.

GAULTHERIA PROCUMBENS.

Wintergreen.

The *leaves* and the *oil* therefrom are a very diffusive, relaxing and stimulating diuretic, carminative and antiseptic. It will relieve flatulence, colic, and assist digestion and diuresis.

This agent is chiefly used as a vehicle for alteratives and other compounds Its taste and odor are both usually agreeable to patients

Ol Gaultheria
" Sassafras   aa. oz 1
" Eucalyptus
" Lavender   aa. oz ss
Thymol   dr i
Carb. Magnesia   oz. ii

Mix the oils, add the thymol, shake the preparation to dissolve. Pulverize the magnesia and add the oils by thorough trituration Then take

Alcohol   oz.xvi
Aqua   oz. XLviii
Sodium Salicylate   dr iii

Shake these last till dissolved and add the former ingredients as above combined.

This is an excellent formula for the making of listerine. It is an antiseptic wash for wounds, abscesses, and for the maintenance of surgical cleanliness.

In chronic conjunctivitis evert the lids and paint the conjunctival surfaces with pure listerine or diluted as the case may require

There are many formulæ for the making of listerine One combines thymus, eucalyptus. baptisia, gaultheria, mentha arvensis and benzo-boracic acid Another formula combines hydrastis, phytolacca. salicylic acid, boracic acid, mentha arvensis, thymus and hamamelis

The Lambert Pharmaceutical Co , of St Louis, have gained a national reputation from the value of their

LAMBERT'S LISTERINE

Is a non-toxic, non-irritating and non-escharotic antiseptic, composed of ozoniferous essences, vegetable antiseptics and benzo-boracic acid; sufficiently powerful to make surgically clean—aseptic—all parts of the human body.

Listerine at 60 degs. Farhenheit is a clear amber-color liquid, but as the temperature is reduced it becomes opaque; this characteristic of Listerine is caused by the partial congelation of its essential constituents,   its brilliancy is resumed at 60 degrees · It is of a slightly acid reaction, a powerful. fragrant aromatic odor and pungent taste, both of which are agreeable; its specific gravity is lighter than water, with which it mixes in any proportion without precipitation or separation of its constituents; this genial compatibility extends to most of the standard remedies of the Materia Medica.   The boracic acid constituent is beautifully exhibited in the atomization of Listerine.

Listerine is a most powerful non-toxic antiseptic; it possesses qualities that are more pronounced in preventing fermentation than in destroying the products thereof, its germicidal value equalling but a five per cent. solution of carbolic acid, although its non-toxic effect, enabling its continued administration or application, renders it of extremely greater value than any dilution of the corrosive and poisonous agents for the destruction of micro-organisms.

As a dressing for wounds, whether accidental or operative, and later in the suppurative stage, Listerine in various degrees of dilution proves thoroughly trustworthy: for treating catarrhal conditions of every locality, Listerine has proven peculiarly acceptable because of its non-poisonous effect, its efficacy as an alterative-antiseptic, and for its detergent, antiphlogistic properties, as well as for the cooling and refreshing effect which its use imparts to the tissues.

Listerine is well adapted for use in the throat or nasal cavities, especially by atomizing or spraying, and for purulent otitis, it is probably unrivaled.

Applied to ulcerous or mucous patches, and in contagious catarrhal affections, Listerine alone or as an adjuvant is a boon to the afflicted because of its freedom from, and power to disguise, objectionable odors.

Listerine is valuable in skin diseases, as urticaria, eczema, pruritus; in eruptive fevers, etc., and in cases where the skin is excoriated or affected with vesicles, pustules or crusts.

Internally, in certain forms of fermentative dyspepsia, Listerine—a true antiferment—is very valuable, and equally so in summer diarrhœas of infants and children.

In typhoid fever Listerine is extensively prescribed, agreeably diluted, both for its antiseptic effect and to improve the condition of the stomach for the reception of nourishment. Listerine by inhalation and by internal administration is a valued means of attaining antiseptic influence in the treatment of phthisis, not only in the later stages during the production and absorption of pus, but also in the earlier process of infection.

GENTIANA LUTEA.

Gentian   .   Europe

The *root* is an intense and permanent bitter, stimulating tonic Though intensely bitter, when given in small doses it is usually well received by the stomach,'and it promotes appetite and digestion, stimulates the circulation, thoroughly tones the digestive organs, and is especially valuable in languid conditions and in that of general debility It is one of the most serviceable of tonics, influencing the secernents as well as the mucous membrane. Its action on the liver is that of a cholagogue rather than to influence in the secreting of bile It influences the portal circulation somewhat similar to hydrastis. It gives good service in biliousness and jaundice. Its tonic powers make it also a good vermifuge, and enable it to slowly promote peristaltic action. It is also somewhat antiperiodic.

The sensitive stomach will receive it only in minute doses without producing a persistent nausea

In general use it is best combined with milder agents

Gentiana Lut.	1
Orange Peel	
Coriander Seed	aa 2

This in infusion forms a good, stimulating and pleasant tonic.

F. E. Gentiana Lut	4
" Citrus Aur Cort	2 .
" Cardamon Sem.	1

This is also a good tonic

Gentiana Lut.	4
Cinchona Cali	8
Citrus Vulg Cort	2
Canella Alba	1

This forms a valuable tonic for languid conditions.

F. E. Gentiana Lut	dr i
Syr Zingiber	q s. oz iv

This is an excellent tonic for a weak stomach and a poor digestion, taken just before meals

GENTIANA OCHROLEUCA.

American Gentian   .

The *root* of this agent possesses somewhat similar properties to those of the European variety, but is usually better received by the stomach. It is a positive, bitter, stimulating tonic. It influences the gastric and intestinal mucous membrane and the liver and gall cyst. As a general tonic, especially if combined with alterants, it exerts a good influence upon the glandular system. Where there is a poor appetite, a weakened digestion and hepatic debility or jaundice and biliousness,'its tonic power is quite valuable. In very debilitated forms of dropsy but few tonics can be used to better advantage and it is one of the most valuable agents to be added to alterant compounds.

F. E. Gentiana Och.   dr. i
"   Euonymous Atr.   dr. ii
'·   Eupatorium Perf.   dr. iv
Syr. Zingiber   q. s. oz. iv

This is a good hepatic tonic for agues.

F. E. Gentiana Och.   dr. i
Capsicum   gr. i
Comp. Syr. Rhei et Pot.   oz. i.

This will break a chill.

Gentian, salicine and capsicum will do the same thing.

F. E. Gentiana Och.   dr. ii
Citrus Vulg.
Coriandrum Sat.   aa. grs. xxx

This made into a syrup is a pleasant tonic.

McCoy, Howe Co., Indianapolis, Ind., make a preparation of which each fluid dram represents,

Gentian
Wahoo   aa. grs. ii
Tr. Iron Chloride   gtta. v

Dr. N. D. Woodward uses this and speaks highly of its efficiency and palatableness, its permanence and its elegant appearance.

GERANIUM MACULATUM.

Cranesbill.

The **root** is a pleasant, positive, tonic astringent. It is only moderately drying, but is persistent and effective. It is one of our most excellent astringent agents. Its chief influence is expended upon the alvine mucous membrane throughout. It is applicable in the treatment of sore mouth or gums, mercurial salivation, spongy gums, catarrhal ophthalmia, leucorrhœa, gleet, dysentery, diarrhœa.

It is a good local and constitutional styptic for hemorrhage from the nose, lungs, stomach, bowels, or uterus.

The fluid extract is a good application to the uvula in case of elongation Apply frequently.

In typhoid fever in case of excessive discharges, whether tæcal or sanious, this agent is one of the most valuable. The addition of a little capsicum will at times be valuable.

Diluted with water or combined with comp. syr. rhei et pot. this agent is one of the most valuable in the treatment of severe cases of cholera infantum.

Geraniin represents this agent quite well, but is less stimulating and more astringent than the herb itself or its fluid extract

GERMS AND GERMICIDES

By ALBERT W. KELLEY, A M., PH. D., M. D,

Professor of Bacteriology, Microscopy and Histology in Chicago Physio-Medical College

In no department of medicine has there been greater advancement than in ætiology. But this knowledge of the cause of disease is of comparatively recent origin; in fact, it is largely the work of the present generation.

The vague notions and theories advanced by former physicians ascribing all disease to impurity of the blood, epidemics, and discrasia of chemical composition, while not without some valid ground, were at best vague and unsatisfactory

With the advent of the microscope, which was invented about the latter part of the sixteenth century, was ushered in a new epoch in this department of medicine. Soon after the introduction of the microscope, minute organisms, which before were unknown, were found in decomposing organic substances. Various conjectures and theories were advanced as to the nature and office of these minute organisms.

As early as 1645 Kircher suggested that diseases might be due to similar organisms, but owing to lack of facilities with which to prove his theory, but little, if any, attention was paid to his teaching About 1710 Anthony Van Leuwenhœck, of Holland, had so improved his microscope that he was enabled to demonstrate the fact that large numbers of micro-organisms existed in normal saliva, in fæcal matter and in vegetable infusions He carried his observations to that extent that he described and attempted to give a classification of some of the more marked varieties.

But it remained for Mueller, of Copenhagen, to give us the first description and classification of bacteria that was in any degree correct. However, it was not until some years later that authentic evidence was obtained connecting germs with disease, when Davanes and Rayer demonstrated the presence of rod-shaped bacteria in the blood of animals suffering with splenic fever. However but little attention was paid to the discovery until Pasteur and others working along the same line published the results of their research, which went far to prove the ætiological nature of micro-organisms.

The researches of Robert Koch upon the history of the bacteria or bacilli of splenic fever have removed all doubts of their ætiological signification. In 1883 Koch startled the medical world by the announcement that consumption was a germ disease and dependent upon the presence, in the affected tissues, of an organism which he named *"bacillus tuberculosis."*

This statement met with strong opposition, both among physicians and the laity; but Koch so fortified his statements, both by experimental and clinical evidences, that it may now be regarded as fully demonstrated. Two years later(in 1885)Koch showed that Asiatic cholera is due to the presence of bacterial organisms—the *"comma bacillus"* Schutz and Lœffer discovered the bacillus of glanders in 1882; Eberth the bacillus which is now generally accepted as the cause of typhoid fever, in 1880; Fehleisen the micrococcus of erysipelas, in 1883; Neissen the micrococcus of gonorrhœa, in 1879. Obermeier announced the discovery of the spirillum of relapsing fever as early as 1868. In 1881 Laveran discovered the micro-organisms of malaria—*malaria plasmodia.* These minute organisms are found in the blood of persons suffering from malaria, and have lately been carefully observed, and according to concurrent testimony they do not belong to bacteria, being really of animal origin, among the protozoa. Pneumonia may also be included with the germ diseases, since the demonstration of Sternberg, Nova and Frankel of the constant presence of the micrococcus Pasteurii in the sputa in that disease. The careful observation and exhaustive experimental research made by those mentioned, as well as that of many others who have devoted years to the development of this department of science, have established the germ theory of disease upon a firm foundation. A large number of diseases are undoubtedly of parasitic origin. Almost daily new facts are discovered which substantiate the germ theory of disease, and as far as the theory is applicable, it eliminates the factor of "accident" from the consideration of ætiology, and disease is assigned a legitimate place in the curriculum of nature

According to the commonly accepted definition, disease is a disturbance of the normal and functional activities of some one or different parts of the organism; the reaction to an unaccustomed influence   According to the germ theory the foreign influence producing functional disturbance is, in many cases, due to the presence of foreign microscopic organisms in the interior of the body, and the number of diseases revealed by the germ theory is constantly growing more numerous.

Especially is this true of that class of diseases generally acknowledged to be contagious. By contagion we mean the transmission of disease from one individual to another, either by direct contact or indirect, as through air, water, clothing, etc

No sharp distinction can be drawn between contagion and infection   Although various attempts have been made to do so, none of the propositions are beyond criticism   The two classes of disease seem to overlap each other, so that no real division occurs.

Infectious disease depends upon a specific agent, as does the contagious, and there is valid ground for the belief that all contagious and infectious diseases depend upon some constant and specific element in each individual disease, this agent in a great majority of cases remains unchanged   However there appears to be an occasional exception; thus the *streptococcus pyogenes* of Rosenbach and the *streptococcus erysipelatis* of Fehleisen, are to all appearance identical, and both are presumed to be the cause of puerperal fever, erysipelas and suppuration. These apparent exceptions will probably disappear when a more definite knowledge of these particular organisms has been obtained.

While no well defined distinction can be drawn between the germs of contagion and those of infection, experience goes to prove that certain germs whose habitat by nature or adaptation is in the human body, and the spores of which can pass from one person to another, where they develop and produce disease.

Another class of germs, those of infection, differ from those of contagion in this, that they have one stage of development in the human body and another in some other media. Thus they cannot reproduce the disease until after they have passed through their second stage of development. This second stage may be in the soil, water or elsewhere. When they have passed through this secondary stage the spores are again ready for the production of disease in man.

In this way a whole section of country may become infected, and persons attacked by the disease who have not been exposed to the sick, or even near them. Such diseases as typhoid, cholera and yellow fever afford good examples of this class of diseases.

The theory of infection has not been satisfactorily demonstrated with each specific germ, but general experience affords adequate proof of the correctness of the theory. We find in the life history of several of the parasitic fungi producing disease in plants, an exact parallel. The common *puccinia graminis*, producing the disease known as *rust,* which appears upon wheat and oats, affords a good example of this cycle of life. The spores found upon the growing grain do not again grow upon the wheat, but grow luxuriantly upon the leaves of certain netted-vernel leaved plants; and the spores formed upon these plants will grow upon wheat or oats, etc., where they produce the disease of rust and thus complete the cycle of life of the fungus.

While the germ theory affords the best and most satisfactory explanation of such facts as are known about infection and contagion, it does not necessarily follow that it satisfactorily explains every occurrence in the dissemination of disease; and it is highly probable that future development will throw new light upon many of these much disputed questions.

Experience has demonstrated that of the large number of distinctive species of bacteria, only a few species are known to be pathogenic; so while the earth, air and water everywhere may be filled with teeming myriads of the minute organisms, only a comparatively few kinds are known to take part in the production of diseases.

The mere presence of *bacteria* is not, in itself, a sufficient cause of disease; but that there are certain kinds of bacteria that uniformly induce disease, when they are inoculated in or gain entrance to the body, is also well known, as well as the fact that certain poisons known as ptomains originate in connection with the disease-producing germs.

These poisons are the product of the micro-organisms, produced in connection by the functional activity of the organism in its process of digestion, growth and excretion, in the same way that alcohol is produced by yeast plant in its remoleculization of sugar.

The ptomains produced by pathegenic germs have been separated from the germs, and when so separated produce the same effect, that of direct poisoning similar to that induced by the poisons from the higher plants. Different species of bacteria produce different poisons—poisons that produce different physiological effects upon the human body. The effects are constant for a given germ, thus furnishing the definite physiological characteristics where. by the germ may be identified. On the other hand we are thus enabled to diagnose the disease from the germ.

It is now quite generally understood that disease is induced not so much by the mere presence of micro-organisms in the body as by their poisonous products, which are formed through changes wrought in the molecular forms of matter.

Bacteria being organic bodies, must of necessity possess the same nutritive functions common to all living bodies, whether plant or animal; viz., digestion, absorption, assimilation, and the formation and excretion of waste products; these are necessary to the life and growth of the organism.

The process of digestion in bacteria, as in other organisms, is accomplished through the agency of soluble ferments, which are elaborated by the organism. In the higher forms of plant and animal life the digestive fluids are produced by specialized cells and found in special organs. In animals it is in the stomach and intestinal tract, where it comes in contact with the food. In the lower forms of life, as in protozoa and protophyte, no specialized organs are found, parts of the simple cell doing the work of the stomach, while other parts of the same cell act in some other capacity at the same time.

All digestive ferments are the direct products of the activity of cell life, whether this digestive fluid be found in the amœba, monad, or in the peptic glands of the higher animals. The function of the ferments primarily, is that

of digestion, which consists quite largely in the remoleculization of certain food substances and the formation of
new compounds.

In the simple celled plants this process is manifest to a
most marked degree, and as all forms of life are supported
by the continued absorption of new matter, the old material must be eliminated, which, in case of the micro-organisms is cast out into the surrounding media, from whence
they obtain their supply of food, so that it is difficult to
determine the exact source of some of the bacterial products, whether they are products of digestion or elimination.

Excretions are classified into two groups: those that
contain much oxygen, and compounds containing but a
small amount. Thus, in animal excretions, carbon dioxide, rich in oxygen; urea, poor in oxygen but rich in nitrogen. In plants we find the same carbonic acid, and in
addition, some free oxygen; and corresponding to urea, we
find the alkaloids and organic acids, all poor in oxygen.

All this goes to show the uniformity of plan in vital
processes, whether manifest by the higher or lower forms
of life. The fact that all bacteria are not pathogenic
shows conclusively that all do not produce the same ptomaines, either by the action of their soluble ferments or
excretions. Nor is their presence in the body in any way
detrimental to health; it is claimed that a large proportion of the non-pathogenic germs are absolutely essential
to the well being of all the higher forms of life, mankind
included. While on the other hand the well-known deadly
effects of pathogenic germs lead us to enquire how we can
best destroy them, or, at least, avoid them.

The development of bacteria, even under the most favorable conditions, cannot continue indefinitely, bacteria can
only grow as long as the favorable conditions continue.
When the soil becomes exhausted their food supply is cut
off. But starvation is not the only cause of their death,
or in many instances bacteria die before the supply of
food is exhausted. Death of the bacteria is brought about
by the accumulation of bacterial products, poisonous to
their producers.

The vinous yeast plant affords a familiar example of the
effects of the bacterial products. When the amount of
alcohol reaches a certain per centage of the solution all
fermentation ceases, although there may still be a large

amount of sugar in the solution, the effect of the alcohol is to check further growth of the bacteria or to destroy them In most spore producing plants resting spores are produced about the time that fermentation ceases These resting spores retain their vitality for some considerable time so that the race does not die out for some time after parent cells are dead

In a media in which bacteria have ceased to multiply it is impossible to rear a second colony of the same kind The nutritive solution seems to possess immunity against a second injection

The cause of this phenomena has been made the subject of special study in the hope of throwing some light on the pathology of infectious diseases Many of this class of diseases due to the presence of micro-organisms have a self-limited duration similar to that observed in bacterial culture, and one attack of such disease gives the body an immunity against subsequent attacks On this subject nothing satisfactory has been learned There is no proof that the limited duration of infectious diseases depends upon either the exhaustion of certain nutritive substances in the animal body or upon the accumulation of poisonous bacterial products Even if this should be the case in reference to the limitation of the acute infectious diseases it certainly could have no direct connection with the immunity against subsequent attacks.

The growth of germs upon dead matter such as are provided for artificial culture cannot be compared directly with their growth and development in living bodies In the latter the germs must compete with living cells, and are subjected to conditions not found in artifical cultures. Any attempt to account for the phenomena of immunity cannot be based exclusively upon a chemical basis but must also take in consideration the properties of living bodies and the functional activities of living cells

Chemical influences which interfere with bacterial life may relate to either the absence of the necessary nutritive elements or to the presence of injurious agents.

Substances which kill bacteria are known as germicides or disinfectants While the term 'anti-septic" as commonly used, does not necessarily imply the power to destroy bacteria. Any agent which has the power to arrest the growth of germs and renders them inactive for a period may be termed antiseptic, or any substance which destroys or neutralizes the poisonous products of bacteria so that it cannot be absorbed into the system is properly termed antiseptic.

The researches of Koch and Wernich have overthrown many of our preconceived notions in reference to the efficiency of various disinfectants and antiseptics.

It has been shown that it is by no means an easy task to destroy germs, while their spores seem to defy most of our so-called antiseptics.

Then it is evident that we should depend upon disinfectants rather than antiseptics. The latter are good, but not so reliable.

Of the long list of antiseptics and germicides, which have within the past few years been highly recommended by physicians and surgeons, but comparatively few have retained the confidence and proved reliable in practice.

While this failure may appear to be due to the lack of germicidal power of the agent, it should be borne in mind that we cannot expect every germicide to serve the same purpose under all conditions, and the choice of the agent to be used must, the same as of other remedies, be governed by existing conditions; for conditions and environments may vary, even more than the agents themselves.

Since all disinfectants are necessarily antiseptic, they may be so classed. The following substances are antiseptic, but in the strength given cannot be considered reliable as disinfectants under all circumstances.

Thymol, - - 1:75000	Pyrogallic Acid, - 1: 100
Bichloride of Mercu-	Boric Acid, - - 1: 600
ry, - - - 1:40000	Salicylic Acid, - 1: 600
Oil of Mustard, 1:30000	Camphor, - - - 1: 400
Permanganate of Po-	Iodine, - - - 1:2000
tassium, - - 1: 3000	Picric Acid, - - 1:3000
Carbolic Acid, - - 1: 600	Sulphate of Iron, - 1: 300
Quinine, - - 1: 1000	Bromine, - - 1:4000
Benzoic Acid, - - 1: 1000	Kreolin, - - 1: 100
Sulphuric Acid, - 1: 1000	Sodium Carbonate, 1: 200
Oil of Cinnamon, 1: 1000	Sulphate of Copper, 1: 400
Hydrastis, - - 1: 500	Nitric Acid, - - 1: 400
Myrrh, - - 1: 1000	Alcohol, - 30 to 95 per ct.
Eucalyptol, - - 1: 2000	Peroxide of Hydrogen, 5 "

The agents named in the above list may be used with satisfactory results in surgical and obstetrical practice as antiseptics, but it should be borne in mind that the great danger in treating cases of this nature comes from carrying the germs to them in the instruments and hands of the operator. In order to avoid contamination from this source the most thorough measures of disinfection are necessary For this purpose it is well to use some of the stronger chemical disinfectants, and where practical heat may be used in order that aseptic conditions may be secured

In all surgical and obstetrical cases the use of antisep tics is of secondary importance to that of disinfectants Nothing short of absolute cleanliness can secure the desired aseptic condition.

In considering the properties of the various germicides and antiseptics, we find that some are valued solely for their germicidal properties. To this class belong bichloride of mercury, carbolic acid, thymol and some of the stronger acids

Bichloride of mercury proves to be one of the most efficient germicides known. No other agent so readily destroys both germs and spores, its action being instantaneous even in very dilute solutions, one part to five thousand; provided, of course, there are no chemicals present with which it unites and thus renders it inert When albumen is present in the solution, the bichloride is decomposed and rendered inactive as a germicide. It is also found that a watery solution of bichloride when allowed to stand for a long time precipitates its mercury salts and becomes inert. This may be prevented by the addition of a small amount of sodium chloride

Some surgeons recommend the addition of a mild organic acid—one that is unduly irritating. The following prescription has given satisfactory results, when used in surgical cases

Hydrarg. Chlorid. Corros.	gr. xv
Acid Tartaric	gr. x vel dr. i
Aquæ Dist	pts. ii

Bichloride solutions are used in strength of 1:1000 to 1:5000 in treatment of ordinary wounds

The objections frequently urged against the use of bichloride of mercury and other chemical germicides, on the ground of their toxic effect upon the human system, are not without valid reasons, but as before stated, we should be governed in our choice entirely by the nature of the individual case, and the special work to be accomplished

In surgical work, where the object is thorough disinfection of the operator's hands, instruments, and the surface of the body to be operated on, we should not hesitate to use some of the stronger germicides, thymol, bichloride, etc.; or if superficial wounds are to be cleansed and rendered aseptic, this class of agents may be used with good results.

However, after thorough disinfection we may with great advantage use the milder antiseptics, which are less irritating to raw surfaces, and are of such nature as to favor the healing process.

Under all circumstances, where deep sinuses or membranous cavities are to be irrigated, avoid the use of those germicides that are readily absorbed by the tissues, such as bichloride, carbolic acid and arsenious acid. When agents of this class are used in deep fissures or in peritonial cavities, toxic symptoms are of frequent occurrence.

We would call attention to the use of *iodoform,* which has little if any germicidal action, yet it occupies a most important place among antiseptics. While iodoform exerts but little influence directly upon the germs, its virtue as an antiseptic lies in its peculiar power of rendering inert the bacterial ptomaines. It decomposes in the presence of germs, and while in a nascent state its elements change ptomaines into innocuous compounds, thus preventing absorption of the poisons by the system, and the formation of pathogenic pus in wounds.

Iodoform is of little, if any, importance in aseptic wounds; its greatest value is in suppurating wounds, where it can be applied directly to the diseased parts. The fact that it does not possess germicidal properties makes it necessary to sterilize it before using, or it may be the means of infection in an otherwise aseptic wound.

A large list of purely sanative non-poisonous antiseptics could be mentioned. To this class belongs hydrogen peroxide, much valued as a disinfectant for suppurating wounds, ulcerated sore throat and diphtheria, but owing to the frequent presence of higher acids is somewhat irritating, it is an excellent cleansing agent to be followed by the milder antiseptics. Hydrogen peroxide may be used in 5 per cent solution up to full strength, according to the requirements of the case.

Boric acid is one of the most important sterilizing agents known for mucous surfaces. When used in a saturated aqueous solution it is an excellent disinfectant, and an antiseptic in weaker solutions

The diluted tincture of myrrh aside from its valuable antiseptic properties acts as a mild stimulant to the circulation and may be used with confidence. Its healing and cleansing qualities are especially manifest in treatment of ulcerated sore throat and nasal cavities For this purpose the pure tincture may be diluted one-half and used as a gargle. In obstetrical and surgical operations it is one of the most desirable antiseptics.

Hydrastis possesses but little power as a germicide but like idoform is one of the most potent agents in its action upon bacterial products. Experience has demonstrated its value not only as an antiseptic but in its benign influence upon mucous membranes. It is one of the best remedial measures that we have for the treatment of choleraic diarrhœa, especially by electrolysis or slow irrigation of the colon and small intestines by way of the rectum. The following prescription may be used for this purpose

Sterile infusion of Chammomile Flowers   1000
Standard Aqueous Solution Hydrastis   50
Gum Arabic   15

Hydrastis like myrrh manifests a tonic influence, and wherever membranes or tissues in wounds or cavities manifest a lowered tone or degenerate condition this agent is indicated. Hydrastis also exerts a very decided anti-malarial influence showing that when taken into the blood it antagonizes the germicidal ptomaines It is also of special value in some forms of chronic dyspepsia where it exerts its peculiar antiseptic properties as well as its influence upon the mucous membranes of the stomach. Hydrastis has long been recognized as an antiseptic and healing agent in the treatment of uterine catarrh, diseases of the bladder and as an injection for gonorrhœa.

GEUM RIVALE AND VIRGINIARUM.

Water Avens, Avens.

The *root* is a pleasant, mild, soothing, tonic astringent It is not drying but soothing to the mucous membrane

It is useful in mild acute and chronic cases of diarrhœa and dysentery In leucorrhœa and gleet it may be used with good effect both locally and constitutionally. It may be used for light hemorrhages from any source Locally it is a good wash for some irritated forms of sore mouth

This article is not best where there is a tendency to constipation without it be combined with some such agent as syr. juglans. Constipation is irritating and diarrhœa is weakening. Avoid both extremes and seek to induce daily regularity. If there be a tendency to diarrhœa use tonic astringents. Such may prevent debilitated conditions. Geum displays its influence to best advantage as a tonic astringent. It is one of the best agents to be used in cases of cholera infantum. It improves digestion and assists assimilation.

The fluid extract is a good preparation, or the powdered root may be boiled in milk.

GILLENIA TRIFOLIATA AND STIPULACEA.
Indian Physic.

The *root* is relaxing and stimulating chiefly to the alvine mucous membrane. Given in small doses in hot infusion it gives an outward flow of blood. If this be continued long or it be given in large doses emesis may be the result. This will also help to equalize the circulation.

Cold preparations chiefly influence the alvine canal and produce catharsis.

This agent is of value in colds, in the incipient stage of eruptive diseases where a good circulation is needed, and not unfrequently catharsis. Such a course is not unfrequently essential in the beginning of the treatment of inflammatory rheumatism.

It may also prove valuable in dropsy.

GLECHOMA HEDERACEA.
Ground Ivy.

The *herb* gives a disagreeable odor, and possesses a bitterish aromatic taste. It is a gently stimulating tonic to the mucous membrane, influencing especially that of the kidneys and of the respiratory tubuli. It will be found of use in cases of chronic bronchitis and phthisis where expectoration is too free.

GLYCERINA.

This is an odorless and colorless fluid obtained from various oils and fats. It has a sweetish taste, remains fluid and can be mixed with water in any desired proportions. Applied to the skin it softens it, but it gives a stinging sensation lasting a few seconds. This however can be avoided if it be previously mixed with a little water

Glycerin is an antiseptic, a solvent and a preservative nearly equal to alcohol For solvent purposes it may be diluted with alcohol to any desired extent

It may be used to partially cover bitter and stimulating medicines, and is frequently used to cover cod liver oil in the forming of an emulsion.

As a solvent more or less diluted with water, it extracts the qualities of drugs and partially covers the excess of bitterness and stimulancy which the same drugs would have, had the menstruum been alcohol

As a wash in eczemas either alone or in combination it is good

| Tr. Iodine | 2 |
| Glycerin | 1 |

To one ounce of this mixture add half an ounce of hyposulphite of soda and apply for barber's itch. Or the following may be used for the same trouble after shaving close·

Prepared Chalk	10
Coal Tar	1 to 4
Glycerin	5
Simple Cerate	50

Or instead of the glycerin and simple cerate, add 20 parts of linseed oil.

Ol Rosæ	gtta xv
Glycerina	oz. i
Spiritus Myristicæ	oz. iii
Ol. Cajuputi	gtta. xx

Apply at night to chapped hands, or the following may be used for the same purpose:

Glycerin	oz ss
Tr Benzoin	dr ss
Aqua Rosæ	oz. iiiss
Aqua Camphoræ	oz iv

M. Apply at night.

Or use the following.

Spermaceti	oz. ss
Ol. Almonds	oz ii
Glycerin	oz i
White Wax	dr. i

Melt together and stir till cold.

Glycerin	oz. i
Tr. Myrrh	dr, ii
Hydrastia Phos.	grs. iii
Rose Water	q. s. oz. iv

In bad cases of sore mouth apply every three hours.

Glycerin	oz. iv
Alum	oz. iv
Mutton Tallow	
Beeswax	aa. oz. ii
Best Pine Tar	oz. i
Carbolic Acid	dr. ii

Dissolve and then stir till cold. It is excellent for piles. As a diluted wash for the head it is cleansing to the surface and nutrient to the hair follicles.

Glycerin	oz. iii
Tr. Capsicum	dr. i
F. E. Quercus Alba	dr, iv
Ess. Bergamot	dr. i

This is a pleasant and effective tonic to the hair follicles after fevers or subsequent to cases of syphilis or wherever there is danger of the hair falling off.

Alcohol	oz. i
Glycerin	oz. ii
Tr. Capsicum	dr. ii
F. E. Verbascum	oz. iii
Ess. Bergamot	dr. ii
Rose Water	oz. i

This is also an excellent hair invigorator. But we do not guarantee either of these recipes to cause bald heads to be covered with a luxuriant growth of hair.

Soften clean glue oz. xiv in cold water oz. xxviii. Make the solution complete in a water bath. Then add oz. ii glycerin. Apply with a camel's hair brush over burns.

Some glycerin diluted may be added to poultices to keep them moist especially during the night.

| F. E. Lobelia Infl. | |
| Glycerin | aa. equal parts |

is a good preparation for the moistening of the wax of the ear and for the relief of partial deafness due to this cause. It is also a soothing and relaxing preparation for caked or inflamed breast.

Glycerin when added to cough syrups promotes expectoration, and when added to cathartics increases their laxative power.

Aqua	32
Glycerin	5
Citric Acid, Lemon Juice or Acetum	1

This is a pleasant and most admirable beverage for the troublesome thirst of diabetes.

Glycozone manufactured by Charles Marchand, of New York, is the chemical result of submitting pure glycerin to fifteen times its own volume of ozone under certain conditions.

This is a good preparation for the prevention of gastric and intestinal fermentation. It heals the gastric membrane, relieves heartburn and gives favorable results in dyspepsia, gastritis and gastric ulcer

After sores have been cleansed by hydrozone or listerine or some other preparation, apply glycozone; it is an excellent fluid dressing.

GLYCYRRHIZA GLABRA.

Licorice.   Southern Europe.

The *root* is a gently relaxing and stimulating, soothing demulcent, influencing chiefly the mucous membrane and especially that of the bronchi. It soothes and relieves conditions attributable to colds It is an excellent adjuvant for bitter medicines; even the taste of quinine and gentian is somewhat disguised by its use. Pills are frequently coated with it and bitter powders are frequently incorporated into it.

If the extract be dissolved and incorporated with lactin or starch and then dried and pulverized, it becomes a splendid vehicle with which to triturate quinine and many other bitter resinoids and stimulants. This is especially excellent where it can be incorporated with medicines that influence the bronchi The fluid extract is also used as a vehicle.

F. E	Glycyrrhiza	
"	Lobelia Inf.	aa dr. ii
"	Aralia Rac.	dr i
"	Sanguinaria Can	gtta xv
Ess	Anise	dr ss
Syr	Prunus	q s oz iv

This for a dry tickling cough is excellent, and so is the following:

F. E. Eupatorium Perfol.
"   Glycyrrhiza Glab.   aa. dr. ii
"   Lobelia Infl.   dr. i
"   Zingiber   gtta. v
Syr. Prunus V.   q. s. oz. iv .

GNAPHALIUM POLYCEPHALIUM.

Life Everlasting.

The *herb* is a mild diffusive, relaxant and stimulant to the mucous membrane. It is slightly demulcent and is soothing to the mucous membrane in whatever part its action is most needed, or as directed by other medicines.

Locally it is a good cleansing wash for either a sore mouth or a foul and irritable vagina.

In the treatment of cystic catarrh it influences the cystic membrane to throw off a large amount of mucous.

In bronchial catarrh it allays irritation and relieves the mucous membrane of its extra accumulation.

The *smoke* of this herb as well as an infusion of the plant yields good results in asthma. Give the infusion and between the doses allow the patient to inhale the smoke. The latter influence is exerted directly by inhalation and the former is directed by the vital force as a necessity for bronchial relief.

In colds in which there is more or less bronchial congestion, a hot infusion of the following is excellent:

Asclepias Tub.   4
Zingiber   1
Gnaphalium   2

Gnaphalium in hot infusion is mildly diaphoretic; zingiber gives it power in diaphoresis.

In gastric catarrh it loosens the mucous discharge, but usually needs some tonic to follow.

Dr. F. G. Hoener recommends this agent in pleuropneumonia, angina, croupy cough, atelectasis pulmonum, bronchiectasis, bronchial catarrh, capillary bronchitis, laryngitis, mumps.

This agent is rendered still more important when combined with verbascum.

GOODYERA PUBESCENS

Spotted or White Plantain.

Dr. F. G. Hoener recommends this agent as excellent for scrofula and chronic diarrhœa

GOSSYPIUM HERBACEUM

Cotton Root.

The **root** is a relaxing and stimulating emmenagogue. In small doses it is antispasmodic and is valuable in dysmenorrhœa where there is usually scantiness of menstrual flow

It is a very improper agent for the use of the pregnant· It may provoke uterine irritation. It will increase labor pains and their intensity hence it is not a proper agent to be used during parturition, especially if the lady be of a hemorrhagic diathesis

In acting as it does on the uterus it also influences diuresis.

Cotton seed *oil* has become quite an industry. It may be used as a substitute for the same general purposes as linseed oil   It may be combined with ulmus as a dressing for burns and irritated sores

GUAIACUM OFFICINALE

Lignum Vitœ   Jamaica, St Domingo

The wood comes to us in the form of chips   The centre wood yields a supply of gum-resin which is its active principle.

Guaiaci resini is a positive stimulating alterative to the general system   The digestive organs all feel its influence and so do the urinary and genital organs.   It stimulates the circulation and induces a good capillary flow.   It is best suited to languid and depressed conditions of the mucous membrane, and a clogged condition of the secernents, as in secondary syphilis, mercurial cachexia and venereal rheumatism   For such purposes however it is best administered with alterants.   For arousing the circulation it is best administered in hot infusion when its influence is felt by the capillary circulation

Asclepias Tub.	4
Zingiber	1
Guaiacum	3

This acts quite fully on the circulation and may be used in syphilitic fever and acute rheumatism.

Cold forms are usually best for chronic diseases.

Guaiacum is not suited to irritated or sensitive conditions. It is too stimulating for such.

The resin may be triturated on lactin or sugar and given dry or in capsule. But the resin does not readily combine with other remedies. The chips are best for the formation of compounds.

        Guaiacum Chips
        Smilax Off.   aa. 2
        Rumex Crisp.
        Arctium Sem.
        Taraxacum D. L.   aa. 3
This is an excellent alterative.
        Guaiacum Chips
        Cimicifuga Rac.
        Phytolacca Bac.   aa. 4 ;
        Xanthoxylum Cort.   1
        Aqua   q. s.
Raise to the boiling point and allow to stand two hours and add sugar q. s. Give three to six times a day for rheumatism.
        Gum Guaiacum   oz. i
        " Myrrh
        " Camphor
        Oil Capsicum   aa. oz. ss
        Alcohol   oz. xxxii
This forms a pain-killer of some importance.
        Guaiacum Resin
        Sugar   aa. oz. ss
        Gum Acacia   dr. ii
Triturate well in one pint of cinnamon water. This forms a good emulsion of this agent.

HAGENIA ABYSSINICA.

Kousso.   Abyssinia.

The *flowers* are an anthelmintic and are used to expel the tape worm. It excites a heat, nausea and sometimes vomiting and thirst. It may be given in powder, infusion or fluid extract after fasting a day. Four hours after giving the dose of kousso give a good large dose of antibilious physic. It usually expels the worm. Occasionally the dose may have to be repeated.

HAMAMELIS VIRGINICA.

Witch Hazel.

The *leaves and twigs* are a pleasant, reliable, mild, soothing diffusive, stimulating. astringent tonic It chiefly influences the mucous membrane

Locally it is much used in gonorrhœa, and in gleet. The aqueous or distilled extract has become a favorite for this purpose It is colorless and when used with colorless hydrastis it makes an excellent injection to soothe the urethra. In the treatment of this disease it gives good results and no urethral contractions follow its use In leucorrhœa it stimulates, astringes and tones the uterus and vagina.

In dysentery and diarrhœa it may be used alone or in conjunction with ulmus or other remedies.

It is a mild remedy for light cases of hemorrhages, rectal, cystic or uterine

In catarrh of whatever part of the mucous membrane it may be, it is a good remedy When needed for vaginal or nasal catarrh it may be used locally. In nasal catarrh it may be used with the nasal douche or be incorporated with vaseline and applied with a camel's hair brush. In vaginal catarrh it may be used by injection, suppository, gelatin capsule, tablet, or upon a pledget of cotton Thus applied it is an excellent remedy for prolapsus uteri.

As a rectal injection it gives favorable results in prolapsus ani and in rectal hemorrhages

In purulent ophthalmia it forms a good wash, and also for sore gums or sore mouth

With a small portion of capsicum it is excellent in cases of menorrhagia Though this agent is an astringent it is not drying but leaves the surface soothed and toned. It influences the nerves in the same manner.

A strong infusion forms a good wash for scaly and other skin diseases

When there is a tendency to hemorrhage it will give relief of after-pains.

Aqueous Hydrastis		dr iii
" Hamamelis		dr ii
Glycerin		oz ss
Aqua	q s	oz iv

This forms a good injection for the inflammatory stage of gonorrhœa.

Aqueous Hydrastis	dr. ii
" Hamamelis	dr. iv
Glycerin	oz. ss
Aqua	q. s. oz, iv

This is best adapted for use as an injection for secondary conditions.

HAPLOPAPPUS BAYLAHUAU.

Hysterionica.   Chili.

The **herb** is covered with a thick balsamic exudation which yields an abundance of fixed oil quite aromatic. It is a soothing, stimulating and somewhat astringent agent influencing the mucous membrane throughout, but especially that of the alvine canal. Its cleansing and toning power makes it an antiseptic of no little importance.

In acute and chronic diarrhœa, in dysentery, the diarrhœa of phthisis and in cholera infantum it is very beneficial, relieving also the tenesmus; nausea and vomiting incident to such conditions. It relieves indigestion and assists in some forms of dyspepsia. In combination with such agents as influence the respiratory organs it increases expectoration, soothes and tones the bronchi.

Its soothing, toning and cleansing power is well marked upon the urinary organs, but it is not a diuretic.

It is stimulating and toning to the generative organs and relieves them of muco-purulent discharges.

It is also beneficial in nasal, gastric and cystic catarrh.

HEDEOMA PULEGOIDES.

Pennyroyal.

This **herb** is an aromatic, stimulating, and relaxing diaphoretic. It is warming to the stomach and sustaining to the capillary circulation. In hot infusion it is a popular agent for the breaking up of colds, and for the relief of the menstrual flow when influenced by congestion. While a diaphoretic, it is no less an antispasmodic nervine and will be found valuable in dysmenorrhœa in nervous ladies, and is of good service in hysteria.

In hot infusion it will be found valuable in eruptive diseases, and may be given very freely when the eruption is slow in making its appearance.

In hot infusion it gives good results in the colic, flatulence, restlessness, peevishness, general nervousness and feverishness of children.

Locally applied a hot fomentation or the local application of steam from an infusion of this agent may be very profitably used to relieve local congestions, whether of head, lungs, stomach, uterus, bladder or kidneys.

The *oil* may be triturated on sugar or lactin and used for the same purposes as the herb. Combined with other agents it forms an excellent application for sprains and for rheumatism.

Dr. F G. Hoener recommends this agent as a specific for sunstroke and for exhaustion from overheat. Give no ice water to drink and place no ice on the head.

HELIANTHELLA TENUIFOLIA.

Helianthella.   Florida.

This is a slender perennial herb bearing showy heads of yellow flowers. It grows about two feet high.

The *root* is an aromatic, relaxing and stimulating antispasmodic, chiefly influencing the mucous membrane, especially of the respiratory organs.

In hot infusion it is diaphoretic and influences the circulation and may be profitably used in colds, bronchitis, phthisis and chronic coughs, in which conditions it is a good expectorant. Large doses may nauseate and may prove emetic.

Cold preparations are somewhat diuretic

HELIANTHEMUM CANADENSE

Frostwort.

This *plant* is a stimulating, astringent, tonic alterative, expending its influence chiefly upon the mucous membrane of the alvine canal, and giving very excellent results in acute and chronic diarrhœa, especially when these are the result of some strumous troubles. It also forms a good wash in either acute or chronic ophthalmia.

For internal use as an alterative it is best combined with other agents of more permanent value, as menispermum or celastrus.

HELIANTHUS ANNUUS.

Sunflower

The *seeds* have a large quantity of oil which may be obtained freely by compression. It is quite nutrient and somewhat mucilaginous. An infusion is rather pleasant, promotes a free flow of urine, soothes the inflamed and

irritable urinary tract. Its influence is largely felt upon
the sabaceous glands quite effectually. Added to diffusives
and diaphoretics it is valuable in scarlatina and in scaly
skin affections. It is claimed for this as for the eucalyptus globulus that when planted freely in malarious regions
it quite effectually does away with malaria. I have seen
several illustrations of this which seemed to favor such a
conclusion. It is also frequently planted near house and
other drains as a means of air purification.

The *root* of the sunflower is a relaxing, moderately
stimulating diaphoretic when given in hot infusion, but
cold preparations act gently on the kidneys and are some-
wha' laxative to the bowels. Both hot and cold preparations may be used with great advantage in bilious and
other fevers, in the former for its diaphoretic influence and
the latter for its influence on the liver, bowels and kidneys.
A strong infusion may produce emesis, which may be no
real disadvantage.

HEPATICA TRILOBA.

Liverwort.

This *plant* is a mild stimulating, demulcent, tonic
astringent. As a patent medicine it has been used for
almost everything; but its main sphere of influence is on
the mucous membrane and the hepatic aparata. It is a
mild soothing remedy and is best used in combination
with other agents of a more positive character.

It forms a good addition to cough syrups, especially
when there is present a torpid liver.

Dr. F. G. Hoener recommends it in seminal discharges
from gleetish affections and weakness of the spermatic
cord and also in nephritis.

HERACLEUM LANATUM.

Masterwort.

The *root, leaves and seed* are a stimulating carminative
and antispasmodic. In hot infusion it influences the circulation, and may be used for the relief of colds, and in
dysmenorrhœa. It produces diaphoresis and quiets the
nervous system. It may also be used in flatulence and
gastric complaints.

HEUCHERA AMERICANA.

Alum Root.

The *root* is a stimulating astringent. It is a good local

styptic, and internally it may be used for hemorrhages and diarrhœa. It gives good results incorporated with vaseline as a local application to hemorrhoids.

For internal use triturate on some saccharine or mucilaginous material, as that of ulmus.

HIERACIUM VENOSUM.

Blood-Wort.

This *plant* is a positive, stimulating astringent. In hot infusion it arouses a full capillary circulation

It is moderately styptic and may be used for hemorrhages from whatever source

It is not a drying astringent but is quite tonic. It is of much importance in dysentery and in diarrhœa, in the treatment of catarrh, and as a gargle for sore throat   Locally it is excellent in chronic leucorrhœa and for a relaxed vagina.

HUMULUS LUPULUS.

Hops.

The *flower and pollen* is a stimulating and relaxing nervine of much power   It mildly influences the secernents and relieves the secernents somewhat as a gentle but thorough alterant   In insomnia the hop pillow is no myth.   It quiets the nerves and soothes the whole system without any shade of narcotism   As a poultice or fomentation it is superior to most other agents for the relief of inflammatory and irritable conditions, whether they be internal or external

It makes a good addition to cough syrups for irritable coughs and restlessness.

It is a superior agent in rheumatism and neuralgia. A hot fomentation may be applied to the parts affected, and with other agents taken internally with the best of success.

In hysteria and dysmeno rhœa it will be found of great advantage whether used by itself or in combination with other agents.

In combination with hepatic tonics it will give good results in nervous depression   It is gently laxative to the bowels and holds a relaxing influence over the liver and gall ducts.

The fluid extract and lupulin both moderately represent the drug.

Lupulin   grs. L

Camphor   grs. XL

Make into 10 suppositories and insert one into the vagina at intervals as needed for pruritus and in cases of nymphomania.

HYDRANGEA ARBORESCENS.

Hydrangea, Seven Barks.

The *root* is an aromatic, stimulating and relaxing diuretic and is very valuable for the relief of calcareous deposits.

Dr. F. G. Hoener says if equally combined with collinsonia canadensis it will dissolve and expel any gravel without pain.

It also gives great relief in severe cases of cystitis.

The Doctor also says that if the juice of black Spanish rettishes be injected into the bladder it will dissolve any hard stone or litho-dialysis and prevent the necessity for the dangerous operation of lithotomy.

HYDRASTIS CANADENSIS.

Golden Seal.

This *root* is the king of tonics to the mucous membrane. It is a mild, positive and permanent stimulating tonic. Its influence, though primarily given to the mucous membrane, extends to all parts of the body, wherever it may be required by the necessities of the vital force or influenced thither by its combination with other agents.

It improves the appetite and assists digestion. In the weak and debilitated stomach, especially if there be nervous disturbances or if the gastric membrane be clogged with congested or catarrhal mucous, and in cases of gastric ulceration, hydrastis given in small and frequent doses will not unfrequently give relief both to the gastric membrane and to the nervous system.

In combination with biborate of soda it makes an excellent wash for children's sore mouth and other forms of sore mouth and sore gums.

Its especial function with the liver is its tonic relief to the portal system. In fact this same class of influence is felt throughout the entire venous system. It is one of the best agents for the sustaining of the venous circulation. Hence its action upon the right or venous side of the heart.

Its influence is also felt by the arterial circulation, but this influence is secondary.

Hydrastis may be made to specially influence the stomach, bronchi, bowels, urinary aparata or genitalia, as it may be influenced by its combination with agents that especially influence any one of these several departments. With aralia, prunus or comfrey it gives tone and vigor to the respiratory organs, with juglans it forms a powerful intestinal tonic, with eupatorium purpureum or capsella its tonic influence is felt upon the kidneys; and with such agents as mitchella it promptly influences the organs of generation

With gentle astringents it is admirable in the gastric and alvine weakness present in cholera infantum, and in diarrhœa generally It tones the membrane and enables it to cast off its accumulated mucous

Locally in female troubles it is unexcelled. Kino or hamamelis may be added as required

In intestinal weakness it may be combined with some preparation of iron, and when alteratives are required to be used the influence of hydrastis is frequently a valuable addition.

It is of great service combined with hepatics for the relief of the portal circulation and for its tonic influence in both the secreting and excreting functions of the liver.

Powdered hydrastis enters into the composition of Dr. Bedford's sore throat powder which has given the doctor so much satisfaction in the treatment of diphtheria and other forms of ulceration of the throat.

Locally the influence of hydrastis is a very superior one In erysipelas, ophthalmia, sore mouth, sore throat, leucorrhœa, vaginal and uterine ulceration, eczema, small-pox. eruptive and syphilitic sores it will do good service.

F. E Hydrastis Can   1
Ol. Lini   8

This is one of the best washes in cases of eruptive diseases to relieve the surface of the itching and burning sensation, in small-pox to prevent pitting, and in scarlatina to prevent the scales from being spread around the room

With hamamelis and glycerin it forms an excellent wash in gonorrhœa

An infusion of hydrastis may be used daily for uterine ulceration.

Prof. E. G. Anthony uses finely powdered hydrastis for ulceration of the cornea.

Pul. Hydrastis	dr. iv
" Myrrh	dr. i
" Capsicum	grs. v to x

In cases of syphilis with bad labial ulcers fill these with the above several times a day.

Remember that hydrastis is an antiseptic as well as a tonic and one of no little power; also a germicide.

Locally applied the following is very beneficial for hemorrhoids:

Adeps	oz. ii
Hydrastis	dr. vi
Tannin	dr. ii
Lobelia	dr. i
Zingiber	grs. xv

For gleet the following has been used with success:

Fld. Hydrastis	oz. iss
Bismuth Subnitrate	dr. ii
Boro-Glyceride, 5 per cent. solution	oz. i
Acacia Mucilage	oz. i

Inject as needed of this, diluted if desirable, three times a day.

F. E. Hydrastis	4
" Phytolacca	2
Acid Salicylic	
Acid Boric	aa. 1
F. E. Mentha Arvensis	
" Thymus Vulgaris	aa. 2
Distilled Hamamelis	5

This forms an excellent wash for the vagina, throat, rectum in cases of hemorrhoids, burns, bruises and sunburns.

McCoy, Howe Co., Indianapolis, Ind., manufacture Golden Liquid Hydrastis, non-alcoholic; representing all the valuable constituents of hydrastis without the dark coloring matter. This is superior to colorless hydrastis in that it not only contains the white alkaloid hydrastine, but also berberine and the volatile principles of the drug. It represents all the medical virtues of the drug, combines with any solution, and is a very valuable preparation.

Hydrastia Sulphate	
Xanthoxylin	aa. 1
Bicarbonate Soda	

Avenia   aa 2

This preparation gives good results in dyspepsia, heartburn and various forms of colic

Phos. Hydrastia	grs xx
Tannin	dr i
F. E. Cinchona	dr. iv
" Dioscorea Vil.	dr iv
" Xanthoxylum	dr ii
Syr Simplex	q s. oz. viii

M. S Use a teaspoonful of this preparation every three
to six hours in cases of lead poisoning.

Hydrastis can

Humulus Lup. aa. equal parts

Use this freely to stimulate, sustain and tone the spinal
nerves.

For washes and injections the aqueous and colorless
preparations may be best on account of preventing the
staining of the linen, yet for general use they are inferior
and do not fully represent hydrastis canadensis

HYDROZONE (Charles Marchand, N Y)

Hydrozone is an antiseptic. a cleanser, a pus destroyer,
and bactericide second to none, and in many respects the
very best. It yields thirty times its own volume of nascent oxygen gas (near to the condition of ozone), consequently it is from two to four times the strength of any
peroxide of hydrogen solution.

It is purer, far more reliable, and should be preferred to
all other preparations sold under the name of peroxide of
hydrogen, hydrogen dioxide, etc

In diphtheria I have made much use of it and always
with gratifying results. It may be gargled or used with
an atomizer freely and frequently. from one to three hours.
After thoroughly cleansing the throat with hydrozone, a
portion should be diluted according to the severity of the
case, and a teaspoonful swallowed

Especially should this be done after the membrane begins to slough. Some portions of this poisonous material
will necessarily fall into the stomach and become deleterious there to the gastric membrane Small portions of
hydrozone taken into the stomach will prove antiseptic
and prevent whatever putrid material may have been
swallowed, from doing any injury to the system.

After gargling or atomizing allow no water or other

drink to be taken for about three to five minutes, when the parts become thoroughly cleansed.

If other agents are to be used to gargle or to atomize the throat, hydrozone is to be used first to thoroughly cleanse the membrane. I have been very successful in the treatment of diphtheria, scarcely ever losing a case.

In tonsilitis, as soon as the pus commences to exude, hydrozone should be used to cleanse the cavity. It gives excellent results.

More or less diluted (according to the degree of sensitiveness of the patient) it may be used with the atomizer in the treatment of nasal catarrh.

In catarrhal conditions of the stomach and bowels it acts like a charm as a cleansing and antiseptic agent.

For cleansing open sores, open abscesses, carbuncles, ulcers, it has no equal. It cleanses thoroughly and innocently. Give plenty of time for the cleansing of the parts before applying any dressing. In otorrhœa I have used it with excellent success. It cleanses, tones and heals.

In diseases of the genito-urinary organs whether of an infectious origin or otherwise, it may be used whenever needed to cleanse the parts. It may be used more or less diluted with water as found necessary.

Per vaginam it cleanses and relieves lecuorrhœa and pruritus and stimulates and tones that organ. In typhoid and bilious fever, typhus, cholera and yellow fever, in more or less diluted form, occasionally it will be very valuable as a bactericide and cleanser of the mucous membrane.

HYPNOTISM.

By G. H. MAYHUGH, M. D.,

Editor of Sanative Medicine, Westerville, Ohio.

History.—Animal magnetism, mesmerism, hypnotism, are synonymous terms for a state or condition, psychic in its character, which has so much of a helpful or harmful influence—in whichever direction it may be turned—upon the physical man, that it has ever justly claimed a large share of the time and effort of medical men.

Frederick Anton Mesmer, after whom this state was termed *mermerism*, did much investigation but he failed to comprehend the subject, and his work was largely initiatory. He saw only physical manipulations and exalted these as the essential elements of its successful production.

The honor of placing the matter on a scientific and rational basis belongs to James Braid an English surgeon, who, in 1842, published the claim that the phenomena did not depend upon the transmission of a fluid (magnetism) from the operator, but that they were due to a peculiar nerve force in the magnetized. This he denominated *hypnotism.*

To Charcot of Paris is due the praise of having done more in recent years than any other one to invest with a therapeutic value the many experiments being made in the field of hypnotism. He made clear the distinctions between the *psychical* and the *physical* in the various phenomena connected therewith and set forth clearly the various stages of hypnotic influence. The results he obtained are now recognized as among the best authenticated points in neural pathology and therapeutics.

Definition and Nature.—Hypnotism is the science of the sleep-like state produced in certain persons susceptible to it by some influence exerted by another or, less frequently, by one's self, which latter is termed *auto-hypnosis.* The study of hypnotism is largely the study of mental philosophy, and this latter seems indeed to be in its infancy. In connection with psychological study are noticed many exceptional-irregular phenomena of mental and nervous states which are difficult of classification, and these we now denominate *hypnotic, somnambulistic, hysteric, lethargic, trance-like.* Hypnotism is proving itself to be one of the primary divisions of a broader and higher field of mental science than has hitherto been known, and investigations are being rapidly pushed therein.

The result of these researches seems to be, that there are various personalities in the same being; that there is an *unconscious* mental life as well as, and consistent with, a *conscious* mental life. It is believed that personality extends no further than consciousness. Hence, we must define *hypnotism* as being, in the light of this idea, that condition in which the normal, conscious self is in abeyance and an inner self is brought out into action. This might be made plainer if, assuming, as previously stated, that personality is limited to the realm of consciousness, we state it that the normal state of mind is that state in which the field of consciousness is unbounded, and the hypnotic state as that in which the field of consciousness is contracted or limited in some particular direction, the attention not being able to take in the normal number of sensations or ideas at once. Every phenomenon of hypnotic suggestion and the various phases of the hypnotic state prove the truth of the proposition above stated; namely, that there are various personalities in the same individual—of course one being chief and the others subordinate to this; but that the *ego*, the normal and supreme self, is, in its totality, made up of various selves, there can be no doubt. True, these selves are limited, split-off, sub-conscious in character, but that they exist no one conversant with the subject under discussion can deny; and the ordinary state of sleep has in its phenomena many corollary proofs of this composite character of the *ego*.

Susceptibility to Hypnosis.—To make hypnotism useful and its application practical, it will be well to very briefly state a few well-ascertained facts as to who can or cannot be hypnotized. Fully ninety-five per cent. of all persons can be hypnotized to a greater or less degree; of these the greater number will be men, so that it is seen that *sex* has a slightly modifying influence. Of greater moment is *age*, those from seven to twenty-one years being most easily hypnotized. *Climate* has a marked influence, those of the tropics being much more easily influenced than people of colder regions. *Race* is a marked factor, the French people being more susceptible than Germans. The Hindoos are the most easily hypnotized of any people on the globe. People of *medium intelligence* are the best subjects of hypnosis. Insanity hinders hypnosis and idiocy renders its accomplishment impossible.

There are many things that hinder or promote hypnosis. Distracting noises, a recent meal, deep mental emotions, strong light, excessive heat or cold—these retard hypnosis; while quiet, rest, moderate light, medium temperature, music, etc., hasten its production, and the operator must watch these points carefully.

Methods of Its Production.—These are various and their special description cannot be here given. All methods are classed as (a) physical and (b) psychical.

The *physical* comprehends all such acts as affect the nervous system through the medium of the sensory nerves—hence there are five avenues open to us in this matter. Of the senses, that of sight is most frequently used. The *psychical* is the method by which the mind is, in various

ways, profoundly and continuously impressed with the
idea of sleep, and depends for its philosophy upon the
principle of "suggestion," of which more will be said
further on.

*Stages of Hypnosis and the Physiological Effects of
Each.*—The stages or grades of hypnosis are the *cataleptic,* the *lethargic* and the *somnambulistic.* Of the *cataleptic* stage, the main feature is muscular immobility, the
person assuming a statue-like attitude eyes are open,
lachrymation is abundantly active, and respiration is less
frequent than normal. The limbs remain in the same position in which they may be placed, but do not resist a
change of position. tendon reflexes are absent and complete
anæsthesia of the surface of the body obtains. Deep muscular sense and vision are partly active. Communicated
positions of the limbs produce corresponding ideas in the
brain.

This state of catalepsy terminates by either a return to
normal or by a change into the state of *lethargy.*

The principal points in this state are, anæsthesia of skin
and mucous membranes, increase of irritability of the motor nerves, and, as a rule, non-susceptibility to suggestion.
The eyes are closed, or half open, the body is relaxed,
mobile, and respiration quickened, tendon reflexes are
increased, and muscular contraction often remains until
released by excitation of antagonistic muscles.

By opening the eyes of the lethargic he is transferred
into catalepsy; by closing the eyes of the cataleptic he is
taken into lethargy.

And a curious proof of the independence of the separate
halves of the brain is found in the fact that the opening or
closing of one eye in the cataleptic or lethargic state, as
the case may be, will cause a change to occur in one-half
of the body in accordance with the rule above stated.

In the third. or *somnambulistic* state there is anæsthesia of skin and mucous membranes, and also, insensibility to pain; the senses are enormously quickened, and
the same is true of the mental faculties. It is on persons
in this state that suggestion works such wonders By
the term suggestion we understand that action by means
of which the operator gains control over the subject operated upon by means of some suggested action or idea To
illustrate. A man whose arm is to be amputated is put
into the *somnambulistic* stage of hypnosis, and it is *sug-

gested to him that he *have no pain.* The operation is
done without pain—suggestion has done its perfect work.
One operator suggested to his lying-in patient that she
have no *pain*: she received it as a suggestion that she
have no *contractions*, and labor ceased till the *suggestion*
was changed.

Its Practical Application.—That the influence of mind
over mind, and that of mind over matter (the body), has in
it a great potentiality for good to the physician and surgeon is being realized more and more. Hypnotism is being
divested of the mysteries that once surrounded it, and in
which the *"faith*-curists" and so-called "christian-scien-
tists" seek yet to envelop it; its application is being
rationally and rapidly systematized, and we have now the
science of Suggestive Therapeutics.

In surgery and obstetrics hypnotism has great utility,
depending upon the anæsthesia it induces. As early as
1829, Cloquet amputated a woman's breast without pain·
by its aid. In 1845, Loysel, of Cherebourg, made a painless amputation of the leg. Velpeau, Broca, and other
French surgeons have made extensive use of hypnosis as
an anodyne in their work. From 1850 to 1860, six hundred
surgical operations were done in the hospital at Calcutta,
in which this agent was the only anæsthetic used. Braid,
in England, used it in the same way. Its use is not so
convenient as is the use of chloroform or ether, too much
time being required to bring most patients under its influence; hence, in this commercial age, where time has such
a monetary value, this fact militates against hypnotic
anæsthesia. It is infinitely more safe than either chloroform or ether, a fact greatly in its favor.

It has been used less frequently in obstetrics than in
surgery, but it certainly has a wide field for its application
in the former.

In mental and nervous disease hypnotism has a more
extensive therapeutic range. Indeed, here it seems to find
its special application. True, many cases of mental derangement are no doubt secondary to some functional,
physical disease, the cure of the latter restoring the mind
to its normal again. But we are persuaded that many
cases of mental aberration are simply pathological states
due to the existence of some abnormal, secondary *ego,*
some perverse consciousness obstinately cherishing its
narrow idea, which, with the normal, supreme *ego* in full

control, would be out of the field of thought and contemplation, but which, in the abnormal state of things, has assumed supreme command of the mind, and inhibits the normal flow of life. Current literature is rich in its record of cures by hypnotic suggestion.

The best plan seems to be to make but one suggestion at a time, thus attacking each hallucination singly, and thereby avoiding confusion. The suggestions are to be given loudly, definitely and precisely. Assurance is thus given that a certain voice, vision or fixed idea will soon vanish, and lo, it is gone!

The range of hypnotic cure among the insane is, unhappily, limited, for not all are susceptible to hypnosis, what per cent we cannot ascertain. Genuine epilepsy seems to bear the same relation to this agent, yet hysterical paralysis, convulsions, etc. come readily under its therapeutic influence, while writer's cramp, chorea and tonic spasms are most readily relieved.

Liebeault has cured a number of obstinate cases of enuresis by hypnotism. Insomnia is said to be very easily cured by this means. Hypnosis has cured many cases of alcoholism.

So we see that bodily suffering and bodily disease can be relieved by hypnosis. And not only this, but the psychical life of man seems equally open to its benign influence, so that bad habits can be overcome and depraved character improved.

Hypnotism is undoubtedly a potent therapeutic force and deserves careful consideration and investigation at our hands.

HYSSOPUS OFFICINALIS

Hyssop.

This *plant* is a mild, diffusive, stimulating and relaxing aromatic. In hot infusion it influences the circulation giving a good outward flow of blood. It is useful for the relief of colds, coughs and bronchial congestions. Inhalation of the steam is a pleasant relief in cases of coryza.

ILEX AQUIFOLIUM AND OPACA

Holly

The **leaves** are a mildly stimulating and relaxing diaphoretic especially when given in hot infusion, and are serviceable in the treatment of colds, feverishness, congestions and inflammations.

ILEX PARAGUAYENSIS.

Paraguay Tea.   Central South America.

The *leaves and twigs* are a soothing, gently stimulat-antispasmodic nervine. The tree is about the size of an orange tree or a little larger and its leaves remain green throughout the year. It is a favorite beverage among the people of Chili, Bolivia, Peru and Southern Brazil. From some of these nations it is a large and valuable export. An effort has been made to cultivate this tree but not with great success. It is more productive in its wild state.

It has a pleasant aroma due to the presence of a volatile oil. It is best in hot infusion, and as a beverage it is superior to Chinese tea. It is more diuretic than coffee and fully as stimulating as tea, but is more soothing and quieting to the nerves than either of them. It allays thirst, relieves hunger, promotes digestion, and stimulates the nervous system producing refreshing sleep.

A hot infusion may be used in feverish conditions, in the eruptive fevers, in pleurisy and in insomnia and general nervousness.

IMPATIENS PALLIDA.

Wild Celandine.

This herb is a stimulating and relaxing alterative influencing the mucous membrane and the secernents throughout. It is of some service in jaundice, dropsy, some forms of indigestion, hemorrhoids, tetter, ringworm and other eczema.

The fresh herb bruised and applied to the surface is said to be a cure for rattlesnake bite.

INULA HELENIUM.

Elecampane.

The *root* is a gently stimulating tonic to the mucous membrane. It is a warming, strengthening, cleansing and toning agent to the gastric, alvine and pulmonary mucous membrane, and is very serviceable in catarrhal conditions of the bronchi, and catarrhal dyspepsia. It is better suited to chronic than acute cases. It is an excellent addition to cough syrups.

In hot infusion its stimulating power gives a good outward circulation.

Elix.	Inula Hel.	oz. i
"	Verbascum Thap.	
"	Polygala Senega aa. oz. iss	
Tr.	Lobelia	oz i

Dr. F. G. Hoener says administer this every 15 or 20 minutes till relieved, in cases of pseudo-membranous croup.

IPOMEA JALAPA.

Jalap.

The *root* is a stimulating cathartic in ordinary doses in from three to six hours. Large doses produce more or less griping and watery stools. In combination with zingiber the griping may to a great extent be prevented. In combination with zingiber and senna it forms a good antibilious physic.

F. E.	Ipomea Jal.	dr. iii
"	Cassia Acut.	dr. iv
Syr.	Zingiber.	q. s. oz. iv

M. S. Teaspoonful or less at night to overcome constipation.

IRIS VERSICOLOR.

Blue Flag.

The *root* is a positive alterative. Its influence extends to the whole glandular system and the lymphatics.

In hot infusion it stimulates a good free outward circulation.

Cold preparations quite freely influence the liver, gall ducts and bowels. Large doses are quite cathartic, and are somewhat nauseating. Its influence is best as an alterant and when combined with other alterants.

It is a most desirable agent in secondary syphilis, scrofula, skin diseases, mercurial cachexia, dropsy, chronic rheumatism and chronic liver troubles. Its best influence is seen in chronic, torpid conditions.

The fluid extract may be used for all the general purposes of the root.

It gives good results in chronic constipation, and it is said to give good results in goitre.

F. E. Taraxacum D. L.   dr. iii
" Eryngium Yuc.   dr. iv
" Iris Vers.   dr. ii
Syr. Zingiber.   q. s. oz. iv
M. S. Teaspoonful three to five times daily for dropsy.

F. E. Iris Vers.
" Smilax Off.
" Rumex Crisp.
" Arctium Sem.   aa. dr. ii
" Xanthox. Carol.   gtta xx
Syr. Simplex   q. s. oz. iv

This forms a good alterant for glandular and skin troubles.

This is an excellent addition to liver medicines, especially when there is more or less impurity of blood and a sluggishness of the circulation.

It is valuable in rheumatism from specific cause. When there are irritable conditions this is not the agent to be used.

F. E. Iris Versi.   dr. vi
" Hydrastis Can.   dr. iv
" Chelone Glab.   dr. v
" Xanthoxylum Frax.   dr. ii
Syr. Simplex   ad. oz. xvi

This has been successful in uterine fibroids.

Irisin is the resinoid and does quite well. It stimulates the lymphatics, absorbents, skin and kidneys. It is a powerful hepatic and stimulating alterant in the treatment of scrofula, syphilis, gonorrhœa, dropsy, rheumatism, glandular swellings, eruptions of the skin, affections of the liver and spleen, and wherever there is a low condition of the excretives.

JATROPHA MACRORHIZA.

Jicama.   Southern States and Northern Mexico.

This plant grows to be about a foot high, and has a short, thick, tuberous *root*, which is a pleasant, comparatively tasteless cathartic. In large doses it may prove drastic and emetic, especially so if the green root be used. These symptoms may be to some extent prevented by the addition of zingiber or mentha piperita. It is both hepatic and cholagogue and need only be used in small doses. It operates in from three to five hours according to the

JEFFERSONIA DIPHYLLA

Twin Leaf.

The **root** is a rather pungent, bitter. stimulating and relaxing alterant.

It influences the mucous membrane and in hot infusion: it induces a good outward circulation and relieves the secernents and the glandular system in general

It is quite stimulating and relieves a torpid condition of the mucous membrane, and is suitable to catarrhal conditions.

With agents that influence the bronchi it stimulates to expectoration With agents that influence the uterine discharge it increases the monthly Its action may thus be also guided toward the kidneys.

It is a very valuable alterant to be used in the treatment of rheumatism. Dr F G Hoener says that he has successfully used it for twenty-five years in cases of rheumatic fever, acute rheumatism, cerebral and chronic rheumatism

It is also valuable in mercurial rheumatism, mercurial cachexia and atonic amenorrhœa, and it may be added to cough syrups when the treatment is for scrofulous or consumptive cases.

F E Jeffersonia Diph
    "   Mitchella Rep   aa dr iii
    "   Liriodendron Tul.
    "   Taraxacum D. L.   aa. dr. ii
Syr. Zingiber   q. s oz iv

This is an excellent alterant where a female tonic is also indicated.

F E Jeffersonia Diph
    "   Dicentra Ex
    "   Phytolacca Bac.
    "   Euonymous At.   aa dr. ii
Syr. Zingiber.   q s oz iv

This is an excellent stimulating alterant.

An infusion of jeffersonia is a good wash for sore mouth and as a wash for the treatment of indolent ulcers.

JUGLANS CINEREA.

Butternut, White Walnut.

The inner bark of the root is more active than that of the trunk, but both are used It yields its properties to boiling water except its astringency, which property is yielded when alcohol is the menstruum used instead of boiling water.

Juglans is an active stimulating hepatic and cathartic. It relieves the portal system, disgorges the liver and cleanses the bowels. For catharsis it usually takes from four to eight hours according to the dose given.

Juglans cinerea tones the entire alvine mucous membrane, but especially that of the lower bowels, influencing peristalsis. The alcoholic fluid extract may profitably be used in diarrhœa and dysentery. It cleanses the surface and leaves the parts toned and astringed. The aqueous extract being free from this astringency may be used to relieve chronic constipation. It is in this sphere one of the most valuable preparations. In relieving the portal circulation it also relieves hemorrhoids and rectal hemorrhages.

In dysentery in small doses it cleanses the bowels, relieves the portal circulation, and tones the mucous membrane.

New Milk   qrt. i
Good Vinegar tablespoonsful 2 to 4

Let it come to a boil. Don't let them eat anything else. This makes a vinegar whey and add juglans and zingiber to suit in cases of diarrhœa.

F. E. collinsonia can. may be added to syr. juglans in the treatment of hemorrhoids and is very valuable in the treatment of rectal hemorrhages.

Solid Extract Juglans Cln.   grs. iii
Capsicum Powd.   gr. ss

may be given at bed-time for chronic diarrhœa; or give

F. E. Juglans Cin.   dr. ii
" Cornus Flor.   dr. iv
Tr. Myrrh   dr. i
Syr. Zingiber.   q. s. oz. iv

M. S. Teaspoonful at bed-time.

To prepare the syrup of juglans gather your bark from the fifth to the twentieth of April in this climate. It is then strongest. Crush or chop fine. Then boil till quite strong and pour off and cover a second and third time to completely exhaust the strength of the drug. Then boil all together and evaporate to three-fourths of equality of one pint per pound of bark. Then for each twelve ounces add alcohol two ounces and sugar four ounces. A small proportion of the fluid extract of zingiber may be added now or when prescribed.

The Syrup Juglans Cin. as kept in stock by Dr. C. T Bedford, made from fresh selected bark and gathered in proper season, according to the formula and practical experience of Prof. G. N. Davidson is the best and most effectual form in which this valuable agent can be given, combining as it does, all the desirable qualities, viz; Reliability, Cheapness and Pleasant Taste. For which it has become favorably known throughout the United States from the Atlantic to the Pacific, from the Lake to the the Gulf.

This preparation is made as above noted by one of the most reliable of pharmacists, and in itself is susceptible of a very wide range of application

In small and frequent doses it may even be used in typhoid fever.

It is well adapted to the treatment of skin eruptions. It is a tonic to both mucous membrane and dermoid tissue and slightly increases the action of the kidneys. It is one of the most valuable agents in the whole materia medica. It relieves the liver, proves gently cathartic and leaves the bowels soluble and toned. These are qualities that can be accorded to but few agents. By the use of this agent the faeces become more or less darkened.

The fluid extract alcoholic may be used in combination with comp. syr. ther et potassæ in the treatment of diarrhœa and dysentery in either adults or children.

Ess. Mentha Pip.	gtta. ii
F. E Hydrastis Can.	dr. i
Bicarb Potas.	dr. ss
Syr Juglans	q. s. oz. iv

This is an alkaline, tonic, hepatic and cathartic valuable in chronic constipation and other atonic conditions of the alvine mucous membrane when there is a tendency to gastric acidulation. Juglans cinerea is a most excellent alterative

The *oil* may be used as an application to irritable sores. It is best triturated with glycerine or vaseline.

JUGLANS NIGRA

Black Walnut.

The *leaves* are a gently stimulating tonic to the mucous

membrane, especially of the generative organs. They also form an excellent fomentation for applying to inflamed and congested surfaces, frozen limbs, or congested lungs.

The *bark* is used very successfully in catarrh, leucorrhœa, prolapsus uteri, relaxed vagina, etc. The fluid extract may be incorporated with vaseline and used with a brush or atomizer in case of nasal catarrh.

A salve made of walnut hulls boiled in cosmoline is a favorite application in cases of eczema rubrum.

The *oil* is excellent in cases of purulent ophthalmia acute and chronic. It cures quite rapidly and scarcely ever disappoints. It is one of the best agents for application to children who become excoriated from urine. If you get all the black out of the hull of the walnut and use for this purpose it is good. It will smart the eyes but little, and may be used for the same general purposes as the oil.

JUNIPERUS COMMUNIS.

Juniper.

The *berries* are a stimulating diuretic, suitable to torpid conditions of the renal apparata. It increases the flow of urine and somewhat influences the uterine function in sluggish conditions. In typhoid fever, dropsy, cystic catarrh, renal congestions, but it is not best in irritated conditions except in combination with eupatorium purpureum in excess.

The *oil* very much resembles the berries in properties and may be used for the same general purposes. With vaseline or glycerine it forms a good wash for irritated surfaces.

The fluid extract is a good preparation.

F. E. Juniperus Com.
" Eupatorium Purpur. aa. oz. ss
Syr. Zingiber. oz. i

This forms an excellent diuretic.

JUNIPERUS SABINA.

Savine.

The *twigs and leaves* are a powerful stimulating diuretic and emmenagogue. The pregnant should not use this agent at all. It is too irritating for internal use, but the *oil* may be incorporated with other ingredients and used upon the surface where a powerful stimulant is required   When used by itself upon the surface of those who are thin skinned it will blister

JUNIPERUS VIRGINIANA.

Red Cedar

The *leaves* contain an essential *oil* which is obtained by distillation   It forms an excellent application for sprains and bruises, painful and swollen joints. Internally, triturated on lactin, it is a stimulating diuretic.

KALMIA LATIFOLIA

Mountain Laurel.

The *leaves* are a mild stimulating and relaxing alterant especially influencing the glandular system

F. E. Kalmia Lat.
" Euonymous Atr   aa dr iii
" Dicentra Ex.   dr. i
" Menispermum Can   dr ii
" Xanthoxylum Carol.   gtta. xv
Syr. Simplex   q. s oz. iv

M. S   Teaspoonful three or four times a day for skin diseases. secondary syphilis, scrofula and glandular swellings

An infusion of kalmia may be used for rheumatism or other conditions indicating irritation of the serous membrane.

The fluid extract is a good preparation and may be used whenever the agent is needed

KRAMERIA IXINA.

Rhatany.

The *bark* contains a large proportion of tannic acid.

The *root* is a mild, pleasant, soothing, stimulating and diffusive, astringent tonic   Though stimulating it is not irritating to the mucous membrane   It is somewhat drying but not intensely so

In the treatment of leucorrhœa, prolapsus uteri and vaginal relaxation it is a valuable wash

It is of much service applied to bleeding surfaces, and internally it is valuable for the relief of hemorrhage, whether it be of the gastric, intestinal, uterine or respiratory organs

Locally it is an excellent application for spongy gums, mercurial sore mouth. It is also of excellent service in the treatment of diarrhœa and in dysentery acute or chronic, and in typhoid fever it is frequently of service.

LACTUCA SATIVA.

Garden Lettuce.

This *plant* is a soothing nervine, whether used as an edible or in the form of an inspissated juice. It is also soothing to the mucous membrane of the gastric and alvine canal. It is pleasant in an irritated or ulcerated stomach and is useful in an irritable dyspepsia.

It is very soothing and quieting to an irritated condition of the nervous system.

Insp. lactuca may be combined with scutelaria and lupulin and used with good results, or the following may be used as a nervine of much value:

Insp. Lactuca
F. E. Humulus   aa. 2½
    "   Scutelaria
    "   Cypripedium   aa. 5½

LAMIUM ALBUM.

Blind Nettle.   Europe, Asia, North Africa.

The *flowers* are a powerful hæmostatic. It is of especial importance in the treatment of bronchial hemorrhage, in the coughing of blood, in uterine hemorrhage and in dysentery.

In metrorrhagia the fluid extract of the blossoms may be combined with some aromatic syrup and given every half hour until the hemorrhage ceases. It may then be given every four hours or as required.

LARIX AMERICANA.

Tamarac.

The *bark* is a mild, stimulating and relaxing alterant, influencing chiefly the skin and secernents. It is best in acute and inflammatory forms of blood and skin diseases. It is not suitable for the treatment of depressed cases, except in combination with more stimulating agents, as iris, dicentra or smilax.

F. E. Larix Am.   dr. iii
    "   Iris Vers.
    "   Dicentra Ex.
    "   Smilax Sar.   aa. dr. ii
    "   Xanthoxylum Car.   gtta. xv
Syr. Simplex   q. s. oz. iv

M. S Teaspoonful from three to six times a day. This is a valuable alterant

LAURUS CAMPHORA.

Camphor

The camphor evergreen is native to Japan and South-eastern Asia. The leaves, stems and trunk yield a so-called gum which is put through a principle of purification. It is very volatile and will evaporate if exposed to the air. To obtain it in fine powder it must be triturated on magnesia, lactin or sugar Camphor is not really a gum, but a concrete oil more or less solidified. It has a penetrating fragrance and a bitter, pungent taste.

Camphor is antispasmodic and rather soothing to the nervous system.

Aqua camphora is made by either of the following formulæ.

Camphor	dr. ii
Alcohol	gtta. xl
Carbonate Magnesia	dr. iv
Aqua	pts. ii

Or

Camphor	dr. ss
Alcohol	dr. vi

Shake these till dissolved, and add by trituration, subsequently filter:

Carb. Magnesia	dr. iss
Aqua	dr. xxvi

One or two grains of camphor will relieve after-pains, or better, the water of champhor may be given. Yet it is not the best thing to be given

Locally it allays muscular soreness.

Ol. Olivæ	4
Laurus Camph. dissolved	1

Or

Laurus Camph	oz iiss
Oil Lavender	dr. i
Alcohol 45 p. c	oz. xvii

Either of the above formulæ is a good application for bruises, sprains or sore muscles

The following is a soothing liniment.

Laurus Camph	oz i
Oil Rosemary	
" Origanum	aa. dr. i

Alcohol	pt. i
Castile Soap	oz. iii

Or

Laurus Camph.	oz. iiiss
Oil Sassafras	
" Cedar	
Tr. Guaiacum	aa. oz. i
" Capsicum	oz. ii
Alcohol	pts. iv

Or

Spts. Camphor	oz. ii
" Origanum	
" Sassafras	aa. dr. ii
" Turpentine	oz. ss

Or

Spts. Camphor	oz. ii
Tr. Capsicum	oz. i
" Guaiacum	oz. ss
Alcohol	oz. iii

Or

Spts. Camphor	dr. iv
" Ammonia	
Oil Sassafras	
Turpentine	aa. dr. ii
Oil Cloves	dr. i

Apply the following for winter eczema:

Gum Camphor	
Oil Origanum	
Oil Cloves	aa. equal parts in vaseline.

To assist in stopping the flow of milk apply to the breasts a few times,

Gum Camphor	oz. ss
Turpentine	oz. iii

The ordinary spirits of camphor is made of gum camphor one ounce to eight ounces of 45 p. c. alcohol.

Camphor, sugar and acacia in equal parts is camphor powder.

Camphor ice is made as follows:

Camphor	oz. ii
Almond Oil	oz. xvi

Dissolve these and melt together

Spermaceti	
White Wax	aa. dr. i

While cooling add

Oil Rosemary   dr. i
Rose Water   oz. xvi

This is an excellent application

Camphor inhaled through the nostrils soothes and stimulates the brain and relieves oppression.

Dr. C. B. Riggs recommends the following for toothache
Tr. Camphor Gum   dr. vi
Oil Sassafras   dr ii

M. Sig. Bathe the gums frequently and fill the decayed tooth with a pledget of cotton saturated with the above compound. When this fails to relieve the aching allow the dentist to extract the tooth or if possible fill it. The tincture of camphor should be a saturated tincture with absolute alcohol.

Spts Camphor   1
Aqua Ammonia   2
Kerosene Oil   4

This will be found valuable for sprains

LAVENDULA VERA.

Lavender.

The *flowers* are a relaxing and stimulating, soothing nervine. It is an antispasmodic and useful in nervous restlessness and the irritation or depression therefrom.

It also forms a good adjuvant for the administering of other agents

The *oil* may be used for the same general purposes, and is best used when triturated on lactin or magnesia.

Lavendula Vera   oz. iss
Cinnamonum Cas.
Zingiber. Off.
Leonurus Card.
Pimpinella Anisum   .   aa. oz. ss

This forms an excellent compound for faintness, palpitation, shock, fright, colic or hysteria It is best administered in hot water.

Oil Lavender
 " Lemon   aa. dr vi
 " Rosemary   dr. ii
 " Cinnamon   gtta. xx
Alcohol 98 per cent   qrts. ii

This is a good cologne for the sick room.

Oil Lavender	M. 245
" Rosemary	M. 61
Cassia Cin.	oz. 1½
Cloves	oz. ⅛
Nutmeg	
Red Saunders	aa. oz. ⅛

Or

Oil Lavender	
Nutmeg	
Cinnamon	aa. grs. 300
Oil Rosemary	M. 20
Red Sandal	grs. 600

Either of these formulæ make good adjuvants for the administering of bitter medicines.

LEONURUS CARDIACA.

Motherwort.

This *herb* is a pleasant, reliable, diffusive, stimulating and relaxing, antispasmodic nervine. It influences the mucous membrane, especially that of the pelvic organs.

A hot infusion promotes a good outward circulation, increases the menstrual flow. It is useful in amenorrhœa and in dysmenorrhœa when congestion is present, and in hysteria and palpitation when the patient is more or less chlorotic.

Leontin	dr. ii
Elixir Wahoo	
Syr. Pepsin	aa. oz. ii

M. S. One teaspoonful after eating and one before retiring for amenorrhœa.

A cold infusion is a good tonic, improving the appetite, assisting digestion, and is somewhat a tonic diuretic.

This is not a proper agent for the pregnant to use, nor for those given to too free menstruation In case of afterpains when the lochia is quite scanty this agent may be used to advantage.

In anæmic and chlorotic nervousness, palpitation, restlessness and insomnia it is one of those mild agents that may be used to great advantage as well as for the relief of the aching back and pelvis in case of tardy menstruation.

F. E. Leonurus Card.	
" Dioscorea Vil.	aa. dr. iii
" Caulophyllum Thal.	dr. ii
Syr. Zingiberis	q. s. oz. iv

This is a good diffusive antispasmodic in cases of dysmenorrhœa

   F. E. Leonurus Card.
     " Senecio Aur.
     " Mitchella Rep.   aa. dr. iii
   Syr. Zingiberis   q. s. oz iv

This is a good nervine tonic for the chlorotic

   F E. Leonurus Card
     " Arctium Lap Sem. aa dr. iii
     " Xanthoxylum Frax.   dr. ss
     " Menispermum Can   dr. ii
   Syr Simp   q. s. oz iv

This may be used by the chlorotic who have some scrofulous or other impurity of the blood current.

   F. E. Leonurus Card.   dr. iii
   Ferri et Pot. Tart.   grs. x
   Hydrastia Sulph   gr. ss
   F. E. Taraxacum D L.   dr iv
   Syr Zingiberis   q s oz iv

This may be used where there is more or less failure of
gastric and intestinal digestion In cases of nervous prostration scutelaria may be added in small quantities.

LEPTANDRA VIRGINICA

Culver's Root.   (Veronica Virginica.)

The *root* is a mild slow but persistent relaxing hepatic
It is very slightly stimulating Its chief influence is exerted upon the liver tubuli rather than upon the gall cyst
It assists in the secretion rather than in the excretion of
bile · In fact it seems to exert but little influence in the
latter direction without being combined with some suitable agent Whenever mild, persistent, relaxing hepatic
influence is needed this agent is reliable and may be used
both internally and externally. But when used externally
it should be combined with an equal portion of capsicum
Thus combined it may be made into an excellent liver pad.

Leptandra, apocynum and and capsicum in equal parts
forms a good liver pad This should be occasionally moistened with the fluid extracts or tinctures of the same.

Leptandra is quite nauseating to some stomachs in some
conditions. In such cases the pad or the application of
the fluid extracts is an excellent substitute

In acute febrile conditions it is best to combine leptandra with more stimulating agents, and in jaundice this

must always be the case, especially if the gall be somewhat solidified. Preparations of the green root are more cathartic than those of the dry root. As a rule leptandra is not a cathartic, yet its relaxing influence is felt upon the whole alvine mucous membrane and through this relaxation of the alvine membrane it dislodges viscid mucous and occasional doses are valued for this cleansing cause in cases of diarrhœa and dysentery. When used as a physic large doses must be given.

In cholera infantum small doses given once or twice a day will cleanse the alvine canal of viscid mucous and assist in the proper secretion of bile, and indirectly by its relaxing influence may also relieve the gall cyst, and thus create a healthy flow of bile, and a healthy condition of the alvine mucous membrane.

In nearly all febrile conditions it is needed, though it is usually best when combined with some diffusive or cholagogue. If it is to be used alone it is best in acute rather than in chronic cases, when it is a necessity that it be combined with more stimulating agents.

In chronic constipation in cases of hepatic failure leptandra may be used, but is best with agents more stimulating and those more cholagogue.

Leptandrin	dr. ss
Oil Capsicum	gtta. x
Lactin	dr. ii

Trit. Make into twenty-five powders. This is a valuable hepatic.

Leptandrin	
Podophyllin	aa. gr. i
Capsicum	
Apocynin	aa. gr. ss

This may be taken in capsule once or twice a day in cases of torpor or congestion of the liver.

In typhoid fever more or less capsicum is needed in small and frequent doses with all hepatics.

Leptandra in combination with some alterants will be found valuable in the treatment of skin eruptions.

F. E. Leptandra Virg.	dr. vi
" Hydrastis Can.	dr. ss
" Gentiana Och.	gtta. xv
Syr. Zingiberis	q. s. oz. iv

This is a good tonic hepatic.

F E. Leptandra Virg.   dr. vi
"   Apocynum And.   dr ss
Syr. Zingiberis   oz. iv

This will influence both sides of the liver about equally.

F E Leptandra Virg.   dr. vi
"   Podophyllin   gr. ii
Syr. Zingiberis   q s oz iv

This will favorably influence both secreting and excreting functions of the liver.

F. E. Leptandra Virg.   dr iii
"   Euonymous Atr.   dr ii
"   Taraxacum D. L.   dr. iv
Syr Zingiberis   q s oz iv

This is a gentle hepatic tonic and forms an excellent base which may be influenced by various other agents.

Leptandrin   grs 1 1-4
Juglandin
Euonymin   aa. gr. 3-4
Apocynin
Sodæ Bicarb.   aa gr 1-16
Ol Res Capsici   gtta 1-40
Ol Mentha Pip.   gtta 1-20

This forms the famous Stimson Physio-Medical Pill, hepatic and cathartic

Leptandrin   gr 1
Podophyllin   gr ½
Irisin   gr. ¼

This forms a good cholagogue. hepatic and alterant.

LIATRIS ODORATISSIMA.

Deer Tongue

This is, a stimulating, astringent tonic, influencing chiefly the mucous membrane It is valuable in the checking of rectal hemorrhages and in dysentery and diarrhœa.

In hot infusion it influences the circulation Its hepatic action is also well marked

Dr F G Hoener recommends the use of this agent in cases of abscesses of the liver and in miliary consumption.

LIATRIS SPICATA.

Button Snake-root.

The **root** is an aromatic. diffusive, stimulating and relaxing diuretic, increasing the flow of urine and relieving irritation

In hot infusion it influences the circulation, gives a good outward flow of blood, soothes the peripheral nerves and the uterus, and is somewhat diaphoretic.

It is a good antispasmodic and may be used to relieve colic, after-pains and dysmenorrhœa, especially where there is a deficient flow.

In hot infusion it is valuable in the fever stage of eruptive diseases. It is quite diffusive and maintains a good capillary circulation.

Used locally and internally it is recommended for the elimination of snake virus, and also for weak sores and chancres. In cases of renal debility or renal and cystic congestion it gives favorable results.

LINDERA BENZOIN.

Spice-bush.

The *bark and berries* are a mild diffusive, relaxing and stimulating diaphoretic. In hot infusion it may be used for the relief of colds and in the eruptive diseases. In relieving the circulation it also soothes and gently stimulates the nervous system and is valuable in the acute stage of rheumatism, gonorrhœa and syphilis.

LINUM USITATISSIMUM.

Flax.

The *seed* are an excellent soothing demulcent, stimulating and toning agent to the mucous membrane of the alvine, respiratory and urinary tracts and is valuable for the relief of irritated and inflamed conditions.

When needed for the respiratory tract, it relieves irritation and promotes expectoration. In hot infusion it may be used for the relief of recent colds and coughs. For such conditions it is best made in syrup form.

When needed for the alvine tract it may be used cold. In dysentery, diarrhœa and cholera infantum it soothes, heals and tones.

When required for the urinary tract it soothes and relieves irritation, but its influence will be more marked when combined with more positive diuretics.

After the oil has to a great extent been pressed out of the ground seed what is left is denominated oil meal. This is frequently used as a poultice. In bronchitis and pneumonia it forms an excellent poultice for the lungs.

It may be frequently moistened with lobelia, verbascum and capsicum combined as desired.

For boils and abscesses it is best combined with ulmus.

The *raw oil* is valuable for many purposes. Internally in sufficient doses it will prove cathartic.

Combined with pulverized ulmus it is a most valuable preparation for the covering of burns I have always had the very best of results with its use. Never allow the surface to become uncovered untill thoroughly healed, It will do its work without leaving any marks, no difference how deep the wound, wipe off any puss that may be present and remove dead flesh and then cover again with this preparation The results of gunpowder accidents I have frequently removed with the same. Of course nervines, cathartics. hepatics or alteratives may be added as needed by the constitution.

An excellent flaxseed tea is made as follows.—

Flax seed .

Rock Candy aa oz. viii

To which add three lemons pared and sliced. Then add two quarts of boiling water, and cool and strain.

Dr. C B. Riggs recommends the following (German Liniment) for burns.

Linseed Oil (raw)

Turpentine __ ...aa oz. xvi

Sulphuric Acid C. P. oz i

Mix the oil and the turpentine thoroughly. Put this mixture into an earthen crock and add the sulphuric acid very slowly, a few drops at a time, then allow to stand twenty - four hours until all the precipitate has formed and pour off and retain the supernatant fluid only.

Keep the burned surface wet with this liniment. The surface may be covered with gauze or cheese cloth and thus kept saturated This forms an antiseptic covering to exclude the air It desirable some agreeable perfume may be added The Doctor says, this is the best thing for burns that he has ever used, and that he has had remarkable results with it, having healed some very extensive burns without ulceration or scar He gives credit to Dr. P Holt for this formula

LIPPIA MEXICANA.

(Lippia Dulcis) Cuba, Central America, Columbia

This is a creeping shrub covered with minute glandular

hairs. It blossoms from November till March.

The *leaves and stalks* are gathered during the flowering season or shortly after. It has an agreeable sweetish taste and is slightly demulcent. It is a pleasant, prompt, stimulating and relaxing, demulcent alterant. It influences the respiratory mucous membrane and is a valuable expectorant. Large doses may be followed by nausea and vomiting.

Care must be taken to have a fresh article. It contains a volatile oil called lippiol, the absence of which renders the agent more or less inert. Much heat must not be used in the extracting of its virtues.

The aqueous extract is devoid of astringency.

In hot infusion it relieves colds, loosens catarrhal secretions, increases expectoration and relieves soreness of the throat and is excellent in the treatment of la grippe. It quickly allays an irritating cough, and is very useful in acute and chronic bronchitis, catarrhal fever, catarrhal phthisis and night sweats. It tones the respiratory mucous membrane and cleanses it of excessive mucous.

LIQUIDAMBER STYRACIFLUA.

Sweet Gum.

From incisions made in the bark of this Southern tree flows a nearly transparent aromatic balsam. Its volatile oil is more or less evaporated upon drying. This resinous *gum* is warming and moderately stimulating and relaxing.

Combined with olive oil or vaseline it forms an ointment for ringworm, scald head, tetter and other irritations of the skin. It rarely fails to cure scabies and is a valuable application for old sores, hemorrhoids and ulcers. Internally it may be used in gleet and other excessive discharges.

The *bark* is a mildly stimulating agent and may be used freely in gonorrhœa, cystic catarrh, dysentery and diarrhœa.

LIRIODENDRON TULIPIFERA.

Tulip-Tree.

The *inner bark* of the trunk and roots is a mild, bitter, aromatic, relaxing and very gently stimulating alterant and nervine.

The green bark is much more positive than the dry.

This agent influences the mucous membrane, the secernents, the nervous system and the generative organs. It improves the appetite, assists digestion and is somewhat laxative to the bowels.

In convalescence it is a mild nervine tonic and is grateful to the stomach.

It is especially soothing and toning to the generative organs and is a valuable agent to be used in the treatment of nervous irritability, hysteria and the irritations sometimes incident to pregnancy.

In influencing the generative system it also influences the urinary membrane and very gently increases the flow of urine.

In combination with such agents as aralia racemosa, symphytum or prunus it influences the respiratory organs and to cough syrups it adds an excellent nervine influence.

F E Liriodendron Tulip
"   Aralia Rac.
"   Symphytum Off
"   Inula Hel   aa. dr. i
Syr. Prunus   q. s. oz. iv
This is a good cough syrup.

F. E. Liriodendron Tul   dr. vii
"   Hydrastis Can.   dr. ss
Syr. Aurantium Cort.   q s oz. iv
This is a good nervine tonic.

F. E. Liriodendron T.   dr iii
"   Caulophyllum Th
"   Leonurus Card
"   Viburnum Op   aa. dr. i
"   Senecio Au   dr. ii
Syr. Zingiberis   q s oz. iv
This is useful in dysmenorrhœa.

F. E Liriodendron Tul.   oz ss
"   Valeriana Off.
"   Caulophyllum Th   aa dr. i
"   Xanthoxylum   gtta. x
Tr. Anisum   dr. i
This forms a good nervine tonic, and so is the following:

F E Liriodendron   dr. iv
"   Convallaria Mult.
"   Euonymous At.   aa. dr. ii
"   Hydrastis Can.
"   Scutelaria Lat   aa dr. ss
Syr. Aurantium Cort.   oz. i
"   Zingiberis   oz. iv

LOBELIA INFLATA.

Lobelia.

The **herb and seed** are relaxant with a moderate degree of diffusive stimulation. More especially in the seed we find an extractive and a volatile oil. It is best gathered when about half ripe, but you will find the plant good at any time of its growth.

Much heat will injure it. To prepare an infusion use a sufficient quantity of boiling water and allow it to stand covered. The seed will not readily yield their properties unless well crushed.

To extract the inspissated juice it must be gathered green and heavily pressed.

When the herb is put up to dry it should be placed upon its root end so as to prevent losing the seed out of the capsules. When once thoroughly dry it should be packed in a close box; or the better way is to make a fluid extract of the fresh herb. For ordinary use this is strong enough.

Lobelia is a relaxant to the mucous, serous, nervous and muscular structures. It influences the glandular system; the fauces and the respiratory tubuli. It increases the flow of saliva; relaxes, cleanses and tones the mucous membrane throughout. To the fauces it is acrid and to the gastric membrane it is nauseating. If small doses be given at regular intervals it will bring the whole body under its influence, and a condition known as "the alarm" produced. Its influence then is complete on the capillaries, the nerve peripheries, the general circulation, and the muscular and glandular systems. In certain acute conditions it relieves the tension of the circulation, establishes the functions of the skin, relaxes the secernents, and relieves the liver, kidneys and bowels.

Lobelia is one of the greatest equalizers of the circulation and gives a full outward flow of blood. Its influence reaches every organ and almost if not quite every tissue of the body, and hence wherever a relaxing influence is needed it will be felt. Medically therefore its range is wide, especially in acute troubles. In influencing the circulation it also influences the nerves, sympathetic, central and spinal.

The muscles thoroughly feel its relaxing power and it becomes one of the best aids in surgery requiring relaxation, especially in dislocations.

Lobelia is abused by Physio-Medicalists more by leaving it out of their prescriptions than in any other way.

It is of great service in croup, pneumonia bronchitis, pleuritis, hepatitis, peritonitis, nephritis, phrenitis, otitis, ophthalmia, rheumatism, and in nearly all the forms of fever. In many cases it is best to add some asclepias and zingiber Such a combination will give quick relief in pulmonary congestions Given in hot infusion it clears out the lungs wonderfully.

Very weak persons can take emetics when they are needed, even an occasional emetic may be given to consumptives Emesis is also valuable in puerperal fever in certain conditions Give to cleanse and stop, and repeat only as required.

Pound the green herb to a pulp and press out the juice into a shallow porcelain vessel and allow to evaporate in the sun to a thick paste and bottle for use. I have heard this plaster recommended as a cure for cancer, but it makes an excellent plaster for swollen joints, sprains, abscesses, boils, etc.

In the beginning of typhoid fever an emetic will prove serviceable in cleansing the system and equalizing the circulation

If necessary you can give the stimulating agents by the stomach and the lobelia by enema. In typhoid cases it takes but little to produce emesis

In the tardy appearance of the eruption in the eruptive diseases an emetic serves a good purpose. It equalizes the circulation, opens the pores and gives free vent for the eruption, usually all that there is in the system, and such cases will make good recovery.

You will find some jaundiced cases that can retain nothing on the stomach. Give them an enema of lobelia and the stomach will soon be emptied of an amount of viscid bile and soon be quieted

An emetic has frequently proven valuable in cases of hepatic congestion

In membranous croup an enema at lobelia to move the bowels and produce relaxation will be of value. Give a strong tea of lobelia per enema and follow with a strong infusion per oram Follow with some diffusive stimulants and relief will be experienced

The enema may also be used in order to produce emesis in cases of malarial fever if required

In dislocations give small doses regularly and frequently and apply also locally, and it will be of great value in relaxing the parts so that the dislocation may be the more readily and easily reduced.

Locally lobelia is of great value applied to abscesses or erysipelas. Hydrastis may be added as needed.

The *oil* of lobelia has less of the stimulating property and is not so likely to produce emesis. To prepare this oil cover the seed with 98 per cent. alcohol, shake this tincture occasionally, and after being well saturated four or five days, then percolate thoroughly, adding alcohol till the strength is exhausted. Evaporate on a water bath and you have the oil. Then water can be added to the percolator and a strong preparation results, to which some glycerin may be added. This will be an excellent addition to cough syrups.

The oil is best for asthma, combined as follows. It seldom fails in hay asthma:

    Oil Lobelia Infl.
    Cincho—Quinine   aa. oz. i
    Sugar (granulated)   oz. ii

Dr. G. H. Mayhugh gives the following for asthma:

    Oil Lobelia
    Cinchonidia   aa. dr. i
    Sacch. Lactin   oz. ii

M. Trit. Sig. Five to ten grains every one to three hours, until relief is had. Then give four times a day till cured.

Dr. F. G. Hoener gives the following for asthma:

    Syr. Scillæ
    Tr. Lobelia
    F. E. Hepatica Tril.
    Syr. Bidens Bip. aa. equal parts.

M. S. Take one dessertspoonful every hour or every two hours till relieved.

    Oil Lobelia
    " Zingiber.   aa. gtta. iii
    Caulophyllin
    Cimicifugin   aa. grs. iss

Trit. on lactin. For hysterical cough give three doses fifteen minutes apart.

    Lobelia Infl.   oz. ii
    Nepeta Cat.   oz. i

Sanguinaria Can.   ' dr ii
Xanthoxylum Frax. Bac   dr i

Add one-half pint saturated tincture of cypripedium Steep in one and a-half pints of water for three hours. Then strain, press and add two pounds of sugar. This is a serviceable cough syrup for the scrofulous and anæmic   :

F E. Lobelia Infl   dr ii
" Cypripedium Pub   dr iv
Tr Capsicum   dr ss
Syr. Simplex   q s oz vi

M S. Terspoonful every half hour in the treatment of puerperal convulsions

In giving lobelia there will be less relaxation if capsicum or hydrastis be added.

In the treatment of congestions some diffusive stimulation should be added

In cases of gastric irritation give minute doses at regular intervals This will allay irritation, prevent emesis, arrest spasmodic conditions and allay sympathetic vomiting.

In spasmodic and membranous croup, whooping cough, asthma, occlusion of the gall ducts, strangulated hernia, rigid os uteri, hour-glass contractions and tetanus, lobelia has no equal.

Emesis is a powerful arrestor of hemorrhages, whether from lungs, uterus or bowels. It casts out impurities and equalizes the circulation.

Lobelia is best suited where and when arterial action is strong and when given in asthenic and more or less putrescent conditions, its continuance usually should be brief, only sufficient to cleanse and then use a more stimulating treatment.

Small doses given at regular intervals and continued for some time will bring on that state known as the alarm, in which condition we examine our patient and find him with a good, full, soft, steady pulse; breathing full and gentle; the secretions of the skin increased; the secernents are all relaxed, and the whole system is in a state of relaxation and rest. The patient rallies from such a condition in an hour or so Usually this time is shortened if some stimulation is given or applied As a result of such condition the skin will be relaxed, there will be a free discharge of urine, of bile and of fæces. The nerves are quieted, the mucous membrane is freed of much mucous, and in every way the whole system and all of its several parts are more completely under the control of the vital force than they had previously been.

In cases of convulsions, lobelia should be combined with caulophyllum.

In tetanus it is best administered by enemata. Give in large doses and give until relaxation occurs, then sustain by appropriate stimulation.

In cases of hemorrhage after emesis follow with astringents.

With ulmus it is valuable in ophthalmia as a wash or poultice.

In surgery it has no equal where relaxation is needed. It quiets the nerves and prevents the vital force from putting forth as much inflammatory effort.

Small enemas may be used to prevent seminal discharges and nocturnal erections.

Lobelia is not best in nervous prostration, paralysis, gangrene or shock.

     Lobelia Inf.   2

     Symplocarpus

     Sanguinaria   aa. 1

This may be prepared into a syrup for croup, asthma and nervous coughs.

     Lobelia Infl.

     Capsicum   aa. dr. iv

     Cypripedium   dr. ii

     Comp. Tr. Myrrh et Cap. (No. 6) oz. viii

This is Dr. Samuel Thompson's Third Preparation of Lobelia. It is a most valuable preparation. In sluggish cases it arouses the system to dislodge semi-putrescent material, and quickly stimulates and equalizes the circulation. It is a most valuable preparation for sick-headache, some forms of dyspepsia and in the incipiency of some forms of apoplexy.

Tincture Lobelia Comp., third preparation, the Physio-Medicalist's sheet anchor, when life hangs in the balance, where effects are required on short notice, the tincture lobelia comp. can be relied upon when made by C. T. Bedford who uses only the best material in its manufacture.

The Oil of Lobelia kept in stock by C. T. Bedford is extra fine being made by the formula peculiar to G. N. Davidson.

     Third Lobelia

     Tr. Lobelia Infl.

F. E. Scutelaria Lat.

"   Valeriana aa. equal parts.

M. S. Three-fourths teaspoonful in warm water every five minutes in a strong infusion of cimicifuga.   Use this in cases of rattlesnake bite.

| Pul. Lobelia Seed | dr. ii |
| Cider Vinegar | pt. i |

The vinegar may be added cold and tinctured for a week, or the vinegar may be raised to the boiling point and added, when it is immediately ready for use.

This is one of the best preparations for croup, whooping cough and asthma. This preparation is best administered in the form of acetous syrup, which is pleasant and very efficient.

To make the syrup fill the bottle two-thirds full of the tincture and add sugar to fill the bottle. Shake until dissolved. Or half the quantity of sugar may be replaced by an equal bulk of honey.

The oil is best administered by being triturated with 16 times its own weight of sugar or lactin, or the two may be combined in equal parts.

Dr. C. B. Riggs recommends the following compound 3-grain Lobelia pill:

Powd. Lobelia Infl. Seed	grs. iss
" Cypripedium Pub.	gr. i
" Capsicum	gr. ss
Extract Boneset	q. s. ad. pill.

Sig. One pill every one to four hours, as the conditions demand. The Doctor says, This is a most excellent preparation where profound relaxation is desired without emesis. It is excellent in peritonitis, lung and bronchial troubles, especially for bronchial cough and painful conditions in any part of the body.

Lobelia seed and tannin in equal parts in vaseline makes an excellent suppository or may be introduced in rectal capsules for hemorrhoids.

Triturate enough lobelia inflata in bicarbonate soda to form a thin paste and this rubbed well into a sore made by a rusty nail or into other inflamed or poisoned sores has been very successful in the hands of Dr. C. R. Phillips. At first put on a paste of this and then keep the surface moist with lobelia tincture. You will be surprised to see how quickly it will cause pain to cease and cure the wound.

Dr. F. O. Broady recommends the following hair tonic:

F. E. Lobelia Seed (made by cold process)	dr. vi
" Bayberry Bark " " " "	dr. ii
Strong Tinct. Capsicum	dr. ii
Glycerin	oz. i
Rose Water	q. s. oz. vi

M. Sig. Apply every morning after having first washed the scalp with a good tar soap. A small quantity well rubbed in is sufficient at each application. I have twice restored my own dying and falling hair with six ounces of this.

LYCOPERSICUM ESCULENTUM.

Tomato. (Solanum Lycopersicum.)

The *fruit* is a stimulating and soothing tonic alterant to the mucous membrane especially of the mouth, stomach and alvine canal. The fluid extract acts on the mucous lining of the mouth and other cavities and is excellent in nurse's sore mouth, canker and ulcerated sore mouth. The dose of the fluid extract is from 30 to 60 drops.

The fluid extract should be made without heat from the ripe tomatoes. Its alterative influence is felt by the lymphatics when they are swollen and hard and when scrofula is present. It assists in the relief of dyspepsia, constipation, catarrh, hemorrhoids, leucorrhœa, spongy gums, decaying teeth.

The tomato is a germicide and a cleanser of the mucous membrane, and may be a means of preventing typhoid fever and diarrhœa.

I have noticed one thing peculiar with the use of the tomato by those who have recently used some form of mercury. There may follow some semblance to salivation, but usually a little hydrastia phosphate and glycerin will quickly relieve this.

LYCOPODIUM CLAVATUM.

Club-Moss. Switzerland, Germany.

The capsules of this moss contain a fine powder called lycopodium which consists of the seeds or spores of the plant. It is exceedingly fine, very light and of a delicate yellow color, tasteless and inodorous.

This powder is a fine absorbent application to excoriated surfaces. It is an excellent baby powder for the preventing or cure of chafing. It may also be used for the covering of burns

LYCOPODIUM COMPLANATUM

Ground Pine.

Dr F G. Hoener says that with this he has cured some very severe cases of erysipelas He gives it internally and applies it as a wash locally

LYCOPUS EUROPÆUS

Bitter Archangel, Bitter Bugle Weed.

This is an extremely bitter, stimulating nervine The *herb* is a powerful antiperiodic and seems to influence the secernents more and the brain centres less than does quinine If it could be properly covered by some vehicle it would be a more valuable agent than quinine Small quantities may be used in large quantities of water as a tonic appetizer

LYCOPUS VIRGINICUS.

Bugle Weed.

The *herb* is an aromatic, soothing, stimulating, astringent tonic, influencing the mucous membrane It is valuable in dysentery, diarrhœa, cholera infantum, in typhoid fever, in hemorrhages of the lungs, gums, bowels, kidneys, uterus.

In hot infusion it influences the capillaries, soothes arterial excitement, strengthens the venous circulation, relieves gastric, alvine and urethral irritation, equalizes the circulation and soothes the nerves

In combination with inula, symphytum or prunus it forms a good tonic cough syrup where expectoration is quite free

Cold preparations influence the kidneys and give valuable assistance in enuresis, cystisis, nephritis and spermatorrhœa.

    F. E Convallaria M.   dr iv
      "   Lycopus Virg
      "   Liriodendron   aa dr. ii
    Syr Aurantium Cort   q. s oz iv
   M S Teaspoonful three times a day for the relief of ovaritis

An injection of lycopus into a fistula is a valuable appli-

cation. It may also be diluted and used in cases of urethral ulceration.

Lycopus is valuable both locally and constitutionally in
hemorrhages.

MAGNESIA.

This name is derived from the name of the district of
country where it was originally obtained. It is one of the
primitive alkaline earths, an oxide of magnesia.

Magnesiæ Sulphas (sulphate of magnesia, epsom salts)
is a mild, pleasant saline cathartic, usually operating in
four or five hours. It may be repeated as needed. If given
in some lemon syrup it forms an effervescent drink.

Magnesiæ Carbonas (carbonate of magnesia) is an
ant-acid and is used much for the relief of heartburn, sour
stomach and nausea, especially during the period of pregnancy. It also assists in keeping the bowels free during
this period. This also effervesces when mixed with some
acid. Magnesia is frequently used to absorb essential oils
by trituration and rendering them capable of suspension
in water, or making the oil more palatable by administering in dry form.

It may also be used as an absorbent or to apply to the
surface to keep it from chafing, or as a baby powder.

It is also used in the manufacture of tablets, pills and
troches.

Magnesia Usta (calcined or burnt magnesia) is obtained
by heating the carbonate and driving off the carbonic acid
gas. This combines with acids without effervescence.
With this exception it is almost identical in practice with
the carbonate.

Liquor Magnesiæ Citratis (solution of citrate of magnesia) is an ant-acid, a liquid preparation, a pleasant, effer-
vescing cathartic.

Milk of Magnesia ($Mg.H_2O_2$) is an excellent ant-acid,
and may be used wherever the use of magnesia is implied.

MAGNOLIA ACUMINATA.

Cucumber Tree.

MAGNOLIA GLAUCA.

Sweet Bay Tree.

MAGNOLIA TRIPETALA.

Umbrella Tree.

The *bark* of the root and trunk of all these species is a

mild aromatic, diffusive, stimulating tonic, influencing the mucous membrane of the alvine and renal tracts It increases the flow of urine and is a gentle laxative to the bowels

In convalescence it is a gentle tonic, improving digestion, and is of value in convalescence from fevers and rheumatism

It is useful in gonorrhœal or other urethral irritation

It is quite soothing to the nervous system and is very sustaining

MALLOTUS PHILIPPINENSIS.

Kamala ,   India

This is an evergreen tree of tropical India   The glands and hair of the capsules come to us in the form of a deep red powder, having but little taste, and insoluble in water.

The berries are gathered and rubbed together so as to divest them of this powder, which is a pleasant anthelmintic.   With occasional failures this brings away the tænia solium.   It causes no colic and needs to be followed by no physic as do other anthelmintics   It is itself rather a brisk physic if given in large doses   It may be given alone or in combination with male fern or kousso in equal parts   An ounce or more of the powder may be given in capsules, in fluid extract or in infusion

MALVA SYLVESTRIS AND ROTUNDIFOLIA.

High Mallows,   *Low Mallows*

These *plants* are demulcent tonics to the mucous membrane throughout.   It relieves irritation, whether of kidneys, bowels, bladder, or stomach   It is of much importance in dysentery, diarrhœa, nephritis, cystitis and urethritis   It may be used externally and internally.   In poultice it is excellent upon inflamed surfaces, and with such agents as aralia, comfrey or inula it gives valuable assistance to the lungs, over which it may also be applied as a poultice

MARRUBIUM VULGARE

Horehound.

This *herb* is a gently diffusive, stimulating tonic to the respiratory organs   In hot infusion it is somewhat diaphoretic, promotes a good outward flow of the circulation and relieves hyperæmic conditions of the lungs, congestions and hoarseness.

In combination with leonurus it relieves the menstrual flow.

Its best influence upon the lungs is in combination with aralia, inula and prunus.

Marrubium decreases the mucous discharge and gives good results in wet catarrh and where expectoration is too free.

MEDEOLA VIRGINICA.

Cucumber Root, Indian Cucumber.

The *root* is a soothing, gently stimulating diuretic. It increases the urinary flow, cleanses the mucous membrane and soothes and tones the urinary passages. It is serviceable in congestions of the urinary tract and in gonorrhœa.

Dr. F. G. Hoener recommends the following as a specific in some severe cases of gonorrhœa:

Medeola Virg.
Agrimonia Eup.
Plantago Major aa. equal parts.

MEL.

Honey.

This is the liquid prepared by the apis mellifica from the juice of certain flowers. The best is made from white clover.

It is stimulating to the mucous membrane, laxative to the bowels, and an expectorant to the bronchi. With sage and boracic acid it forms a good wash for sore mouth, and it is a good addition to cough syrups.

Tr. Lobelia oz. xvi
Oil Anise
" Sassafras aa. gtta. xv
Honey oz xii

This forms a good cough syrup, excellent for croup.

Honey exerts a peculiar influence over some forms of ulcers, especially that produced by the removal of cancers. Here it is one of the best dressings. Spread pure honey all over the sore. It heals quick and does well. It does well as a dressing after cleansing the surface on any ulcer. Cleanse with hydrozone and cover with honey.

Pul. Hydrastis 1
Mel 2

Mix and spread on muslin and lay on the lids in chronic
ophthalmia.

MELALEUCA CAJUPUTI

Cajuput

The *oil* obtained from the leaves is quite pungent and
stimulating Triturated on sugar it is a powerful and
permanent stimulant, quite healing to the stomach, and
influences the circulation toward the surface

Its best use is on the surface, where it is intensely stimulating and may be used alone or in combination with
other stimulating or relaxing medicines as the case may
require Its use will be beneficial in toothache

MELISSA OFFICINALIS.

Lemon Balm.

This *herb* forms a pleasant beverage for convalescence.
It is a strong and soothing, toning nervine.

In hot infusion it is somewhat diaphoretic and may be
used for the removal of colds, and for the restoration of
the menstrual flow stopped by recent cold

MENISPERMUM CANADENSE.

Yellow Parilla

The *root* is a slow, bitter, diffusive, permanent, stimulating alterative It slowly but positively influences the
secernents and the skin, and in diseases influencing such
it is exceedingly valuable as an alterant

It tones the mucous membrane throughout, assists gastric and intestinal digestion, and slowly relieves the liver
and gall ducts

Controlled by agents that have especial influence upon
the respiratory passages it is very valuable in phthisis, in
chronic bronchitis, and scrofulous conditions.

In the treatment of fevers in strumous persons this
agent is one of the best in combination with other suitable
agents

In biliousness, atonic dyspepsia, glandular swellings,
scrofulous and mercurial rheumatism, secondary syphilis
and indolent ulcers, in combination with such agents as
rumex, fraxinus, celastrus, arctium or phytolacca valuable
compounds may be formed

F. E. Menispermum Can.
" Arctium Lap.
" Taraxacum D. L. aa. equal parts.
This is a good hepatic alterant.
   F. E. Menispermum Can.   dr. iii
   " Fraxinus Am.   dr. iv
   " Celastrus Scan.   dr. iii
   Syr. Zingiberis   q. s. oz. iv
This is a good alterant for skin diseases.

MENTHA ARVENSIS.

Japanese Peppermint.   Japan and China.

It is from this plant that we get that useful camphoraceous substance denominated *menthol,* which as an antiseptic is about equal to thymol.

In China and Japan it is considered a specific for headache and is recommended for sciatica and neuralgia.

Menthol camphor put into a carious tooth relieves toothache usually at once.

This comes in crystals deposited from the oil on exposure to cold. It is the camphor of peppermint oil. It is only partially soluble in water but melts at 100 degrees F. and soon volatilizes without decomposition. It will evaporate and disappear at the ordinary temperature of living rooms. It is a camphor and not an oil at such temperature.

Its smell is less pungent than that of peppermint but it has a sharper taste. On the skin it produces a sensation of cold, and yet the temperature may be exalted slightly.

Menthol and iodoform or iodide of potassium combined equally in vaseline may be used for ringworm or tinea capitis.

Menthol may be applied to the head in cases of neuralgia and inhaled for coryza, or combined with albolen it may be atomized. It may be used in this way also in bronchitis, whooping cough, nasal catarrh or asthma.

It is a germicide and antiseptic and is valuable in the treatment of la grippe.

It has been said that 1 to 33000 prevents the development of anthrax bacilli and 1 to 2000 destroys the cholera bacilli.

A 20 per cent. solution may be used for pruritus ani or pruritus vulva. It may be used for the same purposes when combined with olive oil or vaseline

Menthol   grs. xxx
Ess Rosemary or Comp Spts Lavender
Alcohol 45 per cent   aa dr ii
This may be applied to carious teeth.
Menthol   dr. v
Spts. Camphor
Alcohol   aa. oz i

This is usually successful in neuralgia colic and inflamed conditions

Menthol is useful in erysipelas It circumscribes the eruption, allays pain and itching and lessens its duration

Menthol
Alcohol   aa oz i
Oil Cinnamon   gtta. xxx
is successful in facial and intercostal neuralgia.

Menthol may be triturated on sugar or lactin and given in small doses for the vomiting of pregnancy. It may also be combined with syrup and given in small quantities internally for the same purpose, or it may be inhaled.

Menthol may be dissolved in olive or cotton seed oil and used over burns

Combined with sodium salicylate and iodide potassium it will be found useful in rheumatism.

Sprayed into the throat it relieves hoarseness, clears the voice and assists in the treatment of laryngitis.

Menthol is altogether preferable to the ordinary smelling salts.

Menthol must be tightly corked to prevent rapid volatilization

Menthol is claimed to be of much value in sunstroke.

Thymenthol is a good antiseptic preparation of thymol and menthol It is useful where either of its components is useful.

MENTHA PIPERITA.

This *herb* is a diffusive, aromatic, stimulating and relaxing antispasmodic nervine and carminative. It is soothing to the stomach and allays vomiting

Tr Comp Myrrh and Capsicum 3
Ol. Mentha Pip   1

This will arrest chills in the milder forms of ague even after the person has begun to feel chilly. Give small doses every five minutes in some hot water This preparation well diluted may also be used for gastralgia and shock.

F. E Cypripedium Pub.
    "   Dioscorea Vil.   aa 20
Ess Mentha Pip   1
Syr Zingiber.   q. s

This may be used· for colic for babies or adults, also for flatulence, gastralgia, enteralgia, cholera morbus, cholera infantum and chronic diarrhœa

A drop or two of the essence may be added to cathartics and bitter tonics, with the former it prevents griping and nausea and with the latter it partially covers their bitterness

The *oil* is more positively stimulating and warming but is less relaxing and diffusive than the herb.

Oil Peppermint
    " Anise
    " Cajuput
    " Cloves   aa. oz. 1
Alcohol   oz iv

This is a stimulating preparation for either internal use or for external application.

Dr F. G. Hoener recommends the following for delirium tremens

.Elix Mentha Pip   oz. 1
    " Trichostema Dichota   oz. 11
Tr. Ferri   dr iv
Elix. Hydrastis
Oil Bergamot   aa dr. ii

M   S   One tablespoonful four or five times a day. Give hot water or milk to drink

MENTHA VIRIDIS

Spearmint.

This *herb* is a soothing, aromatic, diffusive, relaxing and stimulating diuretic and nervine   It induces free discharges of the watery portion of the urine, relieves flatulence and soothes the nervous system

A weak infusion readily allays nausea and vomiting, the vomiting of pregnancy, and is quieting to the stomach after free emesis.

Mentha Vir.   3
Zingiber   1

forms a good preparation for colic, flatulence and some cases of hysteria.

The *oil* may be used for the same purposes of the herb.

It may be triturated on sugar or lactin for internal use.

Oil Mentha V.
" Rosemary   aa. 1
Tr Lobelia   10

This makes a good application for various aches and pains.

Oil Mentha Pip.
" Mentha Vir   aa. equal parts in Vaseline

forms an excellent application to the nostrils by pencil-brush or by atomization. This protects the mucous membrane, especially when about to be exposed to the cold air. It is very valuable in cases of catarrh It protects the surface, soothes and heals. It is also excellent in hay asthma.

MENYANTHES TRIFOLIATA.

Buckbean

The **root** is a mild, stimulating tonic, influencing the secernents and glandular system

Large doses are somewhat nauseating but are thoroughly hepatic and cholagogue It also increases the flow of urine

In its way it is valuable as an antiperiodic and an alterant It cleanses the secernents and relieves the glandular system generally It will be found useful in scrofula or where there is any impurity in the blood current. It is also quite useful in dropsy, where hepatic, alterative, diuretic and tonic influences are needed to be thoroughly felt.

MICROSCOPY.

By F O BROADY, M. D,

Late Professor of Histology and Pathology in Chicago Physio-Medical College

Only a few hints can here be given on the subject of Microscopy The student is referred for further necessary information to the many excellent manuals published in America and England Chief among these may be said to be Dr. Carpenter on "The Microscope and its Revelations" (cost $6 00); Lionel S Beale's "How to Work with the Microscope" ($7.50); Prof D J Hamilton's "Text Book of Pathology," 2 vols. ($12 50); Stirling's "Histology" ($3 00), a work on common objects. will no doubt be interesting, and M C. Cooke on "Ponds and Ditches" (85 cts.) may be

recommended. With the works of Stirling, Beale, Hamilton and Cooke the foundation for a good microscopical
library has been laid, and with this beginning the charm
of the microscope and its beautiful, useful and wonderful
revelations will never lose its force with the student.

The microscope is simply an aid to the eye, and being a
very delicate aid it is subject to unusual fallacies. A good
instrument should therefore be chosen at first, so that this
outlay of money may not be wasted, but be made the foundation of a complete outfit.

Some of the principal makers of good microscopes are
Zeiss and Leitz of Germany, Beck and Watson of England,
and Bausch & Lomb of America. A good second-hand
stand by Mr. Bullock, of Chicago, is equal with the best,
but Mr. Bullock is now dead. In general, we may say that
the microscopes made by Zeiss and Leitz are carefully
made but none of them are specially arranged for tilting
the instrument. This compels most of the work to be
done with the instrument standing straight up, and is
very tiring to the investigator as well as causing dimness
of vision from retinal congestion. This is a serious fault
with all "continental model" microscopes. Among English makers Watson, of London, is coming to the front; his
beautiful exhibit at the Columbian Exposition attracted
great attention. A satisfactory high-class stand (the instrument without lenses) would be Watson's* "Edinburgh
Student's" microscope, tripod foot, model "H," cost with
case $51.00 in England; with 1 inch and 1-6 inch objective,
two eye pieces, Abbe substage illuminator with iris diaphragm, the cost is $75.00 in England—roughly counting
the pounds at $5.00 and the shillings at 25 cents. In gen-
eral, it may be said that the custom house tariff is at
present 40 per cent. on these instruments, and the express-
age from London to Chicago is $10.00 for 200 pounds. The
services of a custom house broker are needed to get the
goods out of the custom house and shipped to other points;
his charge will be $5.00. A shipment from England is
practical where two or more buyers join in one shipment.

A corresponding American outfit would be Bausch &
Lomb's (Rochester, N. Y.) "Universal Microscope, J,"
two eye pieces, 3-4 inch and 1-5 inch objectives, Abbe condenser, with case, costs $85.00. To either stand a 1-12 inch

---

*W. Watson & Sons, 313 High Holborn, W. C., London, England.

oil immersion lens should be added for advanced work, this is the standard lens for bacteriological work. An excellent lens is sold by Watson for $25 00 in London and a good one by Bausch & Lomb for $44.00 A "nose piece" is next needed to hold the objectives so that a change can be instantaneously made from one power to another. It should be ordered with the stand in order that it may be truly centered to that particular instrument A double nose piece will do (American cost $5.00, English $3 75)

The following list comprises the principal accessories which would make an excellent microscopical outfit with what has already been mentioned· Beale's Camera Lucida (English cost $1.50) for drawing objects and for measurements, dissecting microscope for minute dissections, with objectives 1 inch, ½ inch, ¼ inch (American cost $10 00, English $8 75); stage micrometer, metric system (American $2 00; English $1 25), for measuring size of objects, Rousselet's Live Box (American $2 50, English $2 60) for studying live animalculæ; Cathcart's Microtome, the best of the cheap kind and very useful Watson sells it for $5 25 and it can be used both for ether freezing or imbedding Bausch & Lomb charge $19 00 for practically the same instrument The knife is extra, and Cole's costs $1 12 in England and $3 25 in America Next comes a turn table (American $2.50, English $1 67) for making mountings; dissecting case of instruments (American $3 50; English $2 67), injecting syringe for preparing specimens by Beale's method (American $10 00; English, one pipe less, $3 12); glass shade for protecting the microscope from dust and a great convenience, $5 00 with base This and the following articles can be bought in America to greater advantage The smallest size hand lamp, to be fitted with ground blue glass chimney for evening work, 4-ring retort stand ($1.00); spirit lamp (35 cents), water bath (50 cents); sand bath (50 cents), wash bottle, pipettes, cover glass forceps (50 cents), bell glass (50 cents), for covering work from dust, brass table for heating slides, with suitable lamp ($1 80; a dozen or more each of assorted ebonite and block tin cells (20 cents a dozen), thin cover glasses; ground glass slides, watch glasses; a few staining fluids, as Beal's carmine, eosine, hœmatoxylin (each 20 cents); Bell's cement, Canada balsam, Price's glycerine. two capped bottles (30 cents each) for balsam and glycerine; and Pillsbury's cabinet ($3 25) to preserve your specimens A plain but steady table is also needed. If shipment is made from England it would be very satisfactory to include some of Watson's excellent mounted specimens of human tissue at 25 cents apiece, admitted free of duty.

A good microscope should be steady on its foot; the "field" (that is the surface of the picture presented to view) should be of good size—apparently 2¼ inches in diameter is good; there should be no rings of color around the outer edge of the field if the lens is good; the field should not seem to move or be unsteady as the tube is raised and lowered; and the fine and coarse adjustments should work perfectly smoothly from one end to the other.

Great stress is laid by all teachers of microscopy on the need of the student drawing all that he observes. It is really of the greatest help as it trains the eye to observe closely; it assists in differentiating structures, and the accumulated drawings form a valuable source of reference. It is strongly urged that the student *draw* what he *sees*

In the preparation of the tissues for microscopical examination, but especially in preparing tissues for preservation in cabinets, two somewhat divergent methods are used by microscopists. One class—and they are in the majority—use many different kinds of hardening or softening methods before they color and mount the tissue for preservation. The standard hardening chemicals are chromic, picric, osmic, nitric and formic acids and alcohol; other acids are used for softening. As the hardening power depends upon the power to coagulate albumen and render it opaque, we should also study how to render the tissue transparent after having cut it into thin slices—for which purpose the hardening was done— but no attention is paid to this important step in popular histology. The other method of preparing tissues is by injecting the capillaries with a red and the veins with a blue transparent solution, next doing as little hardening as possible but depending largely upon skill in fine dissections (here the dissecting microscope is necessary), and lastly mounting (preserving) the tissue in heavy (Price's) glycerine. Beale, in his excellent work, fully explains this method, and as he at all times endeavors to alter the tissues as little as possible the student will do well to master Prof. Beale's technique. It is reasonable to expect greater discoveries in the histology of the future from the delicate methods of Prof. Beale than from the harsh methods of

other popular authors, by whom tissues are even boiled
before being mounted

The beginner who, for the first time, attempts to look
through a microscope, may find some assistance in the following instructions: Put the instrument on a steady table
by a north window—never in direct sunlight Tilt the
stand to an angle suitable to the eye of the observer when
comfortably seated   Use either nose piece, but at first
put into the tube the low power objective (1 inch)   Exclude all light from below by a slip of paper and put a dry,
small piece of bread crumb in the Rousselet's Live Box
Rack the tube down till the object is in focus Nothing
but an opaque mass is seen but here and there a glimpse
of more or less transparent pieces appears   Let one or
more of the transparent pieces be in the field and remove
the 1-inch objective, replace it by the ½-inch, and remove
the paper which excluded the light from below. Be sure
to get a beam of light from the concave mirror to pass
through the opening in the stage before focusing Still
but a glimpse of something beyond is seen   Next, raise
the tube and remove the live box On the finger carry a
drop or so of water and carefully apply to the pieces of
crumb. Let them soak a few seconds and gently still more
separate the pieces by means of a needle mounted in any
wooden holder the size and shape of a slim lead-pencil
Needles are useful in microscopy; the slightly curved,
spear pointed surgical needle mounted in a wooden handle
makes an excellent knife for fine dissections Next, gently
press down the cover to the live box, place on the stage,
and focus the tube   We now notice that a number of
small, oval, circular, angular, and perfectly transparent
particles are seen for the first time   Each transparent
particle has a sharp and dark outline and the starch granules are now differentiated. Notice that not until examined in water did the starch granules yield any result;
while looked at in air only opaque masses were seen
Hence we get a hint how the *medium* may be suitable or
not. In the same way examine in air and in water the
thinnest shavings of lead-pencil wood, a thread or two of
cotton, of wool, of linen, of silk, a small pinch of flour,
ordinary starch, pepper, capsicum, powdered mustard,
taking care to let the harder objects soak an hour or so in
water so that they are well penetrated with the fluid.
Next examine moist tea leaves, very thin sections of pota-

to, skin of orange or lemon, cabbage and other vegetables, taking care that in all cases the section is small and thin enough. A razor can be used for this. The beginner will also be greatly interested in examining various specimens of jam and preserved fruits. As these have been long soaked in syrup they have become exceedingly transparent so that the spiral vessels, woody and cellular tissues can be seen without any trouble. Small insects, the proboscis of the mosquito, the flea, lobelia seed, lycopodium, the dust of the wings of moths and butterflies, the scum and ooze of ponds, and many other minute growths yield a rich field for the beginner.

An intimate knowledge of the microscopical appearance of what goes to making up common household dust, mould and debris, is necessary at the very beginning of histological investigation, in order that the observer may not mistake a thread of cotton or wool for elastic tissue of the lungs in tuberculosis. a fibril of linen for shreds of urethral membrane in gonorrhœa, or the sugar mold for tubular casts in nephritis. Also be sure to learn to recognize air bubbles in all kinds of media, as water, oil and gum; oil globules in water and in tissue; and the "Brownian" movements that all finely divided particles, the size of ordinary bacteria or less, show and which may easily be mistaken for life movements.

The beginner will also find that the following precautions will be of advantage in order to save and develop his powers as an observer: Do not work too long at a time, especially with high powers (1-6 inch objective and higher); do not have the object illuminated more intensely than is necessary to see it clearly. Be sure to cultivate the habit of keeping *both* eyes open even though observing with but one, and change from one eye to the other quite frequently to avoid strain. At first work for half an hour only at a stretch, and if this does not tire too much the length of time for observation may be gradually increased; two or three hours a day is the normal length of time for the ordinary observer. If care is exercised a weak eye may be strengthened and made as serviceable as any.

A good microscope with a sufficient supply of accessories is a practical help to the busy practitioner; to the scholar and investigator it is a charming companion and helpful friend. He is dull of wit whose pulses are not stirred at seeing the brilliant, scintillating movements of his own

white blood-corpuscles with the 1-12 inch lens, or the beating heart of some transparent animalcule with the 1-6
inch. A large field of usefulness and discovery in diagnosis and therapeutics as well as in physiology lies before
the medical microscopist But the Physio-Medical investigator will find that the artificial and violent methods of
Allopathy have even invaded microscopy and histology so
that it will be necessary for a member of the only scientific medical school to select from the mass of tissue
destroying Allopathic technique that which is of service,
and on that build a method of his own. Prof. Beale will
probably be of more service than any other popular in-
structor, but as histology has advanced somewhat (though
not as fundamentally as many would make us believe) since
he wrote, there is something to learn from other authors
and more to be developed by Physio-medical investigators.
Let such enter the field with full assurance of rich intel
lectual reward for even the smallest efforts made

REMARKS —An article on Microscopy may seem out of
place in the midst of a Materia Medica, but I think it is
very appropriate. The time has come when microscopy
should be esteemed as one means of determining in some
respects the therapeutical value of the agents we use and
especially of the new ones we seek to choose. It will assist
much in determining whether the agent be sanative or
poisonous, and be a means of purifying our Materia Medica
as well as of guiding in the selection of new agents.
· I hope to enlist the efforts of some willing and efficient
microscopists who will from time to time report the results
of their careful investigations of the various influences of
different agents upon bioplasm as actually observed in the
field of the microscope Prof Broady's article is a very
suitable introduction

MITCHELLA REPENS.

Squaw-Vine

This *herb* is a moderately stimulating tonic nervine ·
Its range of influence is wide and it is one of our most
useful agents. The stomach, bowels, kidneys, uterus,
nervous system and circulation all feel its influence
· It is valued in all kinds of female weakness, but may be
used by males wherever their troubles are similar. In
fact, wherever a good tonic is required, not too stimulat-

ing but permanent, mitchella is in place.   It would be rather difficult to misapply mitchella.

It tones the stomach and bowels, relieves the aching back and stops uterine crampings during gestation.

In nervous feebleness, irritability or prostration, whether in males or in females, it is of superior value.   It is a most important agent in spermatorrhœa, hysteria, and hypochondria.   In leucorrhœa, prolapsus uteri, dysmenorrhœa and all other female weaknesses it is so highly valued as to be denominated a female tonic.   It relieves many an unpleasantness arising during the period of gestation.   It may be taken more or less during this whole period with much benefit to the whole pelvic organism and the lady better prepared for parturition.   There are few if any agents better adapted to the requirements of this period than mitchella.

Mitchella Rep.   9 1-7 or 8
Viburnum Op.   2
Chamælirium Lut.
Caulophyllum Th. aa. 2 2-7 or 2

Each forms an excellent female tonic which will not disappoint you whichever formula you may adopt.

Syrup Mitchella Comp. as made by C. T. Bedford under his improved process of manufacture, gives a syrup which represents the medicinal agents better than any other we know of.

Extract Mitchella   gr. i
Caulophyllin,   gr. ¼
Helonin
Viburnin   aa. gr. ⅛

Form this into a tablet or put into a capsule and use one or two after each meal and before retiring.

If there be any scrofulous or spermatic troubles add menispermum or celastrus as required, or use for spermatorrhœa the following:

Comp. Syr. Mitchella   oz. x
(or F. E. Chamælirium Lut. oz. i)
F. E. Celastrus Scan.
  "   Uva Ursi   aa. dr. iss
  "   Epigæa Rep.   dr. iii

In lung troubles where there is an excessive expectoration the tonic influence of mitchella is very favorably felt.

MITELLA CORDIFOLIA

Bishop's Cap

Dr. F. G Hoener recommends this agent in the treatment of gravel, gonorrhœa and suppressed urine.

MOMORDICA BALSAMINA   :

Balsam Apple.   Tropical.

This is a Southern annual climbing plant The *fruit* is flattened· and narrowed at both ends and orange colored. In the Southern States it is a household remedy for colic pains, cold on the lungs, stomach or bowels In large doses it is emetic. The ordinary dose of fluid extract is one-half to one fluid dram, repeated as needed. Where its influence is needed for.the relief of congestions it should be given in hot water.

The fruit crushed or made into an infusion makes a good covering for burns, bruises, cuts, boils, chilblains and hemorrhoids.

MONARDA FISTULOSA.

Wild Bergamot.

Dr F G. Hoener recommends this agent for spasmodic colics, especially when fever is present, and for the headaches caused by malarial fever

MONARDA PUNCTATA.

Horsemint.

This is a mild, diffusive, stimulating and relaxing antispasmodic nervine and carminative

In hot infusion it influences a good outward circulation and is a diaphoretic, and is useful in the treatment of colds, catarrhal fever and the eruptive fevers It is soothing to the nervous system and somewhat influences the secernents.

It is warming to the stomach, checks nocturnal emissions, relieves the vomiting of cholera infantum and cholera morbus

The *oil* is quite fragrant and makes a good addition to liniments when a stimulating, soothing nervine is needed.

MORUS ALBA, RUBRA AND NIGRA

Mulberry.

The *fruit* is refreshing and laxative Its juice is a

pleasant and grateful drink to convalescents from fever.

The *bark* of the roots is a mildly stimulating and toning diuretic, and is very serviceable in nephritis and albuminaria. It also influences the liver and the alvine canal and is serviceable in jaundice; enteritis and dropsy from hepatic torpor. It tones the stomach, improves digestion; relieves sore mouth and assists in the removal of liver spots upon the face.

MUSA SAPIENTUM.

Banana.

The *fruit* is a pleasant and nourishing food.

The *root* of the banana has given in the hands of some others good results in goitre. I shall report further in some cases now under treatment. It is worth a trial. Dose a teaspoonful of the fluid extract three or four times a day.

MYRICA CERIFERA.

Bayberry.

The *bark* is a positive, diffusive, stimulating, astringent alterative. It arouses the circulation, stimulates all the organs, and brings into greater activity all the secernents. It is one of the best agents to be used in the treatment of scrofula and tuberculosis. It more or less prevents the deposit of tubercle. Though astringent it is more solidifying than drying.

In scrofulous diarrhœa and chronic cholera infantum and goitre it is one of the best agents. Give in large or small doses as required and persist in its use.

Its influence on the uterus is very postive. In prolapsus uteri it is splendid, and in parturition it cannot well be excelled. It induces better contractions and when given near the end of the confinement it will anticipate flooding, and should there be excessive lochia it will assist in stopping the excess. Its influence is also good in excessive menstruation or hemorrhages from other parts of the body and in female weakness.

In hot infusion it gradually arouses the circulation and favors an outward flow of blood. A good free perspiration will follow, which will be more abundant if zingiber be added. It will then be found good in the removal of colds and be serviceable in some acute fevers.

With some persons large doses will induce nausea and

vomiting. In connection with lobelia it is frequently used in producing emesis, which will be very valuable in the treatment of the conditions found in mercurial cachexia, scrofula and secondary syphilis It is an excellent means of ridding the system of impurities. For emetic purposes it should be given in hot infusion

In medical history the name of Dr Samuel Thomson and his composition, his No 6 and his third preparation of lobelia are forever united. His composition is a powerful stimulating astringent preparation of great value in prostrated cases The following were its components

Pul. Myrica Cer		16
" Abies Can		
" Zingiber. Off	aa	8
" Capsicum		
" Cloves		aa 1

Composition, the old reliable compound as recommended by Dr. Samuel Thomson and always used in the crude form i e. powdered state, has been changed by C F Bedford into a reliable fld. ext. which can be quickly converted into an infusion by adding gtts. q s to hot water to meet the requirements. In many cases it is given in capsule and the hot water drank soon after, thus getting rid of the burning and disagreeable taste.

Dr. S E. Carey's formula was as follows

Pul. Myrica Cer		32
" Zingiber. Off		
" Asclepias Tub	aa	16
" Hydrastis		2
" Capsicum		1

Still another formula has been added

Pul Myrica Cer		
" Zingiber Off.		
" Asclepias Tub	aa.	32
" Xanthoxylum Frax.		8
" Capsicum		1

Each of these formulæ in hot infusion are stimulating diaphoretics and may be selected as the conditions require

F. E Myrica Cer.		
" Populus Bal.	aa	dr. iv
Tr Amygdalus Per. Pets		dr i
Syr. Simplex	q s	oz. iv

This is somewhat similar to Dr Samuel Thomson's No. 5 and is a valuable soothing, astringent tonic.

Myricin	grs. v
Oil Xanthoxylum	gtta. iii
Hydrastia Phos.	grs. v

This may be triturated on lactin or given in water oz. iv and used three or four times a day for chronic diarrhœa.

Myrica, hemlock and gum myrrh may be used in infusion by injection for hemorrhoids.

Locally myrica is a good wash for aphthous sore mouth, spongy gums, and upon old and obstinate sores.

Bayberry wax or tallow as it is called is prepared from the berries and is used occasionally in ointments, for ringworm, tetter and other sores.

MYRISTICA FRAGRANS.

Mace, Nutmeg.   Java, West Indies.

This is a mild aromatic, diffusive stimulant, chiefly used as a vehicle for other agents.

NECTANDRA RODICI.

Bebeeru   South America.

The *bark* is a stimulating tonic influencing the gastric and intestinal mucous membrane.

In hot infusion it stimulates the circulation toward the surface and soothes and strengthens the nerves. It is also somewhat antiperiodic. It may be used to much advantage in the treatment of atonic dyspepsia, general debility, hysteria, neuralgia, ague and fevers.

NEPETA CATARIA.

Catnip.

This *herb* is an aromatic, relaxing, slightly stimulating, diffusive, diaphoretic and antispasmodic nervine.

Though considered a very simple agent it is none the less important in children's colic, restlessness, nervous irritability and fevers.

In hot infusion it influences the circulation, soothes the nervous system and relieves irritation, and under proper conditions it increases both menstrual and renal flows. The addition of zingiber increases diaphoresis and intensifies all of the influences of nepeta.

| Nepeta | 5 |
| Mitchella | 1 |

will be found an excellent tonic in some forms of hysteria.

| Nepeta | 10 |
| Dioscorea | 1 |

forms a compound of superior merit for children's colic.

The inspissated juice of the green herb obtained by pressure and evaporated with but little heat forms an excellent antispasmodic for children's convulsions, hysterical convulsions, restlessness and insomnia from irritation of the nervous system This process may be continued to the formation of a solid extract and given in the form of pills

Inspis Nepeta	dr. vi
Ess. Anise	dr. ss
F. E. Valerian	dr. ii
Syr. Zingiber.	q s oz iv

This is suitable for either adults or children as an antispasmodic and for nervine purposes.

A strong infusion made of four pounds of the herb reduced to fourteen ounces, and two ounces of alcohol added, makes a very serviceable fluid extract.

Locally a hot fomentation may be applied to any inflamed parts, over stomach, abdomen, chest or limbs where relaxation is needed. Over the chest it is excellent for the relief of colds.

There is nothing better for the relief of invagination of the bowels than a strong infusion of nepeta Use two or three gallons or as much as is needed till relief is accomplished

NEPETA GLECHOMA.
Ground Ivy

This *herb* is a mildly stimulating, tonic expectorant, chiefly influencing the respiratory organs The secernents all more or less feel its influence and this fact renders this agent of much value as an addition to cough syrups, especially with persons who are inclined to be bilious

In hot infusion it influences the circulation toward the surface and soothes and sustains the nervous system

NYMPHÆA ODORATA AND ADVENA
White and Yellow Pond Lily. (Castalia Odorata)

The *roots* of these two species differ but little medically, though the white is mostly used The root is a demulcent and a mild toning astringent It influences the mucous

membrane throughout, toning but not drying. It materially lessens mucous discharges and is useful in diarrhœa,
dysentery and cystic catarrh.

Locally for leucorrhœa it has few superiors, as also for
prolapsus uteri, ulceration of the cervix, relaxed vagina.

It forms a good wash for purulent ophthalmia.

This is not the best agent to be used when there is a
tendency to constipation.

It forms a good wash for aphthous sore mouth and for
scrofulous sores.

In cases of chafing and excoriations it may be used as a
dusting powder.

ŒNOTHERA BIENNIS.

Tree Primrose, Evening Primrose.

The *leaves* thoroughly influence the mucous membrane
throughout and the nervous system. It is a soothing and
moderately stimulating agent relieving irritable conditions
wherever needed by the vital force. In irritable forms of
dyspepsia, irritation of the urethra, the bladder or the
bronchi wherever it is needed or wherever influenced by
other medicines, its force will be felt for good

It assists in relieving asthma spasmodic dyspnœa, spasmodic coughs and croupal coughs. It assists in relieving
sensitive conditions. It lessens gastric irritation and flatulence, improves the appetite, relieves nausea and vomiting
and the nausea of pregnancy. It cleanses and heals and will
be found useful in typhoid fever and catarrhal dyspepsia.

It may be used in doses of 20 to 50 gtta. 3 to 5 times a
day, it also assists in the relief of hay asthma, angina,
hysteria and whooping cough, epilepsy, spinal irritation
and neurasthenia.

OLEUM EULACHON.

Cod Liver Oil may soon be dethroned from its wonderfully lauded position by eulachon oil obtained from the
candle fish — thaleichthys pacificus, which abounds in the
rivers of British Columbia. This oil is said to be equally
as efficacious in promoting nutrition in scrofulous and tu-
berculous subject. Its flavor is less disagreeable than that of
cod liver oil and may be administerd in the same dose, and
under similar conditions. It seems to furnish equally as
good results.

OLEUM MORRHUÆ.

Cod Liver Oil.

This *oil* is obtained from the fresh liver of the codfish.

The pure oil may be given to infants, they do not seem to object to either its taste or smell as do adults I have given it to many infants and where they are not gone too far with gastric and intestinal indigestion they have done well, and from puny infants they have grown to be healthy and fat.

Adults have more acute taste and smell and the oil must usually be fixed up in some way that there is usually more of other things to form an emulsion than there is present of the oil. With some persons a clove chewed before taking the dose is sufficient to disguise the dose, Some take it in a little wine and some in malt extract.

As a rule it is very questionable as to whether much benefit is derived from the use of cod liver oil I believe proper foods are to be preferred.

OLEUM OLIVÆ

Olive Oil.

This *oil* is nutritious, laxative and cholagogue. It has been successfully used for relief from gall stones. It increases the fluidity of bile and assists in the excretion of the same.

Olive oil is a superior agent to be used in all forms of poisoning from acids, in fact it comes the nearest to being an antidote for all forms of poisoning.

It forms a valuable enema whether it is intended for rectal nutrition or as a rectal laxative In cases where the stomach will not retain food, olive oil, beef extracts and milk may be used by enemata

The oil may also serve as a lubricant to the stomach and bowels in cases of mal-nutrition.

As a cathartic for both infant and adult it is more pleasant than oleum ricini, gives less griping and is more nutritious but is a less active cathartic.

OLEUM RICINI.

Castor Oil

The seeds yield a fixed oil of rather an unpleasant taste and smell and gives a stickiness in the mouth. It is cathartic in from four to five hours. It thoroughly cleanses the

bowels without giving watery discharges. After catharsis the bowels are toned and are left somewhat constipated. In large doses it gripes, but this may usually be avoided by the addition of a drop or two of the essence of mentha
piperita.

It is quite serviceable in acute and chronic dysentery
and diarrhœa and in cholera infantum. It leaves the
bowels soothed and toned. Its taste may be somewhat
covered by milk, essence of peppermint, the yolk of an egg,
sugar, ulmus or acacia.

Ol. Ricini	oz. i
Tr. Cardamon comp.	dr. iv
Ol. Gaultheria	gtta. iv
Pul. Acacia	
" Sacch. Alba	aa dr. ii
Aqua Cinnamon	q. s. oz. iv

This forms an emulsion which disguises the taste of the
oil. The following will also disguise it.

Pul. Acacia	dr. iss
Ol. Ricini	oz. iss
" Cinnamon	gtt. v
Vinum	dr. vi
Lacto-peptine	dr. i
Syr. Zingiber	q. s. oz. iv

In cases of dysentery or diarrhœa the following may be
given in doses of a teaspoonful after each stool or every
three hours.

Ol. Ricini	oz. i
" Anise	dr. i
" Cloves	gtta. iii
Leptandrin	grs. xx
Syr. Simplex	q. s. oz. ii

OLEUM ROSÆ.

Oil of Roses.

This is prepared from several different species growing
in Egypt, Persia, India and Asia Minor.

It is obtained by pressure or by distillation.

Ol. Rosæ	gtta. xx
Carbonate Magnesia	dr. i
Aqua Distillata	oz. viii

Triturate and add water sufficient to make half a gallon or more according to the strength required. This is
pleasant for the sick room.

ONOSMODIUM VIRGINIANUM

Gravel Weed.

The **root** is a demulcent, stimulating diuretic   It soothes the mucous membrane but especially influences the renal department, increasing the flow of urine and toning the organs   It is best in torpid and sluggish conditions where the membrane is more or less clogged with mucous. It cleanses, soothes and tones.

ORIGANUM VULGARE

Wild Majoram

This plant yields an essential *oil* powerfully stimulating, a useful addition to liniments.

Pare your corn close and apply two drops of oil origanum.

Oil Origanum	2
" Cedar	1
Neat's Foot Oil	4

This is a soothing and stimulating liniment.

ORTHOSIPHON STAMINEUS

Java Tea   India, Java, Australia.

This is a perennial plant one to three feet high with *leaves* two to four inches long   They are prepared and come to the market somewhat like other tea. This seems to render the agent more aromatic, and less astringent than are the ordinary leaves   It contains a small percentage of glucoside and the alcoholic extract yields some tannin, but the aqueous extract yields none.

The leaves are a mild, stimulating and relaxing diuretic. A strong infusion acts on the kidneys and bladder, cleanses the mucous membrane, assists in the relief and prevention of gravel, increases the quantity of urine and gives good results in chronic cystitis and ascites.

OSMORRHIZA LONGISTYLIS

Sweet Cicily

The **root** has a sweetish taste   It is a mild stimulating and relaxing antispasmodic, influencing the mucous membrane and is valuable in cough syrups as an expectorant

It influences the gastric and intestinal mucous membrane and relieves flatulence, especially if combined with a small portion of zingiber

OSTRYA VIRGINICA.

Iron Wood.

The **heart-wood** is red and yields a mild, bitter, stimulating, astringent, tonic alterative, chiefly influencing the mucous membrane and the nerves. It soothes, stimulates and tones and is useful in acute and chronic diarrhœa, either per oram or by injection.

Per vaginam it is a good wash for leucorrhœa and female weakness generally. Per oram it prevents miscarriage.

It is quite stimulating to the brain and nerves and is serviceable in some forms of neuralgia. It is a fine antiperiodic and excellent in agues, more permanent than quinine.

It is best combined with some diffusive stimulant, when it will the better influence the circulation and relieve congestive chills. Boil two quarts of the chips thoroughly to make one pint of infusion.

OXALIS ACETOSELLA.

Wood Sorrel.

This **plant** is quite stimulating and somewhat astringent.

By powerful pressure and subsequent exposure to the air a strong extract is made from the application of which as a plaster wonderful successes are reported in the cure of cancers. The addition of a small portion of pulverized ulmus makes such plaster more soothing and enables the patient to keep the plaster on the cancer a much longer time.

Combined with five times its own bulk of vaseline it forms a good salve for application to old sores, especially those of scrofulous origin. It cleanses and heals.

OXYCOCCUS MACROCARPUS.

American Cranberry.

The **berries** form an excellent poultice very valuable in the treatment of erysipelas, or apply the raw juice.

The juice of the cooked fruit is a good acidulated drink where such is required in convalescence.

PÆONIA OFFICINALIS.

Peony.

The **root** is a mild relaxing and stimulating antispasmodic nervine. In hot infusion it may be used for colic, flatus and convulsions of children. Zingiber adds much to its diffusiveness.

PANAX QUINQUEFOLIUM

Ginseng

· The *root* is a mild, aromatic, diffusive, relaxing, tonic nervine.

It soothes and st engthens a weak and irritated stomach, relieves general nervousness, insomnia, light cases of neuralgia, hyperæsthesia and irritable conditions generally.

With aralia and prunus it assists in nervous pulmonary troubles

PANAX SCHINSENG

Chinese Gentian

The *root* is a diffusive, stimulating tonic to the digestive organs. It relieves pyrosis and flatus, and assists digestion and assimilation It does good service in wasting diseases, as chlorosis, consumption, etc

PARTHENIUM INTEGRIFOLIUM

Cutting Almond.

The *root* is a relaxing and slightly stimulating diuretic.

It increases the flow of urine and soothes the entire renal apparata It relieves the aching back, scalding urine and the irritation of gonorrhœa, nephritis, cystitis and urethritis

PASSIFLORA INCARNATA

Passion Flower

This is a reliable relaxing and somewhat stimulating antispasmodic nervine. It relieves excitement of the nervous system, and is of much benefit in spasmodic and neuralgic diseases, insomnia, the delirium of typhoid, the convulsions of children, chorea, dysmenorrhœa, epilepsy. hysteria, la grippe

It also relieves irritation of the brain centres and quiets the general nervous system

PAULINIA SORBILIS

Guarana.   Brazil.

This is a woody climber, bearing a fruit about the size

of a large grape and is nearly filled with one or more nuts about the size of hazel nuts. In the Amazon valley it grows wild, but in the Madiera district it is cultivated and presents somewhat the appearance of a vineyard. They ripen in December and open. The nuts are then gathered, roasted, shelled, ground, and enough water added to allow it kneaded into dougby rolls about a foot long in which state it comes into market.

Guaranin is the alkaloid, a stimulating tonic nervine for sick-headache where the stomach is not much involved.

We are indebted to Mr. K. M. Turner, of the Yale Chemical Co., of Atlanta, Ga., for the most valuable preparation of this agent which he has denominated

SORBILIN.

This is the alkaloid guaranin chemically combined in certain proportions with pure bicarbonate of soda. It is a gently stimulating, soothing and toning nervine.

This is an admirable preparation, an innocent reliever of pain.

In facial, intestinal and cranial neuralgia it is a superior relief. Also in gastralgia, enteralgia and ovarian and uterine pains. It assists much in sciatica, rheumatism and insomnia. It sustains the heart and in angina gives quick relief. It soothes and tones the sympathetic and sensory nerves, and in sick-headache if the stomach is not too much at fault there is nothing better. In such cases it may be combined with a drop or so of Lobelia id. Prep.

Five to ten or more grains of this agent may be used as required.

Dr. John Cooper says: "I have given Sorbilin of the Yale Chemical Co. a very thorough clinical test in typhoid, malarial, irritative and other fevers, also headaches of various kinds, and must say that its effects are very rapid and satisfactory, reducing temperature and relieving headache quickly without any profuse sweating or cardiac depression so common with the coal tar preparations.

"Knowing it to be perfectly harmless I do not hesitate to use it in doses from 10 to 30 grs. every 2 or 3 hours, for any length of time.

"I treated seventy cases of typhoid fever during two months and have used a pound of sorbilin.

"I usually give the doses in the afternoon at one, four and seven o'clock in typhoid fever, with the very best results."

Sorbilin may be combined with salicylate of sodium in
the treatment of rheumatism and be used in fluid extract
of celery seed when needed

PERSEA GRATISSIMA

Alligator Pear   Mexico, West Indies.

This is a tree of moderate size, having leaves four to
seven inches long, and its fruit in the shape of a pear,
pulpy and having one seed.

The *seeds* are a warming, stimulating agent, chiefly valued as an application for intercostal neuralgia, also in
rheumatism, sciatica and ovarian pain

PETROLATUM.

Petroleum.

This is a bland, neutral, protecting dressing

Cosmoline or vaseline (unguentum petrolii) is obtained
from residuum and reduced oils; benzine, naphtha, illumi-
nating and paraffine oils having been removed by distillation by the vacuum process. With iodide potas it forms
an ointment for glandular swellings.

Abolene is a hydro-carbon oil from a new and peculiar
kind of petroleum. It is colorless, odorless, tasteless and
is not affected by exposure to the air or strong acids. It
is a good application for laryngeal and catarrhal affections.

McCoy, Howe Co. manufacture Emulsion Petroleum
with hypophosphites   Each fluid dram contains

Purified Petroleum (medicinal)   m. xx
Hypophosphite Calcium   grs ii
Hypophosphite Sodium   grs. ii
Hypophosphite Potassium   gr i

This is a fine permanent emulsion prepared from C. P.
salts and trituration accomplished by special machinery.
It is used with marked benefit in consumption, bronchitis,
pneumonia, general debility and all wasting diseases. It
may be mixed with wine, milk or water as preferred.

PEUMUS BOLDUS.

Boldo.   Chili

Boldo is an evergreen and fragrant tree. Its whitish
fruit is aromatic, sweet and is eaten in its native country.
Its hard round seeds are sometimes used in making the
beads of rosaries The bark gives a dye material for tanning.

The *leaves* are a soothing, diffusive, stimulating tonic

to the mucous membrane. It is also antiseptic and valuable in atonic dyspepsia, hepatic torpor, biliousness and hepatic congestion. Its influence is also extended to the urinary organs and is useful in cystic catarrh, blenorrhagia and nocturnal erections. It improves the appetite, stimulates digestion and tones the general system.

PHORADENDRON FLAVESCENS.

Mistletoe.

This grows upon a variety of trees and shrubs but seems to prefer oaks and cottonwood. Its appearance is rather peculiar, having greenish yellow, woody, brittle stems. It branches freely and soon forms a dense mass. The leaves are fleshy, of color and brittleness similar to that of the stems. The leaves vary much in size. The flowers are very minute and the fruit is a small whitish berry, very viscid.

The *leaves* are a stimulating and relaxing antispasmodic nervine. It seems to give its especial influence where it is most needed by the vital force. During parturition when the pains are light, it produces prompt uterine contractions and well anticipates hemorrhage.

Besides being an oxytocic it is also valuable in all uterine hemorrhages, and assists much in the expulsion of the placenta when retained after an abortion or miscarriage.

As an antispasmodic it will be found useful in the relief of the extra effort put forth in asthma, epilepsy and other spasmodic conditions.

PHYTOLACCA DECANDRA.

Poke.

The *berries* are a relaxing and stimulating alterant, influencing the mucous, serous and glandular structures. Cook the berries till they burst and pour off the juice without straining. Then cover the berries again with water and cook thoroughly. Now strain off all the juice and boil it down to the consistency of a thick syrup and add the first juice poured off. Bottle for use.

It can also be made into a jelly or into a tincture with 30 p. c. alcohol. Either is excellent for rheumatism. It soothes the serous membrane, relieves the glandular system, solidifies the muscles and throws off the excessive amount of internal blubber as a result of fatty degeneration.

In the treatment of scrofula it relieves the glandular system of its impurities and cleanses the blood current. It increases the flow of saliva, of urine, of perspiration, and frees the alvine canal

Like most alteratives it is slow but persistent, and some time must be given to participate in the full benefits of this agent.

In the early spring the young leaves are frequently used as a popular dish of greens At their maturity the leaves and stalk have much of the same properties as the root and berries.

The *root* in its green state is quite acrid and is quite irritating to the mucous membrane, frequently causing a persistent vomiting. A similar result will follow if the green root be bruised and placed upon the surface of an excoriated or ulcerated part

The green root taken in small and frequent doses will frequently relieve rheumatism

The better way to use this agent is to cut the green root fine and cover with boiling water and allow to boil two or three minutes This preparation may be given in doses of a teaspoonful to a tablespoonful, with but little if any nausea experienced. Two ounces of alcohol to the pint may be added to keep this preparation

The dried root is but of little value

This agent is a good alterant and if applied externally and taken internally for some time it will relieve many a bony and cartilaginous swelling I believe it will avert white swelling, but I have not proved it.

It relieves neuralgia, sciatica and lumbago.

I combine at times the berry juice and this preparation of the root in equal quantities with good results in inflammation or ulceration of the alimentary canal and rheumatism

In case of threatened mammary abscess this preparation of the root may be used internally and locally in hot fomentation or poultice. Treat orchitis and ovaritis in the same way, and so with scrofulous abscess, surface inflammation and inflammatory rheumatism, give large doses and frequently to control at once, else it lingers Phytolacca influences all the deep structures when inflamed and all the serous structures It is a good poultice in case of felon.

The roasted root makes a splendid poultice for inflamed

surfaces. It quickly reduces inflammation and decreases excessive suppuration.

The cooking largely dissipates the naseating tendency so that much more of it can be given than of the green root. But only cook two or three minutes, it is then a better nervine, alterative and laxative.

Phytolacca may be combined with many of the alteratives with much profit.

Take phytolacca roots (green), verbascum thapsus and trifolium pratense in equal parts, cover with boiling water and simmer two or three minutes, than poor off and cover with water, which simmer to one half the quantity, add the two products and simmer to 14 oz. to 1 lb. of the crude, add oz. 4 of sugar to each pint, one dr. of salicylic acid and one ounce of alcohol. Use this for cancer, ophthalmia, scrofula, consumption, rheumatism and overheat.

F. E. Phytolacca Bac.   dr. v
    "   Verbena   dr. iss
    "   Xanthox. Frax.   gtta. xv
    Salicylate Sodium   dr. i
    Syr. Zingiber   q. s. oz. iv
M. S. Teaspoonful every 3 hours for rheumatism.
Bruise the green root and apply to a bunion.
Dr. F. G. Hoener uses the following for acute and chronic rheumatism.
    Succus Phytolacca Bac.   oz. i
    Elix. Betonica Lanc.
    "   Cimicifuga   aa oz. iss

PICRÆNA EXCELSA.

Quassia.   Jamaica.

The *wood and bark* are an intensely bitter, stimulating tonic, influencing chiefly the digestive organs. In languid conditions and in convalescence it improves the appetite and assists digestion. Very small doses only are required. The quassia cup is made out of this wood, and water kept in it for a short time will taste quite bitter, and this water drank before meals is an appetizer and digestant.

    Cardamon Seed   oz. ss
    Cinnamon
    Picræna
    Raisins   aa. dr. vi
This forms a good tonic preparation.

PICRAMNIA ———.

Honduras Bark   (Cascara Amarga) Mexico, Honduras.

The **bark** is a stimulating alterative of especial value in secondary syphilis, syphilitic tubercules, chronic eczemas, gummy tumors, gonorrhœal rheumatism, chronic nephritis, chronic nasal catarrh

Prohibit the use of alcoholics, tobacco and sexual excesses

This agent seems to eliminate the specific virus by way of the skin and kidneys

It improves the appetite and assists digestion. From 30 to 50 drops may be taken of the fluid extract three times daily. Berberis aquifolium and xanthoxylum may be added.

PIMPINELLA ANISUM.

Anise Seed.

The *oil* from the seed is a pleasant, sweet, aromatic, relaxing and stimulating nervine and carminative. It is mostly used as an adjuvant for the administering of cathartics, bitter and nauseating medicines   The oil may be triturated with sugar or magnesia and may then be used in powdered form or combined with water.

PIPER CUBEBA

Cubebs.   East Indies.

The **berries** are a prompt, diffusive, stimulating diuretic, influencing the mucous membrane but chiefly that of the urinary organs.

In hot infusion it influences the circulation.

Their use is not best in acute inflammatory conditions, but in chronic conditions, as gleet and cystic catarrh

This agent is sometimes combined with copaiba for cystic and nephritic congestions, and chronic inflammatory conditions

The *oil* may be used in doses of three to ten drops on sugar, acacia or magnesia

PIPER NIGRUM

Black Pepper.   East Indies.

This is principally used for seasoning food   In hot infusion it stimulates the circulation and tends the flow toward the surface.

The *oil* may be used triturated on sugar or lactin

Piperine is a resinoid used for the same general purposes as the oil.

PLANTAGO CORDATA.

Water Plantain.

The *root* is a mild, soothing, relaxing and stimulating antispasmodic nervine. It is useful in irritable forms of nervous troubles, hysteria, children's convulsions and spinal irritation. It is gently soothing to the stomach especially of the pregnant. In hot fomentation it is a valuable application to swellings, sprains and bruises.

PLANTAGO MAJOR.

Plantain.

The *roots and leaves* are a mild, diffusive, stimulating and relaxing alterant, influencing the entire mucous membrane, but especially that of the urinary tract. The glandular system is thoroughly influenced and it is valuable in cases of scrofula, struma and some eczemas. It mildly increases the quantity of urine, relieves its scalding, the aching back, cystic catarrh, acute and chronic gonorrhœa, and internal and external scrofulous swellings.

A fomentation or wash of the plant is useful for sprains, erysipelas, ophthalmia and other surface irritations.

PLANTAGO VIRGINICA.

The properties of this plant are very similar to those of the cordata.

PODOPHYLLUM PELTATUM.

Mandrake.

The *root* when fresh is quite acrid, nauseating and drastic. The dry root produces much less irritation. It influences the salivary glands, mucous membrane, gall ducts, liver and kidneys. It is decidedly a cholagogue, and a cathartic in from six to ten hours. Large doses leave an uneasy sensation in the lower bowels which soon influences the entire pelvic organism. It is not a proper agent to use much or frequently with the pregnant.

The crude material and the fluid extract have given way to the resinoid *podophyllin*, which is now most used. This is a prompt cholagogue and is a most valuable agent in liquefying the gall in the relief of gall stone, for which purpose it is best triturated with sugar one to fifty or

given in syr zingiberis, or the ingredients may be given
in capsules Give large doses every few minutes. It will
not nauseate nor produce catharsis until the parts become
eased and the gall liquefied. The vital force uses it where
it is most needed. Occasional doses must be given to
maintain a liquid condition.

If this agent is to be used as a cathartic add a little zingiber but use no sugar.

Other agents will give better results if the mucous
membrane is irritated

Podophyllin in small doses is useful in jaundice.

There is one trouble with the use of this agent. After
you have used it for some time, milder agents seem to have
but little effect

POLEMONIUM REPTANS

Greek Valerian, Abscess-Root

The *root* is a diffusive, stimulating and relaxing diaphoretic, antiseptic, nervine and alterant.

In hot infusion it influences the circulation and gives a
prompt flow of blood toward the surface Thus it also
relieves the nerves and the mucous membrane. It is useful in recent colds, pleuritis, tardy exanthems, typhoid
restlessness, nervous prostration, dysmenorrhœa, lingering
parturition, whooping cough and phthisis

It acts prominently on the lungs, the stomach and glandular system

If you can obtain the green herb bruise it and obtain
the strength by hot water and evaporation. Add two
ounces of alcohol to the pint to keep it It is said to relieve of snake virus.

F. E Aralia Rac.   dr. vi   F E. Lycopus   dr. iv
   "   Lycopus V. dr iv   Tr Cimicifuga
   "   Polemonium R dr. ii   " Lobelia
Syr. Prunus   q. s. oz. viii F. E Polemonium aa. dr. ii
                                  Syr. Prunus   q. s. oz. viii
These are both valuable cough syrups

POLYGALA SENEGA

Senega

The *root* is a positive, stimulating alterant, somewhat
irritating to the fauces and salivary glands. It is quite
general in its influence. In large doses it is emetic. To
the respiratory mucous membrane it is a stimulating ex-

pectorant, especially if combined with more relaxing and demulcent agents, as aralia and glycyrrhiza.

In hot infusion it stimulates to a good capillary flow and leads to diaphoresis. It is useful in tardy eruptions, especially of variola, relieves the nerves and circulation and brings the rash out in good shape. In many cases so much stimulation may not be required.

Cold preparations are diuretic and are useful in torpid conditions of the urinary membrane. It is also useful in amenorrhœa, chronic rheumatism, snake virus, mercurial cachexia, secondary syphilis and some eczemas.

POLYGONUM AVICULARE.

Knot Grass, Goose Grass.

This *herb* is a mild, diffusive, stimulating and relaxing, antispasmodic nervine.

In hot infusion it influences the circulation and is diaphoretic, quite stimulating to the capillaries and increasing the periodic flow, especially if a little zingiber be added.

Cold preparations are diuretic and relieve the aching back and bladder.

For irritable coughs it is a good addition to aralia, inula and prunus.

POLYGONUM PERSICARIA.

Heart's Ease.

In hot infusion this *herb* is a diffusive, stimulating diaphoretic, and useful in coughs, colds, glandular swellings and fevers.

POLYGONUM PUNCTATUM.

Water-Pepper, Smart Weed.   (P. Hydropiper.)
(P. Bistorta of Europe.)

This *herb* when green is acrid, but is less so when dried. It is a stimulating and relaxing diaphoretic and nervine.

In hot infusion it is freely diaphoretic, quite stimulating to the circulation and soothing to the nervous system and is slightly emmenagogue.

Cold preparations are diuretic.

In hot infusion it is valuable in recent colds, bronchial and pulmonary congestions, especially if combined with asclepias and zingiber.

Syr	Polygonum	oz. ii	Syr.	Polygonum	oz i
	" Polemonium	oz. i		" Polemonium	oz iss
	" Aralia Rac.	dr. iii		" Prunus	oz ii
	" Hydrastis	dr v		" Aralia Rac.	oz. iss

Either of these combinations forms a good cough syrup for bronchitis and phthisis,

F. E Polygonum Punc.   dr. ii
   " Caulophyllum Thal.
   " Glycyrrhiza Glab.
   " Polemonium Rep.   aa dr. i
Syr. Prunus Virg.   q s oz iv

This may be used for old spasmodic coughs.

In amenorrhœa and dysmenorrhœa when arising from congestion, this is one of our best agents. In parturition when the pains are slow the contractions feeble and the patient fatigued, it stimulates to better contractions and more effectual labor.

In the treatment of swellings, inflammations and congestions, when the green material can be applied in hot fomentation it is one of the very best for peritonitis, pleuritis, hepatitis, cystitis; also for gastric, hepatic, splenic, intestinal, pulmonary, cystic and nephritic congestions. For swellings of the limbs and joints verbascum may be added in hot acetum

Age soon renders this agent inert.

With solidago it is valuable in diphtheria, aphonia, pharyngitis and tonsilitis.

Polygonum combined with alterants makes them of greater value by adding diffusive stimulation and increased arterial force.

An infusion of the fresh herb may be used as a wash for foul ulcers and gangrenous sores

The fluid extract may be used for all purposes of the herb when the fresh material cannot be obtained

POLYMNIA UVEDALIA.

Bearsfoot

This is a coarse looking plant from four to ten feet high. growing in moist fertile grounds in the Eastern and Southern States The leaves are a foot or more in length, and about the same in their greatest width.

The *root* is a stimulating, tonic alterant to the secernents, mucous and serous membranes and glandular system.

It cleanses the mucous surface and increases nutritive
activity.

It is valuable in enlarged spleen, rheumatism, scrofula,
enlarged and tender liver, sore throat, sore chest, inflamed
breasts.

F. E. Polymnia Uv.   oz. i
Adeps   oz ii

This forms an excellent ointment which when applied
over enlarged or sore parts greatly assists the internal use
of the agent, as in rheumatism, spinal irritation, glandular
enlargement, ague cake, inflamed breasts, etc.

POLYPODIUM VULGARE.

Polypody.

The **root** is a soothing, demulcent stimulant, influencing
the mucous membrane of the alvine canal and respiratory
organs. To the bowels it is laxative and to the bronchi it
is an expectorant.

POLYTRICHUM JUNIPERUM.

Hair-Cap Moss.

This **plant** is a pleasant, prompt, relaxing diuretic, and
serviceable in dropsy and the suppression of urine in either
infant or adult. It very materially increases the urinary
flow.

POPULUS BALSAMIFERA.

Balsam Poplar, Balm of Gilead.   (P. Candicans.)

Gather these **buds** in the spring before they become expanded. They are a balsamic stimulant influencing the
circulation and the mucous membrane throughout.

The buds yield an exudation which water dissolves only
in part. They may be tinctured in alcohol, which is then
evaporated and the residuum triturated on sugar. This is
quite stimulating in old coughs and is valuable for debilitated cases. It gives best service with more relaxing
agents. For the kidneys and bladder it should be used
only in cases needing much stimulation. It is best with
relaxing diuretics.

It influences the circulation, but with some diffusive
will do it much better.

It assists in chronic rheumatism, sciatica and lumbago,
but will be better if combined with phytolacca and sodium
salicylate.

Pinus Canaden.
Prunus Virgin.   aa 5½
Populus Balsam
Aralia Rac.   aa 8
Sanguinaria Can.   6
Sassafras   4

This is a good cough compound.

POPULUS TREMULOIDES.

White Poplar.

The buds gathered in winter are very strongly medicinal. The *inner bark and buds* are a stimulating tonic alterant. Its influence is quite general   It promotes appetite and assists digestion when used in lax conditions, and general weakness and depression

In chronic diarrhœa, chronic dysentery, cholera infantum, it is a tonic, not an astringent

It tones the mucous membrane, relieves indigestion and is somewhat anthelmintic

The kidneys and bladder also feel its power   It gradually increases the urine and relieves the aching back

If more or less controlled by uva ursi, it will give good results in cystic and renal catarrh and congestions.

It is also of use in uterine, vaginal and anal weakness, both as a wash and for internal use

It is also a valuable wash for eczemas, purulent ophthalmia, chronic gonorrhœa and syphilitic sores.

Dr. F. G. Hoener recommends the following for cholera morbus:

Elix. Populus Trem.   oz ii
    "   Ambrosia Artem
    "   Monarda Punc   aa oz. i
Dessertspoonful every 15 or 20 minutes

Populus Trem.
Myrica Cer   aa oz ss
Aqua   ·   oz xvi
Inject for anal prolapsus.

Populus Trem
Berberis Vulg
Chelone Glab aa equal parts

forms what is known as Dr. Samuel Thomson's spiced bitters, or No. 5.   It is a fine tonic hepatic.

Dr. Bedford's formula for Spice Bitters differs material-ly from the old formula, making it much more pleasant and palatable. It can be had in powder or fluid extract, the latter being easy of administration: the former may be used in capsule or in hot water as needed, this makes it de-sirable and at the same time economical.

F. E. Populus Trem.   dr. iiss
"   Verbascum Thap.   dr. iv
"   Polygonum Pun.   dr. iss
Syr. Zingiberis   q. s. oz. iv

This may be given three to six times a day for chronic diarrhœa.

F. E. Populus Trem.   dr. ii
"   Berberis Aqui.   dr. i
"   Hydrastis Can.   dr. ss
"   Aletris Far.   dr. i
"   Taraxacum D. L.   dr, iv
"   Xanthoxylum Frax.   gtta. x
Syr. Simplicis   q. s. oz. iv

This forms a good tonic alterant for debilitated cases, especially suited to females.

PORTULACA OLERACEA.

Garden Purslane.

This is an annual succulent plant of our gardens.

It is a gentle, soothing, stimulant to the mucous mem-brane of the alvine and urinary departments. It soothes cleanses and tones and is a quite useful infusion.

Dr, F. G. Hoener uses the following for cholera infan-tum:

Elix. Portulaca Olerac.   oz. ii
"   Monarda Punct.
"   Comptonia Asplen. aa. oz. i

M. S. A half to a whole teaspoonful every one or two hours till improvement.

POTASSIUM.

Potassæ Carbonas Purus is prepared from the lye of wood ashes. It is a strong alkali.

Potassæ Bicarbonas is the result of the absorption of an additional equivalent of carbonic acid gas. This is an acceptable alkali frequently used in various ways and preparations.

Potassa Caustica is also prepared from the carbonate

and is the escharotic, lunar caustic   In the process of obtaining this precipitate we obtain

Liquor Potassœ, which is sometimes used in the mixing of resins or gums with fluid extracts.

Potassa Caustica cum Calce (Caustic Paste) is made by thoroughly triturating caustic potash and unslacked lime This is a somewhat milder escharotic.

Potassœ Chloras is a popular gargle for sore throat, but I believe there are many things better.

Potassae Bitartras, (Cream of Tartar) is occasionally used as a morning drink for constipation and as an addition to physics

Potassae Bisulphas, applied locally and given internally has been successful in some cases of goitre and several cases of pruritus.

Potassii Sulphuretum.

Sulphuret Potas	oz ss
Oil Rosemary	dr i
Aqua	oz. vi or more

Makes a good wash for scabies, pruritus and other itching eczemas

Potassii Iodidum, is a tonic alterant influencing the mucous and serous membranes and glandular system,

Iodide Potas, --- -	dr. iv
Tr. Cimicifuga	
Tr Gentian Comp.	aa (z ii

This used 3 to 6 times a day will give good results in rheumatism.

Iodide Potassium will assist much in the treatment of pneumonia

Locally this agent is valuable for the removal of warts, goitre and eczemas.

Iodide Potas	dr. iv
Pix Liquida	dr. i
Sulphur	dr. iii
Vaseline	oz iv

This is one of the best preparations for tinea capitis.

Iodide Potas.	dr. i
Aqua	oz. ii

A teaspoonful of this may be used 3 or 4 times a day for specific ulceration, scrofula or ophthalmia.

Iodide Potas.	dr i
Tr. Lavender Comp	dr iv

F. E. Serpentaria,   dr. ii.
Syr. Zingiber,   q. s. oz. vi

A teaspoonful every 3 or 4 hours will soon relieve the headache which follows or accompanies puerperal fever.

Iodide Potas,   oz. ss
Aqua   oz. viii

A teaspoonful may be given three times a day in bad cases of nasal catarrh.

McCoy, Howe Co. make a syrup of double strength 2 per ent hydriodic acid. They claim for it exceptional keeping qualities, and absolute purity of ingredients, being kept for months without change.

Potassae Permanganas, is an excellent deodorizer for the sick room, an absorbent of foul gasses and a destroyer of contagia.

Potassae Permanganas,
Manganesii Oxidum,
Acidum Oxalicum, aa. equal parts.

Do not triturate all these together for an explosion may take place. But combine first the oxalic acid and the manganese and then add the permanganate of potassium. Two teaspoonsful of this powder in a dish occasionally diluted with water will be sufficient to thoroughly disinfect a sick room and destroy most atmospheric contagia.

POTENTILLA CANADENSIS.

Cinquefoil, Five-Finger Herb.

This *herb* is a mild, stimulating, astringent tonic, chiefly influencing the mucous membrane, and very serviceable in diarrhoea and dysentery of both children and adults. It is rather pleasant to the stomach and frequently allays nausea and vomiting, and is quite soothing to the nerves.

Locally it is a good wash to either the mouth, the vagina or the rectum, in case of either ulceration or irritation.

It is splendid as a wash for cold sore eyes.

POTENTILLA TORMENTILLA.

Tormentilla.

The *roots* are a mild, stimulating astringent, chiefly influencing the alvine mucous membrane and is serviceable in the ordinary forms of diarrhœa and mild hemorrhages.

PRINOS VERTICILLATOS.

Black Alder.   (Ilex Verticillatos).

This **bark** is a mild, stimulating tonic alterative, influencing chiefly the alvine mucous membrane and the secernents   It is a mild laxative to the bowels and a gentle hepatic and cholagogue   It is of service in biliousness, jaundice, atonic dyspepsia and dropsy arising from secernent failure

The **berries** are more cathartic and less hepatic

PRUNELLA VULGARIS.

Heal All

This **herb** is a mild stimulating astringent influencing the mucous membrane, throughout   To the throat it may be used as a gargle. It is soothing and toning to the urinary organs and will be of service in diabetes. It is a good addition to cough syrups, is serviceable in chronic bronchitis and phthisis where the expectoration is too free.

PRUNUS DOMESTICA.

Prune   France.

This **fruit** is a pleasant nutritious laxative, and may be used in the relief of the habit of constipation, but if used too freely it may occasion flatulence.

PRUNUS INSTITIA RUBRUM

Wild Red Plum.

The **bark** of the root is a relaxing and somewhat stimulating agent influencing the mucous membrane especially of the respiratory organs. A syrup made from an infusion is an excellent agent for asthma

PRUNUS VIRGINIANA

Wild Cherry.   (P Serotina)

The **bark** of the root is the best but the bark of the trunk is as frequently used   This is a mild, soothing, stimulating, astringent tonic to the mucous membrane especially of the respiratory organs and of the alvine canal.

To the former it is a valuable tonic expectorant and to the latter it is a most excellent tonic, very mildly astringent if the alcoholic extract be used.

Its tonic influence is felt by the liver and gall ducts and it is serviceable in the jaundice of children   For this purpose use an aqueous extract, made by putting cold water on the finely-cut fresh bark and frequently shaking for a few hours. Make it frequently fresh and use it very freely. It is successful.

Boiling dissipates the soothing property, but makes an excellent preparation for chronic diarrhœa.

The fresh bark is much to be preferred. Grind or pound up fine the fresh bark and put into a self-sealing jar; pour boiling hot syrup over it and seal it up. Let it stand a few days and then pour it off. You have then the nicest syrup of prunus that can be made. Or it may be made in this way: Take prunus 6 ounces, steep in one pint of hot water three hours. Then strain and add 1¾ pounds of granulated sugar and two ounces of glycerine.

Prunus improves the appetite, enlivens the digestion and tones the whole system. It is one of those agents whose influence may be directed to either the digestive or the respiratory organs, according to the agents with which it is combined, or the necessities of vitality in the individual case.

It quiets nervous irritability and relieves arterial excitement.

In chronic gastritis, weak digestion, typhoid fever, cholera infantum, diarrhœa, convalescence, and in diseases of the respiratory organs this agent cannot be too highly praised. In acute and irritable coughs it is a tonic expectorant of the highest value.

In moist catarrh a fine powder may be used as a snuff or the infusion may be atomized. Thus inhaled it will be of much benefit also to the lungs.

As a wash in ophthalmia it soothes, cleanses and tones weak, irritated and inflamed conditions, whether it be from simple, scrofulous or specific cause.

It is one of the best washes for a weak or inflamed vagina and for the relief of a mild leucorrhœa.

F. E. Prunus Virg.
"   Cornus Flor.   aa. dr. iv
"   Myrica Cer.   dr. ii
"   Xanthoxylum Frax.   gtta. xv
Syr. Zingiberis   q. s. oz. vi
Teaspoonful four times a day for chronic diarrhœa.

Prunus, glycyrrhiza, yerba santa and solidago in equal parts form an admirable troche for weak throat.

Detannated prunus may be consistently mixed with iron preparations

PTELEA TRIFOLIATA

Wafer Ash.

The *bark* of the roots is a mild stimulating tonic. influencing chiefly the mucous membrane, alvine and respiratory

In hot infusion it moderately influences the circulation.

Large and frequent doses are rather irritating to the stomach. Small doses are suited to gastric and alvine torpor, as in diarrhœa, cholera infantum, gastric and intestinal catarrh Also in bronchial catarrh it may be added to cough syrups with a good stimulating result.

Ptelein is the oleo-resin which, triturated on sugar, may be used for the same general purposes as other preparations of this agent.

Ptelea-Pepsin (10 to 30) is a good compound for languid conditions of the gastric and intestinal mucous membrane, as in cholera infantum

PTEROCARPUS MARSUPIUM.

Kino.   East and West Indies.

This *gum* obtained by incisions in the bark of the tree is a positive astringent gently stimulating, soothing and toning rather than drying Its influence upon the alvine mucous membrane makes it an excellent agent in all forms of diarrhœa and dysentery, whether of infant or adult and whether acute or chronic

It is one of the best applications for lucorrhœa, a weak vagina and prolapsus uteri

In hemorrhages, whether from the lungs, stomach or bowels, it renders good service used both locally and constitutionally.

The fluid extract will frequently stop the toothache.

Cold water is very slow in dissolving kino Hot water is much better. For immediate use I like this much better than the tincture or fluid extract, which so frequently gelatinizes and loses its astringency

I have used it a few times successfully in œdema glottidis

PTEROCARPUS SANTILANUS

Red Saunders.   India, Ceylon

This *wood* has but little smell or taste It imparts its

color to alcohol but not to water, being a resinous principle, soluble in hot water and in alcohol, and but slightly
soluble in the fixed oils with the exception of oil lavender
and oil rosemary. Its chief use is that of coloring medicines, especially liniments, to make them more showy
rather than adding any quality.

PUNICA GRANATUM.

Pomegranate.   Asia, Africa, West Indies.

The *bark* of the root is an anthelmintic for the expulsion
of the round, pin and tape worms. A strong infusion may
be used for all these purposes. Large doses may nauseate
hence it should be used in small and frequent doses. Of
course in case of tape worm the patient should fast as long
as he conveniently can prior to taking this dose, and it
should be followed by a full dose of antibilious physic. If
unsuccessful repeat in a few days.

The *flowers* and *rind* of the fruit are quite astringent
and are valuable in diarrhœa and in the night sweats of
phthisis.

PYCNANTHEMUM INCANUM.

Wild Basil.

This *herb* is an aromatic, diffusive, relaxing and stimulating antispasmodic nervine. In hot infusion it influences
the circulation and is useful for colds, catarrhal fever, the
exanthems, malarial fever, infantile convulsions It will
be rendered more diffusive by the addition of a little zingiber.

PYCNANTHEMUM MONTANUM.

Mountain Mint.

This species may be used for the same general purposes.

PYROLA ROTUNDIFOLIA.

False Wintergreen.

The *leaves* are a mild, diffusive, stimulating, astringent
tonic influencing the mucous membrane throughout.

With agents that especially influence the bronchi it is
an expectorant.

With those that influence particularly the uterus and
vagina it stimulates and tones.

In enuresis it gives favorable results, and also in diabetes. It decreases the irritation of the membrane and the amount of the urine

In chronic diarrhœa it tones and astringes the alvine mucous membrane

It is a good wash for cleansing foul ulcers and a good gargle for sore throat.

PYRUS MALUS.

Apple Tree

The *bark* of this tree cooked in lard forms an excellent application for burns and scalds It quickly relieves and heals.

QUERCUS ALBA

White Oak

The *inner bark* of all the oaks yield a large proportion of tannin, and are largely used in the process of tanning leather. It is a stimulating tonic astringent and a powerful arrestor of hemorrhages whether external or internal.

Locally it may be applied to sores, bruises, tetter, ringworm, scaly eruptions and to prevent the falling out of the hair

It forms a good astringent wash for prolapsus uteri, prolapsus ani or relaxed vagina, spongy or bleeding gums, and for hardening them when false teeth are to be used. It is a good gargle for some forms of sore throat, ulcerated or inflamed, and in light cases of diphtheria

Per rectum it may be used for hemorrhoids, fissures and prolapsus ani

Locally it is a good wash for sweaty and tender feet.

Internally it may be used for diarrhœa, acute or chronic. Zingiber, xanthoxylum or capsicum make it more stimulating and diffusive

For night sweats it may be used either locally or constitutionally or both.

F E. Quercus Al.	10
Tr Capsicum	1
Glycerin	20

This is for either external or internal use

The *acorns* are a mild, stimulating, tonic alterative.

QUERCUS LUSITANICA

Nut-Galls.

The excrescences upon the young branches formed by

the puncture of a fly and immediately thereafter the deposit of an egg. The egg hatches, the fly grows and finally escapes. These excrescences are denominated nut-galls and from them is obtained

Acidum Tannicum, a pure astringent without the stimulation. It is a very light powder, readily dissolving in water. Tannin may be used upon a bleeding surface or used internally for hemorrhages and for diarrhœa.

Tannin and powdered lobelia seed in vaseline forms a good ointment for hemorrhoids, or the powders may be enclosed and inserted in gelatine capsules for rectal itching and painful hemorrhoids. The tannin itself may be used in case of prolapsus ani.

Tannic Acid enters into the Pile Suppositories made by C. T. Bedford which a great many of the profession have found very effective in the treatment of rectal troubles.

Tannin and quinine in equal parts in syrup of zingiber forms a good preparation for cholera infantum when the discharge is watery and the patient weak.

Tannin has been successfully used to remove tattoo marks. Cover the parts with a saturated solution of tannin and pick into the skin. Then rub with lunar caustic and allow to turn black. Now wash off the excess. It will pain for some two or three days. In fourteen to eighteen days the scab peels off and leaves a pink surface which disappears in a month or two.

Papoid is said to do this as well as tannin, and milkweed may be used for the same purpose.

In this way many birth marks may be removed, and many may be removed by the use of a sun glass. Burn the surface and heal the wound.

Dissolve tannin in 45 p. c. alcohol and add lint to form a covering for raw and bleeding surfaces. It excludes the air and prevents hemorrhage.

Tannin	dr. ii
Glycerine	oz. i

Apply during the ninth month of pregnancy to toughen the nipples, and in cases of sore nipples.

Tannin	grs. xv
Sulphur Lactate	dr. ss
Petrolatum	dr. v

This is a good application for barber's itch.

Tannin
Pul Acacia Vera   aa. dr. iss
Tr. Arnica Flowers   dr. iiss

Paint the surface with this every five minutes until thick and hard. It will usually abort a boil.

Tannin   grs. x
Sulph. Quinia   grs. v
Aqua   oz. ii

Wash the lids with a little of this in purulent ophthalmia.

Acidum Gallicum is chiefly made from nut-galls and is a pure astringent. It is a good preparation for internal use as it does not act so fully on the mucous membrane and produce so much constipation. It is valuable for gastric, respiratory, cystic or uterine hemorrhages.

QUERCUS RUBRA

Red Oak.

The *bark* of this variety may be used for the same general purposes as that of the other varieties In cancer, as an escharotic use concentrated potash made from the ashes of red oak bark· Apply until the cancer is removed, and then overspread the surface with pure honey.

QUERCUS TINCTORIA.

Black Oak

The *bark* of this variety is more bitter and more stimulating than that of the alba, and is more suitable for very torpid conditions. It exerts about the same astringency as the alba and is a better application for old sores, tetter, ringworm and some eczemas An infusion is the usual method of administering.

Py-oak tannin or blue methyline is a successful application for old ulcers.

RANUNCULUS BULBOSUS.

Butter Cup.

This plant has a solid, fleshy, turnip shaped root. Its flowers appear in May and June in the shape of small cups of a yellow color

The green *root* is quite acrid and stimulating when applied to the surface. An ointment made by simmering the root in lard is useful as an application to glandular swellings and scrofulous sores.

RHAMNUS CATHARTICA.

Buckthorn.

The *berries* furnish a juice which is quite a stimulating cathartic, and in large doses produces nausea, griping and watery stools. But most of these symptoms by being administered in syr. zingiberis are prevented.

RHAMNUS FRANGULA.

Buckthorn.

This is the European variety. It is a mild, stimulating laxative and cholagogue. It leaves a moderate tonic impression. In large doses it is fairly cathartic. For more tonic purposes combine it with euonymous, when it will be valued for habitual constipation arising from indigestion.

RHAMNUS PURSHIANA.

Cascara Sagrada. California.

The *bark* is a very bitter tonic, a slow, mild, stimulating hepatic. Its influence is chiefly expended upon the stomach, liver, gall ducts and bowels. It is of value in chronic constipation, torpor of the stomach and liver and chronic dyspepsia. It influences peristaltic action but is more tonic than cathartic.

F. E. Rhamnus Pursh. oz. i
Syr. Juglans Cin. q. s. oz. iv

This is an admirable hepatic and alvine tonic to be given morning and evening or at night only to overcome constipation.

RHEUM OFFICINALE.

Rhubarb. (R. Palmatum.) Turkey, India.

The *root* is a mild, stimulating tonic to the alvine mucous membrane, the liver and gall ducts. In large doses it is cathartic, but its tonic influence borders on astringency, and hence some slight constipation may follow its use. It is therefore not the agent to assist in overcoming chronic constipation, but its tonic hepatic influence is valuable in the treatment of diarrhœa, dysentery and cholera infantum. Heat somewhat increases its astringency. In such cases it is therefore best boiled or roasted. Calcined radix rhei is prepared by burning the root in an iron vessel till easily pulverized. Give doses of 3 to 5 grs., or use one dram to a half teacup of boiling water. Give a teaspoonful as required from fifteen minutes to three hours for cholera infantum, or use rheum, prunus and mentha piperita in equal parts, with one-fourth part bicarbonate soda. Triturate well and add a heaping teaspoonful to a half cup of boiling water. Give one or two teaspoonsful after each operation of the bowels.

Rheum cleanses the mucous membrane of viscid mucous, and while large doses prove cathartic, small and frequent doses are tonic hepatic. The addition of some alkaline preparation, as bicarbonate soda, bicarbonate potassa or bitartrate potassa, relieves acidity and increases its cathartic power.

Comp. Syr. Rhei et Potassæ is a valuable compound for the making of which many different formulæ are used.

Rheum	oz. viii	Rheum	
Cassia Cin.	oz. iv	Potas. Bicarb.	aa oz. ii
Potas. Bicarb.	oz. i	Hydrastis	oz. i
Hydrastis	oz. iv	Oil Cinnamon	M. 20
Oil Peppermint	M. 30	Oil Peppermint	M. 20

Dr. Bedford has put upon the market a Syr. Rhei et Potassa Comp. composed of the purest Turkey rhubarb made-P. M. formula, but double strength, as suggested by Prof. Geo. Hasty. It is a very reliable neutralizing mixture and an efficient syrup.

He also manufactures a neutralizing mixture according to Prof. Anthony's suggestion of the same agents minus the syrup. In many cases where children are suffering from cholera infantum the syrup is objectionable on account of its fermentative tendency and here the neutralizing mixture acts grandly.

Rheum	oz. xvi
Bicarb. Potas.	oz. vi

Add these to one gallon of strong green peppermint infusion and sweeten to suit. Zingiber and hydrastis may be added if desired.

Rheum, hydrastis, cinnamon and bicarbonate of potassa in equal parts, with one-fifth part pancreatine, may be formed into tablets, of convenient size and be used for some forms of indigestion; or rheum and calcined magnesia in equal parts with a half part of zingiber may be used for the same purpose.

Pul. Rheum	grs. iii
Leptandrin	grs. ii
Hydrastia Sulphate	gr. 1-10

This may be formed into a pill or used in a capsule.
Each pint of the Comp. Tincture represents

Rheum	oz. xvi
Cardamon Seed	
Saffron	
Coriander Seed	aa. oz. ii

Each pint of Rheum, Aromatic, represents

Rheum	oz. x
Cinnamon	
Cloves	aa. oz. ii
Nutmeg	oz. i

Each pint of Rheum, Sweet, represents

Rheum	oz. 6⅞
Glycyrrhiza	
Anise	aa. oz. 2⅞
Cardamon	oz. ⅞

RHUS AROMATICA.

Fragrant Sumach.   (R. Canadensis.)

This bush is of straggling growth three to seven feet high. It has a sweetish and rather pleasant perfume, especially if the leaves be crushed. The flowers are pale yellow; the fruit is globular, clothed with acid, crimson hairs.

The *bark* of the root is a stimulating, astringent tonic, influencing the mucous membrane and especially that of the urinary and alvine departments.

This is a valuable remedy in the treatment of enuresis. Fifteen drops of the fluid extract may be given two to five times a day.

In diabetes 30 or 40 drops may be given as required.

F. E. Rhus Arom.	dr. iii	F. E. Rhus Arom.	
Elix. Aromat.	oz. lss	" Celastrus Scan. aa. oz. i	
Aq. Cinnamon q.s. ad. oz. iii		Syr. Simplex	q. s. oz. iv

These formulæ may be used in enuresis, diabetes or Bright's disease; or use

F. E. Rhus Arom.	oz. ss
Glycerin	oz. ii
Syr. Simpl.	dr. ss
Aqua	q. s. oz. iv

As a tonic astringent it is of much importance in diarrhœa, dysentery and cholera infantum; also in hemorrhages from any organ or part. It is a very serviceable agent during the •menopause with those of hemorrhagic diathesis.

RHUS GLABRA.

Sumach.

The *leaves, berries and bark* are all more or less positive astringents. The leaves are the least astringent, but are valuable in dysentery and hemorrhages of lungs or uterus.

The *bark* is more stimulating, astringing and toning, and is valuable for leucorrhœa, inflammation of the bladder, and for rectal troubles, chronic diarrhœa and rectal hemorrhages. A hot infusion gives a somewhat fuller outward circulation. It is a good wash for aphthous sore mouth and spongy gums.

Dr. F. G. Hoener has with this agent cured several cases of prolapsus ani, and several cases of prolapsus uteri that had by others been pronounced incurable.

The *berries* are a pleasant acid astringent. Fill a vessel full of berries, cover with boiling water and steep a half-hour. Then strain and sweeten to suit the taste. This is a good beverage to allay irritation of the bladder and in the treatment of diabetes and for the relief of bloody urine.

Combined with pineapple syrup it is an expectorant, and is also useful in diphtheria. It may be atomized or gargled. Dr. F. G. Hoener uses the following gargle for sore throat and diphtheria:

    Aci. Rhus Glabra Bac.   oz. iv
    Elix. Phytolacca Rad.
    Syr. Pineapple   aa. oz. i

M. S. Spray the throat as often as necessary, and use internally the following:

    Elix. Betonica Lanc.
      " Eupatorium Perf.   aa. oz. iss
    Tr. Capsicum   dr. ii
    Syr. Simplex   dr. vi

M. S. One teaspoonful or more hourly, and if thirsty drink hot lemonade between times.

RIBES NIGRUM.

Black Currant.

The *fruit* is a pleasant, nutritious, mildly stimulating astringent useful in diarrhœa.

The *root* in hot infusion is a stimulating diaphoretic.

RIBES RUBRUM.

Red Currant.

This *fruit* forms an acidulated drink admirable in convalescence, especially from fevers. It is an appetizer and assists digestion.

The *root* is a stimulating diaphoretic when used in hot infusion, and is very valuable says Dr. Bryson when the eruption of measles is very tardy. An infusion of the *leaves* and *branches* produces nearly as good results as a stimulating diaphoretic.

ROSMARINUS OFFICINALIS.

Rosemary.

The *leaves* are a diffusive stimulant and relaxant. In hot infusion they influence the circulation toward the surface and produce diaphoresis and soothe the nerves. It is chiefly used as a vehicle.

RUBUS CANADENSIS.

Dewberry.

RUBUS VILLOSUS.

Blackberry.

The *roots* of these two varieties are much alike medically. They are a positive astringent tonic, influencing chiefly the alvine mucous membrane, giving good results in acute and chronic dysentery and diarrhœa, prolapsus ani and rectal hemorrhages.

Locally it is a good wash for aphthous sore mouth and bleeding or spongy gums, and to the vagina in leucorrhœa, prolapsus uteri and lax vagina.

The *berries* are a pleasant and nutritious fruit, soothing to weak and irritable stomachs, and useful in diarrhœa and cholera infantum. For this purpose remove the seeds and prepare a cordial as follows:

Juice of Berries	oz. ii	Blackberry Juice	qrt. i
Allspice		Sugar	lb. i
Zingiber.		Nutmeg	
Cinnamon	aa. dr. ii	Cinnamon	aa. oz. ss
Cloves	grs. iii	Cloves	
		Allspice	aa. dr. ii

In either formula bring the berries to the boiling point. Tie the spices in a piece of muslin and put into the berry juice; simmer one hour, covered. Press out the spices and add 1¼ lbs. granulated sugar.

RUBUS STRIGOSUS.

Red Raspberry.

The *leaves* are a mild, pleasant, soothing, diffusive, stimulating, astringent tonic. It allays nausea, sustains the nerves, and tones the mucous membrane. It is effective in acute and chronic dysentery and diarrhœa. It is also of much service in urethral irritation. It soothes the kidneys and urinary ducts. When needed it also sustains the uterus and stops hemorrhage. In ophthalmia it is a first-class wash. In leucorrhœa, gonorrhœa, dysentery and diarrhœa it is a good injection.

No. 6   gtta. x
Infusion Rubus Strig.   oz. iv
will be found useful in diabetes.

The expressed juice of the fruit is very nourishing in convalescence and for weak stomachs.

RUDBECKIA LANCINATA.

Thimble Weed.

The *flowers and leaves* are a moderately bitter, diffusive, balsamic, alterative tonic. It tones the kidneys, increases the flow of urine, is useful in renal congestions, catarrhal cystitis and in the beginning of Bright's disease. It also soothes and tones the digestive and the generative organs, and in hot infusion it influences the circulation and soothes the nervous system.

It is an excellent addition to alteratives. Dr. F. G. Hoener combines it with trifolium pratense flowers in the treatment of gastric cancer.

RUMEX ACETOSELLUS.

Sheep Sorrel.

This *herb* is a positive stimulant which may be made

into a soft extract for application to indolent ulcers and cancers.

RUMEX CRISPUS.
Yellow Dock.

The **root** is a mild, slow, stimulating, tonic alterative. It influences the mucous membrane, the skin and the secernents generally. It is of much importance in all forms of scrofula, skin diseases, syphilis, ophthalmia and glandular troubles.

It is somewhat laxative to the bowels, is both hepatic and cholagogue and assists in the process of assimilation.

The fresh roots of rumex digested in fresh cream or lard and then strained is useful for swellings, irritations, scrofulous sores, scaldhead, eczema, tetter and itch.

Rumex	160	F. E.	Rumex	dr. iv
Celastrus		"	Celastrus	
Ampelopsis		"	Ampelopsis	
Euonymous	aa. 80	"	Euonymous aa. dr. ii	
Oil Anise		"	Syr.Zingiber. q.s. oz. iv	
" Sassafras	aa. 1			
Rosewater	5			

Either of these are good alteratives.

SABBATIA ANGULARIS.
American Century.

This **herb** is a positive, diffusive, stimulating tonic to the heart, stomach, liver, generative organs and nervous system. In hot infusion it promotes the menses and influences a good outward circulation.

Cold preparations increase the appetite, assist digestion and assimilation in languid conditions, chronic dyspepsia and general debility. It is a good hepatic, maintains the portal circulation, but is best combined with more positive agents.

It is a good antiperiodic, and an efficient nervine tonic in nervous prostration, hysteria and general debility, the night sweats of phthisis, in chronic dysentery and diarrhœa, and in convalescence from fevers.

Its tonic power over the stomach makes it a good vermifuge.

SABBATIA ELLIOTTII.
Quinine-Flower.   S. E. United States.

The **root** is a stimulating, tonic nervine; antiperiodic

and anthelmintic. It may be used instead of quinine as an antiperiodic. A hot infusion used freely does well, but where large doses are given patients experience tinnitus aurium similar to that arising from quinine.

SABAL SERRULATA.

Saw Palmetto.   (Serenoa Serrulata.)

The *berries* are a mild, stimulating, tonic alterant, influencing the mucous membrane throughout but especially that of the urinary tract. It is a valuable agent in the relief of renal and cystic catarrh, prostatitis, sexual impotency, masturbation, irritation or inflammation of the renal mucous membraue and painful micturation,

H. K. Wampole & Co's preparation of Saw Palmetto Wine is palatable and efficient. Each teaspoonful representing 30 grs. of the fresh saw palmetto berries. Securing the fresh berries in proper season and by special manipulation, they have prepared a wine, representing fifty per cent. of the fresh berries.

An excellent expectorant, it soothes the mucous membrane in coryza, acute and chronic laryngitis and bronchitis. It increases appetite and digestion, and imparts tone and vigor to the organs of nutrition.

It is soothing and toning to the urinary and reproductive organs in cystitis, urethritis, pyelitis and sexual neurasthenia.

It is valuable in enuresis, in impotence, masturbation and sexual execesses.

Sabal Ser.	20
Carum Petrosel.	3
Cola Acum.	6
Santalum Album.	4
Aromatics	q. s.

This is a good tonic diuretic.

SACCHARUM LACTIS.

Sugar of Milk, Lactin.

Lactin forms only about 5 per cent. of milk. It is frequently used in which to triturate oils and bitter medicines.

SALIX ALBA.

White Willow.

The *bark* is an intensely, bitter, stimulating, tonic nervine, slightly astringent. As an antiperiodic it probably stands near to quinine, and is much less exciting to the nerve centres.

It is useful in general debility, chronic diarrhœa, chronic dysentery, convalesence from fevers, and in hot infusion stimulates the circulation.

An infusion made of the tags is excellent for salt rheum and running sores.

Salacin is an excellent tonic, nervine and antiperiodic. It relieves neuralgia and tones in convalesence. A small portion of capsicum may be added when desired.

It may be used for after pains and rheumatism.

Salacin	grs. x
Xanthoxylin	grs. v
Lactin	grs. xl

Make into five powders and use every four hours for rheumatism.

Acidum Salicylicum is derived from salicin by fusion with potas. hydrate or from gaultheria by saponification with potas, hydrate solution, but mostly treating sodium phenol or carbonate with carbon dioxide gas.

It is odorless, slightly astringent and somewhat irritating to the fauces and increases the saliva. It has but little influence on digestion more than to control fermentation but is quite stimulating to the nerve centers.

A solution of this agent applied once or twice to ringworm usually cures it, and gives good results when applied to soft chancre and syphilitic condylomata, and with lard or glycerine it forms a good ointment, 10 grains to one ounce.

Acidum Salicylicum	32
Cimicifugin	10
Potassii Iodidum	9
Xanthoxylin	2

Triturate on Lactin.

This is a valuable prescription for rheumatism, gout or lumbago.

Sodii Salicylas. To 100 parts salicylic acid with water to form a paste, add 104 parts carbonate of sodium. Carbonic acid gas will be evolved and the salicylate of sodium remain. It acts nearly the same as the acid but is not irritating, is more soluble and is more rapidly absorbed.

Sod. Salicy.   -   dr. i
Potas. Iod.   dr. ss
F. E. Xanthox.   gtta xv
Comp. Gentian.   q. s. oz. iv

M. S. ¼ to 1 teaspoonful in water every three hours for rheumatism.

Sod. Salicy. may be used in some water in doses of 2 to 10 grains every 2 hours for rheumatism.

McCoy, Howe Co., Indianapolis, manufacture Boro-Salicylicum a seventy-five per cent. solution, a powerful antiseptic, germicide and prophylactic, adapted to the use of surgeons, gynecologists, dentists, and the general practitioner.

It is non-toxic, non-irritant, non-corroding, non-escharotic. It is mild, yet powerful. Each fluid ounce represents the antiseptic power of one hundred grains of boric acid and one hundred grains of salicylic acid combined with glycerine in a permanent and soluble form. It is antiseptic and antizymotic, adapted to internal or local use, to create and maintain asepsis, and may be used as a spray, by atomization, irrigation or simple application, and causes rapid, healthy granulation and with but little suppuration. Locally, use ⅛ to ¼ strength; per vaginam ¼ strength; or internally 5 to 20 drops in water three or more times daily.

In chronic cystitis and chronic urethritis it is a valuable local application.

SALIX ERIOCEPHALA.

Swamp Willow.

The *leaves* in hot infusion give good results in enterocolitis.

SALIX NIGRA.

Black Willow,

The *bark* of the roots is a positive, bitter, tonic nervine. It seems to direct its chief influence to the generative organs, where it allays irritation and restores vigor to the entire sexual tract. Taken before retiring it quiets the nerves and prevents lascivious dreams and nocturnal emissions.

Dr. G. H. Mayhugh recommends the following for spermatorrhœa:

F. E. Salix Nigra
"   Celastrus Scan.   aa. oz. ii
Syr. Simplex   oz. iv
M. Sig. One or two teaspoonsful in water four times a day.

The *aments* are a stimulating, astringent tonic especially influencing the genito-urinary organs of both sexes. It is of importance in nymphomania, onanism, seminal incontinence, ovaritis, cystitis, prostatitis, spermatorrhœa and nocturnal emissions. It relieves irritation, soothes the nerves and tones the organs.

SALIX PURPUREA.

Rose Willow.

The *bark* of the roots has about the same properties as nigra,

SALVIA OFFICINALIS.

Sage.

The *leaves* are a pleasant, mild, diffusive, stimulating tonic, slightly astringent. In hot infusion it is gently diaphoretic and quite soothing to the nerves. It cleanses and tones the mucous membrane and may be profitably used in throat troubles from colds and in respiratory, stomach or bowel troubles from the same cause.

Cold preparations are diuretic and excellent in night sweats, and are sometimes used for the removal of the stomach worm.

Infusion of Sage   oz. ii
Powd. Borax   dr. i
Honey to sweeten. Apply to mouth ulcers

SAMBUCUS CANADENSIS.

Elder.

The *flowers* are a mild, diffusive, relaxing diaphoretic and alterant. When given in hot infusion it is excellent for the removal of colds and feverish conditions therefrom, also in measles and chicken-pox. It influences the glandular system and is an excellent addition to some alterative compounds. Its relaxing influence is felt by all the secernents. It is a gentle laxative for children and is very soothing to the nerves.

They form a fine soothing poultice to any inflamed part.
Cold preparations are diuretic.

The *bark* is a stimulating cathartic. It thoroughly arouses the alvine mucous membrane and is excellent for the cleansing and toning of that membrane in cases of gastric and intestinal ulceration and in catarrhal conditions. It is a good gastric tonic and anthelmintic.

An infusion is a good wash for the cleansing of sores.

Boil the green bark till the fluid is a soft extract. Then combine with vaseline and you have an excellent salve for old sores, eczema rubrum, etc.

The *fruit* is nutritive and medicinal. It influences all the secernents and is mildly laxative. It may be made into a wine or jelly and partaken with profit in convalescence.

SANGUINARIA CANADENSIS.

Blood-Root.

The fresh *root* is a very harsh, positive stimulant to the mucous membrane; the dry root is much less so. It influences the mucous membrane, the secernents and the glandular system. Large doses are quite nauseating. As an alterant it is excellent in glandular troubles, scrofula and skin diseases. It is useful in diphtheria internally and externally, and in the cleansing of old sores in preparation for a healing dressing.

It is one of the best additions to cough syrups; it cleanses the mucous membrane, induces expectoration and relieves irritation of the bronchi. With acetous syrup of lobelia, or the 3rd. prep. of lobelia, it is unexcelled in the treatment of membranous croup. The combination must be proportioned to the age of the child and the severity of the case. Give every few minutes until the child vomits and expels the membrane. Then give small doses at longer intervals to prevent a recurrence. In asthma sanguinaria is a valuable addition to lobelia, and in whooping cough a small portion with the acetous syrup of lobelia is a success. Give enough and give frequently enough to compel the spasmodic efforts to cease.

In sluggish cases it is a good emmenagogue.

An infusion of only moderate strength may be used as an injection in case of leucorrhœa but not where the vagina is irritated.

Sanguinaria may be combined with hepatics in torpid catarrhal conditions of the alvine membrane. Toning agents will then be more effective.

The acetous tincture is made by heating acetum oz. xvi to the boiling point and adding to oz. iv of powd. sanguinaria.

Combined with glycerin the infusion or fluid extract will invigorate the hair follicles and prevent the falling out of the hair, whether as a result of fever or other causes; but it will not make hair grow on bald heads. Applied to the skin when inflamed by poisonous contact it will promptly relieve the itching and burning

Sanguinaria and lobelia may be used in equal parts in cases of pruritus.

The nitrate of sanguinaria is an escharotic.

Prof E. G. Anthony makes a pencil of the acetous tr. sanguinaria with starch and tragacanth for application to granular eye lids.

SANICULA, MARILANDICA.

Sanicle.

The *root* is a mild. aromatic, diffusive, stimulating and relaxing agent. Hot infusions are moderately diaphoretic and nervine and may be used for colds with feverishness, whether of the head or the respiratory organs; also in the fever stage of the eruptive diseases, especially in measles.

SANTALUM ALBUM.

Sandal Wood, Yellow or White Saunders.

India, Ceylon.

This evergreen glabrous tree grows 20 to 30 feet high and 2 to 3 feet in circumference, having a brownish bark.

The *wood chips* yield an *oil.* Either is a mild, aromatic, astringent tonic. In pharmacy it is sometimes used to color liquids, especially liniments. It is frequently used as a substitute for copaiba in gonorrhœa, gleet, or other urethral irritations

SARRACENIA PURPUREA.

Pitcher Plant.

The *root* is a mild relaxing and stimulating diaphoretic. When given in hot infusion it is very valuable in measles, scarlatina. small-pox, chicken-pox and other contagious eruptive diseases.

Dr. F. G. Hoener recommends the following for such conditions·

Sarracenia Purp.
Sambucus Can
Eupatorium Perf aa equal parts

SASSAFRAS OFFICINALE.

Sassafras   (S. Variifolium.)

The *inner bark* of the trunk and root is a pleasant, aromatic, warming, stimulating alterative. The wood and bark are frequently used as a pleasant alterant beverage, a popular drink in Spring when the bark has its greatest strength It influences the glandular system, and is valuable in cases of varicose ulcers and those of a scrofulous nature. Give an infusion and poultice the sore with sassafras and ulmus A poultice is also valuable for bruises, congested swellings, and chronic abscesses

In hot infusion it is diaphoretic, nervine and emmenagogue.

The *oil* is used for scabies and other contagious eruptions. It is a good stimulating and relaxing nervine for bruises, sprains, congestions, inflammations, rheumatism and neuralgic swellings.

Oil Sassafras	1	Oil Sassafras
F E. Lobelia		" Cinnamon
" Cypripedium · aa 4		" Cloves in equal parts.

The former is a stimulating and relaxing liniment and the latter a stimulating liniment.

Oil Sassafras   gtta. i
Rain Water   dr. i

forms an application for ulceration of the cornea.

The *pith* in the young shoots in cool water forms a mucilaginous wash of excellent service in acute and chronic ophthalmia It soothes and heals. Gather the pith in spring and allow to dry.

SATUREIA HORTENSIS.

Summer Savory.

This *herb* in hot infusion is a mild, aromatic, stimulating diaphoretic useful in colds, feverishness, and for the relief of the menses when stopped by cold.

SCROPHULARIA NODOSA.

Carpenter's Square.

The *leaves* are a mild, relaxing and gently stimulating

alterative, influencing the secernents and useful in scrofula and skin diseases.

It tones the pelvic viscera, increases the quantity of urine, and soothes and strengthens the generative organs.

SCUTELARIA LATERIFLORA

Scullcap

This *herb* is a positive, diffusive, permanent, stimulating nervine.

It is bitter but not nauseating. Its chief influence is spent upon the nervous system. It is an excellent agent in nervous prostration. In its way it is fully as stimulating as quinia, but its influence is more general than that of quinine. Its stimulation extends to the brain, spinal cord and sympathetic system To all it extends its tonic influence, which is quite permanent.

With lobelia and capsicum, cypripedium and capsicum, or with caulophyllum alone it is an excellent antispasmodic, which may be used in such conditions as chorea, epilepsy, hysteria, puerperal convulsions and other spasmodic conditions of infant or adult I think such combinations would give favorable results in hydrophobia, and I know that such will with delirium tremens and morphia mania It may not cure bad cases of epilepsy but it will help such conditions, especially with alkaline and hepatic preparations. Have such patients abstain from sweets, fats and starches to a great extent.

In the delirium of typhoid and in nervous dyspepsia it is an excellent agent.

In cases of insanity, after getting your patient well under the influence of lobelia and cypridedium put them on scutelaria.

It is also useful in hysteria, hypochondria, general nervousness, insomnia, convalescence from fevers, cranial neuralgia, uterine neuralgia, general female weakness.

A hot infusion renders it more diffusive than is the fluid extract, except it be used in hot water

Scutelarin is a moderate representative

SEMPERVIVUM TECTORUM

House Leek.

The leaves by pressure yield a juice that makes a good

application in acute ophthalmia and for all raw open sores of recent production, and surface swellings.

Internally it is a moderate diuretic.

SENECIO AUREUS.

Life-Root.

This *herb* is a slow, stimulating and relaxing agent, influencing the nervous system and the generative organs.

It gently promotes menstruation, relieves some forms of dysmenorrhœa, the aching back and some forms of hysteria, and tones the generative organs of both sexes.

With sanguinaria it is a positive emmenagogue.

Senecio	dr. iv	F. E. Senecio
Viburnum Op.	dr. ii	" Caulophyllum aa. dr. iv
Caulophyllum		Syr. Zingiber. q. s. oz. iv
Euonymous	aa. dr. i	
Syr. Zingiberis	q. s. oz. iv	

These are good compounds for dysmenorrhœa.

With aralia and prunus it influences the bronchi and may be added to the cough syrups of the chlorotic. It is soothing, cleansing and strengthening to the lungs.

McCoy, Howe Co. prepare Caulo-Senecio, a fine antispasmodic and nervine. Each fluid ounce represents:

Black Haw	
Cramp Bark	aa. grs. XLV
Wild Yam	grs. xxx
Blue Cohosh	
Life-Root	aa. grs. xv

It is very effective in an.enorrhœa and dysmenorrhœa, cramps, colics, cholera morbus, convulsions, hysteria, etc.

SENECIO OBOVATUS.

Squaw Weed.

This is a mild, stimulating alterative.

Dr. F. G. Hoener uses this agent in the treatment of tetter, eczema and chronic skin diseases generally.

SIERRA SALVIA.

Mountain Sage, Sage-Brush. (Artemisia Frigida.)
Western U. S.

This *herb* is a bitter aromatic, diffusive, stimulating diaphoretic, and is also antiperiodic, alterant and nervine. Large doses nauseate and may produce vomiting. In hot infusion it influences the circulation, inducing a

good outward flow of blood and free diaphoresis. It stimulates the entire peripheral circulation and sustains the
heart and arteries. It quite thoroughly influences all the
secernents and the mucous membrane, the liver, the gall
ducts, the kidneys and the bowels. It gives excellent
results in mountain fever, spinal irritation, meningitis;
intermittent, remittent, congestive and rheumatic fevers;
pleuritis, pneumonitis, sciatica, la grippe, scarlatina and
the other exanthemata. Also in muco-purulent leucorrhœa, in phthisis, and in amenorrhœa and dysmenorrhœa
when the results of congestion.

SILPHIUM LACINIATUM

Rosin Weed.

The *leaves* contain a resinous material, a rather bitter
stimulant to the mucous membrane. It lessens expectoration, and lessens the alvine discharges in dysentery and
diarrhœa.

SILPHIUM PERFOLIATUM

Cup Plant.

The *root and leaves* are a diffusive stimulant, influencing the liver, gall ducts and spleen, and is laxative to the
bowels.

In hot infusion it is a gentle diaphoretic and useful in
cases of biliousness, colds, remittent and catarrhal fevers.
It is said also to be an antiperiodic.

SIMABA CEDRON.

Cedron Seed   New Grenada.

This tree grows to the height of about 15 feet. The
stem when about twelve feet ends in a terminal panicle of
flowers covered externally with brownish hairs It then
sends forth side branches which do the same. The fruit
is about the size of a large peach and covered with short
hairs. Each fruit contains one seed having two halves.

The *seed* is a stimulating and relaxing antispasmodic
nervine. By those among whom the tree grows, it is successfully used in the cure of rattlesnake bite and that of
other poisonous reptiles and insects, also in the cure of
hydrophobia. It is used internally and applied to the
surface of the wound, and in hydrophobia it is also used
hypodermically.

Internally from 5 to 30 grains may be used every 3 to 6 hours. Large doses produce in some persons some griping sensations in the bowels.

This agent is also used in spasms, for toothache and as an antiperiodic in agues. As an antiperiodic give two to four grains three to six times during the cold stage.

SINAPIS ALBA AND NIGRA.

Mustard.

The *seed* is quite pungent to the taste and smell, stimulating and acrid. It is prepared for table use and in Spring the young leaves are eaten as greens.

The powdered seed will blister the surface if left on long enough, and if used persistently with food it will irritate the stomach.

It is doubtful whether we can advise the use of an agent that will so quickly destroy a healthy surface. If used to destroy some portion of skin necessary to be destroyed its blistering use would be legitimate. This agent should be used only to stimulate the surface, never allowing it to blister except as above stated.

It is sometimes used internally as a quick emetic in cases of poisoning, but I prefer capsicum, lobelia and bicarbonate of soda for this purpose, but I would give the mustard if nothing better was at hand, a teaspoonful or less in four ounces of water.

It may be used to stimulate over the surface of a congested organ, or over the seat of acute pain, but remove before blistering even if it is reapplied. If some flour and the white of an egg be added it will usually not blister.

Sinapis is sometimes added to a foot bath to stimulate the extremities.

SMILAX CANELLÆFOLIA.

Bamboo-Brier Root.   (S. Pseudo-China).
                                S. E. United States.

The *root* is a stimulating tonic alterative of considerable value in primary and secondary syphilis, rheumatism, scrofula and eczema. An infusion may be used freely.

SMILAX OFFICINALIS.

Sarsaparilla.   Honduras, Jamaica.

The *root* is a mild, pleasant, relaxing and stimulating alterative. In hot infusion it gives an outward circulation of the blood. It is a very mild agent and deserving praise chiefly when combined with other alterants In this way it is of service in scrofula, syphilis and skin diseases.

F. E Smilax Off.
"   Articum Lap
"   Phytolacca Rad.   aa dr. iii
"   Xanthoxylum   gtta. xv
Iodi. Potas.   dr. i

This is valuable for syphilis especially if gummata be present

Sarsaparilla	320	Sarsaparilla	800
Rumex	160	Guaiacum	
Menispermum	80	Iris	aa 80
Oil Sassafras	1	Stillingia	240
		Oil Anise	1

These are good alteratives

SODIUM.

This is the base for a number of alkaline preparations. It is a soft silvery white metal. The hydrate of soda (caustic soda) and quicklime in equal parts form a powder to apply to chancres and warts.

Sodii Chloridum (salt) is a stimulating antiseptic useful in gastric and pulmonary hemorrhages, as a saturated solution inject to relieve pin worms; as a stimulating injection to relieve the bowels; as an application to sprains, bruises, and (envelop the joint in a hot compress of salt water every 3 or 4 hours), in rheumatism and neuralgia; as a wash for weak sore eyes; for cleansing the mucous membrane in nasal catarrh; and for making a salt water bath.

Sodœ Carbonas, (Carbonate of Soda) is as strong alkali used for cleansing and disinfecting. A solution forms a good wash for scaly skin.

Sodae Bicarbonas, (Bicarbonate of Soda.) Baking Soda is a valuable ant-acid, and may be used in cases of poisoning by mineral acids. It is also valuable as a vaginal injection in cases of sterility where such arises from an acid leucorrhœa. This agent is an abortive in tonsilitis if given in the early stage. Give 30 or 40 grains internally and frequently apply to the tonsil by means of a blow-pipe.

Listerine   oz. i
Bicarb. Soda
Biborate Soda   aa grs. xxx

Aqua   q. s. oz. iv

Atomize this in case of catarrh to cleanse the nostrils.

Sodæ Sulphis (Sulphite of Soda) is a good wash for aphthous sore mouth, one dram to an ounce of water. It clears up the trouble in a hurry. In typhoid and other fevers and torpid conditions of the alvine mucous membrane, small doses in solution may be given 3 or 4 times in 24 hours it will readily cleanse the tongue and alvine mucous membrane throughout.

Sulphite Soda	1
Salicylate Lithia	20
Cimicifuga Rac.	30
Cascara Sagrada	30

This combination is suitable for rheumatism.

Sodæ Hyposulphis (Hyposulphite of Soda) is very useful in arresting gastric fermentions, 2 or 3 grains to the ounce of water may be used. A stronger solution is a good wash for sore mouth, and a saturated solution is a good application for ringworm, pruritus and tetter.

Sodae Biboras (Borax) has two equivalents of boracic acid and one of soda and is soluble in ten or twelve parts of water. It is a good alkaline wash for the babe's sore mouth. Salvia, prunus, myrica, kino, rhus glabra or hydrastis may be added. Borax is also a good wash for ophthalmia, granular lids, for cleaning the scalp, tender surfaces and in scaly eruptions.

Borax	dr. i
Glycerin	dr. iv
Phos. Hyd.	grs. iv
Rose Water	oz. iii ss

Use for mouth ulcers.

Borax	dr. iv.
Carbolic Acid	dr. i
Tannin	dr. ii
Glycerin	oz. ii
Alcohol	oz. iii
Rose Water	oz. v

Apply for the removal of pimples and blackheads.

Boracic Acid consists of one equivalent of boron and three of oxygen. A solution of 4 to 10 grains to the ounce of water relieves the burning sensation of gonorrhœa. In resilient stricture and painful cystitis an injection to the bladder of a solution of 8 grains to the ounce of water gives almost instant relief and abates micturition. Wherever used it diminishes muco purulent discharges, whether it be to the vagina for leucorrhœa, to the ear for otorrhœa, or to the eye in conjunctivitis, gonorrhœal ophthalmia, granulated eyelids, catarrhal ophthalmia, corneal congestions, or ulcerated tarsi.

Boracic acid two drams to one pint of water makes a good eye wash. Boracic acid ten grains to simple cerate one dram forms a useful ointment.

Boracic Acid
Tannin aa. grs. x
Glycerin dr. ii
Aqua Rosæ dr. vi

Use a few drops in the eyes every three hours for conjunctivitis.

Boracic acid and acetanilid form a wash for cleansing sores and wounds.

Boracic acid and the aqueous extract of hamamelis in water form a good wash for ophthalmia.

SOLANUM CAROLINENSE.

Horse Nettle, Bull Nettle. (Succus Solanii.)

S. E. United States.

This is the *fresh juice* of the fruit concentrated by exposure to currents of air at a low temperature and preserved by the addition of some alcohol. This is the process adopted by McCoy, Howe Co., of Indianapolis. They prepare it double strength. It is recommended largely in the treatment of epilepsy. If we shall rely upon reports it is very successful. Begin with small doses; increase their size and continue long enough to perfect a cure.

SOLIDAGO CANADENSIS.

Golden-rod.

There are several varieties of this plant, but that bearing a plume-like flower is preferred.

The *leaves and flowers* are a stimulating and slightly astringent tonic antiseptic to the mucous membrane. It is a sanative germicide, and is valuable in the presence of putrescence, as in diphtheria, scarlatina, tonsilitis, pharyngitis or laryngitis. It may be boiled down and made into a confection or troche with sugar, suitable for sore throat of almost any kind, for children or for adults.

Solidago Can.   4
Hydrastis Can.
Myrrha   aa. 2
Chloride of Sodium
Capsicum   aa. 1

This may be made into an acetous infusion for gargling, or for atomizing the throat; or the vinegar may be omitted and the infusion swallowed. In diphtheria and scarlatina there is nothing better. In scarlatina arctium seed should be added. In tonsilitis solidago may be used alone.

Solidago   20
Lobelia
Xanthoxylum   aa. 1

This also may be used for diphtheria and scarlatina. In light form

The Fld. Ext. of Solidago Comp. according to the formula of Prof G. N. Davidson, made by C. T. Bedford is a very excellent combination of agents in the treatment of diphtheria and all forms of ulceration of the throat and mucous surfaces

Here you have the tonic and antiperiodic action of the eucalyptus, the fine stimulation of the xanthoxylum, the relaxation of the lobelia with the slight escharotic action of the solidago made from the green herb.

This comp. proved very effective in the hands of the late Prof. Davidson.

In catarrh and especially in la grippe, solidago is very valuable. It cures quick and completely. I have had more complete eradication of la grippe from the use of solidago, either alone in hot infusion, or in combination with other suitable agents, than with anything else.

In typhoid fever it stimulates and cleanses the alvine mucous membrane very successfully.

In phthisis pulmonalis and bronchial catarrh it is of much value, especially when added to other agents influencing the respiratory organs.

Boiled down to a thin paste and added to vaseline, an excellent salve is formed.

SOLIDAGO VIRGAUREA.

(Virga Latifolia.)

The *leaves* are a stimulating astringent and diuretic. It is valuable in dropsy When given in hot infusion, very freely, it increases freely the flow of urine.

SPIGELIA MARILANDICA.

Pink Root.

The **root** is a domestic anthelmintic. It is usually combined with senna. Large doses produce dizziness, but no such symptoms attend the ordinary dose.

Dr. F. G. Hoener recommends the following as an anthelmintic:

 Syr. Spigelia Mar.
  " Chenopodium Anth. aa. oz. ii
  " Cassia Acut. oz. i
 M. S. A teaspoonful or more four times a day for a few days.

SPIRÆA OPULIFOLIA.

Nine Barks.

The **leaves** are a mild, stimulating, astringent tonic.

SPIRÆA TOMENTOSA.

Hardhack.

The **roots and leaves** are a mild, stimulating astringent, useful in diarrhœa.

STAPHYLEA TRIFOLIA.

Bladder Nut.

The **bark** is a mild, soothing, stimulant and relaxant to the mucous membrane. In hot infusion it influences the circulation and soothes the nervous system. In case of gastric, alvine, urinary and generative irritation it soothes and gently stimulates.

STATICE BRAZILIENSIS.

Baycuru.   Brazil, Paraguay.

The **root** internally is of a reddish brown color, having a thick bark and its pith fully one-fourth of its diameter. The natives use this for all kinds of scrofulous enlargements and glandular swellings. It is a stimulating, astringent alterant. It is used locally as a wash, inhaled and given by way of the stomach. It is used as a gargle in some forms of sore throat.

STATICE CAROLINIANA.

Marsh-Rosemary.

The **root** is a positive astringent, useful in acute and

chronic diarrhœa and that resulting in typhoid fever. It is also valuable in hemorrhages from whatever locality, and whether internal or superficial. It is useful as a wash for sore mouth and spongy gums

STIGMATA MAYDIS

Corn Silk.

This should be gathered immediately after its pollen has been shed It is a demulcent, tonic diuretic. It increases the flow of urine, soothes the kidneys and bladder, and relieves the urine of that strong odor of ammonia which is sometimes present It cleanses the cystic membrane in the relief of cystic catarrh, and of other morbid deposits showing its influence as an antiseptic. It assists in freeing the circulation of urea and is valuable in the treatment of renal and cystic inflammation

Dr. C. B Riggs recommends the following for cystitis.

F E Stigmata Mayd   oz. iss
" Uva Ursi   oz ss
Sodium Salicylate (Wintergreen) grs LX

M. S. Teaspoonful every one, two or three hours This gives relief within a few hours and will give any physician a reputation in this class of cases The Doctor says this has never failed him

STILLINGIA SYLVATICA.

Stillingia.

The **root** is a positive stimulating alterative Large doses are cathartic and emetic and subsequently leave in the stomach and bowels a burning sensation

It stimulates the alvine mucous membrane and the glandular system, and is valuable in the treatment of secondary syphilis, eczemas, ulcers and scrofula It is best adapted to chronic cases and in combination with other agents less stimulating.

F: E Stillingia Syl.   F. E Stillingia Syl
" Dicentra Ex.   " Sarsaparilla Off.
" Iris Ver   " Arctium Sem.
" Chimaphilla U aa dr. ii   " Chimaphilla
" Xanthoxylum C. gtta xv   " Rumex Cr   aa dr ii
Syr. Simplex   q. s oz. iv   " Xanthox Car. gtta x
                            Syr. Simplex   q s. oz iv

Stillingia Syl.	5	F. E. Stillingia	oz. iii
Dicentra Ex.	3	" Sanguinaria	dr. iv
Chimaphilla U.	2	" Iris Versicolor	dr. iss
Xanthoxylum Bac.	1½	Iodide Potas.	dr. iii
Coriander Sem.	1½	Syr. Simplex	q. s. oz. xvi
Iris Vers.			
Sambucus Flowers aa.	1		

These are all good alterative preparations more or less stimulating.

Oil Stillingia	
" Lobelia	aa. dr. ii
" Cajaput	
" Eucalyptol	aa. dr. iii
Alcohol	oz. iii

This is a good liniment for sore throat and wherever needed.

STYLOSANTHES ELATIOR.

Afterbirth Weed.

This *herb* is a soothing, stimulating, tonic nervine especially influencing the pelvic organism. It relieves the irritation and pains frequently present during the pregnant period, prevents miscarriage and quiets the false pains so frequently perplexing just prior to parturition. It is a splendid preparatory to the parturient act, and nicely anticipates a long and tedious labor.

Of the fluid extract 10 or more drops may be given three times a day for a month prior to confinement.

STYRAX BENZOIN.

Benzoin.   East Indies.

This fragrant balsam exudes through incisions made in the bark. This dries to a state of brittleness. An alcoholic tincture is made which may be combined with cough syrups in the treatment of old coughs. In hot water it is quite fragrant and being inhaled will add to its power as a tonic expectorant.

Benzoic acid is quite irritating.

STYRAX OFFICINALE.

Storax.   Southern Europe.

This balsam is a stimulating expectorant.

SULPHUR.

Sulphur Sublimatum is very valuable in the treatment

of diphtheria. After cleansing the throat by the process of gargling or atomizing then use a blow pipe and leave the throat well covered with sulphur. It gives excellent results.

Sulphur burnt in a sick room or through a house is one of the best of disinfectants.

Sulphur may be taken internally but it should be remembered by those who wear jewelry next to the flesh that after taking sulphur a few days the skin will tarnish jewelry. Its chief action is on the circulation and the skin.

Externally and internally it is used as a cure for itch. Triturate sulphur 1, with lard 2 and apply, but sulphuret of potassium is better for this purpose.

Sulphur	dr. vi
Unslacked Lime	dr. iii
Aqua	oz. xvi

Boil the compound till almost a red color. This is the bisulphuret of calcium. A few applications of this will usually cure itch.

SURGICAL ANÆSTHETICS.

BY E. ANTHONY, M. D.

Professor of Surgical Pathology applied, in the Physio-Medical College of Indiana, Indianapolis.

Relative Value of Each —Immediately upon the discovery of ether by Dr. Morton of Boston its use became general throughout the civilized world. Dr. Simpson's discovery of chloroform during the following year robbed Morton, at least for a time, of a portion of his laurels. The influence wielded by Simpson and his friends on the continent, gave chloroform a much greater impetus than ether; but it was soon found that more patients died from the use of the former that from the latter; and this fact caused a reaction, which turned the tide of sentiment in favor of ether. Notwithstanding this chloroform is extensively used by some European nations, especially the Germans. The general effect of these two agents is much the same; but each finds its applicability in the peculiar conditions found in individual cases. Ether is a cardiac stimulant, increasing the force and frequency of the heart, filling up the capillaries and distending the vessels of the brain. This property of ether renders it inapplicabile in persons of a plethoric habit. Also in hypertrophy with irritability of the heart, caused by aoritic stenosis. Its stimulating properties render its use in irritable states of the nasal passages and bronchial tubes very unpleasant, and contra-indicates its use in all well developed cases of bronchitis and organic disease of the lungs. Epileptics are not good subjects for taking ether by inhalation, the increase in the cerebral circulation is liable to bring on the convulsions and such patients sometimes die from this cause. Owing to its liability to cause vomiting it is not highly esteemed in abdominal surgery. Its stimulating effect on the capillaries also favors hemorrhage, the same objection applies to its use in operations about the nose and mouth and in cataract. Its inflammability renders it very dangerous where artificial light has to be employed. Its volatility and bulk contra-indicates its use in armies that are changing places, owing to its inconvenience of transportation. Its odor is very objectionable to many patients, the impression it makes on the nervous system lasts sometimes for several months.

The one redeeming feature is its safety as claimed by its friends, the number of deaths from its use in surgery being less than from the use of chloroform, which, according to statistics, causes one death in ten thousand, while that of ether one in twenty-six thousand. However the mortality from either may not be correct, because the number of these is not known, that may have died from the carelessness or ignorance of the administrators. Even in many well regulated hospitals the administration of the anæsthetic is trusted to inexperienced and careless internes. It is also a part of human nature, from which none of us is exempt, to allow ourselves to become careless. After having administered the agents, perhaps one thousand times without a fatal result, but owing to some little omission a patient may suddenly and unexpectedly die. The life is gone and cannot be recalled. In this more than in other cases, "vigilance is the price of safety." This applies more directly to chloroform than ether, as the former is more certain and potent in action. This may in part explain its greater fatality. The same may be said of its almost universal use by country practitioners, who use it indiscriminately and who are many times compelled to trust its use in the hands of inexperienced men. It is a fact peculiar but nevertheless true that the larger number of patients die when the anæsthetic is given when trivial operations are to be made, such as amputation of a toe or finger, the removal of small tumors and other like trivial proceedures

The explanation of this is, first; experienced men, only, make severe operations; they are aware of the danger, not only of the operation, but of the anæsthetic, and take every precaution to guard the patient against all danger; and when the time comes to make the operation there are no mistakes made. On the other side the operation is trivial, seemingly free from danger, and the operator takes the same view of the anæsthetic, therefore little or no precaution is taken He seems to forget that the anæsthetic is just as dangerous when administered for trivial operations as for severe ones.

The following is an analysis of 21 and 26 cases of chloroform and ether respectively, as taken from the reports at Netley Hospital for the year 1875, and shows the relative time required to bring the patients under the influence The shortest time for chloroform, two minutes and thirty seconds; ether three minutes and thirty seconds Longest time for chloroform, fourteen minutes and thirty seconds; ether, twenty-four minutes. Average time for chloroform, six minutes and twenty-four seconds; ether, eight minutes and ten seconds Average time under its influence—chloroform, twelve minutes and forty-eight seconds; ether, nineteen minutes and six seconds. Smallest quantity used in any one case—chloroform, one dram; ether, two ounces and four drams Largest quantity used—chloroform, eight drams; ether, nine ounces. Average quantity used in any case—chloroform, three drams and nine minims; ether, five ounces and one dram From chloroform vomiting occurred in two cases during or after the use of the drug. From ether vomiting occurred in eleven cases after the use of the drug. Excitement occurred in ten cases during or after the administration of chloroform. During or after the administration of ether there was marked excitement in seven cases

It will be seen from the above analysis that chloroform brings about anæsthesia quicker than ether, that ether holds its influence longer than chloroform; that vomiting is more frequent from ether than chloroform· that it takes four to eight times more ether than chloroform to produce the specific effect.

The temperature of the room has much to do with the

administration of either, as the following table compiled
by Mr. Snow will show. One hundred cubic inches of air
was saturated with ether and chloroform in the following
quantities:

One hundred cubic inches of air at
44 degrees would contain 27 cubic inches of ether vapor
54   "   "   "   24.3 "   "   "   "
64   "   "   "   43 3 "   "   "   "
74   "   "   "   53.6 "   "   "   "
84   "   "   "   66.6 "   "   "   "

One hundred cubic inches of air at
50 degrees would contain 9 cubic inches chloroform vapor
60   "   "   "   14   "   "   "   "
70   "   "   "   24   "   "   "   "
80   "   "   "   36   "   "   "   "
90   "   "   "   55   "   "   "   "

The object of exhibiting the above table is to show that
the temperature of the atmosphere in the operating room
has much to do with the time required to bring the patient under its influence, as the atmosphere will absorb
only a given amount at a certain temperature. A knowledge of this is necessary, because if the temperature is low
it will take too long to get the patient ready for the operation; on the contrary if the temperature is high the
patient may get a fatal quantity. The above is a fair
representation of the opinions of those who prefer ether
in surgery. A brief statement of the representative men
who are not sanguine of the safety of ether, might serve
to put the young practitioner on his guard, as some writers
leave the impression that ether is almost absolutely safe.
The following is extracted from the pen of Joseph Lister,
Esq. At the International Congress at Brussels M. Per-
rin said: "The fact of death resulting from ether cannot
be contested, and accidents, whatever may be said, resemble those from chloroform. Like chloroform, ether exposes
to sudden accidents, impossible to foresee, dependent on
accidental syncope." M. Forget said that "to deny that
every anæsthetic causes sudden death is to refuse to receive
evidence." Kappeler, in summing up the evidence furnished by his table of ether-deaths, says: "From the
foregoing facts, however, it by no means appears that
ether-death in man is essentially different from chloroform-
death, nor that death under the inhalation of ether in

man always commences by disturbance of respiration, and in every case proceeds from the respiratory organs, as experimental physiologists maintain to be the case with animals."

We are forced, then, by clinical evidence, to reject the statement of text-books that ether "never suddenly paralyzes the heart," as well as the latest doctrine that ether always gives warning by the pulse. it becoming "weak and slow, not suddenly but gradually." Nor will the doctrine of Schiff, based wholly upon experiments with animals, that death under ether always begins with the respiratory function, bear examination by the light of clinical experience, while his corollary that the surgeon is always responsible for the death of a patient under ether, is unsound, as it is sure to work if adopted, most serious injury and great injustice to whoever may be so unfortunate as to have an accident with this anæsthetic   The second important fact in regard to ether, is that the dangerous symptoms or death may supervene at some considerable time after the administration has terminated, just as they do after chlorotorm   Whether the fatal event can justly be attributed to ether in such cases as those reported by M. Richet, where a suffocative catarrh began soon after the inhalation, and caused death some days afterwards, remains yet to be determined.   There are cases fully detailed, however, exactly resembling those occurring after chloroform, and in regard to which there can be no question.   The writer is cognizant of a number of such cases, in which the patient was rescued by vigorous measures, and which have never been published.   It is probable that these late appearing accidents are more frequent with ether than with chloroform, from the larger quantity required, its greater solubility in the blood serum, and the slower rate of its excretion.   With present knowledge they are the most inexplicable facts connected with anæsthesia.

The physiological action of ether, although in general resembling that of chloroform, differs in some points so much as to demand consideration, as in its mode of causing death the effect of ether upon the blood-pressure is far from showing in man that entire want of influence which it exhibits in animals, neither does it in man show that invariable and unexceptionable depression of pressure which is characteristic of chloroform   With chloroform, marked depression of the sphygmographic curve is always produced in man while with ether a considerable proportion of cases show no change. Thus, Kappeler gives ten tracings, in three of which there was but slight, if any, change from the normal—an occurrence not presented once in twenty-five observations with chloroform; but in seven of the ten cases "the curve of deep ether-narcosis differed not at all from that of chloroform-narcosis." Deep flushing of the face occurs under the administation of ether. A profuse salivation is a very unpleasant feature, causing cough, efforts at swallowing, and choking sensations. The pupils are not generally so closely contracted as under chloroform, and may remain unchanged. The respiratory action very rarely goes on undisturbed with ether as it often does with chloroform; cough, hawking, catching of the breath are almost always present, and marked irregularity is the general rule. In the length and severity of the stage of excitement there is the greatest contrast between the two agents. With ether irregular muscular action is extreme, and marked rigidity of the extremities, which may extend to the whole body; there are violent efforts to escape from the inhalation, prompted by the distressing sense of suffocation; and, more generally than with chloroform, there are struggles with the arms and legs, attempts to rise from the table, and even get out of the room. The stage of relaxation and complete anæsthesia having been attained, it is maintained with difficulty; the patient readily relapses into a condition of excited intoxication, in which it is impossible for the operator to proceed. Finally, the return to conciousness is marked with more unpleasant symptoms than that from chloroform. A state of excitement like partial intoxication, and various hysterical symptoms are apt to make their appearance, while the smell and taste of the ether may disgust the patient for hours if not days.

The question as to which anæsthetic causes vomiting most frequently afterwards, long undecided, may be said to be settled in favor of the ether by the experience of O'Keith of Edinburgh, whose brilliant success with an operation after which vomiting is especially deleterious is well known. There is no question, however, that this unpleasant effect of ether, as well as the stage of excitement, may be very much and very favorably modified by circumstances fully under control. The quality of the ether should be assured. The mode of administration is very important. When the patient is brought promptly under the influence without saturating the tissues throughout the body, the stage of excitement is less marked, the subsequent vomiting more frequently absent or milder, and recovery from the anæsthetic state is more rapid and less unpleasant.

The relaxation of the vaso-constrictors and consequent accumulation of blood in the arterioles and capillaries of the system generally, renders the use of ether inadmissible in all cases of disease in any of the vital organs where there is dilatation of the blood-vessels and consequent congestion, but especially it is said to be fatal when albumen is present in the urine.

The kidneys therefore should be carefully examined for all organic diseases, and the urine should be tested, not only for albumen, but for all abnormal conditions, and if even slightly diseased, chloroform should be given instead of ether. An impartial study of the above facts will show that there has been but one allegation against chloroform; viz., that it suddenly and without warning causes death, and that in consequence of this disability the rate of mortality is much larger than that of ether; that it does its work so insidiously that the patient is dead before it is known that there is danger. The same may be said of ether, although not to the same extent. By reference to the preceding pages the reader will doubtless see that there is danger to life from the use of any anæsthetic, however carefully administered by even the most skillful hands.

To the writer this subject has been one of deepest interest. The works of all the best writers and thinkers and most practical surgeons of the present and past, as well as the faculty of the Physio-Medical College of Indiana, have been consulted and valuable suggestions received from all. The writer has added to this twenty-five years of close personal observation of the use of anæsthetics, by the most skillful experts in this line, when given by them in the cases upon whom operations were to be made. These cases furnish most convincing proof that although there was not one death in them all, yet in several instances a fatal termination was only averted by the most timely and skillful treatment. The same experience also furnishes proofs that ether and chloroform are both effective anæsthetics, that they both produce death in a greater or less number of cases; that the cause of death may be the same, but that their mode of action may be entirely different. Ether relaxes the vaso-constrictors and allows the blood to accumulate in the arterioles and capillaries, thus causing the blood to be retained in the body longer than natural. This sluggish state of the circulation hinders the normal interchange, in the lungs, of morbific material for oxygen, and the blood assumes a venous appearance.

Death may now occur in either of two ways: first, by this dark and impure blood, which is loaded with material which has been rendered useless in the tissues. and which becomes injurious when retained too long in the system, also absence of oxygen and nutritive material in the blood that circulates in the nerve centres which control the action of the heart. Deprive these centres of their proper stimulus and they cease to influence the heart action, and the organ ceases to move. A second mode of death may be caused by this same kind of impure blood passing through the heart. The proper stimulus to heart action, when applied direct to the heart is a proper quantity and quality of blood; without this the heart action becomes feeble and may cease entirely. Plethoric people have dilated vessels, most frequently in the brain and its membranes. To administer an agent that has the property to dilate these vessels still farther is bad practice, and may result in death by one or the other mode as above described. The same may prove true if the lungs or kidneys are already in a state of engorgement. Chloroform contracts the vaso-dilators, narrows the calibre of the arterioles and capillaries and forces the blood internally upon the large arteries and heart. This contractile power may be sufficient to bring on a tonic spasm, which forces so much blood into the heart that it is unable to keep up its movements. It ceases to act suddenly and death is the result.

This philosophy, if correct, furnishes a separate field for each remedy. Should this be true, and the proper anæsthetic employed, the death rate from anæsthetics might be reduced to a very meagre per cent.; then if the other avoidable accidental causes be prevented, death would be the exception and success the rule. This style of argument would seem to make the anæsthetic responsible for every death; and so it would be if the judgment was infallible and the accidents all avoidable. Such is not the case,

however. It is not possible for the surgeon or the anæsthetist to judge correctly as to the kind of anæsthetic
suitable to each case, neither are the accidents entirely
unavoidable   A proper knowledge of the properties of the
agent used, a prevention of all the preventable causes, a
judicial regulation of the quantity, and a proper attention
to all other circumstances is all that can be expected   If
the surgeon and anæsthetist realize the great responsibility of their position when they are trusted with a human
life, they will be inexcusable if they neglect to prepare
themselves, and fail to take advantage of every measure to
prevent any accident.

It has been a question raised by able men on both sides,
whether the use of chloroform has increased or diminished
the mortality   It was found that the mortality in some
hospitals was greater after the introduction of anæsthetics than before. A solution was found in the history of
the cases. When the properties of ether and chloroform
were published, they became the object of great abuse.
The fear of suffering pain being removed, encouraged patients to desire operations that were entirely improper at
that time. Surgeons also became bold in their conception
of what might be done, and undertook operations for
which they were not well qualified   This filled the hospitals to overflowing.   More patients were crowded into the
wards than they were adequate to contain. Aseptic surgery was then only a dream; ahtiseptsis was thought little
of Sanitary science was not born. It was not a wonder
that patients died—not because of the anæsthetic, but
because of the inexperience of the surgeons in making
operations of so severe a character, and with such bad sanitary surroundings   Then too the use of the agents was
not so well understood, surgeons had to learn much of
their potency, and the accidents to which patients were
liable   Mark the wonderful success in brain surgery, in
abdominal and pelvic operations, and then ask where is
the surgeon that would have the temerity to undertake
these operations without an anæsthetic; and where is the
patient that would brave the knife and submit to any such
operations? And even in general surgery, the writhings
and cries of the patients were more than humanity could
withstand, and few men were willing to undertake to operate under such circumstances   Then for a patient to be
conscious and witness the keen, scathing, lancinating pain

of the glittering knife, and endure the terrible grating of
the saw, or the seething, crisping and scorching effect of
the cautery, would be more than ordinary human minds
can endure. It is doubtless true that a few patients have
succumbed to the influence of the anæsthetic and the operation, but they were patients that could have survived
but a short time at the longest. Contrast these with those
cases where patients have remained for hours under the
influence of an anæsthetic to enable the surgeon to make
long and tedious dissections; which once accomplished, a
human being was saved from impending death.

Much of success depends on care in the administration
of the agent.

In the hands of skillful men the death rate has fallen
very low. Prof. Samuel D. Gross gave chloroform in four
thousand cases without a single death. Of five thousand
cases anæsthetized by Prof. Syme there was not even a
serious occurrence. Prof. Nussbaum never lost a patient
in ten thousand cases. Here are eighteen thousand cases
anæsthetized without one death. It has been said that
Simpson lost only one case in all his large experience. It
is but due to those illustrious men to say that this success
was the result of their skill and care. They took every
precaution, and saw that nothing was left undone that
might add to the safety of their patients. In view of the
fact that anæsthetics were suddenly and universally
adopted by all practitioners, who especially outside the
hospitals and large cities, were without experience in their
use, and with limited means for meeting accidents, the
death rate is exceedingly low. Dr. Gross says: "I ascribe
my own good luck in the use of chloroform to the extraordinary care with which it has been administered in my
practice, and to the purity of the article selected."

The Advantages of Chloroform and Ether.—Anæsthetics not only prevent pain and suffering, but place the
patient in a passive state while the surgeon makes his
operation, or pursues his other manual processes as delib-
erately as if he were operating on the dead body. By its
use all the cavities of the body can be explored. Under
its influence the anus, rectum, vagina, uterus, urethra
and bladder may be painlessly explored. The contents of
the abdomen can be more certainly examined while the
abdominal muscles are relaxed under its influence. Deep
sinuses leading to abscess cavities and diseased bones, can

be readily examined by the probe, or other explorative measures. The exact condition of fractured bones and dislocated joints can be ascertained and the surgeon will be inexcusable if he neglects so important a means of diagnosis in all cases of doubtful character. Delicate operations upon the generative organs of female children and young misses without them being conscious of it, and thus save them the mortification of a personal knowledge of all the procedures

Purity of the Air—The presence of a normal proportion of all the elements of the air, as well as its freedom from foreign substances, has much to do with the success or failure of anæsthetics No excess of carbonic acid gas and other deleterious agents, when present at a time when the proportion of oxygen that should enter the lungs at each inspiration is about to be lessened by the addition of the anæsthetic vapor. An average sized man will give off about six-tenths of a cubic foot of carbon dioxide and from one to one and a-half ounces of water, which is charged with the products of wear of the body. These exhalations are exceedingly offensive to the olfactories and also depress the vital activities of the patient, who already has a surplus of such agents consequent upon the use of the anæsthetic. Particular attention should always be given to selecting a room of proper size, also to the methods of ventilation

Parks and DeChamnout give "6 per 1000 volumes of total carbonic acid gas in the air as the limit of impurity allowable Of this about 2 is derived from respiration and the remainder is the normal quantity present in the atmosphere In order to maintain the air at this standard, an ordinary man requires to be supplied with three thousand cubic feet per hour" This is the minimum quantity, and it is unwise to accept this if more can be obtained From four to five thousand feet should be secured if possible Arrangements for this amount to be changed at least four times per hour should be made This is the maximum number of times that the air can be changed without creating undesirable currents in the room To secure this amount of air, the room should be eighteen by twenty feet, with the ceiling twelve feet high, which is about the maximum size of rooms in private dwellings This space, however, may be increased to twice this size by opening the doors to adjoining rooms.

Attention to ventilation must also be given. So many factors enter into this subject that it is difficult to give any definite rules. First, the height of the column of air —or rather the height of the room; second, the difference between the temperature in the room and that on the outside; third, the rate of velocity of the wind; and fourth, position of the inlet and outlet. If the inlet is on the side from which the wind is blowing it will enter the room more rapidly than if placed on the opposite side. The heating appliances have much to do with the ventilation. Grates are the best ventilators; then come consecutively stoves, heated air from furnaces, and last and poorest, steam heat. All these circumstances must enter into account when arranging the ventilation of a room for anæsthesia. A basis from which calculation may be made is as follows: Take an opening of twenty-four square inches for each individual, or six inches by four; if there are six persons to be in the room, then there should be six such openings. These would aggregate one hundred and twenty-four square inches, which would not give an equal temperature in the room. In private practice the openings or inlets can be arranged by letting the top sash down, and the exact amount estimated in inches or square feet. The windows have the advantage of being lowered or raised according as the amount of fresh air is needed. The operating table should be placed in the room so that a current of cool air can be let in on the patient at any moment should there be any signs of asphyxia. This can be done by placing the patient near a window that can be hoisted at a moment's warning.

Are Chloroform and Ether Poisons?—In the classification of material substances in relation to the human body, there has been great diversity of opinion. In accordance with their inherent properties substances may be arranged in three general classes. First, such agents as are entirely harmless in their action upon the living elements of the body. To the second class belong such agents as water, heat, electricity, a proper proportion of oxygen and nitrogen in the atmosphere, and I may venture to say ether and chloroform, as well as others possessing similar properties that may be found hereafter. These agents have a double action. The human system is so constituted that a certain degree or amount of them is absolutely necessary to health, and life itself may be dependent

upon their presence; and yet in quantities greater than is
necessary to health they become detrimental in their action, and in still greater degrees or quantities destructive
to life. A third class of agents to which the term is applicable, are always, under all circumstances, and in any
quantity destructive to the living elements of the body.
They produce somatic death by destroying such a proportion of the bioplasm as to interfere with, and even cause
the vital functions, (circulations and respirations) to cease.
The exact sphere and application of this word "poison" has
been a matter of dispute among medical men.

It has been contended that there is poison in all substances A better knowledge of chemical laws, however,
has shown that while the elements necessary for the formation of poisons may be found in almost any article of
diet, as well as the human body itself; the organic structure must be broken up and the atoms allowed to arrange
themselves in new and different proportions to form new
compounds Thus, sodium and chlorine may be united in
such atomic relations that sodium chloride (common salt)
is formed. This new substance possesses entirely different
physical properties and exerts a different influence on the
body. The two elements before their combination are
destructive agents, while the compound resulting from
their union is not only harmless in its action upon the
body; but actually is conducive to the highest degree of
health. The most wholesome foods may be partially decomposed either before or after they enter the stomach
and the resulting compounds be virulent poisons, capable
of impairing health and destroying life. A mixture of the
proper proportion of oxygen and nitrogen is essential to
health Any deviation from this gives to the mixture
new properties which are injurious In like manner the
vapor of chloroform possesses properties differing from
those of the liquid Persons may be kept under its influence for hours and if no operation or other procedure is
undertaken that will shock the system, or disturb the circulation, the patient will awake as if from a natural sleep,
and feel as well as usual. If the vapor of chloroform is
destructive to the elementary substances of the body, the
person would surely awake with some feeling of malaise.
Various other forces or influences to which the human
body is subject, may be deleterious, or beneficial according
to circumstances. Light is essential to health and possi-

bly to life at times. The force of gravity holds all matter in proper relation, and all the movements of matter in the universe are divided so that harmony prevails. When the equilibrium of this force is disturbed by bodies being thrown out of their relation to the earth which causes them to be unsupported, they fall to the ground. If a man falls from a building which is fifty feet high and is killed, it cannot be said that he died from the effects of poison. If an engine runs over, crushes the limbs of a man it cannot be said that the engine is a poisonous agent. The word must have some definite application, and must have some special sphere of action. The following definitions are perhaps the most concise, and more nearly express the true relation of that class of agents that are truly poisonous.

This is from Quain's Dictionary of Medicine: "There is no legal definition of the word poison, and the definitions usually proposed are apt to include too much or too little. Generally a poison may be defined as a substance having an inherent deleterious property which renders it capable of destroying life by whatever avenue it is taken into the system." The leading thoughts in this definition are two only; first, the "inherent deleterious property," and second, that the poison must enter the system. There are only two avenues proper by which the poison can enter the circulation, and reach its ultimate destination; viz., absorption from the pulmonary, alimentary, or the cutaneous surfaces. Nearly but not quite all the poisons are taken into the stomach in such quantities as will produce death if absorbed. The second avenue is by lesion of tissue, as by snake bite, stings of insects, or by bringing the virus in contact with an abraded surface. Corrosive substances, such as mineral acids and other chemical agents, unless they possess some element that is capable of being absorbed, cannot be classed as poisonous.

The following definition proposed by Prof. George Hasty, is perhaps the most appropriate that has been given: "Poisons are substances having inherent properties of such a character that when brought into contact with the living matter of the human body, destroy, or tend to destroy the same." The distinctive point in this is, that the poison must be brought in "contact with the living matter." This should be a final test of a poison; viz., that it destroys the living matter. This definition might be more explicit by adding that it destroys or tends to destroy, in infinitesimal quantities. With these agents quantity does not alter quality. This word "poison" has been used in the language of all nations from the earliest dawn of letters. The idea that there is a class of agents that uniformly possesses the power to kill when taken into the body was entertained by several of the sacred writers in a metaphorical sense. The Greeks made use of several words denotive of the poisonous action of some drugs and always in connection with the idea of taking them into the body. Thus they use the word Φαρμακοποσια (Pharmakoposia), the drinking of a medicine, potion, or of a poison; Φαρμακοποτεω (Pharmakopoteo), to drink a medicinal potion or a poison.

In the Latin language is found Potio, a drink, a draught, a potion; from Potare, to drink; Potion, a drink, a draught, especially a liquid medicine.

The French use Empoisoner the Spanish Pongonar, from the Latin Potionare, to give to drink.

The following is from "The Century Dictionary:" "Any substance which introduced into the living organism directly, tends to destroy the life or impair the health of the organism." The above is sufficient to show that all nations recognize a poison as a substance possessing inherent properties capable of destroying living matter when introduced into the body. Do chloroform and ether belong to this class? Do they uniformly kill or tend to kill when introduced into the living organism, and is it brought in contact with the living matter? The answer to this question is probably one of the most difficult connected with the subject under consideration. That patients die while under its influence is unquestioned, but has it an inherent property to kill or tend to kill regardless of all circumstances? Common experience and clinical observation has long since settled beyond a doubt the poisonous character of many substances; but it has only been within the last fifteen years that the power to kill living matter possessed by the agents has been demonstrated by subjecting living matter (bioplasm) to their action. The microscope has shown that infinitesimal quantities destroy leucocytes. Ether and chloroform have not been tested in this way, but there is other evidence which points strongly to the conclusion that they are not poisonous. The properties of opium and its alkaloids have been known to the profession for over two thousand years. Its power to

478

SURGICAL ANÆSTHETICS.

relieve pain has been recognized and tested in all its phases, and while a small dose can be given and stupor produced, yet when well marked the patient shows deleterious results. Complete insensibility cannot be produced without giving enough to cause death. Its effect has been tried in surgical operations and failed. In cases of death from what is called an overdose there will be found a fluid state of the blood, the brain is crowded with dark blood, on the surface there will be ecchymosis produced by effusion; when the brain is cut there will be bloody points on the cut surface. In a case of death from cyanide of potassium bloody points were observed in the brain and spinal marrow. In a case of death from the essential oil of bitter almonds there was general effusion of blood on the brain. In death from alcohol the stomach has been found intensely congested, the mucous membrane presenting in some cases a bright red in others a dark brown color. In death from an overdose of nicotine there was effusion of dark colored blood in the course of the veins of the neck. The membranes of the brain were filled with dark colored blood. In cases of death from strychnia there is a fluid state of the blood and congestion of the brain and upper part of the spinal cord. In a case of death from conium maculatum (hemlock) the lungs were gorged with dark fluid blood, and there were numerous bloody points.

The above are extracts from Taylor's "Medical Jurisprudence." By reference to "The United States Dispensatory," "The National Dispensatory" and Shoemaker's "Materia Medica," it will be seen that there is nothing that contradicts Taylor's statements. He describes these cases as individual cases upon whom he made autopsies and saw for himself. He also describes graphically the symptoms present in cases of death from the vapor of chloroform, but says nothing about the appearances after death. Is it likely that a man in his high position would so minutely describe the post mortem appearances in all other cases and neglect to do so in this one instance? If he made the examination and found lesions would he not have reported them the same as others? May the same not be said of such works as named above, if they had found lesions as in death from other poisons? So far as I know only two observers have found real lesions of tissue after death from chloroform. Tillman quotes Winogradow as saying "that he found granular degeneration of the cells of the brain, spinal cord and ganglia of the heart, both in men and animals."

The following is from "Reese on Toxicology," page 361. ' In death from inhalation (of chloroform) there is very often no lesion discoverable. At times there will be found a considerable congestion of the lungs and bronchial tubes and likewise of the vessels of the brain, together with a dark and fluid condition of the blood."

First as to the statement of Winogradow, it is too general to go into an accurate clinical report. He should have named the specific cases in which he found those postmortem appearances, and stated all the circumstances connected with the administration of the agent, whether the subjects were in good health, etc. He should also have stated the precise points where he found the lesion, as it is not probable that the whole or even a considerable part of any of the organs named were thus destroyed. Until some such accurate report shall be made it cannot be conclusively stated that the anæsthetic vapor caused death in that way.

The second author, Reese, makes the same mistake by not being specific in his descriptions. He also admits that "very often no lesion is discoverable." If lesion is absent in some and present in others, then there must have been some different conditions which he should have discovered and described. That difference might have caused the lesions.

The latest work that the writer has consulted is "Chapman on Toxicology," 1895, Referring to the cause of death from chloroform vapor he says "The postmortem appearances presented in cases of chloroform poisoning are those of death by asphyxia " (Page 229.) The following is from "Garretson's Oral Surgery" (page 436)· "Etherization exhibits to us the entire mechanism of asphyxia: we mean the successive deaths of the various nervous centres. It isolates, just as mechanical experiments do, the intellectual powers, the co-ordination of movements, sensibility, motility, life "

"The autopsy in case of death from chloroform generally reveals little that is characteristic, and often gives no satisfactory explanation of the cause of death. Not infrequently the above mentioned pathological changes in the organs are present and are more or less correctly considered to be responsible for the accident. The blood is ordinarily uncoagulated and dark colored, but microscopic or chemical examination of it has hitherto given no satisfactory explanation for death. It is worth noting, however, that as a result of the disturbance of respiration, the blood is over-loaded with carbonic acid." (See "Principles of Surgery and Surgical Pathology," Tillman, page 31.)

The changes referred to above are "Fatty degeneration of the muscles of the heart, valvular lesions and degeneration of the walls of the vessels. The autopsies of the victims of anæsthesia present nothing positive or characteristic. In such cases death is the consequence of disturbance of the nervous apparatus concerned in the act either of respiration or circulation. The changes which have produced the result are intra-molecular and are consequently beyond the reach of our senses " ("International Surgery," Vol. 1, page 424.) By the same author (page 411): "Keeping in mind the fact that the effect of anæsthetic substances is temporary, it seems more probable that they operate by inhibition of those chemical processes which are associated with the liberation and diffusion of motion throughout the system. Among the protoplasmic molecules the substance acts the part of a screen, like a cloud between the sun and the earth; hindering the energies of one from acting upon the susceptible matter of the other." Anæsthetics are never given to human beings while in health. There is in all cases some lesion of tissue or other abnormal state for which an operation is to be made. These deviations from health may have caused the changes of tissue that they found after death.

As above shown by eminent writers the only conditions uniformly found after death were those resembling asphyxia. It only then remains to learn what is asphyxia. The following from Webster: "Apparent death or suspended animation particularly from suffocation or drowning or the inhalation of irrepressible gases, recently applied also to the collapse state of cholera with want of pulse." Foster's Dictionary: "As now used a state of suspended animation caused by impeded respiration, as by strangulation, smothering, submersion or the inhalation of an irrepressible gas." The above quotations are from men of ability and authority. The definitions are from the pen of the best philologists of the age, and seem to make it clear that death from anæsthetics is caused by asphyxia. In order to determine the difference between

death by asphyxia and that produced by other causes, it
will be necessary to point out the changes that take place
in the tissues of the body. What takes place in asphyxia?

Oxygen is admitted to be indispensable to life by all
physiologists. As above shown, strangulation, smothering, submersion or the inhalation of irrepressible gases,
prevent the ingress of air and consequently oxygen being
one of its constituents, is excluded. The point is made
equally clear that the products of wear are, to a large extent, eliminated from the system through the air as it
passes in and out of the lungs, and life cannot be maintained more than five minutes after these interchanges are
completely arrested. The proper stimulant to the heart's
action is the presence of a proper quantity of blood as well
as a natural quality can only be supplied by the processes
of respiration and circulation. These two functions are
dependent on a natural condition of the nerves controlling
these functions The changes in the blood are absence of
oxygen and the presence in an excessive quantity of the
products of wear. The carbon compounds are largely
eliminated by the lungs When this with the other elements which should also be eliminated are retained and
accumulate in an unnatural quantity and retained longer
than natural, chemical changes take place in the presence
of the blood and carbonic acid gas is evolved. This accounts for the presence of gas in the blood that has been
found by some authors and thought to be the cause of
death; but this has been disproved by other writers who
have found gas in the blood when death had taken place
from other well known causes.

According to the definitions of poisons and other quotations as given above, anæsthetics (chloroform and ether)
do not belong in the category of poisons, since it has been
shown that a poison possesses inherent properties capable
of destroying or tending to destroy life by producing destruction of tissues or living matter of the body. The
inherent properties are as inseparable from these substances as the attractive properties of the magnet, and
cannot be changed without destruction of the form of
matter in which it resides So long as there is a molecule
or an atom unchanged in its structure and relations the
inherent property is present: and this property is exerted
in proportion to its volume or magnitude It follows from
this that a poison when once in the system is as uncon-

trollable as the cannon ball as it escapes from the mouth of the cannon and speeds on its way, producing destruction wherever it comes in contact with other matter. This marks the line indelibly between poisons and that large class of agents whose effect on matter depends on quantity, or are of such a nature that their effect may be prevented, or so modified as to render them capable of accomplishing great good when the law governing them is obeyed, or equally as destructive when the laws are disregarded. Heat, light, electricity, and chemical affinity have long been known to possess such properties; chloroform and ether belong to the same class, but have not been so recognized.

How Do Chloroform and Ether Act?—Rest is an inherent necessity. This proposition is stamped upon all nature. The Creator of the universe, after laboring six days rested upon the seventh, and left the inexorable law stamped upon every molecule of living matter. This means a cessation from action and a period of time when the proper avenues of communication with all external objects is for the time severed. The vegetable world has its period of budding, growing, blooming, and maturing of its fruit, then comes a period of repose. Whether this tendency to repose is inherent or determined by surrounding conditions is not certain; perhaps both are contributing factors. That surrounding conditions do modify the period of repose is abundantly established by gardeners and horticulturists. The gardener can take the seed that matures in early summer, plant it and bring two crops the same season, or he may keep the seed for years by supplying proper surrounding conditions. The horticulturist can convert a biennial into an annual shrub and an annual into an evergreen by supplying necessary conditions to lengthen or shorten this period of repose.

All animal life has its period of rest during which the sensibilities are arrested and motion ceases. It has been thought that the heart never rests; but works on physiology show that it has its period of repose and recuperation. "Taking a cardiac cycle as a unit and seventy-two as the average number of cardiac evolutions per minute, each evolution may be considered to occupy five-sixths of a second, or about eight-tenths, which may be approximately distributed in the following way;

Auricular systole, about .1 plus auricular diastole .7= 8
Ventricular systole about .3 plus ventricular diastole .6= 8
Period of joint auricular and ventricular diastole .4

    plus period of systole of auricles and ventricles .4=.8

If the speed of the heart be quickened, the time occupied by each cardiac revolution is of course diminished, but the diminution affects only the diastole- and pause. The systole of the ventricles occupies very much the same time, whatever the pulse rate." ("Kirke's Physiology, page 186.) By the above we see that the systole and diastole are equal and that the heart rests during the period of diastole, thus proving that the heart rests one-half of the time

A materia medica that is perfect in all its departments must have remedies that will imitate in their action every function of the body. This has to a great extent been supplied. Cathartics imitate the natural movements of the bowels; diuretics increase the secretion of urine, and stimulants promote the circulation Rest is one of the natural functions of the body and sleep promotes rest In this condition the sensibilities are suspended to a large degree, but not entirely, as powerful impressions will arouse the body to activity. There are conditions of the body and states of the mind in which the sensibilities are so completely held-in abeyance that surgical operations can be made without causing any sensation of pain, and that too without drugs From an early date there have been persons who have been so constituted that their co-ordinating and connecting powers have been susceptible of certain influences They may remain clear in their intellectual functions and yet their sentient apparatus be so changed in its relation as to enable them to look calmly on an operation upon their bodies and not experience a sense of pain. In others the intelligence is so disturbed that they are wholly unconscious. This condition has been brought about by certain influences bearing on a susceptible mind. It was this influence that Mesmer exerted on his subjects, and it is the same influence that people call hypnotism at the present time. Chloroform has the same property.

In "Therapeutics, its Principles and Practice," by H. C. Wood (page 140), is the following. "Dr Coleman ('Sansom Chloroform.' page 55, Philadelphia, 1866) states that he has extracted his own teeth without pain; and Dr Snow relates the anecdote of a child who played with his toys during the operation of lithotomy."

The writer had occasion to remove the left half of the inferior maxillary bone for sarcoma in which the horizontal portion from the symphysis to the junction with the ascending ramus was affected; but from that point to the articulation of the bone it was sound. It was thought best to remove the entire piece at the articulation. Prof. C. T. Bedford administered the chloroform and the disarticulation was begun. It was soon found that the anæsthetic was not acting well; symptoms of disturbance of the heart action as well as respiration were observed, and inhalation was discontinued; but the operator continued his work. It was Prof. Bedford's intention to resume the inhalation as soon as it seemed advisable; but the patient soon awoke and did not complain of pain. The further use of chloroform was not required. The operation was completed, the patient all the time talking, but did not complain of any pain until the stitches were being placed, when he said he felt the needle passing through the skin, but said the pain was not great.

The writer was also present where a surgeon was operating for lacerated os uteri. The dissections were completed and the sutures inserted after the patient became conscious and began talking. No more of the anæsthetic was given (which was the usual A. C. E. mixture) and the operation completed without pain.

The following case recorded in the "Journal of a Naturalist" affords a remarkable instance of this general fact. The correctness of the statement having been called in question, it was fully confirmed by Mr. Richard Smith, the late Senior Surgeon of the Bristol Infirmary, under whose care the sufferer had been. "A traveling man, one winter's evening, laid himself down upon the platform of a lime-kiln, placing his feet, probably benumbed with cold, upon the heap of stones, newly put on to burn through the night. Sleep overcame him in this situation; the fire gradually rising and increasing, until it ignited the stones upon which his feet were placed. Lulled by the warmth, the man slept on; the fire increased until it burned one foot (which probably was extended over a vent-hole) and part of the leg above the ankle entirely off; consuming that part so effectually that a cinder-like fragment was alone remaining—and still the wretch slept on!—and in

this state was found by the kiln-man in the morning. Insensible to any pain, and ignorant of his misfortune, he
attempted to rise and pursue his journey; but missing his
shoe, requested to have it found, and when he was raised,
putting his burnt limb to the ground to support his body,
the extremity of his leg-bone—the tibia—crumbled into
fragments, having been calcined into lime. Still he expressed no sense of pain, and probably experienced none;
from the gradual operation of the fire, and his own torpid-
ity during the hours his foot was consuming This poor
drover survived his misfortunes in the hospital about a
fortnight, but the fire having extended to other parts of
his body, recovery was hopeless " ("Carpenter's Human
Philosophy," page 549.)

In the case of insidious shock the body may be horribly
mutilated, either by mechanical injuries or by burns or
scalds, and the patient will be conscious and suffer no pain
while life lasts

These cases are related to show that the sentient part of
the nervous system may be so influenced by circumstances
that exert no evil influences on the living matter of the
centres of circulation and respiration, and yet the function of this part of the nervous system will be entirely
abated for the time being.

An instance has been cited where chloroform vapor arrested fermentation without destroying the vitality of the
ferment or disarranging the organic matter, as evidenced
by its resumption of activity as soon as the anæsthetic is
removed. The sensitive plant was also anæsthetized and
awoke and resumed active growth as soon as pure air was
substituted. In the same manner the human body can be
subjected to the action of those agents and in a very short
time awake and resume all the functions as regularly as
before   Just what action they exert or what changes are
effected it is at present impossible to tell. Henry M. Lyman, A. M., M. D , as above quoted from the "International Surgery," says   "Among the protoplasmic molecules, the substance acts the part of a screen, like a cloud
between the sun and the earth. hindering the energies of
one from acting upon the susceptible matter of the other."
In experimenting with numerous substances upon living
matter, Prof Jacob Redding found that there are agents
which when brought in contact with living matter, would
cause it to relax, spread out and remain motionless as long

as the drug continued in contact with it; but eventually it would resume activities. Another class of agents would cause the bioplast to assume the sperical form; these bioplasts would never resume work, and after some hours would disintegrate and disappear from the field of the microscope. Might not this work the changes that take place in relaxation and paralysis?

It might be urged against this theory that small doses of any narcotic may exert its legitimate effects and then the patient recover, as it is well known that patients recover from the effects of small doses of many poisons, just as they do from small doses of chloroform vapor; and also die from large doses of either. It has been very forcibly shown above that the vapor of chloroform or ether does not destroy living matter, but that poisons positively do. The difference in the mode of death is the only point that is of sufficient importance to discuss. Water is not considered a poison by any one, and yet if its laws are transcended death follows as certainly and promptly as it does from any poison. The body may be immersed in water for an indefinite time, provided the mouth and nose are not submerged; but let these points be covered, the water enters the lungs, excludes the air and respiration ceases. This is purely a mechanical interference with a vital function and one that is preventable. Water is perfectly harmless and conducive to health as long as its laws are obeyed. So we think with the anæsthetics; they are safe while they are kept in their proper sphere of action.

Life then depends on the skill and knowledge of the anæsthetist and on the agent used. The only question then is, how near can these laws be obeyed? Occasionally it will be impossible to foresee and provide against accidental violations of these laws, just as it is in all mechanical pursuits. Sometimes a death will occur and no one could avoid it; but we believe if those laws were better known and greater care exercised, there would be very few deaths—very many less than at this time. This we think cannot be said of any poisonous agent. Whenever any poisonous agent is introduced into the body and comes in contact with the living matter, no amount of skill can prevent its legitimate effect. It either kills or tends to kill, in proportion to the number of molecules of the poison present to those of the living matter.

This may be illustrated by using Sir William Thomson's

hypothesis He has reached a quassi-definite conclusion is follows· ' If a drop of water were magnified, to the size of the earth, the molecules or granules would each occupy spaces greater than those filled by small shot and smaller than those occupied by cricket balls " We cannot even in our imagination enumerate the molecules that, according to this hypothesis, would be found in the blood of a man. Let us suppose now that one grain of morphia could be compressed into a bulk the size of one drop of water and compute the proportion that would :exist between the morphia and the whole amount of blood in the body. It would not seem possible for this amount of morphia to be brought in contact with any large proportion of the blood; but it would kill all the molecules that it could reach, and if it reached a sufficient number so·that the debræ should be so great that its presence would obstruct the circulation of the blood, death would follow; or if a few molecules should reach the vital spot in the medula oblongata and destroy the centres for circulation and respiration, only a few molecules would be necessary to produce death.

This is the reason why a very small amount of some poisons will kill one patient, and will fail, apparently, to injure some other. Although the injury is not apparent at the time, yet it is a destruction of some of the physical organization, and a diminution of the vital properties of the body This calls for the expenditure of some vital effort that lessens the resistive and recuperative powers, and in the end shortens life, or cripples usefulness, just in the same way that a man spends his fortune before he dies. If he has ten thousand dollars and should live ten years. The first year he draws out fifteen hundred dollars and hopes the other eight thousand and five hundred dollars will bring him interest enough to keep up his deposits to the original amount, as a fact it will not do it. At the end of the first year, if the interest is six per cent , he will have as a principal $9010 00; at the end of the second year his principal would be $7960.60; at the end of the eighth year he would have in bank $201 50 Thus it is with the man who habitually or even occasionally takes poison in small doses He does not die after the first, second or even the one hundredth dose; but slowly and imperceptibly, like the man drawing his money from the bank, he is exhausting his reserve powers, and when in old age he is attacked with sickness, he finds his reserve exhausted and he must die several years before his allotted time.

The critic will ask: "Chloroform and ether not being poisons, how do they kill?" The answer is, by inhibition. The anæsthetic restrains bioplasm in the cells in the medula oblong ata, acting the same as it does on the proto- plasm in the cells of the sensitive plant at the base of the petioles. It is a law of the animal economy, especially of man, that if circulation and respiration are prevented for the space of five minutes, death follows as a result. If the anæsthetic reaches the vital spot in the medula oblongata and thus inhibits circulation for the time above men- tioned, the man dies by asphyxia.

Accidents attending the use of anaesthetics.

One of the most common accidents to which patients are exposed is obstruction to respiration caused by the tongue falling back over the glottis   They are exposed to this on account of the position on the back. When the tongue and fauces are relaxed, the force of gravity carries the base of the organ directly over the glottis. The air ceases to enter the lungs, the heaving of the chest deceives the anæsthet- ist, and the continuation of the pulsation at the wrist con- firms the deception. Suddenly the pulse stops, and when death occurs it is attributed to paralysis of the heart. It was the custom of Mr. Syme to disregard the pulse in order that more attention could be directed to the respiration. Mr. Lister also agrees with Mr. Syme and states that the respiration is of more importance than the heart-action. This may be true, but it is the experience of the writer that it is safer to entrust the respiration and circulation to one man and leave the anæthetist to his duties, having only a casual oversight of these vital functions.

The premonitory symptoms of this accident are stertor- ous breathing and vascular disturbances. The former may be caused either by relaxation or spasm of the muscles of the fauces. This latter condition is described by Erich- sen more fully than by any other author, as far as my knowledge extends. He says on the authority of Mr. Lis- ter, that the spasm is at the upper opening of the larynx. The folds of mucus membrane, above the apices of the ary- tenoid cartilages are carried forward till they are in contact with the base of the epiglottis which remains erect, and unchanged in position. The laryngeal stridor that charac- terizes this condition, is of a peculiar character; and re- quires to be heard only once to be recognized ever after.

There is a peculiar effort to breathe and the muscles of the neck and larynx are in a state of rigidity. The respiratory effort is convulsive and the sound is stridulous. This contrasts sharply with the slow, heavy breathing and dull, low pitched stertor of the premonitory stage that preceeds the closure of the glottis in the first condition mentioned.

These two conditions are dangerous in the extreme sense of the word. It shows that the vital spot in the medula is being approached An instant more and the patient may cease to breathe and death takes place either by syncope or asphyxia It is not possible to tell in every case which may be the urgent condition The anæsthetic must be removed from the face at once; all operative proceedures should cease, and the patient be allowed to inhale fresh air. If death by syncope threatens the patient, lowering of the head will favor the return of the blood to the brain. The mouth should be pressed open and the tongue seized with a pair of forceps and drawn well forward If there is spasm of the laryngeal muscles. respiration will be established by reflex action. If respiration is hindered by the tongue falling back, the patient will breathe as soon as there is a free entrance and exit for the air. Should the case be one of asphyxia, and life seems extinct, there may still be hope of recovery The respiration often stops several minutes before the heart ceases to act. Artificial respiration should be instituted; before leaving this part of the subject, I wish to call attention to the manner of drawing the tongue forward. It is necessary to do this, and at the same time see that the larynx and fauces are free. To this end it is well for the anæsthetist, who is supposed to be standing at the patient's head, to grasp the jaws with both his hands and carry them forward, being careful to keep the head in line with the body. This insures a free entrance and exit for air

Artificial respiration is often performed in an irregular and bunglesome manner It is not uncommon to see some one give the patient a punch in the stomach, and I think I have seen very unpleasant results from this rude handling. The patient is likely to be very sore for several days, and sometimes will suffer acute pain in the epigastric region, accompanied with nausea and vomiting It is very dangerous to handle patients roughly The utmost care should be taken in all manipulations lest a sudden movement should stop the heart action and cause death.

To produce insensibility from the use of ether, it is often necessary to exclude nearly if not all the air. Under such circumstances the patient may die from asphyxia, but the heart continues to beat for a short time after all motion of the chest ceases. This is caused by the devitalized, blood filling the capillaries of the lungs, thus excluding whatever small amount of oxygen may have entered with the ether. This condition may first be noticed by a change in the color of the face, especially the lips, which will be livid. Shallow respiration will also mark the onset. Small flickering pulse and dilated pupils, accompanied with convulsive movements of the muscles and distended veins in the neck, may also be present as immediate forerunners of the fatal result. The same treatment as instituted for the foregoing accidents will be proper. Dashing cold water in the face, or pouring it from a height on the chest or abdomen has been found of benefit. Forcibly dilating the spincter muscle with a Pratt's speculum has been attended with good results. Inserting ice in the rectum has been recommended and favorably spoken of. Persons having fatty degeneration of the heart, or a generally soft and flabby muscular system, with a feeble action of the heart and dilatation of the ventricles, are likely to die suddenly if chloroform is used. Ether is safer in such cases than chloroform.

It has been shown that nearly one-half the deaths from ether and chloroform have taken place before full anæsthesia has been produced.

Some anæsthetists have taken extreme ground on the subject of rapidly or slowly bringing patients under its influence. Those on the side of rapidly giving full quantities at once, instruct the patient to take full and rapid breaths. In this case the blood becomes over-charged with the anæsthetic and is carried to the lungs in large quantities, and goes directly to the left side of the heart; a powerful local impression is made on the ganglia of the heart; a portion of this blood goes surcharged to the brain and there makes another powerful impression almost before the general system feels it at all. Under these circumstances the heart may cease to act, or acts feebly; the color of the face becomes pale; the pupils dilate; the respiration is convulsive; and life, if it does not become extinct, is only saved by the most timely and energetic action.

If ether is given, the heart beats violently at first, the

blood fills the capillaries of the skin and gives it a dusky or purple hue ' The brain is crowded with this dark blood, the vessels are engorged, unconsciousness supervenes and death by coma may take place in from two to ten days.

A great amount has been written by some surgeons about death taking place by reflex action in the early stages of anæsthesia. It is difficult for me to understand how an impression of a so-called paralyzing character could make such a profound impression on a distant organ as to cause it to cease to act. I believe that most, if not all the deaths reported to have been caused by reflex action, were in fact caused by suddenly overwhelming the heart as above described The same accident may occur where from some cause the anæsthetic has been removed. The air in the lungs being charged with it already, to resume the anæsthetic in full draughts may over-charge the blood and stop respiration or circulation as above mentioned.

Anæsthetic Compounds —The dangers attending the use of the agents when given singly have induced surgeons to try various methods of compounding them, hoping to modify their deleterious action without impairing their desirable qualities. This effort has met with some opposition. Mr. Snow discards their use and says that a combination of their objectionable qualities is obtained without a full influence of the beneficial. However, the use of any combination has never supplanted either of the great anæsthetics A compound is like any similar substance— it may possess some properties of each of the elements entering into its composition, but those properties are as inflexible as those of the elementary substances Its range of influence may be different, but just as limited. The only scientific rule for forming compounds is the therapeutic indications that call for the use of properties which cannot be found in any elementary substance. These demands are so varied that any compound may contain medicines whose properties are not needed in the case at hand. It is bad practice to allow any agent to go into a compound whose action is not needed If it is a poison, it will certainly prove destructive; if it is not poisonous, it is an embarrassment to a system to eliminate it, as it attempts to, or does cast it out Each compound represents one or many properties, in the same sense as does any single remedy which possesses inherent properties.

The mixture which has been most thoroughly tested is

that consisting of three parts of ether and one of chloroform, known as the "Vienna mixture" and which is said to have been given in Vienna alone eight hundred times without a fatal accident. Bilroth adds to this now, one part absolute alcohol.

Next to this is the alcohol-chloroform-ether mixture—one part alcohol, two parts chloroform, and three parts ether, by measure. These mixtures were especially recommended by the "Chloroform Committee" as being as effective as pure chloroform, and a safer agent when deep and prolonged anæsthesia is to be produced. Although this or any other mixture has been used by only a few surgeons, it is highly recommended by them, and is considered safer and just as effectual as either of the other agents when they are used alone.

The action of anæsthetics is said to have been modified by the use of morphine. The usual method is to give from one-sixth to one-third of a grain at least twenty minutes before commencing the inhalation of chloroform. It is claimed that it lessens the stage of excitement and reduces the amount of chloroform to one-half the usual amount required. The vomiting is less frequent and the patient falls into a quiet sleep. However highly it may be recommended by a few surgeons, it has not been generally accepted by the profession. Tillman recommends it very highly for operations on the face, mouth, pharynx and nose, as the patient retains sufficient intelligence and power to control the muscles of the throat, thus enabling him to keep the blood cleared from the respiratory passages. But he adds: "As objections to the combined morphine-chloroform narcosis, both Kacher and I have noticed that the morphine sleep following the operation has a bad influence upon breathing, and permits the inhalation of foreign matter with a resulting aspiration-phenomena." The authors say that injections of chloral hydrate may be resorted to; that they have a close resemblance to the morphine-chloroform narcosis. In "Moulin's Surgery," by Hamilton, may be found the following: "An injection of morphia before the chloroform is given enables anæsthesia to be produced much more rapidly and without struggling, but it very greatly increases the danger of syncope." Keen, in his "American Text-Book of Surgery," says: "It has been suggested that hypodermic injection of one-sixth of a grain of morphia and one-hundred-and-twentieth of a grain of sulphate of atropia given before the inhalation has commenced, acts beneficially;" but he does not say that he has used it himself. His statement of the fact would imply that he has not used it With the testimony of its friends as to its doubtful efficacy, Physio-Medicalists will have no use for the agent With the stimulants which are at the command of every Physio-Medicalist, reaction from the shock of the operation can be established, and with the nervines and relaxants in the stage of febrile movement, the patient s suffering will be assuaged and sleep procured without any of the risks that accompany the use of the morphia .

In cases where from some cause the stomach is full of food or other accumulations when anæsthesia is begun, the presence of such material interferes with the free movement of the heart and respiration, and may result seriously if not disastrously In the act of vomiting, some of the matter may fall into the larynx and cause fatal asphyxia. To avoid any accident from this cause, when the patient is about to vomit, he should be gently turned on the side being supported by the hands in such a way that there will be free exit for the contents of the stomach Should there be signs of asphyxia, the mouth should be forced open and the fingers carried boldly back of the fauces, for the purpose of exploring the parts, especially the rima glotidis, to see that nothing is resting upon it. If the substance is small, it will probably pass into the trachea In this case artificial respiration should be maintained Failing in this, the trachea may be opened and respiration kept up in that way. Other substances may fall into the larynx Artificial teeth, tobacco, and sometimes the cork that has been used to keep the mouth open Corks, or other small substances used for this purpose, should have a cord attached to them. Sudden death has frequently occurred when patients (either adults or children) have been struggling violently against the use of the anæsthetic. If, they are conscious the spasmodic respiration may carry a large quantity of the vapor into the lungs as stated above; or if semi-unconscious, the air in the lungs being already well charged with the vapor, a deep inspiration such as occurs at times when the lungs are suddenly filled by one deep and prolonged effort, may carry sufficient vapor into the air cells to cause sudden death. The greatest care should be exercised at this time, in order to prevent a sudden ingress of vapor. Vomiting frequently follows the use of the anæsthetic, and may be produced by three separate conditions, all of which are directly attributable to disturbances of the circulation caused by the shock of the operation. The reaction from the vascular disturbances in the abdominal viscera, caused by injury or operations, is attended with nausea and vomiting, which can be promptly relieved by establishing a free and full circulation in all parts of the body. In a second class of cases, the vomiting is caused by an over-distension of the vessels of the brain. This makes pressure on the control centres which, under certain circumstances, influence the centres for vomiting. Vomiting may also be caused by enæmia of the brain, as this condition may be brought about by the use of chloroform, while the former condition is due to the action of ether. In either case there is vomiting, but it may be from opposite conditions.

In the first case, the usual treatment employed by Physio-Medicalists in shock of injury will be proper. In the second and third classes, absolute quiet and rest must be maintained. The patient's room must be darkened and all visitors excluded, allowing no one in the room but the attendants. If the pulse is feeble and soft, and the temperature low, bottles of warm water should be placed at the feet, knees, and along the spine, when it can be done. Weak mustard plasters over the epigastrium and warm applications to the abdomen will often give relief. Hot water by the stomach, in teaspoonful doses, repeated every ten or fifteen minutes, often gives relief from the nausea and adds heat to the body. If the temporal arteries are full and strong, or the head hot, indicating hyperæmia of the brain, bathing the head in three parts warm water and one part alcohol, and dampening the hair with the same. Leaving the head uncovered favors evaporation, and thus tends to reduce the temperature and restore tone to the venous system. Give but little food and medicine by the stomach; medicate and nourish by the rectum, should be the rule, to which there may be exceptions. If medicines are used by the stomach, they should be very mild. After hot water has been used a few hours, if the vomiting is not made worse by it, equal parts of hot milk and water may be allowed, in teaspoonful doses. If the stomach seems hot and there is great thirst, one teaspoonful of calcined magnesia in one-fourth of a glass of cold water and given in teaspoonful doses every half hour, does well. Ten grains of oil of lobelia (prepared by trituration with sugar) may be given once every hour if there is a febrile movement. A weak infusion of mentha vir. or mentha pip. may also prove beneficial; but there is nothing more deleterious than the use of active drugs given in large doses.

Vomiting in the early stage of anæsthesia is caused by a profound influence being made on the nerve centres before the anæsthetic has had time to reach the more remote parts of the system. This need not cause alarm if the stomach is empty. As soon as the vomiting ceases, the agent can be cautiously applied again without any risk. In elderly people and epileptics, there may arise some cerebral disturbance, which can be treated on general principles as the same condition, when it arises in other cases. Hypostatic pneumonia may occur in old people several days after; but it is caused by the inability of the structures to rid themselves of the accumulated blood consequent upon the shock produced by the operation, rather than the effect of the anæsthetic. The same condition may arise in any case whose vital structures are weakened. Fatal syncope may occur when a patient suddenly rises from the table. No patient should be allowed to rise for at least one hour after consciousness has been restored. They should not be left alone—not even for a moment. Austie tells of a case, in his own experience, that rose suddenly, while the attention of the nurse was called to something else, and fell back dead.

Complete Anæsthesia—How to Detect It.—Different writers have mentioned and relied on different symptoms. One surgeon depends on what may be called the arm test. In this test hold up the patient's forearm, and when it falls powerless by the side, the patient is thought to be completely anæsthetized. This test is not reliable, as a patient's mind may be obscured before anæsthesia is established. In such cases they are not sufficiently under the influence to be insensible to pain.

Another surgeon tells us to separate the eyelids and if the pupil is contracted, and insensible to light, and touching the eyeball with a probe gives no response, then the patient is ready for the knife. Dr. Snow, as quoted by Garretson, first called attention to the condition of the eyelashes, which he claims will be the last sensation to

SURGICAL ANÆSTHETICS.

yield, and when they can be touched without giving evidence of sensation, any operation can be made without evidence of consciousness. Dr. Garretson says that he has relied on this test for years, and it has never disappointed him. He says just after unconsciousness is induced, if the eyelashes are touched with a probe they close very strongly, especially in females. If the chloroform is continued the lids gradually lose their sensibility until they fail to respond to any impression.

Pricking the skin with a sharp instrument is sometimes resorted to, but this will fail as sensibility yields first in the anterior part of the body. Operations on the genital organs, rectum, fingers and toes require deep anæsthesia. Plastic operations in which a large amount of the integument is involved, necessitating the insertion of numerous stitches, require more of the anæsthesia than where the dissections are made on the deeper structures.

From personal observation the writer is convinced that each of the above symptoms is of value; but that the anæsthetist should take all the symptoms into account when making a judgment. The general condition of the patient should be considered. The circulation, respiration and condition of the pulse have much to do with the state of anæsthesia. The muscular sense is as reliable as any other single symptom. When a patient is completely anæsthetized it has lost all its tonicity and feels like a dead muscle. If the student will learn the sensation imparted to his hand when feeling the muscles of a cadaver, he will have no difficulty in detecting complete anæsthesia. Again there is something indescribable about a patient under these circumstances which intuitively tells him that the patient is ready for the operation. All the above signs should be given full credit where there is an imperative reason for determining when a patient is anæsthetized.

Incomplete Anæsthesia.—The writer, in common with other members of the profession, has entertained the opinion that it is safer for the patient if he is not profoundly under the influence of the anæsthetic. Especially is this the case when there exists heart disease. Patients partially anæsthetized will writhe, moan and in various ways express signs of pain; but when consciousness returns, they have no knowledge of it. This has been thought to be a safe stage in which to operate. There is, however, a difference of opinion on this point. Many surgeons of

experience advise against the practice. Physio-Medicalists have been very successful As far as I know, there
has never been a death in their hands under these circumstances; yet it is well to give heed to the experiences of
others. Mr Lister relates a case of death that he witnessed "The patient was a man above the middle period
of life He was afflicted with cancer of the penis. Considering the momentary nature of the operation, chloroform was purposely not given to the full extent. The
surgeon now placing his fingers on the pulse and finding
the pulse was good, at once made the amputation almost
instantaneous. I observed," says Lister, "that the passage of the knife through the member was accompanied
by a start of the patient's body The bandage applied on
the organ to restrain hemorrhage was removed, but no
blood flowed from the arteries; he was dead." Lister's
opinion was that he died from the shock operating on a
weak heart, and thinks that if the chloroform had been
pushed to the full extent, he would not have died. It is
probable that it is safer to give the anæsthetic to the degree that was mentioned in a former place, and which so
closely resembles natural sleep It is bad practice to allow
a patient to fluctuate so much as is often seen Patients
who are half conscious and struggling against the pains
inflicted by the surgeon's knife, and the next moment
snoring in the depths of profound anæsthesia, are likely
to have a slow and tedious awakening, together with
troublesome vomiting or other unpleasant complications.

Narcomania,—Persons addicted to the use of morphia,
chloral, cocaine or alcohol, are bad subjects for anæsthesia
Their systems are so inured to influences that so closely
resemble anæsthesia, that they require more than the
others who are not habitual users of those drugs Their
vital capacities being weakened, they are unable to rally
from its influence

Inhalers—One of the chief differences between ether
and chloroform consists entirely in the quantity used
In ether the question is- how nearly can the air be excluded?—while in the other, how little chloroform can be
admitted and yet get its full influence? In the latter case
no instrument is absolutely necessary In fact a handkerchief is claimed to be the best and safest Garretson uses
a sponge. He first wets it in water and squeezes the water
out. Upon this he drops a few drops of chloroform at first,

and in a few minutes he increases it till full anæsthesia is produced. He regards most kinds of apparatus as entitled to no better name than "life traps."

The following is a quotation from Mr. Erichsen (Vol. 1, page 52): "The following is the way in which chloroform may be most safely given on lint or a handkerchief without apparatus of any kind: On a piece of folded lint about three inches square, and about three doubles, a dram of chloroform is poured; and the lint then held about three inches from the patient's nose, so as to admit a free admixture of air with the first few inhalations of the vapor. After the lapse of about one-half minute the lint is brought nearer the patient's nose, to within one inch, but never allowed to touch." Keen uses a handkerchief. Moulin uses a piece of lint and a drop-bottle. He folds the lint upon itself two or three times and then drops a few drops of chloroform on it, and then turns the lint over so that the moistened surface is next to the mouth.

Dr. H. C. Wood read a paper at the Berlin Congress in 1890 in which he called attention to the superiority of "forced artificial respiration." He stated that he had repeatedly resuscitated dogs that seemed to be dead. All the apparatus that Dr. Wood recommends is a face mask, a bellows, and a foot of India rubber tubing. Before applying the face mask a thread should be passed through the tongue, and the organ well drawn out and held in place so that the epiglottis is held up. If the lungs do not expand, an intubation tube should be inserted. He recommends that two sizes be on hand. The lungs should be thoroughly but slowly expanded by each stroke of the bellows, care being taken that too much force is not used, as the air cells might be ruptured. It is essential that the lungs be freed from the residual air as quickly as possible and thus relieve the blood of the chloroform. This apparatus or any other that is complicated will be all right for hospitals or any one who chooses to use it, but in the absence of it, artificial respiration thoroughly performed will accomplish the same result with less risk. Of course it matters not what means is adopted. The operator should see that the throat and larynx are free. To accomplish this the tongue should always be drawn forward. If any apparatus is used, those above mentioned or Esmarch's are the best, and in fact the only ones the writer would recommend. Ether should always be administered with an

inhaler. The Allis or Esmarch's for ether are the best.
The number of inhalers now on the market is very large,
and each has its admirers; but we think that these two
above named are the least complicated, and therefore less
liable to get out of order.

In the absence of any instrument, a very good one can
be made by folding a piece of heavy paper in the form of a
cone, cutting the large end to fit the irregularity of the
face, and then place a napkin, sponge, piece of lint or absorbent cotton in it and secure it with pins Drop the
ether on the under side of this substance and bring it near
the face, but not to touch, for the first few minutes After
the patient has inhaled it lightly for a few minutes, the
quantity of ether may be increased, and the apparatus
brought down close to the face The air may be nearly,
but not entirely excluded   Any signs of asphyxia or failure of the circulation as manifested by the respiration,
pulse or color, should at once be considered a reason for
removing the inhaler until the circulation or respiration
is completely restored. After a patient is fully under
either anæsthetic, the agent should not be continuously
held over the nose. Opportunity should be afforded for a
breath of fresh air every few minutes It requires more
ether to keep the patient constantly at the right stage of
anæsthesia than chloroform   Constant watchfulness is
necessary as the operation proceeds and the room gets
warmer

Anæsthetics During Shock.—This subject has been
under consideration by many eminent surgeons ever since
their (anæsthetics) use in surgery; some recommending
their use, others condemning them. Those who recommend their use claim that they act as a stimulant and
favor reaction Those who oppose their use. do so on the
supposition that they are narcotic poisons. and have a
tendency to add to the shock rather than to act as a stimulant   The unsettled state of this point should cause
Physio-Medicalists to investigate for themselves. This
question, if settled at all, must be done by studying the
cause of pain as well as its influence on the organism.
"Pain the monitor and rest the cure," says Heaton,
"should be recognized by all." Physio-Medicalists have
always considered pain as a friendly monitor, and valued
it as an element in diagnosis They have considered it an
evidence of vital activity, which is no doubt correct; but

does it not also produce debility? And does it not often
add to the gravity of the case? An answer to these questions, either in the negative or affirmative, will probably
determine the advisability of using or not using anæsthetics in shock of injury

Starting with the proposition, as we have, that anæsthetics are non-poisonous, and if properly administered
never produce death or destruction of living matter, our
first inquiry should be, does pain of itself ever produce
prostration or hinder reaction ? For myself, it has been a
matter of common experience that small operations, everything else being equal, cause more shock than major operations do with the use of anæsthetics. Some months ago
Prof Haggard had occasion to remove some small cancer
tumors from the region where he had previously removed
a cancerous mammary gland Cocaine was injected and
two removed without any suffering or apparent prostration. A third one was likewise treated with cocaine, but
owing to the density of the cicatricial tissue the anæsthetic did not reach every part of the structure While
making the last half of the dissection, the lady complained
severely. Her pulse failed and the surface became livid.
Respiration was shallow, and she was on the point of a
collapse when the work was completed, which had not
lasted to exceed three minutes

Only a few weeks ago the writer had occasion to inject
the hernial rings of a large and well formed healthy man.
The operation was followed by severe and prolonged shock.
In about ten days after this, it was found necessary to
repeat the injection, and the patient asked for chloroform,
stating that the operation was too painful   This was not
advisable on account of the risk of vomiting, which would
have defeated the design of the operation Cocaine was
injected by Prof Haggard   The injection was made
equally as thorough as the former one but was not followed by any severe shock   This point, we believe, will
not be controverted by any, as this is one of the principal
reasons why all surgeons use anæsthetics, and forms a
basis for the use of anæsthetics in shock of injury Agents
that will prevent shock while an injury is being inflicted,
ought to be capable of relieving it, at least to some extent,
after it is inflicted   But does pain of itself ever produce
debility ? And can it alone be the cause of death ? I
answer this, in the affirmative and ask the critic what

comparison there is between the extent of lesion in the
case of neuralgia and a cerebral hemorrhage; or between
the pain of angina pectoris and a penetrating gunshot
injury of the lung, when the lesion of tissue is taken into
account? One of the severest kinds of shock is that produced by gunshot injury of the knee, or a crushing of the
bones and joints in railroad accidents It is very difficult
and sometimes impossible to' establish reaction   The
shock is far worse than that from any other injury, notwithstanding the lesion of tissue may be far greater. Is
it not possible that pain is the greatest source of shock in
these cases? If so, and chloroform, not being poison, is
administered, is it not possible that the patient can rally
sooner when not suffering such severe pain, especially if
Physio-Medical remedies are given?

Two forms of shock should be recognized. One in which
the damage is instantaneous, but the effect ceases as suddenly, leaving nothing but the vascular disturbance and
loss of equilibrium of nervous action.   In these cases
prompt Physio-Medical treatment will soon restore them
to a normal state The second class of cases are such as
produce all the above changes in the tissues, and in addition the injured nerves keep up a constant influence on
the nerve centres, and retard reaction   To avoid this
influence becomes at once the important thing to do   Can
this be done without the use of some agent that will prevent these injured structures from transmitting their
deleterious influence to the nerve centres? It is plain to
me that ordinary Physio-Medical remedies will not do this
They are all-powerful to restore circulation and nervous
action, but they have no power to control common sensation   The Physio-Medical materia medica is replete, as I
can testify, with remedies to relieve all the ills of life,
even common sensation may be restored to a normal standard far enough to restore a normal action, but they will
not entirely inhibit the nerves of common sensation when
there is a cause like such injuries as these named above
To expect this of our common relaxants, stimulants and
nervines is as unreasonable as to expect that the same
agents can amputate a limb

All medical men recognize this common law; viz , that
remedies can modify functions, but cannot perform mechanical acts, such as setting bones and dislocated joints;
and so it is with the transmission of sensation to the

centres, while the cause of the irritation continues to
make its impression on the nerve centres. In chloroform,
it is believed there are properties that will do this without
in the least impairing the integrity of the tissues, provided its laws can be obeyed. I am aware of the delicate
ground I occupy as a Physio-Medicalist. Only the desire
to avail ourselves of every agent for the relief of human
suffering that will accomplish that purpose without leaving deleterious conditions on the organism, prompts this
suggestion. To the intelligent, thinking and unprejudiced mind are these thoughts dedicated, with a hope that
our cause (which is of the people), if not benefited, will at
least receive no injury therefrom.

*Why the circulatory and respiratory centers are the
last to be influenced in general anæsthesia.* As I have
stood by the side of patients who were being anæsthetized
and have observed the phenomena, I have asked myself the
question, why is it that every part of the body except the
the circulation and respiration is rendered as insensitive
and motionless as if dead; and yet the heart and lungs perform their part as regularly and harmoniously as if in a
profound sleep? I have wondered if it is an extraordinary
property which anæsthetics possess that accomplishes this
or is it due to some peculiar structure of the nervous or
vascular system? I soon satisfied myself that it could not
be due to the anæsthetics, and turned to anatomy and
physiology for the explanation. A general survey of the
anatomy of the central nervous system and the distribution
of the sympathetic ganglia and nerves, together with the
influence they exert, each upon the other, will furnish a
key to this mysterious condition.

The cerebrum may be regarded as a hollow sphere, having
an internal and an external surface. The latter of these is
all that portion that presents itself to the eye upon a superficial examination. In order to increase the surface it is
every where thrown into folds or convolutions which are
covered in their entirety by gray matter. This matter is
largely made of cells held together by a net work called neu-
roglia which serves as a cement to fix these cells; greater
firmness is also given to this structure by a rich net work
of blood-vessels which break up into a capillary system
that abundantly supplies the cells among which they ramify. This network receives its blood from the vessels in
the pia mater. This membrane is very vascular and

receives its supply of blood from the cerebral arteries, and are branches of the circle of Willis which lies in immediate contact with the base of the brain, and is supplied with blood directly from the heart through the two vertebral arteries and the internal carotids. This arrangement is perhaps the most elaborate provision for the supply of blood to an organ that is found in the human body. The internal surface, or hollow inside the brain communicates with the external surface by the foramen of Magendi This expansion is called the general ventricular cavity, and is divided into five compartments like the rooms in a house. Beginning with the entrance is the fourth ventricle or first room. It is situated on the first floor. The third ventricle corresponds to a room on the second floor and is a narrow, irregularly constructed space situated between the corpora striata in front and the thalami optici behind. Situated above this cavity and communicating with it by the foramina of Munroe are the two lateral ventricles, each extending into a corresponding hemisphere. They are separated from each other like two rooms having a double wall between them Between these two walls is a space known as the fifth ventricle. Ranney not inaptly compares the cavities to rooms in the attic of a two-story house This cavity is supposed to be a continuation of the central canal in the spinal cord, only being contracted at some points and expanded at others This arrangement affords a considerable surface over which the gray matter is extended. This surface is also convoluted, the two principal convolutions being the thalamus opticus and corpus striatum, one for each lateral hemisphere The blood supply for this internal surface of the cerebrum is abundant in proportion to the extent of tissue supplied, and comes more directly from the large trunks at the base of the brain. They may be divided into six groups or sets; two sets are called medial, one anterior and one posterior. The anterior are given off from the anterior cerebrals and anterior communicating artery They supply the anterior extremity of each caudate nucleus. The posterior medial groups are branches of the posterior cerebral arteries and arise from them near their origin from the basilar. These arteries enter the ventricular cavity through the posterior perforated space. They supply the internal parts of the optici thalmi and ramify on the walls of the third ventricle. The antero-lateral group take their origin from the middle cerebral near its origin. They enter the ventricle through the anterior perforate space, and supply the whole of the caudate nucleus except its head. The lenticular nucleus, internal capsule and part of the optic thalamus are also supplied by these branches. The posterior lateral arises from the posterior cerebral artery, and supplies the posterior part of the optici thalami. The posterior cerebral also give branches to the crus and corpora quadrigemina. It will thus be seen that the two surfaces of the cerebrum are well supplied with blood that is sent direct from the heart.

The blood supply of the spinal cord is equally abundant. The arterial pressure, however, owing to the more indirect manner in which it receives its blood, is not quite as great as that of the brain. The blood reaches the cord through the vertebrals, intercostals and lumbar arteries. From the first (the vertebrals) the anterior spinal artery takes its origin by two branches, one from each. From the second, viz., intercostals and lumbar arteries, the blood reaches the cord by a branch which enters the spinal canal through each intervertebral foramen and passes along the nerve root to the pia mater in which they ramify. From these sources the vessels of the cord receive their blood.

These vessels have a peculiar and elaborate arrangement for reaching every part of the cord. The anterior spinal artery as before stated, arises by two branches, one from each vertebral which unite near the junction of the medulla and pons. It extends the entire length of the cord, and receives, as it passes down the cord, reinforcements from each artery that enters the canal through the intervertebral formina. These vessels join the anterior spinal nearly at right angles in the upper part of the cord, but more obliquely as the lower termination is reached. The anterior spinal artery in its course gives off from two hundred and fifty to three hundred branches, which pass along the anterior median fissure to the gray commissure. Each of these branches divides into a right and left branch to supply the lateral half of the gray matter. These again divide into an anterior and posterior branch. Vertically, each of the primary branches gives off two branches, one to the branch above and one to the branch next below; so there is formed a second spinal artery within the cord— the anastomotic artery; from this artery a capillary net-

work supplies the tubular gray matter. The arteries from
the external surface penetrate the substance of the cord.
They supply all the white substance and there is a branch
that enters through the posterior external column to the
posterior horn. This is the posterior cornual artery. Just
on the inner side of the posterior root a small artery enters
the cord and supplies the root and head of the posterior
cornu. A number of small arteries enter with the anterior
root. From the pia mater innumerable branches called
radicular branches penetrate and supply the white matter.
A posterior medial artery extends along the posterior median septum, supplying the columns of Gall on each side.
Another artery situated in the septum between the columns of Gall and Burdoch supplies each of these columns
as they lie in contact with each other. These two arteries
like the anterior medial extends the whole length of the
cord. Thus it may be seen that the cord is richly supplied
with blood from the internal as well as the external surface.

The blood supply of the medulla and pons is derived
from the basilar, vertebral and anterior spinal arteries as
these arteries lie in contact with their anterior (under
surface). They are divided into two sets, median and
radicular. The former of these is a series of branches
given off at right-angles from the vertebrals, basilar and
anterior spinal arteries. They penetrate the substance of
the pons and medulla, passing in direct lines through the
substance of the medulla to reach the nerve nuclei on the
floor of the fourth ventricle, and supply these nerve nuclei
with the greater portion of their blood. The radicular
arteries pass around and on the surface of the medulla to
the roots of the nerves as they emerge from the substance
of the cord. Here they divide into two branches and one
goes to the nerve nuclei. The other follows the course of
the nerve trunk.

By a comparison of the anatomical structure of the cerebrum, spinal cord and medulla, it will be seen that the
latter is very scantily supplied with blood as compared
with the two former, as it only receives blood from the
one source; and that this small supply has to penetrate
the solid structure of the medulla or pass in a tortuous
manner around half its circumference to reach the nuclei
that preside over the two vital functions; viz., circulation
and respiration. It has been shown that the brain has

two surfaces, and that the spinal cord is a cylinder with a canal extending in the centre its entire length; that they both receive blood from the internal as well as the external surfaces. As the spinal cord approaches the upper termination of its course, the central canal is pushed backward by the addition of new matter added for the purpose of supplying new centres with nuclei. At the commencement of the medulla the posterior portion of the cord seems as if it had been split and its substance pushed laterally so that the central canal is exposed and expands into a lozenge-shaped surface—the floor of the fourth ventricle.

Here nestled together are found the nuclei of the most important cranial nerves. In the centre of this little group will be seen the nuclei from which spring the pneumogastric nerves, the other centres clustering around them as if to protect them from external influences. Let us now trace the blood that reaches the nuclei of the pneumogastric nerves. The anterior spinal artery is formed by the union of two branches, one from each of the vertebral arteries. They leave the vertebral trunks at right angles, pass to the surface of the medulla, and then describe a gentle curve downward along the anterior median surface. From this downward trunk the median arteries pass at right angles. This brings the anterior spinal artery parallel with the vertebrals, and the blood flows in opposite directions; viz., upward in the vertebrals and downward in the spinal artery. From this reversed current the blood in the anterior spinal enters the median artery at right angles to the former. The median arteries penetrate the entire thickness of the medulla—one-half inch. These arterial twigs break up into a capillary network, as they arrive at the floor of the fourth ventricle, and supply the nuclei. These are all typical end arteries; i. e., they do not communicate with other arteries. From this brief description of the circulation of the blood in the various nerve centres, as compared with that of the bulb, it may be seen that neither the pressure nor the supply is equal to that of those centres. So much for the structure of the cerebro-spinal axis; but this is not sufficient for our purpose.

The sympathetic or ganglionic system is also an important factor in the circulation of the blood and its structure must receive a passing notice. Anatomically it is divided into ganglia and nerves The principal ganglia form a complete circle consisting of two chains connected by the ganglion of Ribes situated on the anterior communicating artery The lower extremities of these two chains are united by the ganglion impar, which is placed on the anterior surface of the coccyx. These ganglia are divided into pairs except the ganglion impar; this is single. The pairs are named from the region which they occupy. There are four cephalics all connected with the branches of the fifth nerve; three cervical situated in the cervical region; twelve in the dorsal; four in the lumbar; five in the sacral and one (single) in the coccygeal region. These are primary branches and communicate with each other by a superior and inferior branch. They also communicate with the spinal cord by sending branches of communication, one from each ganglion composed of gray matter and receiving one branch of white matter from each spinal nerve Hence the ganglia are composed of gray and white matter (spinal and sympathetic)

The primary branches of distribution in the cervical region are three in number; viz., superior, middle and inferior cardiac They arise from the superior, middle and inferior cardiac ganglia. The branches in the thoracic region are also three in number; great splanchnic, lesser splanchnic and renal splanchnic; all these penetrate the diaphragm The first joins the solar plexus, the second the cœliac plexus and the third unites with the renal plexus In the lumbar region the primary branches of distribution terminate in plexuses corresponding in name to the organ supplied by them; the same is true of those in the pelvic region.

Another set of primary branches of distribution are sent to all the blood-vessels of the body and entwine themselves around the arteries in form of plexuses, from which the arterial coats are supplied The secondary branches of distribution in the thoracic region take their origin from the cardiac plexus and are distributed to the heart. The secondary branches of distribution in the abdominal cavity take their origin from the epigastric or solar plexus and semiluna ganglia, and are distributed through the medium of other smaller plexuses to all the viscera of the abdominal cavity There is, therefore, a complete intercommunication between the cerebro-spinal and the ganglionic nervous system Every organ, and every tissue of an organ, feels the influence of each alternately. Another branch (vaso-motor) takes its origin from the floor of the fourth ventricle, between the calamus scripterius and corpora quadrigemina. These vaso-motor fibres pass down in the substance of the spinal cord. A branch passes out of the spinal column with each anterior root of a spinal nerve, and thence passes to all parts of the body that possess arteries and capillaries. They maintain the tone of the vascular system, and are also called vaso-constrictors. The tenth nerves (pneumogastric) take their origin from two nuclei in the lower half of the floor of the fourth ventricle. They are intimately associated in their origin with the spinal accessory nerves, from which they derive their motor fibres. They also send to and receive fibres from the glosso-pharyngeals and hypoglossals, and have many connections with different branches of the sympathetic. In their range of influence they are the widest; and in their extent of anatomical connections they are the most vital as well as the most important nerves in the human body. Through their connections with the other nerves named above, they influence deglutition, phonation, respiration, circulation and digestion. They are also the inhibitory nerves of the heart.

This double strictural arrangement of the nervous system has its analogue in the muscular system. Every muscle of the body has its antagonistic muscle; thus we have them classed into flexors and extensors, abductors and adductors, rotators and supinators, expirators and respirators, and constrictors and dilators. These two last sets are those whose actions are concerned in respiration and are principally connected in anæsthesia.

When chloroform vapor is inhaled, as has been heretofore described, it is brought into direct contact with the lungs and heart, and were it not for a peculiar arrangement of the muscles and nerves of these structures, those organs would cease to act, and death would supervene before the anæsthetic could reach any other of the nerve centres; because it has been found by experimental physiologists that the heart action will cease when a current of chloroform vapor is directed upon it. The same is true of the lungs—respiration ceases. The lungs are in one sense passive. Inspiration and expiration are carried on by muscles that move the chest, alternately enlarging and diminishing the cavity, in this way producing a tendency to create a vacuum The air rushes in and out and prevents this tendency to a vacuum. The nerves controlling this action have their centres in the floor of the fourth ventricle and near the origin of the pneumogastric nerves Through the influence of this respiratory centre the lungs are kept moving, although they themselves may be bathed in the vapor of the anæsthetic. The same is true of the heart, which, although it is automatic to a limited degree, is under control of the cardiac centres in the medulla The heart and lungs are kept moving to a limited degree by these centres

But by a law of limitation this influence cannot continue beyond a certain degree. This is why anæsthetics should not be pushed too rapidly at the commencement as heretofore stated This danger-point being passed, the vapor is carried by the blood to every part of the body in proportion to the amount of blood circulating in each organ or tissue The cerebrum being better supplied with blood feels the influence first, and intellection, sensation and voluntary motion are first obliterated Operations are sometimes made during this stage. The patient struggles and moans as if suffering the severest pain, and yet after recovery he has no recollection of anything that passed. This is inconvenient for the surgeon, as the struggling interferes with the work and might cause the operator to make an unfortunate stroke of his knife. It is also dangerous to the patient The struggling might cause an arrest of the heart action

The second stage comes when the cerebellum, crura cerebri, pons varolii and spinal cord are anæsthetized All motion and sensation through reflex action cease (See previous pages)

The third stage is characterized by snoring or stertorous breathing, with congestion of the capillaries or the opposite—anæmia, or bloodlessness In some cases, instead of the snore, the respiration becomes deep and labored. In either case the patient is asphyxiated and in a dangerous condition This is an indication that the medulla is being influenced

This condition is produced by an overdose of the anæsthetic, which should be discontinued at once, and the patient allowed to breathe fresh air. Patients should never be brought to this condition, and a skillful anæsthetist will not allow a patient to pass beyond the second stage.

The vaso-motor (constrictor) nerves control all the organs of the body except those immediately connected with the heart and lungs—respiratory and cardiac constrictors. As above stated, the nerves arise from the floor of the fourth ventricle and the point extending above this to the corpora quadrigemina. This is the controlling centre. All the other ganglia connected with this centre are dependent centres.

In anæsthesia by ether the constrictor muscles, which are controlled by the dependent centres, are relaxed and complete insensibility is produced and can be maintained indefinitely without the independent centre being reached. The effect of this dilatation of the capillaries and other blood-vessels is to allow the blood to accumulate in the lungs and brain, and the patient may die from congestion (coma) of the brain or asphyxia, when too much ether is inhaled in proportion to the air. This explanation also shows why persons with pulmonary disease or hyperæmia of the brain should not use ether vapor as an anæsthetic.

Chloroform relaxes the vaso-dilators and allows the vaso-constrictors to narrow the capillaries and other vessels, and force the blood upon the heart so rapidly that the right auricle is distended and the action of the organ is arrested in diastole. This constricting force also drives the blood from the brain and lungs, and patients may die because of the deficient supply of blood, which fails to keep up vital action.

Now for the final answer to the question—Why is the medulla the last centre to be influenced? When patients die as the result of any of the conditions above pointed out, they do so by the anæsthetic inhibiting the vital centres; and this is done either by anæmia in chloroform, anæsthesia or hyperæmia or congestion when ether is used. The medulla oblongata and pons varolii are exempt from these disturbances by reason of the peculiar arrangement of the blood supply, as it has been shown that there is a far greater amount of blood sent to the other centres than to this vital spot. So great is this difference in the supply, that every other part of the body can receive enough to render it entirely insensible without the medulla feeling its influence. Therefore the blood must be surcharged with the anæsthetic in an unwarranted manner before this centre is reached and life is cut off.

A Thorough Qualification Needed.—It is feared that there is not sufficient importance attached to the acquirement of a complete knowledge of the properties of anæsthetics. also to the danger to life if not properly used. It is an indisputable fact that the death rate is very low One death in five thousand from the use of chloroform, and possibly one in twenty-five thousand from the use of ether does not seem alarming, and yet it is not known in what given case it will prove fatal In the Netley Hospital there were twenty-five thousand administrations, and twelve deaths in ten years' use of it; while in the next ten there were over three hundred deaths. It has been shown that death usually occurs suddenly and without warning. In three instances within the past fifteen years there have been four such deaths in this state, three of which were in this city.

It must be a terrible feeling for an operator to find that while he is busily engaged with his work his patient has passed beyond the point of needing his services, and what must be the chagrin of the anæsthetist to know that the life of his patient has been extinguished, perhaps by his negligence It is true that occasionally a patient may die notwithstanding every precaution has been taken to guard against it. It is the duty of every person who assumes this great responsibility to know that nothing has been left undone to insure safety

I fear that there is not sufficient attention given to this subject while at college. Some students get the impression that they may never be called upon to administer these agents; while others, seeing so many cases anæsthetized and that they all come out, will conclude that not very much knowledge is required beyond what they term the use of good judgment. This is a very serious mistake, a knowledge of which may come to the student when he has to regret that a life is lost and that he is responsible. With this conviction on his mind the conscientious student will avail himself of every opportunity to acquire a complete knowledge of this subject, by attendance at every clinic at the hospitals as well as at the college, and close attention to didactic lectures. I have often been astonished at the indifference manifested by students to this subject while patients were being anæsthetized. The attentive student will watch with interest every movement of the anæsthetist as well as the patient, and observe

carefully all the phenomena, and from his text-books learn
the import of each.

Thus armed with all the knowledge it is possible to
acquire, every graduate ought to be qualified to administer these agents. Assuming that he has done all this, and
has mastered all the facts in relation to the more common
accidents to which patients are exposed, we will suppose
that he is now the actor, not the spectator as before. The
operation is to be one of the most serious character. The
surgeon has informed the patient that Dr. B. will give the
anæsthetic. It will be, therefore, proper for him to call
on the patient, and in a short interview endeavor to impress upon his mind that an anæsthetic is entirely safe;
that it produces a quiet sleep from which he will awake
without having felt the pain of the operation. Patients
who can be thus impressed, will quietly take the anæsthetic and pass under its influence without a struggle,
unless there exists some physical impediment. Having
thus by your quiet and dignified manner established their
confidence, and allayed their fears as to results, you then
decide upon the anæsthetic. Will ether, or chloroform be
most appropriate ?

The answer to this will be found in the condition of the
patient. If thin and anæmic, ether will be the proper
agent. If plethoric, or if there are any of the conditions
present heretofore named that would contra-indicate the
use of ether, chloroform should be used. It is necessary,
however, to have both on hand, and only the freshest and
that which has been prepared by the best manufacturing
pharmacists should be used. It should be procured direct
from the retail druggist who has kept it in proper contain-
ers, and away from heat and light. It is not safe to use
ether or chloroform that has been opened and exposed to
light and air in your office. The next thing to do is to
select and procure instruments and appliances with which
to treat the accidents that may arise. This should be
done several days before the time for the operation to be
made. While alone in your office write out an inventory
of what is needed; be sure that you have included all that
will be needed to meet any accidents that may occur in
any case. It is proper to assume that your patient will be
exposed to any accident that ever has happened to any
other patient.

Having reviewed the list and having referred to all the

text-books or notes in your possession, you should at once procure the appliances This should not be deferred till the time of the operation; they should be selected and placed in a proper container at least one day before they will be needed   This should be locked and put in a secure place for use   I once knew an anæsthetist to make all the preparations, leaving the satchel containing the instruments in an accessible place and unlocked.   On the morning of the operation it was hurriedly sent to the house where it was needed   When the patient was on the table it was found that some one had removed the inhaler. An apparatus was improvised, but the absence of the inhaler caused delay and some disappointment on the part of the patient

The following is a list of instruments and medicines that should always be provided. (a) Inhaler, (b) vulselum forceps, (c) hypodermic syringe, (d) common hard rubber syringe, (e) bivalve rectal speculum, (f) electric battery. Medicines—(a) tr., myrrha comp., (b) aqua ammonia. (c) tr. serpentaria tr zingiber. tr lavender comp., aa. dr ii; syr simp., q. s. oz. ʋi. Sig. One teaspoonful from ten to twenty minutes   (d) Vaseline and sponges Napkins and paper will usually be found at the house should it become necessary to improvise an inhaler There should be at least eight ounces of chlorotorm and one pint of sulphuric ether. This is best contained in tin cans, each holding four ounces, which is the best way that manufacturers usually put it up; and the seal should not be broken until needed. Where it is possible, some responsible person should be detailed to look after the pulse, and assist the anæsthetist in any way that might seem to him necessary, should any accidents occur. It should be the duty of the surgeon to see that the room is of proper size, and well ventilated. By reference to the foregoing statement of facts, and the conclusions drawn therefrom, this may be readily determined.

If the patient is greatly reduced in flesh and quite anæmic, with a feeble heart action, ether will be more appropriate than chloroform. If it can be ascertained by the temperature of the head, or by the condition of the arterial or venous circulation, or otherwise, that there is an anæmic condition of the brain, ether will be appropriate, since it has the property of stimulating the arterial system, and will restore a more natural circulation of blood

to the head than existed before. Of course it will be understood that any objections to the use of ether as pointed
out in the preceding pages will be a barrier to it as the
chief anæsthetic. If there is a doubt as to which is the
most appropriate, ether may be given first, and if it produces too much excitement, chloroform may be substituted
until the excitement is quieted. If chloroform is used
first, and the pulse becomes too frequent or irregular, or
respiration shallow or spasmodic, or the face becomes pale
or the lips blue, ether is to be used until the circulation is
re-established. Having in this way settled upon a definite
plan, the anæsthetist will be bet'er prepared for the discharge of his duties. If there is great fear entertained by
the patient, either of the anæsthetic or the success of the
operation, the surgeon should in all proper ways endeavor
to establish confidence in the mind of the patient in the
anæsthetist, by assuring him of the successful use of the
agent in the hands of skillful men. All fears either of
this or of the final success of the operation should be dis-
pelled, and the patient should be *en rapport* both with the
surgeon and anæsthetist. Should such fears exist in the
mind of the patient, the surgeon and anæsthetist should
visit the patient separately, as often as may be deemed
advisable, to see that all fears are allayed, and all preparations are made for the safety and comfort of the patient
and the success of the operation.

To this end the surgeon should see to all the minor details, such as directing the patient to be bathed the day
previous, that the bowels should be cleared out, and that
the patient should not have any food in the stomach when
the time arrives for the anæsthetic to be given. Loaded
bowels, a full stomach, or an inactive or foul skin militate
very much against the successful use of an anæsthetic,
as well as the operation. The skin is a respiratory organ,
next in importance to the lungs, and should be carefully
attended to. The arrangement and size of the room, and
method of ventilation, should be carefully looked after by
the surgeon, for the safety of the patient from the accidents attending the anæsthetic state, as well as for the
convenience of himself. Assuming now that all the preliminaries have been arranged, it will be necessary for the
surgeon to make a visit on the day previous to the operation, to see that all things are ready for the duties of the
following morning, and to him may be assigned the

arrangements for the anæsthetic. The patient should receive all the encouragement possible to allay fears and establish confidence in the success of the operation.

The question of giving medicine to prepare the system for the shock that may result from the combined effect of the operation, loss of blood and the anæsthetic is one fraught with interest. It is the habit of some surgeons to give something on the previous evening, to procure sleep; but it is now too late to accomplish much good in this way; nothing can now be done except to continue such treatment as has been prescribed during the previous time the surgeon has had charge of the case. This treatment should have consisted in such remedies as are calculated to restore or maintain as nearly a natural state as possible. If the case is the result of an accident received the previous day, then the same rule applies as above: restore the circulation, maintain the tone of the nervous system and thus promote quiet, and induce sleep if possible. It is the habit of some surgeons to give a nervine or stimulant a short time before commencing the operation. This can possess no advantages, as whatever effect they produce must be overcome by the anæsthetic, and they promote a flow of saliva that is quite troublesome.

The question of clearing out the stomach and bowels previous to the operation is a matter of importance. No patient should ever be anæsthetized when there are accumulations in the alimentary canal—but the accomplishment of this demands some thought. It is the manner of some surgeons to give a cathartic on the previous evening. This is bad practice. If the patient is strong and robust, a cathartic will be proper; but should be given the evening of the second day before the operation, and then only liquid foods should be taken on the day preceding the operation. On the previous evening a half gallon of water in which an ounce of salt has been dissolved, should be injected into the bowels if the patient can retain it. If the patient is strong and corpulent, this may be repeated in the morning; but if he is feeble, he should not be taxed with anything that will produce exhaustion. If the patient is weak and prostrated, the bath on the previous evening should be made of water that has been boiled, into which salt should be put, the proportion of one ounce to each half gallon of water used; and the enema should be prepared by making an infusion of zingiber, one ounce to two quarts of water, to which is added one pint of milk, and this given slowly, as long as the patient can retain it. This will usually clear out the bowels and strengthen the patient, who, after the salt bath and enema, will procure refreshing sleep. All the above preliminaries being attended to, the patient should be allowed to remain quietly in bed on the morning of the operation, having only a cup of coffee, tea or chocolate; or, if it is preferable, a cup of hot milk with toast, crackers or bread, with only a small amount of butter or fruit jelly; in short, any of the above articles, or anything else in the same line. Whatever is taken should be served at least four hours before the time to make the operation.

In order that the patient's mind shall be free from forebodings, and not harrassed with waiting beyond the time set to begin the operation, the surgeon should arrive early, in order to have all preparations completed at fifteen minutes before the time set to commence the work; at which time all the assistants should be present, and the anæsthetization should begin on the minute. The practice of fixing the time for an operation, say at ten o'clock, and having the surgeon arrive at about that time and then devote nearly one hour to the preparations, is very reprehensible. The patient becomes worried by the mind dwelling on the anticipated pain and suffering; he will grow restless and nervous, and when at last things are ready, they go into the operation nervous and trembling. Such a state is exceedingly unfavorable.

Another point that should be carefully observed: that is not to allow a patient to see or hear the preparation for the operation. When it is possible he should be placed in a room adjoining the operating room, the door between which should be closed, and the work of preparation should be carried forward noiselessly to completion. When the moment arrives for the anæsthetic to be administered, the nurse, who has been with the patient all the time, should make the announcement that the time has arrived, and introduce the surgeon and anæsthetist, who, after a few minutes' conversation, should propose that the anæsthetic be given while the patient is yet in bed. In a few cases the patient, if quite strong and fearless, may be permitted to walk in and take his position on the table; but these are very exceptional ones, and it will sometimes happen that the sight of the table and evidences of preparation

will excite his fears and he will become very weak and
nervous ¯ As a rule he should not be permitted to see the
assistants; only after unconsciousness has been produced
should they enter the room

To return again to the patient who is being anaesthetiz-
ed in bed, after unconsciousness has been produced, he
should be removed to the operating table. The above
method is probably the best for adults but if a child, and
it is able to be out of bed, it should be placed in the arms
of the mother, or some other person in whom it has confidence. The anaesthetic may then be placed on a handkerchief and playfully flitted before the face, or a game of hide
and seek may be indulged in, in which the child is to be
hidden behind the handkerchief, or napkin that is saturated with the chloroform, which soon acts as a stimulant
The little one will soon become dazed and reckless, when
the anaesthetic may be given in sufficient quantities to
produce insensibility It is exceedingly dangerous to undertake to force a child to inhale ether, and in any case for
an anaesthetic to act kindly and safely, the patient's con-
sent must be obtained

For the purpose of getting all the conditions before the
mind of the reader, we will suppose that the patient is a
fairly healthy man, in good flesh but not corpulent, and has
no conditions that contra-indicates the use of ether, and
that agent is to be used The room is of proper size, properly warmed and ventilated

The patient's position on the table will demand some attention As a rule the patient may be placed on the back,
if this position is chosen, the head should rest on a pillow
that is just large enough to fill the concavity which is
formed by the curves of the upper dorsal and all the cervical vertebra, at the end of this curve the shoulders project
backward, at the other end the head extends so far back
that there is quite a sharp curve When the patient is on
the back and the pillow is placed too far forward, under the
shoulders the head falls back and respiration is impeded
by the forcible extention of the muscles on the anterior aspect of the neck, which binds the larynx and trachea down
to the vertebral column If the head is bent too far forward, this also interferes with respiration The most natural position of the head in relation to the body, is that
which it assumes when the body is erect The mouth
should be explored and if artificial teeth are found they

should be removed, as well as any other foreign material
that may be present. The clothing about the neck, and
upper part of the chest should be removed, and these parts
should be freed from anything that hinders free respiration. A light napkin may be spread over the chest, so
that the respiratory movements may be seen, and any failure or irregularity can be detected at once.

The lips and skin about the nose should be anointed
with some soft oil to prevent excoriation, should any of
the liquid chance to fall on the parts. It is also advisable
to pass some of the oil as far up the nasal passages as possible; this will prevent irritation of the mucous membrane by the liquid that may fall about the nose and be
carried back on the nasal passages. Spraying the nose
with some one of the oleaginous preparations which are
used by rhinologists to protect the mucous surfaces from
the action of the atmosphere, will also be of service if
ether is being used, the vapor of which is quite irritating
to the air passages. It has been recently recommended,
probably for the same purpose, to apply cocaine to the
mucous surfaces, as far as it can be carried back, to anæsthetize the nerves. It is said that the death rate is materially lessened when this is done. It is explained that
death often occurs by a paralysis of the heart through
reflex action when the nerves supplying the nasal passages
are powerfully and suddenly impressed by the local action
on them in the early stages of the anæsthetic. It would
seem, however, that the paralyzing influence of the cocaine
would be as deleterious as the influence of the anæsthetic. Shielding those structures from the action of the
agent by covering them over with an impermeable coat of
some soft oil would meet the conditions better than the
cocaine.

The question of giving some form of stimulant just
before commencing the inhalation has been practiced to
some extent. Brandy, whiskey or morphine is recommended by the so-called regular surgeons. Tr. myrrha
comp. and tr. lobelia comp. have been favorites with
Physio-Medicalists. The remedies used by some of the
regulars are not recommended by the best writers; in fact
the morphine has been found injurious, as it prolongs the
recovery from the anæsthetic. Physio-Medicalists have
abandoned the use of stimulants because their use caused

a free flow of saliva, which is very annoying at the time when the patient cannot dispose of it.

We will suppose now that all things are ready, and that the instruments and medicines are all on a stand near the patient's head   The hard rubber syringe is filled with the tr. lobelia comp diluted one-half, the hypodermic syringe filled with the tr. myrrha comp   The physician who has charge of the pulse will be instructed to use them if their use is indicated by the condition of the patient   It is his duty, also, to carefully note the state of the pulse, to listen to the sounds of the heart, and to compare the respirations with the normal standard   These observations enable the physician to judge, at least relatively, of the influence which the prospective operation is exerting on the mind of the patient, and afford an opportunity to give encouragement by a statement that all is well.   All things now being ready, one or two drams of ether are placed in the inhaler   Before the instrument is applied to the face the patient should be instructed to take four or five full inspirations, being careful to force all the air out of the lungs after each inspiration, so that the residual air shall be as pure as possible.   Some anæsthetists instruct patients to take full and even forcible inspirations, at the commencement   This really is a dangerous practice; the patient can in some instances take enough ether or chloroform in this way to produce instant death.   The ether should be given gradually for the first minute or two, in order to allow the mucous surfaces to be slightly influenced by its anæsthetic properties; then the apparatus should be brought down closely to the face so as to exclude nearly all the air, and continued in position until the patient is completely under its influence

Some patients pass under the influence quietly in from five to ten minutes.   If there is no fear or anxiety, and the mind is fully under subjection to the will power, as is the case with most educated persons, there will be no mental perturbations, no positive change in the circulation or respiration; the breathing will be shallow and regular, the pulse will be slightly above the normal standard, and the skin will be slightly redder than natural, thus giving the countenance a light flush if ether is given; if chloroform is used the pulse will be a little below the natural state and the countenance will be paler than the usual color.   The eyes are turned up and the pupils are contracted, the muscular system is entirely relaxed, the body is as motionless as if dead. There is total insensibility to all external objects. Compare this with the sleeping babe and the analogy is so complete that an adept could scarcely point out the difference, which only consists in one thing, and that is the power of transmitting impressions from the nerve peripheries to the central ganglia of the brain, which is instantly aroused to all its wonted activities. Sleep is conditioned upon the unchangeableness of the surroundings. So long as no sounds beyond those existing when sleep comes on, reach the ear, no light penetrates the eye, or no other impressions are made upon the external surface or within the tissues of the body, sleep continues; at least until every cell in the nerve centres has undergone complete repair. As soon, however, as this work is completed, the seeming senseless body becomes a moving, sentient being.

In sleep there are but four signs of life; viz., the respiration, the circulation, the temperature, and the capability of being aroused at any time by impressions being conveyed to the central nerve ganglia from the external surface, or changes made in the tissues of the body, and the impressions being conveyed to the sensorium. In anæsthesia the respiration and circulation are about the same as in sleep, but the temperature falls a little more rapidly and there is total inability to arouse the sensibilities. No sounds arouse the auditory nerve, no light stimulates the eye, the body can be moved in any way, can be cut and mutilated at the will of the surgeon and there is not a single response. A skilful anæsthetist can maintain the above named state of anæsthesia for hours and the patient then awake as from a sleep, provided there has been no operation or mutilation of the body to produce shock. If, however, the ether is pushed farther, the respirations become more frequent and labored. the countenance is disturbed, the color of the face assumes a darker hue, the pulse grows weaker, and when stertorous breathing begins the patient is on the verge of death. If the ether is not at once removed from the face death may take place instantly.

With those who have complete control over their bodies, at least as far as the will is concerned, and in the case of children and old people and all those who are very much reduced, there will be but little resistance

offered at any time, but it will often happen that more or
less resistance will be made in the stage of consciousness,
as well as in the stage of semi-unconsciousness. The ether
will often cause a slight cough and sensation of smothering and the patient will ask to have the inhaler removed,
or will attempt to push it away. There will be a free flow
of saliva that will give rise to great annoyance, and not
unfrequently the tenacious mucous will gather about the
palate, uvula and epiglottis and cause vomiting If the
patient is strong and muscular and not intelligent, or if
there has been the slightest fear or unwillingness to take
the ether, he will probably offer more or less resistance in
the stage of semi-unconsciousness It is at this stage that
he will become almost ungovernable. He will imagine
that some one is trying to do him harm, and will either
attempt to use force and escape, or will resist every
attempt to hold the inhaler over his face. His destructiveness may be aroused and he will attempt summary
punishment on his tormentors This is a critical point in
the process of anæsthesia. If the attempt is made to control him by force, the violent struggling may cause the
rupture of a vessel in the brain, and sudden death may
follow. If he is confined and the ether forced upon him, it
will be necessary to exclude the air entirely and this will
cause death by asphyxia.

Such persons are not proper subjects for the use of ether:
but if the mistake is made, the ether should be discontinued and chloroform used It will happen sometimes that
tetanic spasm may come on: the jaws may be set, respiration may cease in consequence of rigidity of the respiratory
muscles, an arm or a leg may be suddenly thrust out and
stand stiff and immovable. This condition may occur
with the use of either chloroform or ether, and is a very
dangerous condition The anæsthetic should be removed
from the face at once, the jaws should be pried open and
stimulation given, either by emptying the hard rubber
rectal syringe or the hypodermic syringe. The application of heat to the epigastrium, or the dashing of hot
water on the chest may be resorted to. The tongue should
be seized and drawn out of the mouth, and a current of
cool air directed upon the face Such means will generally
restore the vital functions; but should all fail, electricity
may be used perseveringly and attempts at artificial respi-

ration should be made. This will sometimes break the force of the spasm.

It will occasionally happen that there will be an opposite state; respiration will cease, the heart will beat feebly or irregularly, the lower jaw will fall, the pupils will dilate, the limbs lose their tone, and the body will settle down on the table as if dead. Prompt action and well directed effort will be necessary; nothing less than the persevering effort will suffice. The head should be placed lower than the body, stimulants by hypodermic as well as by the rectum, and artificial respiration should be resorted to. The tongue should be drawn well forward, so that the respiratory effort should not be hindered by any mechanical obstruction in the throat. When the patient is resuscitated and consciousness restored, the anæsthetic may be continuously resumed.

Those who say that chloroform or ether vapor is poisonous and destructive to life, say that its use should not be prolonged unnecessarily. This should be the rule and it is eminently proper. No medical or mechanical measure should be continued after the necessity for its use has passed away. Believing as we do that the above named anæsthetics are not poisonous, we would recommend that the operation be not prolonged beyond that which is necessary. Surgeons who use anæsthetics do it for a purpose; and that purpose is usually to render the body insensible while they mutilate it in some way quite sufficient to produce shock, and then attribute all the ill effects to the agent used, and do not for a moment take into account the depressing effect of the operation and loss of blood. When the operation is nearing completion the anæsthetic should be discontinued; but a careful watch should be kept over the patient. As soon as he is able to swallow, some light stimulant should be given. Hot water is preferable. Some patients are restless, and half delirious, as they are rallying from the unconsciousness, and complain loudly of the pain; while others, especially children, may fall into a sound sleep which often lasts for hours. If the sleep is natural, they should not be awakened; but it is imperative that they should be known to be awake before allowing them to sleep; they should, by their answers to questions, give evidence of consciousness and life. After this the sleep may not be disturbed for several hours.

Anæsthesia By the Use of Chloroform.—The general

effect of chloroform is about the same as that of ether, but
it is a much-more potent agent. The laws governing its
use are more rigid and therefore require closer observation
and more positive obedience. It is more pleasant to inhale,
less irritating to the air passages and does not cause that
sense of suffocation that attends the use of ether. From
3 to 4 p c. only can be inhaled without arresting action
There is not that excitement and perturbation of the
mind that results from the inhalation of ether: but they
are more easily disturbed by sounds that reach the ear,
more timid and easily frightened when semi-unconscious
Therefore there should be no loud talking, laughing or
whispering   When it is necessary to speak, the tones
should be subdued but distinct enough for the patient to
hear, and should be confined to the actual necessities of
the case   No remarks should be indulged in that are foreign to the work in hand. The accidents to which they
are exposed are the same as those attending ether; but
they come more suddenly and with less warning, and are
more fatal in consequences. Therefore the anæsthetist
should be alive to the emergencies and fully prepared to
meet them instantly.

The operating table should be made so that the head
can be lowered at a second's warning, as anæmia of the
brain is the accident to which patients are most exposed.
The closest watch should be kept on the respiration, color
of the lips and character of the pulse. If there is any
sudden deviation from the normal condition, the anæsthetic should be removed from the face, and the patient
allowed a breath of fresh air. Should the patient snore,
the chloroform should be discontinued at once. If this
does not suffice, the hypodermic syringe should be used
Should this fail, the rectal syringe may be emptied into
the rectum   It respiration ceases or fails in any way, the
tongue should be drawn forward and respiration established by artificial means   Sometimes breathing may be
established by closing the nose, opening the mouth and
applying the mouth of some other person closely and blowing forcibly into the lungs, alternating this with compressing the chest. In this way warm air is forced in and out
of the lungs, and is more effectual than any other means
When artificial respiration is resorted to, a few drops of
aqua ammonia can be administered the same as the chloroform, and thus apply stimulation directly to the air

passages. Care must be taken, however, not to allow too much of it to mix with the air, as too powerful stimulation might cause spasm of the air cells, or be followed by bronchitis.

Every person present should be as familiar with the management of these cases as the anæsthetist or the operator. They should not wait to be told what to do, but ought to see what some one else is not doing, and do the thing that is proper to do. There is work for all. Thus, one lowers the end of the table, another pulls the tongue out, a third uses the hypodermic, the fourth the rectal syringe, and a fifth opens the windows and allows fresh air to enter the room. There should be no flurry and no loud talking. Everything should be calmly and orderly executed. The patient should be handled gently, and the body as well protected as the circumstances will permit. Warm blankets should be wrapped around the limbs and feet, and bottles of hot water placed at the feet, knees, and along the spine whenever it is possible to do so without interfering with the manipulations for resuscitation.

All this would seem like a great amount of work to be done in a few minutes, and probably more than can be accomplished unless the case is protracted. Occasionally a patient will give signs of life and again collapse, and then revive again, and thus go on for a considerable time, alternating between life and death for some hours. This affords time for all methods of treatment to be instituted. Sometimes a patient will be semi-unconscious and suddenly cease to breathe, or the heart stop, and to all appearances he is dead. In such cases it is proper to make use of all or part of the above methods, for life may not be extinct; it may only be inhibited and the heart may move imperceptibly. If the air in the lungs be gently forced out and a fresh supply allowed to enter, and at the same time be given stimulants by the rectum and hypodermically, together with the application of warmth to the surface, the patient may be resuscitated after he is thought to be dead. Such cases are sometimes abandoned too soon.

SURGICAL USES OF LOCAL ANÆSTHETICS.

By E. M. HAGGARD, M. D.,

Professor of General and Operative Surgery in the Physio-Medical College of Indiana, Indianapolis.

The advantages of a method of procedure which will render only the immediate locality of an operation insensible, and thus enable the surgeon to dispense with the dangers and inconveniences of general anæsthesia, are self-evident. Operations so slight as to scarcely justify the employment of ether or chloroform, with the needful precautions, are frequent, and many of them exquisitely painful, and the risk to life is lessened by the use of an effective local agent which, though more inconvenient, is to be preferred. Patients do not have the same dread of a local anæsthetic as they do for ether and chloroform.

Ice and Salt are local anæsthetics by virtue of the low temperature produced by their mixture. The tissues may be numbed and frozen by them when applied as follows: One-quarter pound of ice wrapped in a towel is crushed into fine bits, add one-eighth pound of salt. This mixture in a gauze bag is laid upon the part to be operated on, which gradually becomes pale, bloodless and insensible, and in about fifteen minutes will be ready for operation. This application should not be continued longer than necessary, else frostbite may be produced.

These materials are obtainable when more convenient anæsthetics may not be had. They give only a local effect.

Usually only the skin is anæsthetized and the effect is not lasting enough for a prolonged operation. The freezing and thawing of the tissues are somewhat painful and the vitality of the tissues is reduced according to the degree and time of exposure to the cold. Better methods of local anæsthesia have caused this to fall almost into disuse.

The Ether Spray is another method by which anæsthesia is secured, through a low temperature produced by the rapid evaporation of sulphuric ether. The ether should be applied by means of an instrument capable of throwing a fine and continuous rather than a coarse spray. A hand atomizer may be used, but a spray attached to a compressed air tank is preferred. If the field of operation is situated on an extremity which can be ligated, anæsthesia may be hastened and prolonged by cutting off the circulation of the part by a rubber band or by Esmarch's method of artificial ischæmia. Evaporation can be hastened by fanning. As in other cases where ether is employed all precaution should be taken to prevent the ether taking fire from a cautery, flame or other source of heat.

When the field of operation is prepared, the spray should be permitted to play upon it. The skin becomes red, then white. When thoroughly blanched and, bloodless, insensibility is complete; then operate.

This method is convenient. The materials are easily obtained. The action is rapid. There are none of the dangers coming from the use of a poisonous drug. Some surgeons prefer this method with Esmarch's constriction, to cocaine and all other methods of local anæsthesia.

The vitality of the tissues may be reduced by too long an application. The freezing and thawing are somewhat painful. The anæsthesia is not lasting, so that the method is only suited to slight operations.

Ethyl Chloride (C_2H_5Cl) operates on the same principle as the ether spray, but is more convenient. It is a clear, colorless liquid with a slight ethereal odor. It boils at 12.5 deg. C., 54 deg. F., and to this low boiling point its efficacy is due. It will produce a temperature of 35 deg. C., 31 deg. F., below zero. At ordinary temperatures it would instantly evaporate unless confined. This tendency to vaporize produces a pressure in the glass tubes in which it is put up, so that when they are opened a fine stream is driven out with some force, and on touching the skin the fluid immediately evaporates and rapidly extracts the heat from the parts. The best and most convenient preparation is that known as ethyl chloride Bengue, made in Paris and sold by all instrument dealers. It is put up in glass tubes holding thirty grammes, which is sufficient for fourteen or fifteen minor operations. The tubes are supplied with screw caps which fit over a capillary opening. This cap is removed and the nozzle of the tube held six to eight inches from the spot to be anæsthetized and on which the stream is directed. The parts become pink, red and then white and are covered with crystals of ice. The skin may be anæsthetized in half a minute and remains in that state for two minutes. As in other operations depending on vaporization, the process can be hastened by fanning or blowing and can be prolonged by any method which will retard or cut off the circulation of blood.

The writer has used the agent with much satisfaction in opening abscesses and other slight operations. It may be used in opening felons, enucleating small tumors, extracting foreign bodies, removal of ingrowing nails and in circumcision. Those who control the sale of the above mentioned preparation in America make the following statements concerning its use in dentistry:

"In dental surgery ethyl chloride Bengue has been used most successfully in all parts of Europe as an anæsthetic in the extraction of teeth, for obtunding sensitive dentine, extirpation of pulps, and for diagnosing peripheral from central neuralgias, etc., etc.

"In extracting teeth the jet should be directed to the dental nerves as near their origins as possible In front of the ear for the upper teeth, behind the angle of the inferior maxilla for the lower ones The spray should be applied for about a minute, but the anæsthesia thus produced is not so complete as when the jet is applied directly to the gums, and as this last method is devoid of danger its use is advised in all cases except those of the last molars, which are not easily reached by the spray.

"In operating on the gums it is advisable, before using the spray, to smear some vaseline over them, after having dried them first, and it is also as well to protect the other healthy teeth with a piece of linen cloth."

Ethyl chloride is also used in dentistry combined with cocaine. After the cocaine injection the gum is sprayed until a thick layer of white crystals is formed. The tooth may then be extracted without pain.

The advantages, disadvantages and limitations of this method are similar to those of the ether spray. It is very convenient and rapid in action, and is perhaps the best of the methods depending on cold for effect.

Cocaine Hydrochloras is the hydrochlorate of an alkaloid obtained from the leaves of erythroxylon coca. It occurs in almost colorless circular crystals or crystalline powder. Its solution in water has a bitter taste and produces on the tongue a tingling sensation followed by numbness.

This agent came into practical use in 1884, and now stands at the head of local anæsthetics. The crystals may be applied directly to the skin or mucous membrane. or in the form of an ointment Solutions are usually more serviceable and act well on the mucous surfaces, where it is more readily absorbed than on the skin Solutions for external use are of a strength of four, ten, and rarely fifteen or twenty per cent They may be painted on or applied by saturating surgical cotton and placing it in contact with the parts to be deprived of sensation. In this latter manner the writer has been enabled to repair a considerable laceration of the penis in a sensitive child

and to perform circumcision in babes without pain.
As a hypodermic injection nothing stronger than a one
per cent. solution is necessary and this must be used with
care. Ligation of an extremity prevents the entrance of
the drug into the general circulation. The writer has
amputated a finger, after ligating it with a rubber cord
and injecting freely the one per cent. solution, without
pain, the patient being an interested spectator as the
parts were severed by knife and bone forceps.

Absorption and injection were combined in the following case of circumcision of an adult by the writer: The
penis being ligated the foreskin was drawn upward and
away from the glans penis. The space thus created was
filled through the narrow preputial orifice with a ten per.
cent. solution of cocaine and secured like the mouth of a
bag by a rubber band around the extreme end of the foreskin. A one per cent. solution was injected into and under
the skin of the penis, and after waiting fifteen or twenty
minutes a painless operation was performed. Considerable quantities of a one per cent. solution may be used in
situations, as above. Much of the injected fluid escapes
from the incisions, and this escape of fluids should be encouraged. The removal of the constricting band may be
delayed and its final removal made gradually, so that any
fluid remaining in the tissues will be taken into the general circulation little by little and will be eliminated
nearly as fast as it enters.

Even with the use of a ligature disastrous effects have
come from a small quantity of a four per cent. solution
injected into a toe. Hence one should use all measures
possible to prevent absorption, and should use the smallest
possible quantity and the weakest effective solution of the
drug.

Drs. Hall and Halsted, of New York, and other investigators have shown that the injection of a solution of
cocaine into a nerve trunk causes a loss of sensation over
the entire area supplied by that nerve for about twenty-
five minutes. This method has been useful in some cases,
but it often fails, probably because of the anastomosis of
terminal nerve fibres. The same area being supplied
partly from one and partly from another trunk, if one
trunk is missed, sensation is only partially lost over the
area of distribution.

Cocaine is used in dental surgery both by absorption and

injection and in combination with ethyl chloride. For injection solutions of one to four per cent. are employed, but much weaker ones would probably be effective. Perhaps the solutions of Dr. Schleich which are given further on in this article would be efficient, and if so, should be used, as cocaine is especially apt to produce poisonous symptoms when used about the head, on account of its rapid entrance into the circulation. The needle of the syringe is inserted parallel to the tooth on either side, before and behind, from two to six punctures being made. The flat side of the needle point may be placed next the tooth, and the needle pushed between the tooth and surrounding tissues till it reaches the bottom of the socket, fluid being slowly forced out as it descends. By the use of ethyl chloride as mentioned above less cocaine is required for the extraction of teeth.

Cocaine has also been used in connection with electricity, though never extensively. The anode, previously dipped in a solution, is placed on the skin a certain distance from the cathode and a galvanic current of from two to four milliamperes turned on. The fluid is carried from one pole to the other, thus cocainizing and anæsthetizing the strip of skin between , .

So many cases of poisoning by the injection of cocaine solutions to the urethra have occurred that many surgeons have abandoned its use in this situation.

Dr W H. Dukeman in the N Y. Medical Journal gives a method of application which he claims is effective and free from danger He speaks as follows: "Two cubic centimetres (thirty-three minims) of a two per cent. solution is amply strong for the relief of pain in deep urethral operations, while in cases of internal urethrotomy of the distal end of the penile urethra not deeper than three inches, I use a four per cent. solution. In both cases the strength is ample. The solution should not remain in the deep urethra more than seven minutes at the utmost. Usually five minutes is enough, while in the distal penile portion it will require seven to ten minutes to completely anæsthetize the urethra It should be seen that the urethra is emptied of the cocaine solution by stripping it so there is no further or prolonged absorption Observing these rules and using weak solutions, I have never seen any alarming or poisoning symptoms from the use of cocaine."

Solutions of cocaine are not permanent, hence they

should be prepared in small quantities and used while fresh. If it is desired to preserve them, a small quantity of carbolic acid or other antiseptic should be added to the solution. Boiling destroys the properties of a cocaine solution. The anæsthetic effect is said to be increased by adding a small portion of sodium carbonate to the freshly prepared solution.

The intensely poisonous character of cocaine forbids its use in any considerable quantity in situations where it will enter the general circulation. Dr. Schleich, of Berlin, Germany, by his infiltration method, has recently overcome this obstacle to a degree and greatly enlarged the field of usefulness of the agent, at the same time diminishing its dangers. Of the three solutions, the one most employed by him has one part of cocaine to about one thousand parts of water.

Anæsthesia is produced by the injection of water alone into the skin. The effect is due to the pressure of the fluid upon the infiltrated tissues driving out the blood and compressing the nerve filaments, and is heightened by the low temperature of the fluid used. But the anæsthesia so produced is transitory and somewhat painful in application. These disadvantages are removed by adding a small proportion of cocaine, which prolongs the anæsthetic effect and is so diluted that a sufficient quantity of fluid to anæsthetize a large area can be injected and received into the general circulation without disaster. The formulæ for the three solutions used by Dr. Schleich are as follows:

	1—Strong.	2—Normal.	3—Weak.
Cocaine Hydrochlorate,	grs. 4	grs. 2	grs. 1-5
Morphine Hydrochlorate,	gr. ¼	gr. ¼	gr. 1-10
Sodium Chloride,	grs. 4	grs. 4	grs. 4
Distilled Water,	fl. oz. 4	fl. oz. 4	fl. oz. 4

Add to each solution three drops of a five per cent. carbolic solution to preserve it. The distilled water should be boiled and the salt heated before preparing the solution, to insure asepsis.

Solution 2 is used in most cases and two fluid ounces may be injected before reaching the maximum dose of one grain of cocaine. Solution 3 will frequently serve and should be used in cases where the operation is not so prolonged and extensive as to require, otherwise, the injection of fluid enough to contain the maximum dose. To get one grain of cocaine the patient must receive twenty fluid ounces of solution 3

When it is considered that this fluid is never all injected at once, and that much of it escapes with blood and other wound fluids, leaving a residue which is slowly absorbed and eliminated, it can be readily understood that the method is much safer and has a wider application than was ever possible with solutions of one per cent and upwards which were formerly employed in a limited field.

For the injection of these fluids the ordinary hypodermic syringe with fine and sharp needles is required. Curved needles are useful in some cases. Both syringe and needle should be boiled in water or alcohol and thoroughly disinfected.

When prepared, the point of the needle is buried in the skin deep enough to cover the opening and fluid is slowly pressed out till a spot about the size of a penny is infiltrated. The affected area becomes white, bloodless and elevated somewhat like the bite of an insect. Anywhere within the affected area the needle may be reinserted and advanced to the edge of the former infiltration and more fluid forced out into new territory. In this manner successive areas may be anæsthetized, covering more skin surface or going deeper into the tissues. Only the pain of the first puncture need be felt, and with sensitive patients this can be avoided by the preliminary use of the ethyl chloride spray for a moment, or by the application of a drop of carbolic solution or cocaine crystals. The pain of inserting a sharp needle is so slight as to seldom cause any complaint.

The operator must take care to inject the fluid into and not under the skin. If the needle is inserted through the skin before the fluid is expelled, the latter will not readily be anæsthetized. Later the fluid may be carried into the deeper structures if desired.

One should not attempt to begin the process in acutely inflamed and sensitive tissue, but in the sound tissue at one side, from which point a gradual advance can be made into, under or around the sensitive parts. It is usually best to cut off the nerve supply by carrying the fluid around or under such a sensitive point rather than directly into it. An acute abscess should be approached in this manner. If it is desired to anæsthetize the interior of the cavity, some of the contents should be permitted to escape first, otherwise the forcing of more fluid inside the abscess cavity will cause an increase of pressure on surrounding parts and lead to intense pain.

Some difficulties were met with by the writer in using this method. While injecting an acutely inflamed toe with ingrowing nail, great pain was caused. The toe was ligated with rubber cord and the skin distended with obstructed blood. Whenever any fluid was injected under the skin, the hydraulic pressure was transmitted to every part of the toe, including the inflamed and sensitive portions, causing intense pain.

The toe should have been rendered bloodless by elevation and the use of a bandage. The injection should then have been thoroughly applied to the sound tissues so as to cut off the nerve supply to the sensitive parts. Another method would have been to leave off the ligature till the toe was well anæsthetized and then ligate; or, if Schleich's fluid was used, the operation might proceed without any ligature; the absence of which would have relieved the hydraulic pressure.

In a deep operation the layers of tissue can be successively infiltrated and divided, or can all be anæsthetized before dividing, by pushing the needle deeper and deeper, continually forcing out fluid from its point till the periosteum is reached, which should also be infiltrated when necessary to sever bone.

The writer has found difficulty in applying this method in the removal of recurrent cancerous tumors of the breast, because the scar tissue left by the first operation was difficult to penetrate with the needle and could not be distended and infiltrated as in the case of normal tissue; hence sensation and pain in that vicinity was not lost completely, as was the case elsewhere.

This infiltration method can be employed in most minor operations, and has been carried by enthusiasts into the field properly belonging to general anæsthesia. Laparotomies, nephrectomies and amputations of the arm have been performed under it. Such operations as the removal of small tumors, opening abscesses or felons, opening the cavities of the body, operations for hemorrhoids, vericocele, hydrocele, injecting hernias, castration, opening of knee joint, opening of pleural cavity, strangulated hernia, tracheotomy, resection of rib, amputations of fingers and toes have been appropriately done under this method.

The advantages of the method are many. In the operation for strangulated hernia vomiting is usually present and the use of chloroform therefore attended with great danger This method of anæsthesia may be substituted and the danger of suffocation from ejected material avoided Operations can frequently be done in the office without assistance Patients who would refuse chloroform or ether will accept this method

The disadvantages are that much time may be consumed in infiltrating and reinfiltrating the tissues during operation. The use of a poisonous drug is always objectionable It is not always desirable to have the patient as a spectator Other objections have been indicated in the foregoing article

The infiltration method is now modified by some surgeons who substitute antipyrine and menthol for carbolic acid in Schleich's formulæ The morphine may also be dropped

There is great variation in regard to the amount of the drug likely to cause death Some persons seem particularly open to its effects while others recover from enormous doses The following rule is commonly agreed on by surgeons of experience Never use more than two-thirds of a grain on a mucous surface nor more than one-third of a grain hypodermically. Schleich's rule in his infiltration method permits the use of one grain as the maximum dose, but this is not all injected at one time and much of it escapes from the wound and never enters the circulation.

In every case the surgeon should take all the precautions enumerated in this article, and should use especial care with each new patient till certain that he has the average tolerance for the drug.

When beginning the use of the drug, the writer had a case of mild cocaine poisoning, but never has observed any since. A bullet was lodged against the scapula; more dissection was required than expected, and the solution was stronger than necessary Had Schleich's method been used a more extensive operation might have been done without any untoward effects In this case it was of distinct advantage to have the assistance of the patient, who could at any time place his finger over the location of the ball when the operator was unable to locate it. The symptoms produced by the drug were pallor, weak, rapid pulse; giddiness; general weakness and tremor. They passed in a short time without treatment.

In more severe cases syncope or delirium, with paralysis or fixation of the respiratory muscles, followed by death, may occur.

The indications for treatment are as follows: In urethral cases, the bladder and urethra should be emptied by catheter and washed out. In all cases the action of the kidneys should be encouraged, as the poison is eliminated by this channel. To this end plenty of fluid should be given. Stimulants of diffusive character may be used. Tr. lobelia compound or tr. myrrh compound by mouth, hypodermically or by rectum will be appropriate. Artificial respiration and inhalations of oxygen are also recommended.

Eucaine is a substance recently brought to notice, and while similar in many respects to cocaine, has some important advantages claimed for it. It is produced by chemical synthesis, and the formula being found to closely resemble that of cocaine, it was surmised that the properties of the drug would be similar, and such may be found to be the case. The drug is used in the same solutions, the same amounts and with the same precautions as cocaine. The intensity, duration and time of setting in of anæsthesia are similar to those of cocaine. The advantages lie in the following points: Eucaine is less poisonous. Animals given a certain dose of it survived, while similar animals died under the same amount of cocaine. Eucaine dilates the vessels locally, instead of contracting them, and decreases the frequency of the pulse instead of accelerating it. Eucaine solutions are permanent and can be sterilized by boiling for a long time, while cocaine will decompose if kept long or if boiled. The drug has been used more in dental than in general surgery, and has received very favorable mention, both in America and Europe. The writer is without experience with the drug.

Menthol —Dr. Tillman, of Germany, in his work on surgery, speaks of having good success with menthol dissolved in lanolin or olive oil. He uses a solution of ten to twenty per cent. hypodermically and sometimes combines it with the ether spray. A mixture of equal parts of lanolin and menthol is applied to the surface with good results. Menthol is not a poisonous drug and seems worthy of further trial and report. If effective, it should have the preference over cocaine. Certainly a non-poisonous anæsthetic is as desirable as a non-poisonous therapeutic agent. It has heretofore appeared to the writer that such an anæsthetic was not possible, because a drug which will strike down or suspend the function of the tissue elements, or a part of the nervous system, must necessarily be de-structive or poisonous If the conclusions and considerations in regard to ether and chloroform in the previous article devoted to general anæsthesia are correct, this position is erroneous, and we should continue to search and test until we find an efficient and non-poisonous local anæsthetic

ANÆSTHESIA IN OPHTHALMIC SURGERY

By E G ANTHONY. M. D.

Professor of Didactic and Clinical Opthalmology, Otology and Rhinology in the Physio-Medical College of Indiana, Indianapolis

Before local anæsthetics were used in ophthalmic surgery, the simpler operations were performed without the use of ether and chloroform. Many surgeons used those drugs only in severe cases and when it became necessary to open the eyeball, there was constant fear and anxiety since the strain from vomiting so frequently resulted dis-astrously to the eye In the last few years rapid advancement has been made in this department of ophthalmology. A better understanding of pathology and new methods of operating with improved instruments, together with the introduction of cocaine, has made the surgery of the eye a most interesting study.

General Anæsthesia:— Notwithstanding the fact that a large number of the operations on the eye can be performed while the tissues are under the influence of a local anæsthetic, the more severe ones which are necessarily prolonged, require general anæthesia. Plastic operations on the lids, tenotomy, enucleation of the eye ball, advancement of the ocular muscles and in many cases, iridectomy can be better performed when relaxation is quite complete from the influence of ether or chloroform. For young people and also older ones, when an operation can be quickly done, chloroform acts well If the individual be weakly and the operation is prolonged, ether does better. In all cases where a large corneal section is to be made, general anæsthesia is not advisable The vomiting which so frequently occurs is likely to destroy the eye by causing intraocular hemorrhage or an escape of the vitreous humor.

Local Anœsthesia:— Either the muriate or the hydrochlorate of cocaine may be used. The rapidity with which the drug acts when applied to the eye depends upon the strength of the solution. Anæsthesia generally lasts about ten minutes. The weaker the solution the slower and less lasting in its action.

When a solution of cocaine is dropped into the eye, a burning sensation is experienced for a few seconds. Then the palpebral fissure begins to appear wider than natural and the conjunctiva looks pale owing to a contraction of its vessels. The pupil soon gets large and when anæsthesia is thorough, mydriasis is complete. Some writers claim that a wider dilatation of the pupil can be produced by the use of cocaine than by any other mydriatic. A test of the various mydriatics will prove the truthfulness of this statement. The accommodation is only slightly impaired. In early life the degree of relaxation of the ciliary muscle produced by cocaine is not sufficient to enable one to adjust glasses accurately. But after forty years of age when the accommodation is naturally weak, and yet interferes with the correction of presbyopia, the drug may be used to advantage. At that age however, it must be used very cautiously. Glaucoma more frequently developes at that period of life. and if the pupil be dilated with cocaine, or any other mydriatic, a glaucomatous attack may be precipitated at once. Before applying the drug then, if the patient be elderly, carefully test the tension of the ball and be sure that all symptoms of glaucoma are absent.

Cataract:-- Operations are best performed under local anæsthesia. Three instillations of a two per cent. solution of cocaine at intervals of two minutes, will produce sufficient anæsthesia to render the making of the corneal section painless. If iridectomy is to be a step in the operation, when the iris is excised, there will be sharp pain unless the drug has been applied a sufficient length of time for it to pass through the cornea and thus anæsthetize the iris. A stronger solution than two per cent, does not act so well. It is more likely to reduce the tension of the ball and soften the cornea. These conditions predispose to collapse of the cornea after the cataractous lens is extracted.

Tenotomy, in cases of strabismus may be performed under local anæsthesia. When the patient is old enough and can bring his will power to bear, this method is preferred. He is conscious and when he makes an effort, can greatly assist the surgeon in controlling the movements of the ball.

Three or four instillations of a four per cent, solution of cocaine will produce anæsthesia of the conjunctiva. After the opening has been made through the conjunctiva and capsule of Tenon, and the conjunctiva freely separated from the sclera at the point of operation, two or three drops of a two per cent solution may be dropped into the wound thus coming in contact with the tendon and muscle This will greatly modify the pain but in no instance should the operator expect the operation to be painless. Traction on the muscle with the strabismus hook will cause pain deep in the orbit at the origin of the muscle where the cocaine can not be applied For this reason in most children under ten years of age, general anæsthesia from the inhalation of ether or chloroform is required The operation can then be performed easily with but little danger of injury to the eye from the patient's resistive efforts.

Enucleation of the eyeball has been performed by some surgeons after having thoroughly applied cocaine Four or five instillations of a four per cent. solution at intervals of two or three minutes anæsthetizes the conjunctiva A two per cent. solution is injected back of the ball by means of a specially devised syringe. After the conjunctiva has been separated from the ball, the two per cent. solution is dropped into the wound. Anæsthesia can not become so complete but that pain is caused by the operation especially where traction is made on the muscle by the hook, and the optic nerve put on a stretch preparatory to section.

I have never enucleated an eye under the influence of cocaine. It requires so much of the drug to produce the necessary anæsthesia, that there is danger of a toxic effect. General anæsthesia from ether or chloroform is preferred.

Iridectomy for optical purposes, may be performed under the influence of cocaine. If a prolonged application of a four per cent solution be made, it passes through the cornea and anæsthetizes the iris An evidence of such anæsthesia is complete mydriasis. Sometimes a drop of a two per cent solution may be injected into the anterior chamber but care must be taken to have the solution free from foreign matter Iridectomy for glaucoma requires general

anæsthesia. The mydriatic effect of cocaine is contra-indicated.

Local anæsthesia is sufficient for operations on the lachrymal passages. Preparatory to *slitting the canaliculus*, a
four per cent. solution of cocaine may be injected into the
tube. A pledget of cotton may also be saturated with the
solution and applied directly over the canal. Anæsthesia
is so complete that but slight pain if any is felt when the
canaliculus is slit. A *lachrymal abcess* may be lanced
after the application of a ten per cent. solution of cocaine
at the point of incision. Sometimes the crystals of cocaine
may be applied directly to the skin covering the abcess.
Stricture of the nasal duct may be incised with a canaliculus knife after the injection into the duct of two or
three drops of a two per cent. solution of cocaine. *Extirpation of the lachrymal gland* is rarely necessary. If
the operation is to be performed, general anæsthesia is required. *Abcess of the lachrymal gland* may be opened
after the application of a ten per cent. solution or of the
crystals of cocaine to the skin covering the gland.

Chalazion or meibomian cyst, requires local anæsthesia
when operated upon. If the cyst be internal, a crucial incision through the conjunctiva into the tumor is necessary.
The part may be previously anæsthetized by everting the
lid and applying a four per cent. solution of cocaine by
means of cotton. If the chalazion be external, the cocaine
crystals may be applied to the skin over the tumor and the
sac removed through an opening in the skin.

Hordeolum or sty, in the stage of suppuration, may be
incised under the influence of a four per cent solution of
cocaine. It is well to remember however, that cocaine has
but slight effect on the edges of the lids and if much anæsthesia is produces in these cases, the drug has to be applied
quiet persistingly.

The *cornea* is quite easily anæsthetized with cocaine.
This makes the drug quite useful in some cases. Ulcera
tion generally causes much sensitiveness to light Sometimes blepharospasm is so great as to prevent inspection of
the ball. Two or three instillations of a four per cent. solution of cocaine produces anæsthesia to such a degree
that the blepharospasm ceases. Then the cornea may be
inspected and whatever agent is indicated can be applied
directly to the ulcer. *Foreign bodies* in the eye may be
easily removed. When they are imbedded in the cornea,

they are very annoying. Under the influence of a 4 per cent solution of cocaine. they may be picked out with a corneal spud without pain. *Paracentesis* of the cornea for temporarily lowering the tension of the ball, for preventing perforation in cases of ulceration of the cornea; and for the removal of pus and turbid aqueous material, may be performed under the influence of cocaine When the actual cautery is to be applied to ulcers of the cornea, general anæsthesia must be produced by the use of ether or chloroform

Pterygium may be operated upon, either by excision, transplantation or ligation, under the influence of cocaine with but slight pain If the operation is prolonged, several instillations may be applied at intervals during its progress

Anæsthesia in the Surgery of the Ear.—Some operations on the ear, such as trephining the mastoid process, and removing tumors from the auricle, require general anæsthesia by the use of ether or chloroform. Others may be made under the influence of cocaine. Paracentesis of the membrana tympani, removal of fungus tissue and polypus tumors and incision of furuncles, may be performed under local anæsthesia. The anæsthetic effect of cocaine upon the drum-head is less marked than upon many other tissues This may be due to its structural arrangement, vascular and nerve supply.

Anæsthesia in the Surgery of the Nose and Throat — Some of the more severe operations on the nose and throat, such as curetting the vault of the pharynx for the removal of adenoid vegetations, require general anæsthesia This operation is only necessary in children, for as age advances the pharyngeal tonsil undergoes atrophy and finally disappears. Less severe operations may be made under the influence of cocaine

Hypertrophy of that portion of the nasal mucosa covering the anterior and posterior extremities of the turbinated bones, may be removed either by cauterization or by the use of the snare. In either case a four per cent. solution of cocaine may be applied. If the hypertrophy be anterior, a pledget of cotton may be saturated with the solution and placed in the nasal cavity between the hypertrophy and septum of the nose in such a way that the cocaine is held in contact with the part to be cauterized or removed. A better plan is to twist the cotton around the end of an applicator and apply in the same manner. Then

there is no danger of the patient drawing the cotton back
into the throat. If the hypertrophy be posterior, two or
three applications may be made back of the palate by
twisting cotton around the end of a curved applicator and
saturating with the cocaine solution. In such cases the
rhinoscopic mirror must be used and some dexterity is
required in bringing the drug in direct contact with the
point desired.

When applied in this way to these hypertrophic masses,
cocaine not only produces anæsthesia, but helps in diagnosis. The action of the drug is to contract the blood-vessels
and produce an artificial anæmia of the part to which it is
applied. If the tumefaction be due to an increased amount
of blood in the part, as is the case in acute coryza and
sometimes chronic rhinitis, it will disappear when under
the influence of cocaine. But if the swelling be due to
hypertrophy of the tissues, the change in the size of the
tumor will be very slight. This enables the surgeon to
decide as to the degree of hypertrophy and at the same
time form an opinion as to how much cauterization is
necessary or how much tissue is to be removed by the
snare.

Polypus tumors, both nasal and post-nasal, may be
removed by means of the snare without pain, after applying a four per cent. solution of cocaine at the point of
attachment. If they are to be removed by evulsion, some
pain will be felt even though the drug has been properly
applied. *Ecchondromata* and *exostoses* of the septum
and *deviation* of the nasal partition, may be operated
upon with but little pain under local anæsthesia.

When *amputation of the tonsils* is necessary, a four
per cent. solution should always be applied. When the
tonsiltome is used the operation may be done quickly. If
the snare be used, the process is slower and the pain
greater. This calls for as thorough anæsthesia as can be
produced.

- Manipulations within the *larynx* are quite easy since
the introduction of cocaine. Before this drug became
known, operations had to be performed in the midst of
gagging and retching. A four per cent. solution applied
to the mucosa of the larynx, so anæsthetizes the part and
prevents muscular spasm, that foreign bodies can be easily
grasped with forceps and removed. A stronger solution
must not be used too freely for there is danger of cocaine

poisoning. *Endolaryngeal* tumors may be cauterized after cocainization Nitrate of silver or chromic acid, if applied cautiously, are devoid of danger. In some cases it is almost impossible to make a laryngoscopic examination, owing to the sensitiveness of the throat and spasm of the muscles An application of a four per cent solution of cocaine to the soft palate and base of the tongue, relieves the spasm and enables the surgeon to proceed with the examination.

Eucaine Hydrochlorate.—This is a local anæsthetic recently introduced to the profession Ophthalmic surgeons who have experimented with it, claim that instead of producing ischæmia, as does cocaine, hyperæmia is developed This affects the entire conjunctival sac and lasts about thirty minutes after the first instillation The drug excites free lachrymation in some cases, but the pupil is not influeuced nor the accommodation impaired

When a solution is dropped into the eye, a burning sensation is experienced for a few seconds. This seems to be more persistent than that produced by cocaine. To avoid this unpleasant effect, it is recommended that a drop of a one per cent. solution be first instilled. This is not painful and soon produces slight anæsthesia Then a drop of a two per cent. solution may be applied. As a rule, two and one-half minutes later anæsthesia is quite complete and lasts from ten to eighteen minutes.

One objection to the use of the drug is its tendency to excite conjunctival hyperæmia. To counteract this action Dr Emile Berger combines cocaine with eucaine as follows

Cocaine Hydrochlorate
Eucaine Hydrochlorate   aa grs iii
Distilled Water, boiled   dr. v
M. Sig. Use as required.

The tendency of cocaine to contract the blood-vessels and produce ischæmia, neutralizes the eucaine, the action of which is to dilate them. Thus we are enabled to produce anæsthesia without exciting hyperæmia of the conjunctiva.

A solution of eucaine does not soften nor dry the cornea. This, together with the fact that it does not cause mydriasis nor impair the accommodation, gives a drug which merits the attention of ophthalmic surgeons, since there are cases requiring anæsthesia in which the mydriatic effect of cocaine is contra-indicated.

Otologists and rhinologists may use a five or ten per cent. solution of eucaine hydrochlorate to advantage.

SWERTIA CHIRATA.

Chirata. (Ophelia Chirata.)

This *herb* is an intensely bitter tonic, influencing the alvine mucous membrane and the liver, promoting appetite and assisting digestion. It is adapted to torpid and sluggish conditions and in small doses is useful in convalescence. Its bitter taste may be partly covered by orange peel.

SYMPHYTUM OFFICINALE.

Comfrey.

The *root* is a soothing, demulcent, gently stimulating tonic to the mucous membrane, especially of the respiratory organs. It allays irritation, increases expectoration and tones the bronchi. It is useful in colds and coughs, and is a valuable addition to cough syrups generally.

The fresh material bruised is a good application to bruises and irritable sores.

Symphytum, rheum, inula, aralia racemosa, symplocarpus and marrubium, of each oz. iss. Boil in one gallon of water. Strain, and boil the liquid to one quart. Add sugar 3 pounds and alcohol 2 ounces. This forms a nervine cough syrup.

SYMPLOCARPUS FŒTIDUS.

Skunk Cabbage.

The *roots and seeds* are a prompt, relaxing and stimulating, diffusive, antispasmodic nervine.

It is good in cases of irritable hysteria, a good addition to cough syrups for irritable coughs, valuable for the restlessness of fevers, in chorea, whooping cough and in general irritation of the system.

SYRINGA VULGARIS.

Lilac.

The *leaves* and *flowers* are a mild bitter stimulating and relaxing agent influencing the mucous membrane, and in hot infusion gives a good outward flow of the circulation.

It is useful in colds with feverishness and is a good addition to cough syrups.

Dr. F. G. Hoener says that the flowers are a specific in whooping cough.

TANACETUM VULGARE.

Tansy.

This *herb* is a bitter, diffusive stimulant. A hot infusion influences an outward flow of the circulation and a moderate free diaphoresis. It is used for the relief of colds and for the relief of the menstrual flow when obstructed by colds. It must not be used by the pregnant. The *oil* is even more dangerous to them.

A poultice of tansy will frequently relieve pruritus vulva.

TARAXACUM OFFICINALE.

Dandelion.   (T. Dens Leonis.)

This *root*, in order that you may experience its best effects, must be gathered during the Summer months after it has accomplished its growth and before the freezing weather of Autumn begins. Boiling impairs its strength. It is a mild, slow, relaxing and stimulating tonic hepatic, influencing slowly the liver, alvine canal and kidneys. It assists digestion and assimilation. It influences the liver in both its secreting and excreting functions. It gives very favorable results in cases of torpid liver, indigestion, constipation, jaundice and dropsy. It needs to be given in large doses and to be frequently repeated. It may be used as an infusion or a diluted fluid extract. It is one of the best of the milder agents. Its influence upon the kidneys is also very favorable.

In typhoid fever its influence is excellent and may be continued any length of time without wearying the system. As a gastric tonic it is very valuable in dyspepsia, and in irritation of the gastric and intestinal membrane, especially when there is torpor of the liver. The presence of zingiber renders it more diffusive.

The leaves form an admirable dish in Spring, served as greens. It is a medicinal food.

TEREBINTHINA.

Turpentine.

Pinus Palustris furnishes the common American or white turpentine.

Pinus Sylvestris furnishes the common European turpentine.

Abies Balsamea is that from which the Canada turpentine is obtained.

Pistacia Terebinthus furnishes Chian turpentine (Terebinthina Chia).

Abies Larix or Larix Europœa furnishes Venice turpentine.

Internally turpentine is volatile, pungent, strongly odorous, quite stimulating to the stomach and strongly influencing the kidneys. Inhaling it produces the same effects, and with some painters leads to jaundice. It is also used externally in liniments.

Oil Turpentine	oz. 50
Oil Origanum	oz. 3
Oil Lavender	oz. 1

Pix Liquida is the turpentine from the pinus sylvestris extracted from the wood burnt under ground and chemically changed by heat. The process by distillation yields pyroligneous acid and leaves the pitch. The oil of tar is a harsh stimulating and somewhat irritating agent.

Pine tar fumes are sometimes used for asthma.

Chian turpentine taken in doses of 2 to 5 grains three or four times a day is reported by several to have cured some cases of cancer of the uterus and of other parts.

It is also reported successful in chorea.

THEOBROMA COCOA.

Cocoa, Chocolate Nuts.

This tree grows in Mexico, the West Indies, and is much cultivated in Venezuela. The nuts have an oily, aromatic, slightly bitter taste and an agreeable odor. They contain a fixed oil which is expressed in considerable quantities and denominated cocoa butter. The shells have been occasionally used as a substitute for coffee. From the kernel a chocolate is prepared which is much used in the culinary art and as a drink at the morning meal.

THUJA OCCIDENTALIS.

Arbor Vitœ.   Northern States, Canada.

The *tops* are a stimulating alterant influencing the mucous membrane, the serous membrane and glandular structures. In hot infusion it influences the circulation and is somewhat emmenagogue and useful in amenorrhœa arising from congestion. Zingiber is a good addition in such cases. It is a rather unsafe agent for the pregnant to use.

In case of spermatorrhœa, nocturnal emissions and the results of masturbation this agent has proven successful.

In various cancerous conditions, especially scirrhous, condylomatous and epitheliomatous varieties, this agent may be used constitutionally and locally. If the os uteri be engaged and there be a tendency to hemorrhage use this freely. It controls capillary hemorrhage. A hot fomentation of the leaves forms a good application in cases of rheumatism

It may also be used for syphilis and applied to venereal warts and sores. It is a good wash for cancerous and gangrenous sores just before dressing them It cleanses and considerably deodorizes

It forms a good application to rectal fissures and it may be injected into hemorrhoids instead of carbolic acid.

It may be used in enuresis with benefit, and in an equal portion of water it may be injected in case of hydrocele into the tunica vaginalis testis.

As an alterative an infusion may be taken very freely.

It may be combined with vaseline and used as a salve.

Dr. C. B Riggs uses the following for eczema.

F E Thuja Oc.‾
"` Hamamelis Virg.   aa oz. ss

M. Sig. Apply frequently to the affected parts, having given first a thorough lobelia and composition emetic. Then follow with a brisk cathartic. Repeat these occasionally as demanded by the conditions present, and continuously use some good alterative compound.

THYMUS VULGARIS

Thyme.

This *herb* is a pleasant aromatic, diffusive, stimulating carminative In hot infusion it is diaphoretic and influences the periods when they have been obstructed from cold. It also aids in the relief of colds and colic.

This plant yields a volatile oil (oleum thymi) which is added to various liniments.

Thymol is from this oil, an antiseptic. It is in large crystals and has an agreeable odor. It is insoluble in water, but readily soluble in oil It is very pleasant to inhale in pulmonary troubles, and is a deodorant for the

sick-room and places not properly ventilated. Prof. J. E.
Roop uses thymenthol in the treatment of uterine troubles.

TOLUIFERA BALSAMUM.

Tolu.

This is a stimulating balsamic especially influencing
the respiratory mucous membrane and giving a warming
impression throughout. It is chiefly used as an adjuvant
in cough compounds and very favorably promotes expectoration.

TOXICOLOGY.

By H. A. HADLEY, M. D.

Professor of Toxicology and Demonstrator of Anatomy, in the Chicago
Physio-Medical College.

Chemistry, Toxicology and Medical Jurisprudence are so
intimately connected that it is impossible to separate
them completely; but as this article is prepared for the
practical benefit of the student and general practitioner of
medicine, toxicology is separated as far as I think to be
practical from Chemistry and Medical Jurisprudence.

To show how inseparable they are; suppose you are called
to treat a case of poisoning and whether death ensue or
not, the poison being administered by some one, other than
the one poisoned, with the intention of committing murder, or if the relatives and friends suspicion such has been
the case, it may become at once necessary to secure the
services of an expert chemist and jurist, (which as a rule
the student and general practitioner of medicine are not,)
in order to be able to bring out the points necessary to sustain a capital charge.

There is a place before this time is reached that the general practitioner will be surely called on to fill and he or she
can fill it whether they be expert Chemists or Jurists, or
not; but the more chemistry and possibly law one knows in
some cases will enable them to administer treatment with
a better understanding and more successfully. What follows is given with the intention of assisting the student
and general practitioner to better fill this place; and all
definitions are made as nearly as possible to conform with
the above ideas.

Toxicology is the branch of medical science that treats
of the nature of poisons, of their morbific effects, of their

antidotes, of their detection in the organs or tissues, and of the treatment at the time of poisoning

While the antidote will form part of the treatment, and a very important part in many cases, and in some no part, there is other treatment to be instituted, hence the latter clause of this definition

To define the substance that creates this branch of medical science, toxicology, is difficult; but for the purposes here intended, I submit the following

A poison is any substance that when taken into the system acts in a noxious manner, by means not mechanical, tending to cause death or serious detriment to health

According to this definition, it matters not by what avenue the poison gains access into the body its ultimate result will be the same. The stomach is the most common method; but the rectum, vagina, ear, nose, lungs, skin, cellular tissue by hypodermic injection, are all channels of entrance. The inhalation of poisonous vapors and subcutaneous injection with the hypodermic syringe act much more quickly than by any other means of introduction, because of their more rapid *absorption.*

Mode of action of poisons —In order that a poison may produce its full morbific effects on the system, it must be taken into the circulation and thus conveyed to all parts of the body, this is done by *absorption*

Corrosives produce local actions generally sufficient to cause death or serious damage to health.

Abundant proof that poisons are absorbed is had by detecting them in the different secretions and excretions of the body, the blood, the different viscera; as lungs liver, kidneys, brain etc Here is an important point in a toxicological examination, to find the poison in the absorbed state in these organs or in the secretions and excretions Rapidity of absorption is remarkable in many cases and is greatly influenced by many conditions, as the solubility of the poison, so long as the poison remains insoluble it can not be absorbed; but some substance insoluble in water are soluble in the fluids of the stomach and intestines. The nature of the surface to which it is applied is a most important factor; the great vascularity of the lungs accounts for the rapid absorption, by this channel of vapors already refered to Some animal poisons as the virus of glanders, syphilis and some others are said to undergo a change if taken into the stomach that renders them innocuous. In the stomach the absorption of poisons is most rapid if the organ be empty. Absorption through the cuticle is slow, but does take place by the application of ointments or washes made from corrosive sublimate, arsenic, opium and other poisons; if these should be applied to an abraded surface absorption will be much quicker.

After absorption into the blood, as the poison passes through the different organs, a portion of it is separated by these organs and then eliminated by the bile, urine, sweat, etc. Another portion is deposited in the organs and is said to be in about the following order as to quantity: the liver, spleen, kidneys, heart, lungs, brain, pancreas, muscles and bones. There is only a small portion of the poison circulating in the capillaries at any one time, yet there is good reason to believe that it is this small portion that proves noxious. Often that which remains in the stomach or other organs is harmless, but is liable to be reabsorbed into the circulation and become active.

In case of death it is a common mistake to attribute the cause of death to the amount of poison found in the stomach, when in fact it has no direct connection with the fatal result, this being caused by the absorbed portion only. Hence in the treatment of a case of poisoning it is important that elimination of the poison be complete.

Classification of Poisons —According to chemistry, are either organic or inorganic, the organic including vegetable poisons and some animal secretions, the inorganic including minerals, many acids and the alkalies.

The classification of most benefit is according to action. If the action of a poison is known the nature of the poison is known, and this is essential to be able to administer treatment intelligently.

According to action all poisons may be divided into two classes:

1. Irritants, which act by causing local irritation; including pure irritants not chemically destructive, as arsenic; and corrosives, which destroy tissue chemically, as mineral acids. The effects of irritants are nausea, vomiting, purging, pain in the abdomen, cramps in the stomach and other parts of the body; the matters vomited and purged being at times mixed with blood.

2. Neurotics, so named on account of their specific action on the nervous centres; these may be divided into narcotics, which cause little or no irritation, as opium;

and acronarcotics, which cause irritation and a neurotic effect also, as aconite The symptoms are altogether distinct from those of irritants, being drowsiness, dizziness, headache, delirium, stupor, coma, and sometimes convulsions and paralysis

A knowledge of the evidences of poisoning constitutes a very important part to the toxicologist, or those called upon to administer treatment in a case of poisoning, or one of suspected poisoning. These evidences comprise. (1) those derived from the symptoms, (2) those obtained from post-mortem appearances; (3) those afforded by chemical analysis, (4) circumstantial evidences; (5) sometimes those obtained by experiments on animals. Attention will be given here only to the first and second of these divisions, as they are the only two that the general practitioner is likely to use very much. the others requiring experts; as for the second, the investigator must be an expert anatomist and pathologist; for the third, an expert chemist; the fourth is best to be left to legal authorities; the fifth is rarely ever used and probably would need the combined efforts and testimonies of all those used in the preceding divisions.

While the evidences afforded by symptoms constitute a very important factor in the diagnosis of poisoning, they alone can never be sufficient to establish the fact, but often furnish a very strong presumption.

There are no characteristic symptoms of any poison; if this were the case there would be no need of a chemical analysis to decide the case To this there may be almost an exception in poisoning from the strong mineral acids and alkalies, the local caustic action being so apparent

As most poisons produce their effects very soon after administration, probably within one hour, some almost immediately, the first point to notice is the sudden occurrence of violent symptoms, especially in a perfectly healthy person soon after taking food or drink.

If poison be given, as it is in some cases, in small quantities and at intervals, the symptoms may come on so gradually that they may readily be mistaken for disease.

The physician should be very careful about mentioning a suspicion of criminal poisoning. if he has such, until he has thoroughly investigated the case by analysis, etc. A suspicion is strengthened if several persons are suddenly seized with the same severe symptoms after partaking of the same food or drink. Even here it might be that some disease, as cholera, especially if cholera be prevalent, would almost simultaneously attack several persons of the same family. Suppose that from two to five hours have elapsed since any food or drink have been taken, without any effect ensuing, any suspicious symptoms coming up are probably due to some other cause than poisoning. The time of the occurrence of symptoms, in relation to any particular meal or partaking of any drinks, is a fact of especial importance in forming an opinion when poisoning is suspicioned.

From what has been said about the symptoms of poisoning it will be observed that it will be difficult to distinguish at times between the symptoms of disease and symptoms of poisoning. The disorders whose symptoms most simulate irritant poisoning are cholera morbus, malignant cholera, gastro-enteritis, peritonitis, ulceration of the stomach and bowels, and strangulated hernia.

Those most resembling neurotic poisoning are apoplexy, epilepsy, inflammation of the brain, tetanus and certain heart diseases. A knowledge of the above facts should put the physician upon his guard against too hastily deciding that a case is poisoning from the symptoms alone, or that the symptoms are due to some disease, when in fact they may be the result of poisoning.

Irritants.—In the consideration of poisons separately, those of most importance only will be given and treated of as briefly as will be consistent with the scope of this article. (The means used to detect the poisons in the organs or tissues being omitted. For these tests reference to some standard chemical text-book is advised.) *Irritants* being considered first, and of this class first *pure irritants.*

Arsenic.—When speaking of poisoning from arsenic, arsenious oxide or white arsenic is always meant, unless otherwise designated. This form is sometimes improperly called arsenious acid, on account of its power to combine with alkalies; the acid reaction is very slight.

Arsenic is one of the most important of all the poisons, on account of its being easily procured and easily administered without being detected. Poisoning often occurs by accident from some of the preparations in common use, as "rough on rats," anilin red, etc.; also from some wall papers, the coloring matter containing arsenic; this is especially dangerous should there be several layers of cheap paper on a wall, which is often the case, in a damp basement. Arsenic is slightly soluble in cold water, and a little more freely so in boiling water. Its solubility is much increased by the addition of an acid or alkali. It is easily held in suspension in tea, coffee, milk or soups, and can readily be mixed with foods without detection.

In large amounts it is said to have a sweetish rough taste, but in small amounts is likely not to be appreciable to the taste.

Symptoms.—The rapidity with which these occur depends somewhat on the form in which the poison is taken and the condition of the person taking the poison; the most favorable conditions are, the poison to be in solution and taken on an empty stomach.

As a rule the symptoms will occur in from half an hour to one hour. There will be, first, faintness, with a constricted feeling of the throat, thirst, nausea, and a burning pain in the stomach increased by pressure; vomiting soon follows, the matter being variously colored but rarely streaked with blood; purging with tenesmus comes on; cramps in the legs are apt to follow, with great depression, cold sweat, intense thirst, and feeble rapid pulse.

This has been mistaken for a severe case of cholera morbus.

The symptoms are usually continuous, although occasionally there are remissions or even intermissions.

Coma, paralysis and convulsions may supervene death. If the patient recovers from the present attack he may suffer for a long time from indigestion, partial paralysis or epilepsy. Symptoms of chronic poisoning usually result from small doses frequently taken, exposure to arsenical vapors, or inhalation of arsenical dust from wall papers. The eyes and mucous membrane of the nose become inflamed and watery, great gastric distress with frequent nausea and vomiting, diarrhœa, headache, jaundiced skin, an eczematous eruption, local paralysis, general emaciation, falling out of the hair, excoriation of mouth and tongue, and death may occur from exhaustion. These symptoms are frequently very obscure and the real cause may not be discovered.

Two grains may be considered the minimum fatal dose for the adult; smaller quantities have produced alarming symptoms, and recoveries have taken place after one or two ounces have been taken.

If death takes place from acute poisoning, it will usually be within twenty-four hours.

Post-Mortem Appearances.—The irritant character of the poison is well shown by the mucous lining of the stomach being highly inflamed, sometimes so uniformly as to present the appearance of red velvet; in other cases there will be patches of dark redness; sometimes there will be a thickened and corrugated condition of the membrane, and frequently white spots of arsenious oxide are found between the rugæ, and when quite a long interval has elapsed before the examination, yellow stains may be found as the result of decomposition into the yellow sulphide. Whether the arsenic has been administered by the stomach, through the lungs, by ointments or lotions, or any other source, the same effect is produced on the stomach, showing that arsenic has a specific action on the stomach, the degree of intensity usually varying in accordance with the amount taken; time elapsed before examination, condition of the patient, etc. This same condition extends to the intestines, only in a less degree.

Treatment.—If vomiting does not exist from the effect of the poison an emetic should be given at once. Myrica compound and lobelia taken in large amounts of warm demulcent drinks; oil and lime water equal parts, or hot greasy water at intervals; any of these are good. If vomiting exists, it should be encouraged by the above means, afterwards giving a large dose of castor oil to thoroughly evacuate the bowels.

If a stomach pump is at hand it will be useful in removing the unabsorbed poison. If the patient is seen soon after taking the poison the above means vigorously applied will probably save the patient, but if not seen early, death is very likely to occur.

After being satisfied that the unabsorbed poison has been removed, a soothing yet sustaining course of treatment will need to be employed, and for a while at least it will be best to administer this mostly by the rectum.

Antimony.—The only preparation of antimony of much toxicological importance is tartar emetic (antimonii et patassæ tartras). This is in the form of large colorless crystals, or in white powder. Poisoning is most likely to occur by accident, as the agent is not certain enough in its effects to warrant its use by the murderer or felo de se.

Symptoms.—A harsh metallic taste is first experienced,

soon followed by nausea and violent vomiting which continues sometimes after the poison has all been ejected, on account of the local irritation in the stomach. There is great thirst, constriction of the throat, burning pain in the stomach and abdomen, purging often violent; sometimes blood is found in both discharges from the bowels and stomach; cramps in the extremities, a feeble rapid pulse, profuse perspiration, with a tendency to syncope. The urine is generally increased in quantity and voided with pain.

Occasionally, if the patient survives three or four days, there is a pustular eruption over the body, similar to that produced by the external application of ointments containing antimony.

A slight corrosive action is sometimes manifested by aphthous ulcerations of the tongue and inside of the mouth.

Besides acting as an irritant to the gastro-intestinal tract it exerts a depressant effect upon the heart.

Fatal Dose.—This has not been determined very accurately and cannot be on account of the emetic properties of the agent; two grains have produced fatal effects, while as much as one ounce has failed to destroy life; in such cases vomiting occurs so quickly that the poison is removed before effects are produced sufficient to cause death. Probably fifteen to forty grains may be considered a minimum fatal dose for an adult.

Fatal Period.—This is also uncertain; it may be in a few hours, or it may be in several days.

Chronic Poisoning.—This occurs by giving small doses at intervals and has occurred several times. The main symptoms being great nausea with vomiting, diarrhœa, often followed by constipation, frequent feeble pulse, loss of appetite, emaciation, difficult breathing, coldness of the skin with clammy perspiration, increased urination, and finally death from complete exhaustion.

Post-Mortem Appearances.—The lining membrane of the stomach and bowels is deeply reddened, softened and covered with a blackish, thick, viscid secretion; the contents of the stomach is of a dark brownish color, sometimes streaked with blood. The throat and esophagus, stomach and intestines also sometimes exhibit aphthous looking spots. The brain and its membranes have been found congested and the lungs are generally congested.

Treatment.—Vomiting should be promoted with warm mucilaginous drinks; also give infusions of some vegetable astringents, as tannic acid, myrica, oak bark, green tea, which produces an insoluble tannate of antimony in water, and thus suspends the operation of the poison; but this is easily soluble in vegetable acids and must be removed by emetics or the stomach pump. It is stated that the usefulness of these antidotes is denied by some. The after treatment must meet the irritated and depressed condition by being soothing and stimulating, and can probably be best given in a vehicle of a mucilaginous character and partly, at least, by the rectum.

Mercuric Chloride (Corrosive Sublimate).—This occurs either in heavy crystalline masses or white powder; is soluble in about thirteen parts cold, or three of boiling water. Alcohol and ether dissolve it more freely, and ether has the power of extracting it from its aqueous solution.

Symptoms.—These usually come on immediately after taking the poison. There is a very strong acrid, metallic taste, often described as a coppery taste, followed by a sense of heat and choking in the throat, which soon develops into a fierce burning pain from the mouth to the stomach. There is nausea with vomiting of a stringy white mucous, often streaked with blood; usually pain in the abdomen, which is also swollen; purging which is sometimes streaked with blood and of a mucous character, accompanied with tenesmus. The pulse is small, feeble and irregular, becoming scarcely perceptible if the symptoms progress. Tongue white and shriveled; skin cold and clammy; respiration difficult; intense thirst; urine scanty or suppressed; salivation may occur, but is not a constant symptom. The external application of the poison will produce the same symptoms as when swallowed

Chronic Poisoning.—This usually comes from small doses taken at intervals. There is loss of appetite, colicky pains, foetid breath, soreness of the gums, increase of salivary secretion, diarrhœa, weakness and emaciation.

Salivation nearly always occurs from chronic poisoning; but it must not be concluded because there is salivation that poisoning from corrosive sublimate exists, for many other drugs will cause the same symptom. A chemical examination of the saliva for mercury will decide this.

Fatal Dose.—Three grains have proved fatal, and recovery has occurred when an ounce has been taken. The circumstances under which it was taken have been such as to cause these varied results and make it impossible to arrive at any definite conclusions as to the size of the fatal dose.

Fatal Period.—This also varies much, but will probably be found to occur in the majority of cases in from one to five days.

Post-Mortem Appearances.—These are usually confined to the alimentary tract; the mouth, throat and esophagus are often softened and of a white or grayish color. The intestines often exhibit the same appearance.

Treatment.—Promote vomiting by the use of warm water in large amounts, at the same time giving albumen as found in eggs, the whites being best. In the absence of eggs, glutin from wheat flour in the form of a paste may be freely given. Milk in a decoction of linseed and warm water has proven very beneficial. While albumen converts the drug into an insoluble albuminate, the object sought is to get it all removed from the stomach.

Oxalic Acid is in the form of colorless, odorless crystals, very much like epsom salt, and is a very powerful poison. Poisoning usually takes place by accident or with suicidal intention.

Symptoms.—These differ very much: in some cases where a large amount—from half to one ounce of the crystals dissolved in water—has been taken, death has taken place so quickly that there was no chance for the symptoms to be observed by a physician. There is an intensely sour taste, followed by a burning sensation from the mouth to the stomach; violent pain in the abdomen, increased by pressure; constriction of the throat almost to suffocation; vomiting of greenish-brown or black matter. If the patient lives, purging of a similar character sets in. Following these symptoms there is a rapid feeble pulse, hurried respiration, intense thirst, cramps and numbness of the extremities, general prostration, delirium and convulsions.

This drug, besides being an irritant proper, in large doses exerts decided corrosive effects, and under all circumstances produces a decided effect on the nervous system and a depressant action on the heart. If much diluted the symptoms do not occur so quickly and are not of such a severe character.

Fatal Dose.—Half an ounce to an ounce may be considered a fatal dose for an adult, although much less has proved fatal; and recovery has taken place when larger amounts have been used.

Fatal Period.—This depends very much on the size and concentration of the dose; probably the majority of cases prove fatal in one hour. It is reported that death has ensued in three minutes, and often in ten minutes.

Post-Mortem Appearances.—The mucous membrane of the mouth, throat and esophagus are usually white, shriveled and easily removed; it may be covered with the dark-brownish matter from the stomach. The stomach, which is somewhat contracted, contains an intensely acid, brown, gelatinous fluid.

If death has taken place rapidly, or if it has been delayed, these appearances are liable to some variation. The intestines will probably not show much change, unless death has been delayed, and then only of an inflamed character.

Treatment.—This must be prompt. It is not best to use much water by itself, as it will aid in the further absorption of the poison; but chalk and magnesia should be mixed with it, or better with milk; these act as antidotes. Scrapings from whitewashed ceilings are good, also limewater and oil. The alkalies, potash and soda, and their carbonates, should not be administered, as they produce compounds, with the acid, more poisonous than the acid.

Corrosive Irritants.—If this class of agents be given in a much diluted form the corrosive properties are generally lost. This then would seem to be only a difference of *degree* rather than of *kind*, between *pure* and *corrosive* irritants; but if those agents already mentioned are administered in either large or small, diluted or undiluted doses, the action is never corrosive but purely irritant, with the exceptions mentioned; hence the division of irritants.

Carbolic Acid (Phenic Acid, Phenol) is a product of distillation of coal-tar. When pure it is in white crystals, and if exposed to light for some time acquires a reddish tinge.

It is soluble in water, but more so in alcohol, ether or glycerol. It has a peculiar creosote-like odor, and is sometimes called coal-tar creosote. If taken in an undiluted state it is a very energetic corrosive, and also produces neurotic effects. Poisoning from this acid is of common occurrence, being generally by accident, or with suicidal intention.

Symptoms —There is intense burning pain in the mouth, throat and stomach; pupils contracted; conjunctiva insensible to the touch; skin cold and clammy; pulse weak and irregular; respiration labored and finally becoming stertorous; vomiting of a frothy mucous sometimes occurs; the mouth is white, and often hardened from the caustic action Coma usually precedes death. The urine has been shown often to be of an olive-green color. Many of these symptoms have been produced by the external application, especially to denuded surfaces Death has occurred within ten minutes after swallowing the acid, but usually will be after an hour or more.

The amount taken, from which death has occurred, has been from half an ounce to an ounce; but a much less quantity would surely prove fatal; dangerous symptoms have occurred from a few drops or grains

Post-Mortem Appearances —The mouth and esophagus are usually white, soft and corroded; but may be hardened and wrinkled The stomach has been found in the same condition, the odor of carbolic acid will be detected in the stomach and even in other viscera. The lungs are usually engorged with blood; the left ventricle is usually contracted, the right flaccid The blood is uniformly dark colored and fluid

Treatment.—Promote vomiting by using warm demulcent drinks with olive oil and castor oil A solution of soap may also be given. Slaked lime with three times its weight of sugar, rubbed together with a little water, or sodium sulphate may be given as antidotes. Never use the stomach pump To avoid collapse, stimulants need to be given.

The Mineral Acids —Sulphuric, nitric and hydrochloric produce effects very similar, and the treatment that answers for one will answer alike for all, and may be considered at the same time, by mentioning a few differences in the physical properties, and some points that may enable a differentiation to be made, without chemical analysis, should it be known that one of these acids had been used and not positively which one

Sulphuric Acid is a heavy, oily liquid, colorless when pure, but as generally seen has a light brownish color If any of the acid gets on the lips, fingers or clothes, the color is changed to red, and afterwards becomes brownish.

By applying ammonia, if the stain is not of too long standing, the original color will be restored.

Nitric Acid is a fuming liquid, colorless when pure, but as found in commerce is generally of a light orange color. If this acid comes in contact with the clothes or skin, they are changed very quickly to a yellow color, and if ammonia be applied to these spots the original color will *not* be restored.

Hydrochloric Acid when pure is a colorless gas, the liquid being formed by passing the gas into water. This solution is usually of a light yellowish color

Applied to dark cloth or the skin, the color is changed to a bright red and will be restored by ammonia. After some days the color of the cloth will be reddish brown.

Poisoning has occurred most frequently from sulphuric and nitric acid, and nearly always from accident or suicidal intentions.

Symptoms.—These are manifested immediately after the acid is swallowed, by a burning in the mouth and throat, with intense pain in the stomach, attended with constant vomiting of a brownish or blackish matter, often mixed with blood and detached shreds of mucous membrane.

The ejected matters are very acid and if they should come in contact with marble will cause effervescence. Thirst is intense. The pulse is small and weak, the skin cold and clammy, respiration difficult, countenance expressive of great anxiety and suffering; the mouth is excoriated, the lips stained and shriveled; if the acid should be poured far back in the throat, the mouth and lips may escape the corrosive action.

Death takes place sometimes without the acid reaching the stomach; here the force is spent on the glottis and death occurs very quickly by suffocation.

The period of death varies from a few hours to weeks or months.

The mental faculties usually remain clear until near death.

The *fatal dose* is very much dependent on whether the stomach be full or empty, or whether the acid be full strength or diluted. If the stomach is full of food, the acid will become mixed with the food and the effect will be exerted on the food, to the saving of the living structures. The amounts, as near as could be determined, that have proven fatal, have been from one dram up, for an adult.

Post-Mortem Appearances.—The mucous membrane of the mouth and tongue are shriveled and eroded; the color may be brownish. yellowish or whitish; generally yellowish in the case of nitric acid The mucous membrane of the esophagus is corroded and easily detached in long shreds.

The stomach is generally contracted, often perforated and containing a dark thickened fluid, sometimes of a yellowish appearance

The intestines are likely to be inflamed, unless death has taken place very quickly. If the contents of the stomach have escaped, through perforation, into the abdominal cavity, the peritoneum will be much inflamed, and dark effused blood will also be found.

Treatment —This must be administered promptly to be of any benefit, especially if undiluted acid has been taken on an empty stomach, A solution of baking soda is probably the best antidote. some objections are raised to alkaline carbonates because C O² is set free and will likely distend the stomach, this is of minor importance compared with the destructiveness of the acid.

Magnesia and chalk-in water are good, a solution of soap, which is always easily obtained, may be used with benefit, if flaxseed tea, barley water or oil can be procured to administer these remedies in, it will also be of benefit. The stomach pump should never be used

Alkalies —Ammonium Hydrate is the only alkali that will receive attention here Potassium and Sodium Hydrate are less powerful than ammonia and the treatment employed for poisoning is the same in each case as the effects are practically the same Ammonia is a gas, it is very soluble in water, and this solution forms the ammonium hydrate, (aqua ammonia) or as usually termed, ammonia of common use The effects on the tissues are similar to those produced by ·the mineral acids, being very caustic in the concentrated form. Poisoning usually occurs by accident; the incautious use of the vapor to resuscitate those in a state of syncope has proven fatal

Symptoms:—In the concentrated form, ammonia causes an acrid nauseous taste, followed by a burning sensation from the mouth to the stomach: severe abdominal pain, increased by pressure; vomiting of mucous matters, streaked with blood; purging, with tenesmus; difficult swallowing, hoarseness and coughing. The pulse is quick and feeble the countenance anxious; respiration rapid and difficult. Death may ensue in a few hours, or not for several months; if postponed for several months, the fatal result is generally due to some secondary cause, as constriction of the esophagus or pylorus, causing starvation.

Fatal Dose:— As with the acids it is difficult to determine this, it probably depends more upon the degree of concentration than upon the amount swallowed. Two drachms of strong ammonia have proven fatal, and recovery has taken place from larger amounts.

Post-Mortem Appearances:— The lining membrane of the mouth, throat and stomach are in a corroded and softened condition. The mucous membrane of the stomach is often blackened from effused blood and may be entirely destroyed.

The larynx and bronchi are very apt to be inflamed.

Treatment:— Diluted vinegar or lemon juice should be given freely at once, followed by olive oil, milk, barley-water, gruel or albumen.

After the poison is neutralized, if collapse occurs, give stimulation by the rectum.

Never use the stomach pump.

Neurotics.—Narcotics.—Opium is a milky exudation from the unripe capsules of the poppy (*papaver somiferum*) rendered concrete and dark colored by exposure to air. The different preparations give rise to almost as many cases of poisoning as all other poisons together, and recoveries are more frequent from this kind of poisoning.

The only important poisonous properties, from a medico-legal view, are due to the alkaloid, morphin, with *meconic acid.*

Opium is not generally used for poisoning, but usually some of its preparations; probably the most common being tincture of opium (*laudanum*) and morphin. It is well to remember that, especially in large cities, many cases of poisoning of children occur from "soothing syrups" containing some preparation of opium; also that laudanum as procured from the drug stores is not of uniform strength.

Symptoms.—If the dose is large, but not so large as to be fatal, there will be first general excitement shown by increased fullness and frequency of the pulse, flushed face, brilliancy of the eyes, and increased activity of the brain.

This is soon followed by calm repose and profound sleep. As the amount of opium is increased this stage is shortened and the more soporific effects manifest themselves sooner. They consist in giddiness, drowsiness, strong tendency to sleep, stupor, which finally ends in profound coma, the person lying motionless with eyes closed as if in a sound sleep. In this stage, before coma, the patient may be aroused by a loud noise, but will speedily relapse into stupor. When the stage of coma supervenes it will probably be impossible to arouse them; the pulse will become weak, respiration slow and stertorous; skin warm and bathed in perspiration, finally cold and clammy; countenance pale and ghastly.

The pupils are usually contracted, and insensible to light; this symptom, together with those already given, is considered diagnostic of opium poisoning.

Sometimes there is vomiting, and if this should occur before stupor sets in, will give great hope of recovery. Convulsions sometimes occur before death; these are more commonly met with in children. The symptoms will usually commence in from half an hour to an hour. If a full dose in a liquid form is taken on an empty stomach, the effects will appear in a few minutes; and if taken in a solid form on a full stomach, the effects may not appear for four or five hours. It is said that intoxication tends to postpone the appearance of the symptoms. Sometimes there will be a partial remission of the symptoms, and the patient gives signs of recovery; but a recurrence follows which terminates in death.

Fatal Dose. —This varies considerably, the circumstances under which it is taken influencing this to a greater or less degree. Four or five grains may be regarded as the minimum fatal dose for an adult, and probably two drams of the tincture.

Recoveries have taken place from twenty grains of opium and one ounce of the tincture. The confirmed opium eater is not taken into account here.

Children are peculiarly susceptible to the effects of this poison; in very young infants death has resulted from two drops of laudanum, and they may become narcotized by the milk of a nurse who has taken opium.

Fatal Period. —The average duration of a fatal case is from six to twelve hours; the extremes being three-quarters of an hour for the shortest, and probably fifty-six hours for the longest period.

Post-Mortem Appearances.—These are neither certain nor characteristic. The vessels of the brain are usually congested; sometimes the lungs are congested. The blood is generally fluid. Upon opening the body the odor of opium may be detected.

Treatment.—The first object to be accomplished is to remove the poison from the stomach; the best means of doing this is by the stomach pump. The stomach should be washed out thoroughly; this prevents a further absorption of the poison. If a stomach pump is not to be had, emetics must be resorted to. Give freely of warm mustard water, or lobelia compound with serpentaria. If the patient cannot or will not swallow (which is sometimes the case), lose no time in giving the emetic by enema. If the patient has lapsed into the lethargic state, shocks of electricity to the head and spine are very beneficial to assist in rousing them; slapping the palms of the hands, soles of the feet, and the back, are also very successful. A very common and useful way of keeping an adult from lapsing entirely into the lethargic state is by having them walk constantly between two attendants; also by dashing cold water over the face and chest. In the case of an infant, one of the best ways is to plunge them into warm water and then swing them through the cool air. All means employed must be persisted in vigorously.

Hydrocyanic Acid (Prussic Acid).—This is one of the most unerring and rapidly fatal poisons known.

The pure acid is not likely to be met with out of the laboratory; there are two varieties which are frequently the cause of death, and are simply solutions of the pure acid in water: (1) The official acid should be two per cent.: and (2) Scheele's acid about five per cent; these are extremely liable to vary in strength. This acid may be obtained from many plants, as the kernels of the peach, apricot, plum and cherry, pips of apples, leaves of the peach, and cherry-laurel, and from bitter almonds. Prussic acid *does not pre exist* in these vegetable substances, but is the product of chemical action. This acid is a colorless, limpid liquid, very volatile, and has the odor of bitter almonds. The vapor of the anhydrous acid if inhaled will cause death very quickly, and even the dilute will cause serious symptoms. The dilute acid is also colorless and retains the odor of bitter almonds.

Symptoms —These will vary some with the size of the dose. When a large dose (half an ounce to an ounce) of the diluted acid is taken, the symptoms may appear during the act of swallowing, or in a few seconds thereafter, and it is rare that their appearance is delayed longer than one or two minutes. They have been described (and even death from the pure acid) as "lightning like."

There is immediate loss of muscular power; the patient will fall and becomes insensible; respiration is hurried and gasping, later becoming slower and sobbing, or convulsive. The pulse is imperceptible; the eyes protruding, glistening, pupils dilated and insensible to light. The jaws are fixed; there is frothing at the mouth; skin cold and clammy; involuntary evacuations of the bladder and bowels may occur; death sometimes takes place in convulsions, or, may be preceded by coma, with stertorous breathing. This last symptom may easily lead to a mistaken diagnosis for apoplexy.

Fatal Dose.—The minimum fatal quantity of the official acid may be taken to be about fifty minims, or twenty minims of Scheele's acid. This is equal to about nine-tenths of a grain of pure acid, from which death has occurred.—Recovery has taken place from one dram of Scheele's acid, equivalent to 2.4 grains of anhydrous acid.

Fatal Period.—Death occurs almost instantly from the anhydrous acid, and varies when the solutions are taken, according to the size of the dose; probably from two minutes to half an hour will include nearly all cases. One or two cases have lived for an hour; but if the patient survives for an hour there is much hope for recovery.

Post-Mortem Appearances —The skin is usually livid, but may be pale; the lips blue; jaws set, with froth around the mouth, sometimes bloody; the eyes are often glistening and staring, with the pupils dilated.

The blood is dark colored and fluid; the lungs, liver, spleen and kidneys are congested; the stomach is usually natural, but the mucous membrane at the cardiac extremity may be reddened. The presence of the peculiar odor of the acid is very conclusive evidence that prussic acid has been taken. It may be noticed in recent cases even before the body is opened, and will be very noticeable upon opening the abdomen, thorax and even the brain; and especially so when the stomach is opened. If the body has lain for some time exposed, owing to the acid being so volatile the odor may have entirely disappeared, or it may be concealed by other odors.

In cases of suicide the vessel from which the poison was taken will nearly always be found close by.

Treatment.—In most cases treatment is of no avail, but a trial should always be made, if the patient is still alive when first seen. Dashing cold water over the face and chest, and letting it fall on the spine from a few feet, have proven successful in a few cases; inhalation of ammonia at the same time is also beneficial. If the power of swallowing is not lost (which usually is, however), large doses of lobelia compound will be of service. This may be given by the rectum also.

Acro-Narcotics —Aconite. From *Aconitum Napellus* (Monk's-hood or Wolf's-bane).—This agent in the form of a tincture is very often found in the household, and used as a remedy to "break up" fevers. There is considerable variation in the strength of different specimens, and what might be considered a "safe" dose of one preparation may not be so of another preparation The root has been mistaken for horseradish.

On account of these facts, accidental poisoning has often occurred from this drug, and if poisoning does occur it is nearly always by accident or with suicidal intentions. The poisonous property is due to the alkaloid *aconitin.*

Symptoms.—These usually appear in a few minutes to an hour. There is dryness of the throat first, accompanied with tingling, numbness, and a burning sensation of the lips, tongue and throat; pain in the abdomen, with nausea and vomiting. The tingling and numbness extend to all parts of the body; there is loss of power to walk, and sometimes the patient is paralyzed, but retains consciousness. There is vertigo, dimness of vision, ringing in the ears, sometimes deafness, frothing at the mouth, a sense of constriction in the throat; a peculiar weight and enlargement of different parts of the body is often complained of, and especially of the face and ears. The pulse becomes slow and feeble, breathing difficult, skin cold and clammy, pupils dilated, and features blanched.

The mental faculties are usually retained until the last; there is sometimes delirium and convulsions. Death is generally sudden and may occur from shock, asphyxia or syncope

Fatal Dose.—This is undetermined owing to the variation in the strength of different preparations Deaths have occurred from probably not more than one-half a dram, and serious symptoms produced from five or six drops of the stronger preparations Aconitin the alkaloid is extremely poisonous, and one-fiftieth of a grain has produced very alarming conditions, and one-tenth of a grain may be considered as a fatal dose. This preparation is often inert

Fatal Period —Death will generally occur in one or two hours, and in most cases within four hours; and if prolonged beyond this time the chances of recovery may be considered more favorable. After death general congestion of the venous system, and especially of the brain and lungs will be noticed

Treatment.—The stomach should be emptied at once, the stomach pump being the most suitable means by which to accomplish this; but in the absence of this means a quick, thorough, stimulating and astringing emetic must be resorted to For this, large doses of lobelia compound, with myrica compound and myrica or tannin are very reliable. Myrica compound (Thomson's) will answer with the lobelia compound

In case of asphyxiation from paralysis of the respiratory muscles, artificial respiration will be beneficial If some time has elapsed since the poison was taken, and it is probable that most of it is absorbed, even if vomiting has occurred a very stimulating emetic will still be of service.

Nux Vomica is obtained from the seed of the *strychnos nux vomica*, and is a very important poison The smallest fatal dose of powder is probably about thirty grains (this is about the weight of one seed) and of the alcoholic extract three grains Nux vomica contains two alkaloids, *strychnin* and *brucin*, which are powerful poisons

The *symptoms* produced by nux vomica and the two alkaloids are practically the same Strychnin being the most powerful and the most frequently met with, will be the one chosen for consideration. While tests have not been referred to, the *color test* for strychnin is so delicate it deserves special mention, and should poisoning from strychnin be suspected, and should the color test (which will not be described) be applied and not give the characteristic reactions, the other alkaloid, brucin, should be tested for, which does not give the characteristic color test for strychnin. From a medico-legal stand-point this may be of much importance.

Strychnin.—This alkaloid, as already said, is found in strychnos nux vomica, and is usually prepared from this variety. It is a white or grayish white powder, of a peculiarly intensely bitter taste, slightly soluble in water, but communicating to it the peculiar bitter taste; soluble in rectified boiling spirit, and in chloroform, but not in absolute alcohol or ether.

This drug is a frequent cause of poisoning, and has gained a fatal notoriety. Poisoning is either accidental, homicidal or suicidal; the latter is probably the more frequent way.

Symptoms.—The action of this drug seems to be mostly on the spinal cord. If taken in solution, the intensely bitter taste will be at once noticed, and there is also a hot sensation produced in the throat, soon followed (usually in from ten to twenty-minutes) by a feeling of restlessness, and a sense of suffocation and great difficulty of breathing. Very soon twitching of the muscles and jerking of the head and limbs set in, suddenly followed by a violent tetanic convulsion which pervades the whole body; the legs become stiff, stretched out and widely separated, the feet arched and usually turned in; the arms flexed and tightly bent across the body, the hands clinched; the head is bent backwards; the body assumes a bow-like form (opisthotonos), resting on the head and heels. The abdomen becomes tense and hard, chest spasmodically fixed and respiration arrested.

The face assumes an anxious aspect, and becomes congested and livid around the lips. The muscles around the mouth are contracted, producing a peculiar grin, *risus sardonicus.* The eyes are prominent and staring, pupils dilated. The pulse is very rapid and feeble. There is great thirst and dryness of the throat, and if the jaws are not fixed, which is sometimes the case, the patient will call for water, and an attempt at drinking will very likely intensify the spasm, causing a spasmodic closure of the jaws and biting of the vessel, and if glass it will be broken. The intellect usually remains clear, even while the patient is experiencing the most terrific spasms, until near death, when consciousness is sometimes lost. The patient can nearly always apprehend the coming of a paroxysm, and will scream and want to be held The special senses are so exceedingly acute that the slightest movement, touch or noise may be sufficient to produce a spasm at any time.

These paroxysms are sometimes so violent as to jerk the patient out of bed. They usually last from half a minute to one or two minutes, but may last six or eight minutes, when a period of complete relaxation occurs, during which there is great exhaustion, and the patient is often bathed in perspiration; the pupils have been noticed to be contracted at this time.

Fatal Dose.- This varies considerably, as there seems to be a difference as to the susceptibility to the action of strychnin One-sixteenth of a grain has proven fatal to a small child and one-half of a grain to an adult. There have been recoveries from enormous doses, seven to twelve grains; these are exceptional From one-half to one grain may be considered as a fatal dose: even this is considerable difference for such a violent poison.

Fatal Period —This varies considerably also Death has taken place in ten minutes (this is after the symptoms have set in) and has been delayed as long as six hours Most cases that terminate fatally will be within two hours.

As a rule, if the case terminates fatally, the convulsions, after once being established, increase in severity and rapidity until death.

Post-Mortem Appearances —These cannot be said to be characteristic However the blood is usually fluid and dark, the lungs engorged, brain and spinal cord congested. The body is usually relaxed at the time of death, but becomes rigid very soon, and in some instances this rigidity passes away before rigor mortis sets in, and at times merges into the rigor mortis. If death should take place during a convulsion, the patient is likely to remain in the state of opisthotonos The rigor mortis is generally prolonged, in some cases lasting for two months. Lividity of the lips, tongue, fingers and toes is frequently noticed.

Treatment.--If the poison has entered the body by the stomach, which is usually the case, a thorough cleansing out of the stomach should be speedily accomplished; the best means of doing this is with the stomach pump, provided the jaws are not already set. As the stomach pump is usually not available, prompt and free emesis should be secured, even though you think the poison is probably all absorbed. Copious draughts of warm mustard water, or myrica compound, lobelia and soda together should be given. Enemas at the same time will also aid in producing emesis. If convulsions have set in it will be difficult to give even emetics by the bowel, and often any attempt at drinking at this time will bring on a paroxysm. It may be by forcibly holding the patient an enema can be given that will produce emesis; while the lightest touch will bring on the paroxysm at times, forcibly holding them will be of much advantage, the patient often calling for this. Inhalations of chloroform are of benefit.

None but the necessary attendants should be around, and perfect quietness insisted upon as far as possible.

TRIFOLIUM ARVENSE.

Curly Clover Weed, Hare's Foot.

An infusion of this plant is very beneficial in chronic cases of diarrhœa, dysentery and watery condition of the bowels in cholera infantum.

TRIFOLIUM PRATENSE.

Red Clover.

The *blossoms* gathered when in the most perfect state are a mild stimulating and relaxing alterant. In hot infusion it influences the circulation to a good capillary distribution. It is mildly laxative to the bowels and soothing to the nerves. The fluid extract combined with acetous, syrup of lobelia is especially valuable in treatment of whooping cough in nervous children and those of scrofulous taint.

The extract has a reputation as a plaster for the removal of cancers. It is a good wash for scaley skin and for indolent ulcers, promoting healthy granulations.

    Trifolium Prat.   16
    Stillingia Syl.
    Berberis Aqui.
    Arctium Rad.
    Phytolacca Rad.
    Cascara Am.   aa 8
    Potas. Iod.   1
    Xanthoxylum Cort.   .   42

This forms a comp. Syr. Trifolium for syphilis buboes and suppurating glands.

Trifolium, rumex and menispermum make a good alterative compound.

TRILIUM ERECTUM.

Beth Root.   T. Purpureum.
                                             T. Sessile.

The root is a soothing, stimulating, astringent tonic, influencing the mucous membrane, especially that of the generative system. It is prompt and persistent but not drying. It is valuable in hemorrhages whether uterine, respiratory, gastric or rectal. A few doses just before the completion of parturition will anticipate extra hemorrhage. It is useful in preventing miscarriage and in female weakness as leucorrhœa, weak vagina and prolapsus uteri. It may also be used in acute and chronic diarrhœa and dysentery.

TRIOSTEUM PERFOLIATUM.

Fever Root.

This *root* is a mild tonic hepatic, valuable in all forms of biliousness with or without fever and in the various forms of dyspepsia. It is mildly laxative.

TURNERA DIFFUSA.

Damiana.   (T. Aphrodisiaca.)
                                             (T. Microphylla.)
                                             California and Mexico.

The *leaves, young shoots, flowers and seed* are all used. In infusion it forms a refreshing beverage of lemon fragrance. It is a stimulating, toning nervine. The Mexicans drink of it freely to enable them to endure hardships and long journeys and to protect them from disease. It slowly but thoroughly stimulates the brain, spinal cord and the sympathetic nervous system, and is very valuable in debilitated conditions of the nervous system; in nervous prostration, paralysis and general debility. In such conditions we usually find an impaired digestion and a more or less impaired condition of the genito-urinary organs. This agent in such cases assists digestion, relieves constipation and stimulates the pelvic organism.

In cases of sexual debility and impotency, spermatorrhœa, masturbation, prostatic troubles, enuresis, cystic catarrh, it slowly but positively relieves constipation, increases digestive powers, strengthens the nerves and improves the general health.

F. E. Turnera Diff.	oz. i
Hydras. Sulph.	grs. v
Sodæ Hypophos.	dr. ss
Syr. Aurantium Cort.	oz. ii
Aqua	q. s. oz. iv

This may be used with benefit in renal and vesical troubles, albuminaria, and diabetes.

F. E. Turnera Diff.	dr. iv
" " Rhus Arom.	dr. i
" " Phytolacca Rad.	dr. iii
Syr. Zingiberis	q. s. oz. iv

This is a good nervine alterant for nervous prostration, prostatic troubles, seminal emissions and sexual impotency.

TUSSILAGO FARFARA.

Bullsfoot.

The *root* is a diffusive stimulant and relaxant. In hot infusion it promotes a good capillary circulation and is soothing to the nervous system. In suitable cough syrups it increases expectoration, tones the bronchi and is valuable in debilitated pulmonary conditions.

ULMUS FULVA.

Slippery Elm.

The *inner bark* forms one of the best demulcents for both internal and external use wherever there is an irritated condition. In constipation, dysentery, diarrhœa or cholera infantum, used both per oram and rectal injection it lubricates, soothes and relieves the intestinal irritation. It is a nutritious demulcent, soothing to the mucous membrane wherever needed and quieting to the nervous system In diphtheria after the throat has been ridded of the decayed membrane it is quite raw, also during the scaling process in scarlatina and measles and at times in typhoid fever; ulmus is then a very important agent.

Ulmus is a good vehicle for capsicum, quinine, gentian, lobelia or hydrastis.

Externally it is a superior agent combined with raw linseed oil for burns, scalds and abraded surfaces. Keep the surface well covered and there is nothing better. With lobelia it forms a good poultice for abscesses and boils.

The ground is best for poultice, the powdered best for

burns and the bark finely chipped for an infusion for the stomach.

It is also used in the formation of pills, troches and suppositions.

URTICA DIOICA

Nettle.

The *roots*, *leaves* and *tops* are a positive, stimulating, tonic astringent; a powerful arrester of hemorrhages whether of the nose, lungs, stomach, bowels, uterus or urinary organs It will also stop hemorrhages when applied locally and relieve painful hemorrhoids. The fluid extract when diluted forms a good wash for some eczemas

Dr. F G. Hœner uses it for atelectasis pulmonum, hæmaturia and asthmatic coughs.

UVULARIA PERFOLIATA.

Bellwort.

Dr. F. G Hœner uses this as a wash for wounds and cold sores, and as a gargle for inflamed gums and larynx

VACCINIUM RESINOSUM

Huckleberry

The *root and bark* are a gently stimulating astringent, influencing the mucous membrane, and useful in aphthous sore mouth, sore throat and leucorrhœa In hot infusion it influences the circulation and assists in the arrest of hemorrhages.

The *berries* are an excellent fruit somewhat diuretic

VALERIANA OFFICINALIS.

English Valerian.

The *root* has a fœtid odor that lasts long and is loud. It is a soothing, diffusive, relaxing and stimulating nervine. It is antispasmodic and useful for relief of irritability of the nervous system, of hysteria. insomnia, and the nervousness of children Essence of anise is frequently used to conceal its taste.

F E Valerian	dr v
" " Dioscorea	dr. ii
Ess Anise	dr. i

Syr Zingiber or Comp. Syr Rhei and Pot   qs oz iv

Use this for colic, diarrhœa and the restlessness of children.

F. E. Valerian, F. E. Dioscorea, F E Caulophylum and

Essence Anise in equal parts in syrup of Zingiber is useful in dysmenorrhœa, convulsions, hysteria, colic and
crampings.

VERBASCUM THAPSUS

Mullein

The *leaves and flowers* are a soothing relaxing and stimulating alterant, influencing the glandular, serous and mucous structures   It is a very useful agent in the treatment
of glandular swellings, hepatization or thickening of lung
tissue, phthisis, asthma, hay-fever, coughs, pleuritis and
in all forms of dropsy.

F. E Verbascum
" " Phytolacca
" " Sambucus Flowers
" " Gnaphalium   aa dr ii
Syr. Simplex   qs oz. iv

F. E. Verbascum   oz. ii
Tr. Lobelia
Capsicum   aa. oz i

Give of the former for bronchitis and croupy cough, and
apply the latter over the lungs

In the treatment of phlegmasia dolens use internally
verbascum 10 and polygonum and hydrastis each 1, and
apply equal parts of verbascum and polygonum.

In dysuria, with or without stricture, you will find of
good service a hot infusion of the root

Externally verbascum is of much value in the treatment
of sprains, bruises, soreness of the chest, painful chronic
abscesses. Many inflamed and painful conditions are relieved by a hot acetous fomentation of this agent   Cover
green or recently dried verbascum leaves with boiling vinegar and allow to simmer, covered, a half hour   Then
strain and add tr capsicum, fld.ext. lobelia and oil sassafras
in equal parts, q s according to the strength of application needed   This relieves painful and swollen joints. It
scarcely ever fails to stop the pain and reduce the swelling

Verbascum   oz. iv . F. E. Verbascum
Lobelia   dr iv Tr. Lobelia
Capsicum   dr. ii Oil Sassafras   aa oz. i
Acetum   qrt. i Mix

Bring the former combination to the boiling point; then

allow to simmer covered for a half hour. Either of these preparations is excellent for rheumatism and stiff joints

F. E. Verbascum	F E Verbascum	oz. iii
" Polygonum	Tr. Capsicum	oz i
Tr Capsicum aa oz i		

. Apply the former in chronic diarrhœa and the latter in peritonitis.

Verbascum	Verbascum
Solidago	Cornus Flor
Cornus Flor aa equal parts.	Hydrastis
	Kino aa equal parts.

Use an infusion of either of these combinations as a vaginal wash

F E Verbascum	F. E. Verbascum	oz iv
Oil Sassafras	Tr. Capsicum	oz. iiss
" Peppermint	" Lobelia	oz i
Tr. Zingiber.	Oil Origanum	dr ss
" Lobelia aa. dr. ii		
Alcohol q. s. oz iv		

Apply the former for periostitis and the latter to drop-sied limbs.

The expressed juice of the green leaves forms an extract or a salve for hemorrhoids that is very beneficial.

Dr. J. H Smith advises the following in dysentery, to be used after each stool

F. E Verbascum Thap	dr ii
" Nepeta Cat	
" Cypripedium Pub. aa dr. iii	

M S · Half teaspoonful to half teacupful tepid water for enema after each stool.

Gather the tops in bloom and subject them to heavy pressure. Apply this to enlarged submaxillary or other enlarged glands It is also an excellent application in some forms of deafness The oil can be obtained by filling a large bottle with the flowers. Use a cork having a hole in it Invert this bottle so that the oil will drip into another bottle below. These bottles must be suspended in the hot sunlight To preserve this a few drops of alcohol must be added. This is splendid in otalgia, scrofulous ophthalmia and in enuresis; it may be given in 10 drop doses, or better, triturated on magnesia

Verbascum Thap .	oz ss
Hydrastis Can.	grs xx

Lobelia Infl. Herb　　　　　dr. i
Aqua Bullens　　　　　　　oz. vi

Filter. Wash the eyes every two hours and cover with a soft cloth wet with the same, in ophthalmia

VERBENA HASTATA.

Blue Vervain.

This *plant* is a bitter relaxing and stimulating nervine. In hot infusion it influences a good circulation toward the capillaries and soothes the nervous system throughout The liver, gall ducts and bowels are all influenced by it. It gives favorable results in biliousness, periodic bilious attacks, and is somewhat antiperiodic Boiling destroys considerable of its stimulating quality and leaves it a relaxing nervine

Dr. F. G. Hoener uses the following for spleenitis.

Elix. Verbena Has.　　　　oz. ii
" Eupatorium Perf.
" Xanthoxylum　　aa oz i

M. S. One tablespoonful every two or three hours
The Doctor also uses the following for myalgia:

Elix. Verbena Hast.
" Betonica Lanc.　　aa. oz. iss
" Cunila Mar.　　　oz. i

M. S. One dessertspoonful every hour until relieved.

Syr. Verbena Hast
" Chelone Glab.　　aa. oz. iss
" Xanthoxylum　　oz i

This is a good tonic hepatic, and the following is splendid for sick headache.

F. E. Verbena Hast
" Scutelaria Lat.
" Euonymous Atr　　aa dr iii
Syr. Zingiber.　　　q. s. oz. iv

In chronic cases this should be given three times daily for some time.

A cold preparation of verbena is excellent in convalescence from fevers and other debilitating diseases.

VERBENA URTICÆFOLIA.

White Vervain.

This *plant* may be used for the same purposes as the

hastata . Dr.. F. G Hoener says it is a specific in the opium and tobacco habits

VERNONIA FASCICULATA

Ironweed.

The **roots, leaves and flowers** are a bitter, stimulating, tonic nervine. In hot infusion it arouses the circulation and soothes the nervous system, and is useful in acute febrile conditions It is antiperiodic, gently hepatic, and useful in convalescence from fevers and other forms of disease.

VERONICA OFFICINALIS.

Speedwell

This *herb* is a mild, relaxing and stimulating tonic alterant In hot infusion it gives a good outward flow of blood and soothes the nervous system. It favorably influences the hepatic and renal organs and gives good results in jaundice, and in hot infusion in acute bronchitis and pneumonia, and with arctium in skin diseases

VERONICA PEREGRINA

Neckweed.

Dr. F. G. Hoener recommends this agent in the treatment of scrofulous tumors, glandular troubles, and scrofulous conditions of the throat and jaws

VIBURNUM OPULUS

Crampbark.

The **inner bark** is an admirable relaxing and stimulating, antispasmodic nervine It quickly relieves the crampings of the limbs due to pregnancy, and also when not due to this condition It quiets pain and uneasiness due to the pregnant period and prevents miscarriage, and is still better when combined with such agents as dioscorea, caulophyllum, mitchella and scutelaria.

Viburnin is only a moderate representative of this agent; the fluid extract is preferable

VIBURNUM PRUNIFOLIUM.

Black Haw.

The *bark* is a soothing, stimulating, astringent tonic, influencing especially the urino-genital organs It relieves after-pains, stops excessive lochia, prevents abortion when threatening, relieves chronic enlargements of the uterus, prolapsus uteri, vaginal laxity, and passive menorrhagia. It is very valuable during the menopause to prevent excessive flow. Dr. F. G. Hoener advises the following.

     Elix. Vib. Pruni   oz iiss
       " Cyp Pub.   oz i
       " Amaranth. Hypoch   oz, i

M. S. One dessertspoonful every hour during period of threatening miscarriage

VITIS VINIFERA

From this vine we obtain from different Mediterranean localities our supply of raisins (uvæ passæ) When eaten they are mildly laxative to the bowels They do not particularly aid digestion, but are chiefly used to flavor different preparations

XANTHIUM STRUMARIUM

Cocclebur, Clotbur

The *leaves* are a mild, diffusive, stimulating, astringent tonic In hot infusion they influence a good capillary circulation, and are valuable in cases of the bites of snakes, tarantulas, centipedes and various poisonous insects Give an infusion very freely and apply a poultice of the boiled leaves.

The green leaves bruised and applied to the surface will blister the surface.

The expressed juice of the green leaves applied to the surface is a valuable local styptic, almost instantaneously producing contractions of the capillaries and the formation of coagulum In cases of bleeding of the nose, stomach rectum, vagina, a spraying or injection of this agent is very useful. In post-partem hemorrhage and in typhoid hemorrhages it should be given internally.

The fluid extract of the green leaves or an infusion of the green leaves or of the burrs, either is excellent for dysuria, strangury, scalding urine, bearing down with painful micturition, gonorrhœa and gleet The infusion of the burrs is nearly tasteless but is very effective

XANTHOXYLUM CAROLINENSIS.

Southern Prickly Ash.

The *bark* and *berries* of this tree are a diffusive stimulating alterant and in hot infusion diaphoretic   In influence it very much resembles the fraxineum, but more fully acts on the secernents and glandular system and is a more serviceable addition to alterative compounds.

XANTHOXYLUM FRAXINEUM.

Prickly Ash.

The *bark* is a positive, diffusive, stimulant, especially inducing a good free capillary and arterial circulation.   It is a valuable addition to alteratives and to diaphoretics It warms the stomach, arouses the skin, and stimulates the salivary glands, the lymphatics and the serous and mucous membrane   It is a valuable addition in all chronic affections, rheumatism, neuralgia and wherever the skin and extremities are cold.

The *seed or berries* are slightly more stimulating than the bark.   In cases of a dry tongue and mucous surfaces use this agent and if need be add a little lobelia   It is one of the best things in the world   It acts slower than capsicum but its effects are more permanent   Give in small and frequent doses,

Xanthoxylum and phytolacca are excellent in rheumatism, syphilis, scrofula, paralysis, aphonia, cholera, cholera morbus, congestions

Xanthoxylin is a moderate representative of this agent The *oil* is much better   Fill a bottle full of the berries then fill it with alcohol.   Allow to stand a week or more Then evaporate the alcohol and you have the oil.   This may be used triturated on lactin 1 to 9.

The dose of xanthoxylum in any form is very small The following may be used for lead poisoning·

Myrica Cer	dr. i
Xanthoxylum	dr ss
Tannin	grs. x
Aqua Bullens	oz viii

M. S   Two teaspoonsful every half hour to two hours as required

XANTHORRHIZA APIIFOLIA.

Yellow Root.

The *root and inner bark* are a strong stimulating tonic and may be used in small portions in convalescence and wherever such tonic is required.

X RAYS, ROENTGEN'S RAYS, CATHODE RAYS

By J M. Thurston, M D ,

Professor of Applied Physiological Anatomy of the Nervous System and Electro-Therapeutics in the Physio-Medical College of Indiana, Indianapolis

The possibilities of this, one of the greatest, if not the crowning triumph of ancient or modern discovery, to furnish incalculable aid to scientific medicine, demands that we here give a careful estimate of its present status from the stand-point of medicine.

Candor compels us to state in the beginning, that so far, the X ray has not attained sufficient practical utility to excite a reasonable hope, much less enthusiasm, in the uninitiated: yet no one who has made any personal progress in the candid study of and practical work with a good working X ray outfit, can fail to become impressed with an abiding faith in the immensity of the final good to medicine that shall come from this wonderful fountain of scientific discovery. To be sure there lies before us an immense chasm of darkest unknown, or X truths if you please, that must be illuminated by most laborious, patient and exact experimental work. But we are on the threshold, the key is within our grasp, and battalions of sturdy, stalwart brain-workers are thundering at the door, vieing with each other as to who shall be first to enter the realms of the mystic light-god, and sack his rich palace of eternal truth.

A study of the history of great discoveries reveals the fact that discoverers, or rather we should say scientific investigators, may be divided into two definite classes— those who work from a purely scientific stand-point, and those who work from the utilitarian stand-point. The one never raises his mental focus beyond the horizon of the laboratory; the other reaches anon out into the practical world to bless the struggling masses with the rich, helpful gifts of science.

This old story is verified in the history of the X rays. In 1831 Michael Faraday developed the induction coil, and the induced currents, which have been named the faradic current in his honor. He also, among many other important discoveries, produced electric discharges and most peculiar fluorescent lights in vacuum tubes containing rarified gasses

Then Geissler followed Faraday, improving upon the vacuum tubes, now called Geissler tubes, sealing in permanent platinum electrodes, producing some new and wonderful effects, and contributing to the science of electrophysics some most important truths. He noted that the fluorescence behaved differently at the anode and cathode, or positive and negative poles; that a most peculiar phosphorescence could be traced to the cathode in the vacuum tube, thus he developed the *"cathode rays,"* which became the centre of interest to scientists in this line of work

Then came Prof Wm. Crookes, who in 1879 commenced publishing a series of papers which astonished the popular mind, and stimulated scientific investigators everywhere in this line of science; though they were familiar with most of the same facts which had already been set forth by Faraday and Geissler, followed by many others of less fame. Crookes further elucidated and improved upon these, adding, to be sure, some important original discoveries. He called it Radiant, or a Fourth State of Matter Though Faraday had spoken of a radiant state of matter, suggesting that in this condition the molecules were in an extremely separated state, as far apart relatively as the molecules of gas compared with those of liquid. The tubes now almost entirely used in producing the X rays are named Crookes tübes.

Hertz experimenting with thin sheets of metal within the vacuum tube demonstrated the power of the cathodic rays to penetrate in straight lines of force solid substances. But his pupil, Paul Lenard. led these rays outside the tubes, by cutting a window in it and inserting an aluminum plate opposite the cathode—negative pole. Through this window Lenard got the rays passing them through opaque substances, and produced photographs; in fact did everything that we are now doing with the X rays. except applying them to human anatomy and surgery; this was reserved for Prof Roentgen, for which he is now receiving the plaudits of *vox populi*, which sinks, for the hour, Faraday, Geissler, Hertz, Lenard. and numerous other patient, earnest and most valuable discoverers, in to eclipse, because he has gotten the attention of the world's doctors with their world of admiring and worshipful clientelle

It was certainly commendable in Roentgen to push aside the "kingly crown" that was offered in christening them

the " Rœntgen Rays", and modestly suggesting the more
scientific name of an unkown radiant quantity, or THE X
RAYS. Of course the improvement made by Prof. Rœntgen
in X ray penetrating power, his deep scientific elucidation
of its physical properties, and above all, his practical contribution to surgery is quite enough honor without the appropriation of others property by calling it the Rœntgen
Ray.

What the X ray really is:— This is a question so strictly
within the province of physical science that we shall only
give a brief statement of Rœntgen's idea which is probably

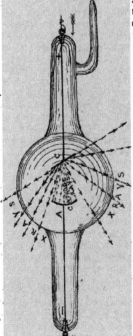

as near correct as the English
theory; remembering the X,
or unknown nature of it,
which will probably remain
so for some time to come.
What the medical profession
want to know is its possibilities.

Reference to the figure which
is Crooke's tube in operation
will aid us in a brief description. The tube is simply a
vacuum, not an absolute nor
even extreme vacuum but
what may better be under-
stood by saying that it contains exceedingly rarified air.
The electrodes are sealed in
the tube, One is circular, cupped, of nickle plated copper
A. The other is square, set
at an angle, and made of al-
uminum.C. These represent
respectively the anode or positive pole, and cathode or
negative pole; a gap is left between them which the cur-
rent jumps in its passage, as
indicated by the arrows at
each pole at ends of the tube
Now a stream is thrown back
from cathode cup A to anode disk C, this is called "the
cathode rays" or "cathode stream. This causes a great

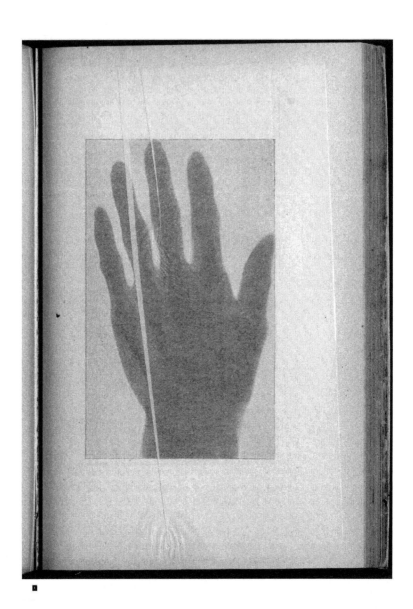

the " Roentgen Rays", and modestly suggesting the more scientific name of an unkown radiant quantity or THE X RAYS. Of course the improvement made by Prof. Roentgen in X ray penetrating power, his deep scientific elucidation of its physical properties, and above all, his practical contribution to surgery is quite enough honor without the appropriation of others property by calling it the Roentgen Ray.

What the X ray really is.— This is a question so strictly within the province of physical science that we shall only give a brief statement of Roentgen's idea which is probably

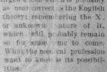

as near correct as the English theory; remembering the X, or unknown nature of it, which will probably remain so for some time to come. What the medical profession want to know is its possibilities.

Reference to the figure which is Crooke's tube in operation will aid us in a brief description. The tube is simply a vacuum, not an absolute nor even extreme vacuum but what may better be understood by saying that it contains exceedingly rarified air. The electrodes are sealed in the tube. One is circular, cupped, of nickle plated copper A. The other is square, set at an angle, and made of aluminum C. These represent respectively the anode or positive pole, and cathode or negative pole; a gap is left between them which the current jumps in its passage, as indicated by the arrows at each pole at ends of the tube. Now a stream is thrown back from cathode cup A to anode disk C, this is called "the cathode rays" or "cathode stream. This causes a great

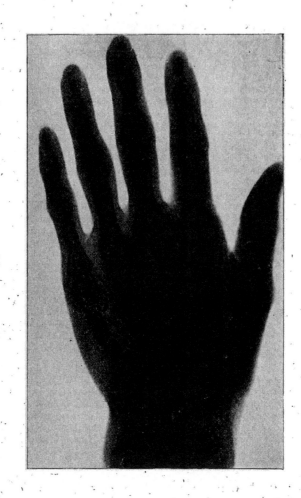

commotion between the molecules of air which by their
rarified condition or separation are easily moved, and are
thrown against disk C, and the tube walls with such force
and friction as to cause efflorescence, and a beautiful soft
greenish blue light illuminates the tube, giving a mild
phosphorescent light inside the tube by which the hands
of a watch can be seen with some difficulty. This is the
cathode light, and was at first thought to be the penetrating rays, hence was called the *"cathode ray"* But Rœntgen has satisfactorily shown, according to present knowledge at least, that the true X rays are those projected
from the slanting aluminum disk C as shown in the figure
by the heavier arrows leading outside the tube

The X rays have a power of penetration much beyond
that of any other form of radiant matter with which we
now are acquainted. To be sure we can, with a strong sunlight unfocused, get illumination of soft tissues, and
shadow outlines of bones, so, also with an electric light,
a photograph may thus be obtained. While in reality they
are a form of electric light, yet a little work with the X
rays will convince any one that they are a newly discovered potency of light that is destined to work a most wonderful revolution in illumination in both art and commerce.

The present status of X rays in relation to surgery —
Practically the X rays offers nothing for general medicine.
But to surgery, rightly directed, it is already a most valu-
able aid.

Its first importance is in locating foreign substances in
the structures Here, as perhaps in all future work in this
line, we must join photography hand in hand with our
new aid Lest the beginner become disgustingly disappointed let us impress him with the importance of a pho-
tographic production above the natural eyesight, that is,
a photograph here, as elsewhere, shows more than we can
discern with the eye Therefore we suggest that you depend more upon the photograph than the eye and the
fluoroscope And as the process is so simple so far as getting a negative, or rather a positive, is concerned we recommend a diagnosis or rather location of a foreign substance by a photograph, rather than by the naked eye, as
we will show by our own experience further on. If you
have a photographer convenient all that is needed is Car-
butts X ray plates, these are ready for work, place the

hand, for instance on the plate without removing the wrapper of black paper, hold it up in front of tube, 4 inches from it with the hand to the light, and from 2 to 5 minutes exposure is sufficient, return the plate to envelope, take it to your photographer who developes, fixes, prints and mounts it in the usual way.

With the static machine, Crooke's tubes and fluoroscope, which can now be bought of G. A. Frei & Co. No 17 Bromfield Street, Boston, Mass., at such reasonable prices that there is no excuse for any Doctor of ordinary means not providing himself with an X ray outfit. We give a friendly warning against the fellows who come along with outfits whose only merit is the exhorbitant demands from the medical profession, on Col. Sellers idea that there are "millions in them" (the Doctors).

Our figure shows a needle in the thumb-muscles which had been there for over 25 years. Of course it was thoroughly encysted and could be felt on deep pressure, but the patient resisted operative proceedure fearing a crippled hand. By thus locating it and especially its long axis, which was impossible except with the X rays, we were enabled to convince her that its removal could be easily effectd without bad results.

A boy 5 years old while crawling at play on the carpet, ran a needle, eye first, into the knee joint, 2 inches in a slanting direction downward above the petella. It passed through the patella-tendon into the synovial-sac, and our first photograph, one week after the accident, showed two thirds of the needle into the sac; 36 hours after, a photograph showed it entirely in the synovial sac; and with the naked eye through the fluoroscope we could see it floating about under the patella in the synovial sac, and could by motions of the knee joint be thrown under patella-tendon to its inner border, where we finally succeeded in forcing the point out so that it could be felt exactly in position shown by the X rays, and we quickly removed it through a short deep incision. Had this remained in the synovial sac, no one can question the loss of the knee joint, and probably the limb, it would have been impossible to locate it without the X rays.

In a valuable little book on X rays, by Dr. Wm. J. Morton, and Edwin W. Hammer, electrical engineer, and published by the American Technical Book Co. No. 45 Vesey Street, N. Y. to produce a shadowgraph to show the aid to bone sur_

gery afforded by the X rays. This picture was made after
a Colles fracture had been put up in splints, the pins in the
bandage plainly show. If the fracture has not been properly approximated and retained the surgeon is thus made
aware of it in ample time to save suit for damage We
recently had such a fracture, a little lower down and quite
oblique, being in a large, muscular, laboring man; it was
enormously swollen from the severe bruise and sprain, so
that we could not have made out the fracture without
the X rays.

Recently a lady applied for treatment of a felon in the end
of the left thumb; as the finger looked peculiar we used
the X ray, and discovered a fragment of needle about one-
fourth of an inch in length penetrating the periosteum
and impinging on the bone The lady then called to mind
that ten years ago she thought she had run a needle in her
thumb, but as it gave her no trouble she had long ago forgotten it. She was etherized, the fragment removed, and
the finger was quite well in three days There is no question about the very serious results had this needle remained
for the inflammatory process would have continued.

We may enumerate the advantages of the X ray in surgery as follows

The Study of Normal Anatomy —The normal anatomical relations of the bony systems can be most thoroughly,
attractively and accurately studied through the fluoroscope, and by the X ray photographs

So also developmental osteology can be studied more accurately; the fœtus at every stage of development en u'ero
will be observed, the new-born infant; and the study continued to the end of full development. It will be found
necessary to change the chapters in anatomy on the development of the bony system when such a systematic study is
made.

Comparative Anatomy —The study of comparative
osteology will find a valuable aid in the X rays; reptiles,
fishes and all the smaller animals can be studied and compared with more perfect accuracy No doubt many material corrections will be made in this science, as well as
that of natural history and zoology

*Location of Foreign Substance in the Human Body,
Fractures and Dislocations.*—These we have already
shown the advantages derived from the X rays To which
we may add the case of a bullet in the palm of the hand,

which the author tried to extract but failed, fifteen years ago; an examination recently with the X rays not only located the bullet, but explained the difficulty of its removal.

Diseases of the Bones.—While of course the X rays accurately reveal the slightest enlargement, and extra growths of bone, yet being only a shadow picture it reveals nothing of the true pathological nature

Anchylosis. Remote Injures to Joints and Bones—The X rays give most valuable aid in differentiating anchyloses In true anchylosis the bony union will be easily and accurately distinguishable

In remote injuries of joints and bones it may be of considerable aid

Medico-Legal—Of no minor import will be the X ray photographs in court, showing most conclusively the location of balls and the nature of remote bone injuries A patient of the author's has now a case in court claiming damages for an injury to the foot, which apparently seems little damaged, but an X ray photograph explains exactly why the man will be a cripple the rest of his life

Dentistry—As the teeth are more dense than the alveolar process, both the tooth and alveolus show distinctly with the fluoroscope, and in photographs, also metal fillings being more dense than either, flaws in fillings, necrosis, and new growths. together with many other dental troubles, may be detected

That Which Medicine Demands of the X Rays, but Which It Cannot as yet Fulfill.—Notwithstanding the brilliant achievements of the X rays for medicine in little over a twelvemonth, as above set forth, yet our miracle-demanding and ever exacting profession must have far greater performances from this wonderful light-ray before its tidal wave of enthusiasm obtains a maximum momentum. Then it will sweep the medical world like an avalanche.

So far this light, with its amazing penetration of solid substances, can give us only a shadow That is, the densest portions like the bones stop most of the rays and consequently cast a shadow in front of them, which is simply a silhouette, hence called shadowgraph, skiagraph, etc The general soft structures, such as cartilage, ligaments, tendons, muscles, etc , though differing in their structural density, seem to have no difference in their ability to

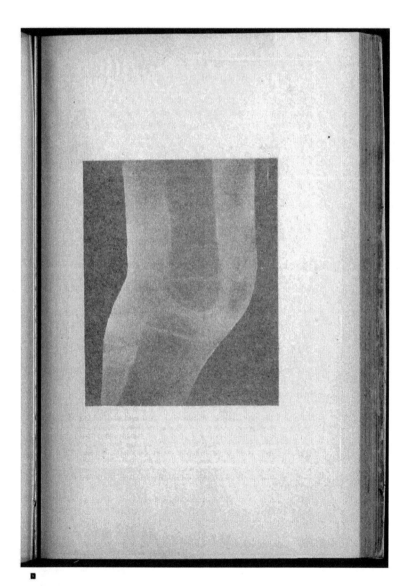

which the author tried to extract but failed, fifteen years ago; an examination recently with the X rays not only located the bullet, but explained the difficulty of its removal.

Diseases of the Bones.—While of course the X rays accurately reveal the slightest enlargement and extra growths of bone, yet being only a shadow picture it reveals nothing of the true pathological nature.

Anchylosis. Remote Injuries to Joints and Bones. The X rays give most valuable aid in differentiating anchyloses. In true anchylosis the bony union will be easily and accurately distinguishable.

In remote injuries of joints and bones it may be of considerable aid.

Medico-Legal.—Of no minor import will be the X ray photographs in court, showing most conclusively the location of balls and the nature of remote bone injuries. A patient of the author's has now a case in court claiming damages for an injury to the foot, which apparently seems little damaged, but an X ray photograph explains exactly why the man will be a cripple the rest of his life.

Dentistry.—As the teeth are more dense than the alveolar process, both the tooth and alveolus show distinctly with the fluoroscope, and in photographs; also metal fillings being more dense than either, flaws in fillings, necrosis, and new growths, together with many other dental troubles, may be detected.

That Which Medicine Demands of the X Rays, but Which It Cannot as yet Fulfill. Notwithstanding the brilliant achievements of the X rays for medicine in little over a twelvemonth, as above set forth, yet our miracle-demanding and ever exacting profession must have far greater performances from this wonderful light-ray before its tidal wave of enthusiasm obtains a maximum momentum. Then it will sweep the medical world like an avalanche.

So far this light, with its amazing penetration of solid substances, can give us only a shadow. That is, the densest portions like the bones stop most of the rays and consequently cast a shadow in front of them, which is simply a silhouette, hence called shadowgraph, skiagraph, etc. The general soft structures, such as cartilage, ligaments, tendons, muscles, etc., though differing in their structural density, seem to have no difference in their ability to

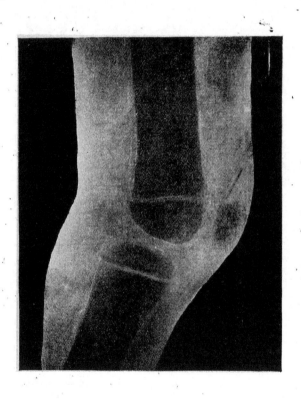

obstruct the X rays; hence, we have in dimmer shadow, an outline shadow-mass of the soft structures. The most important thing to medicine and surgery is totally absent, viz., the details of nerves, blood-vessels, organs, etc.; in short, general tissue and structural differentiation. Then so far as actual diseased conditions are concerned it cannot give us even a hint To be sure growths and destructions of bony structure are readily pointed out, but it gives no clue as to the pathological nature of the new growths, or the destructive processes

The Future Possibilities of the X Rays.—However slight the conservative and skeptical may consider the advantages already afforded our profession by the X rays, the future of this new discovery cannot but be hailed with deepest regard by the candid scientific medical man When we remember it was only a year last December since the attention of medical men was attracted by Prof. Roentgen's discovery that the bones could be seen in the living body, and then bear in mind that the only achievement yet to give us full mastery of the X ray is to gain over it the power of refraction, then shall we have nothing less than microscopic penetration of every tissue element, tissue and structure of the living body. This last step, we confidently prophesy, will be gained within the next twelvemonth. And within the next decade, X ray micro-fluoroscopes will be constructed by which we can view the tissue units, tissues and structures, and their functional activities, in other words, study the living body as we now study micro-organisms in a life slide with our microscopes.

That the general reader may better comprehend us, take an ordinary double convex lense for instance, with a ten-inch focus; ordinary light-rays traveling parallel and striking the surface on either side of the lens are refracted —that is, bent from the periphery towards the centre of the disk—and converge as they pass out on the other side, and finally come to a focus or brilliant spot of light ten inches distant from the lens. Now the X rays will pass through such a lens coming out at the same distance apart on the opposite side, and there is no refraction or bending of them into a focus This is the great difficulty to be overcome And when we shall be able to thus handle the X rays, with their powers of penetration it will be easy to construct a fluoro-microscope by which we can define and magnify the living tissues, as we now do microscopic sections by transmitted light. It is the writer's humble opinion that investigators should get to work along these lines, instead of devising more powerful apparata for stronger light. We already have sufficiently powerful X rays; let us seek to control them by some form of refraction

As to X Ray Outfits.—In this, as everything else pertaining to physicians' supplies, dealers take advantage of every new craze to bleed the medical profession, and outfits are being sold at exorbitant prices

To obtain illumination of a Crooke's tube and its consequent X rays, it is necessary to procure an electric discharge or spark　The distance that the electric current can be made to jump from one electrode to another in this discharge is called a spark-gap; other things being equal, the longer the spark-gap the more powerful the X ray machine.　A seven or eight inch spark-gap is a good machine; the most powerful are ten to twelve inches

At present there are two methods of getting illumination of the Crooke's tube; viz., by an induction coil (the Ruhmkorff coil is used altogether), or with a static machine.　With either of these the only other requisites are a Crooke's tube, a stand or holder for the tube, and a fluoroscope—a pasteboard box, the inside of which is smeared with a fluorescent substance (tungstate of calcium), which enables one to see through opaque substances between it and the X rays

With the Ruhmkorff coil outfit one must have the commercial current from the electric light plant, a storage battery, or a number—from ten to twenty—laclarche cells

For our own part, we prefer static electricity for X ray work, as in our experience it is just as effective as the coil, much more conveniently handled, and far cheaper.　We believe the static to be the ideal current for the X rays

With the Static Machine No 2 furnished by G A. Frei & Co we have been able to do most excellent work.　Our illustrations were taken with this outfit.

Quite recently the writer has found that by using two Crooke's tubes, arranged one immediately in front and a little towards the cathode end of the other tube, the power of X rays may be nearly doubled with the same static machine. One figure was photographed by this arrangement, and will compare favorably with any expensive coil outfit.

ZINGIBER OFFICINALE

Ginger   Jamaica.

The **root** is an aromatic, diffusive stimulant   It is one
of the most useful agents of the materia medica; though
last, it is not least   In hot infusion it is diaphoretic.
When detained by congestion, it relieves the congestion
and assists in reinstating the menstrual flow.   It is one of
the best agents in most grades of feverishness.

In a large majority of compounds it is an excellent aromatic adjuvant   With cathartics it prevents nausea and
griping.

In typhoid and other fevers and in all the exanthems
there is nothing better, and so in bronchitis, pneumonia,
pleuritis and angina.

It relieves flatulence, internal congestions, recent colds,
and is useful in dysentery and diarrhœa.

Zingiber 1, asclepias tub. 4 forms an excellent diaphoretic.
With lobelia, zingiber increases its antispasmodic power.

The fluid extract may be used for all the purposes of the
agent

PHYSIO-MEDICAL.

—x—

PHARMACY.

—o—

By J. M. Thurston, M. D.

Professor of Applied Physiological Anatomy of the Nervous System and Electro-Therapeutics in the Physio-Medical College of Indiana, Indianapolis.

Introductory.

harmacy is the art of preparing remedial agents in the most effective and convenient form for administration in the treatment of disease. The Physio-Medical practice having for its fundamental guidance, a philosophy differing widely from all other schools of medicine, requires a readjustment of all known facts relative to Physiology, Pathology, and Therapeutics to this basic hypothesis, which avers the vital constitution and unity of the physiological whole, in health and disease, rendering all symptomatic, or perverted, as well as normal functional actions, essentially sanative in their intent, by virtue of an *inherent vital force,* whose manifestations through, and only by means of living matter, is always resistive of inimical influences, constructive and regenerative; it therefore follows that a Physio Medical Pharmacopœia, and the subject of pharmacy must be adjusted to this philosophical standpoint.

To this work we address ourself with many misgivings. Not however because of inherent difficulties in adjusting, and rearranging the present known facts, which have been valued by other schools of medicine, or the very large number of established truths that have been discovered and used by Physio-Medicalists, during the last seventy-five years, to the theorem of our school of practice; neither because of the slightest doubt of harmony between Physio-

Medical philosophy, and a single truth of pharmacy and
therapeutics, but we shrink from the task wholly on personal doubts of our ability to fill the requirements of so
great a need as that of a practical working pharmacology
for the Physio-Medical profession.

The Physio-Medical philosophy is interdictory of alcho-
hol as a therapeutic agent, and our pharmacy avoids its
use as a menstruum, claiming for it only preservative properties, and admits only the smallest percentage. It is a well
demonstrated fact that the most potent therapeutic agent
is a *hot infusion* Boiling water, therefore is the most effective and reliable menstruum for obtaining the full remedial
constituency of vegetable drugs, especially. But these infusions do not keep well, they are soon attacked by micro-
organism and fermentative processes, that render them
useless; so that a thoroughly reliable, therapeutically inert, non-alcoholic preservative for a percolate made with
boiling water as a menstruum, is the great desideratum,
in Physio-Medical pharmacy. Such a preservative we shall
endeavor to suggest for many of our fluid extracts, in the
body of this work.

It will be readily understood from the facts set forth a-
bove, that the difference between Physio-Medical Pharmacy, and that of other schools in the preparation of fluid
extracts, especially of the Vegetable Materia Medica, is
quite radical, and will no doubt subject this work to adverse criticism; but as to this we are indifferent, relying
upon the integrity of our principles, and the experience of
our profession, to demonstrate that the source of these
strictures is ignorance, and prejudice.

Owing to the large and wholly unnecessary percentage of
alcohol in the fluid products of the leading manufacturing
houses, whose business acumen rightly prompts them to
pander to the more popular schools of medicine, whose
false and dangerous notion of chemico-therapeutics, or the
idea of the body-functions being the result of chemical disintegration of atoms, thus reasoning that medicines must
also act by chemical equations in the living economy, as
they do in the chemical labratory, has brought into existence numerous "chemical companies," so that the Physio-
Medical practitioner is compelled through the lack of pharmaceutical houses that shall devote proper attention to
our wants, to prepare a large share of his own therapeutic
supplies, or else purchase and use these highly alcoholic

and irritating fluid extracts. Therefore the larger part of this work will be devoted to *Practical Office Pharmacy;* by which we hope to point out an economic outfit, and processes that will draw as lightly as possible upon the busy practitioner's time, also afford him efficient and elegant pharamceutical products

While in some respects, it is desirable to avoid combination of a considerable number of agents, and especially a routine formulæ-practice, yet no experienced prescriber can be induced to confine himself exclusively to single administration of remedies, no more than he could be induced to treat a given disease, through all its phases, and constitutional modifications of various patients, with one single agent. Neither is it possible to find a successful practitioner of several years experience that has not a number of favorite formulæ, which he prizes highly. This is our only apology for concluding this work with a somewhat extensive Formulary.

Partly from necessity, but largely from natural taste for pharmaceutical work, the writer has devoted much time and money to laboratory equipment and pharmacy; which we hope may avail somewhat in presenting to the profession, some originality and individuality in the subject matter of this work that may aid in rendering it of practical value. However we would by no means exclude the large experience, and practical ability of our many friends and co-laborers, and shall present much from others of our own school, and some things of value from other schools of medicine, endeavoring carefully to give due credit to all in the proper place as we go along; the Author's original material standing unaccredited.

FLUID EXTRACTS

The object of pharmaceutical procedure in obtaining a *fluid extract,* is, the solution, in an effective and agreeable form, of the therapeutic principles of vegetable substances, and of inorganic compounds or elements. The two qualities, that of efficiency and elegance, are not always attainable in a pharmaceutical product; indeed, the problem of pharmacy is to overcome this antagonism between taste and therapeutic value; for the practitioner cannot afford to sacrifice the latter for the former. The writer's experience and observation in this direction is, that the tendency of modern pharmacy is sadly in neglect of efficiency, for the sake of elegance In addition to this harmful tendency, is the false notion that the so-called "active principles" and the "inert" constituents should be wholly separated, to the total exclusion of the latter; and to this end analytical pharmacy has been carried to a harmful, not to say ridiculous, extreme *"Organic chemistry"* is a misnomer; *approximate chemistry* is the more appropriate term for the chemical treatment of organic substances, which, at its very first touch, obliterates the vital conditions and physiological continuity of the organic body, leaving us without a supposition as to either the physiological synthesis of the analytical products, or the therapeutic potency of these isolated principles. The fact is that the living matter, which not only constitutes the vital motor of the living plant, but when this same vegetable organism becomes a *materies medica*, it now, in a desiccated form, becomes the essential therapeutic constituent of the drug. This bioplasm is, in the vital living state, matter without atomic characteristics, and therefore absolutely without the pale of chemical law. We have the proof of this in the variance of organic chemical analyses; no two chemists obtain exactly the same results from the same organic substances, the same chemist failing to obtain identical equivalents by different analyses of exactly the same organic body, thus exhibiting the futility of all attempts at scientific accuracy, and impossibility of so-called organic chemistry, so far as it serves physiology, pharmacy, materia medica and therapeutics.

On the therapeutic philosophy that all substances, as they stand in relation to the human organism, are divisible into three general classes, viz , *Food, Medicine* and *Poison,* and that there is a radical difference and distinction between a medicine and a poison, as well as a food and a poison; that a true food substance, when taken up in pabular state by the living matter of tissue-elements, affords materials that can be converted or assimilated by the bioplasm into its own substance, thus losing all atomic characteristics and becoming non-atomic living matter or bioplasm, and eventually tissues and structures In other words, a food is a substance possessed of tissue and structural potentiality—true tissue-building constituency. The difference then between a food and a true medicine, or Physio-Medical remedy, is, the latter is a negative food;

i. e , does not actually afford pabulum and increase of bio-plastic substance, or quality, and consequent tissue-building; but simply modifies and improves the bioplastic conditions, functional potency of the whole tissue unit, and consequently the functional activity of tissues, structures, organs and systems. Hence they are called *sanative agents* or *medicines.* Therefore it follows that the essential nature or quality of Physio-Medical fluid extracts would radically differ from that of the other schools of medicine, even when dealing with the same sanative drugs. So that on the Physio-Medical theorem we regard much of the so-called "inert principles" of vegetable crude drugs essential to a fluid extract, as we require the full normal constituency of the crude article to insure therapeutic efficiency, drug identity, and consequent scientific precision in prescribing. Indeed, as before mentioned, an infusion is the most potent therapeutic form of these drugs; and this is because *it represents in a synthetic state the vital soluble therapeutic constituency of the drug; and this therapeutic potency is the desiccated bioplasm.* We shall therefore give to an infusion, according to Physio-Medical nomenclature, the name of *Normal Fluid Extract.*

Of the theory of bioplasm in a desiccated form constituting the therapeutic potency of vegetable drugs, we scarcely feel called upon to present further argument in defense; but attention is called to the following facts in support. Old and inert vegetable drugs are so because the drying process is carried to the extent of total destruction of the living matter i e , its return to atomic state

The fresh green drug, as a rule, does not furnish as potent infusion or fluid extract, because the fresh bioplasm is not so soluble nor potent as when in a desiccated, partly dried and concentrated state.

Finally, the desiccated bioplasm affords the essential therapeutic potency of these vegetable drugs, because *it furnishes the most assimilable form of pabulum to the bioplasm of the tissue elements,* when administered to the living organism; and it represents the purest type of negative food.

As to the question of inorganic therapeutic agents, and the role that hot water plays in a freshly prepared infusion, this reaches beyond the limits of the present article, into the principles of therapeutics. Therefore, we deem it sufficient to simply mention the facts that cold infusions have equal therapeutic power to hot infusions, only slower in exerting that influence, and consequently more persistent; that inorganic substances are equally efficient in any form, whether cold or hot infusions, or fluid extracts, except rapidity of entering the circulation, afforded them by heat.

While the general rule is, that green fluid extracts, i. e., prepared from the fresh plant, have not met with general favor from the profession, yet there are some agents that furnish certain therapeutic results in the green state, which cannot be obtained from them in the dried form. Phytolacca root, and juglans cinerea, bark of root, are two instances of this kind; the former, in the green state affords an excellent regulator of the vaso-motor nerves of head and face, and is consequently a most valuable remedy in certain forms of facial neuralgia; the dried agent affords no such influence. The fresh bark of green root of juglans cinerea is a prompt and powerful stimulant of the intestinal motor system, and gives a valuable cathartic and hepatic action as a result of this influence; the dried bark of the root yields an astringent and tonic action upon mucous membranes. These will be referred to again in their proper province; we only mention them here to show what these influences above named are because important therapeutic constituency of the drugs have been isolated or dispersed by drying. This fact in no degree constitutes an exception to the general rule already laid down, that a fluid preparation properly made with boiling water as a menstruum, is a *normal fluid extract*, and affords the absolute therapeutic constituency of the drug. Then in order to establish a necessary standard of Physio-Medical fluid extracts, in accordance with the foregoing facts and principles, we would suggest the following general rule:

A Fluid Extract is a fluid preparation whose menstruum is boiling water, or some other fluid that will extract and hold in solution the entire therapeutic constituency of the drug. To which is added the smallest percentage of preservative that will protect the product from fermentative and other deleterious action.

Now we are aware that the inexperienced, and those who have been taught to believe alcohol a powerful menstrium, mistaking the burning, irritating action of the alcohol upon the mucous membranes for "strength," or therapeutic potency of the pharmaceutical product, will deem preparations on the above-formula entirely too "weak" and inadequate. But the experienced Physio-Medical practitioner has proved their reliability, and all who give our fluid extracts, which are conformed closely to this rule, a thorough trial, divesting themselves of all prejudice or preconceived notions, will certainly not be disappointed. They will learn that alcohol is not a menstruum in the true pharmaceutical and therapeutic sense of the term.

Preparing the Crude Drugs.

The proper time to gather vegetable agents is at the stage of full maturity of the part to be used. If the whole plant, which includes roots, is desired, it must be gathered when in full foliage, and bloom, if a flowering plant. If only the roots entire are required, then early spring, when the plant is just shooting above ground. If the bark of the root, then a little later when the sap is starting, so that it peels readily. Barks, and fruits, such as berries, nuts, etc., are gathered in the fall; the bark when the sap is starting down, about the early turning of foliage; fruits at their earliest maturity and ripeness.

Cutting.—The herb-tops, barks and roots should all be cut while in the *green state* into the finest possible transverse sections. Bark of roots should be well washed and scraped, as also the larger roots when used entire. For cut-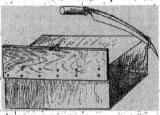ting there is nothing better than the old fashioned hand cutting-box, used by farmers in making chopped feed for horses, which can usually be gotten cheap at hardware and implement stores. A very good cutter can be cheaply made by attaching a corn-cutter to a large square block of wood, having a board nailed on one side, as shown in the figure.

Drying.—After cutting carefully, the materials are dried, at not too high a temperature, in the shade, never

exposing them to the sun, nor in a room the temperature
of which is above 85 deg. F. The atmosphere should be
thoroughly dry and pure. They should be spread out so
as to avoid contact of large masses, which will ferment
and mould. See to it that they dry slowly without injury,
and well protected from dust and insects during the drying process, as well as afterward. Dr. Joseph Weeks, of
Mechanicsburg, Ind., has devised a series of drying racks,
which he lays one upon another, after loading them, and
swings up to the ceiling by ropes and pulleys, out of the
way in the back room of his office, in a most favorable dry-

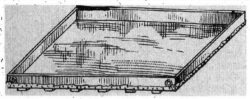

ing atmosphere. They consist, as shown in the figure, of
several box-frames about 3 inches deep, 37x42 inches
square. The bottom is covered by coarse canvas; the sack-
ing used by furniture dealers is best. This is supported
by slats 2x⅜ inches nailed across the frame about 6 or 8
inches apart. After being loaded with the fresh cut drugs
they are piled upon each other, the bottom one, having
rings for the attachment of swinging ropes. Over the top
one is thrown a loose canvas or paper. The contents are
thus thoroughly protected from dust, insects, etc., and yet
a thorough circulation of air i allowed and the drying
process is favored. This is an excellent device, cheap and
convenient.

Comminution.—After the drying process is carried to
the proper extent, the drugs must be reduced to a suitable
degree of comminution, or separation into fine particles
favorable for obtaining in solution their medicinal properties. On a small scale, and especially for plant-tops,
leaves, and the more tender barks, a large iron mortar and
pestle serves the purpose, as it will for all other crude
materials if one is not averse to the free use of muscular
exertion. A good light-running hand drug-mill gives the
most satisfactory results, and should be a part of the
equipment of any considerable pharmaceutical laboratory.

There are quite a number of good drug-mills on the market, and can be gotten from any hardware dealer, ranging in price from $10.00 to $25.00. The Hance Drug-Mill, on the whole, we think is the best one.

Pharmacists vary in their preferences as to grinding of drugs, some using exceedingly fine powder, others very coarse, and others preferring moderately fine powder. When we remember that the process of percolation, the one now universally used - as the best for obtaining the therapeutic values of drugs, depends for its effectiveness wholly on the force of gravity plus the weight of the column of fluid or menstruum as it is called; that after the solvent action of the menstruum is complete, the mere mechanical force of gravity enables it to displace or disengage itself from the drug-residue, and fall from the lower end of the percolator laden with its full complement of extractive constituency, we can readily see that a very fine powder being more compact would render percolation quite slow, and thus restraining the passage through the drug mass deprive the process of the aid afforded by gravity force. Therefore it would seem that after maceration is complete, that is, the full solvent action of the menstruum is spent, rapid percolation through a moderately fine powder should yield the richest percolate; our personal experience, which has been quite extensive in this direction, testing thoroughly the various grades of grinding, is wholly in favor of a moderately fine (No. 50) and moderately coarse (No. 40) powder.

We prefer to not sieve the grindings from a drug-mill. Most all crude drugs of the organic class contain parts more easily comminuted than others; they are mostly the intercellular structures, and these contain the bioplasm of the plant; consequently, as we have before stated, are most potent in medicinal constituency. These more friable parts of the drug will be the finer as the mass comes from the mill, hence sieving separates them readily from the more woody parts, which also contain in many drugs important therapeutic principles, rejecting which, the percolating powder represents only partially the therapeutic value of the entire plant. The entire mixture gives a better powder for percolation.

While beyond question the fresher gathered and prepared the materials, the better the pharmaceutical product, and we strongly urge the physician who can at all, to have them gathered, and prepare all the botanical agents that grow in his immediate locality; yet he will have to depend on the general drug-miller for many valuable foreign agents. He should therefore sufficiently acquaint himself with the physical characteristics of these foreign drugs, and the requirements of first-class materials, to be able to make intelligent selections. As an aid to this end we offer the following general suggestions in purchasing:

Do not buy the crude packed drugs. As a rule they must be very dry to pack well, which over-dry state injures their medicinal value. Such drugs are exceedingly hard to grind, and the labor of comminuting overbalances the difference in price, unless time is of no value.

Deal with a Physio-Medical drug house, as they will be better able to furnish fresh and reliable botanic agents. If such a drug house is not within reach, order direct from the drug-mill.

The grade of grinding drugs is usually indicated by the terms *fine, moderately fine, moderately coarse,* and *coarse.* The United States Pharmacopœia has designated more definitely the degrees of fineness meant by the above terms, in relation to the number of meshes to the linear inch of sieve wire, as follows:

Very fine powder should pass through a sieve of 80 meshes to the linear inch, and is therefore powder *No. 80.*

Fine powder has been sieved through wire of 60 meshes to the inch, and is *No. 60* powder.

Moderately fine powder is sieved with wire of 50 meshes per inch, and is *No. 50* powder.

Moderately coarse powder is sieved with 40-mesh wire, and is therefore *No. 40* powder.

Coarse powder is sieved through wire of 20 meshes per inch, and is *No. 20.*

Thus one can easily indicate to the drug-miller exactly what degree or grade of grinding is desired.

In ordering drugs for percolation always specify, from the mill, *unsieved.* As already explained, the best drug, or in other words the ground product which will represent the full constituency of the plant, is that containing every part of it, and will be made up of different degrees of fineness. The cellular, intercellular and dense ligneous parts each will vary in fineness with the same setting of the mill. The drug-miller knows that the intercellular portions are more easily pulverized, hence he sieves these

finer and. richer parts out, to be taken to the chaser-mill
for pulverization, while the coarser woody, and poorer
medicinally, parts are sold for percolation. Of course the
drug-miller does not know the difference in medicinal richness of these various parts; looking at the matter from a
purely commercial stand-point, he does not think of selling
percolate-powders direct from the mill.

Percolation—Its Purpose, Philosophy and Practical Methods.

The cylindrical vessel for the process of percolation,
made of heavy tin, granite iron, glass or crockery-ware, is
called a *percolator*. The *menstruum* is the fluid poured
on drugs in the percolator; the *percolate* is the liquid
containing the solvent principles which escapes from the
lower end of the percolator; and the process is *percolation,
displacement* or *lixivation*. This process is one of
the very earliest methods of pharmaceutical practice, as
well as one of the most important. The philosophy of
percolation is very aptly set forth in the following, which
we quote from Remington's Practice of Pharmacy, page
228:

"*When a powder placed in a cylindrical vessel
with a porous diaphragm below, is treated from
above with a liquid capable of dissolving a portion
of its substance, that portion of the liquid first in
contact, in passing downward, exercises its solvent power on the successive layers of the powder
until saturated, and is impelled downward by
the combined force of its own gravity and that of
the column of liquid above it, minus the capillary
force with which the powder tends to retain it.*
If the quantity of liquid added is not more than enough to
satisfy the capillarity, no liquid will pass the diaphragm;
but the careful addition of liquid upon the top displaces
that absorbed in the powder without mixing materially
with it, and takes its place, to be in turn displaced by a
fresh portion of liquid."

The above, which undoubtedly is the true principle of
percolative action, is in support of our idea that most powders as furnished by the drug-millers to-day for percolation
are entirely too fine, and when wet they become so dense
as to offer too much resistance to gravity-force, the most
important factor in the process

The Percolator.—Almost every conceivable form of percolator has been devised, both as regards natural percolation, or that by natural force of gravity plus the fluid weight, and special or forced percolation. The history of the development of this most important pharmaceutical process, as well as the various forms of percolator, we have not the time or space here to discuss. We shall confine ourself to the description of but one form of percolator for each process of percolation, that of *natural* and *forced.* With natural percolation, our personal preference, after experimenting with various forms, is the cylindrical vessel with just enough taper from top to bottom to facilitate unloading, with proportion between upper diameter and length of 1 to 4; that is, four inches of length to every 1 inch of diameter at the upper end, with the lower diame-

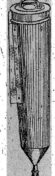

ter inches less; which lower diameter is meant at the commencement of the funnel-shaped part.

This is made of the heaviest grade of tin plate. The upper end is straight for a depth of from 1¼ to 1½ inches, sufficient to receive a closely-fitting lid; from this it tapers gradually to the lower end, which terminates in a funnel extremity, the end of which flares so as to receive a No. 6 or 7 cork, so that it can be thoroughly corked. A diaphragm is fitted so as to lie at the upper part of the funnel at the lower end of the percolator. This should be made of about No. 50 or 60 sieve wire soldered to a heavy iron ring. We do not use a diaphragm except in very resinous drugs, much

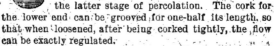

preferring to fill the funnel end with absorbent cotton, packing the drugs directly on it. This gives a filtered percolate, yet allows free escape of the fluid; the only objection being that in drugs with much gum-resin it is liable to become clogged, when hot water is poured on, in the latter stage of percolation. The cork for the lower end can be grooved for one-half its length, so that when loosened, after being corked tightly, the flow can be exactly regulated.

We have three sizes of percolators made. The smallest is 20 inches long; 5 inches upper; 3½ inches lower diameters; and will hold one pound of drugs, leaving ample room above to hold menstruum. The medium size is 30 inches long; 6¼ and 4 inch diameters; and will hold 3 to 5 pounds of drugs. The largest is 53½ inches long; 10 and 8 inch diameters; and will hold from 30 to 40 pounds of drugs, giving room for menstruum above. The first size we use for making fluid extracts of single articles in one quart quantities. The second and third sizes are used for larger quantities of single articles, or for percolating compounds of several articles, in quantities. These percolators are given a heavy coat or two of paint on the outside, and if well cleaned inside after using, they are very durable and will not easily rust or corrode. Of course they will not answer well for green drugs, especially if macerated in the percolator. They can be made to order of glazed crockery, by the potter, but are heavy and must be handled carefully. The best, but most expensive material, would be granite iron ware; these would have to be made by special order at the works. We have heavy tin percolators that have been in use for fifteen years, and many green drugs have been percolated in them, yet they are now bright and clean.

Sometimes the drugs swell after hot water has been poured on them in the percolator, rendering it difficult to

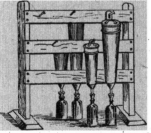

unload the vessel when done. This may be facilitated by blowing forcibly in the lower end of the percolator, with the vessel upside down. A stream from the hydrant turned in the small end works well.

A wooden frame or percolator rack as shown in the figure can be cheaply constructed by any carpenter, and is a most convenient arrangement

The Centrifuge.--Of the special apparata and processes, we desire to call attention only to *centrifugal displacement* as the most thorough and rapid, far exceeding that of any other process with which we are acquainted. An apparatus can be constructed at a moderate cost that answers the purpose admirably.

This figure shows a centrifugal displacer consisting of a heavy iron wheel grooved for a cord-belt, with a handle on one of the arms to turn by hand. A belt from it, guided by a pulley to a small belt-wheel, turns an upright shaft having arms at its upper end, on which is fastened a basket or cylindrical sieve with a solid bottom; it is best made by covering a circular frame-work with No. 80 sieve wire well soldered to it. This is filled with the macerated drugs, secured to the arms of the revolving shaft, and turned at a speed of from 1,500 to 2,000 revolutions per minute, exerting a force two hundred times greater than gravity. The fluid is thus thrown from the revolving sieve

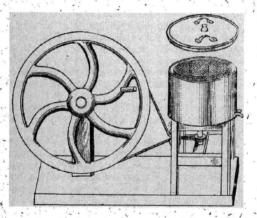

into the enclosing vessel, whose bottom is convex and inclined to one side where the fluid is drawn off through a faucet. The large wheel, as well as small ones, with shaft, arms, frame, etc., can be made by a good carpenter; the seive and vessel can be made by a tinner, and a very cheap centrifuge can be thus gotten up. Any machine shop with foundry can furnish the wheels of iron, and by gearings a higher rate of speed and a more effective machine, either for hand or power, can be constructed.

Maceration.—The essential step of percolation is, *thorough permeation, saturation and solution of the therapeutic constituents of the crude drugs by a menstruum, or solvent liquid.*

There are two ways of macerating the drugs, in the percolator, and in a separate vessel and then transferring to the percolator. The latter, though involving more attention and labor, is much to be preferred.

To macerate in the percolator, the tops of plants, and fibrous barks, in moderately coarse powder is best; however if properly managed any drug in fine and moderately fine powder can be used. With a large piece of absorbent cotton in the funnel part of the percolator, which is uncorked, the drugs are placed in lightly, avoiding the least packing, and the menstruum poured on at first freely till it pours from the lower end of the percolator, which is kept open till all dropping ceases; the menstruum is again returned and allowed to run off freely, returning it the third time the percolator is tightly corked as soon as it commences flowing freely; all the menstruum is now poured on, and the percolator closed tightly at both ends, standing for eight to ten days, when it is percolated.

The most effective method or maceration is done in a separate vessel or vessels, either mixing and changing the drugs thoroughly in the one vessel, or changing them from one vessel to the other, at intervals, so as to bring every part equally in contact with the menstruum, as the more thorough and even the saturation, the more complete will be its solvent action. Several macerating vessels made of heaviest tin plate, holding from one gallon to ten gallons, with closely fitting lids, should be kept for this purpose. The drugs should be sufficiently saturated with the menstruum to drip from them when removed to the percolator after eight or ten days' maceration.

The percolating process varies according to the menstruum used, and the nature of the product desired. If maceration has been in the percolator, and the powder is dense and very fine, percolation should be slow, as it necessarily will be. If a moderately fine or coarse powder, with light drugs, such as leaves and stems, it may be quite rapid, even with percolator maceration.

If maceration has been very thorough, as it will be if properly done in macerating vessels, then rapid percolation is best, because the menstruum being replete with the solvent principles, it only remains to disengage or displace it from the exhausted drugs, and the quicker the better; for a certain amount of evaporation must take place in the open percolator during percolation, which means condens-

ation and precipitation of the solvent constituents, returning to the drugs. Practically the process may be divided
into two stages, viz , *percolating the free menstruum*,
by which is meant that portion of loaded menstruum
which will flow from the percolator by the force of its own
gravity; and *percolating the residual menstruum;*
which is that portion retained by the force of the capillary
attraction of the drugs, after total cessation of flow from
the open percolator

During the first stage of percolation, the escape of percolate should be free and unrestrained, except by the cork
at the lower end of the percolator; the lid should not now
be very tight. as the atmospheric pressure if not fully
admitted to the upper part will restrain the gravity of
the menstruum. The cork should be loosened sufficient to
allow the fluid to drop rapidly, about 35 or 40 drops every
fourth of a minute.

To obtain the *residual menstruum*, the second stage
of percolation, the drugs are removed by some pharmacists
and subjected to high pressure in a drug-press. This process is laborious and not absolutely effective, as a certain
amount of fluid will remain in spite of the highest pressure, which in large quantities of drugs is considerable. By
far the most thorough, rapid and convenient method is
that of displacement in the percolator   If a fresh fluid is
poured on the drugs after the free and fully charged menstruum has escaped, it will take the place of the residual
menstruum, because the capillarity of the drugs will prefer the fresh fluid to that of the denser loaded residual
menstruum. Cold or hot water answers perfectly for
displacing the residual menstruum, and is inexpensive.
Boiling water is much to be preferred for residual displacement, though in drugs containing a large amount of
resinous matter, clogging of the percolator is apt to occur,
and warm or cold water must be used. During this stage,
percolation should be much more rapid, with the lid partly
removed so as to allow free atmospheric pressure; the cork
should be sufficiently withdrawn to allow a small stream
to escape

Centrifugal Displacement.—After thorough maceration, the drugs are placed in the centrifuge and the
machine revolved by hand or power, at its highest speed,
until all the fluid ceases to escape, which will usually take
from three to five minutes; then boiling water is poured

carefully in the centre of the revolving vessel, in quantity
sufficient to make up the total of fluid extract to be obtained, the machine being kept at a speed sufficient to
allow the fluid to gravitate slowly to the bottom of the
vessel while being poured on; then it is worked at its highest speed for three to five minutes longer. In this process
the *residual menstruum* can be almost absolutely displaced and the drugs come out of the machine dry.

The fluid extracts for Physio-Medical use we will designate, with regard to the menstruum used, as *Normal or
Non-Alcoholic, Saturated and Expressed*

Normal Fluid Extracts are those made with boiling
water as the menstruum, to the percolate is added a preservative, and the product is finished. As we have before
explained, boiling water is the only menstruum that extracts the full complement of medicinal constituents of
vegetable drugs as combined in the organic genesis of vegetable growth and development. Hence we call such a
preparation a normal fluid extract.

Alcoholic Fluid Extracts.—According to Physio-Medical philosophy, the formula for alcoholic fluid extracts is,
a menstruum with the smallest percentage of alcohol that
will thoroughly preserve the product; the other constituents of the menstruum being water alone, or in combination with some other solvent. This menstruum is used
for drugs containing resins and gums in considerable quantity, upon which more or less of their medicinal qualities
depend.

Saturated Fluid Extracts.—These are made by a menstruum, alcoholic or non-alcoholic, poured over a definite
quantity of drugs, to the extent of covering the mass, and
allowed to stand closely covered for an indefinite time,
being decanted off as used, or finally filtered off from the
drugs. This process is advantageous for drugs whose
medicinal qualities depend almost wholly on gums and
resins, such as gum kino or gum guaiacum.

Expressed Fluid Extracts are those made from oily or
succulent drugs, such as seeds, fruits, and green plants.
The materials are bruised in a mortar, ground in a drug-
mill, or cooked into a pulp, a greater or less quantity of
some form of menstruum incorporated with it, and the
whole displaced with the centrifuge, or a drug-press.

Formula for Normal Fluid Extracts, e. g. Extractum Scutelariæ. Fluidum Normalis; Normal Fluid Extract Scutelaria Lateriflora.

Scutelaria No. 50 (moderately fine) powder	lb. 1
Boiling Water	fld. oz. 32
Salicylic Acid	oz. av. 1¼
Nitrate Potassium	oz. av. 2
Sodium Sulphate	oz. av. 1¼

Place the powder in a macerator; pour on the boiling water, stirring thoroughly; cover tightly and keep hot in hot water or a steam bath, at a temperature of 160 F., for ten or twelve hours; transfer to a percolator; or much better, the centrifuge, and displace 32 fluid ounces while hot, adding more boiling water if necessary. Mix and triturate thoroughly together the salicylic acid, nitrate potassium and sodium sulphate, and add to the 32 ounces of percolate, after it is cold, let stand 24 hours and filter. Dose 20 drops to a teaspoonful.

These fluid extracts keep well during the hottest weather, in this climate; they mix readily in any quantity of cold or hot water without turbidity or sediment; the preservatives in no way interfere with their action, as alcohol does in many delicate constitutions; in fact they favor the therapeutic potency of many drugs. In testing the strength of these, by taste, compared with the strong alcoholic fluid extracts, as many most erroneously undertake to do, the pungent, irritating effect of the alcohol upon the mucous membrane of the tongue and mouth must not be mistaken for drug-strength; of course if tested by such a misleading method these fluid extracts would indeed seem flat and weak. But a thorough, practical, bed-side test of these preparations by Physio-Medical prescribers will prove them to be quickly and kindly assimilated, without any local irritation of the mucous surfaces, and prompt and efficient in their therapeutic influence. If our physicians will only give these Normal Fluid Extracts, which are distinctively Physio-Medical, a thorough trial, the strong, poisonous, alcoholic fluid extracts of the Alopathic pharmacies would soon disappear from the Physio-Medicalists' shelves.

Almost all of our vegetable agents yield excellent Normal Fluid Extracts. The following list of agents are specially suited to this method of treatment:

Apocynum And., Apocynum Can., Anthemis Nob., Aralia Rac., Asclepias Tub., Arctium Lap., Baptisia Tinct, Berberis Aq., Barosma Cre., Capsella Bursa Pas., Celastrus Scan., Chelone Glab., Caulophyllum Thal., Capsicum An., Collinsonia Can., Cascara Sag., Cypripedium Pub., Cimicifuga Rac., Dioscorea Vil., Eupatorium Perf., Eupatorium Purp., Euonymous Atro., Gentiana Lut., Hamamelis Virg., Helonias Dio., Hydrastis Can., Jeffersonia Diph., Liriodendron Tul., Leptandra Virg., Lobelia Infl. Herb, Lobelia Infl. Sem., Lycopus Europ., Lycopus Virg., Leonurus Card, Mitchella Rep., Myrica Cerif., Nepeta Cat., Nectandra Rod., Phytolacca Dec. Rad., Polemonium Rep., Polygonatum Gigan., Polygonum Hyd., Prunus Virg., Podophyllum Pel., Ptelea Trifol., Quercus Alba, Rhus Glab., Rumex Crisp., Rubus Strig., Senecio Aur., Solidago Can., Salix Alba, Salix Nigra, Stigmata May., Taraxacum Off., Trillium Erec., Turnera Micro., Valeriana Off, Viburnum Pruni., Viburnum Op., Verbascum Thap., Xanthoxylum Frax. Cort., Zingiber Off.

Alcoholic Fluid Extracts are made with a menstruum containing a greater or less percentage of *alcohol as a solvent for certain therapeutic qualities of the drug treated.*

Absolute or undiluted alcohol as a menstruum possesses no solvent action on the medicinal constituents of vegetable drugs, except the resins and pigments. Its action upon the bioplasm and intercellular substances, which constitute by far the most valuable therapeutic constituency, is to so change them both in physical and chemical characteristics, as to render them absolutely inert therapeutically. This is not mere theoretical speculation. The proof of this important fact is not difficult.

Make a section at the apex-node of a growing plant-stem, mount on a microscopic slide with a damp chamber, in Wolf's nutrient fluid, some of the fresh cells, and many naked bioplasts are seen in the free cell-sap. Place under the microscope with a one-eight objective; now add gradually absolute alcohol, and note that the bioplasm, both naked and in the cell-nucleus, becomes contracted into a dense, opaque mass, and that the alcohol has no solvent action on the bioplasm, or other intercellular contents. Prepare another slide in the same manner, but instead of absolute alcohol use hot water; the bioplasm swells, and finally disappears in solution, together with the intercellular contents.

Take a section of the same plant, at the same point, freshly dried and moistened with the same nutrient fluid; place it under the same magnifying power, and note that the bioplasm and intercellular contents are in a semi-transparent and opaque—desiccated—state, having a dull amber color. Now saturate the section with absolute alcohol, and note the contraction of these parts, and the absence of any solvent action upon the bioplasm and cell contents. Proceed in the same way with another slide, except to use boiling water instead of alcohol, and note the prompt solvent action upon these constituents.

Lastly, take a quantity of fresh dried drugs, divide into two equal portions, treat one with absolute alcohol as a menstruum, and the other with boiling water; with equal quantities of each as a dose, test them therapeutically on the same patient, and you will no longer doubt the scientific accuracy of our position.

However, there are important therapeutic constituents resident in the gums and resins, and although boiling water will extract a considerable percentage of both, and quite sufficient for therapeutic purposes in most cases, yet there are some drugs containing quite a large quantity of these gums and resins, that it is desirable to obtain more than can be done by the treatment of normal fluid extracts In such drugs the alcohol answers the double purpose of a solvent and preservative.

Glycerin possesses a far more powerful solvent action upon the *gums* than alcohol, the latter's chief solvent action being upon *resins.* Sugar has a considerable solvent action on gums, when it is dissolved in water in the form of a thin syrup So that it is best to have a menstruum of *alcohol, water and glycerin in equal quantities* for drugs containing gums and resins. Again, where the gums predominate largely, and glycerin is objectionable in considerable quantity, the menstruum is made of *alcohol, water and sugar*

Formula for Alcoholic Fluid Extracts, e. g: Extractum Aristolochiæ Fluidum Alcoholicum, Alcoholic Fluid Extract Aristolchia Serpentaria.

Serpentaria No. 60 powder	lb. av.	1
Alcohol	fld. oz.	16
Water, preferably distilled	fld. oz.	22

Place the powder in a macerator, mix the alcohol and water, and while yet warm from the energy of union pour the whole quantity over the drugs, mixing thoroughly; let stand closely covered for eight or ten days, mixing and changing so as to bring the lower and wetter portions to the top. This is best done by transferring to another macerating vessel. Transfer to the percolator, which has been prepared with a large piece of absorbent cotton saturated with menstruum and placed loosely in the funnel end of the percolator, and covered with a layer of clean moderately fine sand. Packing should be done evenly and slowly, layer by layer. Rinse the macerator out with menstruum and pour on the drugs, after all are in.

Loosen the cork, immediately after the percolator is packed, sufficient to allow a flow of 30 or 40 drops per quarter minute; keep up the percolation at this rate till all the free menstruum has escaped, and dropping ceases; now pour on hot wa'er at about 180 deg. F. until 32 ounces of percolate is obtained, which constitutes the full complement of fluid extract. The percolation may be continued until 12 ounces more is obtained, to which sufficient granulated sugar is added to make 16 ounces. This makes an elixir of considerable strength, and is excellent in dispensing combinations of agents in syrups, etc. The centrifuge may be used instead of the percolator, being more rapid. Dose of alcoholic fluid extract 20 drops to a teaspoonful. Dose of elixir $\frac{1}{2}$ to 1 teaspoonful.

Of the agents best treated by the above method the following are typical:

Abies Can., Amygdalus Pers., Apium Grav., Aralia Rac., Arctium Lap. Sem., Asarum Can., Barosma Cren., Cascara Sag., Chelone Glab., Fucus Ves., Gentiana Och., Glycyrrhiza Glab., Guaiacum Lig., Hamamelis Virg., Hedeoma Pul., Helianthus. Leonurus Card., Leptandra Virg., Mentha Pip., Nectandra Rod., Nepeta Cat., Piper Ang., Polemonium Rep., Ptelea Trif., Rubus Stri., Rumex Cris., Salix Nig., Sanguinaria Can., Senna Alex., Solidago Can., Trillium Erec., Turnera Micro., Valeriana Off., Xanthoxylum Bac., Zingiber Off.

Formula for Glycero-Alcoholic Fluid Extracts,
Extractum Myrrhœ Fluidum; Glycero-Alco-
holic Fluid Extract Gum Myrrh.

Gum Myrrh No. 50 powder ..... lb. av. 1.

Alcohol	fld. oz. 10
Glycerin	fld. oz. 8
Water	fld oz. 20

Place the powder in a macerator; mix the three constituents of menstruum and pour over the drugs, mixing thoroughly. Let stand ten days, changing the drugs so as to insure thorough and even maceration.

Displace with the centrifuge, obtaining 32 fluid ounces of fluid extract. Or transfer to the percolator, with a fine wire diaphragm over the funnel end, filled with absorbent cotton moistened with menstruum, and obtain 32 fluid ounces of fluid extract.

The percolation or displacement may be continued with hot water, obtaining 12 ounces of percolate, in which dissolve granulated sugar a sufficient quantity to make 16 fluid ounces of *elixir gum myrrh*. Dose of *glycero-alcoholic fluid extract* 20 drops to a teaspoonful; of elixir one-half teaspoonful to a tablespoonful.

The following are typical agents for this treatment:

Asafoetida, Balsam, Peruvianum, Balsam Tolutanum, Benzoinum, Gum Guaiacum, Pix Bergundia Pix Canadensis, Styrax.

Formula for Saccharo-Alcoholic Fluid Extract, e. g Saccharo-Alcoholic Fluid Extract Kino.

Gum Kino No. 40 powder	lb. av. 1
Alcohol	fld. oz 10
Water	fld oz. 20
Granulated Sugar	oz. av 10

Mix the alcohol and water and dissolve the sugar in the mixture. Place the powder in a glass percolator, funnel end filled with moistened absorbent cotton. Pour on the menstruum with the percolator tightly corked. Cover the percolator and macerate for ten or twelve days; percolate slowly, obtaining 32 fluid ounces, adding cold water to the drugs if necessary.

The following are some of the drugs that may be treated by this menstruum:

Angelica, Balm of Gilead Buds, Balsam Tolu, Cinnamon, Cloves, Gum Benzoin, Juniper Berries, Myrrh, Orange Peel, Pimenta, Phytolacca Berries dried, Xanthoxylum Berries.

These fluid extracts will be found amply efficient therapeutically, even in the same dose as the strong alcoholic fluid extracts, which are so heavily loaded with resin, largely inert matter, that they are inelegant and unwieldy in dispensing. They cannot be added to even a syrup without rendering it turbid and unsightly. All this class of agents, though largely gum-resinous, it is a mistake to suppose that this constituent holds all their medicinal qualities. These glycero-alcoholic and saccharo-alcoholic fluid extracts represent the total therapeutic values of this class of drugs in their normal genesis. Besides, they are easily handled in prescribing. They mix readily, even with cold water, in most cases without the least turbidity; they combine with syrups and elixirs, making elegant preparations. Dose one-third to one teaspoonful.

Saturated Fluid Extracts, e. g. Saturated Fluid Extract Phytolacca Radix, Green.

Phytolacca Root, green, cut in thin slices	lbs.	5
Alcohol	pts.	2
Water	pts.	3

Put the sliced root in a jug or demijohn of proper size; mix the alcohol and water, and while yet warm from the energy of their union pour over the drugs, cork tightly, and with frequent shaking it is ready for use. After ten to fourteen days the fluid may be drained off by placing the drugs in the centrifuge, or in a percolator, with the funnel end filled with absorbent cotton. Hot or cold water is poured on after dropping ceases, till the full complement of five pints of saturated fluid extract is obtained. Dose 5 to 30 drops.

Aurum Trif. green, Balm of Gilead Buds (Abies Balsamea), Capsella Bursa Past. green, Capsicum An. Pods, Gum Myrrh, Juglans Cin. bark of root, green, Lobelia Sem. whole, Sanguinaria Can. green root. Stigmata Maydis green.

All fluid extracts from the green agents should be made by this formula. They should be cut into the smallest possible transverse sections, pods, berries and seeds being slightly bruised in a mortar.

Expressed Fluid Extracts.

This method of pharmaceutical treatment is suitable for such agents as ripe berries, fruits and succulent green plants. Fruits and berries are used in the fresh state, whole; plants and leaves are cut into fine transverse sections. Digestion or cooking by slow and constant heat, is the essential step of the process; after which the menstruum or medicinal fluid is expressed or displaced by the centrifuge or a drug-press. The centrifuge is the most rapid and fully as thorough as a drug press, and quite as cheap as the regular drug-presses; yet the lard-press, consisting of a screw press turned by a crank, and cog-wheels, which may be gotten at the hardware stores, is cheaper than the centrifuge, and does very well on a small scale of manufacturing.

After thorough digestion by slow heat, the drugs are transferred to a displacer, and the fluid obtained; the product is finished by adding some kind of antiseptic or preservative; in most instances this being sugar, which is also an excellent solvent; it is added before the digestive process.

Of course the medicinal strength of these products is not very definite—no attempt has yet been made at standardization, and fruits and berries especially are difficult to assay. The following formula for different articles and combinations, treated by this method, is aimed to establish a more definite standard; the principle of which is that *one fluid pound of the finished product shall represent two pounds avoirdupois of the agent in its fresh state; e. g. Extractum Fluidum Phytolaccæ Expressidum; Expressed Fluid Extract Phytolacca Berries.*

Phytolacca Berries ripe and fresh	lbs. 16
Water	pts. 2
Sugar, granulated	lbs. 3

Place the berries in a suitable vessel, granite iron preferably, with cover; dissolve the sugar in the water, well heated, and pour over them. Digest, or cook slowly, on steam or hot water bath, for three or four hours. Transfer to the centrifuge, or a drug-press, and obtain all the fluid. If more than one gallon, reduce by evaporation; if less, add boiling water in the centrifuge or press till sufficient is obtained to make a gallon of the finished product. This may be flavored with advantage therapeutically, by essence sassafras, reducing 6 ounces below one gallon and adding that quantity of the essence.

Other drugs that are therapeutically and pharmaceutically compatible may be combined, and a very elegant and convenient product obtained. The following, for example, which is valuable in molecular and nervous rheumatism; it is also efficient as an antifat.

Expressed Fluid Extract Phytolacca Bac. Comp.

Phytolacca Berries, fresh and ripe	lbs. av. 8
Fucus Marina	lbs. av. 4
Senna Alex. No. 40 powder	lbs. av. 4
Water	pts. 5
Sugar, granulated	lbs. av. 4

Dissolve the sugar in the water, hot, and pour over the drugs in a suitable vessel, digest over a hot water or steam bath for six or eight hours; transfer to the centrifuge or drug-press, and obtain the fluid, which, by evaporation, or the addition of boiling water in displacement, must be made to measure one gallon. Flavor with essence sassafras if desired.

Dose, a teaspoonful to a tablespoonful.

Of the fruits that may be treated by this method, the following compound, a valuable tonic laxative, is given as typical:

Expressed Fluid Extract Bromelia Compound.

Pineapples, ripe and fresh	3
Tamarind	lbs. 3
Rhus Glabra Berries, fresh and ripe	lbs. 2
Senna Alex. No. 40 powder	lbs. 2
Water	gal. 1
Sugar, granulated	lbs. 6

Place the tamarind, rhus glab. berries and senna in a suitable vessel, pour on water and digest, closely covered, over steam or water bath, for ten hours. The pineapples are previously cut in thin slices and covered with the sugar, standing closely covered, while digesting the drugs. Incorporate the pineapple with the drugs while hot, as they are transferred to the centrifuge or drug-press, and obtain the fluid, which should, by the addition of boiling water in the press or centrifuge, be made to measure one gallon of finished fluid extract.

Dose a teaspoonful to a tablespoonful.

Agents to be Treated by This Method.

Amygdalus Pers. Fruc., Bromella And., Cassia Fistu., Ficus Car., Fragaria Fruc., Pepo Sem., Phytolacca Bac., Prunus Ar. Fruc, Prunus Dom., Rheum Green Stems,

Rhus Glab. Bac. fresh, Ribes Fruc., Rubus Stri. Fruc., Rubus Vil. Fruc., Senna Alex. green, Xanthoxylum Bac. green.

ELIXIRS.

Practically we divide elixirs into *vehicles* and *medicinal elixirs*. Vehicles or solvents are preparations of water, sugar and alcohol, intended to take up and hold in solution soluble inorganic substances, to act as adjuvants, aiding the therapeutic efficiency of medicinal combinations, and to disguise and render palatable unpleasant agents. These we divide into *simple* elixirs, being the plain combination of alcohol, water and sugar; *aromatic* elixirs, or the addition of aromatic flavoring to a simple elixir; and *adjuvants*, or accessory elixirs, containing substances that aid the therapeutic action of other agents.

Medicinal Elixirs are those which contain the medicinal properties, in definite therapeutic potency, of one or more agents in a menstruum which answers the purpose of an elixir at the same time.

Elixir Simplex;

Distilled Water	pts. 4½
Alcohol	oz. 38
Granulated Sugar	lbs. av. 2¼

Heat the water to boiling point, dissolve the sugar, strain while hot; add the alcohol when cold.

Flavoring for Aromatic Elixir.

Oil of Orange	dr. iv
Oil Caraway	
Oil Coriander	
Oil Cassia	aa. dr. ii
Oil Anise	dr. i
Alcohol	oz. xx

Mix the oils and add to the alcohol.

Aromatic Elixir.

Flavoring	oz. 1
Alcohol	oz. 38
Water, distilled	pts. 4½
Granulated Sugar	lbs. 2¼
Carbonate of Magnesia	oz. ¼

Dissolve the flavoring in 2 ounces of the alcohol and

pour over the magnesia in a mortar, a little at a time, triturating thoroughly; mix the balance of the alcohol with the water and triturate 2 pints of it in successive small quantities with the magnesia in the mortar; filter all into the remainder of the alcohol and water, add and dissolve the sugar; filter through two or three layers of clean white flannel, or coarse filtering paper.

Adjuvant Elixirs; e. g. Elixir Glycyrrhiza Rad.

Peeled Licorice Root, No. 40 powder	lbs. 3
Water a sufficient quantity	
Granulated Sugar	lbs 2
Alcohol	pt. 1

Place the drug in a suitable vessel, dissolve the sugar in 2 pints of water, pour over the drugs and boil gently, well covered, for five or six hours; transfer to the centrifuge or a percolator, and treat with boiling water until 4 pints are obtained, to which when cold add the alcohol and strain through flannel.

This is an excellent base for cough syrups, etc., and is a powerful solvent and disguiser of quinine, salacine, etc.

Elixir Glycyrrhiza.

From Remington's Pharmacy, "unofficinal" list.

F. E. Glycyrrhiza	fld. oz. 2
Alcohol	fld. oz. 4
Syrup	fld. oz. 6
Oil Cloves	min. 10
Oil Cinnamon	min. 5
Oil Nutmeg	min. 12
Water	q. s. fld. oz. 16
Mix.	

Elixir Tolutana.

Balsam Tolu coarse powder	oz. 8
Alcohol	
Water	aa. pts. 2
Granulated Sugar	lbs. 2½

Mix the alcohol and water and macerate the balsam 24 hours, shaking frequently; add the sugar, macerate 10 or 12 hours, shaking frequently, and filter through one or two layers of white flannel.

Elixir Auranti; Orange Peel.

Fresh dried Orange Peel, bruised in
 a mortar to a coarse powder   lbs. av. 2
Water   pts. 2
Alcohol   pt. 1
Glycerin   oz. av. 8
Oil Orange   fld. dr. 2
Pulverized Sugar   lbs. 1½

Mix the water, alcohol and glycerin together and dissolve the sugar in it, reserving 6 ounces of sugar; pour over the orange peel in a macerating vessel and macerate three. days; displace with centrifuge or percolator, using hot water to obtain 4¾ pints. Triturate the oil of orange with the 6 ounces reserved sugar, and dissolve in the percolate, by first rubbing in the mortar by small additions 6 or 8 ounces of the fluid. Strain through white flannel.

Elixir Prunus; Wild Cherry Bark.

Prunus Vir., fresh bark, No. 40 powder   lbs. 2
Water   pts. 2
Alcohol   pt. 1
Granulated Sugar   lbs. 2

Mix the water, alcohol and sugar. pour over the drugs in a macerator, macerate four or five days, and displace with centrifuge or percolator (see saccharo-alcoholic fluid extract), using boiling water, if necessary, to obtain 5 pints.

This is an excellent adjunct to combinations for coughs, colds, and for pulmonary compounds.

Medicinal Elixirs.

The U. S. Dispensatory, and Pharmacopœia, define elixirs to be "aromatic spirituous sweetened preparations containing small quantities of active medicinal substances." This definition of an elixir is incorrect, because it is not in accord with the theory or practice of pharmacy and not consistent with their own therapeutics. For the U. S. Dispensatory, page 537, xv. edition, after admitting that "the object sought in the modern elixir is agreeableness of taste," and to attain this, therapeutic values have been almost wholly sacrificed. says, "their principal activity is due to the alcohol, which has proved in many cases very injurious. These considerations have heretofore prevented an official recognition of elixirs, and the present Pharmacopœia recognizes but one; i. e., elixir of orange, which has been introduced merely as a vehicle. Owing to their extensive use by practitioners all over the country, it becomes necessary to notice some of the most important in this commentary."

The above is one of the many instances of the fallacy, not to say ridiculousness, of sectarian "authority" attempting to dominate the utility of therapeutics. But owing to the extensive preference by the profession all over the country for this valuable product—medicinal elixirs—the U. S. Dispensatory is compelled to give them notice, but pushes them off in the smallest type in an unconspicuous place, because, forsooth, they have not yet received that mystic stamp *"Officinal"*. If these gentlemen could be distracted from the officinal whip, to the demands of advanced medical practice, they might be led to discern the difference between therapeutic value, and pharmaceutical elegance, medicinal potency and alcoholic pungency.

From the Physio-Medical standpoint, as explained in the beginning of this work, we learn that medicinal strength, or more properly speaking therapeutic utility, does not mean concentrated pharmaceutical products. Not to mention the baleful influence of alcohol in the highly alcoholic preparations, even a sanative agent in a highly concentrated form will, especially if its administration be long continued, expend its influence so locally upon the peripheral nerves of the mucous structures of the digestive tract, as to excite violent resistive and repulsive efforts, obstructing its assimilation and broader therapeutic influence, the agent being rejected by the Vital Force, and the physician is thwarted, although his selection of the agent were highly proper. Remembering these facts we realize the value of a fluid preparation affording the broad constituency of the drug in normal proportions, with as much palatableness and elegance as is consistent with these essential therapeutic requirements. Such a preparation w, may have in a properly prepared Medicinal Elixir.

In consideration of these facts we shall define a Physio-Medical Elixir to be, a normal fluid preparation of vegetable agents, with water as a menstruum, containing sufficient alcohol and sugar, as a preservative to also render the product as palatable as consistent with therapeutic efficiency; with a standard strength of one pound avoirdupois of the drug to sixty-four fluid ounces of the finished product. This gives a dosage of 2 grains to the fluid drachm.

Typical Formula for Medicinal Elixirs single agents.

E. g. *Elixir Gentiana Lutea.*

Gentian, No. 50 powder,	lb. av. 1
Water a sufficient quantity.	
Alcohol	pt. 1
Granulated sugar,	lbs. 4

Mix one pint of water with the alcohol and pour over the drugs in a macerating vessel, macerate for 8 or 10 days transfer to the centrifuge, or a percolator, and when all displacement ceases pour on boiling water, setting aside the first quart obtained, continue the displacement with boiling water until 12 ounces are obtained, dissolve the sugar in this, add to the first percolate, and strain through white flannel.

This should measure 4 pints of the finished elixir; if therefore, after adding the sugar it is not enough, more percolate may be added.

Dose one teaspoonful to a dessertspoonful.

Elixir Compounds.

All fluid compounds such as the so called "Compound Syrup of Stillingia," Compound Syrup of Mitchella" etc. which, as they are now made, are not syrups, but elixirs; a true medicinal syrup is a different product. They should be standarized and made as elixirs, We submit the following combinations, so popular with the Physic-Medical profession, made on the standard strength of 1 lb. av. of drug to 64 fluid ounces, 4 pints of finished elixir — 2 lb. of drug per gallon of elixir, and as they have all originated with the Physio-Medical School, we do not hesitate to name them *Standard Physio-Medical Compound Elixirs.*

e. g. *Elixir Mitchella Compound.*

Mitchella, No. 50 powder,	lb. av. 4
Viburnum Op., No. 50 powder,	
Caulophyllum, " " "	aa lbs. av. 2
Cypripedium, " " "	
Helonias " " "	aa lb. av. 1
Water a sufficient quanity.	
Alcohol	pts. 10
Granulated Sugar,	lbs. 20

Place the mixed drugs in a macerating vessel, mix ten pts. of water with the alcohol and pour over them, macerate for 8 or 10 days, changing them every other day so as to insure thorough saturation, transfer to a centrifuge or percolator, after displacement ceases pour on boiling water, set aside the first 20 pints of fluid, continue the displacement with boiling water as menstruum till 12 pints and 10 ounces are obtained in which dissolve the sugar and add to the first percolate, strain through white flannel.

Dose a teaspoonful to a dessertspoonful.

Elixir Stillingia Compound.

Stillingia, No. 50 powder	lbs. av. 3
Iris Vers, " " "	
Corydalis, " 60	"	aa lbs. av. 2
Pipsissewa, " " "	
Sambucus Flow. No. 40 powder	
Xanthoxylum Bac., No. 40 powder	aa lb. 1
Water a sufficient quantity.	
Alcohol,	pts. 10
Granulated Sugar,	lbs. 2

Place the mixed drugs in a suitable vessel and macerate for 8 or 10 days, mixing them every other day, to insure thorough saturation; transfer to the centrifuge, or percolator, and after displacement ceases, continue with boiling water, setting aside the first 20 pints, continue with boiling water till 12 pints and 10 ounces are obtained, in which dissolve the sugar and add to first percolate, strain through a white flannel strainer.

Dose, a teaspoonful to a dessertspoonful.

The following formula we have used for a number of years, and have found it reliable in all scrofulous, and syphilitic troubles.

Elixir Stillingia Compound.

Stillingia, No. 50 powder	lbs. av. 2
Lappa Maj. Rad. No. 50 powder	
Lapp Maj. Seeds, " " "	aa lb. av. 1
Sanguinaria Can., " " "	lbs. av. 1½
Iris vers, " " "	
Pipsissewa, " " "	
Corydalis, " " "	
Coriander, " " "	aa lb. av. 1
Xanthoxylum Ber., No. 40 powder	lb. av. ½
Granulated Sugar,	lbs. 25
Alcohol,	pts. 10
Water a sufficient quantity.	

Mix ten pints of water with the alcohol and pour over the mixed drugs in a macerating vessels let stand for 8 or 10 days mixing frequently, transfer to the centrifuge or percolator, treat with boiling water, set aside the first 20 pints, continue till 12 pints more have passed, in which dissolve the sugar, add to it more percolate if necessary to make 5 gallons when the first percolate is added, then strain through flannel.

Elixir Rhei et Potassæ Compound.

There seems to be no definite standard of strength, or formula for this most valuable and popular compound, like many other of our compounds; and it seems that Physio-Medicalists must wait till the U. S Pharmacopœia sets its "Officinal Seal."

The following we present as a standard formula for a Physio-Medical Compound Elixir of Rhubarb and Potassa.

Elixir Rhei et Potassæ Compound, Neutralizing Mixture, Physio-Medical.

Rhubarb, No. 50 powder	lbs av. 6
Columbo, " " "	
Ginseng, " " "	aa lbs. av 1½
Peppermint, fresh dried herb	lbs. av. 2
Or, Oil Peppermint,	oz. ½
Bicarbonate Potassa,	lbs. av. 2
Alcohol,	pts. 10
Water, a sufficient quantity	
Granulated Sugar.	lbs av 25

Mix the alcohol with 10 pints of water and pour over the mixed drugs in a macerating vessel, macerate for 5 or 7 days, mixing frequently, transfer to the centrifuge or a percolator and treat with boiling water, after first displacement ceases, setting aside the first 20 oz., continue till 12 pints more are obtained, in which dissolve the sugar, adding more percolate if necessary, to make 5 gallons in all, mix with first percolate and strain through flannel. If the oil of peppermint is used, it is to be poured in the absorbent cotton that is placed in the funnel end of the percolator, rubbing, picking, and triturating the oil through it thoroughly.

Dose, one half to one teaspoonful.

The Physio Medical Dispensatory, page 661, gives the

following formulæ for Syrup Rhubarb and Potassa, Neu-tralizing Cordial,

Rhubarb, well crushed, four ounces: dried peppermint herb eight ounces (or the green herb four ounces;) golden seal and cinnamon, each, one ounce. Macerate for two days with one quart of brandy, or with the same quantity of 40 per cent. alcohol. Transfer to a percolator, treat with water and set aside the first pint and a half. Continue the process with water until three quarts have passed, express the dregs, add four pounds of sugar and dissolve at a gentle heat, evaporating until the addition of the first liquid shall make a gallon. When cold, mix the liquors and add one ounce and a half of bicarbonate (not carbonate) of potassa. The addition of the alkali turns the whole syrup deep red: and occasions a flocculent precipitate to remove which the whole may afterward be filtered through flannel; though in practice this sediment may be allowed to remain and shaken up when used, as it contains no inconsiderable power though not so palatable as many desire.

On page 662 it also gives a formula of Dr. H. H. Hill, which has 2 ounces each of rhubarb and carbonate of potassa; one ounce each of golden seal and cinnamon to a gallon of brandy, four pounds of sugar, and twenty drops oil of peppermint.

There is two little rhubarb in both these formulas, and and the large amount of spirits in both, especially brandy, when we remember that this preparation is largely used for stomach and intestinal troubles of children, is most objectionable. Besides the process of treatment particularly the first formula is laborious and yields an inelegant product.

This standardization of our Physio-Medical agents and compounds, into medicinal elixirs, with two pounds of the crude ground drugs to the fluid gallon of finished elixir, will, we feel confident, meet the approbation of the general profession. This gives a preparation of ample strength for ordinary purposes; for extra cases the dose can be increased, or they can be made of double strength, and yet the same proportionate standard maintained. These elixirs are especially adapted to the treatment of chronic cases requiring long continued administration, as they will be tolerated locally by the mucous membrane without unpleasant local effects.

SYRUPS.

Simple and Medicinal.

The object of simple syrups, like that of simple elixirs, is that of a vehicle, solvent, preservative, and to disguise the unpleasant taste of medicines. They are also used as excipients, forming the mass and consistency of pills, suppositories etc

A medicinal syrup, we shall define to be, a fluid preparation in which large quantities of sugar have been added as a preservative to a decoction, which when finished, one pint will represent one pound avoirdupois of the drug used

This establishes sufficient practical difference pharmaceutically and therapeutically, between Medicinal Syrups and Elixirs: and also we have a definite standard strengths medicinally established on a therapeutical basis, instead of the now solely pharmaceutical standpoint, of heretofore vague and indefinite "shot gun" combinations and mongrel pharmaceutical products,

Simple Syrups

Simple syrups may be divided into two kinds, the plain or *simple syrup* and the *aromatic syrup*.

There is much variation among pharmacists as to the quantity of sugar, and method of preparing simple syrups But the most lamentable fact is that the druggists, a very large per cent. of whom, be it said to the discredit of the medical profession who tolerate and patronize them, have never been inside a college of pharmacy, they are the most pretentious class of drug venders Unblushingly they appropriate prescriptions of their physician patrons, and they become famous prescribers, donning the appellation of "Doctor", they gravely undertake to prescribe for the most serious and complicated diseases They are geniuses of marvelous "headache powders", " specifics " for gonorrhœa, syphilis "liver syrups", "antigermicides", and many "magic discoveries" Such druggists pride themselves on " extemporaneous pharmacy ", they can make simple and aromatic syrups in a few minutes by ' cold' percolation ", dissolving dirty sugar in dirtier cold water; in a percolator Cold percolation or any other "cold method" of making syrups is unaseptic, unsanitary and unsafe; and all physicians who have the good of their clientele at heart cannot be too severe in the condemnation of such methods, and druggists.

None but distilled water should be used in making simple and aromatic syrups, and this should always be heated to not less than 212 deg. F. and the sugar dissolved in it at this temperature. Of course in the medicinal syrups, distilled water is the best, for being devoid of nearly all the inorganic constituents it will take up and hold in solution more of the medicinal constituents. However, not being easily obtained in so large quantities as is necessary often in making most medicinal syrups, the continued boiling that is necessary removes nearly all the lime-salts of hard water, renders the process unobjectionable from a sanitary stand point. But when distilled water is not obtainable, good filtered rain water is the next best, lastly well or hydrant water.

As to quantity and quality of sugar, we prefer granulated sugar, of the fine grade, because granulated sugar will be of more uniform dryness, an important point in obtaining accuracy of measurement for one must know the exact increase of fluid bulk on the addition of the sugar. As a rule, with regard to consistency of syrup, *one and one half parts of sugar to one of water is the minimum, and two parts of sugar to one of water the maximum.*

The following formula gives the fluid increase on the addition of granulated sugar to distilled water at a temperature of 212 deg. F. after it has cooled to 77 deg. F.

Distilled water, fl. oz. 8 } = fl. oz. 18
Granulated sugar, oz. av. 16 }

The above formula is important in making medicinal syrups, as one must know the amount of decoction necessary to finish a syrup to the proper quantity on the addition of sugar.

The pharmaceutical object is to obtain a syrup of sufficient consistency to keep well, and yet not crystalize on standing, or become thick and unwieldy in cold weather, that is transparent and easily misceable with other fluids with which it is compatible. Of course it is necessary often, for special purposes, to have a syrup of greater or less consistency, but the following formula will be found a good general working consistency.

Syrupus Simplex.

Distilled water fl. oz. 16
Granulated sugar, oz. av. 24

Heat the water rapidly, closely covered, to the boiling point and dissolve in it the sugar, strain while hot through two thicknesses of white flannel previously wet in boiling water. This should make 32 fl. oz.

This makes an excellent syrup for soda fountains, any of the flavorings or fruit extracts mix readily with it.

In the physicians dispensary a half gallon bottle of simple syrup flavored well with strawberry, pineapple, orange or lemon, will aid materially in taking the 'raw edge" off many of his dispensings

Aromatic Syrups:— These are used for the same purpose as the plain or simple syrup, but are better as solvents and vehicles for the inorganic agents, such as alkalies, acids, and mineral salts generally.

Syrupus Aromaticus.

Simple Syrup,	oz 32
Oil Orange,	dr 2
Oil Caraway,	
Oil Coriander,	
Oil Cinnamon,	aa dr. 1
Oil Anise,	dr. ½
Cotton,	oz ¼

Mix the oils and saturate the cotton, picking and rubbing it thoroughly with the fingers, and finally in a mortar with a little granulated sugar, place in the funnel end of a percolator, first putting in a small pledget of dry cotton, heat the syrup sufficient to make it quite fluid and pour into the percolator on the cotton, letting it percolate freely. If after cooling, some oil globules appear on the surface of the syrup remove with blotting paper, or little pledgets of absorbent cotton.

After the syrup has stopped dropping, a very good light flavoring elixir may be obtained by percolating through the cotton a mixture of 4 ounces of alcohol and 12 ounces of water. A solvent and vehicle.

Syrupus Tolutanus.
Syrup Tolu.

Glycero-Alcoholic Fluid Extract Tolu.	oz. 3
Simple Syrup,	oz 29

Mix and shake thorougly; if any precipitate appear, filter through white flannel previously wet with hot water.

Use as a solvent, or adjuvant for other agents of a

more positive character.

In the above preparation any of the glycero-alcoholic fluid extracts, such as orange, ginger, benzoin, gum myrrh or wild cherry may be added to simple syrup making adjuncts to compounds of other agents and solvents for inorganic substances.

Medicinal Syrups.

Many of the green drugs yield their properties best by this treatment, while others give better results in the fresh dried state. Agents whose influence is required locally upon the functions of the digestive tract, especially the intestinal division of same, such as juglans, cin. green, podophyllum or leptandra should be treated by this process.

With a standard for medicinal syrups fixed at one pound avoirdupois of the drug used to one fluid pound of the finished syrup, whether the drug be green or fresh dried if the selections be made in accordance with therapeutic requirements, the dosage will always be definite.

Syrupus Juglandus, Syrup White Walnut, Bark of Root Green.

Juglans cin. bark of root cut in thin transverse slices,	lbs. 40
Water, a sufficient quantity.	
Granulated sugar,	lbs 60
Salicylic acid	oz. 1
Sulphate of Soda,	oz. 2
Phosphate of Soda,	oz. 1

Place the bark in a granite iron, or common iron kettle and cover with water, boil briskly till about half the water is evaporated, strain off through a common sieve, set aside this decoction, continue covering the bark and boiling down to one half or one third until the fourth time. Mixing all but the first, evaporate by boiling rapidly until with the first decoction 2 gallons 5½ pints are obtained, dissolve in this the sugar while boiling, boil a few minutes. Skim off, and strain through a flannel strainer while hot. After the syrup is nearly cold mix the salicylic acid, and soda-salts, triturate in a mortar, and dissolve in the syrup. This should finish up at 5 gallons.

We have found that the addition of oil peppermint to syrup juglans obviates griping, besides giving it a palata-

ble flavor. To five gallons of syrup, two ounces oil peppermint rubbed in a mortar with a pound of the sugar reserved, add after syrup is cold.

Dose, a teaspoonful to a dessertspoonful.

MUCILAGES, MUCILAGINOUS MIX-TURES, EMULSIONS, BALSAMS, AND HONEYS.

Under this classification we place, 1st., Vehicles which
have no direct solvent action, but simply hold in suspension minute particles of medicinal agents, such as gums,
resins, and inorganic agents. These are mucilages.

2nd., Combinations of gums, resins and inorganic substances with mucilages, making mucilaginous mixtures.

3rd., Intimate combination of oils, and oleaginous gum-
resins in suspension in mucilage. these are emulsions.

4th., Combinations of essential oils, and oleo-resins with
a heavy syrup alone, or in combination with mucilage constituting balsams.

5th., Combinations of essences, of the valatile oils, tinctures, and fluid extracts with clarified honey, these are
called honeys.

Mucilages are made of pure gums containing little or
no resin, and consequently soluble in water, in which they
are dissolved, to a proper consistency.

Mucilago Tragacanthœ, Mucilage of Tragacanth.

Tragacanth, selected, No. 50 powder,   dr. av. 7
Glycerin,   fl. oz. 2½
Distilled water,   oz. 13½

Mix the water and glycerin in a large mouth bottle of a
little more than a pint capacity, set in hot water till near
the boiling point, add the tragacanth, and digest for 4 to 6
hours with frequent thorough shaking, strain through 2 or
3 layers of plain antiseptic gauze, or cheesecloth.

This is a most useful mucilage to have in stock, it keeps
in any weather, excellent for emulsions &c., it answers the
general requirements of a pharmaceutical mucilage better
than any we are acquainted with.

Mucilago Acaciœ, Mucilage of Acacia.

Acacia, select, No. 40 powder   oz. 3½
Salicylic Acid,   grs. 2
Sulphate Soda,   grs. 2
Distilled water, a sufficient quantity.

Put the acacia in 6oz. of water in a large mouth bottle, heat by setting it in hot water to near the boiling point, digest with frequent shaking till dissolved; mix the salicylic acid and soda sulphate, rub well, dissolve in 2 oz. warm water and add to the mucilage, shake well.

A good base for mixtures and emulsions.

Mucilago Cydonii; Mucilage of Quince Seed.

Quince Seed, crushed,	dr. av. 3
Distilled water, a sufficient quantity.	
Salicylic Acid,	gr. 2
Sulphate Soda,	gr. 4

Place the drug in 12 ounces of water, digest on a hot water bath for an hour or two, shaking frequently; mix and triturate the salicylic acid and soda, dissolve in 4 ounces of warm water, add to the mucilage, and filter the whole through two thicknesses of plain antiseptic gauze, or cheesecloth.

This is a very ageeable mucillage, though rather light for emulsions.

Mucilago Ulmi, Mucilage of Elm.

Ulmus, pulverized,	oz. av. ½
Distilled Water,	fl. oz. 16
Salicylic Acid,	grs. 2
Sulphate Soda,	grs. 4

Mix and triturate the salicylic acid and soda, dissolve in the water and add the elm, macerate with frequent shaking until an even mucilage is obtained.

This is a very good general purpose vehicle. With one third part aromatic syrup it completely disguizes quinine and other bitter medicines in powder.

Mucialgo Sassafras Medullæ, Mucilage of Sassa-fras Plth.

Sassafras Pith, coarse powder,	dr. 2½
Salicylic Acid,	grs. 2
Soda Sulphate,	grs. 3
Distilled Water,	oz. 32

Mix and triturate the salicylic acid and soda, dissolve in the water well warmed, and add the sassafras pith, digest in warm water for 3 or 4 hours with frequent shaking, and strain through 2 thicknesses of plain aseptic gauze.

Used largely in cosmetics.

Emulsio Riciniæ, Emulsion Castor Oil.

Castor Oil,	fl dr. 4
Mucilage Tragacanth,	fl oz. 1¼
Simple Syrup,	fl. oz. ½
Oil Orange,	drops 5

Pour the oils in mixed mucilage and syrup, into a bottle sufficiently large to allow free agitation, and shake violently for 20 or 30 minutes.

Dose 1 to 2 tablespoonsful,

Emulsio Copibæ, Emulsion Copaiba.

Copaiba Balsam,	fl oz ½
Mucilage Acacia, or Tragacanth,	oz. 3
Simple Syrup,	oz ½

Mix the mucilage and syrup, add the copaiba, shaking violently for 30 minutes. This can be flavored with oil of peppermint or wintergreen or aromatic syrup, and used instead of simple syrup.

Dose, a teaspoonful

Stimulating Balsam.

Essence of Anise,	
" " Sassafras,	
" " Peppermint,	
" " Pennyroyal,	
Tincture Guaiacum,	
" Capsicum,	a a oz 1
" Myrrh,	dr 4
Simple Syrup (2 sugar to 1 of water)	oz. 6

Mix and shake well.

This is copied from Wilkinson's Botanico-Medical Practice except simple syrup is substituted for "sugarhouse molasses"

Dose from a half to one teaspoonful.

Balsam of Honey.

Tincture Lobelia,	
Essence Anise,	
Essence Sassafras,	aa oz ¼
Strained Honey	oz. 12

Mix.

For emetic in children, whooping cough, asthma and dry coughs Dose not given.—Wilkinson's Practice.

INFUSIONS, DECOCTIONS, and AQUEOUS SOLUTIONS.

When vegetable agents are treated by pouring water either hot or cold, over them and macerated for a short time, and the fluid poured off, it is called an infusion.

When these agents are treated by continuous boiling in water to a more or less concentrated aqueous solution, it is called a decoction.

Aqueous Solutions are obtained from volatile oils, and agents containing oleoresins and resinous principles.

All these preparations alone, without a preservative, are unstable, and belong to "extemporaneous preparations," and the processes of preparing them are denominated "extemporaneous pharmacy;" they are mostly intended for immediate use.

Infusions and decoctions were used almost exclusively by the early practitioners of our school, because of the prejudice of the regular school; aroused by jealousy of many who were brought into competition with the "Botanics," as they were then called, whose success brought them into greater requisition by the people, our pioneers could not, for many years enlist the aid of manufacturing pharmacists, hence we are compelled to rely on their own extemporaneous and crude pharmacy. It is seriously questioned by the older and more conservative heads of the Physio-Medical profession, whether our therapy and bedside practice, have materially gained by the large attention given our materia medica by modern manufacturing pharmacists. Certainly no one who has thoroughly and candidly tested the old, and the new pharmacy, will for a moment hesitate to pronounce in favor of infusions and decoctions when questioned as to therapeutic and practical efficiency.

The only objection being that of our modern homeo-sacchapathic palates. If evidence is needed more than the practical bedside tests of the difference between hot infusions and decoctions, and elegant looking highly alcoholic products of modern pharmacy, we offer in evidence that the U. S. Pharmacopœia, U. S. Dispensatory, and Remington's Pharmacy, all have honored infusions and decoctions with the "Officinal" seal.

While the writer is not the champion of retrograde return to the crude methods of the "tea doctors," as our early practitioners were dubbed, he does advocate the use of infusions and decoctions in all severe cases, and that in such emergencies the physician's better judgment shall not be in abeyance to fastidiousness. For we are sure that by using attractive forms of infusion-cups, nicely decorated and artistically shaped, suggestive cuts of which we herewith append, and in this way utilizing the modern tendency to fads, the hand painted china infusion-cup would do much to popularize and again bring into general use this most effective class of preparations. The *powder triturates* offer an elegant form of material for quick infusions, hot or cold.

Infusion Vessels.

These are designed to effect solubility and suspension in hot or cold water, the therapeutic constituents of medicinal

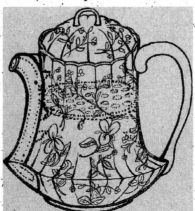

agents as thoroughly and rapidly as possible. Our illustration shows a modification and modernizing of Alsop's infusion jar, one of the earliest forms of infusion vessel the original form of which is shown in Remington's Pharmacy page 291. This is made of queensware or china, the drugs are held, covered by the upper stratum of water on a perforated diaphragm, movable to accommodate any quantity of drugs, and the difference of specific gravity of the heavily loaded fluid carries it to the bottom from whence it is poured off through the spout which commences close to the bottom.

Another illustration from Remington's Pharmacy, shows Squire's infusion mug.

This has a finely perforated colander of queen's-ware which fits in a jar made of the same material, decorated or of silver, or any other material desired; this descends to the bottom, containing the material to be infused upon which the hot or cold water is poured; it is more in the nature of a percolator, and after the drugs are exhausted they can be lifted out without disturbing the infusion.

The physician can have these furnished his patients by some popular queen's-ware merchant, or by a jeweler who can have them made at the factory; or he can have them made and furnish his patients at a good profit to himself. A little push in this direction, and with powder triturates flavored will render these infusions and decoctions really elegant and attractive to his patients, and not only render the practitioner a favorite even with the "*Four Hundred*," but save several four hundred dollars in the purchase by himself or patrons of pharmaceutical preparations, and proprietary medicines, whose gigantic therapeutic claims are only equaled by the enormity of price

The drugs for infusions will vary in degree of fineness; if dried ground drugs are used, from No. 60, fine, for barks; No 50,-moderately fine, for plants whole and brittle roots of small size; to No. 40 for dried berries, pods, and fruits, and for fibrous roots and stems, if leaves alone No 0, coarse powder will do If the green agents, such as stems and fibrous barks or small fibrous roots, they may simply be cut in very small transverse sections. If leaves and small plants especially those containing volatile oils and oleo-resins, they should be thoroughly bruised in a mortar; seed, pods and fruits green, may be infused whole or slightly bruised If powdered drugs are used, and they are much to be preferred, they must be first thoroughly triturated with granulated or powdered sugar, or if sweetness is objected to, then sugar of milk.

The proportion of drug to water varies so widely, both as to the nature and condition of the drug used, and the urgency of the case at hand, that nothing more than a vague general rule can be laid down, either for proportion of drug or length of time for the digesting or "steeping" process, or for the temperature of the water used 'All these things must be left almost wholly to the good judgment of the practitioner which will not fail to properly meet the exigency of each individual case.

The Physio-Medical Dispensatory places the proportion at one ounce of drug to the quart as the common proportion, to two or three ounces to the quart as the maximum, and thirty minutes to two hours for digesting.

Remington's Pharmacy, page 291 gives the following as the

General Officinal Formula for Infusions.
The substance coarsely comminuted, 10 parts,
- or oz. av. 1

Boiling water, 100 parts, fl. oz. 10

To make 100 parts, or fl. oz. 10

We are quite sure that in practice either of these will be found entirely too weak, either with green or dried drugs, unfortunately neither authority specifies the condition of drug as to green or dried state.

We have found by actual measurement, that if the dried

ground drug is used one and one half ounces to eighteen ounces of boiling water to be a good rule; and therefore suggest the following formulas for infusions:—

Standard Physio-Medical Formulæ for Infusions.

The drug dried, ground in fine, moderately
  fine or coarse powder,   oz. av. 1½
  Boiling water,   fl. oz. 18

Place the drugs in a proper vessel and pour over them the boiling water, cover closely, and keep hot in a water bath, on a warm stove or alcohol lamp while using; after 10 minuets it may be used.

Dose, a teaspoonful to a tablespoonful.

Green Drug Infusion.

The drug fresh, green, cut or bruised,   oz. av. 3
  Boiling water,   fl. oz. 16

Place the drug in a proper vessel, pour on the boiling water, cover closely and keep hot while using; after 15 minutes it may be used.

Dose, a tablespoonful to 2 ounces.

Powder-Triturate Infusions.

The drug, powdered, triturated, 2 parts to 1
  of sugar, or sugar of milk,   oz. av. 1½
  Boiling water,   fl. oz. 8

Moisten the drugs with moderatly hot water into a thick paste, place in suitable infusion vessel, pour on the boiling water, cover closely and keep hot while using. If cold water is used macerate ½ to 1 hour.

Dose, one to three tablespoonfuls.

Decoctions.

As we have elsewhere remarked concentration does not always mean therapeutic efficiency, and decoctions illustrate the truthfulness of this rule, for generally speaking they are nauseous and repulsive used alone because they are too much condensed and their influence exerted locally upon the mucous membrane. However there are some agents that necessarily need to be treated in this way to get their proper influence, but even these should be well sweetened with sugar or syrup, when they come more properly under the head of medicinal syrups. Nevertheless those agents that will not readily yield their properties except by considerable boiling, and which the practitioner does not care to keep in the form of medicinal syrup, and whose administration it is desired to continue more especially in cold solution longer than an infusion would keep, may be very advantageously prepared in the form of a sweetened decoction.

From these considerations, and more especially as there seems to be no definite standard of strength, or manner of preparing decoctions. — The U. S. Pharmacopœia giving exactly the same strength and process as for infusions except longer maceration on a hot water bath — two hours; therefore we suggest as more in accordance with pharmacological nomenclature, instead of decoctions, the term *extemporaneous medicinal syrups* be used, and the medicinal strength placed at a standard of one half that of medicinal syrups. Accordingly the following formula is offered;

Extemporaneous Medicinal Syrup.

The drug, dry, ground in moderately coarse
   powder,   oz. av. 8
   Water, a sufficient quantity,
   Granulated Sugar,   lb. 1

Place the drugs in a suitable vessel and pour on 32 oz of boiling water, loosely cover the vessel and boil gently either directly, or on hot water or sand bath till the fluid is reduced to 10 ounces, press off and add to decoction the sugar and evaporate if necessary, to one pint

Dose, a teaspoonful to a dessertspoonful

Aqueous Solutions.

The object of these preparations is the solution in water of the volatile oils, oleoresins, and resins. We have already explained that agents containing the above constituents can be treated either with water alone, or with a very small percentage of alcohol, yielding preparations of sufficient therapeutic potency; because their full therapeutic constituency, ("organic chemistry" so called to the contrary notwithstanding) is not represented in these oils and gum-resins.

Aqueous solutions then, speaking strictly in accord with normal pharmacy and therapeutics, are aqueous solutions representing in part or whole of the therapeutic drug constituency.

They sometimes become actual therapeutic agents, but are most often used as solvents and adjuvants. There are several methods of obtaining aqueous solutions, the process depending on the nature of substance used. The following are typical formulæ for the different classes of agents.

Volatile Oils, e. g. Aqua Anisi. Aqueous Solution of Oil Anise.

Oil Anise,	dr. 1
Carbonate Magnesia,	oz. ½
Salicylic Acid,	gr. 10
Distilled or boiled water,	fl. oz. 16

Triturate the oil of anise with the magnesia and salicylic acid rubbed together first in the mortar, then by successive small quantities add distilled water, triturating at each time, nntill 6 or 8 ounces are mixed with the oil and magnesia, transfer to a filter paper arranged in a funnel, and filter, pouring on the remainder of distilled water.

Aqua Anisi Sem. Water of Anise Seed.

Anise seed, moderately fine pdr.,	oz. 2
Distilled water,	q.
Salicylic Acid,	gr. 10
Nitrate Potassa.	grs. 20

Mix the salicylic acid and nitrate potassa with the drug and rub well in a mortar, add distilled water triturating thoroughly at each addition until six or eight ounces are used, then transfer to a filter paper in a funnel and pouring on the remainder of water obtain 16 ounces in all.

These solutions will keep almost indefinitely if well corked.

The following agents may be treated in this way.

Bay, oil or leaves. Cinnamon, oil or bark. Cloves, oil or berries. Cariander, oil or seed. Eucalyptus, oil or leaves. Fennel, oil or seed. Gum Camphor. Gum Myrrh. Lobelia, seed and oleo-resin. Oil of tar. Peppermint, oil or herb. Spearmint, oil or herb. Xanthoxylum, berries and oil. Yerba Rheuma, fluid extract or leaves. Yerba Santa, fluid extract or leaves.

TINCTURES, ESSENCES OR SPIRITOUS SOLUTIONS, VINOUS PREPARATIONS.

Tinctures, heretofore when little attention was paid to the part alcohol played in their influence upon the system, were largely used. In early pharmacy, whisky and brandy being the principle menstruum, and latter on, under the name of essential tinctures, and so called specific tinctures of the Eclectics.

But modern pharmacy happily has placed them on the back list largely; in which is shown a hopeful tendency also to reduce the percentage of alcohol, as well as drug strength in most of the modern alcoholic fluid preparations.

However, a few of these are still used largely by Physio-Medical practitioners, but they are of a strength that the name tincture is not proper, speaking in strict pharmacology. And from the Physio-Medical stand point they are nothing more than alcoholic fluid extracts. The confusion and impracticability of attempting to work pharmaceutically from a purely "officinal" and untheoretical standpoint is shown in Remington's Pharmacy, where some seventy-three "officinal" tinctures are named, and a table occupying two pages given to show the different menstruum strengths of each, "and other useful data." Percolation, maceration and by solution and dilution, are the various and laborious processes there given for making tinctures. The fact is that nearly all the products recognized by the U. S. Pharmacopœia come more properly under alcoholic fluid extracts already explained, while the drug strength of all these officinal tinctures are so varied that the intelligent prescriber must needs paste the officinal table in his hat to insure any degree of accuracy in dosage, a most serious thing to the patient in view of the free use of such virulent poisons as nux vomica, aconite, belladonna, digitalis or veratrum.

In view of these facts we suggest the following

General Formula for Physio-Medical Tinctures.

The drug dry, ground to moderately
fine powder oz. av. 8
Distilled or boiled water   fl. oz. 25¾
Alcohol,   fl. oz. 10¾

Mix the alcohol and water; pour over the drug a sufficient quantity to throughly moisten, let stand two hours and transfer to a percolator tightly corked, pour over the balance of menstruum, cover the percolator tightly and macerate for three days; percolate slowly until the menstruum has all passed and pour sufficient cold water on the drug to obtain thirty-two ounces of percolate.

As we have already mentioned, experience has proven

that in agents containing volatile, resinous and gum-resinous principles a much more normal therapeutic value is obtained with a menstruum of thirty to forty percentage of alcohol; it is therefore a therapeutic mistake to treat these agents with seventy to full strength alcoholic menstruum. And in view of these facts we suggest a uniform alcoholic percentage of thirty three and a third for all tinctures; and that the process be percolation for all except the resins and gum-resins, and these be treated by saturation and maceration in a suitable vessel for from ten to fourteen days as directed for *saturated fluid extracts.*

Typical Formula for Resinous Agents, e. g. Tinctura Myrrhœ, Tincture of Myrrh.

> Myrrh, moderately coarse powder; oz. av. 8
> Distilled or boiled water,   fl. oz. 25¼
> Alcohol,   fl. oz. 10¾

Place the drug in a large mouth glass bottle of at least two pints capacity, mix the alcohol and water and pour over it, macerate from 10 to 14 days shaking frequently; after 4 or 5 days maceration the tincture may be used, it can be poured off in dispensing without disturbing the drug; after maceration is complete place in a percolator and obtain 32 ounces, using water on the dregs if necessary. Dose 10 drops to a half teaspoonful.

There are several Compounds that are used extensively in the tincture form by Physio - Medical practitioners, which we will give according to above standard, as follows.

Tinctura Myrrhœ Composita, Compound Tincture of Myrrh.

> Number Six (Thompson's name.)
> Myrrh moderately coarse po. oz. av. 7
> Capsicum pods bruised,   oz. av. 1
> Water,   fl. oz. 25¼
> Alcohol,   fl. oz. 10¾

Mix the powders and moisten with sufficient of the menstruum of alcohol and water mixed, transfer to a percolator, pour on balance of menstruum, close the vessel tightly and macerate for six or eight days, percolate adding cold water if necessary, to obtain 32 ounces of tincture.

Dose 10 drops to a half teaspoonful.

Dr. Samuel Thompson's No. 6.

> Gum Myrrh pounded fine,   ℔. 1
> Capsicum,   oz. 1

Put in a gallon of fourth proof brandy; let stand five or six days, shaking it well every day, and it will be fit for use

The following from Botanic Physician published by Wm. Johnson about 1840, is his original formula for No. 6.

Gum Myrrh,	℔ ¼
Golden Seal,	oz 2
Hemlock bark	
Capsicum, a a	oz 1

Put into a gallon of alcohol, shaking once a day for five or six days, let settle, then pour off and bottle for use,

Compound Tincture of Myrrh.

Best Myrrh,	oz. 12
Capsicum	
Balsam of Fir,	
Nutmeg, a a	oz 1
Brandy,	gal. 1

Digest the brandy keeping in a warm place with frequent shaking for ten days; (Howard's Practice 1857.)

From the same author

Simple Tincture of Myrrh.

Myrrh,	oz. 12
Capsicum.	oz. 1
Peach or Cherry Kernels,	oz. 2
Brandy, alcohol or highwines,	gal 1

Digest the drugs in the spirits for 10 days

The author says of these, they are "powerful antiseptics, and highly valuable to wash old foul ulcers that are obstinate to heal" Modern aseptic surgery has fully verified this statement made many years before its advent

We would suggest as a menstruum thirty three and a third per cent. alcohol for all the above, instead of brandy &c

Cost's Domestic Medicine, published in 1859, gives the following compound tinctures which modified somewhat are still largely used.

Nervine and Anodyne Tincture.

Alcoholic extract of cypripedium.	oz 1
Oil of Anise,	oz. ¼
Camphor (gum)	oz ½
Tincture of Garden Lettuce,	lb. 1

Dissolve the first three ingredients in the tincture and keep in tight bottles.

Dose, 10 to 30 drops.

Antispasmodic Tincture.

Lobelia Tincture, (prepared from the seed)
Tincture Myrrh,
Nervine Tincture,   aa pt. 1

Mix. Dose one teaspoonful or more.

Tinctura Lobeliæ Composita, Compound Tincture Lobelia.

Third Preparation, Thompson.

Lobelia Herb, No. 40 powder   oz. av. 4
Capsicum,   "   "   "
Cypripedium,   "   60   "   a a oz. av. 2
Distilled or boiled water,   fl. oz. 25½
Alcohol,   fl. oz. 10½

Mix the alcohol and water and moisten the mixed drugs with a pint of it, after 4 or 5 hours place in a tightly corked percolator and pour on balance of menstruum, macerate for 5 days and percolate, adding hot water if necessary, to obtain 32 oz.

The addition of 3 drachms oil of anise to the tincture renders it more acceptable.

If lobelia seed instead of the herb is used then equal parts of that and capsicum, 3 ounces of each, should be used. Dose, 10 drops to a half teaspoonful.

Do not use the fine powders for these tinctures.

Dr. Samuel Thompson's "3rd. Preparation."

Ground Lobelia Seed,
Capsicum,
Cypripedium,   aa lb. ½
No. 6. best,   gal. 1

Mix and shake well together. Dose from one to three teaspoonsful.

Essences, or Spiritous Solutions.

In accordance with pharmaceutical nomenclature, essences or spirits are simply alcoholic solutions of volatile substances.

These are made in various ways by different manufacturing pharmacists. Remington's Pharmacy, as also the U. S. Pharmacopœia, have five different ways according to the substance treated as follows,

1st. By simple solution 2nd. By solution with maceration. 3rd. By gaseous solutions. 4th. By chemical reaction. 5th. By distillation.

In fact there is but one method and one class of phama-
ceutical essences, viz. those made by solution in an alcoholic menstruum.

Out of twenty-two officinal spirits, Remington's Pharmacy has but five that are made by any other method than
solution, two of which, by distillation, are Spiritus Fru-
menti, Whiskey. and Spiritus Vini Gallici, Grape Brandy.
The trouble is, these authorities loose sight of pharmaceutical laws and group all these preparations under the head
of spiritus, spirits.

The term spirits, therefore in order to avoid this confusion, we shall define as Alcoholic Distillates, Spiritus, as
Alcohol, Whiskey, Grape Brandy.

Essences or spiritous solutions. We shall call alcoholic
or spiritous solutions of volatile substances.

All of the volatile or essential oils and oleoresins, either
singly or in combination are soluble in definite proportions in a mixture of alcohol and water in relation, almost
wholly, to the percentage of alcohol. Full strength alcohol will combine without turbidity with the volatile oils,
such as sassafras, cloves, cinnamon, origanum &c., on the
addition of small quantities at a time, aggitating at each
addition, to an unlimited extent, for when there is more
oil than alcohol it is the same as mixing oil with oil. But
this solubility decreases rapidly on the addition of water
to the alcohol, so that 50 per cent alcohol or equal parts of
alcohol and water will only dissolve 1 dr. of oil to 8 oz. of
the menstruum. However as the object is to combine
these essences with other agents and combinations, and
the lower the percentage of alcohol the more readily the
essence combines with syrups, elixirs &c. and as in this
proportion they are of ample strength for practical purposes, we suggest the standard Physio-Medical essences at
*one dr. of volatile substance to eight ozs. of diluted (50
per cent.) alcohol.*

Typical Formula for Essence.

The Volatile Oil .... dr. 2
Distilled Water,
Alcohol, ... aa oz. 8
Mix the alcohol and water and after they have thoroughly

combined add the oil, shake thoroughly once a day for three days.

Use for flavoring simple syrups, aromatic compounds, medicinal syrups, liniments &c.

Compound Essences. Aromatic Essence of Ammonia. Aromatic Spirits of Ammonia, so called.

Carbonate of Ammonia,	dr. av. 4
Aqua Ammonia,	oz. 1
Essence Lemon,	oz. ½
Essence Lavender,	dr. 3
Essence Pimenta,	dr 2
Alcohol	
Distilled Water,	aa ozs. 7

Mix the alcohol and water and dissolve in it the carbonate of ammonia, next add the essences shaking thoroughly and lastly the aqua ammonia.

Dose: 20 drops to a teaspoonful, largely diluted with water, or simple syrup and water. A valuable antacid and heart stimulant.

Essentia Lavendulæ Compositus. Essence Lavender Compound. "Compound Spirits Lavender."

Oil of Lavender,	dr. 2
Oil of Rosmary,	dr. ¼
Oil of Cinnamon,	min. 10
Oil of Cloves,	min. 5
Oil of Nutmeg,	min. 15
Tincture Saunders,	oz. ¼
Alcohol,	oz. 9½
Water,	oz. 5¼

Mix the alcohol and water, add the tincture saunders, mix the oils and dissolve in the mixture.

Dose, one half to a teaspoonful,

Wines and Vinous Preparations.

In the early days of "botanic medicine," as it was then called, before the immense commercial demand necessitated rapid and large outputs of distilleries and vintages inviting adulterations and artificial methods of production, when pure wines and liquors could be procured, spiritous and vinous medical compounds, wines and bitters were the leading pharmaceutical products of the physicians own manufacturing especially.

But these have fallen largely into disuse, because much

depends upon purity of the spiritous, and more especially
the vinous menstruum which are now villainous artificial
concoctions. As Physio-Medicalists never use the stronger
alcoholics, whiskies, brandies &c., and rarely vinous products therapeutically, except of course in the absence of
all other suitable agents, we would not here give place to
this subject were it not for the purpose of calling attention of the profession to a method of obtaining an unfermented wine, or rather what we shall call *Fruit Essence,*
which we are sure possesses a number of important advantages over all other alcoholic preparations for medicinal
purposes. These advantages are:—

A purely aseptic wine; there is no fermentative process,
it is devoid of the ptomaines and corpses of millions of
micro-organisms, and other debris of fermentation.

It is a pure fruit essence, with a percentage of alcohol in
the menstruum for preservation only, consequently it furnishes in their normal genesis all the nutritive and therapeutic properties of the fruit used.

A low percentage of alcohol, and high percentage of natural properties of the substance treated.

Elegant appearance and delicious taste, retaining in its
native lusciousness the taste and odor of the fruit, it is
transparent and sparkling with the deep rich color of the
fruit used.

It is inexpensive, easily and quickly made by any one.
The physician can make it in quantities, prescribing and
dispensing it to his patients at a good profit, without being liable to the revenue, or temperance law.

These wines are also excellent menstruums for making
medicinal wines and bitters, answering the purpose much
better than any of the "purest" wines and whiskies "sold
for medicinal purposes only." Also a most elegant vehicle
and solvent for unpleasant medicines.

The writer has used these fruit essences in his practice
as above indicated, for twenty years, and feels sure that all
who make them according to the following formula will be
well pleased with the elegance and therapeutic utility of
the product.

*Essentia Fructi. Fruit Essences. e. g. Essentia
Vini. Essence of Grapes. Unfermented Grape
Wine.*

Fresh ripe Concord grapes, three gallon measures
full or   lbs. av 10

Water, distilled or well boiled, cold,	pts. 18½
Alcohol,	pts. 5½
Granulated Sugar,	lbs. 12

Wash the grapes thoroughly in warm water before picking them off the stems, stem and place them whole in a five gallon demijohn; mix alcohol and water, dissolve the sugar in this and pour over the grapes.

To proceed less accurately and more practically, fill the demijohn a little over half full of grapes, and fill full with a menstruum of 75 parts water, 25 parts alcohol in which mixture disolve a little over ¼ pound granulated sugar per pint, which will take about three and a half gallons to fill the demijohn.

Macerate with occasional shaking for 4 or 6 weeks when the fluid may be drained off the grapes, without pressing. In from 4 to 6 days this will do to use. We have often let the fruit and fluid stand together for six months, but usually in seven weeks the grapes will be found tastless, having yielded up their properties to the menstruum.

If sweet catawba grapes are used, less sugar may be employed, say about three ounces to the pint.

While the quantity of alcohol in this menstruum may seem large at 25 per cent, when strong wine has no more than 15 or 20 per cent, yet when the sugar and the grape juice is added it is lowered to about 10 per cent, the smallest quantity that with the sugar will preserve the product from fermentation.

However as the quantity of sugar must be varied in proportion to the amount of acidity of fruit used, and as it may also be varied to suit the desire for a sweet or sour wine, the percentage of alcohol can be lessened in proportion to increase of sugar. The rule is that *the alcohol and sugar together should aggregate at least 40 per cent. of the menstruum.* To this of course is added during the process of maceration the fruit-juice, and we have a preparation that will never manifest the least sign of fermentation, but will improve in richness and elegance by age if kept in jugs or demijohns corked and in a moderately cool place. Though we have kept them loosely corked in jugs in a very hot pantry in summer and very cold place in winter, without the least degree of change.

The fruit must be thoroughly ripe; put into the menstruum whole immediately after they are taken off the stems before any chemical or fermentative change has taken place. Avoid all fruit that is wormy or has the least speck of rot.

The entire list of fruits may be treated by this method, and yield most elegant products. Especially cherries, red raspberries, dewberries, peaches, apricots, catawba, concord, muscatel, and all other varieties of grapes. Cherries, especially the early varieties; wild cherries, currants, and gooseberries thoroughly ripe and wild goose plums.

OILS. SAPONIFIED OILS. FATS. OLEATES. SOAPS.

We shall, for pharmaceutical purposes, divide the oils into *fixed*, and *volatile*. As to source the fixed oils may be divided into organic or vegetable, animal and inorganic or mineral.

The fats, pharmaceutically, may be divided into animal, and vegetable.

Saponified oils, are combinations of fixed or heavy oils, with an alkaline solution, causing a white creamy consistence, the object of which is to render the oil more pleasant of administration, and increase its therapeutic effect.

Oleates.— By this term we mean not the chemical oleate, but oleaginous combinations for the purpose of obtaining misceability of oils with aqueous and other fluids.

Sapo. Soap.— A detergent or cleansing preparation made by boiling fats or oils with a strong alkaline solution, when a thick foamy mass is formed, to which a solution of common salt is added which causes the soap to rise to the top leaving the water underneath. This is called grain or soft soap. Hard soaps are made by evaporating the water instead of adding salt. Finer soaps such as toilet and surgeon's soaps, are made by redissolving grain soap in lye, heating and then adding salt solution. The oftener this is repeated the purer the product, but it necessarily becomes weaker.

The best soaps are made by first boiling fixed vegetable oil, olive oil being mostly used, with purified carbonate of of soda, obtaining the grain soap, and then, purifying as above, and adding tallow sufficient to harden it.

Toilet soaps are made by cutting and kneading grain soap in a machine for that purpose, perfume is added, and then it is pressed into cakes.

Castile soap, which is mostly recommended and used by physicians and surgeons, is simply the purified soap, made as above stated, with olive oil and caustic soda.

Sapo Viridis or green soap is made in Germany and imported, it is made from the lighter fixed oils containing little stearin. It is a soft jelly like soap of a greenish yellow color.

Soaps are used in pharmacy for liniments, plasters, inunctions, and in making pill mass.

Medicated soaps are made by adding various therapeutic agents, such as tar, balsam of tolu, fir, and antiseptics such as carbolic acid, etc. to the purified soap. The object being to combine with its detergent properties that of a local therapeutic application to the skin. While theoretically this seems plausible, practically it is a therapeutic inconsistency; for the detergent effect of the soap would leave nothing of the medicament on the surface. The fact is that so called medicinal soaps have nothing more than aseptic virtues, and in some cases this is quite desirable, yet with modern surgical technique nothing more is desired than a good plain soap.

Volatile Oils.

Volatile or essential oils, are those light ethereal oils whose chief characteristics are odorousness, transparency, fluidity, and the rapidity with which they evaporate when exposed to the air at a very moderate temperature.

They are obtained almost wholly from vegetable agents, mostly existing naturally, sometimes produced by chemical reactions, as destructive distillation, combustion, and by solution of the plant in water.

Pure fresh volatile oils are almost colorless, transparent and should have the odor and taste of the fresh plant or vegetable substance from which they are obtained. If exposed to the air and light or kept a long time in stock, they become thick, opaque, green, yellow, or red, and loose their characteristic odor and taste, becoming terebinthic.

The adulteration of volatile oils is a very common practice by both retail and wholesale druggists. The fixed oils are mostly used as adulterants, being much cheaper. To detect this, pour a few drops of the suspected oil on a piece of clean writing paper, evaporate over a spirit lamp, if adulterated with a fixed oil it will leave a greased spot. The pure volatile oil leaves no stain on the paper. Alcohol is also used; to detect which, place equal parts of oil, water, and glycerin in a test tube shake gently, the alcohol will mix with the water and glycerin leaving a much diminished stratum of oil. Cheaper grades of the same oil are used for adulteration. But practice and experience with the use of the various volatile oils will enable one to readily detect inferior articles.

Volatile oils are chiefly obtained by distillation with water. Some can be distilled directly, a few by expression, and others by solution in some fixed oils. Distillation with water is done by placing the substance in a still, covering with water, and by regulated heat carrying the oil over with the distilled water into a cooler or refrigeratory, where it can be readily skimmed from the surface.

The very lightest volatile oils, that, are readily decomposed, and are not plentiful in the plants containing them, their extraction is best effected by various processes such as maceration, digestion, percolation with some solvent, enfleurage, or by the pneumatic process. The two last processes are for the treatment of delicate perfume laden flowers, and belong to the art of perfumery.

The chief pharmaceutic use of the volatile oils are in liniments, ointments, inunctions, flavoring, and adjuvants to medicinal compounds, being, most of them, diffusive stimulants to the vaso-motor apparatus, both internally and externally administered. The following list comprises the chief volatile oils in general use The oleoresins belong to another class pharmaceutically, and will be found elsewhere.

List of Volatile Oils.

Oil Allspice,	Ol. Pimentæ.	Oil Lavender,	Ol. Lavan iulæ.
" Anise,	" Anise	" Lemon,	" Limonis.
" Bay,	" Myricæ	" Mustard,	" Sinipi.
" Bergamont,	" Bergamii.	" Orange Flo,	" Auranti Flo.
" Birch,	" Betulæ.	" Orange peel,	" Auranti Cor.
" Almonds,	" Amyg. Am.	" Pennyroyal,	" Hedeoma.
" Cajuput,	" Cajuputi.	" Peppermint,	" Mentha Pip.
" Camphor,	" Camphoræ.	" Red Cedar,	" Juniperis V.
" Caraway,	" Cari.	" Rosmary,	" Rosmarini.
" Cinnamon,	" Cinnamomi.	" Rue,	" Rutæ.
" Chomomile	" Anthemidis	" Sandal Wo,	" Santali.
" Cloves,	" Caryophylli.	" Sassafras,	" Sassafras.
" Cariander,	" Cariandri.	" Sabine,	" Sabinæ.
" Dill,	" Anethi.	" Spearmint,	" Mentha Vir.
" Eucalyptus	" Eucalypti.	" Tar,	" Picis.
" Fennel,	" Fœniculi.	" Turpentine,	" Terebinthæ.
" Hemlock,	" Abies Can.	" Wormseed,	" Chenopodii.

Oil Juniper, Ol. Juniperi. Oil Wintergreen Ol. Gaultheria.

The fixed oils, are heavy, transparent or semitranspar-
ent, white, yellow, or greenish. They are thick and greasy
leaving a heavy stain on paper or fabrics. They vary in
taste usually retaining the taste and odor of the substance
from which they are derived.

The medicinal fixed oils are derived chiefly from plants,
nuts and fruits, one or two of much value being mineral.

They are obtained chiefly by expression. The substance
being bruised or ground to a pulp and pressed by powerful
hydraulic presses, either cold, heated or steamed. Some
are best obtained by pressure between hot rollers. The mineral oils exist in a free state or combined with other mineral matters or fluids.

List of Fixed Oils.

Oleum Amygdala Dulcis, Oil Sweet Almond.
" Olivæ, Oil of Olives.
" Ricini, Castor Oil.
" Lini, Flax - seed oil.
" Gossypii Seminis, Cotton seed oil
" Pepo. Pumpkin - seed oil.
" Lycopodium, Oil of Lycopodium
" Myricæ, Oil of Bayberry.
" Juglans Cinerea, Oil of Butternut.
" Juglans Nigra, Oil of Black Walnut.
" Elais, Palm oil.

The fixed oils are used both externally and internally.
Most of them for either use are rendered more efficacious
by saponification, that is, emulsified by an alkali. Especially when administered internally they can be made more
palatable and effective. The following formulæ are for internal use.

Oleum Ricini Saponificatus. Saponfied. Castor Oil.

Castor Oil,
Water, aa fl. oz. 1.
Potassii Carbonas, (Sal. Tartar) grs. 15
Oil Coriander, drops 5

Dissolve the potassa in the water, add the oils and shake
violently for two or three minutes. There will be partial
separation of oil from the solution on long standing but a
little agitation will mix them again.

Dose a dessertspoonful to two tablespoonsful.

Oleum Olivæ Saponificatus.

Olive oil,	fl. oz. 1½
Water,	oz. ½
Potassii Carbonas,	gr. 10
Oil Lavender,	drops 5

Dissolve the potassa in the water and add the oils, shake thoroughly.

Dose one or two tablespoonsful.

Oleum Lini Saponificatus.

Flaxseed oil	
Water,	a a oz. 1
Potassii Carbonas,	gr. 15
Oil Bitter Almonds,	drops 5

Dissolve the potassa in the water and add the oils, shake thoroughly.

Use externally for burns, chilblains, and old sores. Internally for feverish irritated conditions of intestinal tract.

Dose one or two teaspoonsful.

Oleum Pepo Saponificatus, Saponified Pumpkin Seed Oil.

Oil of Pumpkin Seed,	oz. 1
Water,	dr. 3
Oil of Anise,	drops, 5
Potassii Carbonas,	gr. 5

Dissolve potassa in the water, add the oils and shake thoroughly.

Dose one half to one teaspoonful.

Oleum Pepo Saponificatus Compositus. Compound Saponified Pumpkin Seed and Castor Oil.

Oil of Pumpkin Seed,	dr. 2
Castor Oil,	oz. 1
Water,	oz. 1
Aromatic Syrup,	dr. 6
Potassii Carbonas,	gr. 15

Dissolve the potassa in the water, mix the two oils and add to the solution shaking thoroughly, lastly add the syrup.

Dose one to three tablespoonsful. A good tape worm remedy.

Oleum Chenopodii Saponificatus.

Oil of Wormseed,	oz. 1.
Oil of Wintergreen,	drops, 5
Oil of Cinnamon,	drops, 10

Water,   oz. 1½
Potassii Carbonas,   gr. 12
Simple Syrup,   oz. 1

Dissolve the potassa in the water, mix the oils and add to solution, shake thoroughly and add the syrup.

A most palatable and effective vermifuge. Dose one half to one teaspoonful.

Oleum Amygdala Dulcis Saponificatus. Saponified Oil of Sweet Almonds.

Oil of Sweet Almonds,   oz. 1½
Oil of Bitter Almonds,   gtta. 3
Water,   oz. ½
Powdered Borax,   grs. 15

Dissolve the borax in the water, add the oils and shake thoroughly.

An excellent internal application for sunburns, pimples, and freckles. Also an excellent application in diseases of scalp.

Fats.

These are heavy semi-solid and solid fixed oils, derived from the animal kingdom chiefly, though many vegetables are rich in fats. The adipose tissue of all animals yields more or less fat, as also fowls, fish, reptiles, and insects. The chief fats used in pharmacy are,—

Adeps, Lard. Purified lard is obtained by a rather laborious process, and is used for pomades and finer ointments, embrocations. etc.

Fresh well rendered or boiled lard is best in pharmaceutical use, and almost all the mineral salts combine with it better than some of the other fats.

Oleum Adipis, Lard Oil is made by expression at a low temperature of lard. It is colorless, quite fluid, an excellent fixed oil but is difficult to obtain pure in market being usually adulterated with paraffin oil. It is used in making the thinner ointments, and where a heavy absorbent powder is to be incorporated with fat.

Sevum, Suet, Tallow, This is obtained from beef or mutton. Owing to the large proportion of stearin, tallow is dense, white, smoothe and melts at nearly the boiling point of water. Used in making ointments with the lighter oils, such as tar, sassafras etc., and for hardening platters, suppositories etc.

Lanoline. This is a white oily fat, about the consisten-

cy of fresh churned unsalted butter. It is procured from
lamb's wool, by a special and patented process of Oscar
Liebreich's, Berlin, Germany.

This is a most excellent base for incorporating the powdered vegetable agents, and dry mineral powders into ointments, suppositories etc. The following is a most useful
and elegant formula for piles, painful swellings and bruises.

    Lanoline,   oz. 1
    Oil of Sassafras.   dr. 1
    Powdered Valerian
    Powdered Baptisia,   a a dr. 2
    Powdered Ulmus, a sufficient quantity.

Place the lanoline on a glass or marble slab, and with a
spatula first mix the oil sassafras with it, then incorporate the valerian and baptisia, and lastly incorporate powdered elm until the consistency desirable is obtained.

Petrolatum Vaseline. Is a semisolid, reddish yellow,
or clear white fat, obtained as a residue after distillation
of petroleum or coal oil. It is purified by filtration
through animal charcoal.

Any of the vegetable or mineral powders are readily incorporated with vaseline into ointments, plasters etc. A
number of brands or proprietary names for vaseline have
been devised, such as "cosmoline", "malena" etc.

Parafin. This is a solid, waxy substance, inodorous
and tasteless, somewhat harder than tallow, and not quite
so hard as white beeswax. It was at first obtained by the destructive distillation of wood; but is now on a large scale
obtained from petroleum. Parafin is valuable in pharmacy in making plasters, suppositories etc.

Cetaceum. Spermaceti. A 'dense white fatty substance, obtained mainly from the head of the sperm whale,
is used in plasters, ointments, suppositories etc.

Oleum Theobromœ, Butter of Cacoa. This is in yellowish white oblong cakes of an agreeable chocolate smell
and taste. It is obtained from cacao, or chocolate nut, cacoa butter is valuable as a base for suppositories, pastiles,&c

Glycerinum. Glycerin. This most useful pharmacal is
a product of fats and fixed oils. It is thick, syrupy, transparent and very sweet mixing in any proportion with water or alcohol. Originally it was made by its discoverer
Scheele in 1789 by boiling olive oil and litharge in water.

This of course contained lead which was hard to get rid
of sufficiently to fit it for internal administration. Subse-

quently it was found in soap maker's waste; but most of the fat used in the large factories is from dead and decomposing animals, glycerin made from such a source is of a strong odor and unfit for use in pharmacy, notwithstanding it is claimed to be rendered inodorous and pure by a patented process. Pure glycerin for pharmaceutical purposes should be that made from pure olive oil, or fresh pure lard by distillation with super heated steam 400 to 500 deg. F.

Oleates.

It is often desirable to quickly mix or combine a fixed oil or a fat with an aqueous solution or a syrup either in fluid form or an ointment or plaster. For this purpose we present the following formula for reducing these substances to what we shall for want of a better name call *oleates*.

Oleate Lanoline.

Lanoline,	dr. 3
Corn Starch,	oz. 1½
Potassii Carbonas	gr. 10

Mix the starch and potassa, melt the lanoline and adding it to the powder in a mortar in small quantities; triturate thoroughly. A few drops of oil of bitter almonds or any the essential oils during the trituration may be added to give it a pleasant flavor.

Oleate Tar and Sassafras Compound.

Oil of Tar,	
Oil of Sassafras,	a a dr. 2
Corn Starch,	oz. 1½
Pulverized Elm,	oz. ½

Mix the corn starch and elm in a mortar and triturate the oils in successive small quantities.

EXTRACTS. ABSTRACTS. OLEORESINS. RESINOIDS. and ALKALOIDS.

Solid extracts. These were formerly much in use among Physio-Medicalists, but like many other preparations of the fathers of our system, they have yielded to more elegant pharmacy. Before the advent of the machine pill coating with sugar and gelatine, home made pills from solid aqueous extracts were dispensed freely. We are certainly of the belief that solid and semisolid aqeous extracts have been and ever will be powerful therapeutic agents with proper selection of drugs, and careful preparation.

And we earnestly recommend all practitioners who can obtain the fresh green or properly dried drugs to prepare their own extracts. The process is so simple and inexpensive, and one can obtain preparations much superior to that of the large manufacturing houses who have to depend on the general gatherers for supplies which cannot be in good order after long shipments. These extracts can be sent by the home manufacturer to the manufacturers of pills, tablets &c. and made into coated pills, tablets etc. in accordance with your own private formulæ.

The object of extracts is to obtain the medicinal properties of vegetable agents in a solid or semisolid condensed state. and they serve the double purpose of affording a base or mass for other agents in pill, tablet or suppository form, and as a therapeutic auxillary to the product. It seems that no standard either of strength or consistency has yet been established for extracts, and for this reason the physician possessing any kind of facilities for office pharmacy and who can procure the fresh agents should make his own extracts, as those found in market are wholly unreliable as to strength or consistency. Unless kept thoroughly sealed in glass or porcelain jars and in cool, damp place, water evaporates, and the extract deteriorates, becoming hard and inert. The U. S. Pharmacopœia has endeavored to establish a standard of consistency by the term *"pilular consistence,"* but this is no more definite than the term solid extract, as the consistency of a pill mass must depend on the nature and quantity of the powders to be incorporated. The proper way, we think, is to establish a standard of strength representing a definite quantity by weight of the drug fresh green or dried, to commence with, which shall be represented by a definite quantity by weight of the finished extract, which should be always stated on a label upon the container. In this way the druggist or physician could easily ascertain, by weighing, whether evaporation by long keeping, or being loosely stoppered, had reduced the product below the the standard; in which case, if not otherwise deteriorated. sufficient distilled water could be added to bring it up to the required standard of weight and consistency.

With the view of establishing a definite standard of strength for solid aqueous extracts we suggest the following typical formulæ:—

Aqueous Extract of Eupatorium Perfoliatum.
Green. Extractum Eupatoriœ Aquosum.

Eupatorium Perfol, fresh green herb, cut finely lbs. 5
Pure Water, gal. 3

Place the herb in a macerating vessel pour, on one gallon
of water and digest at a temperature of 200 deg. F., closely
covered for 3 hours, strain off the liquid with some pressure, set aside and pour on two gallons of water, simmer
slowly in an uncovered vessel untill the quantity of liquid
is about two-thirds evaporated, press off with a drug press,
or displace while hot with the centrifuge, and mix with
the first liquid, evaporate at a temperature not to exceed
200 deg. F. by direct heat, or over a steam, hot water or
sand bath untill the mass weighs 16 oz. av. Put in a large
mouth glass or queensware bottle, cover with a thin stratum
of glycerin and thoroughly close with a good cork glazing
the top and sides of same with hot beeswax.

Aqueous Extract of Lobelia Herb, Dried.
Extractum Lobelia Aquosum.

Lobelia Herb, No. 30 powder, lbs. 3
Pure or distilled water, gal. 3

Place the drug in a suitable vessel and pour over it one gallon of water. Digest at a temperature of 160 deg. for three
hours, transfer to a percolator or centrifuge and displace
pouring on the other two gallons of boiling water, set a-
side the first gallon; evaporate by boiling the last two gallons to five pints, mix with first and evaporate slowly over
a steam or hot water bath untill one pound of extract is
obtained, put in a well stoppered large mouth bottle, cover
with a thin stratum of glycerin.

Expressed or Inspissated Extracts.

These are made from succulent green plants, which are
bruised to a pulp in a mortar, the juice pressed out with a
drug press or displaced with the centrifuge and evaporated
spontaneously in a warm place. They should be made on
the same standard as aqueous extracts from the green
plant, 5 lbs. of plant to 1 lb. of extract.

Hydro-Alcoholic Extracts.

These are made with a menstruum of alcohol and water.
Some largely resinous agents are best treated in this way;
but the percentage of alcohol need not be large, not exceeding 25 or 30 per cent, for the reason as already stated,

that not all of the normal therapeutic constituents reside
in the resins or gums of these plants, and for the additional reason that the loss of the alcohol, unless one is prepared on a large scale to regain it by distillation, renders
the product unnecessarily expensive. Last but by no
means the least objection, the larger the percentage of alcohol used, the less soluble the extract in the fluids of the
alimentary tract.

The following is offered as a typical formula for a standard hydro-alcoholic extract.

Extract Hydrastis. Hydro-Alcoholic.

Hydrastis, No. 40 powder,	lbs. 3
Alcohol,	pts. 4½
Distilled water,	a sufficient quantity.

Place the drug in a macerating vessel, mix 4 pints of the
water with the alcohol, pour over the drugs and macerate
for five days, transfer to the centrifuge or a percolator and
displace setting aside the first six pints, continue the displacement with boiling water untill two gallons of percolate in all are obtained, evaporate the last percolate by
boiling slowly to a half gallon, mix with the first
percolate and evaporate on hot water or a steam bath to
one pound of extract, put in a well stoppered large mouth
bottle covering with a thin stratum of glycerin.

Alcoholic Extracts, are made with a pure alcohol menstruum. As above stated, such extracts are not desirable
because of their insolubility and expense. Those agents
containing large quantities of gum and resin are treated in
this way under the notion that their medicinal properties
are therein contained. The fact is that the gums as a rule
are sparingly solvent in alcohol, while the resins only partially represent the therapeutic constituency of such
agents.

Abstracts. Saccharated Extracts.

The U. S. Pharmacopœia in 1880 introduced officially under the name *Abstracta*, preparations made by spontaneous evaporation of an alcoholic tincture and adding sufficient sugar of milk so that when dry or powdered the product would be one half the weight of the quantity of drug
used. These preparations had bee n previously made and
sold by a drug firm under the name of saccharated powdered extracts. They were thought to be a great improvement
over the solid extracts both as a standard strength and

therapeutic efficiency, but after an extensive use of them by the profession, for a short time they fell into disfavor as they could not be kept from solidifying and they were found to be insoluble by the digestive fluids.

In place of the above we suggest the following typical formula, the product of which we shall call abstract triturate.

Trituratum Abstractum Scutelariæ. Abstract Triturate of Scutelaria.

Scutelaria, No. 30 powder,	lb. 1
Alcohol,	pts. 1½
Water,	a sufficient quantity,
Pulverized Scutelaria,	" " "

Mix the alcohol with 2 pints of water and pour over the No. 30 scutelaria powder in a proper macerating vessel, macerate 5 days, transfer to a centrifuge or a percolator and displace, adding boiling water, set aside the first quart, continue until three quarts in all are obtained; evaporate by boiling the two last quarts to one pint, mix with first percolate and over a hot water or steam bath evaporate slowly to a very thick extract; transfer to a mortar and triturate with it sufficient powdered scutelaria to make one pound in all; if not reduced to a dry powder, spread it on thin muslin stretched on a frame in a warm place till quite dry, then triturate again adding more powdered scutelaria if necessary to make one pound by weight.

This preparation gives the advantage of first the normal powder of the drug, second, extraction and addition to the normal powder such constituencies as yield most readily to a hydro-alcoholic menstruum, and thirdly rapid and perfect solubility by the gastric and intestinal fluids with consequent complete assimilation of the drug, which constitutes the therapeutic disideratum of a pharmaceutical product.

Oleoresins.

A number of vegetable agents contain a fixed oil which is intimately combined with gum-resinous constituents from which the oil cannot be separated without destructive distillation, while the oil resin and gum can be readily obtained in combination and represents a large therapeutic constituency of the drug. To such a product the name oleoresin is given. Of course an oleoresin however well prepared does not represent the full therapeutic constituency of the drug, nevertheless they are the most concentrated preparations as far as they go in drug constituents of the plant of any other fluid products; but for this reason if no other their therapeutic usefulness is curtailed because such a product must necessarily have a powerful local influence and though from a mild sanative agent may become a dangerous local irritant. Consequently they have from a former rather extensive employment fallen much into disuse amongst Physio-Medicalists, so that a comparatively few oleoresins are now in general use. Another objection is the menstruum which is stronger ether as employed by the U. S. Pharmacopœia, of which it is impossible to rid the product of its principles by the necessarily imperfect spontaneous evaporation.

Still another objection is that it is almost impossible to establish a definite standard strength for these products. As illustrative of what is said above, the following formula is copied from Remington's Pharmacy, page 367.

Oleoresina Capsici U. S. Oleoresin of Capsicum.

Capsicum, No. 60 powder,	100 parts or 32 oz. av.
Stronger Ether,	a sufficient quantity.
To make about	1½ fl. oz.

Put the capsicum into a cylindricle percolator, provided with a cover and receptacle suitable for volatile liquids, press it firmly. and gradually pour stronger ether upon it, untill one hundred and fifty parts [or 4 pints] of liquid have slowly passed.

Recover the greater part of the ether by distillation on a water-bath, and expose the residue in a capsule, until the remaining ether has evaporated. Lastly, pour off the liquid portion, transfer the remainder to a strainer, and, when the separated fatty matter (which is to be rejected) has been completely drained, mix all the liquid portions together.

Keep the oleoresin in a well stoppered bottle.

The oleoresins mostly in use as prepared by this method are.

Oleoresina Capsici.	Oleoresin of Capsicum.
" Lobeliae.	" " Lobelia Seed.
" Cubebæ.	" " Cubebs.
" Lupulini.	" " Lupulin.
" Piperis.	" " Black Pepper.

"   Zingiberis.   " Ginger.

Resinoids or Resins, Resinæ U. S. P.

These preparations were early produced and used by the Botanics and Eclectics together with products containing extractive gums and alkaloidal constituents of plants which were simply crude alkaloids. They became very popular for a time but have given place to the more elegant alkaloids of modern pharmacy. However some of the resinoids have maintained their popularity amongst Physio-Medicalists and are most valuable agents.

Resinoids are made by maceration and displacement with a full strength or high percentage alcohol as a menstruum, and the resin precipitated by adding to the alcoholic solution an excess of water.

These preparations are almost wholly non-therapeutic to use the term, as they represent in an isolated state a single therapeutic constituent of the drug. Consequently their therapeutic range is limited. They simply represent the resinous constituent which is alone soluable in alcohol

The fact of this limited therapeutic range of resinoids, dependent on the absolute alcoholic menstruum, we urge as additional proof of the fact which we have emphasized in the beginning of this article, that an aqueous solution represents the normal therapeutic constituency of organic agents.

Normal Fluid Extracts, Alkaloids.

Under the above name the U. S. Pharmacopœia places what was formerly termed resinoids and alkaloids, of the early Botanics and Eclectics. The fact is that these alkaloids are simply resinoids made by a more perfected method by which the resinoidal inorganic salts of the plant may be isolated. Ether is the principal menstruum.

The resinoids and alkaloids take the name of the original drug with the last syllable terminating in *ine* for the alkaloids, and *in* for the resinoids, thus quinine, salacine, and podophyllin, leptandrin.

The following is a typical formula for resinoids.

Podophyllin, Resinoid of Podophyllum.

Podophyllum, No. 50 powder,   lb. av. 1
Acetic Acid,   oz. 1
Water,

Alcohol, of each, a sufficient quantity. Place the podophyllum in a suitable macerating vessel and pour on sufficient alcohol to thoroughly saturate, cover closely and macerate 4 or 5 days mixing each day so as to insure thorough saturation, transfer to a centrifuge or percolator and displace adding more alcohol until the drug is exhausted (about 1¾ pints of percolate), evaporate or distill off the alcohol till the fluid is thick as molasses; to one pint of water add the acetic acid, cool to a temperature of 40 or 50 deg F. and slowly stir in the thick extract, let stand till all precipitation ceases, decant the supernatant liquid and wash the precipitate by pouring on fresh cold water and decanting two or three times, spread the precipitate on a thin muslin or flannel stretched over a frame and when thoroughly dry reduce to a fine powder.

The alkaloids are made commercially by processes which the manufacturers keep strictly secret, the general plan is to proceed as in the above formula for resinoids, using hydrochloric acid instead of acetic, and after decanting the first fluid it is made alkaline with ammonia or soda and the precipitate returned to it shaking and allowing it to settle, then decanting and washing with cold water. Or the drug in very fine No. 80 powder is mixed into a paste with fresh lime dried and then digested in alcohol decanted and acidulated, then precipitated as in the above formula, washed thoroughly with acidulated cold water, dried and powdered Some agents yield better therapeutic products with the resinoid, while others are better with the alkaloidal treatment.

ERRATA.

Page 79. 9th. line, read no function.
" 128, 17th line, read constitution.
" 151, 9th line from bottom read, sudoriferous.
" 215, after Cyprus add,

Anti-emetic weed was introduced to the profession by
Prof. G. N. Davidson who recomm nded it for its soothing
effect upon the sympathetic nervous system. C. T. Bedford
makes a reliable fluid extract. It not only relieves the
nausea of pregnacny but will be found valuable in those
cases of hemicrania due to reflex action.

Page 279, 13th line read, results.
" 364, at bottom of page add

size of the dose given. It is a valuable addition to other
medicines when the patient is constipated or inclined to
constipation.

The seed are used for the same purposes as the roots.

Page 399, 19th. line read Microtome.
" 400, 13th. line for no read slight.
" 473, 13th. line for no read an.
" 527, 29th. line read acicular.
" 582, 8th. line read Sweet & Lewis No. 11. Also in 9th.
line from bottom in page 586.

Page 588, 5th line from bottom read evolved.
" 591, 19th line and in 6th. and 7th. lines from bottom,
also in 14th line from bottom of page 592 read, Molecular
instead of Atomic.

Page 601, 1st. liue after word displacer adt " for which the
author has applied for a patent. "

Page 605, 6th. line read, 15 grs. 7th. line read, 10 grs. 8th.
line read, 20 grs.

Page 607, 2nd. line from bottom read, 12 oz.
" 612, 1st. line read, muscular.

Add to each formula on this page, Salicylic Acid. dr. 1
Soda Sulph. dr. 2
Pot. Nitrate dr. 3

These should be triturated and dissolved in the fld. extract.

Page 625, 1st. formula for 2½ read 3 and for 13½ read 13.
2nd. formula for 2 grs. read 3 in each line.

Page 626, 1st. formula read 2 oz. for 3 dr. and 3 grs. for 2 grs.
and in 2nd. formula read 1 oz. av.

Page 634, 2nd. formula read 16 fl. oz. distilled water.

Opinions of those who have used the McDannold Chair.

SCRANTON, PA.

The McDannold Chair arrived O. K. My unbiased opinion is that it is the best chair on the market at any price. I would not give it for any other I have ever seen. It is certainly a "gem." E. L. Peet, M. D.

HARRISBURG, PA.

I have had in use for some months the McDannold Chair I purchased from you, and take pleasure in unqualifiedly commending it. It is a chair peculiarly adapted to the needs of the general practitioner, in that it possesses all the necessary features for the treatment of all the special lines of cases, and yet lacks the expensive complications found in so many chairs. I find it most comfortable in operation, both to patient and physician, and regard it as a distinct mechanical advance over its predecessors in the market. Thos. S. Blair, M. D.

ALLEGHANY, PA.

For seven years I have been looking for a chair suitable for general and special work; have found my ideal in the McDannold. For simplicity in adjustment, it cannot be excelled. Dr. L. J. Lyle.

FRANKLIN, PA.

After months of daily use, I take pleasure in saying that I consider the McDannold Chair is complete in all of its appointments, and possesses important advantages over all other chairs that I have ever seen. Its simplicity of construction and perfect ease in its varied adjustments, and the complete control of the operator over the chair in its several movements, make the McDannold surgical and gynæcological chair "par excellence;" and as such I take pleasure in so recommending it to the favorable consideration of the profession. Griffin Reno, M. D.

Lightning Source UK Ltd.
Milton Keynes UK
UKHW022356121020
371445UK00006B/1378